Warman's®
American Furniture

EDITED BY ELLEN T. SCHROY

© 2000 by
Krause Publications

Published by

700 East State St., Iola, WI 54990-0001
715-445-2214
www.krause.com

Please, call or write us for our free catalog of antiques and collectibles publications.
To place an order or receive our free catalog, call 800-258-0929. For editorial comment and further information,
use our regular business telephone at (715) 445-2214

Library of Congress Catalog Number: 00-101577
ISBN: 0-87341-912-X

Printed in the United States of America

Table of Contents

Introduction

Welcome to *Warman's American Furniture*, the newest edition in the fine tradition established by Warman's.

This edition is designed to help our readers understand American furniture. And since it is a price guide, the most valuable part of this edition is the thousands of prices. Valuing antique furniture is an exercise in comparables. First, a reader will have to compare design styles to determine when their particular piece was made. After that determination is clear, they can then read the price listings offered and compare their piece of furniture to those listed. In some cases, an exact match may be found—great! In other instances, perhaps something close will be described, then some adjustment to the value will need to be made, allowing for condition, minor changes, etc. Each reader will have the pleasure of interpreting these values as they see fit, adding value for original finish or hardware. What we can't factor in is any sentimental value a piece of furniture may have; that's strictly up to the reader. That is why we call this a "price guide," understanding that it does its job best when it guides the reader to a conclusion.

Warman's American Furniture is arranged simply, by form. Why? By arranging this edition by beds, chairs, tables, etc., it actually continues the style established more than fifty years ago by Edwin G. Warman in his *Warman's Antiques and Current Prices* and now continued in the popular *Warman's Antiques and Collectibles Price Guide*. The first thing needed to be determined about the piece of furniture is, "What is it?" In many cases, determining how it was originally used will help with that definition. The second question may be, "How long have I had this ___," causing the reader to evaluate the history and perhaps age of the piece. Because furniture is something of value that is often passed from generation to generation, examining a piece's history as part of it's prov-

enance may help determine both age and give valuable clues as to style. Provenance is a fancy term for the history of an object, who made it, when, who has owned it, where was it located, has it been important enough to be displayed prominently for the public to enjoy? As the values of American antique furniture continue to rise, it can be just as fascinating to learn the provenance of a particular piece and understand how that adds to the value.

By using photographs and line drawings, *Warman's American Furniture* helps you understand what style your particular piece of furniture may fall into. It is important to remember that regions and dates mentioned are usually the best estimates available, and unless a piece is signed and dated, nothing is absolute. Descriptions contain regions to help guide you by distinguishing what kinds of woods or variations existed in a particular geographic region. Comparing the woods and design elements will help determine style.

While the title of this edition is *Warman's American Furniture*, you may notice a few examples from other geographic locations included. These are deliberately included to help show differences between regions of the world. Sometimes a style originated in England or another country, and it is important to see how the American cabinetmakers interpreted the style. To better understand furniture from the Chippendale period, for example, you need to recognize that Thomas Chippendale was English. His influence on the furniture styles of his day were great. Today much of the furniture we attribute to that style was created either in England or America. To allow the reader to compare examples is a part of what *Warman's American Furniture* is all about.

Much attention has been paid to the condition of the furniture being described in this edition. Why? Because some collectors only want pieces that still retain their original finish and are willing to pay a premium for it. Other collectors are embracing pieces of furniture with less than a perfect finish, or worn paint, for the beauty of the well-worn patina. You will also notice that sometimes similar examples are listed, with condition being the biggest difference. It would be unrealistic to think that furniture handed down from generation to another has not had repairs. When known, these repairs are noted. As with the original finish, to some collectors these repairs show someone cared enough about the piece to repair it, rather than destroy it. Remember that many of the early period furniture examples described date back to the 1700s and most of us would be showing some wear, too, after all those years.

It would be wonderful if furniture was signed, like china items are. But the fact of the matter is that few pieces are signed. Identification of a craftsmen's work often comes through studying invoices, household inventories, oral histories, etc. Add to that the ability to secure catalogs which show what was made during specific times. Much of what is known about the early craftsmen is hearsay. We know they used pattern books and copied styles that were popular in England and Europe. How quickly these styles changed and how they were reflected by each craftsman is part of the fascination of collecting furniture. One American furniture designer, Duncan Phyfe, is often credited with many more pieces of furniture than he ever made. But, the truth of this is that Duncan was busy during the time of the Sheraton furniture era and his furniture style shifted, as that design style did. Some of the early pieces of documented Phyfe are vastly different than the later works. Because he signed some pieces and was well known, curators and collectors can accurately attribute other pieces to him.

You will notice that there is a deliberate attempt to organize the furniture by period, when possible. And, to make finding examples easier, descriptions are placed in chronological order within a geographical area. How these dates are determined and how the place of origin is determined is a skill that takes years to achieve. Assume that the dates and places given are all approximate, unless the piece is signed and dated.

It is important to learn the specific elements related to a particular design style. To this end, there are many good books available on specific styles. In the bibliography included in this edition, you'll find some of the standard references included. Reading and studying those will enhance knowledge and appreciation for the nature of the elements. Because *Warman's American Furniture* is essentially a price guide, a brief description of styles is included for the different forms, noting what's important to observe, but not exploring the detailed history of each style. To learn that Thomas Chippendale was influenced by the French King Louis XV is interesting, but perhaps not as important as the thought that he developed the classic element of a claw grasping a pearl, hence the "claw and ball" foot so often associated with the Chippendale style of furniture.

Furniture is something we all have, something we live with every day. We acquire it all through our lifetimes, adding or changing to suit our needs. The way we purchase furniture is often quite time consuming as we travel from store to store or perhaps antique dealer to antique dealer in search of that "perfect" piece. What makes it "perfect" is a personal decision, but often it's based on eye appeal, style, color, size, and price tag. To learn more about furniture, it is important to read, observe, and study styles.

When buying American antique furniture, feel free to ask many questions of the seller. "Who made it, when, how long have you had it, where did you obtain it, what do you know of its history, show me the original parts, have you made any changes, etc." By exchanging this type of information, the provenance of the piece is kept alive and possibly enhanced. A good seller will offer to write down this information and include it with the receipt. Make sure that receipt also contains the seller's name and address, date, and price. Keeping records such as these will help establish your ownership and again add to the provenance.

Another good source for buying antique furniture is at auction. Again, don't be afraid to ask questions during the preview of the auction. That's why auctioneers have previews, to allow time for close inspection, questions, etc. before the auction. Many of the prices in this edition are taken from prices realized, provided by many auction companies. Why? Because by using auction prices, it can be assumed that at least two different parties were interested in the particular piece of furniture. Their actions at the auction helped to determine how much each was willing to pay. Some styles of furniture are more popular in one geographic region than another, but these once clear lines are becoming more and more obscured as Americans move around, taking their family heirlooms and treasured pieces of furniture with them. Add to that the current desire to have large homes which we tend to fill with our comforting treasures, sometimes blending in styles from several families, generations, and regions.

To find pure examples of period furniture, take the time to visit some of our nation's real treasures. Visits to historical homes, museums, etc. will guide you to a path of knowledge that will include color and texture as you explore styles and types of furniture used by other generations. Some museums, such as the DeWitt Wallace Gallery in Williamsburg, Virginia, offer tours and lectures led by their curators and feature specific periods or objects. These experiences are excellent opportunities to understand the historical significance of particular pieces of furniture, while more closely examining how a piece was made, perhaps changed through the years, learning what clues and outside references are used to determine provenance.

The other place to learn more about antique furniture is through the wonderful reference books available. Please refer to the separate Reference Listings for some of the books that are terrific places to learn more about furniture, styles, how architecture affected the furniture of the times, and much more.

As I sit at my computer editing *Warman's American Furniture*, I am thankful for all the wonderful pieces of furniture that fill my home. Perhaps if you'd visit my office, you would see a rather plain kitchen-type table under my computer. Yes, you would be correct—it's a fine example of a good drop-leaf table. Yes, it is oak, good and sturdy, as it has lasted for several generations. After a little more examina-

tion, you might discover that it still retains all its original hardware, but that the finish has been redone, years ago, and by a good craftsman, using time-honored refinishing techniques. The secret to this wonderful table is its beautiful legs, turned on a lathe with rings spaced at precise intervals. You'll have to crawl way under the table to really discover the secret of these legs, for they are all attached individually with large bolts, allowing them to come off freely from the top. Why is that so important? It is a major departure from the way most kitchen tables are constructed. The patent dates are also visible when you closely examine the bolts and hardware, giving more clues as to the age of the table. And this feature of free legs allowed me to have the parts carried up to my loft so that I could have a large work space, something difficult to do in an old house with winding narrow stairs. What you can't "see" is that this table also represents a link to my past, for it once belonged to a beloved neighbor. When I was a very little girl, I would get to walk hand in hand with my mother to go visit a wonderful neighbor who often would sit me down at this table with a glass of milk and perhaps some cookies. Years later, it was purchased for me as a gift by my parents when the neighbor's things were sold at auction. Those memories are as important as the gentle curves to the corners of the leaves of the table or those interesting bolts hiding under the straight skirt.

As I further gaze around my office, I see my desk. Usually it is covered with papers, but underneath lies a lovely example of a cherry desk. If I would describe it to you, I'd note the inset leather top, its width, its length, its height. Don't forget to note the banks of four drawers on either side of the kneehole opening, with those interesting drawer pulls—they look like dog's heads frozen in the black cast iron. Somewhere throughout the life of this desk, someone added a cubbyhole back to it, which is perfect to hold the clutter of one's life. But again, it is the provenance of the desk that may be most exciting to our family—the fact my husband's great-great grandfather used this beauty at the family shoe business. How do I know that? By information handed down orally from one generation to the next, but also by a wonderful photograph of great-great grandfather standing by his desk taken in the factory—and even then it was full of papers and documents.

Our home is filled with these kinds of treasures. Many rooms also contain pieces of furniture that my husband I bought together, creating a new line in the provenance of those pieces. How future generations of Schroys will remember these items is something I can help with, by freely sharing what I've learned about them, but also by writing it down in a home inventory, documenting the piece and including a photograph. Because many others have done this same kind of documentation, we have good records of who made pieces of furniture, when, and where, which answers many of the questions we face when trying to determine value.

It is my hope that you will enjoy this edition of *Warman's American Furniture*, that you will find it useful in your discovery of values of objects you hold dear or are trying to evaluate. Preparing this edition has been a joy, for I personally enjoy the aspects of provenance that are so important to furniture. It has served as a refresher course to me as I read about styles, woods, details, details. To the generations past who loved the furniture of their times, we all say thanks for their caring and documentation. To the generations of the future who may next inherit our treasures, we hope they will enjoy them, too—treasure them for their connection to the past, but accept that fact that most antique furniture looks good with a little wear or perhaps a little dust.

Ellen Tischbein Schroy, May 9, 2000

Furniture Styles

1690-1730	William and Mary	1845-1870	Rococo Revival, Victorian
1725-1810	Queen Anne	1850-1914	Naturalistic Revival, Victorian
1755-1790	Chippendale	1850-1914	Louis XVI Revival, Victorian
1790-1830	Federal, Country Formal and Transitional	1855-1885	Neo-Greek Revival, Victorian
1790-1815	Federal (Hepplewhite)	1870-1890	Egyptian Revival, Victorian
1790-1810	Hepplewhite	1870-1890	Eastlake, Victorian
1790-1810	Sheraton	1875-1914	Art Furniture, Victorian
1790-1815	Neoclassic or Greco-Roman	1896-1914	Art Nouveau, Victorian
1795-1840	Duncan Phyfe and Phyfe-Types	1895-1915	Arts and Crafts
1805-1830	Classical (Empire)	1900-1920	Mission, Prairie
1830-1850	French Restauration	1920-1940	Art Deco
1840-1860	Gothic Revival, Victorian	1880-1915	Centennial Revival
1850-1915	Elizabethan Revival, Victorian	1915-1940	Colonial Revival
1850-1880	Renaissance Revival, Victorian	1940s to 1960s	Modernism Era
		1960s to Pres.	Modernism Era, Pop

Furniture Illustrations and Terms

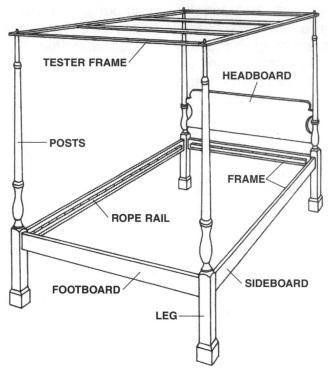

Typical Parts of a Bed

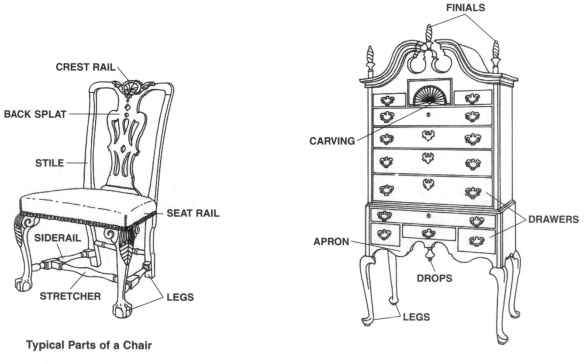

Typical Parts of a Chair

Typical Parts of a Highboy

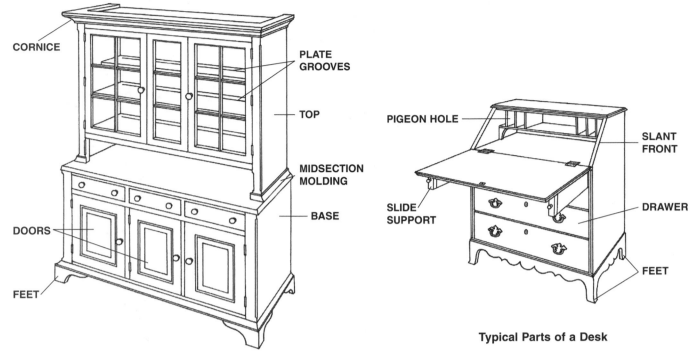

CORNICE

PLATE
GROOVES

TOP

MIDSECTION
MOLDING

BASE

DOORS

FEET

Typical Parts of a Cupboard

PIGEON HOLE

SLANT
FRONT

SLIDE
SUPPORT

DRAWER

FEET

Typical Parts of a Desk

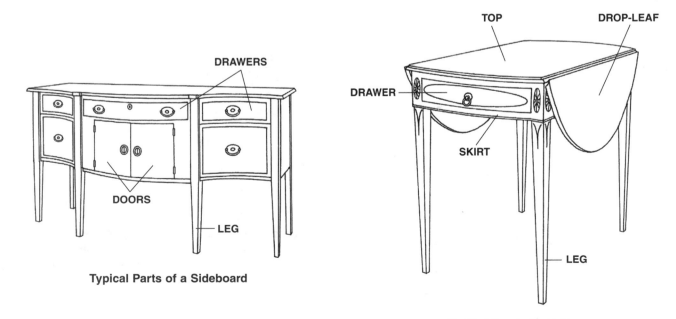

DRAWERS

DOORS

LEG

Typical Parts of a Sideboard

TOP

DROP-LEAF

DRAWER

SKIRT

LEG

Typical Parts of a Table

Construction Details

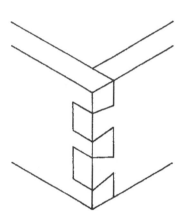

Handmade Dovetail Joint

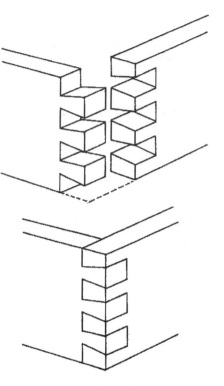

**Machine-made
Dovetail Joint**

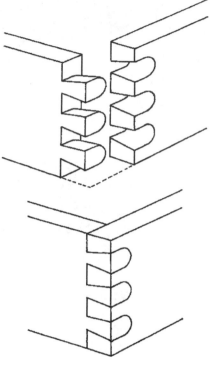

**Machine-made Rounded
Dovetail Joint**

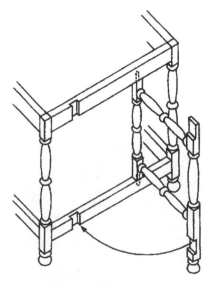

Typical Gateleg Construction

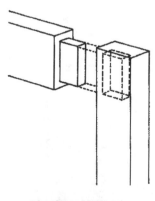

**Mortise-and-Tenon
Joint**

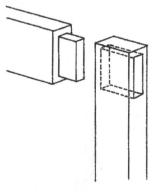

**ThroughMortise-and-Tenon
Joint**

Feet

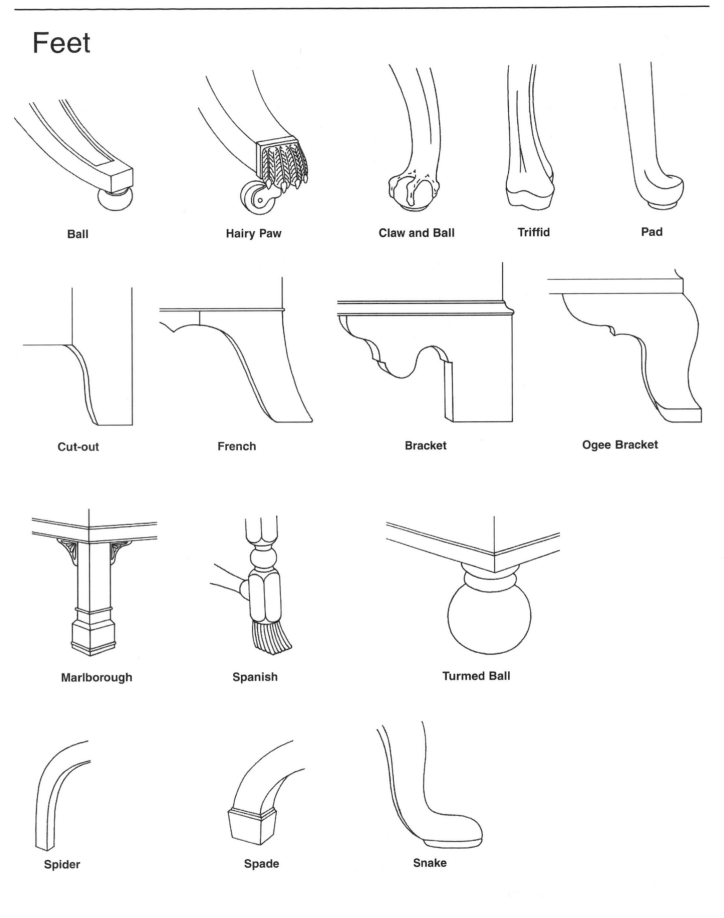

Ball

Hairy Paw

Claw and Ball

Triffid

Pad

Cut-out

French

Bracket

Ogee Bracket

Marlborough

Spanish

Turmed Ball

Spider

Spade

Snake

Legs

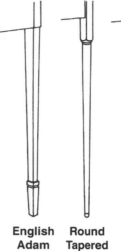
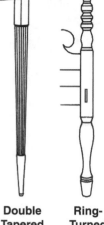
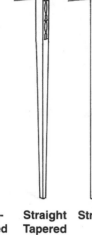

English Adam   **Round Tapered**   **Double Tapered with Reeding**   **Ring-Turned**   **Straight Tapered**   **Straight**   **Cabriole**

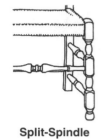

Split-Spindle

Ring-turned

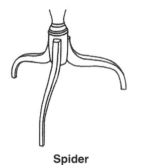

Spider

Snake

Hardware

Bail Handle

Teardrop Pull

Oval Brass

Brass

Pressed Glass

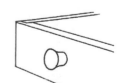

Wooden Knob

Eagle Brass

Beds

A bed can be found in every household and in every furniture style. Inventories of Colonial estates often listed a bed, but gave much more importance to the bedstead or bed hangings. Why? Because often the early beds were rather plain and the wealth of the owner was displayed in the elaborate bed hangings used to disguise this fact. By the Federal period, it was fashionable to have a bedroom on the first floor, primarily to show off one's expensive bed linens and sometimes the more elaborate carved bed. Beds made for southern climates displayed more carving and details earlier, as they were less inclined to be draped with heavy bed hangings that were used in colder regions where hangings were also used to provide warmth in poorly heated rooms. It was not unusual to find more carving and details lavished on the footposts since that was what was easily viewed. Guests were frequently invited into Colonial era bedrooms as a courtesy, perhaps for tea, or socializing. These types of bedrooms were furnished with as fine a piece as the owner could afford, but more emphasis was usually placed on the case pieces used in the room, rather than the bed itself.

Bedroom suites became popular during the Victorian era when furniture was made for every function. By this time, furniture designers were creating beds and accompanying dressers, chests of drawers, chairs, commodes, as well as matching wash stands. As manufactured furniture became more affordable, larger bedroom suites were created and it became a sign of prestige to own a fine bed. Victorian era homes and later architectural styles allowed for larger bedrooms often with higher ceilings that could accommodate massive headboards. These masterpieces were made to not be covered up with bed hangings, but allowed to delight the owner with elaborate carvings, scrolls, and fine woods.

Great architectural changes occurred as the 19th century ended. The Arts & Crafts era, as well as the Mission styles and Art Deco featured houses with smaller bedrooms, causing furniture designers to create beds and bedroom suites which fitted the architectural style. Many of the architects of this area were also furniture designers, creating a complete new environment. One room they often choose to use build-ins and simplified was the bedroom. Beds returned to rather plain styles, more function than design.

Today as the 20th century ends, new architectural styles are again featuring large bedrooms, often with high ceilings. Modern furniture makers have responded by creating masterful bedroom suites to fill those spaces. Headboards are again soaring and large suites include dressers, chests, matching night stands, etc. Traditional styles such as Federal and Chippendale are being updated to fit modern mattress sizes and to again display one's wealth by owning a fine bedroom suite.

Aesthetic Movement

Beds from this design period are bold and highly stylized.

America, c1880, ebonized, gilt incised, and marquetry, 76" l, 64-1/2" w, 73" h........3,165.00

New York, c1870, suite, walnut and burl walnut, full size bed frame, Carrara marble tops on bureau and cupboard, price for suite, mirrored bureau: 55-1/2" w, 24" d, 87-3/4" h; two-door cupboard: 38" w, 17-1/2" d, 32" h; commode: 19-1/2" w, 18-1/4" d, 31-1/2" h 8,500.00

Art Deco

Bedroom furniture from the Art Deco period flows in form. Look for curvilinear surfaces and new types of hardware, such as catalin.

Rohde, designed by Gilbert Rohde, c1933, manufactured by Herman Miller, Zeeland, MI, suite with tall 47" h dresser, mirrored 33" h dresser with catalin pulls, 56" w bed with curvilinear foot board, 14-1/2" d circular night stand, blond finish, some tubular metal supports, sgd by designer and manufacturer 4,890.00

Art Nouveau

Little true American Art Nouveau furniture exists. This example shows how the French influenced and dominated the Art Nouveau furniture market.

Marjorelle Louis, France, c1900, carved and inlaid mahogany, arched headboard with whiplash carved and molded corners, footboard with molded panels, both inlaid with various woods, mother-of-pearl, and copper, stylized poppy blossoms and undulating foliage, 85" l, 69" w, 71-3/4" h 15,500.00

Arts & Crafts

Arts & Crafts beds were typically solid slats with a simplistic look to them. Very little ornamentation is allowed in this design style.

Limbert, Charles P., Grand Rapids and Holland, Michigan, No. 471, alternating wide and narrow slats, orig medium dark brown finish, branded mark, 56-1/2" w headboard.....................3,000.00

McHugh, gatepost headboard and footboard, keyed-through tenon stretchers, orig dark finish, diamond shaped metal tag, single size, 41-1/2" w, 76" l, 38" h 750.00

Arts & Crafts, full size, Gustav Stickley, No. 923, tapered posts, rounded top rail, five broad vertical slats on headboard and footboard, orig finish, branded mark, 78-1/2" l, 56-3/4" w, 48" h, $6,500; leaning at back: three-quarter size, L. & J. G. Stickley, tall tapering posts, six vertical slats on headboard and footboard, orig finish, marked, 84-3/4" l, 51-3/4" w, 54" h, $3,000. Photo courtesy of David Rago Auctions/RagoArts.com, Lambertville, NJ, Lambertville, NJ.

Stickley, Gustav, New York

No. 912, paneled, peaked rail with bowed sides, orig finish, red decal, minor repair to leg, 58" w, 80" d, 51" h...............................7,500.00

No. 923, c1909, full size, tapered posts, rounded top rail, five broad vertical slats to head and footboard, fine orig finish, branded mark, 56-3/4" w, 78-1/2" l, 48" h..........6,500.00

Harvey Ellis design, maple, paneled headboard and footboard, inlaid pewter and hardware design at top and sides, some wear to orig finish, 58" w, 50" h........................9,900.00

Mahogany, "V" crest rails over paneled head and foot board, bowed legs, orig finish, some alligatoring, large red decal, double size, 58" w, 51" h...3,200.00

Twelve spindles under double horizontal top rail at headboard and footboard, branded mark, orig finish, full size, 57" w, 79" l, 49" h.............2,860.00

Stickley, L. and J. G., Fayetteville, New York, three-quarter size, tall tapering posts, six vertical slats to head and foot boards, orig finish, marked, 51-3/4" w, 84-3/4" l, 54" h......3,000.00

Unknown Designer

Arched top rail, wide vertical slat at center flanked by two slats on each side, orig finish, 55" w, 76" l, 56" h 450.00

Oak, full size, five vertical slats at headboard and footboard, orig varnish, 78" l, 57" w, 48" h..850.00

Quarter-sawn oak, three vertical panels in head and foot board, 42" x 53" h headboard, 34-1/2" h footboard............................375.00

Trundle, in style of early Gustav Stickley, slatted back and sides, orig finish, new futon, unmarked, 78" l, 31" d, 33-1/2" h.....5,000.00

Biedermeier

This European style is included as many Biedermeier beds are found in America. Look for curved surfaces and fine woods and veneers.

European, figured mahogany veneer, octagonal posts, turned feet and finials, paneled head and footboards, orig rails, some veneer damage, 38" w, 72" l, 45" h, pr...............750.00

Charles X

This English design period is included as later Victorian adaptations of the sleigh bed are fre-

quently found in the antiques marketplace. Sleigh beds are also popular with today's furniture designers.

English, c1830, sleigh, mahogany, outscrolled headboard and footboard joined by veneered stretcher, block feet, 72" w, 44-1/2" w, 42" h 1,200.00

Chippendale

Most beds found in the Chippendale style are almost plain compared to the case furniture of this period. Chippendale was popular when decorating styles still used elaborate bed hangings.

America, tall post, curly maple, turned posts, scrolled headboard with poplar panel, orig side rails, old mellow refinishing, minor repairs to posts, 60" w, 72" l, 80" h 3,000.00

Ohio, rope, cherry, turned posts with ball finials, scrolled headboard with turned crest, orig rails, cleaned down to old mellow finish, 76-1/4" l, 59-3/4" h 1,210.00

Rhode Island, 18th C, tall post, mahogany, octagonal headposts with lamb's tongue detail continue to sq legs flanking angled headboard joined to fluted and stop-fluted footposts which include lamb's tongue detailing above sq legs joined by rails fitted for roping, accompanying tester frame and bed bolts, old refinish, imperfections, 85" l, 55" w, 79" h..................2,300.00

Chippendale-Style

For compression purposes, here is an example of a modern Chippendale copy and what it sold for at auction recently.

Drexel, mahogany, four poster, carved, 86-1/2" l, 65" w, 67-1/2" h......................850.00

Classical

The Classical period was between c1800 and c1830 and it allowed furniture makers to embrace new curves, scrolls and a much more elaborate design style. More attention was paid to the woods used, the carvings are becoming more realistic and numerous during this style.

Massachusetts, c1825, carved mahogany, vase and ring-turned spiral acanthus leaf and pineapple carved posts, block turned legs, jointed to plain turned tapering head posts, shaped headboard, old refinish, rails extended in length, 78" l, 53" w, 62-1/2" h 1,925.00

Classical, New England, c1830, tiger maple, four vase and ring-turned posts, joined by scrolled headboard and vase and ring-turned foot rail, old refinish, side rails replaced, 52" w, 81-1/2" l, 46" h, $1,850. Photo courtesy of Skinner Auctioneers and Appraisers of Antiques and Fine Art Boston and Bolton, MA.

Massachusetts, c1825-35, carved mahogany, tall post, scrolled mahogany headboard flanked by reeded, carved, and ring-turned posts, acanthus leaf, beading, gothic arches, and foliage carving, reeded and turned feet, orig rails later fitted for angle irons and bed bolts, orig surface, central finial missing, 81" l, 59" w, 98" h...6,900.00

Middle Atlantic States

c1820, post, tall, spiral carved footposts with classical acanthus leaves and beading above dies and turned feet, red painted headposts flank similarly painted scrolled headboards, orig rails with minor additions, tester missing, 78-3/4" l, 55-7/8" w, 81-3/4" h..2,500.00

c1835-45, carved mahogany veneer, low post, scrolled and paneled headboard, leaf carved finials flanked by posts with pineapple finials, acanthus leaves above spiral carved and ring-turned posts, orig rails, bed bolts, and covers, refinished, imperfections, 78" l, 58-1/2" w, 56-1/2" h................1,100.00

c1835-45, carved mahogany veneer, tall post, four turned, carved, and reeded posts continuing to turned feet on castors, flanked by scrolled recessed panel headboard with rolled veneered crest, shaped footboard, joined by flat tester, rails with added angle irons, old refinish, height loss, 61-1/2" w, 72" d, 77-1/2" h..............................2,550.00

New England, c1820, painted, turned tall post, turned and tapering headposts flanking shaped headboard, spiral carved footpost joined by rails fitted for roping, accompanying tester, old red paint, restored, 79" l, 54" w, 60-1/2" h..1,400.00

New England, c1830, tiger maple, four ball top vase and ring-turned posts, joined by scrolled paneled head and footboards, old refinish, side rails replaced, 76" l, 45" w, 43-3/4" h..1,725.00

New England, c1830, tiger maple, four vase and ring-turned posts, joined by scrolled headboard and vase and ring-turned footrail, old refinish, side rails replaced, 81-1/2" l, 52" w, 46" h..1,850.00

New York, c1820-30, carved mahogany veneer, crest rails and supports with water-leaf carving above veneered paneled section over foliate carved ball feet, casters, refinished, 73" l, 33" w, 37" h 2,400.00

Colonial Revival

Colonial Revival is a generic term used to describe furniture that was made to reflect back on styles of the colonial era, but many are not true and incorporate some modern elements. The example included here uses a simple headboard, but the mattress is supported by bed rails, not a rope network.

America, c1920-30, Hepplewhite-style, mahogany, satinwood inlay, bulbous center splat flanked by six slender shaped slats on crested headboard, matching footboard 500.00

America, early 19th C, figured and bird's eye maple, youth, low posts, paneled headboard and footboard, side rails missing, 70" l, 51" w, 42" h..200.00

Cottage

Cottage is a term referring to wonderful American painted furniture that exhibits some ties to Victorian, but dating these pieces is often difficult because not all the expected design elements are present. And, since the pieces are valued for their painted decoration, it is often difficult if not impossible to determine the base wood. Cottage-style bedroom suites show the value of keeping a suite together, adding to the dollar value and preserving a style that was sold as a suite, not individual pieces.

America, suite consisting of double bed, bureau with mirror, wash stand, night stand, chair, and rocker, all grain painted in mustard yellow, with dark brown grained panels decorated with yellow daisies, green leaves, reddish brown scrolled dec, teardrop pulls, some imperfections......................................1,600.00

Country

Country beds are one type of American furniture where always determining the exact style or time of construction is not possible. And, it is also helpful to understand that a lot of rural craftsmen made furniture to design styles they developed rather than their city cousins who used patterns and pattern books.

New England, c1800, block turned posts, painted birch, urn finials, swelled turned legs, peaked headboard, block ring-turned swelled footposts, old red-orange mottled paint, 75" l, 41-1/2" w, 35" h......................................600.00

New England, c1800, block turned headposts, turned slight swelled legs, peaked headboard, low footposts, old red paint, 76" l, 53-1/4" w, 34-1/2" h..............................1,200.00

Pencil Post, walnut, scalloped head and footboards, orig rails and canopy frame, 46-1/2" x 65" mattress size, 76-1/2" h..................4,200.00

Poster, cherry and poplar, America, second quarter 19th C, scrolling headboard, pair of panels supported by turned posts, orig rope posts, 74" l, 53" w, 64" h 450.00

Rope

Curly maple, light natural refinishing, replaced side rails, 47" x 74" mattress size, 54-1/2" h..1,600.00

Curly maple, turned posts and crest rails, paneled head and footboards with raised walnut panel, old varnish finish, replaced walnut side rails, 72" l, 51-1/2" w, 42" h 750.00

Maple and curly maple with good figure, headboard with cutout ends and shaped corners, turned blanket bar on footboard, well turned posts with cannonball finials, turned legs, old worn finish, orig rails, 69" l, 51-1/2" w 775.00

Maple and poplar, light curl in turned posts, goblet finials, refinished, side rails replaced, 76-1/2" l, 52-1/2" w, 44-1/2" h 125.00

Maple, tightly figured, cutout ends on headboard, turned blanket rail footboard, tapered legs and posts with well turned trumpet finials, poplar secondary wood, old worn finish, glued repair to one finial, 69" l orig rails, 47-1/2" w 495.00

Pine, poplar, and maple, turned posts, ball finials, old varnish finish, orig rope pins cut flush with rails, side rails extended, single size, 76" l, 41" w, 33-1/2" h 95.00

Poplar and hardwood, turned posts, trumpet finials, high feet, shaped headboard, blanket rail on footboard, refinished, replaced steel side rails, 76" l, 58-1/2" h 300.00

Poplar, old red paint, turned posts with cannonball finials, paneled headboard with scrolled detail and turned finials, footboard posts cut down, extended orig rails, 78" l, 54-3/4" w, 53" h 750.00

Poplar, turned posts, peaked headboard, pine side rails, red stain, 70-1/2" l, 52-1/2" w mattress, 41-1/2" h, ... 195.00

Poplar, turned posts with elongated ball finials, shaped headboard, blanket roll on footboard, engraved brass plate "Made in 1842 by Matthew Patton for Unity Patton Meharry, Wingate Indiana," old dark refinishing, replaced rails, 75" l, 53-3/4" w, 57" h 375.00

Shaker, mid 19th C, maple, shaped headboard, sq tapering legs, wooden wheel casters, painted green, 74" l, 35-1/2" w 1,750.00

Empire

Empire and Classical are two very similar styles, occurring about the same time frame. Empire often has a more country feel to it which Classical is truer to the European styles of the day. Beds of this era are massive, highly carved, and of fine woods.

These examples of Empire beds were all made in America about 1840.

Canopy, four poster, mahogany, carved acanthus and reeded posts, curved top headboard, 42" w, 87" h 700.00

Empire, 19th C, Zoar, OH, turned posts, scrolled headboard, orig rope rails, only headboard shown, $700.

Full Tester, mahogany, typical manufacture for Southern market, molded tester supported by tapering octagonal posters, paneled headboard with scrolled pilasters, 76" l, 65" w, 104" h 7,000.00

High Poster, birch, rope and acanthus carved turned posts, orig rope rails, arched canopy frame, 72" l, 55" w, 66-3/4" h 1,750.00

Tall Post, curly maple posts, poplar scrolled headboard with old soft finish, turned detail, acorn finials, rails and headboard replaced, 72-1/2" l rails, 57-1/4" w, 89" h 1,650.00

Empire-Style

Beds in the Empire-Style are characterized by some elements taken from the Empire designs, but also more modern elements, like cannon balls.

Cannonball, mahogany, bold detail, replaced headboard with carved eagle, originally rope bed, side rails changed, other repairs, replaced rails, 78" l, 54" w, 59" h 1,200.00

Tall Post, Dauler, Close & Johns, Pittsburgh, PA, early 20th C, deeply carved foliate and turned posts, front posts terminate in paw feet, shaped headboard and foot board, 63-1/2" l, 60" w, 54-1/2" h headboard, 74-1/2" h posts...................................750.00

Tall Post, mahogany, headboard with floral and scroll carved crest flanked by acanthus carved posts, 83" l, 64"w, 99-1/4" h 1,100.00

Federal

Beds from the Federal period are somewhat more decorative than Chippendale, but also still refined. However, bed hangings of this period are becoming a little shorter and more of the elegant posts are being exposed. And, now these sur-

Federal, Massachusetts, Salem, 19th C, carved mahogany veneer, tall post, mahogany veneered flat tester with central rectangular tablets and ovolo corners, spiral and leaf-carved footposts, turned red painted headposts flanking scrolled headboard, some old refinish and height loss, 52" w, 76-1/2" l, 89" h, $4,900. Photo courtesy of Skinner Auctioneers and Appraisers of Antiques and Fine Art Boston and Bolton, MA.

faces can be carved and inlaid, showing signs of wealth in the bed as well as the bed linens.

America, c1810, mahogany, tester, molded shaped rectangular tester, four turned reeded uprights, shaped rectangular headboard, straight side rails, ring-turned cylindrical legs, 77" l, 56-1/2" w, 81-1/2" h.....................2,400.00

America, c1850, tiger maple, four poster, ball finial over ring and spiral turned posts, straight side rails..2,400.00

America, first quarter 19th C, butternut, tester, arched headboards, tapering posts, turned tapering legs, price for pair, twin size, 67" h..1,400.00

America, first quarter 19th C, carved walnut, pencil post, scalloped head and footboards, orig rails and canopy frame, 65" l, 46-1/2" w, 76-1/2" h..4,500.00

America, first half 19th C, cherry, tester, three-quarter, rectangular headboard with

Federal, Massachusetts, Salem, c1820-30, carved mahogany veneer, tall post, reeded posts with leaf carving above turnings punctuated with neoclassical beading over carved Gothic arches and leaves on figured mahogany veneer dies above ring-turned tapering legs, old refinish, height loss, foot board shown, 55-3/4" w, 58" d, 79" h, $6,325. Photo courtesy of Skinner Auctioneers and Appraisers of Antiques and Fine Art Boston and Bolton, MA.

concave side edges, footboard lower, baluster-turned posts continuing to turned legs, rails with rope pegs, 81-1/2" l, 53-1/2" w, 78-1/4" h 500.00

America, first quarter 19th C, mahogany, tester, simple turned post plain headboard, acanthus carved and reeded turned post footboard with some inlay, spade feet, two sets of rails, 66" w, 84" h..................................5,250.00

America, first quarter 19th C, carved walnut, tester, reeded tapering leaf-capped posts rising from reeded urn, square-section pedestal raised on molded plinth base, tester, 82-1/2" l, 58-1/2" w, 83" h....................................4,250.00

Country, c1810, softwood, paneled headboard, low posts with turned acorn finials, 41-1/2" w, 43" h...................................650.00

Maryland or Pennsylvania, c1800, mahogany, tester, large simple turned post, scalloped headboard, large reeded and leaf carved turned post footboard, 58" w, 88" h..........................4,950.00

Massachusetts, c1810-15, carved mahogany, tall post, vase and ring-turned reeded leaf-carved footposts continuing to square tapering spade-footed legs, joined to square tapering maple headposts, shaped headboard, 70" l, 50" w, 89-1/2" h....................................2,100.00

Massachusetts, Salem, c1810-30, carved mahogany, tall post, flat tester frame joining vase and ring reeded and swelled acanthus leaf carved footposts, sq tapering legs, molded spade feet, leaf carved vase and ring reeded and swelled headposts, shaped headboard, old finish, 78-1/2" l, 62" w, 87" h 10,925.00

Massachusetts, Salem, c1820-30, carved mahogany veneer, tall post, reeded posts with leaf carving above turnings punctuated with neoclassical beading over carved Gothic arches and leaves on figured mahogany veneer dies above ring-turned tapering legs, old refinish, height loss, 58" l, 55-3/4" w, 79" h..............................6,325.00

Massachusetts, Salem, 19th C, carved mahogany veneer, tall post, mahogany veneered flat tester with central rectangular tablets and ovolo corners, spiral and leaf-carved footposts, turned red painted headposts flanking scrolled headboard, some old refinish and height loss, 76-1/2" l, 52" w, 89" h..4,900.00

New England, c1800, mahogany, carved and inlaid, tall post, orig rails, replaced testers, refinished, restoration, 54" w, 87" h..............2,950.00

New England, c1815-20, birch, tall post, turned tapering headposts joining to shaped headboard, vase and ring-turned reeded footposts, old refinish, alterations to posts, 68" l, 48" w, 69-1/2" h....................................1,955.00

New England, c1820, painted red, tall post, vase and ring turned and reeded footposts joined to turned headposts and shaped pine headboard, arched canopy frame, old red stain, minor imperfections, 69" l, 48" w, 75" h............2,750.00

New England, c1820, tester, maple, foot posts with carved ring-turned swelled reeded posts joined to more simply turned head posts, refinished, 75-1/2" l, 51" w, 58-1/2" h.....900.00

New England, early 19th C, mahogany, tall post, square tapering headposts flank shaped headboard joined to footposts by rails fitted for roping, flat tester frame, refinished, restored, 78" l, 58" w, 86" h................................2,100.00

New England, early 19th C, painted low post, folding, turned headposts planking shaped headboard, joined to footposts by joined rails fitted for roping and folding, old Spanish brown paint, 77-1/2" l, 52-3/4" w, 33-1/2" h...700.00

Southern, 19th C, tall post, carved mahogany, four reeded tapering tall posts with tapering tall posts with carved wrapped leafage above stylized pineapple carving flanking serpentine headboard, sq tapering fluted and stop fluted legs joined to front posts by molded rails fitted for roping, accompanying tester and bolt covers, old surface, minor imperfections, added angle irons and mattress supports, 78" l, 52-1/4" w, 90" h...................................9,200.00

Federal-Style

The examples shown here include elements found in Federal beds, but are made of woods not usually associated with this period.

Pencil post, hardwood and poplar, old reddish finish, shaped headboard, canopy frame with old worn crewel trim, 72" l, 51" w, 84" h..........220.00

Tester, maple, walnut, and yellow pine, slightly arched headboard raised on square-section tapering posts, four turned posts, tapering and ring-turned, serpentine profile tester, 79-3/4" l, 58" w, 85-1/2" h 1,380.00

Tester, turned and reeded posts, central shell carving with foliage decoration on either side of top of headboard, paneled footboard and headboard with rope edge borders, 82" l, 61" w, 84-1/2" h posts,. 70" h headboard 600.00

George III

An English style from c1800 included here to show the difference between what was being offered as English bed styles compared to the plainer American styles of the day, like Chippendale or Federal.

English, four poster, carved walnut, brass mounted, circular tapered headposts, shaped mahogany headboard, reeded and acanthus-carved footposts, ring-turned feet, casters, 9-1/2" h....................................10,000.00

Hepplewhite

Country, tall post, maple posts, pine headboard, sq tapering posts, orig side rails, refinished with cherry stain, replaced tester frame, 70-3/4" l, 50" w, 75-1/2" h.......................1,350.00

Jenny Lind

This style of rope bed was named in honor of the singer. The name implies spool turned posts, legs, and other decoration. It was a common form of bed, available in several sizes. Some hardwood examples exist, but many were painted disguising the lesser expensive woods used.

Adult's, poplar and hardwood, old cherry-colored finish, tall post, replaced rails, posts have been cut off and reattached, single size, 76" l, 42" w, 69-1/2" h.......................................120.00

Baby's, walnut, old worn finish, turned posts with spool turned details, slats replaced with solid wood board, 38" l, 20-1/2" w, 30" h 115.00

Low Post

A bed to serve the purpose of providing a place to sleep was often adequate for early settlers. These beds were made low and compact and could be disassembled or moved out of the way in small quarters.

New England, northern, c1825-35, grain painted, scrolled head and foot boards flanked by ball topped ring-turned posts ending in ring-turned tapering legs, overall graining simulating rosewood highlighted with gilt stenciling and striping, old surface, minor height loss, 79" l, 52-1/4" w, 45-1/2" h headboard, 46-1/2" h footboard..1,495.00

New England, early 18th C, birch, block turned tapering legs joined by shaped headboard, shorter conforming turned footboard, orig red paint, 75-1/2" l, 49" w, 39-1/4" h 900.00

New England, early 19th C, shaped headboard with orig rails, hinged for folding, attached to footposts with conforming carving, turned finials and legs, orig red paint, rails fitted for roping, very minor imperfections, 74" l, 49-3/4" w, 35-1/2" h................................800.00

Pennsylvania, c1840, posts with acorn turned finials continuing to bulbous vase and ring-turned posts joined by shaped headboard with turned spindles, blanket rail at foot, 72-1/2" l, 58" w, 51" h...........................1,200.00

Pennsylvania, late 18th or early 19th C, walnut, cylindrical turned short headposts, ball-turned finials, center arched headboard, turned tapering legs, conforming footposts and footboard, rails, later hardware added to support box spring, 73-1/4" l, 49-3/4" w, 31" h 725.00

Pennsylvania, early 19th C, dark green and red painted maple and poplar, ball finials on turned posts, centering pitched headboard, shaped footboard, tall turned tapering legs, 47-1/2" h...800.00

Pennsylvania, Berks County, first half 19th C, turned and stained, poplar, ball finials, reel and vase-turned supports centering shaped head and footboard on tall tapering reel and vase-turned legs, peg feet, matching trundle bed with ball finials, similar turnings, centering plain head and footboard, ball feet, 48" w bed...............3,200.00

Mission

Frank Lloyd Wright designed furniture as well as homes. This example shows his desire to provide storage with a piece of furniture, giving it a dual purpose.

Frank Lloyd Wright, Heritage Henredon, No. 2004, mahogany, three sliding storage compartments, central panel having raised concentric rectangular design, Taliesin design to edge, orig finish, red monogram, numbered, king size, 79" l, 12" d headboard, 33" h 4,750.00

Modernism-Era

Beds from this era became quite a statement for the war era brides and their returning husbands. Bedroom suites of all shapes and materials were eagerly bought by the young newlyweds as they settled in their first homes. Furniture makers created styles to reflect the new industrial spirit.

Dunbar, Berne, IN, single size, post war
  Head and foot board comprised of bent wood in zig-zag pattern between slender crest rail and two wide cross rails, leather capped feet, light brown finish, metal tag, single size, 41-1/2" w, 37" h................300.00
  Walnut, curved rect head and foot board joined by three horizontal cross stretchers, medium brown finish, metal tag, 42" w, 38" h 200.00
Nakashima, George, c1957, walnut, headboard block, dovetailed, two sliding doors, flush tenons and dowels, orig finish, 74"n l, 60" w, 46" h 7,550.00
Nelson, George, Thin Edge, manufactured by Herman Miller, birch frame, orig woven caned headrest, white enameled metal legs, 77" l, 38" w, 34" h 4,750.00
Plymodern Furniture, Plywood Corporation, Lawrence, MA, post World War II, suite of four

Modernism-Era, suite, designed by Gilbert Rohde, manufactured by Herman Miller, Zeeland, Michigan, c1933, tall dresser, mirrored dresser with catalin pulls, 56" w bed with curvilinear footboard, circular 14-1/2" d nightstand, all in blonde finish, some with tubular metal supports, signed by designer, manufacturer's label, $4,900. Photo courtesy of Skinner Auctioneers and Appraisers of Antiques and Fine Art Boston and Bolton, MA.

pieces, double bed, large and small chest of drawers, night stand, curvilinear design, inset drawer pulls, color enhanced reddish brown finish, decal mark, minor wear 825.00
Robsjohn-Gibbings, T. H., manufactured by Widdicomb, headboard only, walnut veneer frame, rattan and brass wrapped edge, 80" w, 36" h..200.00
Rohde, Gilbert, manufactured by Herman Miller, suite, ash veneer, leatherette wrapped pulls, two twin beds, cabinet: 30" w, 18" d, 38" h, vanity: 50" w, 16" d, 27" h, pair night stands: 14" w, 12" d, 24" h, stool: 24" w, 18" d, 17" h..1,400.00

Queen Anne

Queen Anne is another simple period for bed styles. Most bed frames were hidden by the ornate hangings.

New England, c1725-1780, field, tester, mahogany and maple, very simple flat board headboard, no footboard, just rail with rope buttons, cabriole legs, pad feet 6,000.00
  Pennsylvania, early 19th C, low poster, turned and painted pine, head and footposts with flattened ball finials, shaped head and footboards, tapered feet, orig rope rails, orig green paint, 48-1/2" w, 74-3/4" h.........3,600.00

Shaker

Shaker furniture is best described as simple, with clean lines. Their beds reflected this style.

New England, first half 19th C, maple and pine, four block turned legs joined by shaped head and foot boards and straight sides, old refinish, 64" l, 29" w, 30-1/4" h 700.00

Sheraton

The Sheraton period from c1790 to c1810 also saw a simple design time for beds. Posts are slender, headboards somewhat plain, and any carving is often found at the foot end on the footposts. Why, again the bed linens were becoming less important, often pulled back to expose the lovely carving.

Canopy
  Carved mahogany, headboard posts simple turned with ring and block turnings, simple headboard, heavily carved footboard posts with spiral turnings and acanthus leaf

bell, sq tester with curtains, 73-1/2" l, 58" w, 88" h without finials..........................3,200.00

Cherry, turned posts and foot rail, shaped headboard, orig canopy and tester......1,500.00

Maple, pine headboard, tapering head posts, turned foot posts, curved canopy frame, refinished, orig rails extended, minor age cracks, 77" l, 54" w, 59" h.........1,750.00

Painted, headboard with D-type cut outs on side, footboard with reeded and turned posts, canopy frame, painted red, 76" l, 52" w, 68" h...750.00

Rope, c1825, maple, goblet finials, side rails, 54" w, 57" h...............................425.00

Tall Post, refinished maple an birch, pine headboard, turned posts with reeded detail on footposts, rope end rails, replaced side rails, curved canopy frame covered in white cotton with floral embroidery, matching bed clothes included, 78" l, 55" w, 66-3/4" h 1,550.00

Tall Post

Like low posts, tall post beds are simple in design. Their name is derived from the high posts found at each corner of the bed, some held tester frames, others were used to simple hold up plain linens or netting.

New England, early 19th C

Birch, four rect tapering posts continuing to sq legs joined by molded peaked headboard and flat tester frame, old surface, 71" l, 51" w, 81" h 17,250.00

Cherry, c1825, four vase and ring turned posts continuing to block vase-turned tapering feet, joined by straight tester frame, scrolled headboard, old refinish, 70" l, 45" w, 90" h 1,955.00

Cherry, four octagonal tapering pencil posts continuing to sq tapering feet, joined by flat tester frame, shaped headboard, old finish, 70-1/2" l, 40-1/2" w, 81-3/4" h 4,200.00

Maple, vase and ring turned reeded tapering footposts joined to hexagonal tapering headpost and arched headboard by straight tester frame, old refinish, minor imperfections, 72" l, 36" w, 83" h...................4,000.00

Victorian

Leave it to the Victorians to ornately decorate their beds. During this time of flourishes and carvings in all furniture, beds grew in height and stature. Woods are generally dark and elaborately carved. Suites were elaborate with dressers with mirrors, chests of drawers, matching night stands, and chairs.

America, refinished walnut, paneled head and footboards with applied scroll and fruit detail, matching crest, orig 73" l side rails, 54" w, 71-1/2" h 450.00

Brass, c1900, straight top rail, curved corners, ring shaped capitals, cast iron side rails, 55" w, 61" h.............................1,200.00

Half Tester, attributed to Prudent Mallard, New Orleans, LA, c1850, carved rosewood, tall arched headboard, shell carved crest, fruit and nuts, scroll carved borders, shaped bordered panels flanked by tall tapering turned headposts supporting upholstered half tester, scroll carved crest, turned finials, paneled sideboards and footboard, turned and carved details, scroll carved corner braces..15,000.00

Eastlake, c1870, walnut and burl walnut veneer, spoon carving, incised lines, applied roundels, 83" l, 58" w.......................1,750.00

Gothic Revival, America, c1850, carved mahogany, tall headboard with three Gothic arch panels, leaf-carved crest rail, flanked by heavy round ribbed posts topped by ring-turned finials, arched and paneled footboard flanked by lower footposts, heavy bun feet 4,750.00

Renaissance Revival, America, c1875

Chestnut and walnut, four pieces, bed, marble-top chest, marble-top washstand, marble-top night stand, each with applied circular panels, case pcs fitted with carved wooden pulls, 81" l, 60" w, 60" h bed, 44" w, 21" d, 32" h chest, 33-1/2" w, 18" d, 29-1/2" h washstand, 19" w, 17" d, 29" h nightstand............. 1,650.00

Stained maple and burled maple, tester, arched headboard with center carved rosette above panel decoration with opposed wing griffins and floral scrolls, panel of suspended palmettos below, gilt incised half round pilasters flanking conforming footboard, side rails, posts, and rounded quarter canopy, minor restorations, headboard: 67" w, 72" h 7,500.00

Benches

Benches represent a form of furniture with many functions. Some benches were made for seating purposes, such as a church pew or window seat. Others were made to assist in the daily living tasks, such as a water bench, designed to hold buckets of water. Benches usually display the same furniture design elements as chairs or tables. Style identification is often attributed by either knowing the original function of the bench or studying the feet or arms.

As furniture styles became more upholstered, benches became settees and sofas, giving the user more comfort. While architectural styles often dictated furniture design, benches and chairs are good examples of how clothing styles affected furniture form. Large wide skirts, full of padding and underlayers didn't require as much padding on a piece of furniture. As clothing styles became sleeker, padding was added to benches in the forms of cushions and pillows.

See Hall and Hat Racks as well as Sofas for more related bench forms.

Church Pew

Collectors and interior decorators have often included former church pews and benches into their decor. Today these usually large benches are usually used for halls, entry ways, etc. Unlike other types of benches, their value is not usually great considering their age and skilled workmanship. However, when sold in the area where the church is known adds greatly to the provenance and value.

Church, carved oak, high back, added cushion, 48" w, 42-1/2" h, $275.

Country, cypress, Louisiana, 19th C, 108-1/2" l, 18" d, 37" h,.. 275.00

Federal, Quaker, attributed to Pennsylvania, early 19th C, flat seat, one board back, cutout ends, 112" l 300.00

Victorian, oak, carved element on high scrolled end, 144" l...............................350.00

Cobbler's

Using a cobbler's bench as a coffee table was a popular decorating scheme in the late 1950s and early 1960s. Today authentic cobbler benches are being recognized for their form, as well as historic significance. Look for signs of wear and usage to make sure a bench is authentic.

America, primitive, pine, varnished, replaced leather seat, replaced case of twelve drawers, under-slung drawer missing, fourteen orig cobbler's tools, 49" l......................................650.00

Conservatory

These benches were frequently used as seating in conservatories, sun rooms, or green house structures.

Victorian, c1880, pine, scalloped crest above spindled gallery, out-scrolled arms joined to plank seat, sq legs, 70-1/2" w, 18" d, 39" h......... 700.00

Country

No country look is complete without a bench. Many are available and come in all kinds of sizes and woods. Look for benches with good construction, appropriate wear, and at a price that suits your budget. Because benches were such a "hot" decorating accessory in the 1990s, many new benches have been made and artificially aged.

Pine, cutout ends mortised through top
Layers of old work repaint, 62-1/2" l, 12-3/4" w, 18-1/2" h 495.00

Old red paint, mortised bootjack ends, square nail construction, embossed "C—an, Dom" on end, 31-1/2" w, 9" d, 8" h 500.00

Old worn and weathered green repaint,

one board top with rounded front corners, beaded edge apron, cut-out feet mortised through top, age crack in one end of top, 104" l, 13-1/2" w 325.00

Original red paint, PA, early 19th C, 96" l, 18-1/4" w, 13" h, ...750.00

Refinished, 35-1/8" l, 12-1/2" w, 14" h...295.00

Poplar, beaded apron, mortised, bootjack ends, scrubbed top, green repaint, 39" l, 13-1/2" w, 18-1/2" h................................365.00

Walnut, curved front corners on seat, soft natural patina, water stains, 63" l, 13-3/4" d, 17-3/4" h..395.00

Hall

Hall benches were convenient places to sit and put on one's coat, boots, etc. Also see Hall Trees for more examples of types of furniture created for entry hall purposes.

Arts & Crafts
Limbert, No. 92, lift-seat, arched top rail and stretcher, six vertical back slats, orig finish, branded mark, 42" w, 18" d, 41-1/4" h......................................4,500.00

Stickley, Gustav, No. 224, paneled back over lift seat compartment, thick slab sides with oval cutout at top, through-tenon construction, refinished, minor repair to back, paper label, 48" w, 22" d, 42" h 5,500.00

Victorian, America, Monks, in the Mediaeval taste, carved poplar, hinged seat flanked by armrests in form of lidded compartments, tri-arched front carved with figural scenes, 42-1/2" w, 30-1/4" h................................475.00

Joint

A joint bench is one generally used to prop up the user's feet or legs. More European examples are found. Americans preferred the smaller stool type benches for the same purpose.

Jacobean Style, late 19th C, oak, rectangular molded top over molded and carved frieze, turned legs joined by stretchers, plain feet, 46" w, 12" d, 19-1/2" h............................700.00

Kneeling

Devote religious practices sometimes encourage the practice of kneeling. Special benches were made for this purpose. Like church benches, their appeal is somewhat limited.

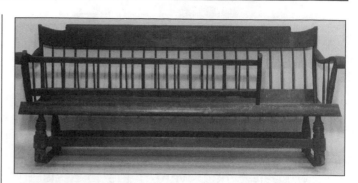

Mammy, Empire, dark finish, traces of orig decoration, spindle back and shaped crest, scrolled arms, "S" scroll seat, turned legs, removable body guard, 82" l, $1,100. Photo courtesy of Garth's Auctions, Inc., Delaware, OH.

Windsor, Country, gray over olive green and red paint, reeded edge top, bamboo-turned legs, splayed base, 36-3/4" l, 6-3/4" d, 6" h 350.00

Mammy

Called "Mammy" after the legions of wonderful women who looked after small children, this type of bench usually contains a small rail to hold in a small child.

Empire, dark finish, traces of orig decoration, shaped crest, spindle back, scrolled arms, boldly detailed with turned legs, "S" scroll feet, removable body guard, 82" l 1,100.00

Federal, New England, c1810, pine, spindle back, scrolled arms, 50" w, 14" d, 30" h 925.00

Windsor, painted black over red, gold stenciling, back crest with stenciled flowers, removable front gate, bench fitted with orig rockers, light brown painted scrolled arms, 48" w, 29-1/4" h...1,000.00

Seat-Type

Another use for benches is to provide seating. Often intended for outdoor use, today benches are finding their way into country homes. Many different design styles are available. Many furniture designers of the Modernism-Era preferred benches over chairs or sofas and fine examples exists from that period. Like the Country Benches listed here, be sure to check for signs of wear as many seating benches were created in the late twentieth century.

Arts & Crafts, Roycroft, Ali Baba, half ash log on keyed-through tenon, quarter-sawn oak trestle base with keyed through-tenon con-

Seat, Arts & Crafts, cast iron semi-circular frame, two bronze panels with Spanish galleons, seven bronze dragon ornamental corbels extend from frame to feet, one dragon missing, feet marked, "M. S. L. Co.," $815. Photo courtesy of Samuel T. Freeman & Co., Philadelphia, PA.

struction, orig finish, carved orb and cross mark, 42" w, 14-1/2" d, 19-1/2" h 13,500.00

Mission, oak, rectangular, flanked by high side rails with five narrow slats, joined by through tenons, lower horizontal stretcher, medium brown finish, edge wear, scratches, 26-3/4' l, 17" d, 28" h 575.00

Modernism Era

Bertoia, Harry, manufactured by Knoll, oak slats, wrought iron Y-base, label, 66" w, 19" d, 15" h 950.00

Frankl, Paul, manufactured by Johnson Furniture Co., cream lacquered cork top above dark mahogany Greek key base, wear to top, 84" w, 21" d, 12" h 2,500.00

Mourgue, Olivier, Djinn, manufactured by Airborne, c1965, tan stretch fabric over foam form, internal metal frame, 48" w, 24" d, 15" h 800.00

Seat, Arts & Crafts, Roycroft, Ali Baba, half ash log on keyed-through tenon, quarter-sawn oak trestle base with keyed through-tenon construction, orig finish, carved orb and cross mark, 42" w, 14-1/2" d, 19-1/2" h, $13,500. Photo courtesy of David Rago Auctions/RagoArts.com, Lambertville, NJ, Lambertville, NJ.

Nelson, George, manufactured by Herman Miller, slats

Birch wood top, ebonzied wooden legs, refinished, 48" w, 18" d, 14" h 1,200.00

Ebonized wooden top, ebonized wooden legs, 72" w, 19" d, 14" h 1,100.00

Robsjohn-Gibbings, T. H. manufactured by Widdicomb

Rectangular upholstered cushion, light walnut X-frame, some wear, 33" w, 18" d, 14" h 775.00

Walnut dowel X-frame, orig tufted green fabric seat, 34" w, 14" d, 22" h............950.00

Unknown Designer, 1940s custom made, upholstered form

Original blue lacquered wood base, needs to be reupholstered, 60" w, 19" d, 16" h...950.00

Rectangular tufted seat, curved dowel legs, orig blue lacquer, needs to be reupholstered, 29" w, 19" d, 17" h 300.00

Unknown Designer, 1960s custom design, tufted tan Naugahyde seat, angular chrome base, 72" w, 20" d, 18" h 700.00

Wormley, Edward, manufactured by Dunbar

Caned seats, orig Larsen fabric cushions, bleached mahogany legs, brass frame, price for pair, 21" w, 17" d, 17" h 1,800.00

Reupholstered top in orange velvet, tapered bleached mahogany legs, unmarked, 40" w, 20" d, 25" h 775.00

Queen Anne-Style, mahogany, needlepoint over-upholstered seat, cabriole legs, pad feet, 23" l, 18" d, 12" h 250.00

Victorian

Gothic Revival, America, c1820-40, carved mahogany, angled over-upholstered seat, carved seat rails centering quatrefoil, facet lancet-carved legs, molded faceted feet, 65" l, 20" d, 15-1/2" h...............1,750.00

Renaissance Revival, America, c1875, satinwood, marquetry, gilt incised, upholstered seat......................................7,200.00

Wicker, painted white, hooped crest rail flanked by rows of dec curlicues, spiral wrapped posts and six spindles, pressed-in oval seat, dec curlicue apron, wrapped cabriole legs, X-form stretcher, 35" w, 31" h 500.00

Windsor, Pennsylvania-Style, deep seat, white cushion, half spindle back, shaped top crest, curved and scrolled arms, eight legs, box stretchers, medium to light brown finish, 19-1/2" d seat, 34" h 1,200.00

Settle

A settle is a wooden framed bench, sometimes found with a seat cushion. Again, they are found in numerous design styles, but often reflect simplicity and ease of use. As for the comfort level offered the user, that's often another matter. Today, settles are often found with more cushions and pillows to soften their lines and add to the comfort level.

Arts & Crafts

Lifetime, Puritan Line, drop-arm form, arched top rail, ten back slats, arched rail under each arm, long corbels on each leg, recovered leather cushion, refinished, paper label, 74" w, 30" d, 37" h......................995.00
    Limbert
        Ebon-oak, three caned panels at back, geometric design of inlaid ebony, caned sides, arched seat rail, new cane, refinished, branded mark, 72" w, 27" d, 39" h 2,750.00
        Oak, open-arm, vertical back slats, corbels, new upholstered drop-in seat cushion, two loose pillows, new finish, branded mark, 74-1/4" l, 26-1/2" d, 37" h 2,000.00
Roycroft, even arm form, two horizontal slats at back and sides, tapered posts, refinished, orb mark, 79" w, 24" d, 38" h...............3,300.00
Stickley Brothers, cube, vertical slats, new blue leatherette cushions, very light over-coat over orig finish, Stickley Bros Quaint metal tag, 76-3/4" l, 29-1/2" d, 31" h 2,300.00

Settle, Arts & Crafts, attributed to Charles Stickley, knock-down cube type, broad vertical slats, drop-in spring seat reupholstered in brown leather, orig finish, unmarked, 79" l, 27" d, 32-1/2" h, $3,000. Photo courtesy of David Rago Auctions/RagoArts.com, Lambertville, NJ.

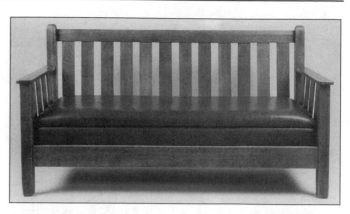

Settle, Arts & Crafts, unknown designer, c1916, oak, tapered posts, horizontal crest rail over twelve vertical back slats, flat arms over four vertical slats, cordovan colored simulated leather seat, storage box, new corner block supports, manufacturer's no. 331, light medium brown finish, wear, 72" w, 30" d, 39-3/4" h, $700. Photo courtesy of Skinner Auctioneers and Appraisers of Antiques and Fine Art Boston, and Bolton MA.

Stickley, Charles, knock-down cube, broad vertical slats, drop-in spring seat, reupholstered in brown leather, org finish, unmarked, 79" l, 27" d, 32-1/2" h 3,450.00
Stickley, Gustav
    No. 205, back with five wide slats, even arm with one wide slat, spring cushion seat, side rails with through tenons, red decal, sgd "Stickley," 56" w, 22" d, 30" h...........3,750.00
    No. 208, even arm form, three wide slats at side, eight back slats, through-tenon construction, replaced seat, over-coated finish with stained varnish, unsigned, 76" w, 32" d, 29" h 5,550.00
    No. 219, vertical bask slats, open arms, short corbels, skinned orig finish, red decal, 71-1/4" w, 26" d, 37-1/2" h...............2,000.00
    No. 225, even arm form, wide horizontal board at back, five slats under each arm, orig finish, sgd, 78" w, 32" d, 29" h 6,850.00
Stickley, L. and J. G.
    No. 229, even arm form, two slats under each arm, wide horizontal back slat, arched seat rail, orig finish, Handcraft decal, 72" w, 26" d, 35" h....................................2,900.00
    Broad vertical back and side slats, arched apron all around, new dark brown leather seat cushion, two matching throw pillows, orig dark finish, "The Work of L. and J. G. Stickley" decal, 72" l, 26" d, 36" h....................3,950.00
    Drop-arm form, twelve vertical back slats, drop-in cushion, recovered in brown

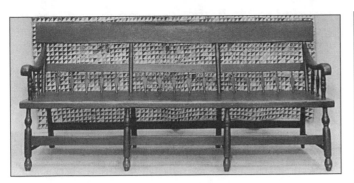

Settle, Windsor, arrow back, wide back crest, half arrow spindles, scrolled arms, plank seat, turned legs, olive green repaint, repairs, 73-1/2" l, $965. Shown in front of pierced quilt made of multicolored triangular pieces, $600. Photo courtesy of Garth's Auctions, Inc., Delaware, OH.

leather, refinished, unsigned, 65" w, 25" d, 36" h... 3,200.00
Unknown Designer

Mahogany, massive construction, through-tenon s at front and sides, seven wide back slats, two slats under arm, orig finish, 82" w, 27" d, 38" h...900.00

Oak, c1912, drop-arm, straight crest rail joining two posts tapered at top, over eleven vertical slats, flat arms tapering toward back over three vertical slats, spring cushion seat, cut-out front seat rail, medium brown, wear, scratches, 81" l, 28" d, 38" h 1,100.00

Oak, early 20th C, canted form, back with ten vertical slats, open arm sides with vertical slats, three plank seat, straight rails, slat repair, 72" w, 26-1/2" d, 36-1/2" h......1,610.00

Oak, early 20th C, rectangular top with raised edge, pierced and arched apron supported by side slabs, scrolled cut-outs at base, refinished top, orig finish to base, 42" w, 14" d, 18" h 1,600.00

Chippendale, Philadelphia, orig red and black graining, yellow and green striping, floral dec, turned legs, worn orig rush seat, scrolled arms, slat back, 48" l..........................1,500.00

Country

America, old mellow refinishing, brown stain, shaped crest, "S" curve arms, half spindle back, plank seat, turned legs, rungs, posts, and spindles, repairs, 71" l.......770.00

Canada, pine, paneled construction, shaped arms, turned spindles, shaped crest, folds open into bed, old worn finish, traces of paint, 68-1/2" l 600.00

Decorated, orig gray paint, light gray seat,

black and dark gray striping, stenciled and freehand flowers and fruit, angel wing crest designs, wide plank seat, S-curved arms, half-spindle back, shaped crest, turned legs and stretchers, minor repair to one arm, 80" l 2,400.00

Pennsylvania, early 19th C, painted yellow pine, rectangular back, hinged seat, straight skirt joining shaped arms, sides with exposed tenons on cutout demilunes, old green over earlier white paint, 60-1/2" l, 18" d, 34-1/2" h..................................2,415.00

Pennsylvania, late 19th C, painted, scalloped crest rail, plank seat, scrolled arms, stenciled black fruit and floral decorations, repainted, 81" l 1,500.00

Mission, Brooks, spindles with wide slats on back and sides, orig reupholstered drop-in spring seat, skinned finish, added braces, unmarked, 82" l, 28-1/2" d, 33-1/2" h........................3,375.00

Provincial, English, c1790 and later, pine, paneled back above wooden seat, one paneled side and on out-scrolled arm, plank legs, 86" w, 20" d, 34-1/2" h............................700.00

Wagon Seat

Wagon seats are a type of seating bench. And, as the name implies, many were actually used to provide more seating in the backs of open wagons. They often served double duty by residing on a porch or parlor until the next time they were required for a wagon. Usually they are found in double width, so that two people could be seated comfortably. The form is not as popular now, but sometimes are included in a country type decorating setting as a novelty.

Massachusetts, ladderback, orig green paint, slat back, shaped arms, replaced rush seat, back feet ended out, 34-1/2" w, 19" d, 30-3/4" h...950.00

New England, late 18th C, painted, two pairs of arched slats joining three turned stiles, double rush seat flanked by turned arms ending in turned hand-holds, tapering legs, old brown paint over earlier gray, 15" h seat, 30" h 1,200.00

Water

Water Benches are also referred to as Bucket Benches. Their name describes their function, as they were designed to hold buckets of water before indoor plumbing was the norm. Look for heavy signs of wear as these benches lived a hard life and were frequently painted.

Pine, attributed to New England, early 19th C, rectangular chamfered top above two short drawers, two shelves joining two cutout ends, old surface with vestiges of old red paint, minor imperfections, 55-1/2" w, 18" d, 40" h...... 4,025.00

Pine, attributed to New England, early 19th C, painted, traces of old red paint, shaped ends, imperfections, 47-1/2" w, 22-1/2" h shelf, 30-1/2" h... 1,825.00

Pine, old blue and green paint, cutout ends, base shelf, crest, 43" w, 18" d, 32-3/4" h.... 300.00

Pine, three tiered layers, refinished.... 300.00

Pine, two shelves, shaped ends, cutout feet, old worn blue paint, 30-1/2" l, 10-1/2" d, 36" h 2,250.00

Pine and birch, rectangular top, plain rails raised on stile ends, bifurcated feet, as found condition, 42-1/4" l 100.00

Shaker, Enfield, CT, oblong top, lead lined drain, straight sides, bootjack feet, orig brown stain finish, 49" l, 16-1/2' d, 33" h........ 1,120.00

Window

Deep windows have long been a favorite place for a seat. Today window benches are not just relegated to life by the window, but serve as seating. Many different types of design styles are available. A few European examples are

Water, country, mid-19th C, old worn blue paint, two shelves, square nail construction, half moon ends, $550. Also shown are assorted baskets and wooden bowls.

included to show the wide range of styles and prices for Window benches.

Classical

Boston, c1835-45, carved mahogany veneer, upholstered seat, veneered rail, leaf-carved cyma curved ends, joined by ring-turned medial stretcher, 48" w, 16-1/4" d, 17-1/2" h... 2,185.00

New England, c1825, rectangular seat with scrolled arms, straight frame and square legs, lacks upholstery, 64" w, 16-1/4" d, 30-1/2" h......................... 1,150.00

New York, c1815-25, mahogany veneer, curving upholstered seat flanked by scrolled ends, scrolled base, old refinish, some veneer cracking and loss, 20th C olive green velvet upholstery, 39-1/2" w, 14" d, 23-5/8" h... 3,500.00

New York, c1820, mahogany and mahogany veneer, upholstered slip seat, veneered rectangular frame, beaded curule legs joined by vase and ring-turned stretcher, old finish, 24-1/4" w, 15" d, 19" h...................... 1,035.00

Classical Revival, mahogany, carved paw feet and lion's heads, maroon velvet cushion, old finish, 16-1/2" l, 29-1/4" w, 23" h 600.00

Federal

New England, c1810, mahogany, upholstered seat and rolled arms, sq tapering legs, H-form stretchers, refinished, minor repair to one leg, 39-1/2" l, 16" d, 29" h.............. 900.00

New York, c1825, figured mahogany, each end with rectangular crotch-figured crest centering removable slip seat, matching seat rail, saber legs, 40-1/2" l.................. 3,500.00

George III, English, mid-18th C, mahogany, rectangular seat, scrolling arms, later velvet cov, straight legs, blind fret craved, H-form stretcher, pr, 38" l 4,750.00

Louis XVI-Style

Carved cherry, overstuffed seat, channeled rails, flanked by molded, overscroll arms carved with beribboned foliate sprays, turned, tapered, and leaf-capped legs............... 200.00

Mahogany, out-curved overscroll arms with X-splats, close-nailed, horsehair upholstered seat, sabre legs with castors, frame reeded and carved with paterae, brass plaque reading, "...Colonial Mft Co., Zeeland, Michigan".............................. 550.00

Blanket Chests

Blanket chests are functional and attractive pieces of furniture. Designed to hold blankets and other bed linens, they were also used as hope or dowry chests. Because of their large storage areas, they could hold a lot of quilts, linens, and other treasures to be used in a young couple's new home upon entering the marriage state. Some blanket chests feature drawers in the base. Many have a till or small box built inside. These tills generally were covered with lids. Some tills were outfitted with locks, and some even contain secret compartments.

The term "six-board construction" refers to the fact that simple blanket chests were often made from six-boards, one for the top, front, back, bottom, and sides. The wider the boards the furniture maker had available, the larger the chest. This type of construction often featured feet cut into the board, commonly referred to as "cutout" feet. Bootjack feet are another common name for a arched foot created by cutting away some of the board. Some six-board blanket chests have turned or bracket feet added at a later date in order to update the style, perhaps to increase height or often to repair damage caused by insects or dampness.

Today, decorators frequently include blanket chests in bedrooms, for storage and even seating. Historically this was true, but many blanket chests were stored in the attic until filled and ready for a child to leave home. While some cultures include the tradition of dowries for young ladies, many young men were sent into the world with a well-stocked blanket chest, too.

When purchasing a blanket chest, look for style, wood, and size. Because blanket chests were not opened every day, like a chest of drawers, expect to find little wear from usage. More likely, wear will be from moving the heavy chest. Many of the early decorated blanket chests have descended in families and are found with relatively bright paint and in good condition. Be sure to ask for the provenance of any decorated piece. Beware that some reproductions do exist and some older blanket chests, which may have had a plain painted surface, have been enhanced with folk art-type painting. Blanket chests found with a cedar lining are generally later. Care should be taken to see if the lining is a later addition. Also examine any hardware, locks, bale handles, etc. as replaced hardware will effect the price.

Also see Miniatures for examples of miniature blanket chests, now very sought after by collectors. Also see Chests, Other, for examples of mule chests, which are similar to blanket chests.

Adirondack

The furniture style known as Adirondack usually evokes an image of a cabin in the mountains. Rustic is another common name used to describe Adirondack furniture. Look for natural twigs, sometimes painted, but often in a form that appears as though the materials were gathered from the nearby forest and nailed together to create the furniture. This truly American style is from the early part of the 20th century.

New York, painted twigs, hinged top, front and side surfaces decorated with applied designs, shaped skirt, old light red paint, 33-3/4" w, 16-7/8" w, 23-1/2" h 750.00

Arts & Crafts

Blanket chests are not a common form in the Arts & Crafts period. Clothing storage was more likely to be a wardrobe or chest of drawers.

Stickley, Gustav, c1901-03, bride's, recessed panels, flat corbels, cast iron strap hinges, fine orig dark finish, large red decal, one corbel replaced, 35-1/4" l, 20-1/4" d, 18" h 25,760.00

Unknown Designer, recessed panels lined in dark brown Japan leather, raised handles, orig dark finish, cedar lined, unmarked, 45-1/4" l, 20" d, 18" h..1,400.00

Arts & Crafts, Gustav Stickley, c1901-03, bride's, recessed panels, flat corbels, cast iron strap hinges, fine orig dark finish, large red decal, one corbel replaced, 35-1/4" l, 20-1/4" d, 18" h, $25,760. Photo courtesy of David Rago Auctions/ RagoArts.com, Lambertville, NJ.

Detail of cast iron work on bride's chest shown above.

Chippendale

Blanket chests of this period, from c1755 to about 1790, represent a good example of a basic form with good storage. The cases are dovetailed, with any details kept simple.

America, walnut, two board top with minor warp, dovetailed case, three dovetailed drawers, apron drop, ogee feet, wrought iron hinges and till, pine and poplar secondary woods, old finish, replaced brasses, minor damage, some separation at seams, 50-3/4" l, 22-1/2" d, 36-1/2" h...3,200.00

Country, America, 19th C

Cedar, six-board dovetailed construction, thumb-molded lid, iron strap hinges, shaped plank feet, cracked bottom board, 44-3/4" l, 17" d, 44-3/4" h..................................490.00

Pine, molded rectangular and hinged top, storage well, front with two simulated drawer fronts over two drawers, molded surrounds, outset molded base with bracket feet, 37-1/2" l, 20" d, 41" h.........................750.00

Poplar, old worn reddish brown paint, dovetailed case, applied edge molding, well shaped dovetailed bracket feet, some edge damage, refinished lid, till lid repaired, 29" l, 14-1/2" d, 18" h...............................1,200.00

Walnut, poplar secondary wood, dovetailed case, two dovetailed overlapping low drawers, dovetailed bracket feet, molded edge till with lid, wrought iron bear trap lock and strap hinges, replaced drawer brasses, refinished, repairs, 48-1/2" l, 23-5/8" d, 26" h 3,300.00

Massachusetts, 18th C, pine, lift top, two faux drawers above two long drawers, bracket feet, refinished, 36" w, 20' d, 43-1/2" h........... 1,120.00

New England, northern, late 18th C, pine, old black paint, scalloped apron, bracket feet, old brasses, 24" w, 12" d, 23" h 6,000.00

Ohio, walnut, dovetailed case, front panel with chip carved floral design, traces of red, green, and yellow paint, old replaced turned feet, 41-1/2" w, 20-1/4" d, 26-1/4" h......6,500.00

Pennsylvania, c1780, pine, green and blue paint, one board top with breadboard ends, dovetailed case, applied lower molding, strap hinges, till with molded lid, ogee feet, 45" l, 19" d, 25-1/4" h 1,450.00

Country

Because many blanket chests were made to hold the hopes and treasures of people settling this great country, they were often made in a rather non-descript style that doesn't quite fall into any design style.

America, 19th C, pine, old red finish, molded edge with staple hinges, end boards with cutout feet, chestnut bottom board, till missing lid,

Painted, Pennsylvania, attributed to Lehigh County, pine and poplar, orig painted decoration, top and ends with brown vinegar graining, blue panel and red trim, blue front panel with stylized flowers and wreath in red and white, "Jong Breing 1776," brown feet and lid edge moldings, dovetailed case, dovetailed bracket feet, till with lid, wrought iron bear trap lock, strap hinges, 50" l, 23" d, 23-1/4" h, $30,250. Photo courtesy of Garth's Auctions, Inc., Delaware, OH.

wear and edge wear, 40" l, 14-1/2" d, 21-3/4" h...900.00

America, 19th C, white pine, hinged rectangular molded top, storage well with lidded till, molded base raised on turned short feet, 50" l, 21-3/4" d, 25-3/4" h 600.00

New England, early 19th C, pine, six-board dovetail construction, hinged top, opening to interior with till and drop panel and drawer, bracket feet, old surface, 39-1/4" l, 21" d, 21-1/4" h..500.00

New York State or Pennsylvania, second quarter 19th C, pine, early red paint, six-board construction, hinged top with molded edge, lidded till, molded base, shaped bracket feet, imperfections, 48" l, 21-1/2" d, 24-1/2" h 1,100.00

Pennsylvania, c1832, pine, robin's egg blue paint, dovetailed case, dovetailed bracket feet, wear and age cracks, repairs to lid at hinge rail, 42-1/4" l, 17-1/4" d, 19-3/4" h.................635.00

Pennsylvania, 19th C, pine, six-board construction, crab lock and strap hinges, interior glove box, two overhanging drawers, French bracket feet, 50" l, 22" d, 28" h............1,350.00

Virginia, c1826, walnut, two board top with applied molding, butt hinges, dovetailed case, base with applied moldings, scalloped dovetailed bracket feet, secret drawer in till, poplar secondary wood, refinished, 42" l, 20-1/2" d, 24-1/2" h...1,200.00

Decorated

Decorated blanket chests with original decoration in tact are the most desirable of the classification of blanket chests. However, the appeal and coloration of the decoration must appeal to the buyer today just as it did originally. Sometimes the name of the original owner is incorporated into the decoration. Do not be surprised to find a man's name as dowry chests were often created for young men, too. Finding a date helps to determine the age and often studying the lettering can yield clues as to the region of origin.

America, cherry and poplar, orig green paint, stenciled white, yellow, and red decoration, dated 1859, lid and base edge molding, dovetailed case, till with two drawers, turned removable feet, spring latches, minor wear, slight edge damage, 48-1/4" l, 20" d, 26-1/2" h.......2,000.00

America, pine, orig black flame graining, red ground, yellow initials "S. S." on lid, added penciled name on lid interior "Susan Stater 1826," beveled edge lid, till with lid, cutout feet, minor wear, 43" l, 16-12" d, 22-1/2" h 1,650.00

America, pine, orig vinegar graining, faded to olive and mustard yellow, black on bracket feet and edge molding, top edge shows orig unfaded red, dovetailed case, till with lid, wrought iron strap hinges and bear trap with key, penciled inscription on lid, 40" l, 18" d, 22-3/4" h...3,300.00

New England, c1820, four (two faux) full length overhanging drawers, shaped skirt, bracket feet, old red finish, 40-1/2" l, 17" d, 38-1/2" h..1,395.00

New England, early 18th C, pine and poplar, molded lift top above half rounded molded case, single drawer, bracket feet, orig paint, 36" w, 18-1/2" d, 37" h.........................4,750.00

New England, 18th C, pine, six-board construction, rectangular molded lift top, dovetail constructed box painted dark blue, front panel with symmetrical floral polychrome designs, imperfections, 42" l, 17" d, 16" h.........2,415.00

Ohio or Pennsylvania, c1840-50, walnut, white pine, poplar, and chestnut secondary woods, punched tulip decoration, painted dec and punched green and mustard highlights, six-board construction, dovetailed case, till with lid, single drawer, later turned feet, minor repairs, 39-3/4" l, 19-1/2" d, 25-1/4" h 3,500.00

Pennsylvania, attributed to Lehigh County, poplar, orig black paint, red trim, white letters "Regina Jaeckein 1805," dovetailed case, two dovetailed overlapping drawers, ogee feet, wrought iron strap hinges, bear trap lock with key, till with lid, three secret drawers, orig brasses, replaced escutcheons, 51-1/4" l, 23" d, 26-3/4" h 7,450.00

Pennsylvania, Berks County, early 19th C, pine and poplar, lift top, two drawers in base, four bracket feet, old green ground paint striped with red, three tablets, center one with uniform, tulips and vines dec on drawers, later paint, flaking, 43-1/2" l, 18-1/2" d, 38-1/2" h 1,265.00

Pennsylvania, Lebanon County, pine, orig painted dec, old repaint on lid and base molding, two arched panels on front in dark blue, pots of bright red and dark blue tulips and large red flowers, dark blue pillars, double hearts down corners, red turned feet, wrought iron strap hinges and bear trap lock, till, 52-1/2" w, 22-1/2" d, 25-3/4" h 1,870.00

Pennsylvania, Mahantango Valley, "Samuel Grebiel 1799," orig paint dec, red, blue, mustard, black, and white, two shaped polygons painted in blue grain painting, identical polygons on each side, two in front with banner above with name and date, interior lidded till, black painted dovetailed bracket base, off-set strap hinges, orig lock, 48-1/2" l, 21" d, 23-1/2" h 3,000.00

Pennsylvania, Pennsylvania German, painted, rectangular molded edge lift top lid, front with two dark panels and name "Anna Schultzin 1802," two drawers below, restored ogival bracket feet, 51-1/2" l, 22-1/2" d, 28-1/4" h 6,000.00

Pennsylvania, Perry County, c1825, dower, poplar dovetailed case, orig lime green rag dec, marked "S. Z."" on front, two bottom drawers, scalloped dovetailed bracket feet with applied wafers and black paint, reeded between drawers, crab lock, sgd "Sarah Zook Bakner" on back, 48" l, 24" d, 29" h 6,000.00

Pennsylvania, c1785, pine, orig blue paint, rectangular hinged lid, opening to well, case with mid-molding above three molded drawers,

molded base, ogee bracket feet, moldings highlighted in red, orig brass handles and escutcheon plate, 51" l, 22-1/2" d, 27-1/2" h 5,960.00

Pennsylvania, late 18th C, pine, orig paint, three tombstone decorated panels on front, one on each side, dovetailed case, bat-wing hinges, crab lock missing, orig feet, replaced till and patches, 52" l, 23" d, 22-1/2" h 1,400.00

Pennsylvania, pine, worn old dark blue and red, three painted panels with polychrome flowers, one board lid with mortised and tenon breadboard ends, molded edge, dovetailed case, till with lid and two drawers, shaped bracket feet, several old repaints, possible orig paint showing in some places, lock missing, wrought iron hinges, age cracks and edge damage, 49" w, 18-3/4" d, 24-1/4" h 1,375.00

Pennsylvania, pine and poplar, orig brown and blue vinegar graining, reserves on front, sides, and lid, front with white heart with star flowers and name and date in red and black, "Johan Witmer 1799," black moldings and feet, dovetailed case, ogee feet, applied case, lid, and base moldings, two dovetailed overlapping drawers, bear trap lock, wrought iron strap hinges, till lid and secret compartment with two dovetailed drawers, minor wear, edge damage, paint wear on lid, 51-1/4" l, 23" d, 27" h 25,000.00

Decorated, Pennsylvania, Soap Hollow, attributed to Jeremiah Stahl, poplar, orig red and green paint, yellow striping, silver and gold stenciled dec of stylized floral designs with birds, initials "S. H." and "1865," dovetailed case, lid edge molding, two dovetailed drawers, reeded molding, dovetailed bracket feet, interior till with lid, minor wear and edge wear, 49" l, 18-3/4" d, 24" h, $19,250. Photo courtesy of Garth's Auctions, Inc., Delaware, OH.

Decorated, Pennsylvania, Soap Hollow, poplar, orig red paint, black and yellow trim, gold stenciled decoration of foliage, flowers, and "Jeremias Wever, 1859, Mf by C. C. B.," dovetailed case with applied moldings, two dovetailed drawers, spacer between drawers with cutout painted yellow heart and circles on black, bracket feet, old glass pulls, replaced inlaid escutcheons, minor repairs to feet, some edge damage and wear, 47-1/2" l, 22-3/4" d, 28-1/2" h, $11,000. Also shown are two decorated boxes, left: pine, orig black case, geometric and floral dec, 15-3/4" w, 7-3/4" d, 6-1/4" h, $2,750; right: dome top, pine, old black repaint, yellow striping, 18" w, 9" d, 9" h, $11,000. Photo courtesy of Garth's Auctions, Inc., Delaware, OH.

Pennsylvania, pine and poplar, orig brown vinegar graining, blue and brown on feet and moldings, blue vinegar graining on drawers, corners picked out in white with black and red diamond design, dovetailed case with applied moldings, lid with applied edge molding, three overlapping dovetailed drawers, bracket feet, till with lid, bear trap lock with key, replaced brass pulls, some damage to feet, nailed repair, 50" l, 22-3/4" d, 28" h 9,900.00

Pennsylvania, pine and poplar, orig brown vinegar graining on yellowish ground, black painted lid edge molding and turned feet, dovetailed case, till with lid, 37-3/4' w, 18-1/4' d, 20-3/4" h 1,265.00

Pennsylvania, pine, old worn orig vinegar graining, tombstone panels, half and whole circles and compass stars in red and white, bluish-green ground, dovetailed case, lid edge and base moldings, turned feet, two dovetailed drawers in till, wrought iron strap hinges and bear trap lock with key, old label on back "H. Sowers, Crestline, Oh," 51-1/2" l, 21-1/2" d, 25-1/2" h 2,200.00

Pennsylvania, pine, orig paint, red and green flat panels with brown grained stiles and rails to resemble curly maple, red lid with green trim, red bracket feet with green trim, till with lid, minor edge damage, one front foot facing damaged, found in Johnstown area, 48-1/2" l, 21" d, 25" h...4,400.00

Pennsylvania, poplar, orig red flame graining, dovetailed case, edge molding on lid and base, turned feet, till with walnut lid, edge damage, lock missing, some wear, 37" l, 18-1/4" d, 23" h..675.00

Pennsylvania, Soap Hollow, poplar, orig red paint, black and yellow trim, gold stenciled decoration of foliage, flowers, and "Jeremias Wever, 1859, Mf by C. C. B.," dovetailed case with applied moldings, two dovetailed drawers, spacer between drawers with cutout painted yellow heart and circles on black, bracket feet, old glass pulls, replaced inlaid escutcheons, minor repairs to feet, some edge damage and wear, 47-1/2" l, 22-3/4" d, 28-1/2" h 11,000.00

Pennsylvania, Soap Hollow, attributed to Jeremiah Stahl, poplar, orig red and green paint, yellow striping, silver and gold stenciled dec of stylized floral designs with birds, initials "S. H." and "1865," dovetailed case, lid edge molding, two dovetailed drawers, reeded molding, dovetailed bracket feet, interior till with lid, minor wear and edge wear, 49" l, 18-3/4" d, 24" h 19,250.00

Federal

Federal blanket chests are identified by their simple lines and their hardware. Many blanket chests identified as "country" may well be from this furniture period, but due to lack of specific dating provenance, and/or replaced parts and hardware, definite attribution is difficult.

America, c1810, hinged rectangular molded edge lid, storage well with till, single long thumb-molded drawer, molded bracket feet, orig brasses, repair to back edge of lid and lock, 45-7/8" w, 32" h...........................1,500.00

Grain Painted

Grain painted blanket chests are examples of decorated or painted blanket chests where a specific type of decoration is used. Graining simulated more expensive woods and usually allowed the maker to use lesser grades of wood.

America, mid 19th C, pine, hinged rectangular and molded lid, opening to storage well with lidded till, molded base raised on turned short legs, traces of brown wood graining on yellow ground, secondary wood poplar, 36" l, 17-3/4" d, 22-3/4" h 500.00

America, second half 19th C, pine, hinged rectangular molded top, opening to storage well with lidded candle till, molded base raised on turned short legs, rich dark brown wood graining, wear, imperfections, 48" l, 21" d, 24" h 750.00

Maine, early 19th C, pine, six board construction, molded top, lidded till, bracket feet, orig red and black paint simulating mahogany, 42" l, 18" d, 23" h 2,400.00

New England, 18th C, pine, early red paint, scrubbed lift top, three graduated faux drawers over long drawer, teardrop pulls, restored, 28" w, 15-1/2' d, 30" h 1,500.00

New England, early 19th C, pine, hinged top, molded leading edge, cavity with open till, single thumb-molded drawer, straight molded skirt, arched sides, all over yellow graining, turned wooden pulls probably orig, minor molding loss, surface mars, 41" l, 19" d, 36" h.............2,400.00

New England, early 19th C, six-board construction, lid opens to cavity with lidded till, straight front, bootjack ends, old surface simulating mahogany, very minor imperfections, 41-1/2" l, 16" d, 20" h 1,725.00

New Jersey, early 19th C, poplar, applied black, subtle red amber mottling, amber faux marble veining, minor imperfections, 32" w, 14" d, 21-1/2" h 900.00

New York, Schoharie County, c1815, molded hinged top, dovetail constructed box, bracket feet, grain painted burnt umber resembles mahogany, initialed "JAS" flanked by yellow flowering vines, 37-3/4" w, 14-1/4" d, 17-1/4" h 1,750.00

New York State, c1830, molded hinged lift top, lidded till, molded bracket black painted base, orig fanciful ochre and raw umber graining, 48" l, 22" d, 29" h...........................1,265.00

Ohio or Pennsylvania, 1830s, pine, six-board construction, hinged top with molded edge, dovetailed case, lidded till, molded base,

turned feet, old red and yellow graining with yellow paint in outline simulating quarter fan inlay at corners, old surface, imperfections, 45" l, 20" d, 28-1/2" h 1,840.00

Pennsylvania, pine, orig brown fanciful graining on faded pink-cream ground, orange-salmon undercoat, black lid trim and feet, molded lid edge, till and secret compartment, dovetailed case, three dovetailed overlapping drawers with orig oval brasses, applied molding above drawers, bracket feet with unusual glue blocks and braces, some edge damage, two drawers with rodent holes, front feet ended out, some touch-up repairs to paint, very worn top, 50-3/4" w, 24-1/4" d, 29-1/4" h 4,000.00

Pennsylvania, poplar, six-board construction, rectangular top with molded edge, till, mid-molding, two short drawers, base molding, splayed bracket feet, allover tones of red and black paint simulating crotch mahogany, pencil inscription on lid interior "Thomas R. Reber Murall 1833 Thomas R. Reber January 16th 1837 C/D Reber Feb. 24-87 bought this chest at Uncle's sale for $3.85. Delivered to Addie May 14/03," orig drawer pulls and brass escutcheons, repairs to front left foot, 49-1/2" l, 22" d, 27-1/2" h 5,250.00

Hepplewhite

The French feet of this blanket chest declare it belongs to the Hepplewhite furniture style.

Pennsylvania, pine, orig red paint, traces of grain painting, case with three dovetailed drawers, French feet, orig locks, wrought iron strap hinges, brass escutcheons, stenciled initials "W. H. G.," 50" l, 23" d, 29-1/4" h 4,000.00

Jacobean

Jacobean is a general name given to heavily carved chests. The example included shows how the price of an antique is affected by repairs and replacements.

America, oak, paneled construction with relief carving, drawer and feet replaced, repairs to lid and molding, old dark finish, 44-1/2" l, 19-1/2" d, 31-3/4" h 825.00

Painted

Like grain painting or decorated blanket chests, painted chests allowed lesser grades of wood to be used to construct blanket chests. This does not mean the chest is any less important and many are constructed as well or better than examples that strictly fit a design style. Fine (expensive) woods could then be reserved for more important pieces of furniture.

Connecticut, Milford, early 18th C, yellow pine, six-board construction, vestiges of painted dec, replaced ball feet, imperfections, 42-1/2" l, 20" d, 26-1/2" h 990.00

Massachusetts, western, 18th C, pine, hinged top with molded edge, lidded molded till, single base drawer, molded bracket feet, old green paint over red, old replaced glass pulls, paint wear on top, 45" l, 17" d, 31-5/8" h..2,650.00

New England, c1780, six-board construction, molded hinged top, dovetail constructed base, bracket feet, orig red paint, minor imperfections, 43-3/4" l, 19" d, 26" h.....................700.00

New England, late 18th C, molded lift top, two thumb-molded drawers on bracket base, old blue paint, brasses and hinges replaced, 36" l, 19" d, 44" h 1,955.00

New England, late 18th C, pine, hinged molded lid, dovetailed box, applied carved ropetwist beading, applied molded base, orig blue paint, 43-1/2" l, 18" d, 17" h.........2,645.00

New England, late 18th C, pine, six-board construction, hinged top with molded edge,

Painted, Pennsylvania, Lancaster Co., dated 1786, decorated after Heinrich Otto, grain painted with green and black paint, two front panels with potted plants and stylized flowers, side panels decorated with lion and tulip design, orig crab lock and key, hinges refastened, interior with glove box, damage to feet, 49" w, 21" d, 21" h, $22,000. Photo courtesy of Alderfer Auction Company, Hatfield, PA.

cavity with lidded till, small shelf, straight front with bootjack ends, early red paint, 51" l, 17" d, 24-1/2" h...1,610.00

New England, late 18th C, pine, six-board construction, hinged top with molded ends, wallpaper lined interior, dovetailed case, molded base, iron carrying handles, old blue green paint, cracks in lid, losses to bottom, 38-1/2" l, 23" d, 20-1/2" h 350.00

New England, late 18th C, pine, six-board construction, hinged lid with thumb-molded edge, cavity with lidded till, carrying handles, old blue paint, paint wear on top, 51" l, 19-1/2" d, 17-1/2" h...1,380.00

New England, early 19th C, painted pine, six-board construction, molded hinged top, cutout ends, old brown-red putty paint decoration, 41-1/2" l, 18-1/2" d, 24" h....................1,150.00

New England, early 19th C, painted poplar, six-board construction, rectangular molded hinged top, dovetail constructed box and bracket feet, center triple arch pendant, painted old apple green over earlier paint, imperfections, 38" l, 18" d, 21-1/2" d.....................575.00

New England, 19th C, orig red paint, cutout bracket feet, repairs, 39" l, 15" d, 21" h...1,250.00

New England, painted, six-board construction, molded hinged lid opens to cavity with lidded till, molded straight skirt with shaped sides, early blue-green paint, minor surface imperfections, 50" l, 19-3/4" d, 25" h..................1,725.00

Pennsylvania, attributed to Lehigh County, pine and poplar, orig painted decoration, top and ends with brown vinegar graining, blue panel and red trim, blue front panel with stylized flowers and wreath in red and white, "Jong Breing 1776," brown feet and lid edge moldings, dovetailed case, dovetailed bracket feet, till with lid, wrought iron bear trap lock, strap hinges, 50" l, 23" d, 23-1/4" h............30,250.00

Pennsylvania, c1780, pine, green and blue paint, one board top with breadboard ends, applied lower molding, dovetailed case, strap hinges, till with molded lid, ogee feet, 45" l, 19" d, 25-1/4" h 1,500.00

Pennsylvania, c1780, poplar, old light blue paint, hinged molded top, interior with till, dovetailed case, two thumb-molded short drawers

Painted, Pennsylvania, early 19th C, poplar, old salmon-orange putty paint over brown pattern, hinged rectangular top, dovetailed case, bracket feet, paint worn, imperfections, 48" l, 41" d, 24-1/2" h, $1,150. Photo courtesy of Skinner Auctioneers and Appraisers of Antiques and Fine Art Boston and Bolton, MA.

with applied horizontal molding, bracket feet, replaced brasses, minor imperfections, 48" l, 22" d, 26-1/2" h 1,725.00

Pennsylvania, early 19th C, poplar, old brownish-red finish, dovetailed case, hinged lid, three dovetailed drawers, dovetailed bracket feet, applied moldings, till with lid, tattered printed Haus Segen fraktur on interior of lid, bear trap lock, 50-14" l, 23" d, 30" h 2,100.00

Pennsylvania, early 19th C, poplar, old salmon-orange putty paint over brown pattern, hinged rectangular top, dovetailed case, bracket feet, paint worn, imperfections, 48" l, 41" d, 24-1/2" h 1,150.00

Pennsylvania, early 19th C, rectangular molded lid, case with two painted framed panels with multicolored stylized stars, three drawers with contrasting decoration, ogee bracket feet, paint refreshed, 52" w, 22" d, 31" h.......4,620.00

Pilgrim Century

Not many examples of this early period blanket chest come to the antiques market. Here is an example sold recently at auction. Being able to attribute the blanket chest to a specific maker further enhances its provenance and also its value.

Connecticut, attributed to Peter Blin, Wethersfield, c1675-1710, carved, painted, and ebonized oak, rectangular hinged lid, storage well with till, front carved with two rectangular inset panels of stylized tulips and leaves, center octagonal panel carved with sunflowers,

ebonized splint balusters, mid molding, two long drawers with egg appliqués, stiles continue to form feet, replaced lid, reduced feet, traces of orig red and black pigment, 47-1/2" l, 20-3/4" d, 34-1/4" h 12,000.00

Queen Anne

Queen Anne blanket chests are identified by having more drawers, or the appearance of more drawers, cabriole legs, and more detailed interiors. Hardware usually is brass and includes handles, locks, and escutcheons. Blanket chests from this time frame are more likely to be finer woods and finished to allow the beauty of the wood to be seen.

Connecticut, mid-18th C, poplar, rectangular hinged molded top above case with two false and two working drawers, applied molding on cutout base, old finish, imperfections, 35-1/2" l, 17-1/2" d, 45" h 2,100.00

Massachusetts, c1740, pine, old red paint, 36" w, 17" d, 31-3/4" h..........................2,400.00

Middle Atlantic States, late 19th C, pine, molded rectangular top, well above two faux short rectangular drawers over long drawer, over two working thumb-molded drawers, bracket feet, valanced sides, arched cutout front, replaced brasses, remnants of blue-green paint, restorations, 21-1/2" l 2,100.00

New England, c1750, marriage chest, pine, hinged rectangular lift lid, upper half faced with faux drawer fronts, brown paint, 35" 4,000.00

New England, 18th C, maple, four aligned drawers, scalloped apron, cabriole legs, pad feet, old refinishing, replaced brasses, 36" w, 18" d, 50-1/2" h 7,200.00

Pennsylvania, c1740-70, cherry, rectangular molded lift top, interior with lid prop and small interior drawer, frame with molded border, large thumb-molded drawer, carved skirt and legs, cabriole legs with claw and ball feet, penciled signature under frame "E. Cope," orig brass hardware on interior compartments, replaced brasses on exterior, working keys for all three locks, some patched repairs to legs, 52" l, 25-1/2" d, 35" h 12,880.00

Pennsylvania, mid-18th C, walnut, molded top over two thumb-molded drawers, upper box with orig locking mechanism, early batwing brasses, scalloped skirt, bracket feet, broken moldings on left drawer, patches on right drawer, repairs to feet, 49-1/2" w, 23-1/2" d, 28-1/2" h..950.00

Shaker

Shaker design incorporates two drawers in the dovetailed case. Instead of purchased hardware, pulls are turned wood. The feet are sturdy, made to take the weight of treasures that eventually will fill a chest like this.

Mount Lebanon, NY, c1840, cherry, rectangular molded hinged top, dovetailed constructed case fitted with two short drawers with incised beading, turned pulls, canted feet, painted white over earlier surface, 43-1/2" l, 17-1/4" d, 25-1/2" h 1,380.00

Sheraton

By the time Sheraton designs were popular, blanket chests were becoming a little more decorative. This example includes a scalloped apron and turned feet and panels rather than flat surfaces.

Country, pine and poplar, orig red paint, molded edge top, paneled front and ends, sq corner posts, mortised and pinned frame, scalloped apron, turned feet, 44" l, 19-1/2" d, 25-1/2" h..900.00

William and Mary

Early William and Mary blanket chests are often paneled and include some decorative elements. Expect to find iron hardware, hinges, and locks on blanket chests of this period.

Connecticut Valley, c1670-1710, joined oak and pine, carved, "S. K." on center panel, two drawers, old refinish, replaced top, 41" w, 17-1/2" d, 45" h 22,000.00

Massachusetts, Boston or coastal region, c1770-1820, pine top, oak six board chest, fielded side pine panels, single drawer, painted panels and drawer outlined with black applied moldings, center yellow painted panel with black decoration, flanked by black tree-like images, bun feet, restored, 44-3/4" w, 19" d, 30-1/4" h..5,000.00

Massachusetts, early 18th C, pine, molded top with pintail hinges above single arch molded base centering panel with carved initials "MG," single drawer, turned ball front feet, sq rear feet, brass teardrop pulls, pierced escutcheons may be orig, imperfections, 42" l, 18-1/2" d, 32-3/4" h 4,600.00

New England, c1700, oak and yellow pine, joined, drawer base, old finish, minor imperfections, 48-1/2" l, 22" d, 32-3/4" h 4,500.00

Rhode Island, early 18th C, tiger maple, rectangular top, two faux drawers, two working drawers, onion shaped front feet, some orig brasses, refinished, minor imperfections, 37" w, 18" d, 38-3/4" h.........................6,000.00

Bookcases

Bookcases are shelved units, often with doors to enclose the shelves. Interiors may have movable or fixed shelving. Because many bookcases are built-in to rooms, finding an authentic free-standing bookcase from early periods is difficult.

Barrister bookcases is a common name for the stacking bookcases popularized in the Victorian era. These can be found in various combinations, some with molded tops, others with drawers in the bases. Several different manufacturers made this type of bookcase.

As with other large pieces of furniture, look for wear in places where doors open, where hands might have rested while looking for a favorite book. Check to see that doors open easily, that all mechanical parts are present and in good working condition. It is not too unusual to find a pane of glass or two replaced over the lifetime of a well-used bookcase.

Also see Secretaries.

Aesthetic Movement

Furniture from this time period usually exhibits fine woods and straight lines.

America, late 19th C, mahogany, upper section with outset molded cornice over three seven-pane astragal doors, outset lower section with three paneled frieze drawers over three cupboard doors with geometric molding, all flanked by fluted stiles, turned short feet 69" w, 20" d, 90" h...1,725.00

Art Nouveau

Furniture reflects the Art Nouveau style of flowing shapes. Much of the Art Nouveau furniture found in today's antique marketplace is of French origin, but American manufacturers also created some lovely pieces.

America, c1900, walnut, dentil molding and brackets in pediment, carved and paneled sides, some loss to finish, some elements missing, 99" l, 94" h.............................1,550.00

Arts & Crafts

Arts & Crafts bookcases have been selling well for the past several years. They are great looking, well made, and very serviceable. Look for original hardware and labels.

Flint Company, No. 607, oak, double doors, leaded glass, three adjustable shelves, orig over-coated dark finish, 36" w, 14-1/2" d, 55" h..1,750.00

Lifetime Furniture, Grand Rapids, MI, early 20th C, oak

Single door, small panels at top, adjust-

Arts & Crafts, Gustav Stickley, New York, c1904, design by Harvey Ellis, mahogany, rectangular overhanging top, square leaded clear glass panels over two divided rectangular panels, arched lower apron, red "Gustav Stickley" mark, wear, 48" w, 14" d, 58-3/4" h, $21,850. Photo courtesy of Skinner Auctioneers and Appraisers of Antiques and Fine Art Boston and Bolton, MA.

able shelves, orig finish, label, 28" w, 13" d, 55" h 1,650.00

Triple door, six panes per door, gallery top, orig finish, paper label, 55-1/2" w, 12" d, 46" h 4,950.00

Two doors, rectangular top with corbel support over two doors with curved shaped top of two short over two long window panels, interior fitted with eight half shelves, copper ring pulls, caned panels on lower front and side, damage to caning, wear, 46-1/2" l, 12-1/2" d, 57-1/2" h...........................1,955.00

Limbert, Charles P., Grand Rapids and Holland, MI

No. 355, single door with six panes over two panels, orig copper hardware, shelves at sides, organic cutout at top, paper label, 33" w, 13" d, 48" h 14,300.00

No. 7242, double door form, three drawers over doors, overlay design in wood of squares above rectangles, refinished, 48" w, 15" d, 55" h 2,800.00

Niedecken, George Mann, mahogany, double door case, leaded glass panels with floral design in green and salmon against amber

Arts & Crafts, Gustav Stickley, New York, c1904, No. 719, oak, gallery top, two doors each with twelve pane, V-shaped pulls, red decal and retailer's paper label "Walter F. Barnes, Broadway, New York," 60" w, 13" d, 56" h, $9,200. Photo courtesy of Skinner Auctioneers and Appraisers of Antiques and Fine Art Boston and Bolton, MA.

Arts & Crafts, L. & J. G. Stickley, Fayetteville, NY, c1910, No. 645, gallery top, double pegged through tenons, twelve panes each door, copper pulls, Handcraft decal. 53" w, 12-1/2" d, 55-1/2" h, $6,900. Photo courtesy of Skinner Auctioneers and Appraisers of Antiques and Fine Art Boston, and Bolton MA.

hammered glass background, architectural tiered base, orig star shaped brass pulls, four orig shelves, orig finish, 48" w, 16" d, 56" h..9,900.00

Paine Furniture Co., three sliding doors, arched leaded glass panel at top with organic design over single pane of glass, eight adjustable shelves, missing backsplash, orig dark finish, sgd with metal tag, 60" w, 14" d, 59" h..2,200.00

Roycroft, East Aurora, NY, overhanging top, chamfered back, five open shelves, bottom drawer with cast pulls, orig light finish, carved orb and cross mark, 34" l, 9-1/4" d, 65-1/2" h...6,500.00

Stickley Brothers, Grand Rapids, MI

No. 303-4784, gallery top, two doors, open section short side slats, single hammered copper ring pull, orig reddish finish, Quaint metal tag/303-4784, 35-1/2" w, 12" d, 50" h 3,750.00

No. 4708, oak, open, gallery top over three open shelves, three sided spindles, medium brown finish, branded Stickley Bros. Co. and "4708," refinished, wear, 26-3/4" l, 12" d, 38-1/2" h 1,050.00

No. 4764, double doors, flush top, eight square panes per door, three adjustable shelves, metal tag, new medium finish, 48" w, 12" d, 48" h 2,750.00

Three-door form, oak, arched gallery top, leaded stained glass at top above two vertical panes on each door, orig copper hardware, orig finish, unsigned, 59" w, 12" d, 60" h 4,750.00

Three-door form, three small panes over two long glass panes on each door, flush top, adjustable shelves, orig finish, unmarked, 59-3/4" w, 13" d, 55" h 3,950.00

Stickley, Gustav, New York

No. 703, designed by Harvey Ellis, double doors each with three leaded panels at top, three vertical windows, arched toe-board, through-tenon construction at sides, orig finish, red decal and paper label, 60" w, 14" d, 58" h 47,500.00

No. 716, similar to 1904-12, gallery top, two doors each with three panes of glass, medium brown finish, large red decal, 41-3/4" w, 12-3/4" d, 56" h, ...9,200.00

No. 717, c1907, oak, gallery top, two doors, eight panes each with through tenons, three interior shelves, V-pulls, Craftsmans Workshops paper label, wear stains, 48" w, 13" d, 56-1/2" h 4,000.00

No. 719, c1904, gallery top, two doors each with twelve panes of glass each, shaped pulls, through-tenon construction, red decal, retailer's paper label "Walter F. Barnes, Broadway, New York," 60" w, 13" d, 56" h, ...9,200.00

No. 719, c1904, wide form, two doors with twelve panes of glass each, orig copper pulls, through-tenon construction, branded mark, refinished, 60" w, 13" d, 56" h 7,700.00

Mahogany, c1904, rectangular top, pair sq leaded clear glass panels over two oak divided rectangular panels, arched lower apron, design by Harvey Ellis, red "Gustav Stickley" mark, some wear, 48" w, 14" d, 58-3/4" h, ...21,850.00

Oak, 1905, gallery top, single door with twelve glass panes, through-tenon sides, orig finish, red decal, remnants of Craftsman label, some replacements at foot board, 35" w, 13" d, 56" h 4,750.00

Oak, 1905-07, gallery top, two doors each with eight panes of glass, shaped pulls, circular device paper label, 43" w, 13" d, 56" h 6,900.00

Oak, early 20th C, V-shaped side panels with through pegged tenons and D-shaped cut-out handles, joined at top by V-shaped rack over medial shelf, medium brown finials, paper Craftsmen label, some wear, staining, 29-3/4" l, 10" d, 30-1/2" h 1,850.00

Stickley, L. & J. G., Fayetteville, NY

No. 232, early form, two doors with twelve panes to each, orig hammered copper hardware, chamfered board back, keyed-tenon construction at sides, orig finish, numbered on back, 53" w, 12" d, 55" h 11,000.00

No. 643, c1912, gallery top, dual exposed tenons, two doors each with eight panes of glass, hammered copper door pulls, labeled "The Work of L. & J. G. Stickley," 36-1/2" w, 12-1/8" d, 55-1/2" h, ...7,900.00

No. 645, c1910, gallery top, double pegged through tenons, two doors each with 12 panes, copper pulls, red Handcraft decal, 53" w, 12-1/2" d, 55-1/2" h 7,000.00

Single door, gallery top, keyed through-tenon construction, chamfered back, light over-coat to finish, Handcraft decal, 40" w, 12" d, 55" h 9,000.00

Two doors, twenty-four mullion windows, chamfered back, through-tenons and keys, orig medium dark finish, thicker wood and nicely grained, red Handcraft decal, 49" w, 12-1/2" d, 55" h..............................12,000.00

Unknown American Designer/Maker

Single door, gallery top, Prairie-style mullion panel over glass paned door, over-coated finish, some stains on top, 36" w, 12" d, 45" h 1,250.00

Single door with 16 panes, oak, c1916, gallery top over four shelves, unsigned, 35" w, 13" d, 56" h, door stripped, hinge hardware incomplete, roughness 1,380.00

Arts & Crafts, unknown designer, chestnut and oak, double door, small glass panes around larger pane, Gustav Stickley copper V-pulls, 42" w, 17-3/4" d, 54-3/4" h, $2,100. Photo courtesy of David Rago Auctions/RagoArts.com, Lambertville, NJ.

Two doors, each with eight panes of glass, hammered copper hardware, slab sides with through-tenon construction, orig finish, 48" w, 13" d, 56" h 3,000.00

Unknown English Designer/Maker, late 19th C, oak and leaded glass, rectangular top over two hinged doors with two short leaded glass panels of striated green and colorless geometric shaped segments over two longer colorless glass panels, four interior shelves, shaped feet, 40-1/4" w, 14-1/4" d, 58-1/4" h 900.00

Viking, oak, four stacking units, single drawer base, orig copper hardware, orig finish, paper label, 34" w, 13" d, 60" h 650.00

Biedermeier-Style

Biedermeier was a popular European furniture style that was frequently copied by American craftsmen.

Inlaid cherry, outset molded cornice with ebonized bead, front with two recessed glazed doors, four shelves, outset molded base raised on black feet, burr poplar panels, ebonized stringing, 53-1/2" w, 21" d, 72" h 700.00

Mahogany, outset molded top, front with two glazed doors, three shelves, sq section stile feet, 35-3/4" w, 15" d, 52" h....................375.00

Chippendale

Architecture in America in the late 1770s followed English examples and so did furniture styles. Because bookcases were often built-in, the example shown below is unusual in its massive size. It also shows some evidence of Chinese Chippendale which was very popular at this time period. Whoever made this bookcase used the latest designs and finest woods.

Maryland or Pennsylvania, 1765-65, mahogany, three sections, upper section with dentiled triangular pediment, plinth with contemporary bust of William Shakespeare, plain veneered frieze; center bookcase with double glazed cupboard doors, astragal mullions, Chinoiserie pattern, molded base; lower section as chest with short thumb-molded central drawer flanked by two similar box drawers, two graduated long box drawers, two graduated long drawers, flanked by fluted quarter columns,

Chippendale-Style, block front, inlaid mahogany, four doors, two bowed center doors, flanked by two flat pane doors, flanked by columns with carved capitals, surmounted by bold urn and griffin floral inlay with Greek key banding, $5,500. Photo courtesy of Alderfer Auction Company, Hatfield, PA.

ogee bracket feet, 44-3/4" d, 25-1/4" d, 106-1/4" h.............................18,500.00

New England, c1770-1800, cherry, two sections, upper section with bookcase with ogival molded cornice, double diamond lattice pattern glaze doors, eight adjustable interior shelves, lower section with double paneled cupboard doors, compartmented and shelved interior, two sliding drawers, molded base, minor restoration, 65-1/2" w, 18-1/2" d, 98-3/4" h 9,500.00

Classical

Classical period bookcases are usually massive pieces of furniture. Look for mahogany and other dark woods, cornices, etc. Many bookcases from this era also have columns as part of the applied decoration.

America, mahogany, rectangular top, cushion-molded frieze, three glazed doors enclosing shelves, three-quarter columns, shaped feet, electrified, 78" w, 17-1/4" d, 58-1/2" h........700.00

America, mahogany, crotch mahogany veneers, top section: large architectural type cornice, two large glass doors with cathedral top muttons, three adjustable shelves; base: eleven drawers, oval brass knobs, applied base molding, two panes of glass cracked, 66" w, 83" h 5,500.00

New York, c1810-30, mahogany, three-part construction, upper section with deeply projecting rectangular cornice over arched frieze; middle section conforming case fitted with pair of geometric glazed cupboard doors, two interior shelves; lower section with rectangular white marble top above bolection-molded frieze drawer, pair of paneled cupboard doors enclosing shelf, centered by engaged colonettes, foliate-carved and gadrooned bun feet, 47-1/2" w, 24-1/4" d, 92-1/4" h 3,500.00

New York or New Jersey, c1825, tiger maple, flat carved molded cornice above two glazed doors, enclosing three shelves, projecting case of two central cockbeaded short drawers flanked by deep drawer and recessed tombstone panel all above three cockbeaded long drawers, flanked by vase and ring-turned columns, sides with recessed panels, old refinish, replaced brasses, imperfections, feet missing, 41" w, 20-1/2" d, 88" h.........................6,000.00

Classical-Style

In a style similar to Classical or Empire, this bookcase also incorporates some elements from a later design style.

America, late 19th C, gilt bronze mounted mahogany, rectangular marble top over drawer, pair of glazed doors enclosing shelves, hairy paw feet, damage to marble, 36" w, 15" d, 53-1/4" h...1,850.00

Country

Books were treasures to be protected and cherished. To accomplish this responsibility, bookcases and book shelves were made. Some bookcases don't have enough design elements of any one furniture style to accurately attribute them, so the generic term of Country is used to classify them.

Cherry, stepback, two pieces, top with dovetailed and molded cornice, double doors, each with fifteen panels of old glass, base with four paneled doors, old mellow finishing, end of cornice restored, 60-3/4" w, 91" h 4,000.00

Walnut, coved cornice, double doors, each with eight panes of glass, rounded arches in top lights, scalloped apron, cutout feet, refinished, 40-1/4" h, 77" h.........................1,200.00

Federal

Bookcases of the Federal period are often called breakfronts. This name is derived from the shape of the case, where it is often stepped back or forward, causing a "break" in the appearance. Other types of Federal bookcases contain drawers, doors, and even writing surfaces.

America, first quarter 19th C, breakfront, mahogany, six parts, flat molded cornice over four Gothic arched glazed and mullioned cupboard doors, lower portion with four paneled Gothic arched cupboard doors, orig glass panes, base missing, 94" l, 22" d, 81-1/2" h..3,950.00

America, c1825, cherry, rectangular top, projecting cornice, glass paneled doors, rectangular case, long drawer above cupboard doors, 47-1/2" w, 23" d, 79" h.........................1,400.00

Middle Atlantic States, early 19th C, mahogany, double glazed doors open to interior of three beaded shelves, lower recessed panel case with double doors, single shelf interior, bracket feet, 53" w, 12-1/2" d, 74" h 4,600.00

New England, c1790, cherry, flat molded cornice above two glaze doors with molded muntins, four interior shelves, two thumb-molded short drawers below, ogee bracket feet, replaced brasses, old refinish, restored, 58-1/2" w, 13" d, 62-1/2" h 4,320.00

New Hampshire, c1820, cherry and mahogany inlaid, flat top with quarter round molding above case with inlaid panel frieze of satinwood and mahogany with stringing and applied reeded band, two glazed doors with beaded muntins enclosing interior of five inlaid drawers and six valanced compartments, lower case with fold-out writing surface and four cockbeaded graduated drawers, four vase and ring turned legs joined by shaped skirt centering satinwood drop panel, replaced brasses, turned wooden pulls, old refinish,

Federal, Middle Atlantic States, early 19th C, mahogany, double glazed doors open to interior of three beaded shelves, lower recessed panel case with double doors, single shelf interior, bracket feet, 53" w, 12-1/2" d, 74" h, $4,600. Photo courtesy of Skinner Auctioneers and Appraisers of Antiques and Fine Art Boston and Bolton, MA.

Federal, Ohio, cherry, molded cornice, one door with four panes of glass, rounded apron, French feet, old finish, pieced repairs, 22-1/2" w, 12" d, 32-3/4" h, $3,200. Photo courtesy of Garth's Auctions, Inc., Delaware, OH.

repairs and imperfections, 37-3/4" w, 18" d, 68" h 5,500.00

Pennsylvania, Philadelphia, 1790-1810, mahogany veneered, four part construction: long rectangular top with detachable molded cornice; two bookcase sections each with pairs of glazed cupboard doors, twelve rectangular panes below top row of arched panes, adjustable shelves interior; lower: center butler's fall-front desk drawer, kneehole area flanked by bands of three cockbeaded short drawers, large paneled cupboard doors, molded base, 119" w, 17-1/2" d, 105-3/4" h 27,500.00

George III

It would be difficult to write a furniture price guide without including at least one example of an English bookcase. This one has been selected since it is so very typical of the period. And, it was sold at an American auction.

English, mahogany, dentil molded cornice over three glazed doors enclosing shelves above three drawers, associated base with drawer fitted with pull-out leather topped writing surface, fitted drawer over kneehole fitted with three drawers flanked by cupboards, ogee bracket feet, 52-1/4" w, 24-1/4" d, 35" h 5,750.00

George III-Style

Stylistically these bookcases are George III, but may be either English or American. The style was as popular with American cabinetmakers as it was with their English counterparts.

Mahogany, carved, glazed, interior fitted with five shelves, 54-1/2" w, 18" d, 85-1/2" h 1,250.00

Mahogany, outset molded cornice, front with three glazed doors, each with simulated eighteen-pane tracery, adjustable shelves, molded plinth base, bracket feet, 71-1/4" w, 15" d, 54-1/4" h.. 600.00

Mahogany, stepped dentiled cornice, four glazed lattice doors, shelves interior, lower section with two small over two wide cockbeaded drawers flanked by twin panel doors, ogival bracket feet, 74-3/4" w, 17-1/2" d, 77-1/2" h.. 2,500.00

Revolving

Revolving bookcases are neat inventions, but usually fail to fall stylistically into a particular furniture period. Most were created during the second half of the 19th century.

Oak, molded rectangular top, five compartmentalized shelves with slatted ends, quadruped base with castors, stamped "Danners Revolving Book Case...Ohio," 24" w, 24" d, 68-1/4" h... 1,100.00

Pine, revolving, four circular tiers, simulated books for supports, quadruped base, 26" d, 60" h, price for pair.............................. 6,000.00

Victorian

The Victorians took their love of ornamentation and nature to great extents with some of their bookcases while keeping others much more plain and business-like.

Mission, gallery top, single-door with mullion panel over glass paned door, over-coated finish, some stains to top, chips to case edges, 36" w, 12" d, 45" h, $1,000. Photo courtesy of David Rago Auctions/ RagoArts.com, Lambertville, NJ.

Globe-Wernicke, barrister type, stacking, oak, glass fronted drawers, drawer in base, metal bands, orig finish 700.00

Macey, barrister type, stacking, oak, leaded glass door, drawer in base, three sections of varying height, needs regluing, 34" w, 11" d 400.00

Eastlake

America, c1880, cherry, rectangular top, flaring bead trimmed cornice, pair of single-pan glazed cupboard doors, carved oval paterae and scrolls across top, adjustable shelved interior, stepped base with line-incised drawers, bail handles, 47-1/2" w, 15-1/4" d, 69-1/4" h........................... 1,200.00

America, c1900, tripartite, walnut, each section with glazed door, period shelves, 55-1/2" w, 14-1/2" d, 54-1/2" h............ 450.00

Elizabethian, c1850, straight front, burl walnut, ormolu mounted porcelain portrait medallion flanked by two glazed cabinet doors enclosing shelves, all over ormolu mounted floral porcelain reserves, bracket feet, 71" w, 17-1/4" d, 43" h 5,375.00

Gothic Revival

c1830, carved rosewood, architectural pediment, two glass doors, 45-3/4" w, 13-3/4" d, 86" h............................... 3,975.00

Boxes

Collectors and decorators have long used boxes as wonderful accessories. Today beautiful boxes are treasured for the craftsmanship of their style, as well as the storage they offer. Included in this section of *Warman's American Furniture*, you will find examples and prices for the most desirable forms of boxes in today's antique marketplace. Boxes are listed below, divided by their function. However, it is often difficult to determine what the original usage was. Many boxes also defy clear stylistic lines. No matter what they were originally used for, boxes are charming additions to many rooms. Collectors today eagerly seek colorful, well-made examples.

Band

The term "band box" refers to a box that is usually covered in wallpaper or hand painted. Most band boxes are oval. Because their wallpaper covering is usually delicate, few examples exist in perfect condition. Reproduction band boxes are available. Some craftsmen today are creating wonderful examples of band boxes.

Davis, Hannah, early 19th C, wood construction, wallpaper covering

Green, white, and beige floral paper, lined with old newspaper, labeled "Band Boxes made by Hannah Davis, Jaffery, N.H.," wear, 14-3/4" l 715.00

White floral decoration on blue ground, losses, wear, 12" l, 9" d, 9" h 635.00

Pennsylvania, early 19th C, black and white sponge painted on dark blue ground, minor wear, 6-3/4" l, 3-3/4" d, 5-1/2" h 920.00

Unidentified Maker, poplar and ash, worn orig wall paper covering water fowl in shades of blue, wear and edge damage, 13-1/2" w, 17-1/2" l, 11" h...750.00

Bentwood

Bentwood boxes are available in all sizes, shapes, and colors. Look for good construction and little shrinkage or damage where the seams join or overlap.

Carrying type, round, lapped seams, copper tacks, lid, swivel handle, old patina, 15"d, 7" h..475.00

Shaker, oval, maple and pine, three fingers, gray paint, wear, abrasion, 11-1/2" l, 8" w, 4-3/4" h...1,265.00

Storage, oval, orig black graining, varnished, Hersey type finger construction, iron tacks, lid glued, 5-1/2" l 200.00

Storage, round, covered

Black paint, olive-gold stenciled decoration with hearts, one nailed finger on both lid and base, some wear to black paint, alligatoring on top, 5-1/2" w, 3-3/4" d, 1-3/4" h..............250.00

Old dark green repaint, lapped seams on base, finger construction on lid, 8-3/4" l, 4-1/4" h 750.00

Old green paint, lapped seams, some traces of black paint on lid, 13" l.........615.00

Old light blue paint, lapped seams with steel tacks, 9-1/4" d, 5" h....................600.00

Old light blue paint, lapped seams with steel tacks, signed on bottom "P. C. Burr," minor edge damage, 10-1/2" d, 5-3/4" h 495.00

Old light green paint, lapped seams, wear, 10" d 150.00

Old olive gray paint with star like design in black on lid, lapped seams with iron tacks, 6-1/4" d..420.00

Bible or Book

Bible or Book boxes are named to represent their use. Examples found today usually contain carving or decoration of some type.

America, 19th C, carved pine, incised decorations of hearts and other symbols on cover, painted dark brown, 4-1/4" w, 1-1/2" d, 7" l 460.00

America, late 19th C, poplar, old black paint, gold polychrome floral spray, red design, wear, 12" l...365.00

America, late 19th C, walnut, old varnish on cover and marbleized paper interior, dovetailed construction, minor age cracks, edge damage, 12-1/2" l 395.00

England, 18th C, carved oak, molded hinged lid, carved curvlinear and floral decoration to front and side facade, forged iron hasp and lock plate, brass plat on lid inscribed "David Alexander Hume," losses, separation, wear, 27-3/4" l, 18" d, 7-3/4" h 800.00

Bonnet

Bonnet boxes were used to store precious bonnets and also to transport them during travel. Today, Shaker bonnet boxes are the most sought after, but other fine examples exist.

Shaker, painted cylindrical form, ash and pine, single lap, bail handle, attached with square shaped wooden pegs

Gray paint, repair to lid, 10-1/4" d, 8-1/4" h 230.00

Red paint, age splits, losses to bottom, 10-1/2" h, 8" d 490.00

Bride's

Bride boxes are usually identified by their brightly colored decorations. Usually made of bentwood, look for decoration that is bright and shows some signs of wear.

Bentwood pine, orig floral decal on side, birds on lid, laced seams, 15-1/4" l 675.00

Pine, worn orig polychrome paint, floral band on sides with white, red, yellow, and black tulips, full length portrait of man and woman on lid, damage to laced seams, very worn 19" l..440.00

Candle

Candle boxes were used to store the necessary candles in early households. The most typical form is a rectangular box with a sliding cover. However, examples of hanging candle boxes are available and treasured by collectors.

Hanging

America, pine and chestnut, traces of old red, carved compass designs on front boards, scratched carved compass design on crest, 12" w, 8-1/2" d, 15-1/4" h 1,100.00

Candle, Ohio, attributed to, poplar, orig brown and green decoration, dovetailed, molded edge on rim, raised panel on sliding lid, minor edge damage, 10-1/2" w, 6" d, 4" h, $5,775. Photo courtesy of Garth's Auctions, Inc., Delaware, OH.

America, poplar, layers of old yellow paint, two compartments, hanging crest, 11-1/4" w, 5-1/2" d, 16-1/2" h.............................3,300.00

Table Top, sliding lid

America, decorated, pine, orig brown graining, four sides and sliding lid with light colored reserves of daubed paint, orange, brown, and black, dovetailed, 13-1/4" w, 8" d, 5-1/4" h 2,430.00

America, hardwood, old dark worn paint over blue, dovetailed, molded lid, end missing on lid, square knob replacements, 10-1/4" l, 6" d, 4" h..............................385.00

America, pine, old worn red paint, tab handle on lid, 8" l 420.00

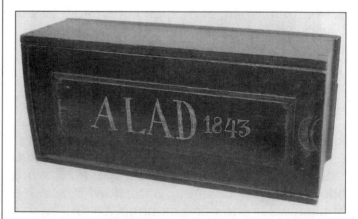

Candle, Illinois, attributed to, original dark red paint, dovetailed, lid inscribed "ALAD 1843" in white on relief carved panel, molded edge around base with wood pegs, pencil inscription in interior "Mrs. Lina Anderson Batavia, Ill. 1901," 14" w, 6-1/2" d, 4-1/2" h, $1,650. Photo courtesy of Garth's Auctions, Inc., Delaware, OH.

Candle, country, c1800, pine, traces of orig red paint, hand carved shell for pull, $400.

Ohio, attributed to, poplar, orig brown and green decoration, dovetailed, molded edge on rim, raised panel on sliding lid, minor edge damage, 10-1/2" w, 6" d, 4" h...5,775.00

Illinois, attributed to, original dark red paint, dovetailed, lid inscribed "ALAD 1843" in white on relief carved panel, molded edge around base with wood pegs, pencil inscription in interior "Mrs. Lina Anderson Batavia, Ill. 1901," 14" w, 6-1/2" d, 4-1/2" h 1,650.00

Pennsylvania, attributed to, elaborate decoration in gold, black, red, and yellow, deep blue ground, small area of touch-up on rim, minor age crack, 7-1/4" w, 4-1/4" d, 3-1/2" h 8,500.00

Chess and Backgammon

Boxes designed to hold game pieces and often serve as playing boards are always popular. Here is an example of a combination board and box. See Miscellaneous for Game Boards.

Victorian, lacquered, rectangular, Chinoiserie gilt-dec on sides with figures and foliate borders, chess board on outside with various figures on each black square, interior of backgammon board with central gilt foliate and red polychromed details, associated backgammon pieces, 19-1/2" x 9-3/4" x 3-3/8" closed.. 400.00

Chocolate

Before the advent of paper boxes, wooden boxes served the purpose of transporting all kinds of goods, including chocolate and candy. Today these boxes are valued for the decorations and the beauty of the wood.

Victorian, lacquered wood, rectangular, applied enameled brass decoration at corners, hinged lid cornered with conforming applied decorations, centered by domed medallion, 8-1/2" l, 5-3/4" d, 4" h 200.00

Cigar Humidor

Cigars have always been valued and only a proper humidor will do to keep cigars at their peak. Cigar boxes found in high-style designs and made of exquisite woods are found in the antiques marketplace. Most of those are English or Continental in nature.

Arts & Crafts, style of Shop-of-the-Crafters, oak, cast strap hinges, zinc lining, orig finish and patina, felted bottom, 15" w, 12-1/2" d, 8-1/2" h..900.00

Cutlery Tray

Cutlery trays or knife and fork boxes are rectangular boxes often found with a center handle that served as storage and tote box for tableware utensils. Today collectors are looking for unique handles, decorations, original painting or interesting construction.

America, mid 19th C

Carved and inlaid walnut, center divided carved in patriotic motif, eagle heads at handle, flags flanking heart, wreath on reverse, canted sides inlaid with various woods as stars and shields, corners and applied molding at base are painted black, minor surface wear, two strips of molding missing, 13" l, 9" w, 5-1/2" h..........2,550.00

Carved and painted pine, shaped divider with cutout handle, molded base whimsically painted with black scribed compass stars and circles, dots, and wave lines on mustard ground, minor paint wear, losses, 12-3/4" x 11-1/4" 8,625.00

Country, walnut, old finish, dovetailed drawer in base, divider with heart-shaped cut out, 12-3/4" w, 22" l, 11-1/2" h 1,375.00

Grain Painted, America, early 19th C, pine, dovetailed and nailed, rectangular, shaped divider handle with scrolled ends, some paint loss, wear, 11-1/2" l, 8" w, 6" h 150.00

Handmade, worn varnish finish, divider with cutout handle, 16" l, 11" w 140.00

Painted wood, two compartments, divider with shaped cutout and curved handle, molded edge and base, repainted blue, traces of old red paint, minor age splits, 13-1/2" l, 9-1/2" w, 4-3/4" h 980.00

Walnut, dovetailed drawer in base, divider with heart shaped cutout, old finish, 22" l, 12-3/4" w, 11-1/2" h 1,375.00

Decoupage Decorated

Boxes were frequently an important part of a gift of presentation. During the middle to late 19th C, the technique of decoupage or the pasting of small cutouts onto a surface was very popular. Layers and layers of varnish or another type of protective surface was put over the cutouts. It was a way for an individual to customize an otherwise plain box into something fanciful for the recipient. The following example is quite typical of the decoupage decorated boxes available today in the antiques marketplace.

America, mid to late 19th C, painted pine, dovetailed construction, decorated with printed paper cutouts of small figures, animals, scenes, and objects, orig lock, dovetailed repair under left hinge, minor losses, 13" w, 8" d, 7-1/2" h 300.00

Dough

Large families required large quantities of bread and baked goods. Dough boxes were commonly used to mix and store rising yeast breads. Usually rectangular, some were so important, they were placed on frames or legs. Look for rather primitive construction—these were boxes made to be used, not necessarily adorned.

Country, poplar, cherry finish, turned splayed legs with button feet, one board top, 20-3/4" w, 35-3/4" l, 27-1/2" h 420.00

Pennsylvania, poplar and pine, old mustard paint over earlier red, one top cleat repositioned, section of side molding missing, 34" w, 16-1/4" d, 12-1/2" h 330.00

Goodie

The term "Goodie" box refers to a stylistic box created only during the Arts & Crafts period.

Arts & Crafts, Roycroft, mahogany, copper hinges and handles, orig finish, carved orb and cross mark, minor split to top, 23" l, 12-1/2" w, 9-1/2" h 1,100.00

Knife

Knife boxes are upright cases where a household's precious silver knives were kept. The more elaborate the knife box that rested on a sideboard, the more effluent the family was. English examples are eagerly sought by American collectors. It is often quite difficult to determine the country of origin on these elegant boxes.

Federal, England or America, early 19th C

Flame Mahogany, hinged, deep rectangular top opening to storage well, cockbeaded lip, outset plinth base, 12-1/4" w, 12-1/4" d, 16" h 500.00

Inlaid mahogany and mahogany veneer, serpentine front, slant lid top with shell inlay, string inlay at edges, three shaped feet, minor veneer damage, age split, price for pair, 8-1/2" w, 15" d, 11" h 3,800.00

Inlaid mahogany and mahogany veneer, serpentine front, slant lid top with silver fittings, fitted interior with inlaid dec, repairs, imperfections, 9" w, 11" d, 15" h 1,100.00

Inlaid mahogany and mahogany veneer, shaped front slant lid top, silver fittings, fitted interior with inlaid dec, missing lock plate, veneer damage, 8-1/2" w, 13" d, 14-3/4" h 690.00

Inlaid maple, serpentine front, slant lid top with shell inlay, fitted interior with inlaid dec, age cracks, warping to lid, 8-1/2" w, 11-1/2" d, 15-1/2" h 690.00

Hepplewhite, mahogany veneer with inlay, convoluted serpentine facade with segmented edge inlay, interior baffles (old replacements) have inlaid design, veneer damage, price for pair, 9-1/2" w, 11-3/4" d, 15" h 2,310.00

Lap Desk

Lap desks or boxes are boxes usually with

slanted lids that contained stationery, ink, and writing implements.

America, 19th C, burl, chestnut bottom, dovetailed construction, old finish, repairs, 21-1/2" w, 15-1/2' d, 9-1/2" h 1,380.00

America, 19th C, pine, lift top, shaped gallery top over slanted lid, dovetail joinery on box, turned feet, interior fitted with mirror, wear, 12-1/2" l, 12-3/4" d, 9-1/4" h 175.00

English, c1845, brass mounted oblong mahogany, interior fitted with gilt-tooled black leather writing surface, pair of silver-plate capped cut glass ink bottles, covered nibs compartment, open compartment, pen tray, large, splint to writing surface 275.00

English, c1850, mahogany, interior fitted with gilt tooled green leather writing surface, brass fixtures, mounted on later mahogany stand to form chair side table, 16" w, 9-3/8" d, 23-1/2" h 400.00

Regency, c1820, mahogany

Case brass bound, shaped brass plaque, opening to writing surface and storage compartments, fitted with concealed side drawer, later stand of sq legs, 22" w, 11" d, 25-1/2" h 900.00

Double Action, case brass bound, central shaped brass plaque, opening to interior fitted with leather document folder, storage compartments, hinged front opening to writing surface, later stand of sq legs, 20" w, 10-1/2" d, 24" h 700.00

Victorian, c1860

Black lacquer, abalone inlaid and painted castle decoration on top, folds out to reveal blue velvet writing surface which opens to inner storage compartment, gilt scroll work and abalone inlaid molded sides, later stand, lacquer chips, lid detached, paint faded, gilt worn, 20-5/8" w, 17-3/4" d, 4-3/4" h 400.00

Burl walnut, brass bound top, leather writing surface, storage compartments, later circular stand, tapering reeded legs, toupie feet, 13-3/4" w, 10-1/2" d, 23" h 475.00

Liquor Chest

Just as spices were a precious commodity, so was liquor. The example listed here is interesting in that it was probably made in England, but destined to appeal to American tastes or perhaps was some sort of presentation piece.

England, attributed to, c1795, mahogany inlaid, rectangular box with hinged top, inlaid with great seal of the United States of America, brass and polychrome stained wood centered by interrupted line and crossbanded border, inlay repeated on front and sides, front with inlaid drapery above ivory diamond escutcheon with flanking brass handle, interior fitted with six gilt colorless glass decanters, two wine glasses, and spill tray, one decanter damaged and fitted with early cork make-do stopper, minor imperfections, 11-7/8" w, 7-1/4" d, 8-3/4" h 9,200.00

Paint Decorated

Thousands of generic boxes were made in America from the early to mid-19th century. Because they were durable, they often outlived their original contents. Considering that it was probably the spice, coffee, or tea that was really desired, many boxes were painted. The boxes were often mass produced by small factories all over the country and were used for various usages. Today collectors eagerly seek these colorful boxes and enjoy them for their size and uniqueness.

Basswood, mustard and red decoration, green finger swirled vinegar background, orig brass bale pull on lid, minor wear and age cracks on lid, 15" w, 7-1/2" d, 6" h 2,475.00

Decorated, optic block pattern on lid and three sides in gilt, red, and black, shield-shaped escutcheon, interior fitted with three-section compartments, 19th C, 13" l, 11" d, 6-1/2" h, $3,740. Photo courtesy of Skinner Auctioneers and Appraisers of Antiques and Fine Art Boston and Bolton, MA.

Basswood, old dark green paint, red and green foliage on top and front, lighter green shows beneath, dovetailed, orig brass bale pull on lid, iron hasp lock on front, 18" w, 8-1/2" d, 6-1/2" h...1,320.00

Cherry, painted with black, red, yellow, and off-white graining, gold borders, dovetailed, hinged lid opening to interior divided into six small and one large compartments, orig lock, ivory escutcheon, very minor paint loss, old repair inside, 13" w, 7" d, 4-1/2" h...4,900.00

Curly Maple, academy painted box, hand painted pink and green floral and seashell decoration, sgd "Maria" within banner on reverse, dovetailed, bun feet, 9-3/4" w, 6-1/2" d, 3-1/2" h..4,025.00

Hardwood, orig salmon red paint, black, white, and green foliage dec, turned, round, minor age cracks, 4-3/4" d, 2-1/2" h.......440.00

Maple, green and yellow border, black and brown sponged ground over earlier red, top initialed "C. W.," fitted interior, brass lock, 12-1/4" w, 7-1/2" d, 4" h 415.00

Pine and poplar, orig red paint, black, red, green, yellow, and white dec, star ornaments on lid, stylized vine on base trim, till with secret drawer, homemade wire and tin hinges, pen-

Decorated, orig red paint, eagle and banner, and "Hannah Miller" on lid, front with pheasants with cornucopia, ends with birds kissing on one end, apart on other, yellow, green, gold, and black, interior lined with work orange paper, small areas of touch-up, found in Vermont, 9" w, 4-5/8" d, 4-3/4" h, $12,100. Photo courtesy of Garth's Auctions, Inc., Delaware, OH.

Decorated, pine, dome top, orig black paint, blue edge striping, stenciled decoration in red and silver, freehand red and yellow flowers on lid, brass bale handle and lock with hasp, minor edge wear, New England, possibly MA, 10" w, 6-1/2" d, 5" h, $5,225. Photo courtesy of Garth's Auctions, Inc., Delaware, OH.

ciled inscription inside lid, found in NY state, 16" w, 8" d, 7" h.................................4,400.00

Pine, Chinoiserie gold and black dec, red repaint, brass bale pull on lid, brass tacks, interior lock, 12-1/2" w, 6-1/2" d, 5" h...........300.00

Pine, dome top, orig black paint, blue edge striping, stenciled decoration in red and silver, freehand red and yellow flowers on lid, brass bale handle and lock with hasp, minor edge wear, New England, possibly MA, 10" w, 6-1/2" d, 5" h 5,225.00

Pine, dome top, old black repaint, yellow striping over earlier red, orig brass bale on lid, additional bales on ends, found in Maine, 8" w, 9" d, 9" h..11,000.00

Pine, dome top, old green paint, wooden peg construction, applied base molding, wire hinges, found in Kingston, MA, 10-1/2" w, 7" d, 6" h..350.00

Pine, dome top, old green paint, wire end handles, staple hinges, age crack in lid, 10-1/2" w, 5-3/4" d, 4-3/4" h 300.00

Pine, grain painted with yellow borders, stenciled fruit, dovetailed, slide top, minor abrasions, slight imperfections, 8-1/4" l, 5" w, 5-1/4" h...2,185.00

Pine, hinged lid, applied molding, top painted with scrolling leafy border, red ground, minor paint loss, 11-3/4" l, 7-1/4" h, 6-5/8" h 750.00

Pine, old brown and black grained decoration, yellow line borders, dovetailed case, lid with molding around edge, four styles of graining inside, ivory diamond shaped escutcheon, bracket feet with arched aprons, lift-out tray and interior with old blue, 10-1/2" w, 7" d, 6" h 715.00

Pine, orig black painted ground, two baskets of fruit on front panel, lid with four shells in gold, red, and white, tulips on each end, inset panels, gold lined borders, ball feet, ring pull, lock with brass escutcheon, Massachusetts, 10" w, 6-3/4" d, 5-1/2" h 7,700.00

Pine, orig black paint, white, red, yellow, and red geometric and floral decoration, dovetailed case, wire hinges, penciled inscription "Douglas 1822, Massachusetts" on inside lid, 15-3/4" w, 7-3/4" d, 6-1/4" h 2,750.00

Pine, orig black paint, red, olive, and yellow striping, divided interior with powdery blue paint, dovetailed, 10" w, 5-1/2" d, 4-1/2" h 990.00

Pine, orig brownish red flame graining, dovetailed case, minor damage at hinges, 12" w, 7" d, 7" h..250.00

Pine, orig brownish red paint, dovetailed case, domed top, molded bracket feet, cutout, penciled names on bottom, small patch and varnish, Pennsylvania, 13-1/4" w, 8-3/4" d, 8-3/4" h..1,100.00

Decorated, pine, inset panels, gold lined borders on orig black ground, ball feet, tulips on each end, two baskets of fruit on front panel, lined with four shells in gold, red, and white, ring pull and lock with brass escutcheon, Massachusetts, 10" w, 6-3/4" d, 5-1/2" h, $7,700. Photo courtesy of Garth's Auctions, Inc., Delaware, OH.

Decorated, poplar, dome top, grained repaint, yellow and red lined borders, painted fans in corners, gold initials "A. H." on lid, fitted lock, minor age cracks, 10-1/2" w, 6-1/2" d, 5" h, $715. Photo courtesy of Garth's Auctions, Inc., Delaware, OH.

Pine, orig brown over red decoration, fine dovetailing, lid with early brass with feather design, ring pull, 11-1/2" w, 8" d, 4-1/4" h 385.00

Pine, orig dark brown, green, and yellow paint, dovetailed case, lined with period wallpaper with leaf design, shades of green, maroon, gray, and white, orig brass ring handle, 14" w, 10-1/2" d, 6" h 550.00

Pine, orig green paint, black line detail around edging and faint fans on lids, dome top, dovetailed, orig brass bale pulls on ends, hasp lock, found in Maine, 22" w, 10-1/2" d, 9" h.........360.00

Pine, orig green paint, red, gray, and black swags and tassels on front and sides, top with yellow, black flowers, red and white border, green interior fitted with lock and till, dovetailed, 10-1/2" w, 5-3/4" d, 5" h..........10,175.00

Pine, orig red and black graining, dovetailed, brass lock and hasp, brass bale, emb oval escutcheon, wire hinges, some wear, 10" w, 5-1/2" d, 5" h 330.00

Pine, orig red paint, black border, stenciled gold leaves and fruit, dovetailed, orig brass bale pull on lid, wrought iron hasp lock on front, sgd in pencil "L. B. Lawrence 2-19-08" inside, 12" w, 6" d, 5-1/2" h..............................3,850.00

Pine, orig red sponge dec, dome top with orig brass bale pull, brass lock with hasp, 14" w, 9" d, 6" h......................................990.00

Pine, orig yellow paint, stenciled leaves on black border, dovetailed, wire hinges, wire hasp, 10-1/2" w, 6-1/4" d, 5-1/4" h 2,310.00

Pine, painted in optic block pattern on lid and three sides, gilt, red, and black, hinged rectangular box, shield-shaped escutcheon, interior fitted with three-section compartment, 13" l, 11" d, 6-1/2" h...3,740.00

Pine, stenciled in gold with eagle, hunter, deer, and leaves on top and front, dovetailed rectangular, brass ring handle and hasp, lacks divider and support inside, wear, 10" w, 5-3/4" d, 4" h 375.00

Pine, worn old blue paint, molded edge lid removable, wooden cleats engage hinge rail, applied base molding, some edge damage, separation in bottom board, 11-1/2" w, 7-1/4" d, 7-1/4" h..440.00

Poplar, grained repaint, yellow and red lined borders, painted corner fans, gold initials "A. H." on lid, fitted lock, dome top, minor age cracks, 10-1/2" w, 6-1/2" d, 5" h 715.00

Poplar, old black checkerboard design, dark varnish, dovetailed, 14" w, 6-3/4" d, 6-1/4" h 275.00

Poplar, orig graining in imitation of rosewood, stenciled gold decoration on lid, yellow striping brass lock, orig brass bale pull on lid, 1910 pencil inscription in lid, 19" w, 8-1/2" d, 7" h...900.00

Poplar, orig green paint, black and yellow striping, brass knob, label inside from 1974 exhibition at Art Institute of Chicago, 9" w, 5" d, 4" h...1,760.00

Decorated, sliding lid, gold, black, red, and yellow decoration on deep blue ground, small area of touch-up on rim, minor age crack, attributed to PA, 7-1/4" w, 4-1/4" d, 3-1/2" h, $8,250. Photo courtesy of Garth's Auctions, Inc., Delaware, OH.

Poplar, orig red line detail, blue border and sprigs, light green ground, interior with open till, lock with key, attributed to Dauphin County, PA, some edge wear, 9-1/2" w, 6" d, 5" h 770.00

Poplar, orig red paint, dome top, brass lock with hasp, brass bale handle with two studs, 10" w, 5" d, 4" h...660.00

Poplar, orig red paint, yellow line and white flower decoration, domed lid, square nail construction, interior with partial 1839 New York newspaper lining and stains, age cracks, 22" w, 9" d, 8-1/2" h..............................2,530.00

Poplar, orig red repaint, stenciled grapes and leaves, yellow lined borders, replaced ring pull, embossed brass escutcheon, interior lock, 11" w, 6-1/2" d, 5" h................................250.00

Poplar, orig red paint, yellow border stripe, dovetailed case, chamfered edge top, replaced ivory escutcheon, period floral wallpaper on lid interior, 8" w, 5" d, 4-1/2" h...................1,265.00

Poplar, orig yellow paint, black and red striping, gold monogram on lid, dovetailed case, two dovetailed drawers, interior and drawers lined in red paper, black and white lithograph landscape on inside of lid, orig embossed brass hardware with ring handles, 11-3/4" w, 7-3/4" d...3,850.00

Tulip Poplar, orig dark brown graining, yellow ground, orig brass bale handle, 14" w, 8-3/4" d, 6-1/4" h..500.00

Undetermined type of wood

Orig red paint, eagle and banner, and "Hannah Miller" on lid, front with pheasants with cornucopia, ends with birds kissing on one end, apart on other, yellow, green, gold, and black, interior lined with work orange paper, small areas of touch-up, found in Vermont, 9" w, 4-5/8" d, 4-3/4" h.........12,100.00

Orig red swags and abstract foliate dec, red and black cardinal on front, over light green painted ground, imperfections, 11" w, 5-1/2" d, 5" h....................................4,900.00

Pantry

Boxes were often used in Colonial-era pantries. Today collectors seek these well used boxes. Expect to find some wear on these handy household relics. The boxes listed below are all American, mid 19th C, round

Pantry, c1870, round, lapped sides, drop handles, left in orig blue paint, $500; right with orig putty-colored paint, $475.

examples. *Probably some of the other boxes listed here under headings like "Painted Decorated" were also used as Pantry boxes.*

Ash, hand-painted stylized dec in white, green, and black, minor wear, 10-1/2" d, 5-1/2" h...230.00

Staved construction, fastened with two woven lap hoops, carved initials on cover "R. P. F.," minor paint loss to green paint, 14-1/2" d, 6-1/2" h...865.00

Pipe

Hanging pipe boxes were fixtures in Colonial households, usually kept near the fireplace to keep the pipes and tobacco dry. These long boxes are perhaps the hottest area of box collecting at this time.

America, early 19th C

Cherry, chestnut and pine secondary wood, scrolled top rim and crest, one dovetailed overlapping drawer, molded bottom edge, old refinishing, orig gray paint on interior, incomplete drawer bottom, 19-1/4" h.............................3,850.00

Cherry, pine secondary wood, scrolled top edge with lollipop crest, molded corners, one dovetailed drawer, molded edge base, turned pull, old finish, some edge damage, age cracks, 18-1/2" h.......................2,950.00

Mahogany, pine secondary wood, scrolled top edge with tulip crest, one dovetailed drawer, molded edge base, turned pull, old

varnish finish, minor edge damage, small old repair, 20-3/4" h.............................2,200.00

Mahogany stained poplar, nailed construction, shaped top edges at front, sides and extended backboard, thumb-molded drawer front, brass knob, molded base, minor wear, 4-3/4" w, 5" d, 22" h.........................2,645.00

Pine, canted sides, pierced back, single drawer, includes six clay pipes, repair, minor losses, wear, 6-1/4" w, 5-1/2" d, 18-3/4" h......................................1,955.00

Pine with old red wash, nailed, shaped edges at opening, expended backboard with hole for hanging, lower section with drawer, brass knob, thumb-molded base, repairs, 5-3/4" w, 4" d, 21-1/4" h...................2,990.00

Pine with orig dark reddish brown paint, one drawer with dovetailed and nailed construction, front board has decorative circle designs forming initials "I. S.," and edging carved medallion, deeply scrolled top edges with lollipop crest, minor edge damage, some old renailing, 17-1/4" h...........5,225.00

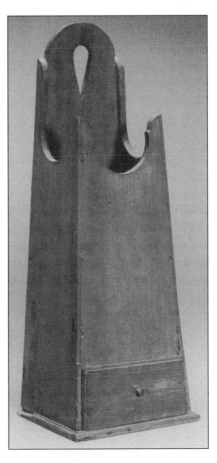

Pipe, 19th C, pine, canted sides, pierced back, single drawer, repair, minor losses, wear, sold with six clay pipes, 6-1/4" w, 5-1/2" d, 18-3/4" h, $1,955. Photo courtesy of Skinner Auctioneers and Appraisers of Antiques and Fine Art Boston and Bolton, MA.

Pipe: pine with red stain, elaborately scrolled crest, two compartments with finely cut scalloped edge, three cutout hearts, one dovetailed drawer, molded bottom edge, 16-3/4" h, $4,950. Photo courtesy of Garth's Auctions, Inc., Delaware, OH.

Pine with orig red paint, chip carved edge on open top and fish tail crest with compass star designs, one drawer with molded edge, bracket feet, early wide dovetailing, minor edge damage, 18-1/2" h 8,800.00

Pine with red stain, three cut-out hearts and elaborately scrolled crest, one dovetailed drawer, two compartments with finely cut scalloped edge, molded bottom edge, back of drawer scratch carved inscription "January 13, 1813, John ___," minor repairs, small hanging hole added above top heart, 16-3/4" h 4,950.00

Poplar, old gray-blue over red paint, well detailed scalloped backboard and crest, one nailed drawer, 19-1/2" h.................16,500.00

Connecticut, cherry, old finish, applied carved heart, scrolled edges and crest with applied pinwheel-like flower, one dovetailed overlapping drawer in base, minor edge damage, wear at hanging hole in crest, 20" h 3,850.00

Salt

Salt boxes were another type of box frequently kept near the kitchen fire. Like early spices, salt was a precious commodity.

Mahogany, hanging type, old finish, applied base molding, hinged slant front lid and shaped crest, old replaced pine bottom board, attributed to PA, 7-3/4" w, 6-1/2" d, 10" h 440.00

Oak, crest, dovetailed, lift lid, divided interior, old finish, 11-1/2" w, 7-1/4" d, 9" h..........200.00

Sewing

Sewing boxes full of sewing implements are frequently handed down through families. Today collectors value them for the interesting designs, as well as their provenance.

America, mid-19th C, painted red and black, attached lid, molded edge, landscape scene with two large buildings, trees in background, 9-1/4" w, 6-1/2" d, 2-3/4" h 5,175.00

America, mid-19th C, poplar, hanging, natural and ebonized finish, cutout and chip-carved designs, crest with work pincushion, two semi-circular shelves for holding thread, hinged-line compartment in base, 20-1/4" h 850.00

Chinese Export, 19th C, lacquer and gilt, 8-sided ftd box, dragons and figural motifs, fitted compartments with ivory sewing implements,

Sewing, MA, pine, orig stencil dec, green borders, silver and gold stars, red lines, smoke ground, sliding lid with flower and leaf design, brass pull, pencil inscription, "Mary Houghton Stowe who was born in Hubbardstone, Mass. In 1808," ball feet, minor wear, 9" w, 6" d, 4-1/4" h, $5,225. Photo courtesy of Garth's Auctions, Inc., Delaware, OH.

lower drawer and brass handles, minor wear, one broken handle, 14-1/4" l, 11" d, 6-3/4" h 1,735.00

Massachusetts, mid-19th C, painted wood, small hinged box with thread holes on top of larger box with feet, drawer hosing till, outside painted brown with black edging, yellow borders, urn and eagle on top, smaller box opening to reveal painted scene of fox in uniform having drink and cigar, partially obscured inscription reads "S (?) Richardson in uniform presented to h(?) by me (illegible)," on bottom written "Rosalind Webster from Grandma and Grandpa Webster 1953 Was Grandma Webster's Familys - the Alger Brooks Family of Medford, Mass," minor paint loss, 11-1/4" w, 9" d, 8-1/2" h 920.00

Tramp Art, pincushion frame top, drawer, orig dark finish, 9-1/2" l 175.00

Shirtwaist

A shirtwaist box is a special storage box. The name is derived from the term denoting a popular clothing style about the same time the Arts & Crafts period was developing. Because these boxes were often cedar lined, they were the perfect storage boxes for off season clothes.

Arts & Crafts, Gustav Stickley, c1912, oak, cedar lined, red, hammered copper lift handles, branded mark, 32" w, 17" d, 16" h.......9,775.00

Shirtwaist, Arts & Crafts, Gustav Stickley, New York, c1912, oak, cedar lined, red, hammered copper lift handles, branded mark, 32" w, 17" d, 16" h, $9,775. Photo courtesy of Skinner Auctioneers and Appraisers of Antiques and Fine Art Boston, and Bolton MA.

Spice

Spice boxes are favorites among collectors. They usually contain small drawers or divided interiors. However, beware of reproductions and fakes made to deceive buyers as antique. Check carefully for signs of wear, old nails, repairs, etc. and even smells to indicate what kind of spice was kept in a box. Also see Chests, Other, for larger Spice Chests.

Hanging

Cherry, crest with hole for hanging, dovetailed case, three dovetailed drawers with divided interiors, old worn finish, some edge damage, 9-1/4" w, 5-3/4" d, 13" h....1,320.00

Pine, America, 19th C, heart-shaped pierced back, slanted lift-top lid attached with wooden pegs, two-compartment box over single drawer with six sections, 8-1/2" l, 9-1/2" d, 13-1/2" h..............................490.00

Pine, America, 19th C, orig salmon pink paint, black, yellow, and red striping, polychrome paint decoration on lid, edges, and front surface, scrolled crest, divided interior, hinged lid, two nailed drawers with porcelain pulls, heavily alligatored over varnish, poplar secondary wood, 13" w, 7-1/2" d, 15-1/2" h..................................... 19,500.00

Table Top

Country, pine, orig cream colored paint, red striping, stepped case with twelve drawers with porcelain pulls, repaired break on scrolled crest, 20" w, 11-1/2" d, 16-1/2" h 2,860.00

Walnut, sliding lid, dovetailed case, four part divided interior, old finish, 7" w, 5" d, 2-1/2" h 825.00

Storage

Again, another generic term to describe the function of a box. Whatever the original intended item that was stored in these larger boxes are generally gone, leaving the lovely box to delight today's collectors.

America, early 19th C, painted, maple, turned cylindrical form, hardwood base with incised lines, green, yellow, and black leafy vine decoration, red ground, pine lid incised with lines, initials "K. F." in center circle, foliate border, two age splits, break at lower band, 14-1/8" d, 6-1/4" h 7,575.00

Storage, early 19th C, painted maple, turned cylindrical form, hardwood base with incised lines, green, yellow, and black leafy vine decoration on red ground, pine lid with incised lines, initials "K. F." in center circle, foliate border, two age splints, break at lower band, 14-1/8" d, 6-1/4" h, $7,475. Photo courtesy of Skinner Auctioneers and Appraisers of Antiques and Fine Art Boston and Bolton, MA.

America, mid-19th C, grain painted pine, dome top, dovetailed construction, later gold painted highlights, painted iron lock, brass handle on lid, minor paint loss, 12" l, 6" d, 6" h................230.00

America, mid-19th C, grain painted pine, yellow striping, iron lock and hasp, interior lined with remnants of early fabric, minor paint loss, 28" l, 12-1/2" d, 9-1/2" h.........................350.00

America, late 19th C, mahogany inlaid, dovetailed construction, lift top decorated with exotic wood star inlay in center, star points at corners, lid interior with ripple molding, case with two half drawers, banding, escutcheon with contrasting inlay, imperfections include wear and age cracks, 13" l, 10" w, 20" h..........................850.00

America, late 19th C, walnut, molded edge lid and base, additional applied moldings, lock and key, 11" w, 5-1/2" d, 5-1/4" h 250.00

Massachusetts, early 19th C, carved and painted dec, rectangular hinged top with applied carved crouching cat handle, box carved in relief with full figure of woman wearing lace cap, white ruffled collar, yellow dress trimmed in red-orange, holding yellow flower on leafy stem, flanked by large tree with red fruit, gray dog stands to right, red and green bird in flight, 16-1/4"w, 8-3/4"d, 11-1/2" h 26,450.00

Wall Boxes

The last of the generic box categories. Wall boxes were often hand made to the specifications of the housewife or for the intended use. Today these interesting looking shapes and colors catch the eye of collectors. Also see Cupboards, Hanging.

America, 19th C, cherry and mixed woods, scalloped back with two holes for hanging, slant lid, dovetailed, lower drawer, 12" w, 7" d, 12" h...850.00

America, 19th C, grain painted and stenciled, nailed and dovetailed, lower drawer, shaped backboard pierced for hanging, red and black graining, bronze stencil dec, repaired crack in backboard, bottom board, surface wear, 12-3/4" w, 7" d, 10" h.............................1,850.00

America, 19th C, painted red, slanted lift top lid, single drawers, damage, 13-1/2" h 1,610.00

America, 19th C, pine, dovetailed and nailed construction, backboard shaped into two half circles, each pierced for hanging, imperfections, 13" w, 71/4" d, 9-1/4" h 550.00

America, 19th C, pine, painted, rectangular form, shaped back, two pierced round hangers, old yellow paint, wear, reinforcements, 12-3/4" w, 5-1/2" d, 8-1/2" h 375.00

America, 19th C, poplar, traces of green paint, square nail construction, three stepped compartments, four board back with few nails missing, refinished, age crack in one side, 10-1/4" w, 5-3/4" d, 20-3/4" h 300.00

Pennsylvania or Connecticut, c1830-40, carved and painted walnut, arched cornice

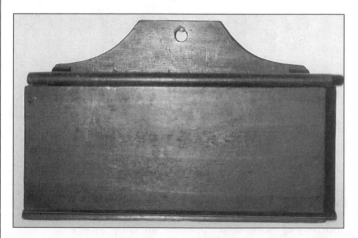

Wall, hanging, c1830, pine, orig green paint, $600.

molding flanks carved device, tasseled pendants, curving sides continuing to form box with carved vines and leaves flanked by cross-hatching, arched mirror back, dark red-brown stain, old black paint, minor imperfections, 12" w, 4-1/8" d, 20-1/4" h 1,955.00

Watercolor Paints

Understanding that there is a collector for every type of box, here's an interesting example of something that you may not associate with being sold in a box, much less one with a fitted drawer. However, to early artists, these boxes were useful to carry their implements and paints.

Mahogany, fitted interior with drawer, some orig contents, orig printed and hand colored label "Reeves & Inwood, London," 8-3/4" w, 4-1/4" d, 2-1/2" h 450.00

Wood

A wood box was designed to be kept on a porch, perhaps in a keeping room or kitchen to store cut wood, all ready for use in the fireplace or stove. Because these boxes received a lot of hard use during their lifetimes, look for signs of wear, numerous coats of paints, etc. Today they are getting all cleaned up and taking on new life as collectors discover new ways to use them.

America, 19th C, grain painted, two lift lids, some damage to lids, 70" l.....................950.00

Writing

Writing boxes include boxes designed to contain stationery and writing accessories. Some more sophisticated boxes are similar to small desks with fitted interiors. Writing boxes differ from lap desks in that a writing box usually has a flat top, while a lap desk has a slanted top and is more comfortable to write while seated in a chair. Secret compartments are rarely found in both writing boxes and lap desks. Writing boxes tend to be of finer woods and display a finer workmanship than lap desks.

Mahogany, old finish, dovetailed drawer in base, one external dovetailed drawer, brass bale handles, 16" w, 10" d, 6" h 385.00

Mahogany, old finish, dovetailed case, tambour top made to open when dovetailed drawer is pulled out, lift-top lid, partial paper label "Mrs. Anna M. McIntosh...New York," orig brass bales on ends, repairs to hinge rail, cloth backing of tambour deteriorated, 16" w, 10" d, 6-3/4" h..700.00

Mahogany, old finish, one dovetailed drawer in end, orig brass bale, fitted interior with two old inks and pen, writing surface recovered with green felt, 9-1/2" w, 15-3/4" l...........600.00

Mahogany, old finish, fitted interior with one external dovetailed drawer, brass bale handles, 16" w, 10" d, 6" h 385.00

Pine, old worn olive brown graining over red, dovetailed case, fitted interior with four pigeon holes, two drawers, orig brass bales, hinges and lock replaced, age crack in lid, edge damage, 20" w, 10-1/4" d, 9" h......................275.00

Rosewood veneer, gilded brass trim, fitted interior, 14" l 375.00

Cabinets

Cabinets of all shapes and sizes have been created through all styles of American furniture. Many were design to accommodate a specific social function, while others were designed for storage purposes. As with other forms of furniture, today's collectors of American furniture enjoy the history of why a piece was created, but many choose to use their cabinets for a slightly different use. Because many cabinets are small, they are easily fit into many room settings. Cabinets are different than stands or tables in that they have a door to access storage areas.

Comments about design elements relating to a particular style are not included, as it often is difficult to determine by the cabinet style. Many times usage, types of materials used, or other clues are more beneficial to determining age.

Additional examples of furniture with storage capacity are found in Blanket Chests, Boxes, Chests of Drawers, and Cupboards.

Bar Cabinet

Also referred to as liquor cabinets, bar cabinets were unique creations designed to hold liquor bottles and usually the stemware associated with the favorite beverages of the era. Sometime high-style designs contained work surfaces on which to create the perfect drink.

Art Deco, walnut, sarcophagus form, two doors, square top with drop-front cabinet on left, mirrored bar, small drawers on right between two open bays, 48" w, 21" d, 54-1/2" h 600.00

Arts & Crafts

Stickley Brothers, Grand Rapids, Michigan, attributed to, flush top, two door compartment with pull-out copper tray, single drawer, second two door cabinet, orig dark finish, unmarked, 27-1/4" w, 16" d, 51" h 2,700.00

Stickley, Gustav, New York, No. 87, single drawer over cabinet door, both with hammered copper pulls, interior compartments with rotating bottle holder, red Ali Ik Kan decal, 22" w, 16" d, 39-1/2" h 3,750.00

Cabinet on Stand

A cabinet on a stand is just what the name implies. A small cabinet that rests on a stand, perhaps to ease accessibility while sitting or to elevate the precious contents.

Queen Anne, c1700, black lacquer, two doors and eleven interior drawers decorated with Chinoiserie decorated exotic landscapes and creatures, later mahogany blind fretwork stand, 40" w, 20-1/4" d, 68" h 2,750.00

Cellarette

A cellarette is a unique cabinet form which facilitated the chilling of wines and beverages.

Arts & Crafts

Stickley, Gustav, New York, single drawer and door, hammered copper pulls, arched apron, red mark, new finish. 20" w, 15" d, 29" h 4,000.00

Stickley, L. and J. G., Fayetteville, NY, overhanging rectangular top, pull-out shelf, two cabinet doors, hammered copper strap hardware, new medium finish, unmarked, 32" w, 16" d, 36" h 5,000.00

Unknown Designer

Oak, c1905, drop front inlaid with copper, interior fitted with racks and porcelain cylinder, single door, hammered brass hardware, interior of lower door fitted with insulating metal, 21-3/4" w, 13-3/4" d, 43-1/2" h 550.00

Oak, early 20th C, hinged lift top with copper lining, single drawer, cupboard door, interior shelf and fitted compartments, replaced pull, 23-1/2" w, 17-1/4" d, 43" h 2,415.00

Classical Revival, New York, c1825, mahogany and mahogany veneer, shaped base with canted corners, flattened ball shaped feet, 16-1/2" w, 15" d, 33" h 1,200.00

China Cabinets

China cabinets appeared on the decorating scene when it became important to display one's wealth by displaying the finest china. Originally designated for dining rooms, china cabinets were often part of dining room suites. Some china cabinets were made to compliment existing future styles and blend in nicely. Today collectors often feature china cabinets in other rooms to house their collections of all types of things. Another common name for a china cabinet is china closet. Expect to find grooved plate rails in many of the shelves of china cabinets, to facilitate horizontal display of china plates.

Aesthetic Movement, New York, c1880, carved mahogany, arched crest, carved tendrils and leaf tip lunettes, open platform with pierced undulating foliate frame work, poppy carved stiles, rectangular beveled and mirrored glass door, short cabriole legs with tendril pierced spandrels, wired for interior lighting, 35-1/4" w, 98" h 3,750.00

Arts & Crafts

Limbert, Charles P., Grand Rapids and Holland, MI

China, Arts & Crafts, Lifetime, double door, through tenon top and gallery, paneled back, orig hardware, orig finish, unmarked, 55" w, 16" d, 54" h, $4,000. Photo courtesy of David Rago Auctions/RagoArts.com, Lambertville, NJ.

China, Arts & Crafts, Gustav Stickley, designed by Harvey Ellis, New York, c1904, oak, rectangular overhanging top, arched single door, arched rail below, 36" w, 15-1/4"d, 60" h, $8,625. Photo courtesy of Skinner Auctioneers and Appraisers of Antiques and Fine Art Boston and Bolton, MA.

#1466, arched and notched top rail with corbel details under overhanging top, two doors with orig copper strap hinges and hardware, eight panes of glass to each, four panes at sides, arched and notched toe-board, through-tenon construction, orig finish, branded and numbered, 48" w, 16" d, 56" h 7,250.00

Double door, through tenon top and gallery, paneled back, orig hardware and finish, 55" w, 16" d, 54" h 4,000.00

Stickley, Gustav, New York

No. 822, single door with sixteen glass panes, gallery top, hammered copper V-pulls, refinished, two replaced panes, remnants of paper label, 35-1/4" w, 13" d, 58-1/4" h 5,500.00

Designed by Harvey Ellis, NY, c1904, oak, rectangular overhanging top, arched single door with glass pane, arched rail below, shelved int., 36" w, 15-1/4" d, 60" h 8,625.00

Designed by Harvey Ellis, NY, c1904, oak, rectangular overhanging top, arched single door with glass pane, orig iron hardware, arched toe-board and bowed sides, fine orig light finish, red decal, remnant of paper label, 33" w, 16" d, 60" h...................8,850.00

Unknown Designer

Double door form, gallery top, eight glass panes to each door, Gustav Stickley hammered copper ring pulls, orig finish, unmarked, two glass panes missing, 42" w, 15-1/4" d, 66" h.................................4,200.00

Double door form, orig copper hardware at back, corbels at sides, orig finish, 47" w, 15" d, 55" h 1,750.00

Trapezoidal, flaring sides, two lower front doors with butterfly joints, orig ebonized finish, replaced door without glass, unmarked, copy of early Gustav Stickley design, 35-1/4" w, 15-1/4" d, 65" h 7,500.00

Colonial Revival

Breakfront, early 20th C, two sections, molded cornice with four glazed and mullioned doors, three shelves over two central cupboard doors, flanked by six drawers, oval brasses with embossed eagles, 78-1/2" w, 16-1/2" d, 83-1/2" h...........................2,250.00

Chippendale Style, c1940, walnut veneer, breakfront, scrolled broken pediment, center urn finial, pr of glazed doors and panels, long drawer over two cupboard doors, 44" w, 15" d, 76" h 600.00

Edwardian Style, curved glass sides, single flat glazed door, illuminated interior, mirrored back, 42" w, 16" d, 64" h 1,100.00

Hepplewhite, inlaid mahogany, leaded glass, velvet lined interior, 43" w, 21" d, 75-1/2" h..700.00

Modernism Era

Frankl, Paul, manufactured by Johnson Furniture Co., mahogany top with three glass shelves, above seven drawers and two

doors, mahogany and lacquered cork, 72" w, 21" d, 74" h 1,000.00

Marx, Samuel, manufactured by Quigley, c1940, eight doors with parchment wrapped front, 62" w, 24" d, 87" h 5,500.00

Parzinger, Tommi, manufactured by Charak, 1940s, contrasting light and dark mahogany, two doors, brass pulls, upper cabinet with lattice glass doors, 36" w, 17" d, 81" h 950.00

Rohde, Gilbert, manufactured by Herman Miller

Checkerboard walnut veneers, two doors beneath sliding glass top, refinished, 36" w, 14" d, 50" h 750.00

Pickled veneer, sliding glass doors above two doors with cutout pulls, tubular metal legs, 36" w, 13" d, 50" h.......................775.00

Victorian, oak, bow front, leaded glass, amber glass diamonds in top panels, 37-1/2"w, 14-1/2" d, 61-3/4" h 600.00

China, Victorian, Jacobean Revival, c1880, carved oak, mask head acanthus carved cornice, single glazed cabinet door, flanked by figures of herm, winged figural supports, platform base, bun feet, $6,000. Photo courtesy of Samuel T. Freeman & Co., Philadelphia, PA.

Corner Cabinets

Not wishing to waste any important storage space, corner cabinets were created in many design styles. Also see Cupboards, Hanging, Corner.

Classical, mid to late 19th C, hanging, mahogany, arched top with carved scrolls, shell and ribbon carvings, carved urn finials to pediment, molded cornice over beveled glass door, flanked by fluted sides, molded base with carved skirt, three shelves cut in same offset corner manner as case, 25-1/2" w, 14" d, 39" h 900.00

George II Style, oak, incorporating period elements, cavetto molded triangular top, front with pair of bi-paneled doors opening to two shaped shelves, outset molded base with bracket feet, 37" w, 20-1/2" d, 46-3/4" h 800.00

Victorian, **Gothic Revival**, burled walnut, Gothic style mullioned glass door top, base with cupboard door, damage, 29-1/2" w, 18-1/4" d, 78" h 220.00

Display Cabinets

Like china cabinets, display cabinets are meant to display a collection or things that indicate the owner is wealthy or possesses good taste. Another name for display cabinet is "vitrine." Many furniture designers created display cabinets to be included in living room or den settings. Many display cabinets are lighted to further enhance their contents. If modifying an antique display cabinet with lighting, take into consideration what the heat and light rays will do to your objects.

Aesthetic Movement, America, fourth quarter 19th C, rosewood and marquetry, two sections, upper section with galleried top, pair of glazed cupboard doors, lower section with floral carved panels over pair of glazed cupboard doors, turned feet, 54-1/2" w, 20-1/2" d, 109" h 2,750.00

Art Deco, teak

Continental, molded rectangular top, rounded corners, two glazed cupboard doors, shelved interior, above two paneled cupboard doors, stepped block feet, 36" w, 17-1/2" d, 69-1/2" h 400.00

Dutch, shaped and molded cornice, carved square geometric designs over single glazed paneled door with serpentine edge, shelved interior, two small drawers, molded and shaped plinth base, 36-1/2" w, 17-1/2" d, 75" h 450.00

Arts & Crafts

Shop of the Crafters, overhanging rectangular top, three inlaid doors, three open shelves, some enhancement to orig finish, unmarked, 31-1/2" w, 16-1/4" d, 63" h 5,500.00

Unknown Designer, two display sections, recessed beveled mirror, two drawers between two glazed display sections, over two larger paneled base doors, sq faceted wooden pulls, over-coated finish, unmarked, 49-1/2" w, 20-1/2" d, 62-1/2" h 2,100.00

Classical, Middle Atlantic States, c1815-15, mahogany and mahogany veneer, rectangular top with cockbeaded pediment backboard over two glazed doors flanked by turned half engaged columns, turned legs, refinished, 28-3/4' w, 12-1/2" d, 33" h 2,000.00

Edwardian, c1900

Mahogany and boxwood inlay, rectangular, Gothic-style mullioned glazed doors, square tapering legs, spade feet, 41-1/2" w, 14-1/4" d, 63-1/4" h 1,200.00

Satinwood, paint decorated, breakfront top, glazed doors, interior shelves, splayed legs, 42" w, 15" d, 48-1/2" h 950.00

Edwardian-Style, mahogany, inlaid decoration, three glazed doors, adjustable shelves, mirrored back, price for pair, 51" w, 16" d, 63" h 1,750.00

Federal-Style, cherry, rectangular top, curved crest, glass case, blown glass panes, twelve reverse graduated drawers, bracket feet, 36" w, 15" d, 62" h 1,750.00

French-Style, Paines Furniture Co., late 19th C, gilt bronze, kingwood, and marquetry, galleried bowed top, glazed front and sides, two glass shelves, cabriole legs, orig paper label, 28" w, 17" d, 61" h 2,645.00

Modernism Era, George Nelson, manufactured by Herman Miller, walnut veneer, sliding glass doors and shelves, price for pair, 34" w, 12" d, 24" h... 525.00

Napoleon III, gilt bronze mounted walnut, upper part with molded frame over gilt-bronze mounted frieze, glazed panel door opening to interior fitted with one shelf, flanked by two tapering columns mounted with lions heads, outset lower part centered with single drawer, supported by pr of double turned columns, platform base, toupie feet, 29" w, 21" d, 80" h..1,200.00

Queen Anne-Style, early 20th C, burl walnut, molded double-domed bonnet above two astragal glazed doors, two long drawers below, paneled tapering legs, shaped stretchers, bun feet, 39" w, 12" d, 77-1/2" h..................2,100.00

Victorian, Eastlake, c1870-80

Walnut and walnut veneer, step molded cornice over single glazed door, ebonized moldings, interior with five narrow shelves over four wide shelves, upper compartment missing, 32-1/4" w, 16" d, 67" h.......1,235.00

Walnut, trapezoidal, galleried top, flat reeded columns topped by spool turned capitals surrounding single glazed door, glazed canted sides, carved triangle and dot borders, five interior shelves, Medieval style brass hinges and lockplate, 44" w, 17" d, 58-3/8" h..3,360.00

William IV-Style, carved mahogany, molded cornice with projecting ends above two astragal glazed doors, flanked on either side by engaged pilasters headed by acanthus carved Ionic capitals, plinth base, glazed sides, 54" w, 19" d, 85-1/2" h.........................1,210.00

Filing Cabinets

Before the advent of steel filing cabinets, those who designed offices created wooden filing cabinets to help take the clutter of business and get it organized.

Arts & Crafts, unknown designer, c1910, golden oak, plain vertical stack, five drawers, orig brass nameplates and pulls 600.00

Linen Cabinets

Similar in function to a sideboard or linen press, a linen cabinet may be found in the dining room or pantry and holds table linens and other small accessories in its large drawers. Also see Cupboards, Linen Press, and Sideboards.

Federal, New York, carved mahogany veneer, rectangular top over two small cockbeaded drawers over two recessed panel

doors flanked by reeded panels, opening to four interior drawers, two front carved paw feet, two ring-turned rear legs, some restoration, 44-1/2" w, 22" d, 44-1/2" h 1,495.00

Map or Print Cabinet

A cabinet specially designed to hold maps or prints usually consists of multiple drawers, wide enough to hold maps and narrow enough to hold only a few maps at a time. Today's modern architect's or plan files are modern adaptations of this type of cabinet. Map and print collecting is not a new phenomena and the lovely Victorian-era map cabinets testify to the thought that collectors have long been enjoying the details and vibrant colors of early maps and prints.

Victorian, second half 19th C

Oak, outset rectangular top over front with five graduated and scribed drawers, recessed bail handles, sides double paneled, outset molded plinth base, 40-1/2" w, 27-1/2" d, 30-1/2" h..............................700.00

Music, Arts & Crafts, Gustav Stickley, New York, c1912, No. 70W, oak, gallery top, rectangular paneled door, branded mark, 20" w, 16" d, 46" h, $7,475. Photo courtesy of Skinner Auctioneers and Appraisers of Antiques and Fine Art Boston and Bolton, MA.

Music, Neo-Classical, c1860, ebonized rosewood case with slate top, single drawer over one door, paneled sides, door, and drawer, intricate gilt carved ornamentation and composition inlay flanking the central door with gilt bronze plaque of putti, molded base with stylized bracket feet with conforming gilt decoration, minor loss, 40" w, 19" d, 44" h, $2,200. Photo courtesy of Alderfer Auction Company, Hatfield, PA.

Oak, top with inlaid ebonized banding and diamond pattern, six long drawers, all with like banding, brass pulls, label holders, bracket feet, 47" w, 33" d, 36" h 1,100.00

Music Cabinets

Just as maps and prints deserve their own special storage cabinet, so does sheet music. Also see Stands, Music.

Art Nouveau, hardwood, cherry finish, crest with beveled glass, paneled door, applied decoration, 19" w, 13-1/2" d, 49" h...............200.00

Arts & Crafts

Gustav Stickley, c1912, No. 703, oak, gallery top, rectangular paneled door, branded mark, 20" w, 16" d, 46" h, ...7,475.00

Victorian, inlaid mahogany, bow front, single drawer over door, inlaid with instruments and flowers, some loss to finish on door 650.00

Pedestal Cabinet

A pedestal cabinet is another functional usage of a unique piece of furniture. Furniture makers of the second quarter of the 1800s wanted to provide some storage while giving space to hold up a favorite statue or perhaps a large jardiniere filled with a plant.

Empire, c1825, mahogany, circular gray marble top, cylindrical body, door enclosing shelves, plinth base, 16" d, 29" h...........800.00

Side Cabinets

Side cabinets are small cabinets used by the side of a chair, sofa, or perhaps in a bedroom. Also see Stands, Side and Tables, Side.

Aesthetic Movement

America, fourth quarter 19th C, ebonized and marquetry, mirrored, 40-1/4" l, 16-1/2" d, 62-1/4" h...2,400.00

New York, attributed to Horner, credenza, ebonized, marquetry inlaid, shaped inset marble top, ormolu bronze figural mounts, two drawers over two doors with concave sides, side panels inlay with flowers on green ground, front door panels inlay with baskets of flowers with bow tie ribbon, int. fitted with shelves, 67-1/2" w, 19-1/2" d, 41" h 8,000.00

Side, Country, New England, c1820-40, pine, orig blue-gray paint, dovetailed gallery, two cupboard doors, bracket feet, white porcelain knob, wear to paint and edges, $2,250.

Art Deco, French, early 20th C, Breche d'Alep marble top above case fitted with single paneled cupboard door, flanked on either side with free-standing column ending in carved paw feet, whole painted saffron with ebonized and green faux-marble accents, price for pair, 35-1/2" w, 18-1/2" d, 36-1/2" h 7,700.00

Empire, mid-19th C, mahogany, outset rectangular top with arched and molded backboard flanked by spindle galleries, front with outset cockbeaded frieze drawer raised on free standing Ionic columns flanking recessed cupboard door with lancet panel, opening to shelf, plinth base raised on ball feet, brass stringing throughout, secondary woods mahogany, poplar, and white pine, 24-3/4" w, 24" d, 53-1/4" h..550.00

French Restauration, New York, c1820, console, mahogany and mahogany veneer,

Side, Modernism-Era, George Nelson, Thin Edge, miniature, c1956, teak veneer, four drawers, rosewood fronts, white lacquered door, miniature porcelain pulls, marbleized French paper interior, orig swagged leg base, 20" w, 13" d, 27" h, $14,500. Photo courtesy of Treadway Gallery, Inc. of Cincinnati, OH.

rectangular marble top, center swell front drawer over pair of molded cupboard doors flanked by plain columns, capped with gilt capitals terminating in turned squatty bulbed feet, 42" w, 17-1/2" d, 36" h.........................1,950.00

Louis XVI Style, amaranth and satinwood, porcelain and gilt metal mounted, superstructure surmounted by rectangular top with convex ends, pierced three-quarter gallery, front with pair of paneled doors, porcelain panels painted with floral urns, opening to shelves, all flanked by conforming open shelves, outset lower section with similarly rounded ends, conforming frieze centered by a drawer inset with three further porcelain plaques painted with floral sprays and garlands, tapering octagonal legs with toupie feet joined by shaped cross stretcher, gilt metal mounts, 41-1/2" w, 12-3/4" d, 51-1/2" h 2,600.00

Mission, Frank Lloyd Wright, Heritage Henredon, No. 2005 with cradle base, mahogany, two doors each with raised concentric square design, bordered by Taliesin design, one adjustable shelf, orig finish, numbered, red monogram signature, 34" w, 20" d, 26" h 6,600.00

Modernism Era

Eames, Charles, manufactured by Herman Miller

ESU 200, c1952, rectangular black laminated top with primary colored masonite pulls, zinc angle iron frame, three drawers, perforated metal panel, 47" w, 16" d, 33" h...11,000.00

ESU 400, c1954, primary colored masonite panels in chrome angle iron frame, two drawers, perforated metal panel, X-stretchers, replaced sliding dimple doors, some wear, 47" w, 17" d, 48" h................6,500.00

Knoll, Florence, manufactured by Knoll International, credenza

Rectangular white marble top over four drawers, two doors, rosewood veneer, chrome base, roughness to drawers, 75" w, 18" d, 26" h 4,250.00

Walnut veneer, four sliding doors, black leather pulls, interior shelves and drawers, 72" w, 18" d, 28" h 1,325.00

Walnut veneer, two doors, four drawers,

chrome metal base, 75" w, 18" d, 26" h 700.00

Lowey, Raymond, DF 2000, manufactured in France, 1960s

Eight drawers, one door, plastic fronts, chromatic shades of red, white metal frame, 61" w, 20" d, 30" h 2,000.00

Nine drawers, one door, chromatic plastic fronts in neutral tones, 81" w, 21" d, 30" h 1,900.00

McCobb, Paul, manufactured by Calvin, from Erwin Collection, bleached mahogany, four drawers, brass base, orig label, refinished, price for pair, 36" w, 19" d, 34" h 1,450.00

Nelson, George, manufactured by Herman Miller

Birch veneer, four drawers, silver-plate pulls, ebonized wood legs, 36" w, 19" d, 30" h 1,750.00

Birch veneer, five drawers, silver-plate pulls, ebonized wood legs, 24" w, 19" d, 40" h 1,450.00

Coral lacquer, light walnut case, three drawers, one door, label, scratch to front, 56" w, 19" d, 30" h 1,600.00

Coral lacquer, light walnut case, four drawers, label, light wear, 24" w, 19" d, 30" h 1,100.00

Orange lacquer, walnut case, three drawers, wooden pulls, label, minor wear to top, 24" w, 19" d, 30" h 1,320.00

Rosewood veneer, three doors, lift-up top sections, white coated pulls, cast aluminum legs, interior shelves, 56" w, 20" d, 41" h 7,700.00

Thin Edge, miniature, c1956, teak veneer, four drawers, rosewood fronts, white lacquered door, miniature porcelain pulls, marbleized French paper interior, orig swagged leg base, 20" w, 13" d, 27" h 14,500.00

Thin Edge, three doors, rosewood veneer, white pulls, cast aluminum legs, label, top refinished, 34" w, 19" d, 31" h 2,860.00

Thin Edge, three doors, four drawers, white pulls, cast aluminum legs, label, worn finish, 80" w, 19" d, 33" h 2,300.00

Thin Edge, four drawers, two drawers, white pulls, cast aluminum legs, worn finish, 67" w, 19" d, 33" h 2,400.00

Walnut veneer, four drawers, one door, orig forest green lacquer, silver-plate pulls, 34" w, 19" d, 30" h 2,100.00

Walnut veneer, two doors, orig forest green lacquer, silver-plate pulls, some wear to top, 34" w, 19" d, 30" h 1,980.00

Woodgrain laminate top, two black sliding doors, tubular legs, repairs to top, 60" w, 18" d, 26" h 950.00

Parzinger, Tommi, manufactured by Charak, 1940s, contrasting light and dark mahogany, two doors, brass pulls, marked, 25" w, 15" d, 34" h 775.00

Rohde, Gilbert, manufactured by Herman Miller, pickled veneer, two doors with cutout pulls, tubular metal legs, 36" w, 13" d, 29" h 1,200.00

Robsjohn-Gibbings, T. H., manufactured by Widdicomb, walnut veneer, rattan wrapped handles, cast brass legs

Four drawers, refinished, 35" w, 21" d, 41" h 850.00

Six drawers, 68" w, 21" d, 32" h 750.00

Wegner, Hans, walnut veneer case, roll top front, wear, 28" w, 20" d, 27" h 50.00

Wormley, Edward, manufactured by Dunbar

Dark mahogany, three drawers, three sliding doors, woven fronts, nickel plated base, 62" w, 18" d, 38" h 3,000.00

Side, Victorian, Neo-Georgian, attributed to New York, c1870-90, breakfront, later added faux marble top, ebonized case, central glazed cupboard door flanked by urn inlaid and beveled wood banded cupboard doors, four fluted flat columns with ormolu capitals, 66" l, 14-3/8" d, 39-1/8" h, $1,525. Photo courtesy of Samuel T. Freeman & Co., Philadelphia, PA.

Pair, seven drawers, curved wooden handles, white lacquer, brass feet, gold tag, 34" w, 21" d, 47" h 1,500.00

Victorian

American, last quarter 19th C, Asian taste, stained pine, rectangular top with heavily carved and reticulated iris gallery, drawer and cabinet door enclosing shelves, all with similar carved reticulated paneling, 35-1/2" w, 16" d, 66-1/2" h 700.00

Gothic Revival, first quarter 20th C, carved oak, molded rectangular hinged top over paneled door carved with Gothic tracery, flanked by columnar stiles surmounted by mediaeval statues, sides and back similar, columnar legs joined by platform stretcher, fitted with phonograph, 19-1/4" w, 19-1/4" d, 51-1/4" h....................900.00

Neo-Georgian, attributed to New York, c1870-90, breakfront, later added faux marble top, ebonized case, central glazed cupboard door flanked by urn inlaid and beveled wood banded cupboard doors, four fluted flat columns with ormolu capitals, 66" l, 14-3/8" d, 39-1/8" h 1,525.00

Renaissance Revival, America, late 19th C Walnut, marble top over molded rectangular top, three drawers, cabinet doors, shaped plinth base, 53" l, 18-1/2" d, 38" h.......1,450.00

Walnut, marquetry, rectangular top, center cupboard door with large center medallion flanked by pair of cupboard doors, acanthus leaf molding, teardrop hardware, 65" l, 19-1/2" d, 43" h........................2,400.00

Rococo Revival, third quarter 19th C, walnut, demilune, bowed Carrara-marble top, case fitted with four mirrored cabinet doors, shaped base, 60" w, 19" d, 33-1/2" h..............................1,650.00

Smoking Cabinets

Smoking cabinets, as well as smoking stands, were designed to hold a smoker's implements, usually a large ashtray, place for cigarettes and cigars, matches, often a pipe holder and tobacco storage area. Also see Stands, Smoking.

Arts & Crafts

Limbert, Charles P., Grand Rapids and Holland, MI, single door, orig copper hardware over lower shelf, refinished, branded mark, 12" w, 12" d, 36" h 1,100.00

Unknown designer, oval top, corbelled sides, single paneled door, square hammered copper pull, cleaned finish, interior shelves missing, 20" w, 13-1/4" d, 29-3/4" h....... 450.00

Somno Cabinet

This is a unique cabinet style designed and crafted by Gustav Stickley. Thanks to the catalogs and research available from this period, the name Somno has been retained. A Somno is a half-sized wash stand. Because Stickley designed his with a drawer and a door, often his version of a Somno is used in living rooms as a side cabinet or accent piece.

Arts & Crafts

Gustav Stickley, New York, square top over single drawer with orig wooden pull, paneled door with orig copper V-pull, orig interior with one shelf, orig finish, branded signature, 16" sq, 28" h 7,800.00

Spice Cabinets

Spice cabinets were made to hold spices that were so very precious to early settlers. They usually feature small drawers and to further insure their safe keeping, many have doors that enclose the drawers. Because spice cabinets were thought to be one of the "must haves" by those who began to collect antiques several generations ago, they were also early forms to be reproduced. Be sure to carefully examine any spice cabinet before purchase. This should be an example of using all the senses to determine authenticity. Many drawers continue to retain a bit of the fragrance of the spice it once held. Some may retain a stain from the color of a spice like paprika. Look carefully for signs of consistent wear and years of handling. Also see Spice Chests (Chests, Other)

Chippendale-Style, mahogany and mahogany veneer, single door with arched tombstone panel, interior with seven nailed drawers, brass ring pulls, arched pigeonhole center, molded base, bracket feet, old finish, oak and pine secondary woods, reconstructed, 17" w, 11-3/4" d, 23" h..990.00

Country, New England, 19th C, painted pine, traces of orig paint, imperfections, 7-3/4" w, 4" d, 10" h.............................1,950.00

Spice Cabinet, oak, maple, mahogany, and walnut, molded cornice with Greek key frieze, paneled door with inlaid sunburst, dovetailed interior drawers, bracket feet, hinges replaced, repairs, 13-3/8" w, 19-1/2" h, $6,875. Photo courtesy of Garth's Auctions, Inc., Delaware, OH.

Federal

America, c1810, cherry, walnut top, single raised panel door, scalloped dovetailed bracket feet, interior with one shelf, refinished, 19" w, 8" d, 23-3/4" h 3,000.00

Maryland or Virginia, walnut, interior divided into cubby holes, lower drawer, one rear foot replaced, 15" w, 9" d, 18" h.................2,950.00

Sheraton, oak, maple, mahogany, and walnut, molded cornice with Greek key frieze, paneled door with inlaid sunburst, dovetailed interior drawers, bracket feet, hinges replaced, repairs, 13-3/8" w, 19-1/2" h...............6,875.00

Spool Cabinets

Spool cabinets were designed for the display of multicolored thread on store countertops. Collectors today enjoy their wide drawers for a variety of uses. Most spool cabinets have either two or four drawers. The better the advertising and the better the original condition, the higher the value.

Victorian, walnut, four drawers, orig labels covered with wallpaper, composition foliage pulls, one pull cracked, 24" w, 14" d, 12" h...450.00

Vice Cabinets

The Arts & Crafts have provided us with several interesting styles of cabinets. This one, as its name implies, takes care of your vices,

Vice, Arts & Crafts, Lakeside Crafters, two doors with brass strap hardware, zinc-lined section, glass holders, pipe stand, orig finish, over-coat to top only, paper label, 13-1/4" sq top, 31-3/4" h, $650. Photo courtesy of David Rago Auctions/ RagoArts.com, Lambertville, NJ.

mainly smoking and drinking. Also see Cabinets, Smoking.

Lakeside Crafters, zinc lined section, glass holders, pipe stand, two doors with brass strap hardware, orig finish, top over-coated, paper label, 21" w, 14" d, 31-3/4" h...................750.00

Stickley, Gustav, drawer, door under flip top, copper shelf, rotating bottle holding, wine glass notches inside, new finish, red decal, 18-1/2" w, 18" d, 35-1/2" h 4,750.00

Wall Cabinets

Wall cabinets put more storage at the disposal of their owners. Also see Boxes, Wall, and Cupboards, Hanging.

Federal, pine, single door with four glazed panels, two glazed panels on angled sides, spoon rack shelf, 25" w, 24" h.............1,200.00

Victorian, c1870-90, mahogany, pentagonal form, flat top, carved molded cornice, floral rosettes and reeded columns flank two glass doors over braided carved base, three adjustable shelves 700.00

Candlestands

Candlestands are lovely furniture accent pieces whose original function has been outlined by its unique style. Designed to hold a candle or lamp, these small tables were easily moved around a room. Their high cabriole legs allowed them to be placed close to chairs or tables, with that sweeping foot even tucked under a chair when necessary, plus the tripod base was a sturdy base on which to place a lighted candle or fluid lamp. Although the basic design of a candlestand is simple, often great care and craftsmanship was exhibited in the elaborate turnings of the center column. Wealth was exhibited by displaying exquisite vasiform columns with detailed feet.

Some candlestands were made with a tilting mechanism so that the top could be turned to facilitate placing the stand closer to a wall when not it use. The term "tilt-top" is the common name for this type of mechanism. The phrase "bird cage support" refers to a tilting device made up of small turned posts that resemble a bird cage. The term pedestal, post, column or support generally refer to the central area between the top and the base. Remember, most candlestands were used in the eras where it was a popular practice to have one's furniture around the perimeter of the room, only bringing forward those pieces that were needed

Today, candlestands function as small end tables as well as their original intended usage. Reproductions of this popular form abound. Look for signs of wear, age to the wood, and original period finishes. Well made repairs generally do not detract much from the value of a candlestand.

Centennial

The Centennial held in Philadelphia in 1876 inspired a lot of furniture to be made in earlier styles, including this example.

Hepplewhite-style, mahogany, elongated pentagonal top, tripod base, old base repairs 375.00

Chippendale

During the Chippendale period, candlestands were very useful pieces of furniture, used in many rooms. Some feature mechanisms to allow the top to tilt so that they could be placed against the wall of a room. The tops range from round to square and are found in different sizes. Columns were turned on a lathe, allowing the maker some control in the design and style. All Chippendale candlestands have three feet, called a tripod base. Most of these feet end in snake feet, which are small pointed feet.

America, birch, orig red paint, oval, tilt top, turned column, tripod base, snake feet, repair at base of column, 14" w, 19" l, 27-3/4" h..5,300.00

America, birch, orig red paint, square top with ovolo corners, shaped turned column, tripod base, snake feet, old mellow refinishing on top, age crack in top, 15-3/4" w, 16" d, 25-1/2" h..1,980.00

America, cherry, round one board top, urn and rings turned column, tripod base, snake

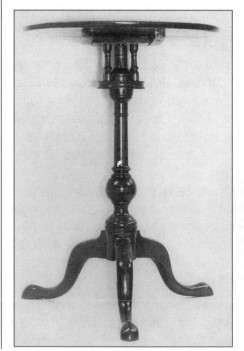

Chippendale, Chester County, PA, tilt top, mahogany, one board round top, turned column with pronounced ball turning, cabriole tripod base, snake feet, $4,500.

feet, old mellow finish, repaired split to top, 37-1/2" h..385.00

America, cherry, round one board top, urn turned column, tripod base, snake feet, old finish, old repairs to base of column, 17-1/2" d, 27-1/2" h..990.00

America, cherry, round two board top, turned column, tripod base, snake feet, worn orig finish, wrought iron support on base, column restorations, 17-1/2" d, 26-1/2" h 1,540.00

America, cherry, round two board top, turned column, tripod base, snake feet, old dark finish, 18" d, 25-1/2" h 4,100.00

America, cherry, round two board top, turned vasiform column threaded to screw into cleat, tripod base, well carved legs, snake feet, old nailed repairs at base, 17-3/8" d, 27-3/8" h.......1,375.00

America, cherry, square checkerboard top, old red repaint over green, details on rings of vasiform turned column, tripod base, snake feet, repairs on base an leg, 13-3/4" sq, 25-1/2" h..3,575.00

America, cherry, square shaped scalloped top, turned column, tripod base, snake feet, old refinishing, repair to column, 16" sq top, 27-1/4" h..1,760.00

Chippendale, Salem, Massachusetts, 18th C, tilt top, mahogany, serpentine top with molded edge, turned pedestal, cabriole legs, pad feet, minor imperfections, 16" w, 27" h, $5,420. Photo courtesy of Skinner Auctioneers and Appraisers of Antiques and Fine Art Boston and Bolton, MA.

America, cherry, square one board top with applied edge, one dovetailed drawer with brass pulls, urn turned column, high tripod base, well shaped legs, snake feet, old dark finish, poplar secondary wood, 17" sq top, 26-3/4" h 4,125.00

America, cherry, square two board top with scalloped edge, slender turned and tapered column, tripod base, snake feet, some restoration at base of column, 17" sq, 28" h...........1,540.00

America, Dominican mahogany, dish turned tilt top, turned column, tripod base, snake feet, old finish and over-varnish, repairs to base, age cracks to column, repairs to hinge block, 21" d, 27-1/2" h 1,750.00

America, mahogany, one board dish turned top, turned column, tripod base, snake feet, old finish, 15-1/2" d, 26" h..........................2,860.00

America, mahogany, one board round top with small band inlay border, birdcage support, urn pedestal, snake feet, early repair to one leg, some inlay missing, 18" d, 27" h...........1,350.00

America, maple, figured square top, well shaped turned column, tripod base, snake feet, old dry red surface, old repair at base, brace added, short split in top, 15-1/8" sq, 23-1/2" h..3,300.00

America, walnut, birdcage, round dish top, revolving four pillar birdcage, bulbous shaft with ring turnings, downswept legs ending in snake feet, orig tilting mechanism, small piece missing from one leg, 21-1/2" w, 27" h...............8,960.00

America, walnut, round one board top, turned column, tripod base with snake feet, old alligatored varnish finish, crack in base of column and one leg, old metal brace added, 16" d, 25-1/2" h 660.00

America, or England, c1780, mahogany, tilt-top, dished circular top, spiral carved base and ring turned pedestal, tripod cabriole legs, pad feet on platforms, old refinishing, imperfections, 21" d, 27" h................................1,380.00

Connecticut, Connecticut River Valley, late 18th C, cherry, old refinishing, minor imperfections, 17" w, 16-1/2" d, 25-1/2" h.......16,400.00

Connecticut, Hartford, late 18th C, cherry, shaped top, vase and ring-turned pedestal, tripod cabriole leg base, arris pad feet on platforms, old refinishing, imperfections, 25" h 1,150.00

Connecticut, Litchfield, late 18th C, carved cherry, old black paint, gilt striping, 145-1/4" w, 15-1/4" d, 25-1/2" h 3,200.00

Connecticut, late 18th C, cherry, circular molded top, bulbous vase and ring-turned post, tripod cabriole leg base ending in pad feet, old refinishing, repairs, 15-1/2' d, 26' h.......1,495.00

Massachusetts, 18th C, mahogany, dished top, turned pedestal, cabriole legs, pad feet, old finish, 14" d, 27-3/4" h 2,100.00

Middle Atlantic States, 18th C, birch and pine, circular top, vase and ring-turned post ending in turned drop pendant, tripod turned leg base, old refinishing, imperfections, 23-1/2" d, 16" h 350.00

Middle Atlantic States, 18th C, walnut, octagonal lipped top, chamfered underneath, hexagonal pedestal, cabriole legs, snake feet, 12-1/2" d, 28" h 6,600.00

New England, late 18th C, dish-top, cherry, turned pedestal, cabriole legs, pad feet, refinished, 18-1/4" d, 26-3/4" h....................2,185.00

New England, late 18th C, tilt top, refinished walnut, one board dish turned top, turned column, tripod base, snake feet, hinge block and latch are old replacements, pieced repairs on top, minor age cracks, 21-3/4" d, 29" h 935.00

New Hampshire, attributed to Samuel Dunlap, old refinishing, birch, painted red, imperfections, 16-1/2" w, 16-1/8" d, 26-1/2" h..2,950.00

New York State, drop-leaf, old black repaint with of Victorian striping, pine top with D-shaped leaves, single dovetailed drawer, turned column, four spider legs, minor insect damage, restoration, 17" w, 12-1/2" d, 5" leaves, 25-3/4" h.............................2,200.00

Pennsylvania, Lancaster county, c1800, walnut, tilt-top, one board circular dish top, birdcage with turned posts, turned column, tripod base, snake feet and pads, refinished, age cracks in column, top flange cracked, short age cracks on top, 19" d, 29" h...................2,500.00

Pennsylvania, Lehigh County, c1700, figured maple, tilt-top, square top, birdcage support, urn form standard, three cabriole legs, slipper feet, repairs to birdcage hinge and standard, 15-1/2" d, 27-1/2" h 750.00

Chippendale, New England, 18th C, maple, molded to, turned pedestal, cabriole legs, pad feet, old surface, minor repairs, 14-1/2" d, 26" h, $1,725. Photo courtesy of Skinner Auctioneers and Appraisers of Antiques and Fine Art Boston and Bolton, MA.

Pennsylvania, Philadelphia, c1750, mahogany, tilt-top, circular dish top, birdcage over ring-turned vasiform standard, tripod cabriole legs, slipper feet, 21-1/2" d, 28-1/4" h.............9,000.00

Pennsylvania, Philadelphia, c1750-80, mahogany, birdcage, raised dish rim on circular top, swiveling birdcage, compressed ball and ring-turned pillar, cabriole legs, pad feet, orig birdcage mechanism and brass clasping hardware, old repair to one leg, 20-1/2" w, 28-1/4" h.......................................32,480.00

Pennsylvania, c1760-80, mahogany, circular dished top, ring turned ball pedestal and tripod cabriole base, pad feet on platforms, old finish, imperfections, 16" d, 29" h 8,150.00

Pennsylvania, c1760-80, mahogany, tilt-top, circular molded top, birdcage support, turned post on tripod cabriole legs, pad feet on platforms, old refinishing, imperfections, 21-3/4" d, 27-1/4" h..5,175.00

Pennsylvania, late 18th C, walnut, circular molded top, turned birdcage support, vase and ring-turned post, tripod cabriole leg base, pad feet on platforms, old refinishing, 20-1/2" d, 29" h...3,450.00

Rhode Island, attributed to John Goddard, Newport, 1760-90, carved mahogany, molded top, contoured cleats, turned pedestal, cabriole leg base ending in carved five-toed pads, old refinishing, minor repair, 32" d, 28" h.......3,450.00

Chippendale to Hepplewhite, transitional

When a piece of furniture clearly evolves from one period to another, it is called "transitional." This example combines the turned column of the Chippendale period, but with an added urn shape more commonly found in the Hepplewhite period.

America, paint decorated, hard wood, old black repaint, yellow stringing, earlier red shows beneath, oblong eight sided top, urn turned column, tripod base, snake feet, one board has age cracks, 22" w, 15-3/4" d, 26-1/2" h..........1,320.00

Classical

Candlestands of the Classical period show more turnings on the column. This example shows how the maker wanted to make sure it appeared like cherry and added a red wash to enhance the graining.

New England, 1830, red washed cherry, octagonal top, vase and ring turned post, tripod spider leg base, 15" w, 17" d, 27" h.......375.00

Country

Because candlestands were such necessary items in a household, many local craftsmen made their own versions. Some display elements found in other period styles, but because their origin is known to be from a more rural location or other elements, many are simply referred to as Country.

Adjustable, New England, late 18th/early 19th C, maple, oak, and ash, shaped double candle support on threaded shaft, dished top with turned pedestal, circular base, three splayed turned legs, remnants of salmon-orange paint, 14-1/4" d, 44" h 1,955.00

Birch, old red wash and yellow striping, square top, tapered turned column, tripod base, high snake feet, base restoration, cleat is cracked, 14" w, 26-3/4" h 1,430.00

Birch and hardwood, replaced one board top with cut corners, turned column, tripod base, snake feet, nailed repairs to base, refinished, 19" w, 18-1/4" d, 26-1/4" h 250.00

Connecticut, late 18th C, stained cherry, tilt-top, dished top, ring-turned swelled pedestal, cabriole lets, pad feet, old surface, 20-1/4" d, 28-3/4" h...3,220.00

Decorated, poplar, round top, orig red and black graining, gilt stenciled fruit compote decoration, turned column, turned tripod base, 17-1/2"h, 28-1/4" h 300.00

Painted poplar, round one board top, turned column, tripod base with snake feet, old green repaint over black, 19" d, 25" h 950.00

Pine and maple with some curl, round one board top, bowling pin shaped column with some ring turning at top and base, tripod base with turned feet, repainted, 13-1/2" d, 26" h...450.00

New England, southeastern, late 18th C, cherry and maple, circular top, vase and ring turned post and tripod base, three tapering legs, remnants of old dark green paint, imperfections, 12" d, 25" h 1,150.00

Empire

By the Empire period, candlestands are becoming less apparent, replaced by stands of other natures and small tables. Lighting is evolving to lamps. These examples show a finer grade of wood used in their construction and larger more detailed tops.

Continental, first quarter 19th C, mahogany, circular cockbeaded top, twist-turned standard, triangular platform base with concave sides, paw feet, 12-3/4" d, 27-1/2" h.................250.00

New England, 1815-25, tiger maple, square top with shaped corners, elaborate ring-turned pedestal, incurvate legs, refinished, light tigering, 16-1/2" w, 16-1/2" d, 28-1/2" h 1,265.00

Federal

Candlestands of the Federal period are also numerous. However, now the tops are becoming a little more stylized, and different shapes are found, like octagons and rectangles. More tilting tops are encountered. Columns tend to be a little more elaborate than Chippendale columns. Most of the bases are still tripods, but feet are now pad-type feet. Many types of wood are used. The type of wood used often

Federal, attributed to Nathan Lombard, Southern Worcester County, Massachusetts, c1800, cherry inlaid, square top with inlaid corners and stringing in outline, turned pedestal, shaped cabriole leg base, pad feet, losses, surface imperfections, 17-1/2" w, 17-1/4" d, 26" h, $10,350. Photo courtesy of Skinner Auctioneers and Appraisers of Antiques and Fine Art Boston and Bolton, MA.

gives a clue as to the region of origin.

America, first quarter 19th C, tiger maple, rounded corners on rectangular top, three out-curving legs, circular medial shelf, 24" w, 18" d, 28" h 1,400.00

America, c1810, mahogany, tilt-top, octagonal top, early maple pillar with urn, ring, and bulbous turnings, tapered mahogany legs, tripod base, old repairs to two legs, 22" w, 41" h...300.00

Connecticut, c1790, cherry, circular top, vase and ring turned pedestal, tripod cabriole leg base, pad feet, old finish, minor imperfections, 21" d, 28" h 1,495.00

Connecticut, c1790, cherry, square top, applied beaded edge, vase and ring turned post, tripod cabriole leg base, pad feet, refinished, 18" w, 17" d, 27-1/2" h 1,380.00

Connecticut, c1790, cherry, square top with ovolo corners, vase and ring turned post and tripod cabriole leg base, pad feet on platforms, refinished, minor imperfections, 16-1/2" w, 16-1/4" d, 28" h 1,495.00

Connecticut, c1790, mahogany, square top, chamfered platform with drawer, vase and ring-turned post on tripod cabriole base ending in arris pad feet on platforms, old refinishing, 14-3/4" w, 14-1/2" d, 29-1/2" h 3,200.00

Connecticut, c1815-20, cherry, rectangular top, single drawer, straight sides, joined by corner posts ending in turned drops on vase and ring turned post and arris cabriole legs, pad feet on platforms, refinished, 19" w, 19-1/2" d, 25-1/2" h..750.00

Connecticut River Valley, late 18th C, painted, circular top, vase and ring-turned post, tripod cabriole leg base, pad feet, painted brown with contrasting elliptical panel on top, imperfections, 17-1/4" d, 26" h 325.00

Massachusetts, c1780, mahogany, tilt-top, circular dished top, vase and ring-turned pedestal, tripod cabriole legs, arris pad feet on platforms, old refinishing, top warped, 19-1/2" d, 27-1/4" h 875.00

Massachusetts, c1790, mahogany, circular top, vase and ring-turned pedestal, cabriole tripod base, pad feet, old refinishing, 13-3/4" d, 25-1/2" h..5,225.00

Massachusetts, c1790, mahogany, serpentine top, vase and ring-turned pedestal, cabriole tripod leg base, arris pad feet on platforms, old finish, very minor imperfections, 19" w, 19-3/4" d, 27" h 5,550.00

Massachusetts, c1800, attributed by Nathan Lombard, southern Worcester County, cherry inlaid, square top with inlaid corners and stringing in outline, turned pedestal shaped cabriole leg base ending in pad feet, losses, surface imperfections, 17-1/2" w, 17-1/4" d, 26" h............10,350.00

Massachusetts, c1800, mahogany inlaid, tilt-top, molded octagonal top, old refinishing, 23" w, 15-3/4" d, 28-3/4" h 1,500.00

Massachusetts, c1800, mahogany, octagonal tilt-top, vase and ring-turned post, tripod spider leg base, spade feet, refinished, 21-1/4" w, 15-3/4" d, 29-1/2" h 1,500.00

Massachusetts, c1800, mahogany, serpentine tilt-top, square corners, vase and ring turned post and tripod cabriole leg base, pad feet on platforms, refinished, minor imperfections, 19-1/2" w, 19-1/2" d, 25-1/2" h 2,300.00

Massachusetts, c1810, mahogany, tilt-top, octagonal top, vase and ring-turned pedestal and tripod spider leg base, old finish, 15-3/4" w, 21-3/4" l, 28" h....................1,265.00

Massachusetts, c1810, mahogany, tilt-top, oval top, vase and ring-turned post and tripod base, spade feet, old finish, imperfections, 13" w, 21-1/2" l, 29" h.........................1,380.00

Massachusetts, c1815-25, birch, octagonal top, vase and ring turned pedestal, tripod cabriole leg base, pad feet, old finish, imperfections, 14-1/2" w, 18-1/2" d, 28-3/4" h...................920.00

Massachusetts or New Hampshire, c1800, birch, oval shaped tilt-top, urn shaped pedestal, curving legs, spade feet, old refinishing, top slightly warped, 22-3/8" w, 14-1/4" d, 28" h........................950.00

Massachusetts, western, late 18th C, cherry, octagonal top, vase and ring turned post, tripod cabriole leg base, old varnish, 15-1/4" w, 15-1/8" d, 25" h 2,300.00

New England, c1790-1810, mahogany, tilt-top, octagonal top, vase and ring turned post and tripod vase, spade feet, old refinishing, 18" w, 18" d, 27-3/4" h.........................2,100.00

New England, c1800, cherry, dish top, old finish, minor imperfections, 15" d, 27" h.....2,500.00

New England, c1810, cherry and birch, rectangular top with shaped corners, vase and ring-turned post, tripod base with shaped legs, old finish, imperfections, 16" w, 13" d, 28" h 490.00

New England, c1790, maple, octagonal top, vase and ring-turned post, tripod cabriole leg base, pad feet, old finish, imperfections, 15" w, 15-1/8" d, 27" h 1,610.00

New England, c1825, mahogany, shaped tilt top, vase and ring turned post, tripod spider leg base, old finish, imperfections................400.00

New England, early 19th C, painted, octagonal shaped top, outlined in black, painted checkerboard and four gilt scrolled flourishes dec, pedestal, cabriole legs with similar Victorian dec, 18" w, 17-3/4" d, 29" h........12,650.00

New Hampshire, c1800, labeled "Jeremiah Gooden Cabinetmaker Milford," cherry and tiger maple, sq top with ovolo corners, vase and ring turned pedestal, tripod spider leg base, old refinishing, minor imperfections, 16-1/8" w, 16-1/4" d, 28-1/4" h 4,600.00

New Hampshire, c1810-20, maple, carved tilt top, swelled reeded post, chip-carved detail, old red varnish, minor imperfections, 20" w, 15-3/8" d, 29-1/2" h 1,200.00

New York, c1810, mahogany top and legs, rect top with cut corners, curly maple column, tripod base with scimitar legs, turned button

feet, refinished, minor imperfections, 17" x 23" x 26" h...715.00

Rhode Island, c1790, mahogany inlaid, sq top with string inlaid edge, vase and ring turned pedestal, tripod cabriole leg base, ending in pad feet, refinished, 17-3/4" w, 17-3/4" d, 28" h...1,265.00

Rhode Island, c1810, mahogany, tilt-top with serpentine sides and square corners, vase and ring-turned pedestal, tripod cabriole legs, arris pad feet, old refinishing, 20-1/2" w, 28-1/2" h...750.00

Hepplewhite

Candlestands of the Hepplewhite period closely resemble those of the Federal period, but are usually a little more ornate, have more turnings on the columns, more delicate legs, etc.

America, birch, rectangular one board tilt top with cut corners, well-turned column, spider legs, high feet, old varnish feet, dark varnish stain on base, 14-1/2" w, 21-1/4" l, 28" h 950.00

America, cherry and maple, one board top with cut corners, turned column, tripod base with spider legs, refinished, 16-1/4" x 17-3/4" top, 27-3/4" h..350.00

America, cherry, octagonal top, turned column, tripod base, high spider legs, old worn reddish brown finish, restoration to base and one leg, 17-1/2" w, 19" d, 26-1/4" h........660.00

America, cherry, one board octagonal top, turned column with chip carving, tripod base, spider legs, old refinishing, minor damage, old repair, 17-1/4" x 18-1/8" top, 27" h.........500.00

America, cherry, one board rectangular top with applied gallery, well turned birch column, tripod base, snake feet, old finish, repair at base of column, 16-3/4" w, 19-1/8" d, 25-1/4" h...775.00

America, cherry, rectangular top with scalloped edge, boldly turned column, tripod base, spider legs, old mellow finish, old repair to one leg, 16-1/4" w, 19-1/2" d, 27-1/2" h 935.00

America, mahogany, rectangular one board top with cut corners and good figure to wood, curved ends, turned column, tripod base, spider legs, old finish, 17-3/4" w, 25-3/4" d, 28-3/4" h...2,530.00

America, mahogany with inlay, cut-corner top with banded beaded edge and conforming inlay medallion, turned column, tripod base with spider legs, stringing on edge of top and legs, old finish with wear, 13-1/2" x 19-3/4" top, 27" h...1,375.00

Connecticut, Wethersfield, cherry, one board top with cutout ovolo corners, urn turned column, tripod base, snake feet, orig finish on underside of top, rest refinished, minor age cracks, 15-3/4' w, 16-3/8" d, 27-3/4" h..................................1,995.00

New Hampshire, maple, vining inlay on oval top and post, sq tapering column, four spider legs, refinished, damage and old repairs, 12-7/8" w, 17-3/8" d, 29-1/4" h 1,450.00

Primitive

This hand-made example is included to show how the form varies. Adjustable candle arms are found in a few other design styles, including Federal and William and Mary.

America, early 19th c, 40" h, wooden, adjustable candle arm, dark brown patina.......715.00

Queen Anne

The gracefulness of the Queen Anne style is very apparent in the shape of candlestands. The cabriole legs often sweep gently into slipper feet. The center column is turned and shaped with gentle curves. Tops of candlestands in this period are of different shapes. One of the most interesting is one called "pie crust" there the edges may be shaped or have additional moldings to create a tiny lip or edge, like the crust of a handmade pie.

America, cherry, squared top, turned shaft, cabriole legs, slipper feet, orig finish, repairs, 28"h..950.00

Country, mahogany, pie crust tilt top, center turned pedestal, graceful legs, pad feet, 20" d, 28-1/2" h..275.00

New England, late 18th C, cherry, round top, turned and shaped pedestal, cabriole leg base, arris pad feet, old refinishing, imperfections, 18" d, 26-1/2" h 900.00

New England, late 18th C, maple, square top, shaped pedestal, cabriole legs with worn pads, refinished, 17" w, 16-3/4" d, 25-1/2" h..920.00

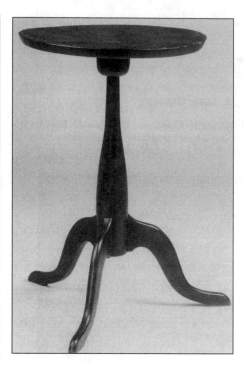

Shaker, Mount Lebanon, New York, c1830, cherry, round top, turned pedestal, thin iron plate beneath, tripod base, old dark stain, imperfections, 16" d, 24-3/4" h, $1,150. Photo courtesy of Skinner Auctioneers and Appraisers of Antiques and Fine Art Boston and Bolton, MA.

Vermont, 18th C, cherry, circular top, vase and ring turned post, tripod cabriole leg base ending in arris pad feet on platforms, old refinishing, 15-1/4" d top, 25-3/4" h............1,150.00

Shaker

Since the Shakers lived a simple life, their candlestands reflect this in their plainness. The Shakers used candlestands, but also invented other clever ways of bringing light to their work with built-in candle-slides in case furniture, hanging candleholder, etc.

Mount Lebanon, New York community, c1830, cherry, round top, turned pedestal with thin iron plate beneath, tripod base, old dark stain, imperfections, 16" d, 24-3/4" h.........................1,150.00

Windsor-Style

The truly American Windsor style found in chairs also extended to candlestands. Look for bamboo turnings like those used in chair spindles and legs. Additional candle sockets allowed the users to obtain even more light from this functional piece of furniture.

America late 18th C, mixed woods, top fitted with threaded column with adjustable cross-section and two candle sockets, square column with dovetailed center shelf, tripod base with turned legs, old refinishing, 44" h.............385.00

Chairs

Chairs are a common form of furniture found in every design style and in every room setting. Simple ladderbacks were used as kitchen chairs, elegant suites of chairs graced the dining room, while easy chairs waited by the fire for their occupants. Bedroom suites frequently included several matching side chairs and perhaps a rocker to match the bed and case pieces. A good chairmaker was an important member of early Colonial communities and found his work to be in demand. His craft was taught to apprentices and often they closely followed the examples at hand. Early design books were used as guides, but American ingenuity often adapted styles to suit woods available, etc.

During many of the early furniture styles, such as Chippendale, Federal, and Queen Anne, it was assumed that large pillows would be used on the seat, adding a little more comfort. Later styles, such as Arts & Crafts, featured cushions included as part of the design and often making a statement by their use of leather, or other coverings. As furniture making became factory made, American furniture makers made many chairs to meet the ever-increasing demand for affordable furniture. Today, furniture buyers can choose from well-made craftmen chairs that reflect early styles, mass produced chairs readily available at furniture stores and interesting designs by custom manufacturers.

To help identify chairs in this edition of *Warman's American Furniture Price Guide*, we have divided chairs into major classifications, such as arm, dining, side, etc. Then the chairs are listed by design styles. However, it is hard to determine whether a side chair began life as a dining room chair, bedroom chair, etc. One way to determine if chairs were originally sold as a set is to carefully examine the interior frame for signs of numbers. Often Roman numerals were used to indicate that it belonged to a set. These numerals were sometimes incised into the frame, while others were simple chalk markings.

Brief descriptions of what design elements to expect are listed for arm chairs; expect to find similar elements for dining, side, and other types of chairs.

Some terms that relate to chairs are:

Crest rail: the top rail on the back.

Side rail: side rails extending from the crest rail to seat.

Stretcher base: the structural members that extend from leg to leg, adding stability. An H-stretcher looks like its name implies. A box-stretcher is a bar from leg to leg. An X-stretcher goes across the base and the stretcher bars cross, sometimes joined together.

Splat: the decorative part of a back between the crest rail and seat. When shaped like a vase, it can be known as a "vasiform splat."

h seat: Seat height is often noted to help determine the original usage of a chair. This kind of information is important to consider to understand if a chair has been shortened because of damage, wear, removing casters, etc.

Back height: This "h" dimension indicates the height at the center of the back of the chair.

Over-upholstered: Upholstered section that appears to be overstuffed.

Also see Benches, Hall, and Sofas for additional forms of seating furniture.

Arm Chairs

Arm chairs are defined as chairs that have two arms to the side of the chair. Many design styles of furniture are determined by the crest, back, or legs. However, in arm chairs, one more element can be used to determine the style, by closely observing the arm. The supporting arm structure and how it's connected to the back and seat frame are often important clues as to age and method of manufacturing.

Aesthetic Movement: Aesthetic Movement furniture is often sleek looking and was on the cutting edge of new designs.

America, late quarter 19th C, heart-shaped back surmounted by carved and pierced crest, scrolling half-upholstered arms, turned and tapered legs, casters, price for pair, 24" w, 23-1/2" d, 41" h 550.00

Art Deco: Art Deco chairs typify the transition from stuffy "straight" chairs to sleeker, more modern designs. Look for clean lines and use of fine woods or metal.

Brune, New Orleans, early 20th C, Marlborough, mahogany, padded back and arms joined by downswept uprights to padded seat, sq legs joined by H-form stretcher, 38-1/2" h 350.00

Frankl, Paul, c1930s, streamline form, reupholstered in back leather, white wool seat and back, 36" w, 37" d, 28" h 2,200.00

Lloyd, Kem, attributed to

Manufactured by Lloyd, 1934, streamline design, tubular chromed metal with reupholstered black leather cushions and wooden armrests, 28" w, 40" d, 29" h...........4,400.00

Manufactured by Mueller Furniture Co., 1940s, knockdown construction in wood after design of famous airline chair, price for pair, 23" w, 26" d, 33" h...........3,300.00

McArthur, Warren, manufactured by McArthur Industries, c1930, tubular anodized aluminum frame, channeled sling seat, reupholstered in off-white fabric, 31" w, 22" d, 32" h 4,500.00

Art Nouveau: Chairs from this design period feature scrolls and floral carvings.

America, c1900, giltwood, tall upholstered rectangular backs, scrolled arms, acanthus leaf and floral carvings, gilt stretcher base, price for pair, 26" w, 50-1/2" h..........1,990.00

Arts & Crafts: Arts & Crafts chairs are functional, no-nonsense seating. They look sturdy and well made and have lasted well. Look for examples in good condition, but with some wear. Original maker labels, brands, and signatures add to the value.

Kendall, David Wolcott, oak, caned back and seat, flat arms with sq vertical supports to the floor, 29-3/8" w, 34-1/4" h, caning damage, minor wear, price for pair 1,840.00

Limbert, Charles P., Grand Rapids and Holland, MI

Arts & Crafts, David Wolcott Kendall, oak, caned back and seat, flat arms with square vertical supports to the floor, caning damage, minor wear, price for pair, 29-3/4" w, 34-1/4" h, $1,840. Photo courtesy of Skinner Auctioneers and Appraisers of Antiques and Fine Art Boston and Bolton, MA.

No. 931, three vertical back slats, recovered orig drop-in cushion, refinished, branded signature, 28" w, 23" d, 36" h 700.00

No. 1935, slightly shaped top rail, five vertical back slats, wooden saddle seat, refinished, 26" w, 20" d, 39" h 600.00

Arched top rail over two horizontal back slats, recovered seat, orig finish, branded mark, 25" w, 2" d, 39" h...................425.00

Caned back and side panels, inlaid ebony at back and legs, arched seat rail, new cane, refinished, sgd, 25" w, 26" d, 39" h...1,200.00

Four vertical back slats, long corbels under each arm, recovered orig cushion, orig finish, branded mark, 28" w, 23" d, 36" h...850.00

Two sq cutouts to back slats, flat tapered arm rests, new black leather drop-in seat cushion, orig finish, branded mark, small repair to back leg, 27-1/2" w, 24-1/4" d, 38-1/2" h.......................4,250.00

McHugh, heavy ladder back, orig rush seat, Mackmurdo feet, fine orig finish, unsigned, 24" h, 34" d, 37" h 450.00

Morris, William, attributed to, mahogany, two arched top rails, three vertical back spindles, each with central rectangular detail, orig finish, 20" w, 19" d, 30" h.............900.00

Roycroft, East Aurora, NY

Ladderback, two horizontal back slats, apron carved "Roycroft," inset tacked-on

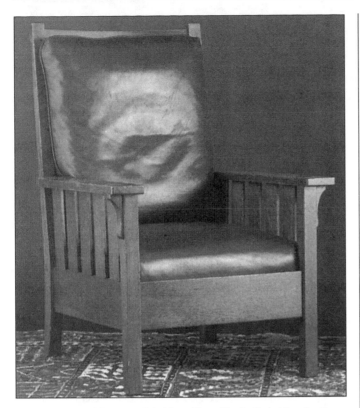

Arts & Crafts, Gustav Stickley, New York, fixed back, five vertical slats on each side, drop-in leather spring seat, reupholstered loose back cushion, orig finish, branded mark, 29" w, 32" d, 42" h, $2,600. Photo courtesy of David Rago Auctions/RagoArts.com, Lambertville, NJ.

hard set, light cleaning to orig finish, new leather seat, 25" w, 22-1/2" d, 38" h 2,600.00

Oversized, narrow back and side slats, broad flat arms, reupholstered brown leather loose seat cushion on slatted base, light over-coat to orig ebonized finish, carved orb and cross mark, few shallow holes, 32" w, 24-1/2" d, 38-1/2" h 2,000.00

Tall back, short slats under arms, Mackmurdo feet, new tacked on leather back and loose seat cushions, carved orb and cross mark, refinished, 28-1/2" w, 26-3/4" d, 47-1/4" h 3,000.00

Stickley Brothers, Grand Rapids, MI

No. 577-1/2, early form, caned panel at back over six vertical slats, caned seat, refinished and recaned, numbered, 25" w, 22" d, 40" h 300.00

No. 917-1/2, deep form, double horizontal rail, three vertical back slats, orig finish, unsigned, 30" w, 35" d, 36" h 1,200.00

Cube Chair, narrow arms, mortised through front legs and vertical slats, orig loose seat cushion, orig finish, unmarked, 27-1/2" w, 30" d, 33-1/4" h 3,795.00

Stickley, Gustav, New York

No. 310-1/2, three horizontal back slats, orig leatherette seat and tacks, orig finish, red decal, price for pair, 25" w, 21" d, 36" h..2,250.00

No. 318, vertical back slats, open arms, short corbels, skinned orig finish, red decal, 27" w, 25" d, 37-1./2" h.........600.00

No. 324, large form, five slats under each arm, originally had rope foundation, seat has been altered, re-coated orig finish, red box mark under arm, 29" w, 29" d, 40" h..1,760.00

No. 353A, Harvey Ellis design, three vertical back slats, orig rush seat, arched seat rail, orig finish and rush, branded signature, 25" w, 22" d, 41" h 4,700.00

No. 2592, 1902-04, oversized, four horizontal back slats, top slat arched, tacked-on orig red Japan leather seat, orig dark finish, early red decal, 29-1/4" w, 25" d, 41" h..4,500.00

No. 2626, five vertical back slats, canvas foundation, orig loose cushions, orig finish, early red decal, 28" w, 23" d, 38" h 6,000.00

Fixed back, five vertical slats on each side, drop-in leather spring seat, reuphol-

Arts & Crafts, L. & J. G. Stickley, Fayetteville, NY, c1918, Model No. 942, gold and red label on front stretcher, price for set of four, 21-3/4" w, 37-1/2" h, $3,220. Photo courtesy of Samuel T. Freeman & Co., Philadelphia, PA.

stered brown leather loose back cushion, orig finish, branded mark, 29" w, 32" d, 42" h...2,600.00

Spindled back and sides, long corbels, through-tenon side rails, orig finish, casters, replaced canvas sling seat, no seat cushion, replaced spindle, unmarked, 28" w, 23-1/2" d, 50" h 4,500.00

V-back, five vertical back slats, corbels, orig tacked-on brown Japan leather seat, orig square tacks, worn orig finish, wear to seat, red decal, 25-3/4" w, 20-1/2" d, 36-3/4" h 1,150.00

Stickley, L and J. G., Fayetteville, NY

No. 422, c1912, V-back over six vertical slats, spring cushion seat, L. & J. G. decal, 38" h, 27-3/4" w, 20-1/2" d 460.00

Fixed back, five slats on each side, corbels, and new brown drop-in leather seat and back cushion, orig finish, branded "The Work of L. and J. G. Stickley," 31-3/4" w, 36" d, 41-3/4" h 4,450.00

Ladderback, arched apron, corbels, and new upholstered drop-in spring seat, new finish, "The Work of..." label, 27-3/4" w, 22" d, 40-1/2" h 425.00

Mahogany, ten vertical back spindles, orig finish, breaks to orig drop-in rush seat, unsigned, 24" w, 21" d, 42" h 990.00

Open arm chair, matching footstool, chair with four horizontal back slats, drop-in spring seat, reupholstered in tan leather, orig reddish-brown finish, sgd "The Work of L. and J. G. Stickley," 29" w, 28" d, 49" h.....21,000.00

Tall back, four vertical back slats, drop-in spring seat, minor enhancement to orig finish, Handcraft label, 28" w, 24" d, 44" h 1,450.00

Unknown Designer

Heavy construction, three wide back slats, three under each arm, orig spring cushion, orig finish, unsigned, 29" w, 25" d, 35" h 425.00

Mahogany, flared rail above ten slats, eight slats under each arm, reupholstered orig cushions, orig finish, labeled "Geo. C. Flint," 29" w, 24" d, 37" h.................775.00

Oak, curved and arched crest rail over six back slats, shaped arms with long cor-

bel supports, curved seat, front, and side stretchers, spring cushion seat with oatmeal colored upholstery, 26-1/4" w, 24" d, 37-1/2" h 230.00

Oak, cutout back over recently upholstered seat, splayed slab legs with keyed-tenon construction, refinished, 28" w, 20" d, 32" h 425.00

Oak, six vertical back slats, four vertical under arm slats, recovered orig cushions, orig finish, 28" w, 27" d, 36" h 850.00

Oak, wide crest rail over three back slats, spring cushion seat, orig dark finish, marring, roughness, 29-1/4" w, 24-1/4" d, 34-1/2" h 200.00

Centennial: The Centennial style of chairs have produced some interesting examples, with the most famous named for Martha Washington. Look for elements of earlier styles blended together.

Chippendale-Style, Martha Washington-style, shaped crest rail, upholstered arms with molded forearms, square molded front legs, flat stretchers, raking rear legs, gold silk upholstery, 26-1/2" w, 30" d, 40" h 900.00

Hepplewhite-Style, Martha Washington type, open arms, worn beige upholstery, 20th C reproduction 200.00

Chippendale: Dating from 1755 to 1790, many chairs were made during this period. Look for fine woods, squared elements. Seats tend to be upholstered and slipped into the frame. Some are rushed or splint, or solid wood.

America, wing-back, mahogany and other woods, arched rectangular padded back flanked by wings continuing into padded, out-scrolled arms, bow-front, loose cushion seat raised on square-section legs joined by H-stretcher.......................................1,150.00

Massachusetts, Boston or Salem, c1755-85, mahogany, pierced splats, over-upholstered seats, front cabriole legs, high pad feet, old refinishing, minor repairs, price for pair, 37-1/2" h 8,200.00

New Hampshire, c1790, carved maple, shaped crest rail above vase splat, scroll-carved arms, trapezoidal splint seat, square beaded legs joined by cutout seat rail and box-stretchers, old refinishing, some imperfections, 17-1/2" h, 41" h 900.00

Chippendale-Style: Imitating the popular American Chippendale style, this example shows some of the design elements, but was made much later.

America, mahogany, carved crest, pierced splat, needlepoint seat, cabriole legs, claw and ball feet.......................................495.00

America, mahogany, shell carved crest rail, pierced vasiform splat, shaped scrolled arms, upholstered seat, Marlborough legs..325.00

English, early 20th C, mahogany frame, old worn moss green velvet upholstery, 36-1/2" h...220.00

Classical: Classical furniture styles all tend to have scrolls and a sweeping form. Chairs follow this definition with scrolled terminals and interesting feet.

America, c1825-35, deeply tufted barrel back, arm trim with dark mahogany finish, turned feet, reupholstered, 41-1/2" h......800.00

America, c1825-35, mahogany, upholstered rectangular back, bowed seat, square tapering legs, price for pair, 23" w, 20-1/2" d, 35" h 2,950.00

America, c1840, reeded crest rail with scrolled terminals, cabriole arm supports, reeded rail on splayed legs, paw feet, wooden rosettes on front, burgundy velvet upholstery, 34" w, 25" d, 32-1/2" h......950.00

Federal: The Federal period extends from c1790 to c1815. The style is typified by fine woods, inlay, and several different styles of legs. Feet found on Federal chairs vary from diminutive feet to more pronounced Spanish feet. Seats can be rushed, caned, or solid wood.

America, c1790-1810, maple, straight crest rail over pieced shaped splat, outscrolled arms ending in paws, drop-in seat, sq molded legs 425.00

Massachusetts, c1800, inlaid mahogany, shield back with bellflower and wheat sheaf sprigs, pierced splat, serpentine seat, scrolled arms, sq molded tapered legs with H-stretcher.......................................1,500.00

New England, c1775-1800, curving crest above raked terminals, vasiform splat,

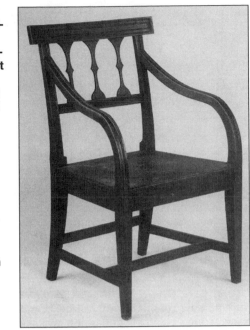

Federal, New England, c1790-1800, carved birch, rectangular beaded crest above three shaped incised splats, paneled beaded stiles with shaped arms continuing to square tapering legs, joined to raked rear legs by square stretchers, wooden seat painted black, 16-1/4" h seat, 34-3/4" h, $825. Photo courtesy of Skinner Auctioneers and Appraisers of Antiques and Fine Art Boston and Bolton, MA.

downward scrolling arms, block and baluster turned front legs ending in Spanish carved feet, joined by boldly turned front medial stretcher, old splint seat, old red paint, imperfections, 17-1/4" h seat, 35-1/2" h 8,050.00

New England, c1790-1800, carved birch, rectangular beaded crest above three shaped incised splats, paneled beaded stiles with shaped arms continuing to square tapering legs, joined to raked rear legs by square stretchers, wooden seat painted black, 16-1/4" h seat, 34-3/4" h 825.00

New York or Southern New England, c1810-20, orig black ground paint, gilt and green neoclassical embellishments, central urns, rush seats, urn shaped spindles under each arm, ring-turned legs, front stretcher with plaque, minor surface imperfections, price for pair, 18" h seat...................3,150.00

Pennsylvania, Philadelphia, c1790-1810, carved mahogany, molded shield-shaped arm and upholstered back, flanked by short shaped arms with carved rosettes over curved and molded supports, over-upholstered seat, reeded apron, sq tapering reeded legs with carved rosettes, several old repaired breaks, 35-3/4" h.............12,700.00

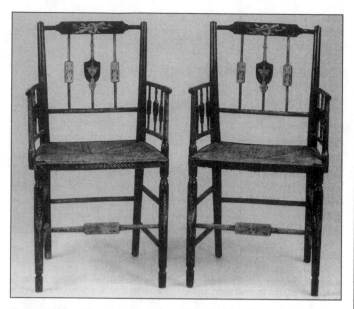

Federal, New York or Southern New England, c1810-20, orig black ground paint, gilt and green neoclassical embellishments, central urns, rush seats, urn shaped spindles under each arm, ring-turned legs, front stretcher with plaque, minor surface imperfections, price for pair, 18" h seat, $3,150. Photo courtesy of Skinner Auctioneers and Appraisers of Antiques and Fine Art Boston and Bolton, MA.

Mission: Famed architect Frank Lloyd Wright included designs for furniture and accessories in his unique house style.

Purcell, Feick and Elmslie, designed for Merchants Bank of Winona, MN, c1911, flat even arm over vertical side spindles separated by bands of cubes at top and bottom, recessed and framed in stepped molding, ball feet, orig green leather upholstery, brass tacks, unsigned, 24-1/4" w, 23" d, 36-1/4" h 14,500.00

Wright, Frank Lloyd, from Robert Winn House, Kalamazoo, MI, 1953, cherry finish, refinished, recovered, descended in Winn family, 33" w, 22" d, 29" h 2,250.00

Modernism Era: The Modernism-Era spans from the 1940s to the 1950s. During this time, furniture designers experimented with new materials and shapes. Today collectors are starting to discover these chairs and enjoy them for their form.

Bertroia, Harry, manufactured by Knoll International, Diamond Chair, white plastic wire construction, green seat pads, price for pair, 33" w, 25" d, 31" h 250.00

Eames, Charles

Low Wire, manufactured by Herman Miller, black Naugahyde upholstered fiberglass shell, zinc struts, 26" w, 26" d, 24" h 600.00

Soft Pad chair, set of six, manufactured by Herman Miller, channeled red fabric upholstery, cast aluminum frame, tilt and swivel mechanism, casters, wear to arms, 23" w, 23" d, 32" h.........................2,800.00

Frankl, Paul, manufactured by Directional, c1966, sculptural bronze exterior in abstract design, orig gray fabric, price for pair, 28" w, 29" d, 26" h 2,520.00

Nakashima, George, solid walnut, Windsor back, plank seat, price for pair, 25" w, 18" d, 27" h......................................1,000.00

Nelson, George, manufactured by Herman Miller

Flexible back in gray fiberglass, rubber and stainless steel fittings, tubular swag leg base, label, 28" w, 20" w, 34" h...1,500.00

Swagged Leg, molded charcoal fiberglass seat, adjustable back, metal base, label, 28" w, 26" d, 33" h 2,200.00

Thin Edge, upholstered in blue fabric, cast aluminum legs, price for pair, 36" w, 32" d, 30" h 2,650.00

Norell, Arne, Sweden, walnut and leather, sq shape, tapered cylindrical posts, leather sling-back arms and seat on through-stretchers raised on cylindrical legs, maker's label, price for pair, 26" w, 26" d, 28" h 1,265.00

Panton, Verner, manufactured by Plus-Linje, c1958, Cone Chair, chromed wire cone form

Circular seat in green fabric, 25" d, 30" h 2,970.00

Reupholstered in red wool, swiveling chrome base, 21" d, 33" h............1,500.00

Platner, Warren, manufactured by Knoll International, 1966

Bronze wire construction, orig orange fabric, label, 25" w, 22" d, 30" h 325.00

Metal rod construction, upholstered back rail over welded steel rod sides, upholstered seat raised on pedestal base, 1966 American Institute of Architects

International Award, set of four, 28-3/4" h 800.00

Rohdes, Gilbert, manufactured by Herman Miller, white leather upholstery, curved wooden legs, 25" w, 25" d, 34" h 750.00

Wormley, Edward, Riemerschmid, manufactured by Dunbar, set of four, sculptural form, dark mahogany, reupholstered seats, refinished, unmarked, 24" w, 20" d, 31" h 2,700.00

Modernism Era, Pop: The later segment of the Modernism-Era, these chairs are even more outstanding in their free-form designs and use of color.

Mazza, Sergi, Toga chair, manufactured by Martemide, Milan, molded red fiberglass form, impressed marks, price for pair, 28" w, 25" d, 24" h 1,320.00

Paulin, Pierre, manufactured by Artfort, two piece upholstered form, orig red fabric, white pedestal base, 28" w, 21" d, 26" h 275.00

Sottsass, Ettore, Mandarin chair, manufactured by Knoll International, c1986, black enameled tubular metal frames, cream leather upholstery, price for set of six, 26" w, 22" d, 33" h 900.00

Queen Anne: Chairs made in the Queen Anne period frequently include a style referred to as a banister back, which features upright back slats and turned elements. Chairs were frequently painted, but many were also made from fine woods. Seats can be slip, splint, rush, or solid wood.

America, late 18th C, banister back, traces of old black paint, turned posts, legs and finials with half turned slats, old woven splint seat, feet ended out, 17-1/2" h seat, 45-1/2" h 1,265.00

Connecticut, late 18th C, banister back, shaped crest, scrolled handholds, old splint seat, boldly turned medial stretchers, old red stain, some height loss, 16-1/4" h seat, 48-1/4" h 4,025.00

Country, birch and maple, yoke crest, vasiform splat, scrolled arms, replaced rush seat, turned legs, Spanish feet, turned front stretcher, refinished, traces of old red paint, repaired split on back leg, 17-1/2" h seat, 40-1/2" h 2,200.00

Country, four vertical ribbed slats on back, well turned posts and finials, shaped arms with scrolled hand rests, sausage turned front posts, stretcher base, turned feet, old black repaint, restorations to feet, arms and woven seat replaced, old black repaint, 18" h seat, 46-1/2" h 690.00

Massachusetts, mid 18th C, maple, shaped crest rail, vasiform splat, scrolled arm rests, rush seat, turned legs, Spanish feet, turned front stretcher, old refinishing, 42" h 2,995.00

Massachusetts, mid 18th C, maple, shaped yoked crest rail, chamfered vasiform splat flanked by raked and blocked rounded stiles, scrolled arms, trapezoidal slip seat, frontal cabriole legs, pad feet, racked block turned rear legs, turned stretchers, old refinishing, repairs, alternations, 42" h 3,200.00

New England, found in Portland, Maine, old black repaint with yellow striping, crest with relief carved detail, arms with scrolled hand rests, beaded edge sides, contemporary rush seat, restorations, ended out feet, 43-1/4" h 1,540.00

New York, Hudson River Valley, c1750-80, maple and ash, shaped crest, solid vase form splat, shaped arms, rush seat, turned

Queen Anne, Pennsylvania, Philadelphia, c1740, walnut, balloon seat, shaped crest rail with volutes, vasiform back splat, flaring arms ending with carved knuckles, slip seat, cabriole legs, webbed pad feet, $40,000. Photo courtesy of Samuel T. Freeman & Co., Philadelphia, PA.

tapering legs joined by stretchers, pad feet, later brass platforms 1,950.00

Queen Anne-Style: These examples take the curved back and urn-shaped splat of Queen Anne and adds Spanish feet usually found in other design periods.

America, walnut, back scrolled crest rail, open vase shaped splat, out scrolled arms, drop-in seat, concave seat rail centered with shell carving, cabriole legs, shell carved knees, pad feet, 19th C 1,720.00

Country, pegged construction, relief carved scallops on crest, molded and curved back with urn shaped splat, molded arms with well developed scrolls, rush seat, Spanish feet, well turned front stretcher and arm posts, old refinishing, small chips on foot, 17" h, 43-1/2" h.................................1,430.00

Victorian: Victorian chairs were certainly designed for more comfort than many earlier styles. As machine carving become more prevalent, furniture designers incorporated it into chairs. Woods found in Victorian chairs are generally fine. Seats are often upholstered, but can be of other materials. Look for more sweeping lines in this design period, which stretches from c1830 to c1915.

America, third quarter 19th C, carved mahogany, cartouche-shaped padded back within conforming frame surmounted by flower carved crest, out-curved scroll arms with padded elbow rests, serpentine-fronted overstuffed seat with shaped conforming rails continuing into cabriole legs with scroll feet, frame carved throughout with flowers and foliage, price for pair....................700.00

America, third quarter 19th C, simulated rosewood, button back, cartouche form back within conforming frame surmounted by carved swags of autumn fruit, out-curved arms with elbow rests and back-curved supports, serpentine front, over-stuffed seat with shaped conforming rails continuing into cabriole legs with caster, frame molded throughout 500.00

America, late 19th C, carved walnut, padded over-scroll back, downswept scroll arms, over-stuffed seat, turned tapering and ring-turned legs.................................125.00

Eastlake

c1875-90, mahogany, open arms resting on carved eagle supports rising into rolled upholstered back, resting on stretcher base, 27" w, 34" d, 34" h...................450.00

c1880-90, walnut, line carved back with embossed and brown painted cardboard backing, cane seats with embossed cardboard overlay, ring turned front legs and stretchers, price for set of four, 22-1/2" w, 21" d, 41-3/4" h 300.00

Elizabethan Revival, George Hunzinger, New York, arched crest with spindles, inlay cloth covered woven metal back and seat, marked "Hunzinger NY Pat March 20, 1869, Pat April 18, 1876," 18" w, 17-1/2" d, 37" h 1,450.00

Gothic Revival, c1850, walnut, carved, upholstered seat and arms 5,450.00

Renaissance Revival

c1865, ebonized and gilt incised, orig velvet and needlepoint upholstery, minor losses, 46-1/4" h 400.00

c1870, carved rosewood, carved and incised gilt back, inset bronze maiden plaque crest, carved female head on arms, turned incised carved legs, casters, 29" w, 25" d, 43-1/2" h 850.00

c1870, carved walnut, bust carved crest rails, small bust on carved arms, turned legs, wooden casters, striped silk upholstery, price for pair, 22-1/2" w, 20" d, 40-1/2" h 425.00

c1875, oak, carved and pierced backrest and front stretcher, block and cylinder H-stretcher base, some repairs and loss, 58"h..300.00

Rococo Revival, walnut, scroll carved frame, floral crest, open arms, repairs to frame, reupholstered in velvet, well executed tufted back medallion, 38" h............................330.00

William and Mary: William and Mary chairs are rather strict looking, but incorporate rushing and caning. Loose cushions often were used with this style of chair. Some hand carving is found. Turning of finials and legs is popular, as well as Spanish feet.

America, first quarter 18th C, cane back, molded crest rail and stiles, out-curving arms, upholstered seat, ring and block turned front legs ending in Spanish feet, turned stretchers, caning damaged, losses to inner stiles, later upholstery, left arm repaired, 24-1/4" w, 20-1/4" d, 43" h....................................4,480.00

America, early to mid-18th C, banister back, painted, bowed crest rail with four molded banister slats supported by turned posts, straight tapered arm supports, rush seat, turned arrowhead stretchers, turned legs on peg feet, older red paint finish, bottom of legs replaced, slats replaced, 24" w, 18" d, 47-1/2" h....................................420.00

America, 18th C, walnut, shaped, pierced, and bird carved crest rail flanked by ball stiles, pierced floral carved and caned back splat, shaped ring turned round supports, cane seat, floral carved apron, scroll feet 1,120.00

Connecticut, early 18th C, turned and carved, banister back, damaged, 49" h 875.00

Delaware River Valley, 18th C, maple, slat back, turned stiles, turned ball finials joining reverse arched slats to shaped and scrolled handholds, vase and ring-turned legs ending in ball feet, bulbous turned front stretcher, plain turned double side stretchers, old refinishing, imperfections, 16-1/2" h seat, 46-1/2" h 9,225.00

New England, c1730, slightly arched upholstered backrest, outward curving arms, baluster turned arm supports, rectangular upholstered seat, baluster turned legs, bulbous turned front stretcher, feet restored, repairs...2,750.00

Pennsylvania, 18th C, walnut, shaped crest rail, three molded vertical slats flanked by shaped arms, baluster turned supports, solid plank seat, block-and-cylinder-turned legs, box-stretcher, rear feet pierced, seat restored, 42-1/2" h..........................58,500.00

William and Mary-Style: This example includes some elements of William and Mary, but scrolled legs are not typical of this style.

America, 20th C, scrolled legs, turned legs, reupholstered in off-white raw silk, 20th C reproduction, 45-1/2" h 415.00

Windsor: Windsor chairs have been popular with Americans from the early periods and con-

Windsor, bow back, New England, c1800, maple, old black paint decoration, shaped seat, bulbous legs and H-stretcher, $2,500.

tinue to fascinate craftsmen who create wonderful masterpieces today. Different variations on the back help define the type of Windsor, such as bow back, bird cage, sack back. While we treasure these chairs today, many were made to be used on porches and outdoors. Consequently, many were painted and repainted through the years. One unique feature of a outdoor Windsor is a small channel on the seat, called a rain gutter, that served the purpose just as named. The term "bamboo turnings" refers to chair parts that were lathed to resemble bamboo. Expect to find wear on old Windsors. Well done repairs are acceptable to many collectors. Sometimes a signature is found and that adds greatly to the value.

Bird Cage Crest, seven spindle back with three through crest, bamboo turnings, round seat, stretcher base, refinished, restored crack in seat, some height loss, 15-1/2" h seat, 34-1/2" h 200.00

Bow Back

Bowed crest rail, spindle back, turned arm posts, shaped arms, saddle seat, splayed base with turned legs, H-stretcher, old worn dark green repaint, 17-1/2" h seat, 38-1/2" h 3,520.00

Bowed crest rail, spindle back, turned arm posts, shaped arms, saddle seat, splayed base with bulbous turned legs, H-stretcher, dark brown repaint, ended out legs, one ended out stretcher, one partially replaced arm post, 17-3/4" h seat, 38-1/2" h 1,045.00

Molded bow, seven spindle back, scrolled arms, bamboo turnings, well shaped round seat, stretcher base, repaired crack in seat with bow-ties on underneath side, unreadable signature, Pennsylvania, alligatored black paint over earlier colors, 16-3/4" h, 36" h.........935.00

Molded bow, seven spindle back, scrolled arms with incised line borders, mortised through bow, shield shaped seat with rain gutter, splayed base, refinished, 17-1/2" h seat, 37-1/4" h 495.00

Reeded bow, scrolled arms and spindle back, bamboo turnings, shaped seat with edge carving, turned arm posts, splayed base and rungs, old worn black paint, repairs, 18-1/2" h seat, 36" h 475.00

Shaped arms and spindle back, turned arm supports, shaped seat, splayed base, bulbous turned legs, H-stretcher, worn old black over green paint, arm posts don't match leg turnings, one doweled repair, 17" h seat, 34-1/2" h 990.00

Windsor, bow back, Pennsylvania, black repaint with yellow striping, nine spindle back with molded bow, scrolled arms, shield shaped seat with rain gutter, splayed base with bulbous turned legs and H-stretcher, one spindle broken below bow, age cracks in seat, some height loss, minor repairs, 16" h seat, 37-1/2" h, $500. Photo courtesy of Garth's Auction, Inc., Delaware, OH.

Brace Back

Connecticut, c1796-1840, continuous arm, old dark finish, trace of paint, shaped arms with turned posts, shield shaped seat, splayed base, well turned legs, H-stretcher, faintly signed "A. D. Allen" (Amos Denison Allen, South Windham,) repair at bow in arms, age cracks in seat, price for pair, 18-3/8" h seat, 38-1/2" h 4,620.00

New York, c1770-90, black paint, yellow dec, oak scrolled crest rail, hickory back posts and five spindles, maple arms, legs, and stretcher, poplar seat, 26" w, 19-1/2" d, 17-1/4" h seat, 43" h 9,500.00

Rhode Island, blue-black repaint, beaded edge bow, turned spindles, mahogany scrolled arms, turned arm supports, shaped seat, splayed base, turned legs, H-stretcher, underside of seat initialed "A. K" in white chalk, iron brace on one arm, tail piece replaced, 16-3/4" h, 36" h..725.00

Braced continuous arm, CT, 1780-1803, chestnut and maple, branded "E. B. Tracy," crest with beaded edge continues to shaped hand-holds over shaped seat with extended piece to receive bracing above deeply incised splayed legs joined by H-stretchers, 17" h seat, 37" h 1,100.00

Comb Back, New England, early 19th C

Continuous arm, pine and maple, remnants of old resin varnish surface, rockers added, height loss, 15" h seat, 44" h
....750.00

Writing arm, painted, shaped crest rail, five spindles, shaped back, writing surface with two drawers beneath, shaped seat with drawer, splayed bamboo turned legs joined by stretchers, old black paint, restoration to drawers, 17" h seat, 42-1/2" h 4,025.00

Continuous Arm

America, molded crest continues to shaped arms, bamboo turnings, shaped seat, splayed base, worn old dark finish, 17-3/4" h seat, 37" h 1,430.00

Connecticut, attributed to Ebenezer Tracy, Jr., New London, c1800, shaped crest rail continuing to hand holds above 7

Windsor, continuous arm, Connecticut, attributed to Beriah Green, Windham County, old brown finish, oval seat, turned arm posts, bamboo spindles and shaped arms with beaded edge, splayed base with distinctive turned detail, "H" stretcher, price for pair, one with 16-1/2" h seat, 37" h back, other 17-1/4" h seat, 39-3/4" h, $5,225. Photo courtesy of Garth's Auctions, Inc., Delaware, OH.

spindles, vase and ring-turned arm supports, shaped saddle seat on splayed swelled ring-turned tapering legs joined by stretchers, old salmon red painted surface, 17" h seat, 35-1/2" h............3,200.00

Connecticut, attributed to Beriah Green, Windham County, old brown finish, oval seat, turned arm posts, bamboo spindles and shaped arms with beaded edge, splayed base with distinctive turned detail, H-stretcher, price for pair, one with 16-1/2" h seat, 37" h back, other 17-1/4" h seat, 39-3/4" h 5,225.00

New England, c1780, comb back, extended serpentine top above bowed crest rail continuing to carved knuckle hand holds, vase and ring-turned legs joined by stretchers, dark green over early paint, 17" h seat, 42-1/2" h............2,550.00

New England, early 19th C, pine and maple, shaped incised seats, turned splayed legs, refinished, 35" h, price for pair 1,100.00

New Jersey or Pennsylvania, c1790-1810, painted, crest rail above nine spin-

dles, scrolled arms on vase and ring-turned supports, carved saddle set, splayed bamboo turned swelled legs joined by stretchers, old salmon red paint over earlier paint, imperfections, 17" h seat, 37" h.....................................2,300.00

Fan Back

New England, c1780, painted, serpentine crest with scroll-carved terminals above 9 spindles, shaped arms ending in scrolled carved hand holds on vase and ring-turned supports, carved saddle seat and splayed vase and ring-turned legs joined by vase and ring stretchers, 17" h, 43-1/2" h 5,465.00

New England, c1790, ash and maple, shaped crest rail above eight spindles, shaped handholds over vase and ring-turned supports, carved saddle seat, splayed vase and ring-turned legs, joined by stretcher, refinished, 17" h seat, 40" h 3,800.00

New England, late 18th C, ash and pine, serpentine crossbanding in carved terminals above raked tapering spindles, serpentine arms ending in knuckled handholds, incised seat, bulbous turned splayed legs joined by stretchers, refinished, minor repairs, 17" h seat, 43" h 5,750.00

Windsor, decorated, old tan repaint, dark red striping, simple floral designs, scrolled crest, spindle back, bamboo turnings, shaped seat, scrolled mahogany arms, underneath of seat signed "L. Stevens," wear, repairs to arms, minor edge damage, 17" h seat, 35-3/4" h, $385. Photo courtesy of Garth's Auctions, Inc., Delaware, OH.

Nutting, Wallace, old natural finish, branded and paper label, 18" h, 44" h 1,100.00

Rhode Island, c1780, brace back, carved serpentine crest rail with scrolled terminals above 5 spindles on vase and ring-turned stiles joined to shaped arms in carved knuckle hand holds, vase and ring-turned supports, carved saddle seat, splayed vase and ring-turned legs joined by turned stretchers, 16-1/2" h, 43" h 7,475.00

High Back, Pennsylvania, 1770-80, painted, serpentine crest terminates in carved scrolls above spindles, open arms ending in carved knuckles, shaped incised seat, bulbous turned legs joined by swelled stretchers, old red paint, 18-1/2" h seat, 39-3/4" h 6,325.00

Hoop Back, early 19th C, various woods, arched back enclosing seven bamboo turned rods, scroll arms with spindle-turned supports shaped slab seat raised on splayed, bamboo turned legs with similarly turned H-stretcher, stained, imperfections 250.00

Sack Back

America, six spindle back, well turned arm supports, shaped seat, splayed base

Windsor, fan back, Wallace Nutting, old natural finish, branded and paper label, 18" h seat, 44" h, $1,100. Photo courtesy of Garth's Auctions, Inc., Delaware, OH.

Left: Windsor, sack back, mixed woods, bulbous stretcher, 21" w, 38" h, $900; right: Windsor, comb back, mixed woods, shaped crest rail, bulbous stretcher, 20" w, 38" h, $1,870. Photo courtesy of Richard Opfer Auctioneering, Inc., Timonium, MD.

with turned legs, H-stretcher, refinished, restoration, replacements, 17" h seat, 37-1/2" h 385.00

America, seven spindle back with shaped arms, arm supports match legs, oval shaped seat with rain gutter, splayed base with well turned vase and ring legs, H-stretcher, old refinishing, base restoration, replacements, 16-1/2" h seat, 37-3/4" h 475.00

America, spindle back with shaped arms, bowed crest rail, turned arm supports, shaped seat, splayed base, turned legs, H-stretcher, old refinishing, seat formerly cut for potty and plugged, other old repairs, 16" h seat, 37-1/2" h 450.00

Massachusetts, c1780, ash, pine, and maple, molded bowed crest rail above eight spindles, carved knuckle handholds on vase and ring-turned supports, shaped saddle seat on splayed vase and ring-turned legs joined by turned stretchers, old finish, imperfections, 17" h seat, 39" h 2,185.00

New England, c1780, maple and ash, bowed crest rail above seven spindles, shaped arms, vase and ring-turned supports, shaped saddle seat, splayed vase and ring-turned legs joined by stretchers, old varnish, repair to crest rail, 16-1/2" h seat, 38" h 2,185.00

New England, c1790-1810, chestnut and ash, arched crest, shaped handholds, sheet with incising and pommel on ring-turned splayed legs joined by swelled stretchers, old refinishing, 17" h, 38" h 1,495.00

New England, late 18th C, painted, bowed crest rail above seven spindles, shaped arms, vase and ring-turned supports, shaped saddle seat, splayed vase, ring-turned legs joined by swelled stretchers, old black paint, 17" h seat, 35-1/4" h 2,300.00

Southern New England, late 18th C, later rosewood graining and yellow outlines, old surface, 17-5/8" h seat, 38" h 1,500.00

Tablet Back, New England, early 19th C, maple, ash, and pine, crest with two horizontal concave rails enclosing tablet above seven spindles, bamboo turnings, bow shaped incised seats on splayed legs joined by stretchers, old refinishing, imperfection, price for assembled set of six, two arm chairs, four side chairs, 17" h, 33-1/2" h 2,300.00

Writing, attributed to Ebenezer Tracy, Lisbon, CT, c1770-80, comb-back crest with six spindles above shaped arm rail with scroll arm terminals and writing surface, drawer on vase and ring supports, turned spindles, ring-turned legs joined by turned stretchers, shaped saddle seat and suspended drawer, old refinishing, restorations, 17" h seat, 46" h..................5,175.00

Windsor-Style, brace back continuous arm, dark green paint, reproductions by D. R. Dines, in Tracy style, price for set of ten, 17-1/2" h seat, 37" h..3,850.00

Corner Chairs, Roundabouts

Just as cabinets and cupboards were made to fit into a corner, so were chairs. The name "Roundabout" is used in several parts of the country to describe these interesting chairs. It is possible to find corner chairs with deep skirts that were used in bedrooms as commodes. However, not every corner chair served this function. Many styles of corner chairs are actually quite comfortable, as they have ample seat-

ing space and the height of the arms generally conforms to the sitter's natural arm height.

Centennial, Chippendale-Style, c1880-1900

Mahogany, carved crest rail with mask, three fluted columnar supports, two pierced and carved splats, all four legs have carved knees claw and ball feet, orig blue velvet upholstery, 25-1/2" w, 27" d, 32" h......500.00

Walnut, carved lion's head mask crest rail, two pierced splats, low crest rail slip seat, sq legs, paw feet 250.00

Chippendale

America, mahogany, curved back centered by shaped over-scroll crest block, continuing onto out-scrolled arms, turned and ring-turned posts interspersed by pierced sheaf splats, drop-in seat raised on acanthus-capped cabriole legs with pad feet....................700.00

America, walnut, low crest rail, vase shaped splat, scrolled arms, turned arm supports, upholstered slip seat, sq legs, box stretcher, refinished, 30" h...................500.00

Massachusetts, 1770-1800, roundabout, walnut, shaped crest on scrolled arms, shaped splats, slip seat in molded frame, frontal cabriole leg ending in pad feet, three turned legs ending in small turned feet, old refinishing, repairs, 17" h seat, 30" h 10,350.00

New England or New York State, 18th C, mahogany, scrolled crest above pierced splats, molded seat frame, front cabriole leg with pad feet joined to turned legs by X-stretchers, old refinishing, restoration, 19-1/2" h seat, 30-1/2" h..................2,645.00

New England, late 18th C, maple, crest with shaped terminals, cyma curved horizontal splats, rush seat, turned legs, button feet, joined by turned stretchers, refinished, minor imperfections, 17" h, 31" h...............2,185.00

Queen Anne

America, c1740-60, walnut, plain three-piece crest rail terminating in volutes, solid vasiform back slats, upholstered drop-in seat, deep scalloped skirt, short cabriole legs, trifid fore foot, 24" d, 31-3/4" h 20,160.00

Country, mid-18th C, maple, turned posts with arched slats and curved arms, old replaced rush seat, front duck foot, turned rear

Corner, Queen Anne, New England, late 18th/early 19th C, maple, scrolled arm terminals above vasiform splats, molded seat frame, slip seat, deep shaped skirt, frontal cabriole leg ending in pad foot, other turned feet, old refinish, imperfections, 15-1/2" h seat, 28-1/2" h, $2,185. Photo courtesy of Skinner Auctioneers and Appraisers of Antiques and Fine Art Boston and Bolton, MA.

feet, refinished, tops of posts and feet have been ended out, 17" h seat, 31" h 495.00

Maryland, western, c1750-60, mahogany, comb back over shaped crest continuing to flat hand holds, three vase and ring-turned stiles, two vase splats at angle to center back stile, needlepoint seat, frontal cabriole leg with claw and ball foot, three ring-turned legs, 26" w, 46" h 2,750.00

Massachusetts, Boston, 1752-60, walnut, shaped crest continuing to scrolled hand holds above three vase and ring-turned stiles and two vase splats on molded shoes, slip compass seat on frontal cabriole leg ending in pad foot, three straight turned tapering legs ending in pad feet, all joined by cutout seat frame above block, vase and ring-turned cross stretchers, old surface, imperfections, 17" h seat, 30" h............................ 43,700.00

New England, Southeast, c1740-60, chamber, cherry, shaped crest rail continues to scrolled arms, vase and ring-turned supports, shaped splats on molded shoes, upholstered slip set and three block and turned tapering legs, button feet, joined by deep skirt, front cabriole leg ends in high pad foot, old finish, 16-1/2" h seat, 28" h..........................4,325.00

New England, c1775, maple, shaped arms, turned supports, turned legs, two

turned box stretchers, traces of red paint, 19" h 500.00

New England, late 18th C, old red paint, repairs and imperfections, rush seat badly deteriorated, 17" h seat, 30" h 1,750.00

New England, late 18th/early 19th C, maple, scrolled arm terminals above vasiform splats, molded seat frame, slip seat, deep shaped skirt, frontal cabriole leg ending in pad foot, other turned feet, old refinishing, imperfections, 15-1/2" h seat, 28-1/2" h 2,185.00

Rhode Island, last half 18th C, walnut, orig Spanish brown paint, shaped crest projects above scrolled back rail ending in circular handholds on block, vase and ring-turned stiles continuing to turned slightly swelled legs, frontal cabriole leg ending in pad foot on platform supporting ballooned slip seat, joined by block, vase and ring-turned cross stretcher, minor imperfections, 17-1/2"h seat, 30-1/2" h 4,650.00

Queen Anne-Style, fruitwood, heart-shaped splats, crewel-work seat, cabriole legs, pointed pad feet 300.00

Windsor, Connecticut - Rhode Island border region, 1790-1800, painted maple, spindled crest above pillow back lower crest ending in scrolled terminals over shaped horizontal splats, rush seat, turned legs, feet joined by stretchers, old black paint, very minor imperfections, 16-1/2" h, 38-1/2" h...............4,600.00

Desk Chairs

Most desks are designed so that the user is in a seated position at a comfortable writing height. However, few arm chairs are designated specifically for that purpose. More than likely, the chair was of the same style and period of the desk. Some examples from the Arts & Crafts period are listed below to show the range of prices for this chair form. It is important to remember that decorators of the Arts & Crafts period wanted to achieve a total look and frequently designed an entire room, including the furniture, hardware, lighting, and textiles to coordinate, match, or make a statement about the owner.

Arts & Crafts

Limbert, Charles P., Grand Rapids and Holland, Michigan, c1912, horizontal H-back over single slat, orig leather seat, branded mark, 35" h 550.00

Roycroft, East Aurora, NY, mahogany, hourglass back slat with initial "H," tacked-on Japan leather seat, Mackmurdo feet, orig finish, carved orb and cross mark, 17" w, 17" d, 43-1/2" h 1,400.00

Stickley, Gustav, New York

No. 362, horizontal top rail, orig leather and tacks on back and seat, orig finish, swivel mechanism needs repair, paper label, 18" w, 18" d, 35" h 1,150.00

No. 398, low H-form back, recovered leather seat, orig finish, 17" w, 16" d, 33" h..1,650.00

Swivel, arms, new tacked-on burgundy leather upholstery, some refinishing, unmarked, 26" w, 21" d, 36-1/2" h 1,400.00

Stickley, L. and J. G., Fayetteville, NY, swivel, five vertical back slats, drop-in seat cushion, skinned orig finish, paper label, 27" w, 22" d, 39" h 1,200.00

Dining Chairs

Many of the arm chairs and side chairs found in today's antique furniture market began life as dining room chairs. And, as the dining room was an important room for entertaining in colonial eras, it was equally important to have impressive furniture. Lavish dinners and long dining room tables demanded exquisite chairs in multiples. When not being used for dining, these chairs often were found waiting at the sides of the room for their next function.

Most dining sets of chairs contain at least one arm chair, usually for the master. If a second arm chair is included, it was meant for the hostess. Dining room chairs should be carefully examined for a number that may be inscribed on the interior of the frame, indicating that it is a part of a larger set.

Arts & Crafts

Limbert, Charles P., Grand Rapids and Holland, Michigan

Arm, two vertical back slats, fabric covered drop-in seat cushion, dry orig finish, branded mark, 25" w, 17" d, 36" h 295.00

Set of four, one arm chair, three side chairs, single back slat, arched back rail,

orig worn drop-in leather cushions, orig finish, branded mark, some imperfections, 24" w, 21" d, 36" h.........................1,450.00

Set of ten, #1711, one arm chair, nine side chairs, arched top rail, two back slats, orig drop-in cushions with some wear to orig leather, 17" w, 17" d, 36" h....5,500.00

Roycroft, East Aurora, New York

Arm, Grove Park Inn, crest rail with carved "GPI" over single broad vertical panel, orig tacked-on leather seat, orig finish, carved orb and cross mark, 25-1/2" w, 16-1/2" d, 41" h 4,750.00

Set, one arm chair, five side chairs, two horizontal back slats, new upholstered fabric seat covers, orig finish, carved orb and cross mark, arm chair: 24-3/4" w, 22-3/4" d, 37-3/4" 9,750.00

Side, hourglass back slats, orig tacked-on Japan leather seats, orig finish, unmarked, from estate of Wm Roth, Roycroft designer, 17-1/4" w, 18" d, 40-1/4" h, price for set of six.........................8,000.00

Stickley Brothers, Grand Rapids, Michigan

Set of four, one arm, three side, chevroned crest rail over two cutout slats, back panel and seat tacked-on with blue Japan leather, orig finish and upholstery, unmarked, arm: 25-1/2" w, 22" d, 42-1/4" h 3,500.00

Set of five, two vertical back slats, tacked-on old fabric seats, new finish, branded mark, 17-1/2" w, 16" d, 37-1/2" h 1,475.00

Stickley, Gustav, New York

..No. 370, set of six, two arm chairs, four side chairs, ladderback, three horizontal back slats, recovered drop-in cushions, orig finish, red decal, arm chair: 25" w, 23" d, 36" h; side: 17" w, 16" d, 36" h 3,300.00

No. 1299, Thornden, two wide horizontal back slats, new rush seat, orig finish, unsigned, 16" w, 18" d, 36" h 2,200.00

Stickley, L. and J. G., Onondaga Shop, Fayetteville, NY

Tall back, spindled, fine orig hard leather seat, 17-1/2" w, 16" d, 41-1/4" h, ... 1,200.00

Tall back, three vertical back slats, drop-in seats cov in new brown leather, new finish, wear to back legs, price for pair, 19-1/4" w, 19" d, 46" h 600.00

Three vertical back slats, arched front rail, new rush seats, orig dark finish, Handcraft label, price for set of four, 20" w, 16-1/2" d, 36" h 3,000.00

Majestic Chair Co., attributed to, tall back, three long vertical back slats, orig worn inset rush seat, new finish, unmarked, 17" w, 17" d, 49-1/2" h................................1,900.00

Unknown Designer

Set of six, two of three vertical back slats corseted, replaced tacked-on red vinyl seat, orig ebonized finish, unmarked, 18" w, 18" d, 38" h........................1,950.00

Set of twelve, arched top, four vertical back slats, solid seat, some wear to orig finish, 17" x 17" x 36" 1,200.00

Chippendale

English, two armchairs, six side, mahogany, rectangular back with shaped crest rail over pierced tracery splat, drop-in seat with molded rails, molded sq section legs joined by U-stretcher, price for set of eight 6,000.00

Maryland, c1770-85, one armchair, three side, carved mahogany, serpentine crest with carved floral devices, similar pierced horizontal splats, molded trapezoidal set frames, square legs with molded outside edges joined by square stretchers, refinished, restoration, price for set of four, 17" h, 37" h 4,325.00

New England, c1760-1800, two armchairs, six side, maple, serpentine crests which end in raked molded ears above pierced splats, trapezoidal rush seats, square legs joined by square stretchers, price for assembled set of eight, arm: 17-1/2" h seat, 38-1/2" to 41-1/2" h, side: 16-1/2" to 17-1/4" h seat, 37-1/4" to 40" h 2,300.00

Chippendale-Style, early 20th C

One arm chairs, five side chairs, veneered, pierced splat, slip seat, cabriole legs, paw feet, price for set of six 950.00

Two arm chairs, four side chairs, mahogany, pierced splat backs, straight tapered legs, H-stretcher, upholstered slip seats, price for set of six, 20" w, 17" d, 38" h........1,800.00

Two arm chairs, four side chairs, mahog-

any, shaped crest above pierced splat, slip seat, cabriole legs, ball and claw feet, price for set of six, 37-1/2" h.....................1,400.00

Two arm chairs, six side chairs, hardwood with old brown finish, carved ribbon back slats, needlepoint upholstered slip seats, molded legs, price for set of eight, 19" h, 37" h 1,150.00

Two arm chairs, six side chairs, cherry, arched crests, vasiform pierced splat, slip seat, sq legs, price for set of eight............... 2,400.00

Two arm chairs, six side chairs, mahogany, fiddle backs with leaf carved ears, molded rect front legs, needlework seats, price for set of eight, side: 21-3/4" w, 19" d, 39" h 10,350.00

Two arm chairs, eight side chairs, carved mahogany, scrolling and acanthus carved crest, elaborately carved and pierced splat, slip-in seat, cabriole legs headed by acanthus carving, ball and claw feet, price for set of ten, 37-1/2" h 3,500.00

Two arm chairs, eight side chairs, carved mahogany, serpentine crest rail above elaborately pierced and carved splat, slip seat, sq blind-fretted legs, joined by like stretchers, price for set of ten, 38-1/2" h 2,750.00

Two arm chairs, eight side chairs, mahogany, pagoda form crest above elaborately pierced and carved ribbon splat, slip seat, molded legs, price for set of ten, 28" h arms, 42" h 3,900.00

Four side chairs, mahogany, arched scrolling crest rail, pierced interlaced splat, slip seat, Marlborough legs, stretchers, price for set of four 1,800.00

Classical

Massachusetts, made by Eben White, Boston, September 30, 1826, one arm chair, eight side chairs, bird's eye maple, rectangular scrolled crest, splat with carved rosettes and scrolled ends, joining curving stiles, saber legs and cane seats, old surface, minor repairs, provenance includes original bill of sale in the manuscript collection of the Peabody-Essex Museum, Salem, MA, price for set of nine, arm: 17-3/4" h seat, 30-3/4" h, side: 17-1/2" h seat, 31" h 23,000.00

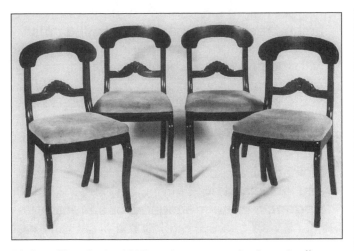

Dining, Classical, c1825, mahogany, arched crest rail over fan carved horizontal back splat, upholstered seat, sabre legs, price for set of eight (four shown), $1,100. Photo courtesy of Samuel T. Freeman & Co., Philadelphia, PA.

Middle Atlantic States, c1820, four side chairs, mahogany, wide crest rail with cut scrolled ends, outswept front legs, needlepoint seat, price for set of four, 17" h seat, 33" h 850.00

New England, c1830, tiger maple, wide crest rail, caned seat, old refinishing, labeled "From Ryther Place in Bernardston," price for set of six, 17-1/2" h seat, 43" h 2,225.00

New York State, c1835, tiger and bird's eye maple, lyre-shaped seat, caned seat, refinished, repairs, price for set of eight, 17" h seat, 33-1/4" h 3,000.00

Classical Revival

c1910-40, mahogany, shaped back splats, saber legs, price for set of five, 35" h .500.00

20th Century, two arm chairs, six side chairs, vasiform back splats, saber legs, price for set of eight, side: 18" w, 19" d, 34-1/2" h 2,185.00

Edwardian, in the style of Thomas Chippendale, c1900-1910, carved mahogany, damask upholstered slip seats, price for set of four, 42-1/4" h..700.00

Empire

America, 19th C, mahogany, foliate carved top rail, scroll-cut splat, saber legs, 18" w, 18" d, 35" h 200.00

America, c1800, two arm chairs, six side chairs, mahogany and walnut, rolled mahogany top rails, incurvate sides and center walnut panels, horizontal walnut slat, tapered trapezoidal pad seats, fluted edge frame, tapered reeded legs with pear form feet, joined by slightly baluster X-form stretchers, price for set of eight.........................4,320.00

Federal

America, two arm chairs, four side chairs, stained beech, tablet crest rail, pierced foliate splat, caned seat, saber legs, price for set of six 1,950.00

Massachusetts, c1790-1800, two arm chairs, six side chairs, mahogany, inlaid, shield back with rays terminating in sunset-type carving, upholstered seats with decorative tacks, straight tapered legs and cross stretchers, price for set of eight, 17-1/2" h seat, 37" h 15,500.00

New England, c1800, three arm chairs, four side chairs, maple and hickory, bead turned spindle backs, notched crest rails, rush seats, turned front legs, all skinned, assorted restorations, price for set of seven, side: 18-1/2" w, 16-3/8" d, 34-7/8" h 3,565.00

Rhode Island or Salem, MA, c1795, set of four side and matching arm chair, carved mahogany, shield back with molded crest and stiles above carved kylix with festoons draped from flanking carved rosettes, pierced splat terminating in carved lunette at base above molded rear seat rail, seat with serpentine front rail, sq tapering legs joined by stretchers, over-upholstered seats covered in old black horsehair with scalloped trim, old surface, price for set of five, 16-1/2" h seat, 37-3/4" h................23,000.00

Hepplewhite, Maryland, six side chairs, mahogany, shield back, upholstered slip, tapered grooved legs, H-stretcher, provenance from Smith Plantation, Pikesville, Maryland, price for set of six, 20" w, 38" h 6,820.00

Mission, Frank Lloyd Wright, Heritage Henredon, No. 2002, set of four, mahogany, low upholstered back with Taliesen design to edge, recovered upholstered seat, retailers label, orig finish, 20" w, 22" d, 32" h 1,200.00

Modernism Era

Bertoia, Harry, manufactured by Knoll International, white plastic wire construction, blue seat pads, label, price for set of four, 21" w, 20" d, 30" h 500.00

Komal, Ray, manufactured by J. G. Furniture, 1949, Model #939, one piece molded plywood frame, nickel connector, tubular metal frame, price for set of four, 21" w, 19" d, 28" h 2,200.00

Rohde, Gilbert, manufactured by Herman Miller, pickled bentwood frames, reupholstered in black wool, some wear, price for set of eight, 18" w, 20" d, 30" h 265.00

Robsjohn-Gibbings, T. H., manufactured by Widdicomb, two arm and four side chairs, curved slat backs, orig orange upholstery curved legs, price for set of six, 23" w, 20" d, 35" h 1,650.00

Saarinen, Eero, manufactured by Knoll International, c1948, black fiberglass back, orig tan Naugahyde seat, satin chrome base, price for set of six, 22" w, 21" d, 22" h 3,750.00

Wegner, Hans, c1950, walnut, bent back and arm rail, plank seat raised on tapered circular legs, price for set of six, 30-1/2" h 900.00

Wormley, Edward, manufactured by Dunbar

Set of six, two arms and four side chairs, dark mahogany frames, orig Jack Larsen patterned fabric, big "D" label, some fading to fabric, 19" w, 20" d, 39" h 1,750.00

Set of six, two arms and four side chairs, dark mahogany frames, rattan backs, 22" w, 18" d, 33" h 1,650.00

Set of eight, walnut frames, curved tapered legs, rattan backs, black and white vinyl cushions, refinished, 24" w, 21" d, 33" h 1,400.00

Wright, Frank Lloyd, manufactured by Henredon, two arm chairs, four side chairs, mahogany, upholstered back and seat, carved Greek key pattern trim, price for set of six 1,200.00

Queen Anne-Style, America

Set of eight, two armchairs, six side chairs, walnut, dipped crest rail over vasiform splat, needlepoint overstuffed seat with shaped rails, cabriole legs with hairy-paw feet, carved flower heads and foliage 3,000.00

Set of eight side chairs, walnut, open arched rectangular back with dipped crest rail over vasiform splat, padded drop-in seat with molded rails, cabriole legs, pad feet 500.00

Set of twelve, two armchairs, ten side chairs, walnut and maple open rectangular back with vasiform bend splat surmounted by yoke-shaped crest rail, padded drop-in seat with molded rails, cabriole legs with lappets and pad feet joined by H-stretcher 2,750.00

Regency, inlaid mahogany, open rectangular back with curved, over-scroll crest rail inset with flame mahogany panel, curved crossbar, slip seat, molded saber legs, price for set of six...2,200.00

Regency-Style, two arm chairs, eight side chairs, mahogany, rope twist crest, horizontal splat, centered inlaid patera, splayed legs, price for set of ten, 26" h arms, 32" h..4,000.00

Rustic, cedar, barrel form, burled details under peaked and spindled top, re-coated finish, dated 1938, 28" w, 22" d, 31" h 850.00

Sheraton

Set of six, Center County, Pennsylvania, late 19th C, rod back, painted olive green, crest with red, yellow, and green floral design, black and gold striping, price for set of six, 32" h......................................3,315.00

Set of eight, two arm chairs, six side chairs

Maple, bamboo turned arms, backs with crossed supports, rush covered horseshoe-shaped seat, reeded front legs, price for set of eight, 33" h.....................2,860.00

Painted, old worn cream colored paint with gold and black, turned legs and posts, outward curving feet, balloon seats, shaped arms and ladderbacks, replaced paper rush seats, minor repairs, price for set of eight, 33-1/2" h...................1,980.00

Victorian

America, walnut, rectangular crest, carved back, splat, damask upholstered seats, saber legs, price for set of four...........425.00

Eastlake, c1870, one armchair, six side chairs, mahogany, fan-carved crest rail, reeded stiles and stretchers, block carved front legs, minor damage, price for set of seven, 35" h...875.00

Renaissance Revival, four armchairs, four side chairs, heavily carved frames surmounted by heraldic lions, center coat of arms, spiral and spool-turned supports, price for set of eight 6,000.00

Rococo Revival, walnut, shaped back, button-upholstered seat, cabriole legs, price for set of six, 35-1/2" h 1,200.00

Easy Chairs (Wing)

Not all American seating furniture was austere. The easy chair was introduced during the William and Mary period. Because easy chairs are upholstered and frequently padded and feature large wings at the back, they are also called "wing" chairs.

Centennial, c1876, mahogany, arched crest rail, serpentine wings, out-scrolling arms, molded square tapering legs, raked rear legs conjoined by straight stretchers, 32-5/8" w, 32" d, 46" h...800.00

Chippendale

America, c1750-80, mahogany, arched crest rail, serpentine wings, out-scrolling arms, molded square tapering front legs, raked rear legs, conjoined by straight stretchers, repairs to rear legs, 32-3/8" w, 28" d, 46-1/2" h..............................3,600.00

America, c1770-90, mahogany, Marlborough legs, H-stretcher, old needlepoint fabric, 34" w, 46" h.................................2,420.00

America, c1770-90, mahogany, notched corner legs, H-stretcher, old needlework fabric upholstery, 34" w, 45" h 3,500.00

America, c1770-90, mahogany, straight legs, H-stretcher, reupholstered, 32" w, 43" h 4,200.00

Connecticut, East Windsor area, c1770-80, mahogany and cherry, arched back with ogival wings, out-scrolled arms with conical supports, serpentine seat rail with upholstered seat, cabriole legs, claw and ball feet joined by stretchers, wear to upholstery...........40,000.00

New England, late 18th C, mahogany, serpentine back and shaped arms, straight seat on square legs joined to raked rear legs by box-stretchers, old finish, repairs, 19" h seat, 45" h 990.00

New England, late 18th C, mahogany, serpentine crest, out-scrolled arms, tight seat, square legs joined by H-stretchers, old surface, restored, 15" h seat, 46-1/2" h 1,265.00

New England, late 18th C, mahogany, serpentine crest, shaped wings, scrolled arms, square front legs joined by square stretchers to rear raking legs, old dark stained surface, repairs, wear to upholstery, 14" h seat, 48" h 3,800.00

Pennsylvania, Philadelphia, 1750-80, mahogany, molded straight legs joined by stretchers, 20th C upholstery, old refinishing, 17" h seat, 48-1/2" h 3,500.00

Pennsylvania, c1770-90, mahogany, shaped back, shaped wings, out-scrolled arms, upholstered with brass tack trim, molded front legs, refinished, restoration, reupholstered, 17-1/2" h seat, 48" h 2,750.00

Chippendale Style

Late 19th C, walnut, upholstered, claw and ball feet, 33-1/4" w, 31" d, 44-1/2" h ...300.00

Early 20th C, mahogany

Canted back with shaped crest flanked by outward flaring wings and scrolled arms, cabriole legs, claw and ball feet, upholstered in yellow fabric, 28" w, 23-1/2" d, 43-1/2" h 125.00

High back, slightly shaped seat, front cabriole legs with shell carved knees, claw and ball feet, 30" w, 52" h 750.00

Leather, H-stretcher, well worn, 29" w, 45" h...1,100.00

Reproduction, 20th C, reupholstered in light colored linen, worn, 40-1/2" h..200.00

Tall back with shaped crest flanked by wings and out-scrolled arms, sq legs joined by H-stretcher, light blue damask upholstery, 24" w, 23" d, 48" h 250.00

Colonial Revival, Queen Anne-style, hardwood cabriole legs, turned stretcher, upholstery removed, old dark finish, 46" h......900.00

Federal

New England, c1815-20, upholstered, serpentine crest above outward flaring arms, straight skirt, vase and ring-turned tapering legs, sq raked rear legs, all on casters, 19" h seat, 47-1/2" back........................4,600.00

Easy, Federal, New England, late 18th/early 19th C, upholstered, serpentine crest above scrolled arms, serpentine front seat rail, square tapering front legs, square raking rear legs, old surface, 45" h, $4,890. Photo courtesy of Skinner Auctioneers and Appraisers of Antiques and Fine Art Boston and Bolton, MA.

New England, late 18th/early 19th C, mahogany, upholstered, serpentine crest above scrolled arms, serpentine front seat rail, square tapering front legs, square raking rear legs, old surface, 15" h to seat frame, 45" h 4,890.00

Hepplewhite

New England, c1790-1800, cherry, serpentine upholstered back flanked by ogival wings, out-scrolled arms, upholstered seat, sq tapering legs joined by stretchers, center stretcher restored 2,950.00

New England, c1790-1800, mahogany, serpentine upholstered back flanked by shaped wings, out-scrolled arms, upholstered set cushion, molded square tapering legs joined by stretchers, 47 h.........4,600.00

New England, early 19th C, mahogany, serpentine upholstered back flanked by shaped wings, out-scrolled arms, upholstered seat, sq tapering legs joined by stretchers, refinished, reupholstered, 17-1/2" h seat, 46-1/2" h..................1,450.00

Queen Anne, America, 18th C, maple frame, shaped back, out curved wing, walnut cabriole legs, stretchers, pad feet over flattened ball feet, 46" h 29,000.00

Queen Anne-Style, mahogany, padded back, wings and out-scrolled arms, over-upholstered seat, cabriole legs, pad feet, ring and block turned stretchers............................500.00

Sheraton, Pennsylvania, Philadelphia, c1795, mahogany, serpentine upholstered back flanked by ovigal wings, out-scrolled arms, upholstered serpentine seat fitted with loose cushion, tapering legs, spade feet, H-stretcher, brass casters 25,000.00

Victorian

America, walnut base, burl veneer trim, turned legs, relief carved detail, reupholstered in royal blue velvet, price for pair, 34-1/2" h 495.00

English, c1880, walnut and green leather upholstery, scrolled back, padded neck, loose bowed seat, short turned legs on casters, scuffing, 37" h............................2,185.00

Folding Chairs

Folding chairs are certainly a form that folks in the 20th century are familiar with. But, did you know they have been around for years? Just as our popular folding chairs do today, early examples folded for ease of carrying and storage.

Arts & Crafts, church, Boston, c1895, back and sides carved with stylized flowers and leaves, eight keyed through-tenon joints on X-shaped base, orig finish, unmarked, 27" w, 22" d, 5" h..1,500.00

Modernism Era, Russel Wright, manufactured by Samson Co., 1940s, molded plywood seat, back, and arms, orig salmon lacquered metal frame, orig labels, price for set of four, 25" w, 26" d, 31" h...............................2,875.00

Victorian, Elizabethan Revival, George Hunzinger, New York, walnut, Berlin work upholstered seat and back.....................750.00

Gondola Chairs

Like corner chairs and tub chairs, a gondola chair is a figural type of chair. The shape resembles a sleek gondola and frequently the form is found in rich woods with embellishments. The form is only represented in the more romantic type styles.

Classical, late

Massachusetts, c1830-50, mahogany, molded arched peaked crest above baluster flame splat flanked by bull cutouts, serpentine seat rail, saber legs, matching crotchwood veneer on crests and splats, repairs, imperfections, price for set of four, 18" w, 17-1/2" d, 31-1/2" h..............................920.00

New England, c1825, mahogany and mahogany veneer, concave scrolled cresting, vasiform splat, raked stiles, patterned horsehair upholstered slip seats, frontal saber legs joined by bowed seat rail, refinished, orig upholstery in fine condition, price for set of four, 32-1/2" h 1,750.00

High Chairs

The high chair was a clever invention to elevate a child to the correct table height. Wonderful early examples exist and usually show signs of generations of users. Many types of chair styles have been adapted to create a high chair.

Arrow Back

Country, mixed woods, arched crest, turned arms and supports, rabbit ear posts, well shaped incised seat, splayed base, light varnished finish, replaced foot rest, 22-1/2" h seat, 34" h 200.00

Pennsylvania, 1800-20, old dark green paint, plank seat, bamboo turned splayed legs joined by similar stretchers, surface imperfections, wear to paint, 21" h seat, 33" h 375.00

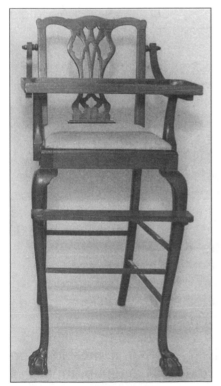

High, Chippendale-Style, early 20th C, mahogany, shaped crest, pierced splat, shaped arms, slip seat, cabriole legs, claw and ball feet, hinged tray, old finish, 38-1/2" h, $440. Photo courtesy of Garth's Auctions, Inc., Delaware, OH.

Chippendale Style, early 20th C, mahogany, pierced splat, shaped crest, slip seat, shaped arms, cabriole legs, ball and claw feet, hinged tray, old finish, 38-1/2" h.............440.00

Ladderback

Middle Atlantic States, 18th C, maple and ash, old refinishing, 18" h seat, 34" h..825.00

New England, late 18th C, maple and ash, surmounted by vase and ring form finials, back rails composed of shaped horizontal slats, arms fitted with cylindrical handholds, cylinder and ring-turned stiles, arm supports, joined by stretchers, old surface, imperfections, front seat rail missing, 17" h seat, 37-1/2" h............390.00

Slant Back

Massachusetts, mid-18th C, maple, turned finials, stiles, posts, and stretchers, worn rush seat, old finish, some height loss, 20" h seat, 33-12" h 1,610.00

New England, 1820s, black painted surface, legs with gold stenciled highlights, red and black taped seat, considerable paint loss, 20-1/2" h seat, 33-1/2" h 750.00

Windsor

America, dark brown repaint with red line decoration, four spindle back with rabbit ears, round seat, turned arms, bamboo turnings, 36" h...475.00

New England, early 19th C, rod back, painted, incised tapering spindles, 21-3/4" h seat, 33-1/2" h 980.00

Invalid Chairs

Several different types of chairs were developed to assist in the care of invalids. Some were designed to assist in getting the invalid from place to place, while others were used to seat an invalid during meal times or leisure times. Easy chairs were often favored as invalid chairs, as they offered a little more warmth.

Victorian, America, 19th C, walnut, rounded top rail continuing into half-upholstered arms mounted with swiveling directional knobs, shaped legs flanked by two front and one back wheel, folding foot rest, 26-1/2" w, 26" d, 43" h...1,100.00

Victorian, Eastlake, walnut, high back, cane seat, flat arms, flat foot supports, cast iron wheels, cast iron handle on back for pushing, 50" h..1,200.00

Ladderback Chairs

"Ladderback" refers to the horizontal slats which form the backs of these distinctive chairs. Production of this style spanned several furniture periods, but they are generally thought of as ladderback rather than a furniture style, like Chippendale. Ladderbacks tend to be sturdy chairs and were used in kitchens and less formal areas of a house.

America, various hardwoods cleaned down with red stain, three arched splats, turned arm posts and finials, shaped arms, turned feet, old worn splint seat, feet ended out, 16-1/2" h seat, 46-1/4" h..360.00

New England, late 18th C, mixed woods, urn shaped finials, four slat back, turned legs, 40" h..550.00

New England, late 18th C, old black repaint, four arched slats, turned finials, old woven splint seat with wear, turned legs, stretchers and posts with shaped arms, 17" h seat, 46-1/2" h..550.00

Pennsylvania, Delaware Valley, 18th C, cherry and oak, five arched and graduated slats supported by cylindrical posts with ovoid finials, tapered arm supports with scrolled terminals, turned legs with ball/peg feet, rush seat, boldly turned front stretchers, one slat repaired, bottom of legs replaced, 22-1/2" w, 18" d, 49" h..415.00

Lolling Chairs

A lolling chair is similar to an easy chair, in that it is upholstered and often padded. A lolling chair will frequently have an exposed wooden frame and some have decorative wooden design elements or decoration. Lolling chairs generally have low seat heights, tall backs, and deep seats allowing the user to rest with a little more relaxed posture.

Chippendale

America, c1780, upholstered back, serpentine crest above shaped and beaded arms, concave molded supports continuing to molded Marlborough legs joined by stretchers, restored, 16" h, 37-1/2" h 1,695.00

Massachusetts, c1780, carved mahogany, serpentine crest above two shaped arms continuing to molded beaded concave supports and sq tapering legs joined by raked rear legs, box-stretchers, refinished, imperfections, 15" h seat, 43" h.......4,900.00

Federal

Massachusetts, c1785-95, mahogany inlaid, upholstered serpentine back above serpentine arms, curving arm supports, H-stretcher base, sq line inlaid legs, casters, old surface, upholstered, imperfections, 15-1/2" h seat, 43-1/2" h................12,900.00

Massachusetts, Newburyport, c1790, open arm, mahogany inlaid, orig label for Joseph Short, old surface, minor imperfections, worn upholstery, 17" h, seat, 44-1/2" h...... 18,200.00

Middle Atlantic States, c1800, mahogany, upholstered back and seat, sq tapered legs, H-stretcher, restoration, imperfections, 16" h seat, 41-1/4" h 975.00

New England, c1810, mahogany, arched crest, rectangular back, shaped arms, molded supports, frontal ring turned tapering legs, brass casters 3,200.00

Hepplewhite

America, cherry and birch frame, open arms with molded top edge, back frame with mortised vertical slats, sq tapered legs, old worn brocade upholstery, refinished, 44-1/4" h..1,950.00

America, mahogany frame, sq tapered legs, mortised and pinned H-stretcher, refinished, repairs to frame, arms replaced, added casters, reupholstered, 43-1/2" h 1,000.00

Massachusetts, Eastern Shore, 1790-1800, mahogany, inlaid, serpentine upholstered back, shaped arms, line and bellflower inlaid down curving arm supports, serpentine upholstered seat, molded sq tapering legs, minor repair to right arm 15,000.00

Massachusetts, c1800-16, mahogany, upholstered serpentine back, shaped arms, molded down-curving arm supports, upholstered seat, molded sq tapering legs joined by H-stretcher, one stretcher replaced..7,500.00

New England, 1790-1810, mahogany, serpentine upholstered back, shaped arms, down-curved arm supports with beaded edges, upholstered seat, sq tapering legs joined by stretcher, 17" h seat, 45-1/2" h 3,750.00

New England, early 19th C, mahogany, inlaid, serpentine upholstered back, shaped arms, outline stringing on down-curved arm supports, upholstered seat, outline stringing on sq tapered legs, joined by stretcher, caters, refinished, restored, reupholstered, 18" h, 36" h 2,500.00

Victorian, second half 19th C, upholstered, walnut veneer, arched crest rail, ogee shaped arms descending short cabriole legs, carved rosettes mid leg, shaped apron, front brass casters, some veneer loss, loose rear right leg, missing rear casters, missing some applied decoration, 24-3/4" w, 34" d, 37-1/4" h 100.00

Lounge Chairs

A lounge chair is a chair which again offers comfort, may be upholstered or include cushions. It is a form found in the less formal styles. The Modernism-Era movement designers gave this type of arm chair a more whimsical feel with their free-form designs, bold use of color and metal framing.

Adirondack, Old Hickory, slanted form, orig woven seat and back, pine pole construction, orig finish, 24" w, 36" d, 40" h 1,100.00

Modernism Era

Aalto, Alvar, manufactured by ICF, bentwood

Lounge, Art Deco, Heywood Wakefield, c1935, rattan, curvilinear arms, gold Naugahyde seats, left with fitted arm to hold newspaper, wear, price for pair, left: 40" d, 30-1/2" h, right: 31" d, 30" h, $825. Photo courtesy of Skinner Auctioneers and Appraisers of Antiques and Fine Art Boston and Bolton, MA.

birch frames, orig black canvas strapping, label, price for pair, 24" w, 27" d, 35" h 1,850.00

Bertoia, Harry, manufactured by Knoll International, c1958, Bird Chair, black diamond pattern metal rod back, rubber mounts, orig upholstery, rod base, manufacturer's tag, 38-1/2" w, 39-1/4" h chair, 14-1/2" x 23-3/4" footstool, two chairs and foot stool 950.00

Breuer, Marcel, manufactured by Isokon, c1937-38, chaise lounge, molded plywood seat within bentwood frame, purple fabric upholstered cushion, thru-tenon construction to seat, repairs, 55" w, 24" d, 28" h 5,500.00

Eames, Charles, manufactured by Herman Miller

Aluminum Group, channeled charcoal Naugahyde upholstery, cast aluminum frame, wear to arm, chair: 26" w, 26" d, 37" h, matching ottoman, 21" w, 22" d, 18" h 550.00

No. 650 chair and ottoman, black leather upholstery, molded rosewood plywood shells, cast aluminum base, orig label, chair: 33" w, 28" d, 33" h, ottoman: 26" w, 21" d, 16" h 3,500.00

No. 670 chair and ottoman, molded rosewood plywood shells, tufted black leather upholstery, early down filing, label 2,900.00

Soft pad, green fabric, cast aluminum frame, 24" w, 26" d, 35" h 250.00

Heywood Wakefield, bentwood maple frame, cushions reupholstered in vintage fabric, 30" w, 33" d, 30" h 300.00

Jacobsen, Arne, manufactured by Fritz Hansen

Egg Chair, sculptural fiberglass shell, reupholstered in purple wool, cast aluminum base, matching ottoman, chair: 32" w, 24" d, 41" h, ottoman: 21" w, 15" d, 17" h..2,925.00

Swan Chair, c1957, orig purple wool upholstery, cast aluminum base, 30" w, 28" d, 31" h 1,430.00

Jeanerette, Pierre, manufactured by Knoll International, Scissors Chair, c1947, birch wood frame, chrome plated steel bolts, reupholstered in red fabric, 24" w, 28" d, 32" h 750.00

Knoll, Florence, manufactured by Knoll International, square form, tufted seat and back, orig light tan leather, bronze base, price for pair, 32" w, 32" d, 30" h 2,325.00

Laverne, Erwin and Estelle, manufactured by Laverne International, c1957, Invisible Group, molded Lucite form, circular cushion, 30" d, 23" h 1,500.00

Mourgue, Olivier, Djinn Chair, manufactured by Airborne International, c1965, sculptural form, orig purple upholstery, price for pair, 28" w, 24" d, 27" h 2,320.00

Nakashima, George, New Hope, PA, walnut, curved crest rail over eleven spindles, low plank seat, price for pair, 32-1/2" h 4,600.00

Nelson, George, manufactured by Herman Miller

Cantinary, orig channeled wool upholstery, chrome strut base, orig label, price for pair, 30" w, 28" d, 29" h...........2,400.00

Coconut Chair, triangular white enameled metal shell, orig blue Naugahyde upholstery, chrome strut frame, 40" w, 32" d, 32" h 14,500.00

Coconut Chair, triangular white enameled metal shell, reupholstered in blue wool, welded chrome strut frame, some wear to chrome, 40" w, 35" d, 33" h 2,900.00

Panton, Verner

Heart Chair, manufactured by Plus-Linje, c1956, metal form, orig blue wool upholstery, chrome base, 40" w, 24" d, 36" h...13,200.00

Wire Cone Chair, manufactured by Plus-Linje, c1960, chromed wire construction, circular seat reupholstered in blue wool, 25" d, 30" h..........................1,750.00

Platner, Warren, manufactured by Knoll International, 1966, bronze wire construction, orig yellow woven wool fabric, label, chair: 41" w, 35" d, 39" h, matching ottoman: 24" d, 16" h...............................2,860.00

Risom, Jens, manufactured by Knoll International, 1940s

Brown canvas strapping to molded birch frame, reupholstered, 20" w, 26" d, 29" h..750.00

Original tan leather strapping to birch frame, orig label, 21" w, 26" d, 29" h..1,550.00

Sarrinen, Eero, manufactured by Knoll International

Grasshopper, upholstered seat, molded birch frame, 26" w, 34" d, 36" h.......770.00

Womb Chair, sculptural fiberglass form, reupholstered in red wool, black metal frame, chair: 29" w, 32" d, 36" h, matching ottoman: 25" w, 20" d, 15" h 2,200.00

Van Der Rohe, Mies, manufactured by Knoll International, Barcelona Chair, stainless steel X-frame, tufted black leather seats, label, wear to leather, price for pair, 30" w, 30" d, 29" h 2,420.00

Wormley, Edward, manufactured by Dunbar

Chaise Lounge, Listen-To-Me, orig channeled blue-green fabric upholstery, walnut frame, brass and wire stretchers, gold metal tag, 72" w, 26" d, 26" h 13,200.00

Curved seat and back, reupholstered in orange velvet, tapered bleached mahogany legs, price for pair, 28" w, 26" d, 32" h...2,325.00

Dark mahogany frames, tilt back, caned sides, upholstered seats in patterned fabric, gold metal tag, price for pair, 26" w, 22" d, 27" h 1,200.00

Rectangular back, reupholstered in blue fabric, bleached mahogany base, marked, 28" w, 28" d, 34" h...........................200.00

Upholstered seat and back, dark walnut frame, reupholstered in ochre felt, 26" w, 28" d, 30" h 650.00

Modernism Era, Pop

Paulin, Pierre, manufactured by Artifort, c1965, Ribbon Chair, sculptural form, white lacquered wood base

Original blue wool fabric, matching ottoman, orig label, chair: 36" w, 24" d, 28" h, ottoman: 29" w, 19" d, 16" h.........2,800.00

Original purple upholstery, 38" w, 24" d, 28" h..2,650.00

Ponti, Gio, manufactured by Pallucco, Rome, 1971, satin chrome frame, upholstered vinyl seat and back, 24" w, 24" d, 32" h 2,650.00

Woodard, chaise, 1960s, extruded aluminum frame, tufted upholstered, 55" w, 24" d, 28" h, needs reupholstery...................770.00

Morris Chairs

Morris chairs are chairs with broad backs, seats, and arms. Most featured an adjustable back frame, allowing the user to slightly recline. The first chair of this type was made by Morris, Marshall, Faulkner & Company in London. The design is credited to William Morris, one of the founders of the English Arts & Crafts movement. The design was quickly embraced by the American Arts & Crafts community.

Arts & Crafts

Handcraft, oak, slant back, leather seat and back cushions, six vertical slats on each side, orig rectangular label on back, price for pair, 32" w, 26" d, 39-1/2" h 3,000.00

Knaus, flat arms, five slats and corbels under each arm, orig finish, recovered in tan leather, 31" w, 36" d, 38" h 2,970.00

Lifetime Furniture, Grand Rapids, MI, No. 569, flat arms over five wide slats, through-tenon construction, orig cushion recovered in leather, orig finish, 33" w, 38" d, 42" h 3,750.00

Stickley Brothers, Grand Rapids, MI, open arm, drop-in spring seat, loose back pillow upholstered in beige ultrasuede, new dark finish, unmarked, 31" w, 39-1/2" d, 36-1/2" 2,100.00

Stickley, Gustav, New York

Morris, Arts & Crafts, similar to Gustav Stickley's No. 637, lady's, oak, flat arm with corbel support over twenty square spindles, rails with through tenons, unsigned, 34-1/2" d, 27-1/2" w, $5,750. Photo courtesy of Skinner Auctioneers and Appraisers of Antiques and Fine Art Boston and Bolton, MA.

Morris, Arts & Crafts, L. & J. G. Stickley, similar to No. 774, lady's, flat arm with corbel, supports over five vertical slats, 27-1/2" w, 30-1/2" d, 39" h, $2,415. Photo courtesy of Skinner Auctioneers and Appraisers of Antiques and Fine Art Boston and Bolton, MA.

No. 332, early form, flat arm over five wide slats, heavy through-tenon construction, orig cane foundation, recently refinished, 32" w, 38" d, 38" h 7,500.00

No. 332, early form, flat arm, slats to floor, orig seat frame, new woven support, orig dark finish, red decal, cushions missing, 31-1/2" w, 39" d, 38-1/2" h 16,000.00

No. 336, bow arm, recovered orig spring cushion, fine orig finish, red decal 13,200.00

No. 369, bent arm form, five vertical slats under each arm, through-tenon construction, orig adjustable pegs, replaced seat, old refinishing, branded signature, 33" w, 38" d, 40" h........................8,500.00

No. 369, drop arm, five vertical slats to sides, orig Japan leather drop-in spring seat and back cushion, minor tear to seat cushion, unmarked, 33-1/4" w, 37-1/2" d, 38-1/2" h 16,000.00

No. 2340, c1902-04, open bow-shaped arm, sgd with red decal in box, webbing missing, 37" d, 23-3/4" h, ...19,550.00

Bow arm, four horizontal back slats, red leather drop-in seat cushions, orig finish, red decal, replace peg on back, some repairs to rear arm, 30-1/2" w, 36-1/2" d, 42" h...6,725.00

Spindled sides and corbels under slanted arms, drop-in seat cushion recovered in white muslin, light over-coat to orig finish, few scratches, replaced pegs,

unmarked, 27-1/2" w, 37" d, 36-1/2" h
....7,500.00
Stickley, L. and J. G., Fayetteville, NY

No. 470, early form, adjustable back, open under arm, orig black finish, replaced cushions, some wear to feet 2,600.00

Flat arm with corbel supports over five long vertical slats, 27-1/2" w, 30-1/2" d, 39" h..2,415.00
Unknown Designer

Lady's, similar to Gustav Stickley, No. 367, NY, c1907, spindle-sided, flat arm with corbel support over twenty sq spindles, rails with through tenons, unsigned, 34-1/2" d, 27-1/2" h.......................5,750.00

Oak, adjustable slat back, two hinged-lid compartmented arms, S-shaped side supports, carved knot design on legs, square feet, replaced cushions, 34" w, 28" d, 39" h 1,450.00

Mission

Unknown Designer, Prairie School design, paneled sides and back, refinished, some veneer loss on legs, 31" w, 40" d, 40" h
....2,500.00
Young, J. M.

Flat arms, slats to floor, shoe feet, orig drop-in spring seat with new leather, orig fin-

Arts & Crafts, Gustav Stickley, New York, c1912, No. 370, oak, three horizontal back slats, reupholstered slip seats, branded mark, two shown of five piece set, 37" h, $2,185. Photo courtesy of Skinner Auctioneers and Appraisers of Antiques and Fine Art Boston and Bolton, MA.

ish, partial paper label, 30" w, 36" d, 36" h
....4,750.00

No. 186, similar to Gustav Stickley No. 332, flat arm form, five slats under each, through-tenon construction, recovered orig cushions, orig finish, unsigned, 32" w, 36" d, 40" h 3,750.00

Parlor

Parlor chairs of the Victorian period reflect a desire to show one's statue by having fine furniture in a modern style. Often part of a suite, the following are examples of what has been sold recently in the auction market.

Victorian

America, third quarter 19th C, rosewood, spoon back, button-upholstered, cartouche form back within serpentine fronted overstuffed seat, shaped rails, continuing to cabriole legs with casters, frame molded throughout 1,200.00

Rococo Revival, John Henry Belter, NY, c1860, laminated and carved rosewood, Rosalie pattern, undulating cresting with flowers, leaves, and trailing fruit and vines, serpentine seat rail similarly carved, molded cabriole supports, blue silk upholstery, price for pair 3,450.00

Potty Chairs

Before indoor plumbing was popular, this natural part of life had to be attended to. Chairs were often fitted with chamber pots and discreetly placed in bedrooms and other living spaces. More examples of children's chairs exist, but occasionally a nice example of a full size chair can be found.

Sheraton-Style, 19th C, oak, slatted back joined to hinged seat, out-scrolled arms, sq legs, 27-1/2" w, 18-1/2" d, 41" h.............300.00

Sewing Chairs

A sewing chair is generally a small chair with short legs that was designed to be comfortable to sit by the fire and sew. Often these shorter chairs were used by quilters sitting at a large frame where the shortened height facilitated their ability to reach under the frame to perform their delicate stitching. Also see Rockers, sewing.

Ladderback, hardwood, old red finish, three

slats, turned finials, short turned legs and stretcher, replaced blue and ecru tape seat, 10-1/2" h seat, 31-3/4" h 200.00

Side Chairs

The easy definition of a side chair is a chair without arms. However, this fails to recognize those chairs designed to be used in dining rooms, in bedrooms, at desks, and all throughout early homes. It is more than likely some of the chairs listed below started their useful lives as sets or suites.

Some furniture styles of side chairs are often referred to as "gentleman's chairs," as they allowed a gentleman to sit comfortably with his sword attached to his belt and resting to the side. This type of side chair has a back, seat, and foundation of legs and possibly stretchers. A "lady's chair" can also be a side chair, but with small supports added between the back and seat, ideally to support the hip areas of ladies. The term "straight chair" often refers to side chairs to, especially those with a straight back and no upholstery.

Aesthetic Movement, late quarter 19th C

America, walnut, upholstered back above foliate carved panel, over-upholstered seat, ring-turned legs ending in casters, gold velvet upholstery, restorations, price for pair, 33-1/2" h 460.00

Bedford, MA, cherry, foliate carved back, twisted slender splats, caned seat, slender tapered legs, partial paper label "The Marble & Shattuck Chair Mfg...Bedf.," price for pair, 34-1/4" h 230.00

Art Deco

McArthur, Warren, manufactured by McArthur Industries, tubular anodized aluminum legs, brown Naugahyde seat and back, price for set of four, 17" w, 16" d, 34" h 4,750.00

Unknown Designer, shaped over-scrolling top rail, padded rectangular curved backrest, overstuffed seat, saber legs, price for set of six 750.00

Arts & Crafts

Limbert, Charles P., Grand Rapids and Holland, MI, set of six, two back slats, recovered padded seat, refinished, branded mark, 17" w, 16" d, 36" h 2,000.00

McHugh, heavy ladderback, orig rush seat, Mackmurdo feet, fine orig finish, unsigned, 24" w, 23" d, 40" h..............450.00

Roycroft, East Aurora, New York

Ladderback, raised posts, tack-on tan leather seats, tapering legs, carved orb and cross mark on apron, refinished, 17" w, 16" d, 36-1/2" h 1,500.00

Ladderback, two back slats, cloud-lift apron carved "Roycroft," inset tacked-on hard old, (non-orig) leather seat, over-coated finish, 18" w, 18-1/2" d, 38-3/4" h 1,300.00

Stickley Brothers, Grand Rapids, MI

No. 312-1/2, side arched top rail, three back slats, molded plank seat, orig finish, numbered, 16" w, 14" d, 38" h 345.00

No. 479-1/2, notched top rail, three vertical back slats, recovered drop-in cushion, refinished, 18" w, 1" d, 37" h............400.00

Stickley, Gustav, New York

No. 308, c1912, H-back, rush seat, branded mark, imperfections, 40-1/4" h 175.00

No. 335, designed by Harvey Ellis, 1904, tiger maple, three vertical back slats inlaid with copper, pewter, and wood floral motif, arched apron, new inset rush seat, refinished, red decal, 16-3/4" w, 16-1/2" d, 39-1/4" h 4,750.00

No. 353, three vertical back slats, rush seat, arched apron, red decal, orig medium finish, scratches, roughness, 39-1/4" h 460.00

Ladderback, chestnut, V-form crest rail, arched rail, orig webbed seat construction, replaced loose cushion, cleaned orig finish, unmarked, 19" w, 18" d, 37" h 2,000.00

Maple, designed by Harvey Ellis, three vertical slats with inlaid design in copper and pewter as back, rush seat, arched seat rails, cleaned orig finish, two with orig rush seats, some refinishing, two signed, price for set of six, 17" w, 16" d, 40" h 23,000.00

Stickley, L. & J. G., Fayetteville, NY, oak, slightly curved crest rail over three vertical slats, leather seat, Handcraft decal, 15-3/4" w, 18" d, 37-1/4" h..................350.00

Turner & Co., England, c1910, oak, shaped crest rail over four vertical slats continuing to lower stretcher, plank seat, maker's tag, 13-1/4" w, 12-1/2" d, 21-1/4" h 520.00

Centennial

Chippendale-style

America, 19th C, mahogany, pierced splat, sq legs joined by stretchers, slip seat, old finish, price for set of five............3,000.00

America, late 19th C, carved mahogany, shaped shell carved crest rail, pierced vasiform back splat, balloon slip seat, shell carved apron, cabriole legs, leaf-craved knees, claw and ball feet, price for pair 900.00

America, late 19th C, mahogany, shaped crest rail and back splat, Marlborough legs, 21-1/2" w, 19" d, 39" h 100.00

Pennsylvania, Philadelphia, c1876, assembled set, mahogany, carved crest rail, pierced splat, beading on rails and straight front legs, interior corners of all legs chamfered, some glue blocks replaced, price for set of seven, 22" w, 20" d, 38 to 39" h 7,850.00

Colonial Revival, carved mahogany, shaped shell carved crest rail, pierced vasiform back splat, balloon slip set, shell carved apron, cabriole legs, leaf-carved knees, claw and ball feet, price for pair...................825.00

Chippendale

America, c1750-80, mahogany, carved crest rail, pierced and carved splat, beading

Chippendale, mahogany, crest with carved ears, relief carved center medallion, fluted back posts with pierced and carved splat, molded edge seat frame with shaped apron, orig slip seat frame reupholstered, cabriole legs, carved knees, claw and ball feet, orig finish, repairs to one back foot, repairs to splat, 39-5/8" h, $5,500. Photo courtesy of Garth's Auctions, Inc., Delaware, OH.

on rails and straight front legs, old repairs to splat and left stretcher, 21-1/2" w, 19" d, 38" h 1,910.00

America, c1775, carved mahogany, splayed rectangular back, tri-arched crest rail over pierced gothic tracery splat, over stuffed seat with shaped and molded rails, cabriole legs, claw and ball feet, claws with back-swept talons, frame molded throughout, crisply carved with acanthus foliage 1,300.00

America, c1780, carved mahogany, fluted back posts with pierced and carved splat, crest with carved ears and relief carved center medallions, molded edge seat frame with shaped apron, orig slip seat frame, cabriole legs, carved knees, ball and claw feet, orig finish, reupholstered seat, repairs to one back foot, corner crack in seat frame, 39-5/8" h 5,500.00

America, c1785, carved mahogany, pierced splat and shaped crest, molded edge seat frame, square legs, molded corner and inside chamfer, H-stretcher, old finish, slip seat missing, later rockers have been removed from legs, 16" h seat, 36" h 440.00

America, late 18th C, walnut, shaped crest, vasiform splat, slip seat, sq legs, H-stretcher, refinished, some damage, replaced pins in mortise joints in base, 18" h seat, 38" h 525.00

Connecticut, late 18th C, cherry, serpentine crest, pierced vasiform splat, rush seat, molded legs, box stretcher, price for set of six 3,000.00

Country, maple with some curl, shaped crest, pierced vase shaped splat, square legs, mortised and pinned stretcher, refinished, replaced rush seat, 16-1/2" h seat, 37-1/2" h 440.00

Maryland, Baltimore, 1775-90, mahogany, serpentine crest terminates in scrolled back molded ears, pierced elaborate arched splat, molded trapezoidal seats, square legs with molded edges, joined by square stretchers, slip seats upholstered in white, old refinish, price for pair, some repairs, 17-3/8" h seat, 37-1/4" h 2,300.00

Massachusetts, Boston or Salem area, 1750-1800, carved mahogany, serpentine crests include central shells with flanking chip carving, terminating in raking molded ears, strapwork patterns splats ending in scrolls, trapezoidal slip seats, molded frames, cabriole legs with arris knees, frontal ball and claw feet joined to rear raking sq legs by block ended turned stretchers, old refinishing, imperfections, 16-1/2" h seat, 37-1/2" h, price for pair 27,600.00

Massachusetts, Boston or North Shore, c1755-85, mahogany, serpentine crest terminates in raked molded ears, pierced splats, trapezoidal over-upholstered seats, cabriole legs with arris knees ending in paw feet, joined to sq chamfered rear legs by block ended side stretchers, old refinishing, very minor imperfections, 18" h seat, 38" h, price for set of three 5,500.00

Massachusetts, Boston, c1760-90, attributed to George Bright, mahogany, serpentine crest rails with scroll-carved terminals above pierced spats with carved scrolls flanking floral devices, on molded shoes, trapezoidal slip seats on straight molded frames joining sq chamfered legs and molded box stretchers, missing brackets,

Chippendale, Maryland, Baltimore, 1775-90, mahogany, serpentine crest terminates in scrolled back molded ears, pierced elaborate arched splat, molded trapezoidal seats, square legs with molded edges, joined by square stretchers, slip seats upholstered in white, old refinish, price for pair, some repairs, 17-3/8" h seat, 37-1/4" h, $2,300. Photo courtesy of Skinner Auctioneers and Appraisers of Antiques and Fine Art Boston and Bolton, MA.

other minor imperfections, price for pair, 16-1/2" h seat, 36-1/4" h..................3,480.00

Massachusetts, Boston, c1780, mahogany, serpentine crest rail centering carved foliage device with scrolled terminals, pierced carved intertwining splat flanked by raked stiles trapezoidal overupholstered seat on cockbeaded sq legs joined by stretchers, old refinishing, minor imperfections, price for pair, 17-1/2" h, 37" h 8,625.00

Massachusetts, c1780, carved mahogany, carved pierced back splat, upholstered drop-in seat, old refinishing, minor imperfections, 17-1/2" h seat, 38" h 1,200.00

Massachusetts, c1780, carved mahogany, serpentine crest rail with carved terminals, pierced splat, raked stiles, trapezoidal slip seat, frontal cabriole legs ending in pad feet on platforms, chamfered rear legs, old refinishing, 37" h..............................2,400.00

Massachusetts, c1780, mahogany, carved crest with shell and ears, pierced and carved splat, upholstered seat, cabriole legs, claw and ball feet, turned H-stretchers, wear to base and feet, minor repairs to knee brackets, minor repairs, reupholstered, 16" h seat, 37-3/4" h 2,225.00

Massachusetts, c1790, mahogany, shaped crest rail, pierced splat, rush slip seat, straight legs, box stretcher, old brown finish, 39-1/2" h...................................525.00

Massachusetts, Concord, last quarter 18th C, dark stain, serpentine crest, raked molded terminals, pierced splat, upholstered slip seat, sq legs, front legs with molded outside edges, jointed by sq molded stretchers, imperfections, 17-3/8" h seat, 39" h....885.00

Massachusetts, Newburyport, attributed to Sewall Short, 1760-80, carved mahogany, shaped crest rail with carved leafage above pierced splat flanking raked stiles, trapezoidal over-upholstered seat, cabriole frontal legs with acanthus leaf and scroll carving, carved ball and claw feet joined to chamfered rear legs by block and ring-turned stretchers, old refinishing, some imperfections, 17-1/2" h, 37" h 3,800.00

Massachusetts, 18th C, mahogany, ribbon back, pierced horizontal splats with beaded edges, joining molded tapering stiles also with beaded edges, slip seats, square legs joined by stretchers, old surface, imperfections, price for pair, 16-3/4" h, 39" h.............1,150.00

New England, 18th C, carved mahogany, ladder back, serpentine upholstered seat, molded stiles and chamfered legs, old surface, minor imperfections, 17" h seat, 37-1/2" h..500.00

New Hampshire, Portsmouth, c1780, carved mahogany, shaped crest with incised edge, pierced vase form splat with Gothic arch, over-upholstered seat, square molded legs joined by stretchers, price for pair 7,200.00

New York, Long Island, early 19th C, straight molded crest, pierced slat, slip seat, square legs joined by square stretchers, old surface, price for set of three, 17" h seat, 35-1/2" h..460.00

North Carolina, c1760-80, carved mahogany, shaped crest rails above pierced splats and raked stiles with trapezoidal slip seats on frontal cabriole legs with carved scrolled returns, claw and ball feet, raked rear legs, old finish, some imperfections, price for pair, 18-1/2" h, 40-3/4" h...........................5,750.00

Pennsylvania, c1760-80, carved mahogany, serpentine crest rails with central carved shells terminating in scrolled back notched ears above interlaced splats, scrolled volutes flanked by fluted stiles, rounded backs, molded trapezoidal seat frames, central carved shells above cabriole legs embellished with foliate and leaf carving, ball and claw feet, old dark surface, imperfections, 17-3/4" h seat, 39-1/2" h, price for pair.....................................80,600.00

Pennsylvania, c1760-80, walnut, arched crest rail with ears, pierced splat, shaped seat rails, cabriole legs ending in claw and ball feet, orig glue blocks missing, replaced by iron strap reinforcements, seat rail with "II," 23-1/2" w, 20-1/2" d, 38-1/4" h 1,290.00

Pennsylvania, Philadelphia, c1750-80, carved mahogany, serpentine crests end in scrolled back ears, carved central shells and beaded edges, reverse curved interlaced scroll splats flanked by similarly spooned stiles with beaded edges and rounded

Left: Chippendale, Pennsylvania, Philadelphia, c1760-80, walnut, shell carved crest rail with scrolled ears, pierced splat with scroll carving, shaped front and side rails, cabriole legs with boldly carved knees, ball and claw feet, marked with "V" on front rail, 23-1/2" d, 21" d, 38-3/4" h, $2,100; right: Chippendale, Pennsylvania, Philadelphia, c1760-80, walnut, shell carving flanked by scrolls and carved ears on crest rail, pierced splat, shaped skirt with inverted carved shell and shaped side rails, cabriole legs with C-scrolls, ball and claw feet, front rail with "I," bottom 2" of both rear legs replaced, 21" w, 20" d, 40" h, $3,920. Photo courtesy of Samuel T. Freeman & Co., Philadelphia, PA.

backs, shaped molded trapezoidal seat frames with carved applied central shells over shell carved cabriole legs with scrolled knee brackets, ball and claw feet, old dark surface, 17-1/2" h seat, 40-1/2" h, price for pair 47,150.00

Pennsylvania, Philadelphia, c1760-80, carved walnut, serpentine crest ends in scrolled back ears, central shell above vasiform splat, raked stiles joining to molded trapezoidal slip sea, centers another carved shell above frontal cabriole legs, ball and claw feet, old finish, minor repairs, losses, 17-3/4" h, 40" h................................6,325.00

Pennsylvania, Philadelphia, c1760-80, walnut, shell carved crest rail with scrolled ears, pierced splat with scroll carving, shaped front and side rails, cabriole legs with boldly carved knees, ball and claw feet, marked with "V" on front rail, 23-1/2" d, 21" d, 38-3/4" h 2,100.00

Pennsylvania, Philadelphia, c1760-80, walnut, shell carving flanked by scrolls and carved ears on crest rail, pierced splat, shaped skirt with inverted carved shell and shaped side rails, cabriole legs with C-scrolls, ball and claw feet, front rail with "I," bottom 2" of both rear legs replaced, 21" w, 20" d, 40" h 3,920.00

Pennsylvania, Philadelphia, c1780, carved mahogany, open rectangular back, tri-arched crest rail over Gothic tracery splat, drop-in seat with molded rails, sq section legs joined by H stretcher 850.00

Pennsylvania, Philadelphia, c1785, carved mahogany, open rectangular back with tri-arched crest rail surmounting pierced vasiform splat, drop-in seat with molded rails, molded sq section legs with pierced brackets..400.00

Rhode Island, Newport, c1775, walnut, pierced splat and yoke crest, carved cross hatching and carved ears, balloon seat frame, turned H-stretcher, cabriole legs, claw and ball feet, old finish, reupholstered, some repairs, 17-1/4" h, seat, 38" h 5,500.00

Rhode Island, c1780, mahogany, serpentine crest rail centering scratch carved punchwork quarter fan above pierced vase shaped splat, square raked stiles, trapezoidal upholstered slip seat on sq legs joined by stretchers, old refinishing, 17-1/2" h seat, 39" h 1,380.00

Chippendale-Style

Mahogany, owl's eye splat, upholstered seat, acanthus carved cabriole legs, claw and ball feet...250.00

Mahogany, scroll carved crest rail, pierced vasiform splat, upholstered seat, Marlborough legs 350.00

Mahogany, shell carved crest rail, pierced vasiform splat, upholstered seat, Marlborough legs 225.00

Chippendale to Federal Transitional, New England, c1790, cherry, Chippendale style ears on crest rail, pierced central plat with urn and scroll designs, resting on pedestal, tapered legs, inside seat rail numbered "IIII," 20" w, 19" d, 38" h 1,950.00

Classical

Maryland, c1820, attributed to John and Hugh Finley, painted light yellow, gilt and

Classical, New England, c1830-40, bird's eye maple, shaped scroll-back rest, vasiform splat, rolled front seat, turned tapering legs joined by stretchers, old cane seat, early surface, price for set of six, 17-3/4" h seat, 34-3/4" h, $1,840. Photo courtesy of Skinner Auctioneers and Appraisers of Antiques and Fine Art Boston and Bolton, MA.

black painted ruit filled compotes flanked by scrolls bordered by contrasting black and green striping, caned seats, surface imperfections, price for pair, 32" h 950.00

Massachusetts, Boston, c1820, mahogany, carved Grecian-style, figured mahogany crest above drapery carved splat, scrolled anthemion decoration flanking molded stiles, acanthus carved molded front legs, old refinishing, minor patch to crest, 32-1/2" h............ 1,200.00

Classical, Pennsylvania, c1830-40, painted and decorated, old brown paint, stenciled decorations on crest and front rail, gold striping, wide curving crest, shaped splats, flanked by raked stiles, rolled plank seat, ring-turned tapering legs, joined by stretchers, price for set of six, 17" h seat, 31" h, $920. Photo courtesy of Skinner Auctioneers and Appraisers of Antiques and Fine Art Boston and Bolton, MA.

New England, c1830, bird's eye maple, horizontal back splats and front stretchers, rush seat, saber legs, spindle sides and back stretchers, general wear, price for set of four, 17-1/2" w, 16-3/4" d, 32-3/4" h 1,680.00

New England, c1830-40, bird's eye maple, shaped scroll-back rest, vasiform splat, rolled front seat, turned tapering legs joined by stretchers, old cane seat, early surface, price for set of six, 17-3/4" h seat, 34-3/4" h 1,840.00

Empire, America

c1820, maple and bird's eye maple, open rectangular back with over-scroll crest rail over vasiform splat, caned seat with over scroll front rail, turned tapering legs joined by box stretcher, price for pair 250.00

c1825, walnut, flat top rails with reverse carved molding, three slats between peaked top openings, sides with slightly baluster turned standards, upcurving caned seats, supported by plain incurvate front legs, tapered back legs joined by slightly bulbous stretchers, price for set of four 400.00

c1830-40, Pennsylvania, painted and decorated, old brown paint, stenciled decorations on crest and front rail, gold striping, wide curving crest, shaped splats, flanked by raked stiles, rolled plank seat, ring-turned tapering legs, joined by stretchers, price for set of six, 17" h seat, 31" h 920.00

c1835, Pennsylvania, decorated, orig gray paint, black and green striping, angel wings or leaves in gold and egg-like medallions with green leaves on shaped crest, plank seat, turned posts, turned legs, price for set of four, 17-1/2" h seat, 32-3/4" h 1,550.00

c1835, mahogany, curved crest rails, slender horizontal splat, applied upholstered seats, saber legs, price for set of five 500.00

Last quarter 19th C, tiger-maple, open rectangular back with curved over-scroll crest rail, pierced foliate cross-bar, seat with convex rails, turned and ring-turned legs, splayed feet, turned box stretcher, price for set of four 1,200.00

Late 19th C and later, mahogany, vasiform back splat, saber legs, 18" d, 16" d, 32-1/2" h 200.00

Federal, New England, c1775-1810, ribbon back, mahogany, serpentine crests with beaded edges, horizontal pierced splats flanked by stiles with beaded edges above over-upholstered seats, square beaded legs joined by stretchers, old surface, repairs, price for set of five, 38" h, $2,530. Photo courtesy of Skinner Auctioneers and Appraisers of Antiques and Fine Art Boston and Bolton, MA.

Early 20th C, mahogany, gondola form, foliate carved top rail, saber legs, 18" w, 20" d, 38" h 200.00

Federal

Connecticut, c1780, mahogany, pierced vasiform splat, urn finial, upholstered seat, straight tapering legs, replaced rear corner braces 750.00

Maryland, c1780, mahogany, pierced shield-shaped splat, straight tapered legs, H-stretcher, needlepoint slip seat, 20" w, 39" h. 775.00

Massachusetts, c1790, inlaid mahogany, shield back, arched rail, carved foliate pendant above pierced and fluted splat, flared seat, sq molded legs 1,250.00

Massachusetts or Rhode Island, c1780, mahogany inlaid, shield back, arched molded crest above five molded spindles and inlaid quarter fan, overupholstered seats with serpentine fronts, molded tapering legs joined by stretchers, price for pair, 17-1/2" h seat, 37" h 5,475.00

Massachusetts or Rhode Island, c1790, carved mahogany, beaded shield back with fan carving, molded stiles, joined to over upholstered shaped seat on square tapering molded legs joined by stretchers, old refinishing, minor imperfections, 18-1/2" h, 27-1/4" h 2,645.00

New England, 1775-1810, ribbon back, mahogany, serpentine crest with beaded edge, horizontal pierced splats flanked by stiles with beaded edges, over-upholstered seat, square beaded legs joined by stretchers, old surface, repairs, price for set of five, 38" h 2,530.00

New England, c1800, cherry, rectangular back enclosing four vertical spindles bordered by inlaid stringing over trapezoidal slip seats, inlaid sq legs joined by stretchers, old refinishing, price for set of three, 35-5/8" h 1,400.00

New Hampshire, Portsmouth, attributed to Langley Boardman, 1774-1833, mahogany, sq back, reeded on crest rail, stiles, and stay rail, over upholstered serpentine seat, molded sq tapering front legs, sq stretchers and rakes rear legs, refinish, minor imperfections, 18" h seat, 36" h 1,035.00

New Hampshire or Massachusetts, c1800, square back, refinished, reupholstered, price for pair, 17-3/8" h seat, 36" h 8,900.00

New York, c1810-20, burled mahogany, rectangular crest, scroll back, carved rococo scrolls and floral designs in splat, sloping molded side rails descend to tapered legs, 19th C handwritten ink tag reads "This belonged to Gen. P. M. Wetmore Born 1798 Died 1876," price for pair, 33" h 1,400.00

Pennsylvania, Philadelphia, c1805, carved and satinwood inlaid mahogany, molded shield back, pierced flower head and bell-flower carved splat, satinwood inlaid fan, over upholstered seat, sq molded tapering legs, feet extended, price for pair 4,500.00

Pennsylvania, Lehigh County, c1810, paint and stencil decorated, horizontal crest flanked by projecting stiles, four arrow-form spindles, serpentine sided bow front seat, turned tapering legs, ball feet, joined by stretchers, decorated with flowers and foliage, green highlights, yellow ground 750.00

Pennsylvania, Philadelphia, c1810, grain painted and stenciled decoration, horizontal reverse scrolling crest, shaped crest rail decorated with C-scrolls and palmettos, rush seat, ring-turned tapering legs, tall peg feet, joined by stretchers, stenciled fruit and foliage, black and yellow ground, gold and red highlights 2,200.00

Pennsylvania, c1855, brown painted, stenciled, arched crest and tapering stiles, vasiform splat, balloon form seat, ring-turned tapering legs joined by stretchers, fruit and flowers in green, blue, and red with cream and gold highlights decoration, price for set of six 2,250.00

George III, English, late 18th/early 19th C, mahogany, shield back with sheaf of wheat carved splat, bowed upholstered seat, circular tapering stop-fluted legs, damages, restorations, price for pair, 37" h 690.00

George III-Style, English, late 19th C, paint dec mahogany, shaped backs with urn-form splats, upholstered seat, saber legs, exotic birds and foliage dec, restorations, price for set of four, 34" h 4,600.00

Hepplewhite

America, mahogany, shield back, rush seat 320.00

Maryland, mahogany, shield back, molded members, well detailed Prince of Wales feather and draper swags, slip seat, sq tapered molded legs, H-stretcher, reupholstered, refinished, two added glue blocks, 17" h seat, 37-5/8" h 750.00

Massachusetts, Salem, mahogany, shield back, molded members, inlaid fan, sq molded tapering legs, H-stretcher, old finish, reupholstered seat, price for pair, 37-3/4" h 2,750.00

North Carolina, Charleston, c1780, attributed to Benjamin Frothingham, carved by Samuel McIntire, shaped crest rail over pierced urn and floral swag carved back splat, carved fruit basket base, upholstered seat, molded tapering legs, joined by stretcher, price for pair 24,000.00

Hepplewhite-Style, pierced splats, square legs joined by stretchers, price for set of six, 38-1/2" h.. 660.00

Hitchcock, Hitchcockville, CT

c1800-50, black painted, open splayed rectangular back, turned crest rail centering by block, pierced scroll cross-bar, woven rush seat raised on splayed turned and tapered legs joined by turned box stretcher, stenciled gilt highlights, price for pair.................... 600.00

c1825-30, black painted, stencil dec, gilt and polychrome dec, turned crest rails, horizontal splats with fox hunting scenes, flanked by raked tiles, rush seats, ring-turned legs joined by stretchers, imperfections, price for pair, 18" h, 33-1/2" h..........................1,150.00

c1835-50, orig red and black graining, yellow and green striping, gilt stenciling, black painted balloon rush seat 375.00

c1850, black painted, stencil dec, gilt and polychrome dec, cane seat, general wear, 34-1/2" h 200.00

Hitchcock-Type

New England, first half 19th C, painted, splayed rectangular open back surmounted by curved crest rail with incurved ends and painted foliate motifs, over two turned crossbars, saddle-shaped slat seat raised on turned and tapered legs joined by double U-form stretcher, decorative front stretcher, sepia highlights on lemon-yellow ground, price for set of three............................350.00

New York, first half 19th C, splayed rectangular back surmounted by scroll-painted crest rail, two cross bars over five spindles, saddle-shaped solid seat raised on turned and ring-turned splayed legs joined by turned box stretcher, painted throughout with umber highlights on lemon-yellow ground, price for set of six 500.00

Klismos, Classical, America

c1820-30, mahogany, concave crest rail with carved shells on each end centering crotchwood panel, single horizontal splat with carved shells and panel, spool turned front legs ending in peg feet, some minor restorations and repairs, price for set of six, 17-5/8" w, 18" d, 33-1/4" h...............5,650.00

c1825, ebonized, gilt scrolling foliate detail, pink upholstered slip seats, price for pair, 17-5/8" d, 32-3/4" h......................650.00

c1830, painted, concave rectangular crest rail, pierced horizontal splat, ribbed seat rail, carved stretcher and pegged feet, rush seat, black paint, gild decoration, price for pair, 18-1/2" w, 20" d, 32" h 750.00

Ladderback

America

Country, sausage turned posts with turned finials, four arched slats, turned legs and stretchers, feet ended out, wear to rush seats, old finish, price for pair 275.00

Early old black repaint, sausage turned posts with large finials, four arched slats, replaced rush seat, front legs with button feet, well turned stretcher, 17-1/4" h seat, 43" h...825.00

Early old black repaint, three arched back slats, tapered posts with well turned finials, worn splint seat, 14-1/2" h seat, 38-1/4" h 250.00

Hardwood, four graduated arched slats, turned finials, old rush seat, turned legs, bulbous front feet and stretcher, refinished, 42" h......................................800.00

New England, late 18th C, maple and ash, painted Spanish brown over earlier red paint, early hickory splint seats, minor imperfections, price for pair, 16" h, 39-1/2" h 950.00

Pennsylvania, c1840, painted green, four slat back, replaced rush seat, bulbous turnings terminating in arrows 2,200.00

Shaker

Early 19th C, attributed to Harvard, Massachusetts, painted, slat back, three arched slats joining turned stiles, tape seat, turned legs joined by stretchers, old red paint, 15-1/8" h seat, 40" h 460.00

Mid 19th C, maple, curved back with three arched cross-bars flanked by posts with finials, woven bark seat raised, turned legs joined by turned double-box stretcher
....600.00

Mission, Frank Lloyd Wright, from Robert Winn House, Kalamazoo, MI, 1953, cherry finish, refinished, recovered, descended in Winn family, 24" w, 22" d, 29" h....................3,500.00

Modernism Era

Eames, Charles, manufactured by Herman Miller

DCM, molded ash plywood back and seat, metal frame, 19" w, 19" d, 29" h..........120.00

DCM, molded walnut plywood back and seat, chrome frame, black plastic feet, price for set of four, 19" w, 18" d, 29" h
....750.00

DCM, original red aniline dye, patterned upholstered seat and back, orig upholstery label, 19" w, 19" d, 29" h.................925.00

Eiffel Tower, c1951, black wire construction, early screw-on footpads, gray fabric bikini pads, price for set of four, some repairs 1,200.00

LCM, molded walnut plywood seat and back, chrome frame, price for pair. 22" w, 24" d, 27" h 750.00

LCW, molded ash plywood seat, back, and frame, 22" w, 23" d, 27" h 1,400.00

LCW, molded birch plywood seat, back, and frame, 22" w, 22" d, 27" h 850.00

McCobb, Paul, dowel ladder back, plank seat, wrought iron frame, price for pair, 18" w, 20" d, 34" h 600.00

Nelson, George, manufactured by Herman Miller

Caned seat and back, wood frame, white metal base, price for set of four, c1956, 18" w, 19" d, 33" h 1,700.00

Sculptural birch frame, seat and back reupholstered in purple fabric, label, c1954, refinished 600.00

Van Der Rohe, Mies, manufactured by Knoll International, brown leather seat, tubular polished chrome frame, unsigned, price for set of eight, 19-1/4" w, 27-1/4" d, 31" h 1,650.00

Modernism Era, Pop

Cherner, Norman, manufactured by Plycraft, molded walnut plywood seat and back, bentwood legs, label, price for set of four, 17" w, 19" d, 32" h 800.00

Gehry, Frank, Easy Edges, c1972, corrugated cardboard construction, masonite edge, water stain, 16" w, 21" d, 32" h 850.00

Saarino, Eero, manufactured by Asko, Pastille, c1968, molded white fiberglass forms, price for pair, 36" d, 20" h 900.00

Queen Anne

Albany County, 18th C, maple, fiddle-back, crest rail over vasiform splat, rush seat, turned tapering legs, pad feet, old refinishing, repairs, price for pair, 17" h seat, 40" h 920.00

America, banister back, old brown grained repaint, scalloped crest, three turned half spindles back, old rush seat with some damage, bulbous turned front stretcher, chips on turnings, 15-1/2" h seat, 42" h 1,165.00

America, banister back, old green repaint, three turned half spindles and bulbous turned front stretcher, replaced rush seat, 17-1/2" h seat, 41" h 495.00

America, banister back, urn shaped splats, bulbous turned front stretcher, button feet, old dark alligatored finish, price for pair, 15-3/4" h seat, 39" h 1,650.00

America, banister back, "U" shaped crest, urn finials, four molded back spindles, old replaced rush seat, turned posts and front stretcher, old refinishing, damage to rear leg, old repairs and replacements, 16" h seat, 40-3/4" h 385.00

Connecticut, attributed to John or Samuel Durand, Milford, back repaint, Victorian gold line detailing, vase shaped splat, worn rush seat with traces of black paint, cabriole legs, boldly turned front stretchers, 16-1/2 seat, 41" h 675.00

Connecticut, attributed to Samuel Durand, Milford, urn shaped splat with crest, cabriole front legs with bold turnings, replaced rush seat, old alligatored red and black repaint, 16-3/4" seat, 40-3/4" h 900.00

Connecticut, attributed to Samuel Durand, Milford, York, boldly turned posts and front stretcher, old worn rush seat, alligatored finish, 16-3/4" h seat, 40-1/2" h 550.00

Country, hard and softwood, shaped crest, vasiform splat, replaced rush seat, turned

Queen Anne, Massachusetts, attributed to Boston, walnut, yoke crest over curved back posts, vase splat, balloon seat, cabriole legs with duck feet, turned stretchers, old refinishing, slip seats reupholstered in green floral damask, price for pair, 39-1/2" h, $11,550. Photo courtesy of Garth's Auctions, Inc., Delaware, OH.

legs and rungs, bulbous front stretcher, old mellow finish, feet ended out, 17" h seat, 40-1/2" h 1,200.00

Country, hard and softwood, yoke shaped crest, vasiform splat, old worn rush seat, turned legs and posts, bulbous front stretcher, old dark finish, feet ended out, 38-1/4" h 625.00

Country, maple, old dry red paint, shaped crest, urn splat over contoured back, splint seat with old light green painted surface, seat 17" h, 42-1/4" h 1,100.00

Country, old black repaint, Victorian gold decoration, urn shaped back splat, well turned posts, replaced rush seat, cabriole front legs, 16-1/2" h seat, 39-7/8" h 715.00

Country, three half turned posts on back with faint incised compass stars and heart crest with finials, woven splint seat, turned front legs and stretcher, well turned rear posts, some loss of height to legs, 15" h seat, 40-3/4" h 450.00

English, 18th C, mahogany, yoke back and vasiform splat, slip seat, cabriole legs joined by stretchers, pad feet, price for set of four, 39-1/2" h 950.00

Massachusetts, Boston, c1740-50, carved walnut, serpentine spooned crest rail, vasiform splat, raked stiles, trapezoidal slip seat, frontal cabriole legs, pad feet, joined to rear chamfered legs by turned stretchers, shaped seat rail, old finish, 40" h 4,750.00

Massachusetts, Boston, c1740-60, maple, shaped crest above vasiform splat, slip seat over scrolled seat rail, cabriole legs ending in pad feet, joined to raked rear legs by block and baluster turned stretchers, old refinishing, repairs, 16-3/4" h seat, 40" h.............5,100.00

Massachusetts, Boston, c1740-65, walnut, double arched crest, central carved shell above vasiform splat, balloon shaped over-upholstered seat, cabriole legs joined by block and baluster turned H-stretchers, padded disc front feet, old surface, imperfections, 17" h seat, 40-1/2" h 8,050.00

Massachusetts, Boston, c1750, walnut, vase shaped splat and curved back posts with yoke crest, balloon seat, cabriole legs with duck feet, turned stretchers, old refinish-

ing, reupholstered slip seats, price for pair, 39-1/2" h 11,500.00

Massachusetts, c1750, painted, solid vasiform back splat, rush seat, Spanish foot, bulbous front stretcher, old Spanish brown paint, minor imperfections, 17-3/4" h seat, 41-3/4" h 2,120.00

Massachusetts, c1750, walnut, solid vasiform back splat, crewel upholstered seat, cabriole legs joined by turned stretchers, front frame inscribed by previous owner "Timothy Thornton Ipswich 1775," provenance included to show chairs descended in family, price for pair, 17" h seat, 39-3/4" h..................15,000.00

Massachusetts, 18th C, maple, shaped crest, vasiform splat, rush seat, block and baluster turned legs, Spanish carved feet, old refinished surface, minor repairs, 17" h, 39-1/2" h 1,035.00

Massachusetts, 18th C, maple, spooned crest rail above vasiform spat and raked chamfered stiles joined to trapezoidal slip seat by scrolled frame, two frontal cabriole legs ending in pad feet, raked rear legs joined by block vase and ring-turned stretchers, refinished, imperfections, 18-1/2" seat, 40" h 2,100.00

Massachusetts, 18th C, painted, yoked crest rail above vasiform splat, raked stiles, rush seat, block vase and ring-turned legs

Queen Anne, Massachusetts, 18th C, maple, shape crest and vasiform splat, block and baluster turned legs, Spanish carved feet, old refinished surface, minor repairs, 17" h, 39-1/2" h, $1,035. Photo courtesy of Skinner Auctioneers and Appraisers of Antiques and Fine Art Boston and Bolton, MA.

on Spanish feet, bulbous turned front stretcher and square side stretchers, old surface, 17" h, 41" h 1,150.00

New England, 18th C, painted, shaped carved crest rail above vasiform splat and molded raked stiles, rush seat on block vase and ring-turned legs joined by bulbous turned stretchers, old burnt sienna and dark brown paint with yellow pin-striping, 16" h, 41" h 1,495.00

New England, last half 18th C, grain painted, yoked crest rail above vasiform splat, rakes stiles, rush seat on block vase and ring-turned legs, carved Spanish feet, joined by bulbous turned front stretcher and side stretchers, old brown grain paint, 17" h seat, 39-3/4" h 920.00

New England, northern, 18th C, maple, shaped crest and splat, rush seat, block and baluster turned legs ending in Spanish feet, old refinishing, imperfections, 18" h seat, 42" h 425.00

New Hampshire, hard and soft wood, yoke crest, vase shaped splat, paper rush seat, turned rungs, turned legs, Spanish feet, good

Queen Anne, New York, Albany County, 19th C, fiddleback, maple, crest rails above vasiform splats, rush seats, turned tapering legs, pad feet, old refinish, one of two front pieced feet, price for pair, 17" h seat, 40" h, $920. Photo courtesy of Skinner Auctioneers and Appraisers of Antiques and Fine Art Boston and Bolton, MA.

old worn dark patina, traces of old red paint, minor scratches, repairs, 71" h.............850.00

New Hampshire, Portsmouth, attributed to, 1730-70, maple yoke crests, vasiform splats flanked by stiles, rear chamfering above trapezoidal over-upholstered seats, cabriole legs with arris knees, pad feet, joined by block ended stretchers, old refinishing, minor surface imperfections, price for pair, 18" h seat, 37-1/2" h 4,890.00

New York, attributed to Jacob Smith, 18th C, cherry and ash, shaped crest rail, vase shaped splat, arched seat rail, flanked by vase and ring-turned stiles, rush seat on vase and ring-turned tapering legs ending in pad feet on platforms, joined by bulbous turned front stretchers and plain turned double side stretchers, old refinishing, 18" h seat, 41-1/2" h 750.00

Pennsylvania, Philadelphia, c1750, walnut, shaped crest rail, scrolled vase shaped splat, balloon seat with needlepoint, cabriole frontal legs, straight back legs, repairs to crest and back, 20" w, 18" d, 41-1/2" h 6,850.00

Pennsylvania, Philadelphia, 18th C, walnut, squared crest rail, vase shaped splat, trapezoidal slip seat with shaped skirt, cabriole legs with pad feet, imperfections, price for pair 850.00

Rhode Island, Newport, or Boston, Massachusetts, c1740-50, carved walnut, shaped crest rail centering carved shell, vase shaped splat joining rounded raked stiles, slip balloon seat, frontal cabriole legs ending in pad feet on platforms, joined to rear chamfered legs by turned stretchers, old finish, 40-1/2" h 36,000.00

Queen Anne-Style

America, walnut, shaped upholstered back and seat, front cabriole legs, saber rear legs, slipper feet, price for pair, 39-1/2" h 400.00

Queen Anne to Chippendale Transitional

America, c1740, mahogany, shell carved crest, balloon seat, drake feet, repairs 2,950.00

America, c1740-80, cherry, shaped crest rail with carved ears, carved and pierced vase shaped splat, balloon seat, cabriole legs with claw and ball feet, fan carving at knees, turned H-stretcher, old finish, edge wear and damage, price for pair, 16-3/4" h seat, 38-1/2" h 2,420.00

Pennsylvania, Philadelphia, c1740-70, mahogany, incised crest with carved shell, bold ears, pierced vasiform splat, inverted carved shell on skirt, cabriole legs with shell carved knees ending in pad feet with unusual turnings, rear legs have chamfered corners, seat rail incised "IIII," 23" w, 21" d, 40" h 5,100.00

Pennsylvania, Philadelphia, c1750-60, walnut, shell carved crest rail with double scrolled volutes, continuing to carved rounded stiles, vasiform splat, balloon fitted slip seat supported by two shell carved cabriole legs with two volutes, ending in claw and ball feet, square back legs, rear to splat lock reglued, front seat rail inscribed with two strokes, balloon seat frame inscribed "IIIII," indicating chair was part of a set, back seat rail contains letters "SM" in white chalk, letters similar to others found on chairs belonging to Samuel Morris, 19" w, 16-3/4" d, 41" h 336,000.00

Sheraton, decorated

American, c1800, polychrome decoration, slightly curved crest rail, five vertical and three horizontal bamboo turned spindles, rush seat, bamboo-turned tapering cylindrical legs, double stretchers, orig red, gold,

Sheraton, Pennsylvania, Philadelphia, c1800, carved mahogany, straight crest rail over floral and swaged interlaced back splat with center urn, upholstered seat, molded taping legs joined by stretcher, price for pair, $5,000. Photo courtesy of Samuel T. Freeman & Co., Philadelphia, PA.

white, and yellow floral decoration on black ground 375.00

Country, curly maple, slightly curved crest rail, slightly curved splat, rush seat, turned legs, 34-3/4" h 300.00

Country, old worn red and black graining, yellow striping, gold floral design on crest, refinished seat with added yellow striping, price for set of four, 17-5/8" h seat, 34-1/2" h 990.00

Country, Ohio or PA maker, orig worn paint, touch-up and black repaint, stenciled splat and crest, branded label "Ara. Howe," price for set of six, 17-3/4" h seat, 33-1/4" h 990.00

Middle Atlantic States, c1815-25, grained and paint dec, Grecian style, simulated rosewood, gold striping, rush seat, old surface, minor imperfections, price for set of six, 18" h, 33-1/2" h..................................650.00

Victorian

America, late 19th C, carved walnut, open rectangular back with pierced and arched crest rail centered by flower head, lyre-shaped pierced splat hung with festoons, overstuffed seat with molded rails, baluster turned legs with casters......................125.00

Eastlake, c1870, lady's, walnut, Minerva head carving on crest, incised lines, applied burl veneer panels and roundels decoration, shaped hip brackets with conforming decoration, shaped reupholstered back and seat, turned front legs, 36" h..........................450.00

Elizabethan Revival, George Hunzinger, New York, ebonized, back stamped "Hunzinger, NY, pat March 30, 1869," 34" h 300.00

Naturalistic Revival, New England, first quarter 19th C, bamboo turnings, turned raked stiles joining three parts of horizontal spindles, rush balloon seats, outward flaring ring-turned legs joined by stretchers, refinished, price for set of six, 17-3/4" h seat, 33-1/2" h 900.00

Renaissance Revival

c1850, walnut, balloon back, foliate and cabochon carved back rest, serpentine seat, cabriole legs..........................165.00

c1850, walnut, balloon back, kidney-shaped scroll carved crest, paisley upholstered slip seat, rocaille caved serpentine skirt, 37" h 175.00

c1850-70, upholstered, carved crest with pair of hounds and wild boars head, spiral turned legs and stretchers, carved floral rosettes, peg feet, imperfections, price for pair, 19" w, 17-1/2" d, 18" h 300.00

c1870, walnut, spindle inset backrest, foliate incised frame, caned seat, turned legs 90.00

c1875, plank seat and back, carved stretcher, some loss of finish, price for set of ten..900.00

Rococo Revival, c1850-65

Laminated hardwood, New York, back pieced with leaves and fruit foliate craved apron, cabriole legs, pink upholstered back cushion and seat, repaired crests, price for pair, 19-1/2" w, 16" d, 38" h 920.00

Laminated rosewood, arched back with foliage and scroll dec upholstered serpentine seat, cabriole legs on casters, 35-1/4" h 575.00

Turkish Revival, c1880, reupholstered in aqua marine velvet and fringe, 27" w, 28" d, 34" h...300.00

William and Mary

America, c1700, oak, scroll carved crest rail flanked by turned stiles, baluster finials, three vertical molded slats, recessed plank seat, short baluster-turned and block legs, turned stretchers, price for pair, 43-1/2" h 7,200.00

Delaware Valley, c1690-1730, ladderback, cherry, turned ball post finials, five graduated arched slats, front legs with modest turnings, compressed ball feet, straight circular stretchers, old rush seat, left leg cracked near top, possibly cut down, 18" w, 14" d, 43-1/2" h................................1,190.00

Massachusetts, Boston, c1700, maple, molded rest with molded back posts and upholstered splat, old black leather upholstered seat, bulbous turned front stretcher, mortised and pinned back and side stretchers, turned front legs and feet, old nailed repairs, seat needs upholstery, old mellow refinishing, 43-1/8" h........................6,900.00

Massachusetts, c1700, turned oak and maple, upholstered back and seat, old finish, 19" w, 15" d, 36" h 5,550.00

Massachusetts, Boston, c1720, painted and carved, shaped back with shaped slender cane section in back, caned seat, scalloped apron, turned and block carved legs, bulbous turned stretchers, elongated Spanish feet, 19-1/4" h seat, 45" h 750.00

New England, 18th C, maple, banister back, refinished, old repairs, 45-1/2" h..500.00

Pennsylvania, c1710-30, walnut, shaped crest rail, three vertical molded slats flanked by rectangular tapering stiles, plank set, block and ball-turned legs, paired baluster-turned front stretcher, restored seat, 40" h................ 600.00

William and Mary-Style, walnut, pieced carved fan and floral crest rail, floral velvet upholstered seat, inverted trumpet form legs, shaped stretcher, bun feet 375.00

Windsor

Arrow Back, decorated

Original black graining, red ground, green border details, stepdown crest with restoration, wear, 18" h seat, 34" h 375.00

Original decoration of olive green and gold fruit and leaves on crest, highlighted with olive green and gold on yellow ground, bamboo turned legs joined by stretchers, paint loss and minor repairs, price for assembled set of six, 17" h seat, 33-1/2" h 2,300.00

Original red decoration, yellow and green foliage on crests, shield shape seats, bamboo-turned legs, some wear to seats and rungs, price for set of four, 18-1/4" h seat, 35" h 3,000.00

Balloon Back

Pennsylvania, c1860, chair back stencil decorated with basket of fruit on crest, vase shaped splat with stenciled eagle and shield "Union," gilt vine stenciled border, stiles, seat, and legs with yellow and salmon painted striping, some paint wear, price for pair, 18" h, 33-1/2" h 500.00

Pennsylvania, Muhlenberg Township, Berks County, hooped crests, vasiform splats highly decorated with red, green, and gold stenciled front in a basket, gold flourishes and striping, all orig red-brown painted ground, painting striping, minor surface imperfections, price for set of six, 18" h seat, 34" h...........................1,955.00

Birdcage

America, old worn brown repaint with yellow striping, bamboo turnings, shaped seat, repairs, price for set of four, 18" h seat, 33-1/4" h................................900.00

Massachusetts, Daniel Abbot, Newbury-port, c1809-11, painted black, six spindles, bamboo turnings, branded "D. Abbot & Co.," 16-1/2" h seat, 33" h...............230.00

Bow Back

America, molded bowed crest rail, seven spindle back, saddle seat, splayed base with turned legs, H stretcher, old refinishing, some repairs and size variation, price for set of five, 16" h, 34-1/2" h.....................1,450.00

America, molded bowed crest rail, seven spindle back, saddle seat, splayed base with turned legs, H-stretcher, old worn dark green repaint, 16" h seat, 36-1/4" h
....550.00

Connecticut, New London County, or Plainfield, New Hampshire, c1810-15, painted, bowed crest rail above nine spindles, carved saddle seat, splayed bamboo turned legs joined by stretchers, old painted surface, branded "S. Tracy," 17" h seat, 36" h...690.00

Massachusetts, Boston, 1790, maple and ash, branded "S. J. Tuck,"" bowed beaded crest above nine tapering incised singles, incised shaped seat, swelled splayed legs joined by H-stretchers, refinished, 18-1/2" h, 38" h...................1,100.00

Massachusetts, Boston, old red repaint over white, well formed bow with molded edge, seven spindle back, bamboo turnings, shaped saddle seat, price for pair, 18-1/4" seat, 37-3/4" h..................1,480.00

New England, c1780, braced, bowed crest rail above eight swelled spindles, shaped saddle seat, splayed vase and ring-turned legs joined by turned stretchers, painted old green over earlier dark green, 17" h seat, 35-1/2" h 750.00

New England, c1810, bamboo turnings, shaped saddle seat, assembled set of six 1,955.00

New England, early 19th C, painted, arched crest, tapering spindles, incised seat, splayed bamboo turned legs joined by similar turned stretchers, allover old black paint with gold highlights in incised areas and bowed crest, very minor imperfections, price for set of eight, 18" h seat, 36" h... 18,400.00

Brace Back

Molded bow, seven spindle back, shield shaped seat, splayed base with bulbous turned legs, H-stretcher, old refinishing with good patina, minor age cracks, price for set of three, 16-1/4" h seat, 34-3/4" h 1,850.00

Spindle back, saddle seat, splayed base with bulbous turnings, H-stretcher, old refinishing, good color, leg turnings vary slightly, old repairs, 17-3/4" h seat, 37" h..700.00

Curved Crest, New England, 1830-40, yellow painted ground embellished with stenciled green and raw umber fruit and leaf designs, gilt highlights, dark striping, three horizontal slats, four ring-turned spindles from lowest rail to shaped seat, bamboo turned legs with stretchers, imperfections, old paint, price for set of six, 17" h seat, 33-1/2" h..............3,220.00

Fan Back

America, curved yoke crest, eight spindle back with turned posts, saddle seat, splayed base, bulbous turned legs, H-stretcher, old refinishing, pieced repair on crest, repairs to seat, one cross stretcher replaced, 17-1/2" h seat, 36-3/4" h 275.00

Connecticut, 1790-1810, old green paint, serpentine crest over nine spindles, incised shaped seat, bulbous turned splayed legs joined by stretchers, worn paint, 18" h seat, 40" h.................3,450.00

Connecticut River Valley, c1790-1810, curved yoke crest rail, spindle back, saddle seat, shaped legs, H-stretcher, Spanish brown finish, 36" h.....................950.00

Connecticut, Lisbon, late 18th C, Ebenezer Tracy, branded "E. B. Tracy," old finish, imperfections, 17" h seat, 34-1/2" h 450.00

Country, shaped crest, shaped set, splayed base with H-stretcher, old worn refinishing, faint brushed name on underside of seat, 17" h, 35-1/2" h..........295.00

New England, c1790, painted, shaped concave crest rail above seven spindles, vase and ring-turned stiles, shaped saddle seat, splayed vase and ring-turned legs joined by stretchers, old grain paint with yellow and green pin striping, mustard yellow seat, minor imperfections, 18" h seat, 37" h...7,500.00

New England, early 19th C, painted, curving crests, tapering spindles, shaped seats, splayed legs, repainted dark red, 35-1/2" h, price for set of four 3,200.00
Hoop Back, America, early 19th C

Bamboo-turned spindle back, saddle seat, rakish legs, H-form stretcher, painted green..700.00

Caldwell, I., late 18th/early 19th C, mixed wood, saddle seat, ring-turned splayed legs, H-stretcher 750.00

Maple, seven spindles back, plank seat, turned legs with similar stretchers, price for set of four................................1,955.00

Mixed woods, bamboo turned rods, bamboo turned legs, assembled set of six, 17" w, 19" d, 37" h........................1,785.00
Rod Back

Dalton, William, Boston, c1800, slightly concave crest rail, seven spindles, bamboo-turned stiles, shaped incised seat, splayed legs joined by stretchers, old dark brown surface, branded "W. Dalton," price for set of six, 17" h, 33" h.............4,325.00

New Hampshire, c1800-20, rosewood graining, price for set of four, 17-1/2" h seat, 34" h....................................2,650.00

Steel, Anthony, Philadelphia, c1810, painted, double rod crest rail with central medallion over seven bamboo turned spindles and two posts, dish seat, four bamboo turned legs and stretchers, 19th C mustard paint with black highlights and gilt flower to medallion, branded mark "A. Steel" on seat, repair to crest rail, some

Windsor, yoke back, shaped seat, bamboo turnings, refinished, wear, $750.

losses to paint, 16-3/4" w, 16" d, 34-1/8" h 375.00
Step Down

New England, c1810, shaped crest above seven spindles and raked stiles, shaped seats, splayed bamboo turned legs joined by stretchers, old refinishing, later painted decoration, some repairs, price for set of six, 15-1/2" h seat, 33" h........................ 1,200.00

New England, 1820-30, painted yellow ground, green and red stenciled leaf and berry dec, green accents, shaped plank seats, splayed bamboo turned legs, some repaint, price for set of four, 17" h seat, 33-1/4" h 900.00

Windsor-Style, birdcage, worn yellow repaint, saddle seat, bulbous turned legs, splayed base, H-stretcher, laminated seat has painted over paper label, some age, but not period, 35-1/2" h....................................275.00

Slipper Chairs

A slipper chair is an armless chair, usually found in a bedroom, to be used to put on one's slippers.

Aesthetic Movement, attributed to Herter Brothers, New York, c1870, ebony inlaid maple, India Rubber Co. casters, restorations, 29-1/4" h..750.00

Hepplewhite, Philadelphia, Haines Connolly School, mahogany, back with four carved spindles with flame tops, middle with square rosettes, reeded sq tapering feet, casters, 32" h..400.00

Victorian

Renaissance Revival, c1870, mahogany, carved, shaped fan-carved crest rail, ivory upholstered shield back and crest, bulbous and reeded tapering legs, casters.................250.00

c1875, walnut, marquetry, part ebonized, price for pair, 36" h 2,600.00

Rococo Revival, America, second half 19th C, walnut, pierced back with scrolling carved arabesques, surmounted by grapes and leaves, 18" w, 18" d, 40" h 200.00

Suites

A suite of chairs is any grouping of chairs. Often there are several arm chairs and matching armless chairs. Dining chairs are another example of suites of chairs. Look for matching upholstery and trim, as well as design elements in suites.

Arts & Crafts, Gustav Stickley, NY, c1907, No. 354-1/2, oak, one arm chair, four side chairs, V-shaped crest rail over five vertical slats, leather seat with copper tacks, some with paper labels, 36" h, price for set of five 6,325.00

Sheraton, America, c1800, two arm chairs, six side chairs, polychrome dec, well executed old repaint, red and black graining, yellow striping, gold stenciling, old rush seats, price for set of eight, 16" h seat, 34" h 3,600.00

Windsor, Maine, c1810, one armchair, three side chairs, birdcage, bamboo turnings, seven spindles, shaped seats, splayed legs joined by stretchers, old black paint, price for set of four, 16-3/4" h seat, 31-3/4" h 1,575.00

Tub Chairs

A tub chair is a rounded chair, usually with the back and arms at a level to encourage the user to relax when using a chair of this nature. It is a form much more common in European furniture styles.

Empire-Style, 19th C, ormolu-mounted mahogany, shaped splat to arms raised on ormolu caryatids, tapering sq legs ending in ormolu paws, 30" h 550.00

Wing, See Easy Chairs

Chests of Drawers

Chests of drawers are a furniture form found in all design styles. Sizes, woods, and ornamentation vary from style to style.

The phrase "overlapping drawer" refers to a slight extension on the face of the drawer that covers the drawer opening tightly when closed, thus overlapping the case. The phrase "graduated" means the drawers are different in size from one to another, usually the smallest drawer is in the top, the next one slightly larger, etc. Both "cockbeaded" and "thumb-molded" refer to different types of molding that was used as decoration. The terms "bow front" and "serpentine" describe the shape of the front of a chest of drawers. A "bow front" is generally slightly swelled, or bowed, in the center. "Serpentine" describes a more shaped top, often having several curves. Both bow front and serpentine chests of drawers will have a flat back.

Because chests of drawers was a popular piece of furniture, many homes had more than one, resulting in many examples available to the antique marketplace. Some of these beautiful chests of drawers were made by early local craftsmen and a few are signed or easily identified with a maker or geographic region. As furniture became mass-produced, chests of drawers kept their appeal and the form remained popular.

Chests of drawers offered a cabinetmaker an opportunity to use fine woods and elegant brass hardware. When a description includes the phrase "...secondary wood," that refers to the wood used on the interior of the drawers, perhaps the back, or areas that are unseen. This practice allowed the cabinetmaker to keep his costs down by using only expensive wood for the exterior case. It is also theorized that this practice allowed the cabinetmaker to use lesser-quality native woods that he had readily available, saving the expensive mahogany for the front and tops. Today, by studying the secondary woods, dealers and auctioneers gain an important clue as to the region of origin for a chest and sometimes the time frame.

Some other names for chests of drawers are dressers, chests, or bureaus, usually depending on the geographic nature of language rather than a difference in style.

Aesthetic Movement

Furniture from this brief furniture style is exciting when found in the antiques marketplace. Look for elements that are pre-cursors to the sweeping changes brought in by the Arts & Crafts movement.

New York, fourth quarter 19th C, maple, triangular cornice over open archwork over rectangular mirror plate, flanked by molded columns, galleried candle brackets, rectangular marble top over case with three graduated drawers, elaborate pulls, casters, 50-1/4" w, 22-1/2" d, 84" h 2,400.00

Art Deco

Art Deco chests of drawers are bold examples of this new furniture style that hit the American scene about 1920 and lasted until the 1940s when even more modern styles became popular.

America, c1935, mahogany, rectangular raised panel mahogany top over three canted and zigzag drawer fronts and sides, square patinated metal drawer pulls, tapered angular legs in lighter shade of mahogany, scratches, wear, 30-1/2" w, 20" d, 35-1/2" h 1,850.00

Quigley, France, c1925, parchment covered, rectangular top, three tapering drawers, pyramid mirrored stiles, bracket feet, back branded, 44-1/2" x 35"..2,750.00

Arts & Crafts

Chests of drawers of the Arts & Crafts period are as well built as other case forms of that period. Some experimenting with different configurations of drawers, doors, and mirrors occurred. Most chests were made in oak, but some other woods were also popular. Copper and wrought iron was the material most often used for hardware. A good original finish, intact hardware, and a maker's label or branded mark will add value.

Roycroft, East Aurora, NY, c1910

Chiffonier, mahogany, backsplash with shaped ends, rectangular top, case with two short drawers over four long drawers, hammered pulls, four shaped feet, branded mark centered on lower drawer, 41-5/8" w, 23-1/2" d, 58-1/2" h...........................3,850.00

Dresser, rectangular mirror, case with two small drawers over four graduated long drawers, hammered copper rectangular pulls, mint orig ebonized finish, carved orb and cross mark, mirror brackets missing, minor water damage to drawer face, 41" w, 24" d, 52" h to top 7,500.00

Arts & Crafts, Gustav Stickley, New York, c1912, No. 905, oak, swivel mirror, rectangular overhanging top, two short drawers over three long drawers, large hammered brass ring pulls, branded mark, 48" w, 22" d, 62" h, $9,775. Photo courtesy of Skinner Auctioneers and Appraisers of Antiques and Fine Art Boston and Bolton, MA.

Arts & Crafts, Gustav Stickley, New York, c1912, No. 906, oak, rectangular top, two short and four long drawers, hammered circular pulls, branded mark, 41" w, 21" d, 48" h, $13,800. Photo courtesy of Skinner Auctioneers and Appraisers of Antiques and Fine Art Boston and Bolton, MA.

Stickley Brothers, Grand Rapids, MI, attributed to Timothy A. Conti, c1903, case with six drawers, gallery top of four panels inlaid with ebony and pewter in Glasgow rose motif, orig finish, unmarked, 34" w, 22" d, 56" h 7,550.00

Stickley, Gustav, New York

No. 622, c1902, oak, case with two short drawers, four long graduated drawers, panel construction sides, large red Gustav Stickley decal with "Stickley" outlined, 41" w, 22-1/2" d, 50" h.................................4,750.00

No. 902, oak, arched back rail, case with two top drawers, four long drawers, oval hammered pulls, red decal in top right drawer, 39-3/4" w, 22" d, 53-1/2" h 4,500.00

No. 905, c1912, oak, swivel mirror on rectangular top, case with two short drawers over three long drawers, large hammered brass ring pulls, branded mark, 48" w, 22" d, 62" h 9,775.00

No. 906, c1912, oak, rectangular top, case with two short drawers and four long drawers, hammered circular pulls, branded mark, 41" w, 21" d, 48" h 13,800.00

No. 909, oak, case with two short drawers, three graduated drawers, panel construction sides, red Gustav Stickley decal in top right drawer, paper label, 37-1/4" w, 19" d, 42" h 2,750.00

No. 911, Harvey Ellis influence, orig mirror with butterfly joint construction on supports, case with two half drawers over two full drawers, orig wooden knobs, arched toe-board, branded signature, 48" w, 23" d, 67" h 7,700.00

No. 913, Harvey Ellis design, case with six half drawers over three full drawers, orig wooden pulls, arched toe-board, bowed sides, fine orig finish, branded signature, 36" w, 20" d, 47" h 15,450.00

Arts & Crafts, Gustav Stickley, New York, c1912, No. 911, oak, rectangular overhanging top, swivel mirror with butterfly joints, two drawers over two long wide drawers, round wooden pulls, arched toe board, red decal, paper Craftsman label, new finish, mirror: 43-1/4" w, 33-1/4" h, chest: 48" w, 22" d, 33" h, $4,000. Photo courtesy of David Rago Auctions/RagoArts.com, Lambertville, NJ.

Tall, in the style of Harvey Ellis, case with six half-drawers over three long drawers, wrought copper hardware, orig dark brown finish, paper label, red decal, 36" w, 20" d, 50" h 15,000.00
Unknown Designer, manufactured by Dunbar, Berne, IN

Chest, rectangular top, case with eight half drawers, black leather pulls, tapered angular feet, metal tag...................................1,380.00

Dresser, case with two half drawers over two full drawers, wooden knobs, orig swivel mirror with corbel supports, re-coated orig finish, 42" w, 23" d, 70" h....................950.00

Chippendale

The period corresponding with Chippendale furniture, c1755 to c1790, represents an important building period for young America. Construction of houses was occurring in every state. New homes required furniture and the craftsmen responded with all types of goods. Case furniture, like chests and cupboards, were made in all types of fine woods. While the claw and ball foot is easily identified with Chippendale, other types of feet, like bracket, were used on case pieces.

America, birch, rectangular top with bowed front and molded edge, beaded frame, case with four dovetailed drawers, orig oval brasses, pine secondary wood, refinished, stains in top, crack in foot, 39" w, 21-3/4" d, 36" h ...4,500.00

America, cherry, rectangular overhanging top, dovetailed case with five dovetailed drawers, molded base, bracket feet, poplar secondary wood, refinished, replaced brasses, age cracks in top, feet with edge damage, 39-1/2" w, 48" h..................................1,950.00

America, cherry, replaced two board top with scalloped edge, case with four dovetailed drawers with molded edges, scalloped bracket feet, replaced brasses, pine secondary wood, refinished, repairs to feet, 36-3/4" w, 25" d, 39" h..1,100.00

America, decorated, curly maple and pine, orig red flame graining, molded edge top, case with three dovetailed overhanging drawers, top deep drawer (with two drawer fronts), one board ends with cutout feet, backboards signed "L. L. 1807" and "P.P.H.G.—(grained), 1847," replaced

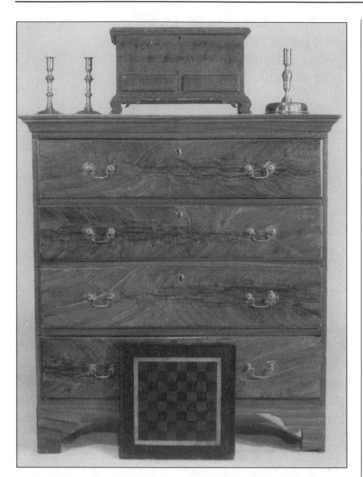

Chippendale, decorated, curly maple and pine, orig red flame graining, molded edge top, three dovetailed overhanging drawers, top deep drawer (with two drawer fronts), one board ends with cutout feet, backboards signed "L. L. 1807" and "P.P.H.G.—(grained), 1847," replaced brass bails are in orig holes, pine secondary wood, 36" w, 22" d, 42-1/4" h, $6,100. Also shown are English Queen Anne brass candlesticks, $1,870, miniature decorated Chippendale blanket chest, 11" h, $24,200; Spanish brass candlestick, $550, and decorated checkerboard, $1,595. Photo courtesy of Garth's Auctions, Inc., Delaware, OH.

brass bails are in orig holes, pine secondary wood, 36" w, 22" d, 42-1/4" h 6,100.00

America, walnut, case with four overlapping dovetailed drawers with beaded edge, full dust shelves, ogee feet, old refinishing, poplar secondary wood, replaced feet, replaced brasses, 38" w, 20-3/4" d, 40-1/4" h 1,250.00

Connecticut, c1780, cherry, rectangular overhanging top with molded edge, inverted corners, case with four graduated cockbeaded drawers, ogee bracket feet, old refinish, restoration, 39-1/4" w, 19" d, 33-1/2" h 2,750.00

Connecticut River Valley, c1775, serpentine front, birch, thumb-molded top, case with four

dovetailed drawers set in beaded frame, well shaped bracket feet, pine secondary wood, replaced brasses, refinished, age crack, repaired breaks in top, 34" w, 22-1/2" d, 32-3/4" h 8,800.00

Connecticut River Valley, c1780, carved cherry, rectangular top with applied molded edge, case with four graduated cockbeaded drawers flanked by ring-turned spiral carved quarter columns, ogee bracket feet, replaced brasses, restoration, 39" w, 19" d, 34-1/4" h 4,500.00

Country, curly maple, rectangular overhanging top, case with four dovetailed drawers, bracket feet, refinished, bottom backboard and feet replaced, brasses replaced, 41-1/4" w, 19-1/2" d, 37-1/2" h 2,450.00

Country, maple, projected top, case with four dovetailed drawers, orig brass pull handles, applied cutout feet, refinished, 35-3/4" w, 32-3/4" h..950.00

Country, walnut, case with four dovetailed drawers, bracket feet, refinished, pine secondary wood, feet replaced, replaced brasses, 36" w, 20-1/2" d, 40" h.............................990.00

Chippendale, Massachusetts, block front, mahogany, thumb-molded top, four dovetailed drawers set in beaded frame, conforming base molding, apron drop with carved fan, ogee feet, orig brasses, pine secondary wood, old finish, minor base repairs, 33" w, 21" d, 30" h, $25,300. Photo courtesy of Garth's Auctions, Inc., Delaware, OH.

Maryland, mahogany, four graduated drawers, ogee bracket feet, possibly feet replaced, 33-1/2" w, 20" d, 33-1/2" h 5,500.00

Massachusetts, c1720, wavy birch, overhanging molded top, cockbeaded case with four graduated drawers, bracket feet, replaced brasses, old refinish, 35-1/4" w, 19" d, 32-3/4" h..2,990.00

Massachusetts, Boston, c1750-90, block front, mahogany, thumb-molded shaped top, conforming case with four graduated drawers, molded base, bracket feet, old refinish, replaced brass, rear foot missing, backboard inscribed "G. Russell" (George Russell, 1800-1866, born in Providence, RI, married Sarah Shaw, and died in Manchester, MA,) 33" w, 19-1/4" w, 29-1/4" h..........................46,000.00

Massachusetts, Salem or Marblehead, c1760-80, figured mahogany, reverse serpentine, thumb-molded overhanging reverse serpentine top with end blocking, conforming case with four graduated drawers also with end blocking separated by beading, molded base, large claw and ball feet, old surface, orig brasses, minor imperfections, 38" w, 21" d, 32-3/4" h..79,500.00

Massachusetts, c1770-80, birch, overhanging molded top above cockbeaded case, four graduated drawers, bracket feet, replaced brasses, old refinishing, minor imperfections, 36" w, 17-1/4" d, 34" h..........................6,785.00

Massachusetts, c1770-80, cherry, rectangular molded top, case with four graduated thumb-molded drawers flanked by engaged turned and reeded quarter columns, ogee bracket feet, replaced brasses, refinished, restorations, 38" w, 20" d, 34" h 2,990.00

Massachusetts, c1770-80, maple, flat molded cornice, case with two graduated thumb-molded short drawers over four graduated long drawers, bracket feet, most brasses orig, old refinishing, 36-3/4" w, 18" d, 44-1/2" h 4,025.00

Massachusetts, c1775, block front, mahogany, thumb-molded top, case with four dovetailed drawers set in beaded frame, conforming base molding, apron drop with carved fan, ogee feet, orig brasses, pine secondary wood, old finish, minor base repairs, 33" w, 21" d, 30" h..25,300.00

Chippendale, Massachusetts, attributed to Connecticut River Valley, serpentine front, birch, thumb-molded top, four dovetailed drawers, beaded frame, bracket feet, refinished, pine secondary wood, replaced brasses, age crack and repaired breaks in top, 34" w, 32-3/4" h, $8,800. Also shown are pair of Queen Ann brass candlesticks with old repairs, $275, Hepplewhite shaving mirror, mahogany and mahogany veneer, three dovetailed drawers, ogee feet, brass pulls, 17-1/2" w, 8-1/2" d, 23-1/2" h, $1,320. Photo courtesy of Garth's Auctions, Inc., Delaware, OH.

Massachusetts, c1780, bow front, carved mahogany, overhanging top with inlaid edge, cockbeaded case, four graduated drawers, carved claw and ball feet, old refinishing, replaced brasses, imperfections, 37-3/4" w, 22" d, 34-1/2" h 5,500.00

Massachusetts, c1780, reverse serpentine, mahogany, case with four graduated drawers, bracket feet, old replaced brasses, refinished, restorations, 36-3/4" w, 20-1/4" d, 31-1/4" h 9, 775.00

Massachusetts, c1780, serpentine front, birch, serpentine overhanging top with molded edge, conforming cockbeaded case with four graduated drawers, central drop pendant, bracket feet, old brasses, refinished, 40" w, 21-1/2" d, 36-3/4" h 3,750.00

Massachusetts, c1790, serpentine front, mahogany, thumb-molded top, case with four dovetailed drawers with edge beading, base moldings, ogee feet, pine secondary wood, orig brasses, old finish, old repairs, 35-1/2" w, 32" h...14,300.00

Massachusetts, c1780, maple, rectangular overhanging molded top, case with four graduated thumb-molded drawers, ogee bracket feet on casters, old brasses, old refinishing, restoration, 36" w, 19-1/2" d, 31-1/2" h 2,300.00

Massachusetts, Boston, c1780, serpentine front, mahogany, molded edge top, case with four dovetailed drawers, beaded frame, base edge molding and apron drops, ogee feet, old brasses, old finish, 42" w, 24-1/4" d, 31-1/2" h......7,150.00

Massachusetts, Boston, c1780, serpentine front, mahogany, thumb-molded top, case with four dovetailed drawers, beaded frame, high bracket feet with well-shaped scroll work, old replaced period brasses, old finish, minor repairs to feet, 20-1/2" x 37-3/4" top, 34-3/4" w, 32-1/2" h..23,100.00

Massachusetts, Boston, 18th C, oxbow, cherry, shaped top with molded edge, conforming case with drawers, beaded surrounds, molded base with central scrolled drop pendant, claw and ball feet, orig brasses, surface with old dark stain, 44" w, 21" d, 36" h 6,900.00

Massachusetts, Newburyport, late 18th C, oxbow, carved birch, shaped top with molded edge, conforming case with four drawers with molded drawer separators, molded base with central fan-carved drop, flanking scrolls, claw and ball feet, refinished, replaced brasses, imperfections, 38" w, 21" d, 33" h 9,795.00

Massachusetts, late 18th C, bow front, pine, birch, and apple wood, bowed molded top, case with four gradated drawers, molded straight bracket base, old surface, replaced brasses, one foot replaced, 38" w, 18-1/4" d, 32" h...1,725.00

Massachusetts or New Hampshire, late 18th C, painted birch, rectangular overhanging top with molded edge, case with four drawers with beaded surrounds, molded shaped bracket base, old Spanish brown paint, replaced braces, imperfections, 36" w, 18" d, 36" h 2,645.00

Middle Atlantic States, mahogany, rectangular top with applied molded edge, case with four graduated drawers, fluted quarter columns, ogee bracket feet, some early repairs, 37" w, 20" d, 34-1/2" h.........................6,250.00

Middle Atlantic States, walnut, rectangular top with applied molded edge, case with four graduated drawers, scalloped bracket feet, some early repairs, refinished, 32" w, 17" d, 30" h..6,000.00

New England, southeastern, c1770, maple, flat molded cornice, case with two thumb-molded short drawers over five long drawers, tall bracket feet, old brasses, old refinish, 35" w, 17-1/8" d, 62" h.........................4,900.00

New England, c1770-1790, maple, rectangular molded edge top, conforming case with four dovetailed long drawers, molded base, straight bracket feet, orig brasses, 39-1/2" w, 18-1/4" d, 32-7/8" h...4,950.00

New England, c1780, birch, tall, flat molded cornice, case with six thumb-molded graduated drawers, bracket feet, replaced

Chippendale, Massachusetts, Newburyport, late 18th C, oxbow, carved birch, shaped top with molded edge, conforming case of four drawers with molded drawer separators, molded base with central fan-carved drop, flanking scrolls, claw and ball feet, refinished, replaced brasses, imperfections, 38" w, 21" d, 33" h, $9,795. Photo courtesy of Skinner Auctioneers and Appraisers of Antiques and Fine Art Boston and Bolton, MA.

brasses, old refinish, imperfections, 36" w, 18" d, 51" h 3,150.00

New England, c1780, cherry and maple, overhanging cove-molded cornice, case with five graduated thumbnail-molded drawers, bracket feet, replaced oval brasses, old refinishing, imperfections, 39-1/2" w, 19-3/4" h, 49" h.........3,200.00

New England, c1780, cherry, rectangular top with applied molded edge, case with four cockbeaded graduated drawers, bracket feet, old replaced brass pulls, old refinishing, imperfections, 41-1/8" w, 20" d, 35" h 1,265.00

New England, c1780, maple, rectangular molded top, case with five graduated thumb-molded drawers, bracket feet, centering drop pendant, replaced brass bail pulls, refinished, repairs, 36-1/2" w, 17" d, 41-1/2" h 1,610.00

New England, c1790, bow front, mahogany and mahogany veneer, slightly projecting top, case with four graduated drawers, ogee bracket feet, brass handles and escutcheons, restoration, 38-1/4" w, 20" d, 33" h......3,200.00

New England, Southern, c1810, bow front, cherry, rectangular top with bow front, conform-

Chippendale, Pennsylvania, c1750-80, mahogany, rectangular top with molded edge, four graduated cockbeaded drawers, case flanked by fluted quarter columns, ogee bracket feet, period brass bail handles, oval key escutcheons, cedar secondary wood, 40-1/2" w, 21-1/2" d, 34" h, $7,280. Photo courtesy of Samuel T. Freeman & Co., Philadelphia, PA.

ing case fitted with four cockbeaded graduated drawers, ogee bracket feet, old oval brasses, old refinishing, minor imperfections, label inscribed "this bureau was made for Hannah Child wife of Dr. Charles Eldridge 1810," 42-1/2" w, 24" d, 37" h..........................4,600.00

New England, 18th C, maple and pine, lightly tigered top, case with four thumb-molded drawers, shaped bracket feet, old refinishing, orig brasses, 40" w, 17-1/2" d, 39" h 2,100.00

New England, late 18th C, apple wood, rectangular overhanging top with beaded edge, case with four drawers with cockbeaded surrounds, molded bracket base, refinished, replaced brasses, repairs, piece of foot missing, 37-1/2" w, 19-1/2" d, 35" h............2,100.00

New England, late 18th C, maple and birch, rectangular top, case with five drawers, shaped bracket base, orig brasses, old refinishing, restoration, 37" w, 17-1/2" d, 34-1/2" h 2,530.00

New England, southeastern, late 18th C, maple, molded cornice, case with six thumb-molded drawers, top one visually divided into thirds, central fan carving, bracket base, replaced brasses, refinished, 37" w, 17-1/2" d, 57" h...4,900.00

New England, late 18th C/early 19th C, maple, rectangular overhanging top, case with two beaded drawers over three long drawers, ogee bracket feet on platforms, refinished, restored, 38" w, 17-1/2" d, 32" h 2,415.00

New Hampshire, 1760-80, maple, flat molded cornice, case with five graduated thumb-molded drawers, bracket feet, center pinwheel carved pendant, brasses missing, old refinishing, minor imperfections, 38-1/2" w, 18" d, 49-1/4" h 4,000.00

Pennsylvania, c1750-80, mahogany, rectangular top with molded edge, case with four graduated cockbeaded drawers, case flanked by fluted quarter columns, ogee bracket feet, period brass bail handles, oval key escutcheons, cedar secondary wood, 40-1/2" w, 21-1/2" d, 34" h 7,280.00

Pennsylvania, c1750-80, mahogany, rectangular top with molded edge, case with four graduated thumb-molded drawers, case flanked by fluted quarter columns, ogee bracket feet, pine and poplar secondary woods, period brass bail handles, beaded escutcheons, minor patch repairs, 35" w, 22" d, 34-1/2" h............14,560.00

Pennsylvania, c1750-80, walnut, rectangular top with molded edge, case with four gradu-

Chippendale, Pennsylvania, c1750-80, walnut, rectangular top with molded edge, four graduated thumb-molded drawers flanked by fluted quarter columns, molded base, ogee bracket feet, orig pierced brass handle and key escutcheons, minor patched repairs, 34" w, 21-1/2" d, 34" h, $9,250. Also shown are Aaron Willard shelf clock, c1795-1800, $12,320; and Tucker pitcher, $6,720. Photo courtesy of Samuel T. Freeman & Co., Philadelphia, PA.

ated thumb-molded drawers flanked by fluted quarter columns, molded base, ogee bracket feet, orig pierced brass handle and key escutcheons, minor patched repairs, 34" w, 21-1/2" d, 34" h 9,250.00

Pennsylvania, c1750-80, walnut, rectangular top with molded edge, case with four graduated thumb-molded drawers, molded base, ogee bracket feet, replaced brasses, one back foot restored, 37" w, 20" d, 33" h.........2,580.00

Pennsylvania, c1750-80, walnut, rectangular top with molded edge, case with two thumb-molded drawers over three graduated thumb-molded drawers, molded skirt, ogee bracket feet, replaced brasses, key escutcheons, and bracket feet, 36" w, 19-1/2" d, 33" h 2,250.00

Pennsylvania, c1760-80, mahogany, rectangular molded top, case fitted with four graduated thumb-molded drawers flanked by fluted quarter columns, molded base, ogee bracket feet, minor repairs to feet and case, replaced brasses, cedar secondary wood, carved initials "BL" on underside of case, faint chalked inscription, 42" w, 22" d, 34" h.............6,720.00

Pennsylvania, c1760-80, mahogany, rectangular molded top, case fitted with four graduated thumb-molded drawers, two frontal carved claw and ball feet, ogee bracket rear feet, old replaced brasses, refinished, imperfections, 36" w, 21" d, 32-1/2" h 9,200.00

Pennsylvania, c1770, cherry, cove molded cornice, case with five small and four long graduated thumb-molded drawers, bracket feet, brass bail handles, escutcheons, and lock plates, 47" w, 23" d, 70" h 6,000.00

Pennsylvania, c1770, mahogany, rectangular lipped molded top, case with four graduated wide lip molded drawers, quarter round fluted corners, ogival bracket feet, old brass bails, 39" w 4,650.00

Pennsylvania, c1770-80, carved cherry, rectangular molded top, case with four graduated thumb-molded drawers flanked by fluted lamb's tongue corners, bracket feet, replaced brasses, refinished, minor imperfections, 41-1/2" w, 19-1/4" d, 34" h 4,140.00

Pennsylvania, c1770-80, mahogany, case with four graduated thumb-molded drawers, flanked by fluted corner columns, ogee bracket feet, some drawer lips missing, 35-1/2" w, 20" d, 33" h...11,000.00

Pennsylvania, c1770-80, walnut, walnut veneer drawer fronts, rectangular top with banded inlay, case with four graduated cockbeaded drawers, case flanked by fluted quarter columns, base with matching band inlay atop ogee bracket feet, pine and poplar secondary woods, replaced beaded brass bails and key escutcheons, 40-1/2" w, 21-1/2" d, 36" h 6,160.00

Pennsylvania, c1770-90, cherry, molded rectangular top, case with five graduated drawers, case flanked by fluted quarter columns, scalloped apron, squat cabriole legs which are 19th C additions, drawers completely rebuilt.................490.00

Pennsylvania, c1775, walnut, molded cornice, case with seven graduated dovetailed drawers, fluted quarter columns, molded base, ogee bracket feet, poplar secondary wood, refinished, replaced brass handles and escutcheons, 38" w, 60" h 5,750.00

Pennsylvania, c1775, walnut, molded cornice, case with five small and five long dovetailed drawers, ogee bracket feet, poplar and chestnut secondary wood, 40-1/4" w, 70-1/2" h...........6,975.00

Pennsylvania, c1780, carved mahogany, rectangular molded top, case with four cockbeaded graduated drawers, flanked by fitted quarter columns, ogee bracket feet, replaced brasses, old refinishing, restoration, 40" w, 19-1/2" d, 35" h 6,325.00

Pennsylvania, c1780, walnut, heavily molded top and cornice, case with three small drawers over three larger graduated drawers, all thumb-molded, flanked by fluted quarter columns, molded base, ogee bracket feet, replaced brass bail handles, key escutcheons, and feet, 39" w, 22-1/2" d, 38" h 2,100.00

Rhode Island, c1770-80, cherry, overhanging molded top, case with two thumb-molded short drawers and four graduated long drawers, ogee bracket feet, replaced brasses, old refinishing, restorations, 36-1/2" w, 18-1/2" d, 42" h..2,415.00

Rhode Island, Newport, c1770-80, attributed to Townsend-Goddard School, serpentine, mahogany, case with four graduated drawers, bracket feet, early surface, orig brass pulls, minor surface imperfections, 39" w,

20-3/4" d, 34-1/2" h 24,000.00

Rhode Island, c1780, maple, molded cornice, case with two thumb-molded short drawers and six graduated long drawers, bracket feet, old brasses, old refinishing, restored, 36" w, 19" d, 53-1/2" h.........................3,450.00

Chippendale to Federal Transitional

As one style fades out of fashion, it was often still present as the craftsmen translated the old style into the newer designs. These examples of chests of drawers show definite elements of both periods.

America, serpentine front, mahogany, serpentine top with thumb-molded edge, case with four dovetailed drawers with inlaid stringing, bandy feet with claw and ball details, pine secondary wood, refinished, old replaced period brasses, age cracks in ends, 42-1/4" w, 25-1/2" d, 39-3/4" h 5,775.00

Maryland, mahogany, rectangular top with applied molded edge, case with two small drawers over three graduated long drawers, all with line inlay, ogee bracket feet, refinished, 33-1/2" w, 19-1/2" d, 35" h 22,000.00

Chippendale-Style

Examples of chests of drawers which have elements relating to Chippendale, but also later influences.

America, mahogany, molded rectangular top, case with three small drawers, central drawer fan carved, over three long drawers, ogee-molded bracket feet, 44-1/2" w, 21" d, 35" h..200.00

America, mahogany, molded rectangular top, four graduated long drawers, bracket feet, some 18th C components, 37" w, 19-3/4" d, 31-3/4" h..500.00

America, southeastern, late 18th C, mahogany, two small drawers over three graduated drawers, bracket feet, refinished, replaced brasses, minor imperfections, 19" w, 31-1/2" d, 31-1/2" h..3,950.00

Classical

The Classical style of furniture extends from c1805 to c1830. Furniture made during this time

period is also often referred to as "Empire." Design elements include fine woods, some veneers, beadings and moldings to drawers and edges. Feet can be as simple as bun or bracket feet or as ornate as hairy paw or lion feet.

America, c1820-1840, mahogany veneer, case with two overhanging cockbeaded drawers over three wide graduated cockbeaded drawers, flanked by applied reeded half columns, bun feet, wooden pulls, one pull broken, 42-3/4" w, 21" d, 40-5/8" h 600.00

American, c1830, ebonized mahogany, gilt stenciled, step back fitted with swing mirror, three small drawers, lower section with single beveled drawer over two deep drawers, circular wood pulls, flanked by half-ebonized columnar sides, ring-turned legs, ball feet, 38-1/2" d, 21-1/2" d, 45" h 1,400.00

America, c1830, mahogany veneer, case with two small cockbeaded drawers over three

Classical, New England, c1810, cherry and bird's eye maple, architectural crest, turned and pineapple carved half column pilasters, seven dovetailed drawers with solid bird's eye maple fronts, replaced turned front feet, replaced brass feet, 45-1/2" w, 22-1/2" d, 58-1/2" h, $935. Photo courtesy of Garth's Auctions, Inc., Delaware, OH.

graduated cockbeaded drawers, flat reeded panels terminating in spool turned feet, later brass pulls, some veneer patches, 42-1/2" w, 20-3/4" d, 41-3/4" h 850.00

America, c1830 and later, mahogany, top with scroll-cut gallery, case with pair of shallow drawers, turned legs, 42" w, 19" d, 49" h 550.00

America, c1840, mahogany, two parts, upper section with recessed row of drawers beneath pair of columns supporting rectilinear mirror plate, base with two over three drawers, 41-1/2" w, 22" d, 88" h............................800.00

America, c1840, pine and poplar, old red finish, case with two dovetailed overlapping drawers with edge beading, cutout feet, drawer knobs replaced, 23-3/4" w, 12-1/4" d, 20" h 1,375.00

America, c1850-60, mahogany veneer and hardwood, overhanging top drawer with ogee front, case with three dovetailed drawers, turned free-standing pilasters, turned feet, old worn mahogany finish, old replaced brass hardware, old repairs and veneer damage, 40-3/4" w, 19-1/2" d, 42-1/2" h 425.00

America, c1860, mahogany, top with scrolling gallery, case with pair of drawers, four drawer base with scroll columns, 42" w, 19-1/2" d, 54" h 450.00

America, second quarter 19th C, mahogany, rectangular mirror plate on chamfered swing-frame suspended between obelisk form posts, base with two drawers, outset chest with rectangular marble top over outset ogee molded drawer raised on scrolled pilasters flanking two long drawers, scroll feet, 42-1/2" w, 22" d, 80-1/2" h...550.00

America, first quarter 19th C, pine, outset rectangular top surmounting front with outset frieze drawer raised on corbel and reeded stiles flanking three recessed graduated and cockbeaded drawers, platform base raised on ball feet, secondary wood poplar, 42-1/2" w, 20-1/2" d, 45" h 400.00

America, second quarter 19th C, cherry and pine, rectangular top, case with four drawers, upper drawer molded en arbalette, turned short feet, as found condition, 43-1/4" w, 18-1/4" d, 43-1/2" h..250.00

Country, cherry, case with four dovetailed drawers, half column pilasters, replaced fruit and foliage pulls, height lessened, added casters, repairs, 52-1/2" w, 21-1/4" d, 45-1/2" h 250.00

Maine, pine, orig red and black graining, yellow and green striping, old brasses, edge damage, top poorly executed replacement, 41" w, 21-1/4" d, 40-1/2" h 350.00

Massachusetts, c1820, bow front, mahogany

Classical, New England, c1820, mahogany, recessed superstructure fitted with two small drawers over straight front, four cockbeaded drawers, brass lion mask head ring pulls, flanked by spiral turned outset corner columns, 42" w, 20" d, 49" h, $2,000. Photo courtesy of Samuel T. Freeman & Co., Philadelphia, PA.

and mahogany veneer, case with four small drawers, four long drawers, fluted quarter columns, turned legs, refinished, 44" w, 23-3/4" d, 39-1/2" h..950.00

Massachusetts, Northshore, c1825, carved mahogany and mahogany veneer, scrolled backboard over three short drawers on projecting case with two half drawers over three long drawers, flanked by recessed panels and pineapple, acanthus leaf and spiral carved columns continuing to turned feet, replaced glass pulls, refinished, imperfections, 42-3/4" w, 22" w, 45" h..1,000.00

Massachusetts, Northshore, c1825, carved mahogany and mahogany veneer, shaped backboard, case with two small drawers over four aligned long drawers, spool and spiral carved posts, glass knobs, scalloped apron, short turned legs, old brass, refinished, minor imperfections, 38-1/2" w, 19-1/2" d, 49-1/2" h..1,400.00

Classical, New England, c1820, crotch mahogany, rectangular stepped back top fitted with three small drawers, swing mirror, straight front fitted with three wide graduated drawers, circular pulls, scroll feet, 34-1/4" w, 17-1/2" d, 67" h, $900. Photo courtesy of Samuel T. Freeman & Co., Philadelphia, PA.

New England, c1825, tiger maple, rectangular top, case with large top drawer over three graduated incised beaded drawers, flanked by ring-turned columns, turned posts, casters, old refinishing, old emb brass pulls, 47" w, 22-1/2" d, 49-3/4" h 2,750.00

New England, c1830-50, bow front, pine, ormolu mounted scrolling back board, spool turned pilasters, 43" d, 20" d, 44" h........700.00

New York, c1825, mahogany and mahogany veneer, rectangular black painted and foliate stencil decorated framed mirror on scrolled acanthus leaf carved supports over three short drawers, projecting case with convex drawer and two long drawers flanked by free standing columns continuing to turned feet, star inlaid wooden drawer pulls, inscribed in pencil "Augustus Ozul Yonkers NY," minor imperfections, 36-1/2" w, 22-1/2" d, 63" h.........3,000.00

Ohio, 1830-40, bird's eye maple veneer, rectangular overhanging top, case with four cockbeaded drawers, recessed paneled sides, turned tapering legs, old refinishing, replaced brasses, imperfections, 41" w, 20" d, 43" h...........1,955.00

Vermont, Shaftsbury, c1816, maple, cherry, and tiger maple veneer, rectangular top with molded edge, case with two short drawers over four graduated drawers, inscribed, "Made by Asa Loomis in the year 1816," 42-1/2" w, 19-3/8" d, 45" h 6,450.00

Classical-Style

This chest of drawers looks like a Classical or Empire-style chest, but the ebonized wood indicates that it may have been made at a later date.

Mahogany and ebonized wood, rectangular top, case with four drawers flanked by pilasters, down curving feet, 46" w, 22" d, 42" h........900.00

Colonial Revival

Colonial Revival is the term used to describe furniture made in the early part of the 20th century that reflected back to earlier styles. This furniture was made by machine, rather than the hand-crafted techniques used during the historic period.

Hepplewhite-Style, c1920, solid mahogany, inlay on drawers and back rail, case with two small drawers over two long drawers, eagle brasses, 42" w, 19" d, 38" h 450.00

Federal

Chests of drawers made during the Federal period, c1790-1815, are generally made of mahogany, maple, birch, or cherry, and veneers. Inlays were popular and the contrasting woods were used as stringing, bands, bellflowers, and other types of decoration. Legs are generally straight with tapering to various types of feet, including bracket, bulbous, or spade.

America, c1800, cherry, mahogany molding on top edge, case with four dovetailed drawers with applied edge molding, scrolled apron, reeded stiles, paneled ends, turned feet, banded inlay around base, poplar secondary wood, refinished, old brass pulls, 39-1/2" w, 20" d, 41-1/4" h 1,500.00

America, c1800, cherry veneer, rectangular top, straight front, case with four graduated cockbeaded drawers, oval brass bail handles, escutcheons, lock plates, shaped apron, French bracket feet, veneer loss to feet, 42-1/2" w, 20-1/4" d, 39-1/2" h 950.00

America, c1800, inlaid cherry, outset rectangular ogee molded top with stringing, case with three graduated drawers, shaped skirt continuing into splayed bracket feet, secondary woods poplar and white pine, imperfections, 15-1/2" w, 12-3/4" d, 24-1/2" h 865.00

America, c1800, butler's, inlaid mahogany, molded rectangular top with crossbanded edges, front with secretaire drawer opening to interior fitted with felt-lined writing surface and arrangement of six drawers and seven valanced pigeonholes, over three long graduated cockbeaded drawers, shaped skirt continuing to splayed bracket feet, ebony stringing throughout, secondary wood white pine, 46-1/2" w, 22-1/4" d, 46-1/2" h 2,400.00

America, c1800-15, mahogany, outset rectangular top surmounted by front with two short over three long graduated and cockbeaded drawers, flanked by reeded stiles, raised on turned short legs, secondary wood white pine, old refinishing, imperfections, 43-1/2" w, 22-1/2" d, 40" h 200.00

Marshmallow Sofa, Modernism-Era, George Nelson, manufactured by Herman Miller, 1957, circular cushions in orig Alexander Girard fabrics, sample version, made to illustrate range of fabrics available, eighteen cushions each in a different fabric, satin chrome and black enamel frame, 51" w, 32" d, 30" h, $15,400. Photo courtesy of Treadway Gallery Inc. of Cincinnati, OH.

Pair of Coconut Chairs, Lounge, Modernism-Era, George Nelson, triangular white enameled metal shell, original blue Naugahyde upholstery, chrome strut frame, 40" w, 32" d, 32" h, $10,450 each; matching ottoman, original blue Naugahyde, chrome base, original upholstery label, 24" w, 19" d, 16" h, $5,225. Photo courtesy of Treadway Gallery, Inc. of Cincinnati, OH.

Trundle bed, Arts & Crafts, in the style of early Gustav Stickley, slatted back and sides, original finish, unmarked, new futon, 78" l, 31" d, 33-1/2" h, $4,250. Photo courtesy of David Rago Auctions/RagoArts.com, Lambertville, NJ, Lambertville, NJ.

Settle bench, Arts & Crafts, attributed to George W. Maher, solid posts with pyramidal tops, broad vertical back slats, new tacked on tan leather seat, refinished, 78" l, 28-1/4" d, 40-1/2" h, $2,700. Photo courtesy of David Rago Auctions/RagoArts.com, Lambertville, NJ.

Settee, Arts & Crafts, Gustav Stickley, New York, No. 165, mahogany, tapering posts, curved back slats, new dark brown mohair pillows, orig finish, few minor scratches, no visible mark, 61-1/4" w, 28-1/2" d, 41" h, $17,000. Photo courtesy of David Rago Auctions/RagoArts.com, Lambertville, NJ.

Sideboard, Arts & Crafts, L. & J. G. Stickley, Fayetteville, NY, replaced plate rack, two cabinet doors flanking four drawers, long linen drawer, original finish, "The Work of L. & J. G. Stickley" decal, some stains to top, 72" w, 25" d, 49-1/4" h, $4,500. Also shown are a copper coal scuttle, $425, and hammered copper American beauty vase, $600. Photo courtesy of David Rago Auctions/RagoArts.com, Lambertville, NJ.

Armoire, Victorian, Classical Revival, c1870, burl walnut and ebonized, flat step molded cornice with fan and spherical finials, shaped center mirrored door flanked by leaf decoration, ebonized columns flanked by two panel doors with column sides, step molded base fitted with single drawer, 91" w, 23" d, 104" h, $7,000. Photo courtesy of Samuel T. Freeman & Co., Philadelphia, PA.

Child's blanket chest, from the workshop of Ernest Batchelder, California, oak, front panel decorated with pyrography of stylized yellow daffodils, feet with square cutouts, orig finish, unmarked, break to one foot, 27-1/4" l, 14" d, 15" h, $8,500. Photo courtesy of David Rago Auctions/RagoArts.com, Lambertville, NJ.

Desk, left, Arts & Crafts, Gustav Stickley, designed by Harvey Ellis, New York, No. 706, drop-front, rectangular overhanging top, paneled front inlaid with copper, pewter, and wood floral decoration, full gallery interior, lower shelf, faintly visible mark on back, two splits in back boards, new finish to top, 30" w, 13" d, 44" h, $28,000. On the right is a side chair, Arts & Crafts, Gustav Stickley, New York, c1904, No. 335, tiger maple, three vertical back slats inlaid with copper, pewter, and wood floral motif, arched apron, new inset rush seat, red decal, refinished, 16-3/4" w, 16-1/2" d, 39-1/4" h, $4,000. Photo courtesy of David Rago Auctions/RagoArts.com, Lambertville, NJ.

Left: drop-front desk, Arts & Crafts, Limbert, Grand Rapids and Holland, Michigan, slant-front, gallery top, fitted interior, single drawer with square hammered copper pulls, original finish, branded mark, ring stain on top, 33" w, 18-1/4" d, 34-1/2" h, $1,100. Right: library table, Arts & Crafts, Limbert, Grand Rapids and Holland, Michigan, rectangular overhanging top, single drawer with square hammered copper pulls, arched apron, original finish, branded mark, 48" w, 28" d, 29" h, $1,400. Arts and Crafts lamp also shown. Photo courtesy of David Rago Auctions/RagoArts.com, Lambertville, NJ.

Left: Magazine stand, Arts & Crafts, Stickley Brothers, Grand Rapids, Michigan, five shelves, slatted sides, and back, original finish, taped on Stickley Bros. paper label/4602, 15-1/2" w, 12" d, 47" h, $1,200. On the right is a bookcase, Arts & Crafts, Stickley Brothers, Grand Rapids, Michigan, gallery top, open section with short side slats above two doors, single hammered copper ring pull, orig reddish finish, Quaint metal tag/303-4784, 35-1/2" w, 12" d, 50" h, $3,500. Photo courtesy of David Rago Auctions/RagoArts.com, Lambertville, NJ.

Chests of drawers, Federal, New Hampshire, Portsmouth, c1805-15, mahogany and flame birch, edge of birch top outlined with patterned inlay, case of four cockbeaded drawers, each visually divided into three panels by flame birch veneer outlined in stringing and banded mahogany veneer, flame birch veneer drop lane pendant centering veneered skirt, elongated French foot, original brasses, old refinish, 40-1/4" w, 21-1/8" d, 36" h, $83,900. Photo courtesy of Skinner Auctioneers and Appraisers of Antiques and Fine Art Boston and Bolton, MA.

Chests of drawers, Federal, Massachusetts, c1800, attributed to Nathan Lombard, Southern Worcester County, inlaid cherry, overhanging top with serpentine front, square corners, two lines of chevron stringing joining quarter fans at corners centering urn and flowering vine motif, edge with chevron stringing and mahogany banding, back edge with applied beaded strip, conforming case below four cockbeaded drawers with vertically grained cherry veneer bordered by chevron stringing and mahogany feather banding, faux keyholes surrounded with leaf and husk inlay, flanking concave columns with husk and dot inlay above leaves and husks and inverted icicles with leaves, carved pointed arched capitals and bases carved with stylized leaves surrounded by chevron stringing, bracket feet with C-scroll cusp and bead shaping, bordered by chevron stringing, replaced brasses, old possibly original finish, very minor imperfections, 42-3/4" w, 19-3/4" d, 36" h, $365,500. Photo courtesy of Skinner Auctioneers and Appraisers of Antiques and Fine Art Boston and Bolton, MA.

Miniature chests of drawers, Victorian, three dovetailed drawers, applied ornamentation, arched mirror top with leaf and column ornamentation, repaired back leg, minor loss, 8" w, 5" d, 18" h, $770. Photo courtesy of Alderfer Auction Company, Hatfield, PA.

Highboy, Queen Anne, New England, c1740-60, cherry, flat top, step molded overhanging cornice, four wide graduated drawers, base with one wide drawer over three small drawers, center fan carved, scalloped skirt with two pendant drops, cabriole legs, pad feet, later butterfly brasses, one drawer front chipped, two repaired, 40" w, 20-1/8" d, 70-1/2" h, $16,800. Photo courtesy of Samuel T. Freeman & Co., Philadelphia, PA.

Tall Chest, Chippendale, Pennsylvania, c1800, walnut, molded cornice, dovetailed top, three short drawers over five long graduated cockbeaded drawers, flanked by quarter columns, ogee bracket feet, 42" w, 20-1/2" h, 65-1/4" h, $6,875. Photo courtesy of Alderfer Auction Company, Hatfield, PA.

Secretary, modern Chippendale-style reproduction, Walnut with inlaid stars, 40" w, 94-1/2" h. Did not meet auction reserve, and therefore was not sold at that particular auction.

Secretary, Chippendale, Pennsylvania, cherry, two piece, upper: broken arch pediment, boldly carved floral rosettes, turned and carved finials, double doors each with seven panes of glass in geometric arrangement, fluted quarter columns, applied reeded detail, base: slant top lid with fully developed fitted interior of eight dovetailed drawers with serpentine fronts, center door with blocking and carved fan with five graduated drawers with serpentine fronts, eight pigeonholes each with hidden drawers and fan carving, two letter drawers with fluted columns and reeding, four overlapping dovetailed drawers, fluted quarter columns, ogee foot, original eagle brasses, H-hinges, and latches, original finish, minor repairs to feet and some replaced glue blocks, 38-1/4" w, 20-3/4" d, 90" h, $88,000. Photo courtesy of Garth's Auctions Inc., Delaware, OH.

Corner chair, Queen Anne, America, c1740-60, walnut, plain three-piece crest rail terminating in volutes, solid vasiform back slats, upholstered drop-in seat, deep scalloped skirt, short cabriole legs, trifid fore foot, 24" d, 31-3/4" h, $20,160. Photo courtesy of Samuel T. Freeman & Co., Philadelphia, PA.

Side chairs, left: Chippendale, America c1750-80, mahogany, carved crest rail, pierced and carved splat, beading on rails and straight front legs, old repairs to splat and left stretcher, 21-1/2" w, 19" d, 38" h, $1,910. Right: Queen Anne to Chippendale transitional, Pennsylvania, Philadelphia, c1740-70, mahogany, incised crest with carved shell, bold ears, pierced vasiform splat, inverted carved shell on skirt, cabriole legs with shell carved knees ending in pad feet with unusual turnings, rear legs have chamfered corners, seat rail incised "IIII," 23" w, 21" d, 40" h, $5,100. Photo courtesy of Samuel T. Freeman & Co., Philadelphia, PA.

Side chair, Queen Anne to Chippendale Transitional, Pennsylvania, Philadelphia, c1750-60, walnut, shell carved crest rail with double scrolled volutes, continuing to carved rounded stiles, vasiform splat, balloon fitted slip seat supported by two shell carved cabriole legs with two volutes, ending in claw and ball feet, square back legs, rear to splat lock reglued, front seat rail inscribed with two strokes, balloon seat frame inscribed "IIIII," indicating chair was part of a set, back seat rail contains letters "SM" in white chalk, letters similar to others found on chairs belonging to Samuel Morris, 19" w, 16-3/4" d, 41" h, $336,000. Photo courtesy of Samuel T. Freeman & Co., Philadelphia, PA.

Tea table, Queen Anne, Massachusetts, coastal northern, or New Hampshire, c1730-60, mahogany, molded tray top overhangs straight molded frieze, scrolled skirt, cabriole legs, scrolled knee returns, pad feet on platforms, old refinish, imperfections, 30" w, 19-1/2" d, 27-1/2" h, $41,400. Photo courtesy of Skinner Auctioneers and Appraisers of Antiques and Fine Art Boston and Bolton, MA.

Dining Table and Chairs, Modernism-era, T. H. Robsjohn-Gibbings, radiating walnut veneer toped table with dowel legs, three leaves, label, 48" d, 29" h, $2,310; set of six chairs, two arm chairs, four side chairs, curved slat backs, original orange upholstery, curved legs, 23" w, 20" d, 35" h, $1,650. Photo courtesy of Treadway Gallery, Inc. of Cincinnati, OH.

Card table, Arts & Crafts, Gustav Stickley, New York, c1902, No. 447, two side drawers with faceted wooden pulls, stretchers mortised through legs, keyed through-tenon center stretcher, original finish, early red box decal, minor stains on top, 30" w, 18" d, 28-3/4" h, $20,000. Photo courtesy of David Rago Auctions/RagoArts.com, Lambertville, NJ.

Dining, Arts & Crafts, unknown designed, rectangular top, elaborately carved trestles, unmarked, new finish, 71-1/2" l, 35-3/4" d, 30" h, $1,200. Photo courtesy of David Rago Auctions/RagoArts.com, Lambertville, NJ.

Library table, left, Arts & Crafts, Limbert, Grand Rapids and Holland, Michigan, trestle, triple corbels on each side, lower shelf mortised through legs, original medium finish, unmarked, 49-3/4" l, 28" d, 29-1/4" h, $2,600. Also shown is Henry J. Cleveland hand-wrought copper lamp base with screen and parchment shade, $1,400. On the right is a Morris arm chair, Arts & Crafts, L. & J. G. Stickley, Fayetteville, NY, fixed back, five vertical slats under each arm, corbels, new brown drop-in leather back cushion and seat, original finish, lighter color to arm tops from normal wear, branded "The Work of L. & J. G. Stickley," 31-3/4" w, 36" d, 41-3/4" h, $4,000. Photo courtesy of David Rago Auctions/RagoArts.com, Lambertville, NJ.

Chests of drawers, Chippendale, Massachusetts, Salem or Marblehead, c1760-80, figured mahogany, reverse serpentine, thumb-molded overhanging reverse serpentine top with end blocking, conforming case with four graduated drawers also with end blocking separated by beading, molded base, large claw and ball feet, old surface, orig brasses, minor imperfections, 38" w, 21" d, 32-3/4" h, $79,500. Photo courtesy of Skinner Auctioneers and Appraisers of Antiques and Fine Art Boston and Bolton, MA.

Chests of drawers, Federal, Ohio, attributed to North Jackson, Trumball County, decorated, poplar, original red graining on yellow ground, ebonzied detail, well-shaped scroll crest, four dovetailed drawers, half column pilasters, high turned feet, replaced hardware, some period brasses with embossed eagle heads, 41-3/4" w, 20-1/2" d, 53-1/2" h, $7,150. Photo courtesy of Garth's Auctions, Inc., Delaware, OH.

Crib, Arts & Crafts, Gustav Stickley, New York, each side entirely spindled, orig finish, no visible mark, 55" l, 35-1/2" w, 34" h, $8,000. Photo courtesy of David Rago Auctions/RagoArts.com, Lambertville, NJ.

Wall cupboard, Federal, Pennsylvania, Soap Hollow, c1861-65, poplar, two pieces, original red and green paint, red and yellow striping, gold and silver stenciled decoration with birds, etc., upper section with molded cornice, double doors each with six panes of old glass, center panel with three panes, over pie shelf, base section with three dovetailed drawers over two doors and center section, all with raised panels, dovetailed bracket feet, turned quarter columns on both sections, bottom rail of upper section with stenciled label "Manufactured by Peter K. Thomas," pieced repair to cornice, two drawer fronts replaced, touch-up repair to paint, 63-3/4" w, 86-1/2" h, $35,200. Photo courtesy of Garth's Auctions Inc., Delaware, OH.

Left: lamp table, Arts & Crafts, L & J. G. Stickley, circular overhanging top, lower circular shelf on arched cross-stretchers, unmarked, refinished, chip to one leg, 24" d, 29-1/4" h, $750. Also shown is a Dirk Van Erp hammered table lamp. Center: arm chair, Arts & Crafts, Gustav Stickley, New York, V-back, five vertical back slats, corbels, orig tacked-on brown Japan leather seat, orig square tacks, worn original finish, red decal, tear to seat, 25-3/4" w, 20-1/2" d, 36-3/4" h, $900. Right: bookcase, Arts & Crafts, Gustav Stickley, New York, c1905, single door, twelve glass panes, gallery top, through tenon side, original finish, red decal and remnant of Craftsman label, repairs to base, 35" w, 13" d, 56" h, $4,500. Also shown are two pieces of American art pottery. Photo courtesy of David Rago Auctions/RagoArts.com, Lambertville, NJ.

Tea table, Chippendale, New England, 18th C, apple wood, tilt-top, serpentine top, cabriole leg base, pad feet, refinished, one foot pierced, 35" w, 34" d, 27-1/4" h, $460.00.

Blanket chest, Federal, American, c1800, polychrome, brown feather painting, front with twin incised painted panels, lion and flat tulip after Heinrich Otto, side panels with flat tulip and parrot, red polychrome straight bracket feet, 44" l, 19-1/2" d, 18-1/2" h, $6,500. Photo courtesy of Samuel T. Freeman Co., Philadelphia, PA.

Sofa, Victorian, Rococo Revival, Méridienne, attributed to John Henry Belter, c1850, rosewood, elaborate C-scrolls, shell, grape, foliate, and floral carving, shaped and carved apron, carved cabriole legs, upholstered back and seat, one of a matched pair, $25,000.

America, c1810-20, straight front, mahogany, case with four graduated drawers, small oval brasses with figural cartouches, bail handles stamped with figural cartouches, ball handles stamped verso "H. J.," tall bracket feet of later date, 38-1/2" w, 19-1/4" d, 35" h 2,465.00

America, c1825, elliptical front, mahogany, most surfaces veneered, case with four graduated drawers with inlaid diamond shaped key escutcheons, brasses with stamped concentric oval designs and are signed "H. J." on bails, bulbous legs with ball and ring turnings, 39-1/2" w, 22-3/4" d, 39" h 1,200.00

America, c1825, swell front, bird's eye maple, case with four graduated wide cockbeaded drawers, half-round columnar corners, short turned feet, paneled sides, 41-1/2" w 2,750.00

American, early 19th C, bow front, cherry, rectangular overhanging reeded edge top, case with four graduated dovetailed drawers with applied edge beading, paneled ends, shaped apron, turned feet, inlaid shield shaped escutcheons, old finish, pieced repairs to drawer edges and bottom drawer, 42-5/8" w, 20" d, 39" h..1,650.00

America, early 19th C, bow front, mahogany, cherry, and flame birch veneer, bowed top with inlaid edge, case with four dovetailed drawers outlined in flame birch veneer bands, veneered and scrolled front skirt with similar side shaping, old brasses, old refinishing, 43" w, 19" d, 37-1/2" h..1,380.00

Connecticut, c1790, inlaid cherry, rectangular overhanging top with molded edge, case with four incised beaded graduated drawers with inlaid quarter fans and stringing, ogee bracket feet, old refinishing, 38-1/4" w, 18" d, 34-1/4" h..7,200.00

Connecticut, c1800, inlaid cherry, rectangular overhanging top with string inlaid edge, case with four graduated drawers with mahogany veneer bordered by stringing and interrupted line inlay on slightly splayed French feet, inlaid valanced skirt, brasses appear to be orig, old refinishing, minor imperfections, 39-1/4" w, 18-3/4" d, 36-3/4" h 5,700.00

Country, cherry and curly maple, top with reeded edge and scalloped gallery, deep top drawer, three dovetailed drawers with cock-beaded edge, turned and rope carved pilasters, paneled ends, chestnut secondary wood, refinished, 41" w, 53" h............................975.00

Country, curly maple, molded top edge, case with four dovetailed drawers with applied beaded edge, paneled ends, turned feet, poplar and chestnut secondary wood, replaced brass pull handles, 41" w, 21" d, 48-3/4" h.............1,100.00

Country, mahogany and mahogany veneer, rectangular top, outset corners, case with four long drawers, compressed spherical carved capital over reeded column, turned feet, plain frieze, refinished, replaced brasses, 41" w, 21-1/2" d, 43" h 995.00

Country, mahogany and satin wood veneer, biscuit corners, "D"-shaped facade, four dovetailed drawers with applied edge beading and inlay, turned and reeded feet and pilasters, ring turned posts, turned wooden pulls, backboards mkd "J. J. Drew, Norwalk, O," repairs, some veneer and edge damage, age cracks in top and side panels, 45-1/2" w, 23-5/8" d, 37-3/4" h.........2,000.00

Massachusetts, c1800, attributed to Nathan Lombard, southern Worcester County, inlaid cherry, overhanging top with serpentine front, square corners, two lines of chevron stringing

Federal, Massachusetts, c1800, cherry, molded rectangular overhanging top, case of four graduated beaded drawers, molded bracket feet, replaced brasses, refinished, restored, 41-3/4" w, 19" d, 33" h, $2,415. Photo courtesy of Skinner Auctioneers and Appraisers of Antiques and Fine Art Boston and Bolton, MA.

joining quarter fans at corners centering urn and flowering vine motif, edge with chevron stringing and mahogany banding, back edge with applied beaded strip, conforming case below four cock-beaded drawers with vertically grained cherry veneer bordered by chevron stringing and mahogany feather banding, faux keyholes surrounded with leaf and husk inlay, flanking concave columns with husk and dot inlay above leaves and husks and inverted icicles with leaves, carved pointed arched capitals and bases carved with stylized leaves surrounded by chevron stringing, bracket feet with C-scroll cusp and bead shaping, bordered by chevron stringing, replaced brasses, old possibly original finish, very minor imperfections, 42-3/4" w, 19-3/4" d, 36" h 365,500.00

Massachusetts, c1800, bow front, inlaid cherry, rectangular top with elliptical front crossbanded and string inlaid, case fitted with four graduated cockbeaded drawers bordered by mahogany crossbanding, crossbanding base with flaring French feet jointed by cutout skirt, emb oval brass pulls may be orig, old surface, imperfections, 38" w, 22" d, 34-3/4" h...................6,900.00

Massachusetts, c1800, bow front, inlaid mahogany, overhanging top with bow front and inlaid edge, conforming case with four cockbeaded drawers with bird's eye maple panels bordered by stringing and mahogany crossbanding, tall cutout feet, old finish, orig brasses, minor imperfections, 38" w, 21" d, 34" h...................................5,500.00

Massachusetts, c1800, bow front, mahogany, overhanging bow front top, conforming case with four cockbeaded graduated drawers, flaring French feet joined by valanced skirt, brass pulls and escutcheons appear original, old refinishing, imperfections, 40" w, 19-3/4" d, 38-1/2" h...3,800.00

Massachusetts, c1800, bow front, mahogany and mahogany veneer inlaid, case with four graduated drawers, outswept feet, refinished, replaced brasses, imperfections, 39" w, 21-1/2" d, 34-3/4" h 2,195.00

Massachusetts, c1800, bow front, mahogany and mahogany veneer, bowed front shaped top, conforming case, four graduated cockbeaded drawers, flaring French feet, shaped skirt, old refinishing, orig brasses, 40-1/2" w, 20-3/4" d, 35-1/4" h 2,600.00

Massachusetts, c1800, cherry, molded top overhangs case with four beaded graduated drawers, molded bracket feet, replaced brasses, refinished, restored, 41-3/4" w, 19" d, 33" h..2,415.00

Massachusetts, c1800, cherry, rectangular overhanging top, cockbeaded case with four graduated drawers, inlaid base, flaring French feet, shaped skirt, old refinishing, replaced brasses, very minor imperfections, 37-1/2" w, 19-1/2" d, 37-1/4" h 2,100.00

Massachusetts, c1800-10, birch, rectangular overhanging top, case with four graduated drawers on cutout feet, orig oval brass pulls, old surface with red wash, minor imperfections, 38-1/2" w, 18-1/2" d, 38-3/4" h 1,955.00

Massachusetts, c1800-10, mahogany and mahogany veneer, rectangular overhanging top, case with four cockbeaded graduated drawers, flaring French feet, orig oval brasses, refinished, imperfections, 43" w, 23" d, 37-1/4" h..4,315.00

Massachusetts, c1805-15, attributed to Alden Spooner and George Fitch, bow front, cherry and bird's eye maple veneer, case with four graduated drawers, shaped apron, turned legs, orig brass handles, refinished, 38" w, 20" d, 42" h..5,200.00

Massachusetts, c1810, bow front, cherry inlaid, conforming case with four drawers, scalloped apron, old finish, replaced brasses, minor imperfections, 42-3/4" w, 20" d, 41-1/2" h...1,925.00

Massachusetts, c1810, bow front, mahogany inlaid, overhanging top, swell front, inlaid edge, case with four cockbeaded drawers, flaring French feet, old refinishing, old replaced oval brass pulls, repairs, 38-1/2" w, 22" d, 34" h..2,300.00

Massachusetts, Salem, c1810, bow front, mahogany and flame birch veneer, birch bowed top, case with four graduated drawers veneered with flame birch surrounded by mahogany crossbanded veneer, flanked by colonettes and reeding, terminating in ring turned feet, shaped skirt outlined with starts burned into the wood, replaced brasses, old refinishing, minor imperfections, 36-3/4" w, 20-1/4" d, 37" h 14,950.00

Massachusetts, Salem, 1810-15, bow front, mahogany veneer carved, case with four cockbeaded drawers, spiral carved engaged flanking columns topped by colonettes and C-scroll carvings, shaped veneered skirt and orig inlaid turned pulls, old refinishing, imperfections, backsplash missing, 38" w, 19-1/2" d, 39" h 1,495.00

Massachusetts, c1815, bow front, carved mahogany and mahogany veneer, shaped top, ovolo corners, beaded edge, conforming case with four graduated beaded drawers flanked by quarter-engaged ring-turned reeded columns continuing to ring-turned swelled legs, old refinishing, orig brasses, imperfections, 41-3/4" w, 22-5/8" d, 41-3/4" h...............................1,450.00

Massachusetts, c1815, bow front, mahogany and mahogany veneer, rectangular bow front top with ovolo corners and crossbanded inlaid edge, conforming case with four cockbeaded drawers, quarter engaged ring-turned beaded posts continuing to tapering ring-turned reeded legs, arched crossbanded skirt, circular brass pulls, old refinish, 41" w, 21-3/4" d, 39-1/2" h 1,840.00

Massachusetts, c1815-20, bow front, mahogany and mahogany veneer, top with bow front and ovolo corners above conforming case with four cockbeaded drawers, flanked by quarter-engaged ring-turned columns ending in vase and ring turned legs, joined by cutout apron, old brass pulls, old refinishing, minor imperfections, 37-1/2" w, 19" d, 39" h 2,500.00

Massachusetts, c1815-20, mahogany inlaid, rectangular top with ovolo corners, inlaid edge, case with four cockbeaded drawers bordered with tiger maple crossbanding, flanked by quarter engaged ring-turned reeded posts continuing to vase and ring turned legs and joined by shaped apron with tiger maple banding continuing around legs to sides, replaced old brasses, old refinish, veneer losses, 43" w, 20" d, 41-1/4" h 1,610.00

Massachusetts, c1815-25, bow front, mahogany and tiger maple, top with bow front and ovolo corners, crossbanded edge over case with four cockbeaded graduated drawers, central tiger maple panel flanked by mahogany panels and borders, contrasting stringing and crossbanding,

quarter engaged ring-turned reeded posts continuing to swelled feet, old refinishing, turned pulls, minor imperfections, 40-1/4" w, 20-3/4" d, 38-1/4" h..............................2,650.00

Massachusetts, c1820, bow front, cherry, bird's eye maple, and mahogany veneer, rectangular top with bowfront, case of four cockbeaded graduated drawers veneered with bird's eye maple panels and bordered by mahogany crossbanding, flanking ring-turned legs joined by scrolled maple and mahogany veneered skirt, sgd "Samuel Stonington," replaced brasses, old refinish, imperfections, 40-1/2" w, 21-1/4" h, 40" h 4,500.00

Massachusetts, c1820, bow front, mahogany and mahogany veneer, rectangular top with bowfront and ovolo corners, conforming case with four cockbeaded graduated drawers flanked by quarter engaged ring-turned reeded posts continuing to turned legs joined by cutout skirt, turned wooden pulls, old refinish, sun bleached, other imperfections, 40" w, 18" d, 38-1/2" h...1,650.00

Massachusetts, c1820, mahogany and mahogany veneer, rectangular top, ovolo corners and carved edge, case with four graduated cockbeaded drawers, flanked by ring-turned reeded legs ending in turned swelled feet, old replaced pulls, old finish, imperfections, 40-3/4" w, 19-1/2" d, 41" h.........1,950.00

Massachusetts, c1820-30, cherry, rectangular top with ovolo corners, overhanging case with four scratch-beaded drawers, flanked by reeded quarter engaged columns, ending in turned tapering legs, orig turned wooden pulls, old refinishing, 43-1/2" w, 21" d, 39-1/4" h 1,150.00

Massachusetts, c1825, bow front, carved mahogany and mahogany veneer, scrolled backboard above two cockbeaded glove drawers with flanking ovolo corners and quarter engaged vase and ring-turned columns, projecting case with four thumb-molded drawers with flanking ovolo corners and quarter engaged vase and ring-turned spiral carved columns continuing to turned feet, old brasses, old surface, minor imperfections 1,725.00

Massachusetts, c1825, carved mahogany and mahogany veneer, scrolled backboard, two cockbeaded short drawers flanked by quarter-engaged vase and ring-turned columns, projecting bow front case with cockbeaded graduated drawers, flanked by ovolo corners and quarter-engaged vase and ring-turned spiral-carved posts, turned legs, wooden pulls, old finish, imperfections, 37-1/2" w, 17-1/4" d, 44-1/2" h 1,495.00

Massachusetts, early 19th C, bird's eye maple, ovolo corners, case with four drawers, reeded columns, turned feet, orig brasses, old surface, 40" w, 19-1/2" d, 41" h 1,500.00

Massachusetts, early 19th C, bow front, cherry veneer, bowed top with inlaid edge, case with four cockbeaded drawers, outline stringing, veneered skirt with central flame birch veneer lunette, four French feet, old surface, oval brasses appear to be original, imperfections, 39-3/4" w, 17" d, 37" h 3,795.00

Massachusetts, early 19th C, tiger maple, rectangular overhanging top, case with four scratch beaded graduated drawers, cyma curved skirt flanked by curving French feet, orig brasses, refinished, imperfections, 39-1/2" w, 18" d, 35" h........................3,800.00

Massachusetts, North Shore, early 19th C, bow front, mahogany veneer, bowed top, carved concentric circles above engaged reeded columns, turned feet, old refinishing, orig brasses, height loss, 40" w, 22-1/2" d, 38" h..1,265.00

Massachusetts or New Hampshire, c1820, bow front, inlaid wavy birch, shaped top with ovolo corners, conforming case with four drawers, two satinwood panels bordered by mahogany crossbanding and cockbeading flanked by one-quarter engaged ring-turned and reeded columns, swelled legs, joined by valanced skirt with center satinwood panel, old refinishing, imperfections, 39-1/2" w, 22" d, 41-5/8" h 3,600.00

Massachusetts or New Hampshire, early 19th C, bow front, mahogany veneer, top with recessed edge, bowed case with cockbeaded drawers, cyma curved veneered skirt flanked by French feet, old refinishing, replaced brasses, imperfections, 41" w, 19-14" d, 33-1/2" h..3,355.00

Middle Atlantic States, serpentine, mahogany, shaped serpentine overhanging top, case with four block ended line inlaid drawers,

Federal, New England, c1820, mahogany inlaid, rectangular top with outset corners set with octagonal framed swing mirror, inlaid swan form harp decorated stiles, bowed front and top with string and banding inlay, brass bail handles, openwork escutcheons and lock plates, flanked by flat fluted columnar sides, ring turned tapered legs, peg feet, 34" w, 22" d, 70" h, $3,590. Photo courtesy of Samuel T. Freeman & Co., Philadelphia, PA.

chamfered corners with leaf and vine inlay, scalloped bracket feet, refinished, 40" w, 21-1/2" d, 37" h 6,500.00

New England, c1790, cherry, rectangular top, barber pole inlay over straight front, case with four graduated cockbeaded drawers, flanked by recessed pin line inlay columns, shaped apron with center fan decoration, French bracket feet, 41-1/2" w, 20-3/4" d, 27-1/2" h..4,500.00

New England, southeastern, c1800-10, cherry, rectangular overhanging top , case with four cockbeaded graduated drawers, flaring

French feet, old brass pulls, old finish, 36-3/4" w, 19" d, 36-1/2" h 4,600.00

New England, c1810, tiger maple, rectangular top, cockbeaded case with four graduated drawers, cutout base with applied reeded molding, refinished, old oval brasses, 40-1/2" w, 19" d, 39-3/4" h 5,750.00

New England, c1810-20, bow front, mahogany and tiger maple veneer, overhanging shaped top with ovolo corners, case with four cockbeaded tiger maple graduate drawers, flanking quarter-engaged vase and ring-turned reeded posts continuing to vase and ring-turned legs, joined by shaped skirt centerline inlaid tiger maple panel, replaced oval brasses, old refinishing, restorations, 40" w, 22-1/2" d, 37" h......................................2,185.00

New England, c1820, maple, rect top with ovolo corners, ring-turned columns ending in turned tapering legs, flanking four reverse graduated drawers, refinished, replaced brasses, 41" w, 18-1/2" d, 41" h................................ 900.00

New England, c1815-20, cherry, painted, rectangular top with ovolo corners, case with four cockbeaded graduated drawers with flanking quarter engaged vase and ring turned reeded posts continuing to turned legs, replaced brasses, old red repainted surface, minor imperfections 3,250.00

New England, c1815-25, carved mahogany and mahogany veneer, rectangular top with ovolo corners, case with four cockbeaded graduated drawers flanked by quarter engaged ring-turned reeded posts continuing to vase and ring-turned legs, replaced brass pulls, old refinishing, 42-3/4" w, 19-3/4" d, 43-1/4" h................ 1,035.00

New England, northern, c1820, bow front, birch and mahogany veneers, overhanging top with bow front and square corners, conforming case with four drawers bordered with crossbanding and stringing flanked by square posts on vase and ring turned feet, old refinishing, replaced brass pulls, imperfections, 40-1/2" w, 21-1/2" d, 41-1/2" h 1,850.00

New England, c1820, birch and mahogany, rect overhanging top, case with four bird's eye maple cockbeaded graduated drawers, ring-turned swelled legs, refinished, replaced brasses, 39" w, 18-1/2" d, 38-3/4" h..................................1,720.00

New England, early 19th C, bow front, cherry, four cockbeaded graduated drawers, veneer cyma curved skirt, orig brasses, old refinish, surface imperfections, 41-1/2" w, 21-3/8" d, 37" h 2,875.00

New England, early 19th C, bow front, cherry inlaid, bowed top edged in inlay, case with four cockbeaded drawers, skirt outlined in veneer, flaring platform feet, casters, orig brass pulls, old refinish, 38-3/4" w, 22-1/4" d, 38-1/2" h 3,000.00

New England, early 19th C, painted, slightly overhanging rectangular top, case with four drawers on cutout feet, old red paint with fanciful dark brown graining, replaced oval brasses, 36" w, 18-1/2" d, 38" h.........................3,220.00

New England, early 19th C, wavy birch, rectangular overhanging top above cockbeaded case, four graduated drawers, bracket feet, refinished, replaced brasses, 38-1/2" w, 19-1/4" d, 35" h 2,200.00

New Hampshire, Portsmouth, c1805-15, mahogany and flame birch, edge of birch top outlined with patterned inlay, case with four

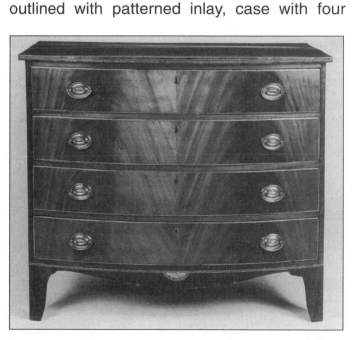

Federal, New Hampshire, Concord, New Hampshire, Concord, early 19th C, bow front, mahogany veneer, bowed top with inlaid edge, conforming case of mahogany veneered drawers outlined with stringing, shaped skirt with central lunette inlay outlined in banding, flanked by French feet, old refinish, orig brasses, imperfections, 39-3/4" w, 17-3/4" d, 37" h, $4,990. Photo courtesy of Skinner Auctioneers and Appraisers of Antiques and Fine Art Boston and Bolton, MA.

cockbeaded drawers, each visually divided into three panels by flame birch veneer outlined in stringing and banded mahogany veneer, flame birch veneer drop lane pendant centering veneered skirt, elongated French foot, orig brasses, old refinishing, 40-1/4" w, 21-1/8" d, 36" h 83,900.00

New Hampshire, c1810-15, attributed to Joseph Clark, Portsmouth or Greenland, birch inlaid, rectangular overhanging top with bow front, case of four cockbeaded drawers with mahogany veneer flanked by contrasting inlaid stringing and wavy birch panels, all bordered by mahogany cross-banding, flaring French feet, center rectangular drop panel of wavy birch bordered by checkered and contrasting inlaid banding, old refinishing, orig brasses, 39-1/2" w, 20-3/4" d, 38-3/4" h 8,200.00

New Hampshire, c1820-30, cherry, bird's eye maple, and mahogany, rectangular overhanging top, case with four cockbeaded graduated drawers outlined in stringing, shaped veneered skirt, inlay accents on over-turned legs, replaced brasses, 38-5/8" w, 19" d, 40-3/4" h..4,100.00

New Hampshire, Concord, early 19th C, bow front, mahogany veneer, bowed top with inlaid edge, conforming case with mahogany veneered drawers outlined with stringing, shaped skirt with central lunette inlay outlined in banding, flanked by French feet, old refinishing, orig brasses, imperfections, 39-3/4" w, 17-3/4" d, 37" h 4,990.00

New Hampshire, early 19th C, wavy birch, overhanging top with beaded edge, case with drawers with beaded edges, curving skirt, high bracket feet, orig brass, old refinishing, remnants of red paint, minor imperfections, 39-1/2" w, 18" d, 38" h 1,850.00

New Hampshire, early 19th C, bow front, mahogany and bird's eye maple veneer, bowed top with inlaid edge, case with four cockbeaded drawers, bird's eye maple veneer surrounded by crossbanded mahogany veneer, scrolled front skirt with side shaping, curving feet, orig brasses, old refinishing, minor imperfections, 39-3/4" w, 22" d, 37" h 9,775.00

New York, upstate, 1815-25, mahogany inlaid, case with cockbeaded drawers, bracket base, possibly orig brasses, old refinishing, imperfections, 45-1/2" d, 21" d, 39" h 1,725.00

New York, early 19th C, mahogany and mahogany veneer, crossbanded top, case with four drawers, brass pulls, French feet, 46-1/4" w, 23" d, 44-1/2" h 2,250.00

Ohio, attributed to North Jackson, Trumball County, decorated, poplar, orig red graining on yellow ground, ebonzied detail, well shaped scroll crest, case with four dovetailed drawers, half column pilasters, high turned feet, replaced hardware, some period brasses with embossed eagle heads, 41-3/4" w, 20-1/2" d, 53-1/2" h 7,150.00

Pennsylvania, c1790-1800, cherry inlaid, flat cove molded cornice with dart inlaid band around case with three cockbeaded short drawers and five cockbeaded graduated long drawers, flanked by inlaid lambrequin corners on inlaid bracket feet, replaced brasses, old refinishing, some loss to height, 40-1/2" w, 21" d, 60-3/4" h 3,500.00

Pennsylvania, c1800, tiger maple, rectangular overhanging top, case with two cockbeaded drawers over four graduated long drawers inlaid with diamond form escutcheons and stringing, flaring French feet, joined by shaped apron, refinished, replaced brasses, restoration, 38-1/2" w, 20-1/2" d, 53-1/2" h 4,200.00

Pennsylvania, c1810, bow front, inlaid figural cherry, oblong top with line inlaid edge, case with four graduated cockbeaded long drawers flanked by line inlaid canted corners, splayed bracket feet, patches to cockbeading, feet replaced, 41" w, 24-1/4" d, 38-1/2" h 1,200.00

Pennsylvania, western, c1815, bow front, mahogany inlaid, contrasting crossbanded veneer surrounds, case with four drawers, orig brasses, minor imperfections, 43-1/2" w, 23" d, 38-1/2" h...2,400.00

Pennsylvania, Lehigh County, c1820, bow front, cherry, shaped top with reeded edge, case with four cockbeaded long drawers, shaped apron, splayed bracket feet, 39-1/4" w, 22-1/4" d, 37-1/2" h 1,750.00

Rhode Island, c1815-20, mahogany inlaid, rectangular top with ovolo corners, case with four graduated cockbeaded drawers flanked by quarter engaged ring-turned reeded columns ending in vase and ring-turned legs, ball feet, joined by shaped skirt, brasses may be original and include portrait likeness of Napoleon, old refinishing, imperfections, 44" w, 23-3/4" d, 38-1/4" h..2,185.00

Vermont, 1815, paint decorated basswood, rectangular top, case with four graduated thumb-molded drawers, cutout feet, orig painted dec to simulate exotic wood bordered by stringing and crossbanding, shades of tan and light brown, orig oval brass pulls, signed "Henry Davist...Readsboro Feb...1815 $7.50," 41" w, 19" d, 42" h..............................7,500.00

Vermont or New York State, 1815-20, tiger maple veneer, rectangular top with tiger maple veneered edge, case with four cockbeaded veneered drawers, curving skirt flanked by angled feet, replaced brasses, old refinishing, imperfections, 45" l, 22-3/4" d, 46" h 2,875.00

Virginia, c1810, serpentine, walnut veneers, case with four drawers, inlaid, pine and poplar

Federal, Vermont or New York State, 1815-20, tiger maple veneer, rectangular top with tiger maple veneered edge, case of four cockbeaded veneered drawers, curving skirt flanked by angled feet, replaced brasses, old refinish, imperfections, 45" l, 22-3/4" d, 46" h, $2,875. Photo courtesy of Skinner Auctioneers and Appraisers of Antiques and Fine Art Boston and Bolton, MA.

secondary wood, period brasses stamped "H. J.," refinished, foot professionally restored, 38" w, 22-1/2" d, 40-1/2" h................................5,225.00

Virginia, c1810-15, walnut, molded edge top, case with four dovetailed cockbeaded drawers, splayed feet, pine secondary wood, replaced brass handles, refinished, 38-3/4" w, 43-1/4" h 1,200.00

Federal, late

When a style is referred to as "late," it means the style is similar to that of the period, but the piece was probably constructed after the date generally thought to end the period. This is easily explained when it is considered that craftsmen continued to make whatever style and forms that they had orders for, what was popular in their region.

America

Mahogany, rectangular top, open molded splashboard, case with four long drawers, turned legs, 41" w, 22" d, 52" h 475.00

Walnut, rectangular molded top, case with four long drawers, turned tapering legs, replaced brasses, 46" w, 21" d, 44" h 400.00

Federal-Style

Federal-Style indicates that the same type of design elements are used for this Federal-looking piece, but it is made by a modern manufacturer.

Kittinger, Old Dominion, pattern 2023 HC, molded top, case with four serpentine form long drawers, burl inlaid shaped skirt continuing into shaped legs, 37" w, 22" d, 34" h 500.00

French Restoration

Few examples of this interesting furniture style exist. The period was limited from c1830 to 1850. As the name implies, it was influenced by the French designers. It incorporates swirls, circles and flourishes.

America, c1840-50, mahogany veneer, case with four long drawers, carved pilasters, flat sides, paw feet 400.00

George III, late

George III and Georgian chests of drawers are included, even though they are English, as examples of what influenced American crafts-men. These examples all sold at American auctions recently, so it is apparent there is some interest in this furniture style.

English, early 19th C

Mahogany and inlay, rectangular molded top, case with two short drawers, central secret drawer over three graduated drawers, bracket feet, 52-1/4" w, 21-3/4" d, 39-1/2" h 4,350.00

Mahogany, bow front, bowed top, case with four graduated cockbeaded drawers, French feet, restorations, 41" w, 23" d, 34" h 1,035.00

Georgian

Determining whether these chests of drawers are English or American is quite difficult. Stylistically they fit the profile of Georgian furniture, but walnut would have been a more American choice of wood.

c1790 and later, bow front, mahogany, banded top above case fitted with two small drawers over three long graduated drawers, scalloped apron, bracket feet, 40-1/2" w, 20" d, 40-1/4" h..1,750.00

c1800 and later, walnut, banded top inset with burled oyster panels and inlaid with satinwood stringing, case fitted with three long graduated drawers inlaid en suite, bracket feet, 42" w, 20-1/2" d, 34-1/2" h 2,500.00

c1810, mahogany, fitted with flame veneered frieze above two short drawers over three long graduated drawers, bracket feet, 46" w, 20-1/2" d, 45" h 1,400.00

c1810, mahogany, rectangular top with reeded edge, case fitted with two short drawers over three long graduated drawers, bracket feet, 43" d, 22" d, 41-1/2" h 1,875.00

c1810, oak, top with molded edge, case fitted with two short drawers over three long graduated drawers, shaped bracket feet, 40-1/2"w, 20-3/4" d, 39" h 1,100.00

c1810 and later, mahogany, rectangular top with molded edge, case fitted with three long graduated drawers, bracket feet, 40" w, 20-1/2" d, 32" h...1,100.00

c1830, mahogany, rectangular top with molded edge, case fitted with two short drawers over three long graduated drawers, bracket feet, 38" w, 19-3/4" d, 38-1/2" h 900.00

c1840, blond mahogany, rectangular top with molded edge, case fitted with four long graduated drawers, shaped bracket feet, 43" w, 21-1/2" d, 42-1/2" h 1,400.00

Hepplewhite

The Hepplewhite period is often closely associated with the Federal period. The chests listed here show some similarities to that period, but feature even more inlays, more curving to the

Hepplewhite, serpentine, cherry with inlay, four dovetailed drawers with edge molding, choice matched flame grain veneer, scrolled apron, French feet, inlaid banding around top edge and base, and escutcheons, refinished, feet restored, replaced brasses, 37-1/4" w, 20-3/4" d, 40-1/2" h, $2,860. Also shown are brass and copper tea kettle, $300, Hepplewhite shaving mirror with serpentine front, inlaid mahogany, three dovetailed drawers, adjustable mirror, $360, canary child's mug and creamer, $220, clear Astral lamp (repairs), $2,310. Photo courtesy of Garth's Auctions, Inc., Delaware, OH.

case or feet. French feet and more elaborate brasses define the period.

America, bow front, cherry, facade of curly maple and mahogany veneer and inlay, four dovetailed drawers, banding around base, drawer edges, and top, inlaid diamond escutcheons and oval medallion on top drawer with urn, scrolled apron, French feet, turned mahogany pulls, old refinishing, some repairs, damage to veneer, top has been reworked, 43" w, 22" d, 39-1/2" h..........................3,500.00

America, bow front, cherry, front edge of bowed top has curly maple banding, case with four dovetailed drawers, shaped apron, high French feet, oval medallion on apron, stringing, and invected corners on drawers inlay, orig oval brasses with emb flowers and foliage, poplar secondary wood, old varnish finish, edge damage and age cracks in apron, old repair, 36" w, 20-3/4" d, 43-1/4" h 3,300.00

America, bow front, curly maple and cherry, line inlay, shaped apron, French feet, period brasses, 39-1/2" w, 21-1/2" d, 38" h 1,200.00

America, bow front, mahogany veneer, case with four dovetailed drawers with applied edge beading, French feet, old replaced period eagle brasses, dust shelves, edge and veneer damage, old repairs, 34-1/2" w, 19-1/2" d, 37" h 1,750.00

America, curly maple, case with four overlapping dovetailed drawers, chamfered corners, applied top end with inlaid stringing, scalloped apron with inlay, French feet, poplar secondary wood, replaced oval thistle brasses, refinished, 41-1/2" w, 21-1/2" d, 45-1/2" h................4,200.00

America, inlaid cherry, banded top edge with corner fans, case with four dovetailed drawers with cockbeading and stringing, high cutout feet, scrolled apron, banding and inlaid medallion on apron, old finish, replaced brasses, poplar secondary wood, some edge and veneer damage, 44" w, 25-1/4" d, 43-1/2" h 4,850.00

America, inlaid cherry, case with four graduated finely dovetailed drawers with stringing, chamfered corner posts with three line inlay, scalloped apron, French feet, banded walnut inlay around base, minor edge repairs, refinished, walnut secondary wood, minor repairs, 42" w, 21" d, 38-1/4" h..........................2,865.00

America, mahogany, inlay, case with five dovetailed drawers, applied edge beading, ogee feet, poplar secondary wood, replaced brasses, worn old French polish finish, pieced repairs to case, 37-1/2" w, 21-1/2" d, 45-1/2" h................1,250.00

Country, pine, red stain, solid bird's eye maple drawer fronts with natural finish, four dovetailed drawers, cut out feet and apron, old brass knobs, refinished, age cracks in front feet, 37-3/4" w, 35-3/4" h......................1,100.00

Middle Atlantic States, walnut, case with four drawers, foliate and double-line inlay in each top corner, top center foliate medallion, herringbone stem and barber pole inlay on edge with mahogany crossbanded on top edge and drawer fronts, chamfered quarter columns with vine and leaf inlay over cup with two green colored leaves, barber pole and herringbone inlay at base over orig French bracket feet, pine secondary wood, new brasses, refinished, partial restoration to bottom inlay, 38-1/2" w, 18-1/2" d, 38-1/2" h 4,200.00

Pennsylvania, walnut, molded edge top, case with four cockbeaded drawers, dovetailed case, French bracket feet, 39-1/2" w, 22-1/4" d, 34-1/2" h...3,250.00

Bow front, refinished cherry, figured cherry veneer drawer fronts and mahogany veneer along top edge, four dovetailed drawers with applied edge beading, French feet, replaced brasses, some damage to feet, 40" w, 22-3/4" d, 38-1/2" h...2,200.00

Mission

The term "Mission" and "Prairie" are used to describe the same time period. It is generally thought of as a little later than the American Arts & Crafts period, extending to the 1920s.

Frank Lloyd Wright, Heritage Henredon

No. 2000, chest of drawers, mahogany, case with six drawers and two cabinet drawers, Taliesin design top edges, cruciform base, orig finish, numbered, red decal, 37" w, 20" d, 53" h 2,500.00

No. 2000, dual dresser, mahogany, case with series of eleven drawers, recessed handles, bordered by Taliesin design, orig finish, red monogram and script signature, 62" w, 20" d, 29" h 3,100.00

Modernism-Era

Chests of drawers were not very popular with the designers in the 1950s. Most chests were sold en suite with bedroom suites. Sideboards and cabinets were a more popular storage form in this period.

Dunbar, Berne, IN, manufactured by mid-20th C, rectangular top, case with five graduated drawers, recessed handles, platform base, light finish, metal tag, scratches, wear, 28" l, 18" d, 31-1/4" h 865.00

Nakashima, George, c1957, walnut, block dovetail top, dowel construction, eight drawers, two walnut slab legs, orig finish, 72" w, 20" d, 32" h...6,000.00

Queen Anne

This design style is best thought of as curving. Chairs exhibit cabriole legs, and chests of drawers from this period often include carved scallops, reflecting the use of curves.

Country, attributed to Pennsylvania, cherry, molded edge top, case with four dovetailed overlapping drawers, apron drop, high bracket feet, cleaned down to old red, pine secondary wood, one front foot ended out, some edge damage, two backboards replaced, red color enhanced, 36" w, 17-3/4" d, 44" h 2,550.00

New England, southeastern, c1700, painted oak, cedar, and yellow pine, rect top with applied edge, case of four drawers each with molded fronts, chamfered mitered borders, separated by applied horizontal moldings, sides with two recessed vertical molded panels above single horizontal panel, base with applied molding, four turned ball feet, old red paint, minor imperfections, 37-3/4" w, 20-1/2" w, 35" h...26,450.00

New England, southeastern, c1760, tiger maple, flat molded cornice, case with two thumb-molded short drawers, four graduated long drawers, bracket feet, refinished, replaced brasses, 36" w, 19-1/4" d, 46" h 3,600.00

New England, c1780, maple, slightly projecting top, case with four graduated drawers, shaped skirt, short cabriole legs, pad feet, brass handles, refinished, 38-1/2" w, 20" d, 38-1/2" d..1,250.00

New England, 18th C, maple, flat molded top, case with two thumb-molded short drawers, four graduated long drawers, bracket feet, old refinishing, replaced brasses, restoration, 36" w, 18-3/4" d, 44-1/2" h 3,950.00

Queen Anne-Style

The Queen Anne style remained popular, but the delicate cabriole legs may not have appealed to designers in the later time frames.

c1820, walnut, later veneers, top quarter-veneered and with herringbone banding, case with short drawers, three long graduated drawers, banded en suite, bun feet, 41-1/2" w, 20-1/2" d, 39-1/2" h 1,000.00

c1820 and later, walnut, banded top quarter-veneered with oyster panels, case fitted with two short drawers over two long graduated drawers, all banded en suite, bun feet, 32-1/2" d, 18" d, 31" h...1,800.00

c1840 and later, walnut, banded top with elaborate concentric inlay and oyster veneered panels, case fitted with two short drawers over two long graduated drawers, all banded and veneered with like panels, bun feet, 38" w, 20-1/2" d, 33-1/2" h 2,000.00

Sheraton

Sheraton closely resembles Federal styling and is often used to refer to more country adaptations of that style.

America, bow front, mahogany and mahogany veneer, case with four drawers with applied edge beading, molded stiles with reeding, turned feet, pine secondary wood, old finish, orig oval brasses, wear and minor edge damage, filed age cracks in top, one foot with age crack, 41-3/8" w, 23-1/2" d, 38-1/2" h 1,100.00

America, cherry, rectangular top, case with four dovetailed drawers, solid ends, scalloped apron, ring-turned legs, poplar secondary wood, old refinishing, pierced repairs, edge damage, replaced brasses, 38" w, 21-1/2" d, 44-1/2" h..950.00

America, mahogany, rectangular top with cookie corners, shaped backsplash, three quartered reeded corner columns, shaped apron, turned feet, orig hardware, 42-1/2" w, 39-3/4" h..1,50.00

America, c1825, swell front, bird's eye maple, case with four cockbeaded graduated wide drawers, half-round columnar corners, short turned feet, panel sides, 41-1/2" w 2,650.00

Country, attributed to Stark County, OH, cherry, banded inlay around top edge, case with four dovetailed drawers with edge beading, scrolled apron, solid ends, turned feet, banded inlay around base, diamond inlaid escutcheons, old soft finish, replaced brasses, poplar secondary wood, 40" w, 19-1/4" d, 45-3/4" h..3,575.00

Country, attributed to Massachusetts, bow front, cherry with mahogany veneer facade, turned pilasters and biscuit corners, case with four dovetailed drawers with applied edge

Sheraton, New England, c1790-1810, pine, orig brownish red graining, stepback to with two dovetailed drawers, four dovetailed drawers, slender turned legs, crest missing, 39" w, 43-1/2" h, $1,100. Also shown are two mismatched pairs of hog-scraper candlesticks, $110 and $250, cut silhouette with full length portrait of man in top hat, ogee bird's eye veneer frame, $360, and gilded brass eagle, attached to stone base, $165. Photo courtesy of Garth's Auctions, Inc., Delaware, OH.

beading, high turned feet, pine secondary wood, replaced brasses, 41-1/4" w, 21-1/4" d, 40-1/2" h..3,200.00

Country, bow front, birch, reeded columns, turned feet, refinished, 42" w 900.00

Country, bow front, maple and cherry, curly and bird's eye veneer, case with four dovetailed drawers with applied edge beading, paneled ends, turned feet, scalloped apron, refinished, 39-3/4" w, 44" h 3,000.00

Country, cherry and curly maple, case with four dovetailed drawers with edge beading, pine end panels, turned feet, refinished, 47" w, 18-1/2" d, 45-1/4" h 750.00

Country, cherry, case with four dovetailed drawers with cockbeading, paneled ends, scrolled apron, turned feet, poplar and walnut secondary woods, refinished, 39-1/4" w, 19-3/4" d, 39-1/2" h 800.00

Country, maple and cherry, bow front, curly and bird's eye veneer, case with four dovetailed drawers with applied edge beading, paneled ends, turned feet, scalloped apron, refinished, 39-3/4" w, 44" h 2,550.00

Mahatanga Valley, cherry, old yellow and brown graining over red, rectangular top with molded edge, case with four overlapping dovetailed drawers, paneled ends, reeded stiles, turned feet, inlaid ivory escutcheons, pine secondary wood, brasses replaced with wooden knobs, 37-1/8" w, 19-1/4" d, 36-1/2" h................................1,200.00

New England, c1790-1810, pine, orig brownish red graining, stepback top with two dovetailed drawers, case with four dovetailed drawers, slender turned legs, crest missing, 39" w, 43-1/2" h 1,100.00

New England, c1820, pine, plain rectangular case fitted with three graduated drawers, painted overall with linear and curved watermelon and bead design in gray and shaded black over beige washed ground, hand cut scalloped apron base, bracket feet cut from side panels, replacement metal pulls, back inscribed "1827/Murcy Willey/Pike," attached written label "Mrs. Henry Willey, Flat Station, Ogle Co., Ill," 41-1/2" w, 17" d, 45-1/2" h 16,100.00

Ohio, c1820-30, walnut, case with four graduated drawers, scratch bead and inlaid diamond escutcheons, double lined inlay on stiles

Sheraton, New England, c1820, pine, plain rectangular case, fitted with three graduated drawers, painted overall with linear and curved watermelon and bead design in gray and shaded black over beige washed ground, hand cut scalloped apron base, bracket feet cut from side panels, replacement metal pulls, back inscribed, "1827/Murcy Willey/Pike," attached written label "Mrs. Henry Willey, Flat Station, Ogle Co., Ill.," 41-1/2" w, 17" d, 45-1/2" h, $16,100. Photo courtesy of Butterfields.

and on top board, white pine secondary wood, 41-1/2" w, 20" d, 46-1/4" h 1,650.00

Pennsylvania, cherry, inlay, top section with rounded top and five dovetailed drawers, center doors with star inlay and three interior drawers, base with seven dovetailed drawers, paneled ends, scrolled apron, turned feet, brass pulls, old finish, poplar and oak secondary woods, some edge damage to feet, repairs to base, mismatched top, 41-1/2" w, 21" d, 69-3/4" h...3,025.00

Pennsylvania or Ohio, poplar, old red finish, two small drawers over three graduated dovetailed drawers with edge beading, turned feet, scrolled front and side aprons, paneled ends, replaced brass pulls, 33-1/4" w, 19-3/4" d, 40-3/4" h..3,750.00

Virginia, c1810, serpentine, walnut veneers, case with four drawers, inlaid, broken front,

period brasses stamped "H. J.," pine and poplar secondary wood, refinished feet professionally restored, 38" w, 22-1/2" d, 40-1/2" h 4,900.00

Sheraton-Style

Like many other popular styles, Sheraton-influenced pieces were made well after the period ended. This example takes the veneered drawer fronts and adds columns, an element more closely associated with Classical.

America, mid-19th C, bow front, inlaid mahogany, case with four banded drawers, circular mahogany pulls, flanked by ring-turned round reeded column supports, 46" w, 23-1/2" d, 40-1/4" h...2,750.00

America, early-20th C, mahogany veneered drawer fronts and top, case with five graduated drawers, flat fronts with bowed centers flanked by twist carved three-quarter columns ending in leaf carved pegs, pierced brasses with bail handles, mirror missing, 44" w, 22" d, 46-1/2" h 550.00

Victorian

Victorian chests of drawers are typically thought of as having lots of carvings, moldings, and applied elements. Some types of Victorian are more architectural in nature.

America, rosewood, ivory inlaid, rectangular top, case with four short and four long drawers, free standing reeded columns, inlaid base, turned feet, restoration on base molding, 51-1/2" w, 20-3/4" d, 43" h 6,500.00

America, rosewood, ivory inlaid, rectangular top, case with four short and four long drawers, free standing reeded columns, inlaid base, turned feet, restoration on lower left base molding, 41-1/2" w, 20-1/4" d, 45" h..............5,775.00

America, serpentine front, poplar, mahogany veneer facade, serpentine top drawer, two serpentine stepback drawers, case with five dovetailed drawers, applied beading, worn finish, 40" w, 19-3/4" d, 47" h...........................330.00

America, walnut, figured wood drawer fronts, applied moldings and carvings, two stepback handkerchief drawers, case with three dovetailed drawers, casters, mirror missing, 38-1/2" w, 17-3/4" d, 41-1/2" h.................................. 420.00

Pennsylvania, Soap Hollow, cherry, reddish stain, black ebonized trim, rounded edge rectangular top, case with six dovetailed drawers with edge beading, paneled ends, turned feet, scrolled apron, locks with shield shaped escutcheons, replaced wooden knobs, poplar secondary wood, may have had crest, 36-3/4" w, 44-1/2" h 2,750.00

Eastlake, curly walnut, burl veneer, carved detail, scrolled crest, case with four dovetailed drawers, two handkerchief drawers, well detailed molded panel fronts, refinished, 39" w, 17-1/2" d, 46" h 750.00

Gothic Revival, Cottage Style, MA, late 19th C, pine, pediment and molded scalloped cornice over rectangular mirror flanked by frame with candle plateaus, shelf under mirror, case with four drawers, brown and orange comb-graining, black and gold accent striping on olive green, rose and gold floral motif on top, painted round reserve with landscape scene on front, casters, orig brass and paint, 38" w, 18-3/4" d, 76" h 950.00

Renaissance Revival, c1870, walnut and burl walnut, gray veined marble top, stepped base, case with two small drawers and three

Victorian, Rococo Revival, oak, burl veneer, marble top, pierce carved crest with foliage and grape clusters, inset mirror, four bracket shelves, two dovetailed drawers over two doors, applied carvings and fruit, door hardware replaced, wear, applied carvings have edge damage, silvering worn on mirror, 54" w, 18-1/2" d, 96-1/2" h, $2,695. Also shown are pair of Quimper swan shaped bowls, $690, and Quimper hexagonal plates, $270 for set of four, Photo courtesy of Garth's Auctions, Inc., Delaware, OH.

long drawers with paneled fronts, brass strapwork pulls, intricate carved mirror frame back with four candleholders, molded plinth base with inset paneled sides, casters, 46-1/4" w, 22-1/2" d, 37-1/4" h 1,120.00

William and Mary

The rectangular lines associated with William and Mary are clearly illustrated with this chest of drawers. Using several different kinds of wood for chests of drawers also allowed the craftsman to use woods readily available, something that was important in the early settling of America.

America, c1700, walnut, rectangular, case with four graduated drawers, bulbous onion feet, replaced brasses, restoration, 36-1/2" w, 24-1/4" d, 36" h 2,285.00

America, bachelor's, burl veneer, case with five dovetailed drawers, pull-out shelf, worn finish, veneer damage, replaced base molding, turned feet, and backboards, orig brasses, 30" w, 19" d, 35" h 1,980.00

America, oak, molded edge top, case with five dovetailed drawers, facade with applied moldings, bracket feet, old worn finish, orig engraved brasses, repairs, feet replaced, 36" w, 35-3/4" h 1,350.00

Massachusetts, southern, or Rhode Island, tiger maple, graduated drawer construction, two over four drawers, applied moldings to top and bottom, turned turnip feet, old grunge finish, three escutcheon plates present, rest of hardware missing, some repair, 36-1/4" w, 18-1/4" d, 48" h 2,950.00

New England, southeastern, c1700, painted oak, cedar, and yellow pine, joined, rectangular top with applied molded edge above case with four drawers each with molded fronts and chamfered mitered borders, separated by applied horizontal panels above a single horizontal panel, base with applied molding and four turned ball feet, old red paint, old replaced feet, 37-3/4" w, 20-1/2" d, 35" h 13,800.00

Pennsylvania, c1720-40, walnut, rectangular top, applied cove molding, two short drawers over three graduated long drawers, molded base, compressed ball-turned feet, 39-1/4" w, 21-3/4" d, 40" h 40,000.00

Chests of Drawers, Other

Several forms of chests of drawers are found in the antique marketplace. Among these are highboys, lowboys, chests on chests, and tall chests. Included in this section are all of these types of chests of drawers and more.

Many of these chests were made in two or more pieces. This was done to facilitate moving the large pieces and it was probably easier for the craftsman, too. While it is quite normal to see highboys and other large chests in museums and restored historic properties, it is important to remember that these were often originally made for storage and intended to be used in bedrooms, as well as other rooms. Because architecture has changed as much as furniture styles, consideration had to be given to how these big pieces would get up stairs, etc. Look for signs of carrying handles on many of the large two-piece chests.

As in bedrooms, the ability to "show-off" one's important furniture was important to our colonial ancestors. These massive pieces of furniture were clear signs of one's wealth and statue in the community. The best hardware was used, careful attention was paid to the maintenance of these large case pieces, too. With the current trend for original finishes in today's antique marketplace, what we often fail to remember is that many times these pieces were made of lesser woods then the fine mahogany used so often in smaller chests of drawers. Elaborate finishes were created trying to duplicate the graining of mahogany and other expensive woods. Many of these original finishes have been removed over the years. How much the original finish adds to the provenance and value of the piece is very much determined by a potential buyer.

Some of the early craftsmen who created these masterpieces did sign their work. Look closely at the backboards or in drawers or even under drawers for such a signature. Finding a documented craftsman's name will add greatly to the value. As in other types of furniture, styles and woods used varied from one geographic region to another. By carefully studying these changes, auctioneers, collectors, appraisers, antique dealers, and curators are able to discern where a particular piece originated.

Also see Chests of Drawers for similar pieces of furniture, including dressers.

Apothecary Chest

Before the advent of pharmacies and easily available medicines, home owners frequently stored basic medical preparations and herbs to treat illnesses. These chests are known as "Apothecary" chests. Look for chests with small compartments; some may retain labels or stains indicating what their original contents may have been.

America, chestnut, pine side panels, top-lift compartment, seven drawers, Rockingham pulls, short turned feet, 17-1/4" w, 8" d, 27-1/2" h...725.00

America, pine, applied lid edge and base moldings, nine dovetailed drawers with turned pulls, turned feet, worn refinishing, stains, minor repairs, 19-3/4" w, 10-1/2" d, 23-3/4" h...2,500.00

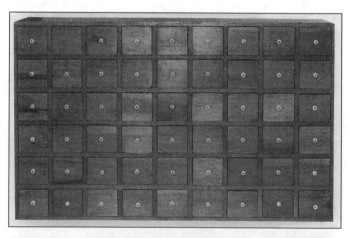

Apothecary, country, poplar, 54 drawers with porcelain pulls, late wire nail construction, refinished, 59-1/4" w, 13" d, 37" h, $1,210. Photo courtesy of Garth's Auctions, Inc., Delaware, OH.

America, pine, old dark repaint with red and blue showing underneath, one board door with applied molding, four dovetailed drawers with divided interior, molded edge top and base, turned feet, pine, cedar, and mahogany secondary woods, some edge damage, 9" w, 6-3/8" d, 11-7/8" h 2,200.00

America, pine, eighteen overlapping drawers with locks, old mellow refinishing, feet and backboard added, replacement knobs, repairs, 45" w, 13-3/4" d, 24" h............................825.00

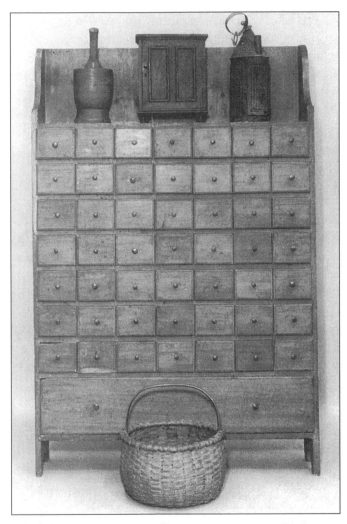

Apothecary, New England, pine, orig bluish-gray paint, high back with shelf, forty-nine small drawers over one large drawer, all with molded overlapping edge and brass pulls, some with old penciled or ink labels, bootjack feet, orig brass knobs of varying sizes, 37-3/4" w, 19" d, 57-1/2" h, $24,200. Also shown are turned mortar and pestle, $275; small apothecary chest, pine, old dark repaint with red and blue showing underneath, one board door with applied molding, 11-7/8" h, $2,200; punched tin candle lantern, $300, woven splint basket, $550. Photo courtesy of Garth's Auctions, Inc., Delaware, OH.

America, poplar, nine drawers, wooden pulls, wire nail construction, old red paint, one back board replaced, 7-1/2" w, 11" d, 11" h 600.00

America, poplar, nineteen drawers with square nail construction, old finish, some damage to back boards, 21" w, 7" d, 24-1/2" h 1,045.00

New England, pine, orig bluish-gray paint, high back with shelf, forty-nine small drawers over one large drawer, all with molded overlapping edge and brass pulls, some with old penciled or ink labels, bootjack feet, orig brass knobs of varying sizes, 37-3/4" w, 19" d, 57-1/2" h..24,200.00

Butler's Chest

This unique style of chest features a desk section for a butler's use. Usually the section is hidden behind a drawer front that discreetly hides this extra function of the chest. Also see Secretaries, Sideboards, and Desks for other examples of furniture fitted with compartments for a butler's use.

Classical, America, c1835, mahogany, fall front, fitted interior, five drawers with brass escutcheons, pair of cupboard doors, finely carved acanthus leaf and scroll designed columns, hairy paw feet, 53-1/4" w, 33-3/4" d, 53" h...2,000.00

Chest on Chest

Chests on chests are easy to identify, as they appear just as their name implies, one chest of drawers stacked upon another chest of drawers. Such a structure afforded the owner lots of storage. Most chest on chests feature a molding or some way of making sure the two chests mated together. Watch for "married" chest on chests, where both the chests may be vintage but did not start life together.

Chippendale

America, c1790, mahogany, two sections, upper section with dentillated cornice above case fitted with two short drawers over three long graduated drawers, flanked on either side by canted pilaster, lower section fitted with three long graduated drawers, bracket feet, 43" w, 21-1/2" d, 67-1/2" h.......8,500.00

America, c1795-1810, cherry, molded cornice, dovetailed cases, nine dovetailed overlapping drawers, scalloped apron, bracket feet, pine secondary wood, old mellow refinishing, interiors of drawers varnished, old brasses in orig holes, repairs, age cracks, 77-3/4" h 13,200.00

Connecticut, attributed to London County, cherry, two sections, upper section with bonnet top, carved rosettes, flame finial on shell plinth, seven drawers, carved shells on drawers in top and base. Base section with five dovetailed overlapping drawers, scrolled and carved apron that conforms to curve of four cabriole legs, ball and claw feet, replaced brasses, pine secondary wood, old mellow finish, signed "A. H. Landon," on upper right hand drawer, 37-1/4" w, 21" x 40" cornice, 84" h.................................49,500.00

Massachusetts or New Hampshire, c1760-80, maple, two sections, upper section with flat cove molded cornice, case fitted with five thumb molded graduated drawers, lower case of four thumb molded graduated drawers, bracket base with center drop pendant, old bail brass pulls, refinished, minor repairs, 36" w, 18-1/2" d, 76" h 14,950.00

Massachusetts or New Hampshire, mid 18th C, maple, two sections, upper section with flat cove molded, dovetailed case with graduated

Chest on Chest, Chippendale, Pennsylvania, c1750-80, walnut, highly figured drawer fronts, rectangular flat top with molded cornice, three thumb-molded drawers over seven graduated thumb-molded drawers, molded skirt ending in ogee bracket feet, poplar and cedar secondary woods, feet replaced, 41-1/2" w, 23-1/2" d, 76" h $8,960. Photo courtesy of Samuel T. Freeman & Co., Philadelphia, PA.

thumb-molded drawers, lower section with bracket base, old refinishing, orig brasses, 38-1/2" w, 18-1/2" d, 76-1/2" h 12,250.00

Massachusetts or New Hampshire, 18th C, married, maple, cornice molding above upper case of five graduated thumb-molded drawers, lower case of four graduated thumb-molded drawers, heavy molded base, arris knees, ball and claw feet, replaced brasses, refinished, 38-1/2" w, 17" d, 77-1/2" h 5,750.00

New England, mahogany two sections, upper section with bonnet top, central urn finial on column, concave inlaid fan central drawer flanked by two small drawers, over four graduated drawers, three graduated drawers in base section, ogee bracket feet, some early drawer repairs, 37" w, 21" d, 85" h 12,100.00

Pennsylvania, c1750-80, walnut, highly figured drawer fronts, rectangular flat top with molded cornice, three thumb-molded drawers over seven graduated thumb-molded drawers, molded skirt ending in ogee bracket feet, poplar and cedar secondary woods, feet replaced, 41-1/2" w, 23-1/2" d, 76" h 8,960.00

Pennsylvania, Lancaster County, mid 18th C, walnut, boldly detailed, molded cornice, top case with seven dovetailed overlapping drawers, fluted quarter columns on top and base, one dovetailed drawer in base, base moldings, ogee feet, old finish, some edge damage, wear, 47-3/4" w, 21" d, 65" h............. 14,300.00

Chippendale-Style, walnut with inlay, molded cornice arched to accommodate three arched top drawers, three long drawers with stringing, three dovetailed overlapping drawers in base, cabriole legs with small feet, shaped apron with scalloping, pine secondary wood, refinished, some additions to top, base later reconstruction, replaced brasses, 39" w, 20-1/2" d, 67-6/8" h 1,760.00

Georgian, Hepplewhite-Style, c1790, mahogany, dentillated cornice above case fitted with two short drawers over three long graduated drawers, bracket feet, 41-1/2" w, 22" d, 73-1/4" h 4,500.00

Queen Anne

Connecticut, c1780, carved cherry, two sections, upper section with molded and scrolled crest with carved urn finials, dentil molding, three thumb-molded short drawers, central short drawer with pinwheel carving, four graduated long drawers, flanking engaged quarter columns; lower section: three graduated drawers, flanked by engaged quarter columns gadrooning below skirt with pinwheel carved pendant, four cabriole legs ending in pad feet, replaced brasses, restored, 37-1/2" w, 18-1/2" d, 48" h 9,200.00

Pennsylvania or Delaware Valley, walnut, crown molded cornice, fluted chamfered corners, dovetailed base, moldings around base, and sections, bracket feet, worn orig finish, originally had pin brasses, Chippendale period bat-wing bail brass replacements, pine and oak secondary woods, carved date inside bottom of upper section "1738+3 mo.," some edge damage on back edge of top chest, 22-3/8" x 40-3/4" cornice, 37-3/4" w, 69-1/4" h 42,500.00

Queen Anne-Style, c1860 and later, walnut, two sections, upper section filled with plain frieze over two short drawers, two long drawers, all banded and inlaid with oyster veneer panels, lower section fitted with two short drawers over three long graduated drawers, all banded in inlaid en suite, bun feet, 36-1/2" w, 16-1/2" d, 73" h 3,000.00

Regency, c1820, mahogany, over-hanging cornice with applied ebonzied rings, case fitted with two short drawers over three long graduated drawers, lower section with modified Greek key banding over three long graduated drawers, shaped bracket feet with scroll and foliate carvings, 48" w, 21" d, 78-1/4" h 3,850.00

Commodes

Commodes are small chests of drawers, often with a cupboard door or lift-lid, where a chamber pot could discreetly be stored between usage. Other items needed for personal hygiene could also be stored in this type of chest.

Classical, America, country, mid-19th C, mahogany, lift top, single drawer cupboard base, 29" w, 16-1/2" d, 32" h 200.00

Classical-Style, c1860, bedside, ormolu-mounted mahogany, fitted with plain frieze

Chest on Frame, Chippendale, Pennsylvania, attributed to Lancaster County, walnut, top dovetailed case with wide molded cornice, seven dovetailed drawers, fluted quarter columns on top and base, single dovetailed overlapping drawer in base, base moldings, detailed ogee feet, old finish, pine secondary wood, replaced brasses, some edge damage, drawer edge repair, 40-3/4" w, 21" d, 65" h, $14,300. Photo courtesy of Garth's Auctions, Inc., Delaware, OH.

above paneled cupboard door, flanked to either side by engraved pilasters headed by ormolu maiden's heads and ending in block feet, 20-1/2" w, 15-1/4" d, 33" h 750.00

Federal

America, c1800, inlaid mahogany, converted to lidded chest, outset rectangular lid opening to storage well, front with two simulated drawer fronts, square-section tapering legs, 19-1/2" w, 16-1/2" d, 18" h 600.00

Massachusetts, Salem, c1800-15, mahogany, demilune top, conforming case, central cockbeaded molded drawer flanked by similar hinged compartment drawers, double cupboard doors with molded panels, three sliding trays, flanked by similar cupboard doors, shelves interior, scalloped apron, French feet, 55" w, 32" d, 40" h 48,000.00

Georgian, c1820, mahogany, bedside, top with full scalloped gallery, fitted with three carrying handles, lift-top compartment, lower section now converted to deep drawer, sq legs, 21" w, 19" d, 32" h 2,200.00

Victorian

America, walnut, single dovetailed drawer with applied moldings, double doors, scrolled apron, cutout feet, applied fruit and foliage pulls, back replaced, crest loose, some refinishing, 31" w, 15-3/4" d, 29-3/4" h..........220.00

Eastlake, walnut, three drawers, single door, marble top, backsplash missing, 30-1/2" w, 14" d, 27-3/4" h 350.00

Chest on Frame, Queen Anne, Newburyport, 1750-80, maple, cornice molding above upper case of four graduated drawers, lower case with one drawer, central fan carved drop pendant, four cabriole legs ending in high pad feet, old refinished surface, replaced brass, imperfections, 36" w, 15-1/2" d, 56-1/2" h, $8,100. Photo courtesy of Skinner Auctioneers and Appraisers of Antiques and Fine Art Boston and Bolton, MA.

Highboy

This popular style of high chests of drawers was first popularized in England. However, it did not take long for American craftsmen to start designing and creating exquisite examples of impressive chests of drawers. As the name implies, the chest towers to the ceiling, some with high bonnets and decorative cresting, while others have flat tops with decorative moldings. The bases usually contain additional drawers and are raised up on legs that help determine the furniture style. Like well-made desks and secretaries, some highboys have been found to be hiding secret compartments. Other names for highboys include chest on frame and chest over drawer. Before purchasing a highboy, carefully examine it. Pull out all the drawers and see that all the dovetailing is exactly the same. Drawers should move in and out smoothly. Allow for some shrinkage of the wood and wear through the years. Check to see if all the brasses are of the same period.

Centennial: Because early highboys were often expensive, stylistic copies were made through the years. Many were created about the time of the Philadelphia Centennial, c1876. This furniture style is identified by use of lesser woods, some decorative elements of the period being copied, plus often other enhancements, too.

Chippendale-Style

New England, c1876, mahogany, flame finials, central fan carved drawer flanked by two small thumb-molded drawers over four graduated thumb-molded drawers, butterfly brasses with bail handles, lower section with two thumb-molded drawers over three drawers, central one being fan carved, cabriole legs, claw and ball feet, finials repaired, 41-1/2" w, 19-3/4" d, 87" h...............2,250.00

Pennsylvania, Philadelphia, early 20th C, mahogany, scroll molded top with pinwheel terminals and three flame urn finials, shell carved drawer flanked by two small drawers, three thumb-molded drawers, frame base with molded edge, one drawer over shell carved drawer flanked by two smaller fluted quarter columns, scalloped skirt with shell carving, cabriole legs with carved knees, claw and ball feet, one chipped drawer front, 39" w, 20-1/2" d, 82" h 1,225.00

Chippendale: Most highboys available in the antiques marketplace are from the Chippendale or Queen Anne period. It was a terrific way to display wealth, while having a functional piece of furniture for storage purposes. Architects of this time period did not include many closets in homes. Look for elaborate skirts, cabriole legs, and claw and ball feet. Some examples are found with other variations. Drawer configurations vary slightly from region to region.

America, third quarter 18th C, walnut, upper section with outset cavetto cornice over front with arrangement of three short over two half over three long graduated drawers, lower section with waist molding over single long drawer, drawer fronts with overlapping molding, shaped skirt continuing into cabriole legs with claw and ball feet, secondary woods poplar, white pine and yellow pine, 43-1/2" w, 23" d, 74-1/2" h 4,900.00

Connecticut, attributed to New London County, Colchester area, third quarter 18th C, cherry, bonnet top, top with architectural designs with fluted pilasters, molded and dentilated goosenecks with relief caved rosettes, flame finial on shell plinth, three small drawers over four dovetailed graduated overlapping drawers, carved shells on two drawers, base with five dovetailed overlapping drawers, four cabriole legs, scrolled carved apron which conforms to curve of cabriole legs, claw and ball feet, old mellow finish, replaced brasses in orig holes, pine secondary wood, sgd "A. H. Landon" on upper right hand drawer, probably an unrecorded journeyman in the Benjamin Burnham-Samuel Loomis shop, 37-1/4" w, 21" w, 84" h...........49,500.00

Connecticut, curly maple, dovetailed case, molded cornice, eight overlapping dovetailed drawers, scalloped drop and chip carving, ogee feet, old worn refinishing, replaced brasses, 40-1/4" w, 20-1/2" d, 81" h..................16,000.00

Massachusetts, attributed to Eliakim Smith, Haldey, c1760, carved cherry, molded bonnet top with three turned finials above cockbeaded case, central fan-carved drawer flanked by short drawers, four graduated drawers below, all flanked by vine-carved pilasters on stop-fluted bases, lower cockbeaded case of long drawer and central fan-carved drawer below flanked by short drawers with valanced apron and two drop pendants joining four cabriole legs, old refinish, brasses may be original, legs cut off, 39" w, 19-1/4" d, 76" h..............................23,000.00

New England, c1770-80, maple, two sections, upper section with flat top, molded cornice, top drawer faced to simulate five drawers with pinwheel carved center drawers, lower section with two long drawers, one long drawer faced to simulate three short drawers, angular cabriole legs, claw and ball feet, 37-1/2" w, 18-1/2" d, 70" h...9,250.00

New England, 18th C, carved cherry, serpentine cove molding above upper case of thumb-molded drawers, central one fan carved, lower case with similar drawers, central fan carved drawer, skirt with front and side shaping, cabriole legs, pad feet, some replaced brasses, refinished, repairs, missing finials and pendants, 38" w, 19-1/2" d, 84" h.............37,950.00

Pennsylvania, c1750-80, walnut, rectangular molded top, three drawers, molded base, cabriole legs, ball and claw feet, entire frame base and legs old replacements, replaced brasses, old finish, patched repairs, 39-1/2" w, 22-1/4" d, 56-3/4" h............920.00

Pennsylvania, Philadelphia, c1750-80, walnut, swan neck cresting with flower head terminals, carved shell and foliate shell, fluted quarter columns, scroll carved apron, acanthus carved cabriole legs, claw and ball feet, 44" w, 95" h...............................7,200.00

Queen Anne: Queen Anne highboys can be as majestic as those found in the Chippendale period. Look for flat molded cornices and tops rather than the bonnet tops found in the Chippendale period. The feet of Queen Anne highboys tend to be more delicate than the claw and ball of the Chippendale period.

America, c1760, walnut, flat molded cornice, straight front, three small over five wide graduated thumb-molded drawers, brass bail handles and block plates, flanked by quarter-reeded columnar sides, lower section with

Highboy, Chippendale, Connecticut, attributed to New London County, Colchester area, third quarter 18th C, cherry, bonnet top, top with architectural designs with fluted pilasters, molded and dentilated goosenecks with relief caved rosettes, flame finial on shell plinth, three small drawers over four dovetailed graduated overlapping drawers, carved shells on two drawers, base with five dovetailed overlapping drawers, four cabriole legs, scrolled carved apron which conforms to curve of cabriole legs, claw and ball feet, old mellow finish, replaced brasses in orig holes, pine secondary wood, sgd "A. H. Landon" on upper right hand drawer, probably an unrecorded journeyman in the Benjamin Burnham-Samuel Loomis shop, 37-1/4" w, 21" w, 84" h, $49,500. Photo courtesy of Garth's Auctions, Inc., Delaware, OH.

shaped apron cabriole legs, trifid feet, 43" w, 22-1/2" d, 69-1/4" h...........................9,500.00

America, maple, curly facade, molded cornice, top dovetailed case with seven overhanging dovetailed drawers, four overlapping dovetailed drawers in base, scrolled apron, cabriole legs with trifid feet, orig brasses, refinished, pine secondary wood, base reworked, several brasses incomplete, one escutcheon missing, 35" w, 20-7/8" d, 70-1/4" h..........................7,500.00

America, maple, flat top, six short and five long drawers, fan carved upper and lower drawer, shaped apron, cabriole legs with duck feet, refinished, replaced hardware, 32" w, 20-1/4" d, 73-1/2" h.............15,500.00

American, walnut with figured veneer, herringbone cross banding on drawers, applied moldings, top: molded cornice, dovetailed

case, five dovetailed drawers, scrolled apron with turned drops and three dovetailed drawers, cabriole legs, duck feet, old refinishing, replaced brasses, cornice and molding between sections replaced, facade veneer has damage and restoration, apron drops replaced, other repairs, 35-1/2" w, 22" x 39-3/4" cornice, 21-1/2" d, 38-1/2" w base, 64-1/4" h...3,300.00

Connecticut or Massachusetts, c1760, maple, flat top with molded cornice, five thumb-molded graduated drawers, set into lower section with long thumb-molded drawer over three short drawers, valanced apron, cabriole legs ending in pad feet on platforms, orig brasses, old refinish, minor imperfections, 37-1/2" w, 70-1/2" h 18,400.00

Country, maple, top with dovetailed case, molded cornice, six dovetailed overlapping drawers, three dovetailed drawers in base, scrolled apron, cabriole legs, duck feet, refinished, repairs, mismatched, cornice replaced, molding between sections replaced, brasses replaced, 36-1/2" w, 69-3/4" h...........3,850.00

Country, walnut, dovetailed chest, seven dovetailed overlapping drawers, inlaid initials "M. E." on top drawer, base with scalloped apron, cabriole legs, and duck feet, repairs to drawers, cornice replaced, brasses replaced, replaced base, refinished, 40-1/2" w, 20-1/4" d, 58-1/2" h.........1,650.00

Country, walnut facade, maple legs, pine sides, molded cornice, dovetailed case, seven molded edge dovetailed drawer, scrolled apron, cabriole legs, duck feet, orig base, refinished, replaced cornice, 34" w, 19-1/2" d, 56" h................................5,000.00

Massachusetts, c1730-50, figured walnut veneer, cornice molding above blind frieze drawer, two thumb-molded short drawers, three graduated long drawers, lower section with one long and three small drawers, flat arched cyma-curved skirt, drawers with figured walnut veneer outline in herringbone veneer above cabriole legs ending in pad feet, old darkened surface, old replaced brasses, repairs, 34-1/2" w, 18-1/4" d, 70" h.................19,950.00

Massachusetts, c1750, cherry, two sections, cornice molding above upper case of five graduated drawers, lower case with three small drawers, cabriole legs ending in pad feet, old refinish, old replaced brass, repairs, 34-1/2" w, 17-1/2" d, 64" h...............19,550.00

Massachusetts, Newburyport, 1750-80, maple, two sections, cornice molding above upper case of four graduated drawers, lower case with one drawer, central fan carved drop pendant, four cabriole legs ending in high pad feet, old refinished surface, replaced brass, imperfections, 36" w, 15-1/2" d, 56-1/2" h..........................8,100.00

Massachusetts, c1760, maple, two sections, upper section with flat molded cornice, case with two thumb-molded short drawers, four graduated long drawers; lower case with one long drawer over three short drawers, four cabriole legs, pad feet on platforms, valanced apron, replaced brasses, old refinish, imperfections, 38" w, 21" d, 72" h....9,775.00

Massachusetts, c1760, maple, two sections, upper section with flat molded cornice, case with two thumb-molded short drawers, and four long graduated drawers, base with three small drawers, shaped apron with two drop pendants, cabriole legs, pad feet, refinished, 35-3/4" w, 22" d, 69-1/2" h 9,625.00

Massachusetts, c1760, maple, two sections, top with overhanging cornice and two short drawers, above four graduated thumb-molded long drawers, lower section fitted with mid-molding and one long drawer above two short drawers, valanced apron with acorn pendants joining cabriole legs, ending on hocked pad feet on platforms, replaced brasses, old refinish, restored, 38" w, 19" d, 72-1/2" h 8,100.00

Massachusetts, c1760, tiger maple, two sections, upper section with flat molded cornice, case with four thumb-molded graduated drawers, base with long drawer and central fan carved concave drawer flanked by drawers, cabriole legs, valanced apron with two turned drop pendants, old refinish, orig brasses, 37-3/4" w, 16-1/2" d, 69-1/2" h 29,750.00

Massachusetts, Salem, c1760-75, carved walnut, cornice molding above three small drawers, central one with fan-carving, four

thumb-molded graduated drawers, lower case with one long drawer above three small drawers, central one fan-carved, scrolled skirt, cabriole legs ending in arris pad feet, old brasses, refinished, two replaced moldings, 37" w, 19-3/4" d, 72-1/4" h................16,100.00

Massachusetts, c1770, maple and birch, two sections, top with flat molded cornice, five thumb-molded graduated drawers, set into lower section of single thumb-molded drawer over fan carved central drawer flanked by short drawers, cabriole legs, pad feet joined by valanced concave carved skirt, brasses appear to be original, old refinish, repairs, 38-1/4" w, 19" d, 73-1/4" h................10,350.00

Massachusetts, North Shore, 18th C, walnut and maple, cove molding, five graduated thumb-molded drawers, lower case with small drawers centered by fan-carved drawer, shaped skirt, cabriole legs, pad feet, some old brasses, old refinish, restoration, 37" w, 19-3/4" d, 72" h 8,100.00

Massachusetts, 18th C, cherry and maple, molded cornice, nine dovetailed overlapping drawers in top, four in base, scrolled apron with block carving that conforms to carved fan on center drawer, cabriole legs, duck feet, replaced Ball & Ball brasses, refinished, several repairs, two sets of apron drops included, 35-1/2" w, 76-3/4" h..........8,525.00

Massachusetts, 18th C, carved tiger maple, flat top with molded cornice, upper case with four graduated thumb-molded drawers, lower case of similar drawers, one long over three short, center fan-carved drawer, flat arched skirt with drop pendants, cabriole legs ending in pad feet, old refinish, some replaced brasses, two rear legs pieced, small piecing to front pads, 35" w, 18-1/2" d, 69-1/4" h........................18,400.00

Massachusetts, mid-18th C, salmon-red painted pine and maple, molded hinged top, double arch molded case, single drawer, applied molding at base, shaped skirt joining four cabriole legs, pad feet on platforms, orig engraved brasses, 35-1/2" w, 16" d, 40-1/2" h.....................................54,625.00

New England, c1740-60, cherry, flat top, step molded overhanging cornice, four wide graduated drawers, base with one wide drawer over three small drawers, center fan carved, scalloped skirt with two pendant drops, cabriole legs, pad feet, later butterfly brasses, one drawer front chipped, two repaired, 40" w, 20-1/8" d, 70-1/2" h..................................... 16,800.00

New England, c1740-60, cherry, flat top, step molded overhanging cornice, five graduated drawers over molded base with one long drawer over three drawers, fluted chamfered corners, shaped skirt with fish tail center ,cabriole legs, pad feet, 44" w, 21" d, 73" h.................................. 11,550.00

New England, c1740-60, mahogany, bonnet top, three flame finials on urn plinths, carved rosettes, three small drawers with center carved fan over four graduated drawers, molded mid section over long drawer over three small drawers with center fan carved, straight apron with center drop roundel and two pendants, cabriole legs, 40" w, 20" d, 81" h.................................... 11,500.00

New England, c1750, cherry, two sections, upper section with flat molded cornice, cove molded corners, bow straight front, four graduated thumb-molded drawers, lower section with

Highboy, Queen Anne, New Hampshire, curly birch, two sections, upper portion with detailed molded cornice, dovetailed case, five dovetailed graduated overlapping drawers; lower portion with four dovetailed overlapping drawers, well developed blocked and carved fan, scrolled apron with acorn drops, cabriole legs, duck feet, old mellow finish, pine secondary wood, orig brasses, minor edge repair, apron drops replaced, 37" w, 22-1/2" d, 73-1/4" h, $55,000. Photo courtesy of Garth's Auctions, Inc., Delaware, OH.

one wide over three small molded drawers, brass bail handles, escutcheons, and lock plates, shaped apron with acorn drops, cabriole legs, pad feet, 38" w, 21" d, 68" h........5,900.00

New England, c1750, cherry, two sections, upper section with flat molded cornice, two small over three long graduated thumb-molded drawers, lower section with one long drawer over three small drawers, shaped apron, cabriole legs, pad feet, 37" w, 19" d, 66" h 4,750.00

New England, southern, c1750-80, maple, two sections, upper section with cornice molding above upper case of five drawers, lower case of three small drawers, cabriole legs ending in pad feet, replaced brasses, old refinish, repairs and losses, 36" w, 20" d, 63-1/2" h...5,750.00

New England, c1760, tiger maple, rectangular molded top, five graduated drawers over long drawer over three small drawers, scalloped apron, cabriole legs, spoon feet, replaced glass pulls, refinished, restored, 37-1/4" w, 17-1/4" d, 73" h...............5,500.00

New England, south eastern, early 18th C, painted maple, cherry, oak, and pine, top with flat molded cornice, double arch molded case, two short drawers, frame with valanced skirt, four ring turned legs, disc feet, old engraved brasses, old Spanish brown paint, imperfections, 35" w, 19" d, 54-1/2" h.............. 3,500.00

New England, last half 18th C, maple, pine, and cherry, rect molded slightly overhanging top, case with five thumb-molded graduated drawers, frame with skirt and drop pendant, cabriole legs, pad feet on platforms, replaced brasses, refinished, restoration, 36" w, 19" d, 52-1/2" h 1,380.00

New England, 19th C, maple, two sections, cornice molding on upper case, five graduated thumb-molded drawers, lower case with similar drawers, shaped skirt, cabriole legs, high pad feet, replaced brasses, old refinish, minor restoration, 38" w, 17" d, 70-7/8" h...................12,650.00

New England, period elements, walnut veneer, bonnet top, broken arch pediment, brass finials, fan carved top drawer over two narrow over three graduated wide drawers, lower portion with one wide over three narrow drawers, fan carved central drawer, claw and ball feet, sides split, loose molding pendant drops missing, new brasses, 38-1/2" w, 20-3/4" d, 81" h...............................6,440.00

New Hampshire, curly birch, two sections, upper section with detailed molded cornice, dovetailed case, five dovetailed graduated overlapping drawers; lower portion with four dovetailed overlapping drawers, well developed blocked and carved fan, scrolled apron with acorn drops, cabriole legs, duck feet, old mellow finish, pine secondary wood, orig brasses, minor edge repair, apron drops replaced, 37" w, 22-1/2" d, 73-1/4" h..55,000.00

New Hampshire, walnut and birch, two sections, upper: dovetailed case with eight overlapping dovetailed drawers with carved shells, turned finials, molded cornice, base: five overlapping drawers with carved shells, scrolled apron, cabriole legs, duck feet, orig brasses, old finish, some old repairs, 36" w, 20" d, 84" h.....................................15,400.00

Highboy, Queen Anne, New Hampshire, walnut and birch, two sections, upper: dovetailed case with eight overlapping dovetailed drawers with carved shells, turned finials, molded cornice, base: five overlapping drawers with carved shells, scrolled apron, cabriole legs with duck feet, orig brasses, old finish, some old repairs, 36" w, 20" d, 84" h, $15,400. Photo courtesy of Garth's Auctions, Inc., Delaware, OH.

New York, Long Island area, 18th C, tiger maple, cornice molding above upper case of two small over three long graduated thumb-molded drawers, cove cornice molding over base with long thumb-molded drawer over small center drawer flanked by larger drawers, cyma curved skirt, cabriole legs on pad feet, old refinish, restoration, 35-1/2" w, 17-3/4" d, 70" h..............................16,100.00

Pennsylvania, c1760-80, walnut, two sections, top with flat molded cornice over case of three thumb-molded short drawers, two half drawers, three graduated long drawers, four cabriole legs, carved pad feet, valanced apron, old finish, orig brasses, detailed Quaker provenance, 38" w, 22" d, 65" h.................28,450.00

Pennsylvania, walnut, pine secondary wood, bonnet top with seven dovetailed overlapping drawers with carved fan and flame carved finials, four dovetailed overlapping drawers with carved fan, scrolled apron with acorn drops, cabriole legs, duck feet, old replaced engraved brasses, old finish, repairs to bonnet top, 36" w, 83-1/2" h........18,700.00

Rhode Island, 1830-40, grain painted pine, molded lift top, single drawer, shaped bracket base with high arched sides, orig red and yellow paint simulating tiger maple, orig turned pulls, old dry surface, 39-3/4" w, 20" d, 36" h......................................2,100.00

Queen Anne-Style: This modern interpretation of the Queen Anne style captures the most important elements, plus the grace of the style.

Kindel Furniture, cherry, two sections, upper section with swan neck pediment, center fan cut drawers flanked by two drawers over four graduated drawers, lower section with long drawer over center fan cut drawer, flanked by two small drawers, 36" w, 20" d, 77" h......................................1,200.00

William and Mary: Highboys of the William and Mary period are just as massive as those found in the Chippendale period. They feature more applied decoration and sturdy legs and supports.

America, walnut and pine, burl veneer facade, two sections, upper section with molded cornice, five dovetailed drawers, lower section with three dovetailed drawers,

Highboy, Queen Anne, Pennsylvania, walnut, pine secondary wood, bonnet top with seven dovetailed overlapping drawers with carved fan and flame carved finials, four dovetailed overlapping drawers with carved fan, scrolled apron with acorn drops, cabriole legs with duck feet, old replaced engraved brasses, old finish, repairs to bonnet top, 36" w, 83-1/2" h, $18,700. Also shown is dome top box, fabric on wood, painted decoration, green marbleized paper interior, 19" l, $415. Photo courtesy of Garth's Auctions, Inc., Delaware, OH.

scalloped apron, herringbone cross banding, turned legs and feet, scalloped edge stretcher base, replaced legs and stretchers, beaded edge molding on apron and facade molding on base, some veneer and molding repairs to top, old replaced engraved teardrop brasses, 34-1/2" w, 20" d, 61-1/2" h..............................9,775.00

New England, southeastern, early 18th C, painted pine, two sections, upper section with flat molded cornice, single arch molded case with two short drawers and three long graduated drawers, base with three short drawers, four turned legs joined by flat shaped stretchers, turned feet, brasses may be orig, painted dark brown, restoration, 33" w, 18" d, 55" h 16,100.00

Pennsylvania, Philadelphia, c1715-30, stained cedar, two sections, upper section with elaborate molded cornice, bolection molded frieze drawer over case of three short drawers, three graduated long drawer, double bead molded dividers, lower section defined with mid molding over short central drawer flanked by two short deep drawers, ogival arched apron, short baluster and ring

turned legs, molded arched stretcher, 42" w, 23" d, 67-1/4" h..............................57,000.00

Lowboy

A lowboy is best thought of as a companion to a highboy, but smaller in scale. Expect to find the same stylistic characteristics as those found on highboys, i.e. claw and ball feet on Chippendale examples. As architecture dictated some forms of furniture, clothing styles also changed and that effected how furniture was used too. A lowboy offered storage for necessities such as gloves, hose, and smaller articles of clothing. Also see Tables, Dressing.

Chippendale
Middle Atlantic States, mahogany, rectangular top with notched corners, single long drawer over three smaller drawers, scalloped skirt, cabriole legs, claw and ball feet, 35" w, 19-1/2" d, 29" h 3,300.00

Pennsylvania, c1765, carved and inlaid walnut, oblong quarter-veneered top, notched corners, four molded drawers, fluted quarter columns, volute and shell-carved skirt, shell-carved cabriole legs, claw and ball feet, restorations, stamped "J. Hooten" on underside of center drawer, 33-1/2" w, 21-3/4" d, 28" h..............................19,500.00

Chippendale-Style, tiger and bird's eye maple, claw and ball feet 1,250.00

Queen Anne
America, burl walnut, molded edge top, matched veneer rectangles, bordered in two borders with matching veneers, front has two sq drawers flanking central drawer with burl walnut veneer, center with shaped apron, four cabriole legs, pad feet, old brasses, 29-1/2" w, 18-3/4" d, 28" h...............3,000.00

America, curly maple, thumb-molded rectangular top, two dovetailed drawers, cabriole legs with exaggerated slipper feet, scrolled apron, made from highboy base, minor repairs, drawer returns repaired, brasses replaced, pine secondary wood, 37-3/4" w, 35-3/4" h.............................1,760.00

America, walnut, satinwood inlay, rectangular molded edge top, three drawers, scalloped apron, round tapered legs, pad feet, 32" w, 19-1/2" d, 28-3/4" h...............2,750.00

Lowboy, Queen Anne, Pennsylvania, figured walnut, pine and oak secondary woods, thumb-molded one board top with cut corners, case with scrolled apron with carved shell, quarter columns with carved foliage, four dovetailed drawers, cabriole legs with carving on knees, stocking legs, trifid feet, orig brasses, old finish, age crack in top, possible reshaping to apron, 33-1/4" x 20" top, 29-3/4" h, $19,800. Also shown are brass candlesticks, $635 and 10-1/2" d Oriental porcelain bowl with underglaze blue and polychrome dec, $1,540. Photo courtesy of Garth's Auctions, Inc., Delaware, OH.

America, c1740-60, walnut, rectangular top, case with one wide drawer over three small drawers, flanked by fluted quarter columns, brass bail handles, scalloped apron, cabriole legs terminating in trifid feet, refinished, top replaced c1913, 36-1/4" w, 19-1/2" d, 30-1/4" h..........................7,280.00

Connecticut, cherry, thumb-molded top, three dovetailed overlapping drawers, scalloped apron, slender cabriole legs, duck feet and pads, pine secondary wood, old finish, professionally restored feet, knee returns and apron drops missing, replaced brasses, age cracks, 33-1/2" w, 20-1/2" d, 29-1/4" h.......................................2,400.00

Massachusetts, c1720-50, walnut, rectangular top, molded edge, three drawers with molded surrounds, shaped beaded skirt hung with turned pendants, circular tapering legs, pad feet, 33-1/4" w, 20-1/2" d, 30" h..7,500.00

Massachusetts, c1750, cherry, poplar secondary wood, carved fan and thumb molded top with cutout corners, four dovetailed overlapping drawers, scrolled apron with acorn drops, cabriole legs, duck feet, orig brasses, old finish, pristine condition, 20-3/4" x 34-3/4" top, 30-1/4" h.....................34,100.00

Massachusetts, c1750, walnut and maple, rectangular top, single long drawer over three drawers, drop pendants, cabriole legs, old brasses, old refinish, minor imperfections, 30" w, 20-1/2" d, 31" h.........12,000.00

Massachusetts, attributed to North Shore, c1750-70, walnut, thumb-molded two board top, six dovetailed drawers with banded inlay, center drawer with concave blocking with inlaid compass star, scrolled apron with turned drops, cabriole legs, duck feet, pine secondary wood, replaced brasses, old mellow finish, age cracks in top, interior stains, back painted black, 34-1/2" x 25" top, 32" h......................................15,400.00

New England, c1750, rectangular molded top, three small thumb-molded drawers, shaped apron with maple banding, cabriole legs, hoof feet, 35-1/2" w, 21-1/4" d, 27-1/2" h.......................6,000.00

Pennsylvania, figured walnut, pine and oak secondary woods, thumb-molded one board top with cut corners, case with scrolled apron with carved shell, quarter columns with carved foliage, four dovetailed drawers, cabriole legs with carving on knees, stocking legs, trifid feet, orig brasses, old finish, age crack in top, possible reshaping to apron, 33-1/4" x 20" top, 29-3/4" h.............................19,800.00

Pennsylvania, Philadelphia, c1750-80, attributed to William Savery, two-piece curly maple top with notched corners, maple case with one wide drawer over two small drawers, chamfered fluted corners, scalloped apron, cabriole legs with lambrequin carved knees, trifid feet, butterfly brasses, 35-1/2" w, 22" d, 30" h..................................392,000.00

Rhode Island, c1760, mahogany, rectangular molded top, notched corners, one long drawer over three small drawers, shaped

Lowboy, Queen Anne, Pennsylvania, Philadelphia, c1750-80, attributed to William Savery, two piece curly maple top with notched corners, maple case with one wide drawer over two small drawers, chamfered fluted corners, scalloped apron, cabriole legs with Lambrequin carved knees, trifid feet, butterfly brasses, 35-1/2" w, 22" d, 30" h, $392,000. Photo courtesy of Samuel T. Freeman & Co., Philadelphia, PA.

apron with turned drop pendants, cabriole legs, pointed slipper feet, imperfections, 34-1/2" w, 21-1/2" d, 30-1/2" h.........3,500.00
Queen Anne-Style, walnut, carved shell in skirt, drake feet....................................1,400.00
William and Mary
   America, burl walnut, herringbone cross banding, molded edge top with geometric veneer pattern, scrolled apron, acorn drops, applied facade moldings, three dovetailed drawers, turned legs and feet, undulating cross stretcher, legs and stretcher old restorations, old replaced engraved teardrop brasses, 31" w, 23-3/8" x 36-1/2" top, 29-1/4" h.......................................14,250.00
   Pennsylvania, c1730-60, walnut, rectangular lift top, deep compartment, cast with two horizontal fielded panels over two thumb molded short drawers, inverted baluster turned legs, ball turned feet joined by molded box stretcher, 48-1/2" w, 24-1/2" d, 40-1/2" h 5,500.00
William and Mary-Style
   Oak, projecting top, shaped apron with

drawer, turned inverted cup legs, X-stretcher, 23" w, 29" h......................1,980.00
   Walnut faced, three drawers, turned legs, X-stretcher, 33-1/4" w, 21" d, 29" h.....750.00

Mule Chest of Drawers

Mule chests of drawers are a cross between blanket chests and chests of drawers. The height of a mule chest is greater than blanket chest. This type of chest features a lid that lifts, usually hinged, with a deep interior well. Drawers below offered more storage. Often a small interior drawer, or till, was included in the well. Most Mule Chests available to today's collectors were made by craftsmen rather than machine made. They cross over furniture styles in their simplicity and lack of ornamentation. Because of this, they are often hard to date or determine their origin in a specific geographic region.

Mule Chest, Empire, America, oak and pine, hinged lid with six false drawer fronts, two dovetailed overlapping drawers, scrolled apron, bandy feet, replaced brasses, refinished, repairs to feet, apron, and lid, 47-3/4" w, 21" x 50-1/2", 42-1/2" h, $2,200. Also shown are folk art carving of Indian head by Popeye Reed, $525, country writing box, pine with old worn olive brown graining, 20" w, 10-1/4" d, 9" h, $275, yellow ware teapot with brown sponging, applied flowers, chips, hairlines, lid missing, $140. Photo courtesy of Garth's Auctions, Inc., Delaware, OH.

Country

America, pine, lift lid, two dovetailed drawers, cutout feet, till with lid, dark stain finish, repairs, some loss to height, front facings replaced, hinge tail restored, hinges replaced, replaced brasses, 39-1/4" w, 18-1/2" d, 37" h 650.00

America, pine, old red and black graining, lift lid over two false drawers, two drawers with wide early dovetailing, one board ends with cutout feet, base molding, replaced brass teardrop pulls, wrought iron strap hinges, till with replaced lid, feet old replacements, 36" w, 18-3/4" d, 36-1/2" h 1,550.00

America, pine, old red repaint, molded lid with battens beneath at either end, two long dovetailed graduated drawers with cock-beaded edges, high bracket feet, scalloped apron on front and sides, replaced oval brasses, interior compartment fitted with iron lock and hinges, minor age cracks, 36" w, 17-1/2" d, 35-1/4" h 2,585.00

America, poplar, lift lid over one false drawer, three overlapping drawers, cutout feet, scrolled apron, refinished with brown stain, replaced brasses, minor repairs, 37-3/4" w, 44-3/4" h 800.00

Massachusetts, decorated, pine, orig gray-blue vinegar graining, gray-olive ground, black and yellow edge striping, lift lid with applied molding over two false drawers, two dovetailed drawers, high cutout feet, scrolled apron, bottom signed "Daniel," 42-3/4" w, 19-3/8" d, 41-3/4" h 7,700.00

Empire

America, decorated, pine, old red repaint, black combed graining, lift top lid, two early dovetailed drawers, bracket feet, early brasses, repairs to feet, some side scratches, 41-1/2" w, 17-1/2" d, 44-1/2" h 825.00

America, grain painted, pine, orig red flame graining, six board top construction, two dovetailed overlapping drawers with molded edge top, high cutout feet, cutout apron, staple hinges replaced with butt hinges, minor repairs to feet, lid broken and glued, replaced brasses, 43-1/2" w, 20" d, 42-3/4" h 990.00

America, oak and pine, hinged lid with six false drawer fronts, two dovetailed overlapping drawers, scrolled apron, bandy feet, replaced brasses, refinished, repairs to feet, apron, and lid, 47-3/4" w, 21" x 50-1/2", 42-1/2" h 2,200.00

America, pine, thumb-molded top, two overlapping dovetailed drawers, bracket feet, old dark finishing, int. lined with 1875 Boston newspaper, pierced repairs to feet and drawer fronts, 40" w, 18" d, 34-3/4" h 700.00

New Hampshire, decorated, pine, orig reddish brown imitation flame figured wood graining with line inlay, black turned feet, molded edge lid over two false drawers, two dovetailed drawers, turned pulls, pine sec-

Mule Chest, Empire, America, grain painted, pine, orig red flame graining, six board top construction, two dovetailed overlapping drawers with molded edge top, high cutout feet, cutout apron, staple hinges replaced with butt hinges, minor repairs to feet, lid broken and glued, replaced brasses, 43-1/2" w, 20" d, 42-3/4" h, $990. Also shown are two tolé bread trays, $440 and $110 (small splits), miniature Sheraton chest of drawers, cherry, 12-3/8" h, $440, Ohio red and yellow clay lion, $275. Photo courtesy of Garth's Auctions, Inc., Delaware, OH.

ondary wood, minor edge damage, 38-1/2" w, 40" h 1,650.00

Queen Anne, pine, old brownish red paint, lift lid top, three false drawers, three overlapping drawers with wide early dovetailing, high cutout dovetailed feet, replaced hinges and braces, 37-1/2" w, 18-1/2" d, 52-1/4" h 2,650.00

William and Mary
America, c1730-60, walnut, lift top, deep compartment, two horizontal fielded panels over two thumb-molded short drawers, inverted baluster-turned legs, ball turned feet jointed by molded box stretcher, 48-7/8" w, 24-1/2" d, 40-1/2" h...........................6,000.00

Spice Chests

Spice chests are small chests with multiple drawers that were used to store expensive spices. Some of these chests also feature a door to encase the drawers, adding security against invading insects and humidity. It is not unusual to find stains or odors remaining from the spices once contained in these chests of drawers as their oils and fine textures often found their way into crevices in the wood of the drawers. Spice chests are also known as Spice Cupboards. Also see Boxes, Spice.

America, 19th C, pine, six drawers, three tiered construction, overhanging molded edges, shaped backboard, round wooden pulls, painted red, minor wear, 15-1/2" w, 6-1/2" d, 12-3/4" h 1,840.00

America, mid-19th C, oak, bird's eye maple drawer fronts, six drawers, turned wooden knobs, sq nail construction, 14-1/2" w, 7-1/2" d, 17-3/4" h...385.00

Middle Atlantic States, mahogany, single raised panel door, some shelves missing from interior, possible foot replacements, 17-1/2" w, 9-1/2" d, 22" h 1,100.00

Pennsylvania, c1780-1800, walnut, dovetailed, cove-molded cornice, raised panel hinged door, opens to interior of eleven small drawers, brass pulls, molded base, old surface, 15-1/2" w, 11" d, 18-1/4" h.................14,950.00

Sugar Chests

Sugar chests are generally found in southern climates. Like Spice Chests, they are generally small as both sugar and spices were imported and not sold in large quantities. They were created to store sugar against humidity and invading pests.

Classical, Kentucky, c1830-40, cherry, two sections, upper section with two board top, applied molded edge, lower section with one drawer, turned legs, poplar, and white pine secondary woods, minor repair, refinished, 29-1/2" w, 17-3/4" d, 34" h 4,500.00

Country, Missouri, c1830-50, walnut, dovetailed case, two boards on each side, turned feet, two section interior, refinished, replaced feet, lid and baffle, 31-1/2" w, 19" d, 30-1/2" h 1,200.00

Sheraton, walnut, fine turned legs, single drawer in base, interior divided into three sections, fine dovetailed construction, signed "Read Atlanta GA" old refinish, 29" w, 18-3/4" d, 39" h 3,200.00

Tall Chests

Tall chests are large storage units designed to hold clothing. As fashions included more layers, such as vests, it became necessary to have some additional storage. Tall chests of drawers were a practical solution to this problem. Because tall chests were designed to be functional rather than decorative, look for feet that can support the weight of the chest and the contents. Plus, these chests were used on a daily basis, so look for signs of wear and patinas that reflect generations of usage. Some have cornices and bases with moldings that can be removed easily. Stylistically expect to find the same elements as those found in highboys.

Chippendale: Expect to find molded cornices on Chippendale tall chests. More often, they will have bracket feet, as the feet are generally substantial enough to carry the weight of the chest.

America, 18th C, cherry, rectangular top, projecting cornice, case with three aligned drawers, five graduated drawers, bracket feet, 46-1/2" w, 21" d, 63-1/2" h..........900.00

America, 18th C, maple, molded cornice, dovetailed case with five overlapping dovetailed drawers, bracket feet, pine secondary wood, old mellow refinishing, old but not orig

Tall Chest, Chippendale, curly birch, molded cornice, dovetailed case, six overlapping drawers, top drawer with three drawer front and carved fan, scrolled apron with carved fan, bracket feet, refinished, replaced feet and cornice, 35-1/4" w, 20" d, 52" h, $2,200. Photo courtesy of Garth's Auctions, Inc., Delaware, OH.

brasses, age cracks, 35-1/8" w, 19-1/4" d, 54-1/2" h 4,500.00

America, 18th C, tiger maple, projecting cornice top, case with six graduated drawers, bracket feet, 42" w, 19-1/2" d, 51-3/4" h 3,750.00

America, 18th C, walnut and poplar, molded cornice, dovetailed case, nine molded edge dovetailed drawers, fluted quarter columns, replaced ogee feet, pine secondary wood, refinished, repairs and replacements, 42" w, 24" d, 69" h 1,870.00

America, late-18th C, maple with some curl, molded cornice, six dovetailed graduated drawers, scalloped bracket feet, refinished, replaced brasses and escutcheons, backboards renailed, cornice and feet replaced, 35-3/4" w, 18" d, 52-1/4" h................2,475.00

Maryland or Virginia, late 18th C, walnut, applied molded cornice, three over two over four graduated molded drawers, brass escutcheons, brass pulls stamped "H. J.," chamfered and fluted quarter columns, ogee feet on wafers, poplar secondary wood, refinished, minor repairs, 43" w, 21" d, 65" h.........9,400.00

Massachusetts, Worcester County, c1790, cherry, flat molded cornice above applied beaded molding, case of six beaded graduated drawers, bracket feet, replaced wood pulls, old refinish, 37-1/4" l, 17" d, 53-1/4" h 11,500.00

Massachusetts, 18th C, pine and maple, cornice molding above case of five graduated drawers, turned pulls, bracket feet, refinished, imperfections, inscription in top drawer "Goodale Marlboro, Mass," 37" w, 18-1/2" d, 46" h................................3,220.00

Massachusetts, late-18th C, cherry, flat molded cornice, five thumb-molded gradu-

Tall Chest, Chippendale, Massachusetts, 18th C, pine and maple, cornice molding above case of five graduated drawers, turned pulls, bracket feet, refinished, imperfections, inscription in top drawer "Goodale Marlboro, Mass," 37" w, 18-1/2", 46" h, 3,220.00.

ated drawers, bracket feet, replaced brasses, refinished, stained to resemble tiger maple, 36-1/2" w, 17" d, 52" h 4,600.00

Massachusetts, southeastern, or Rhode Island, late 18th C, tiger maple, cornice molding above seven thumb-molded drawers, bracket base, some orig brasses, refinished, repairs to feet, 36" w, 18" d, 57-1/2" h 5,465.00

Massachusetts or New Hampshire, 18th C, maple and birch, flat molded cornice over case with five thumb-molded graduated drawers, top drawer with faux three drawer facade with center carved fan, tall bracket feet, replaced brasses, refinished, imperfections, 38-1/4" h, 19-1/4" d, 49-3/4" h 1,955.00

New England, c1780, sycamore, flat molded cornice above case fitted with six graduated drawers with incised cockbeading, bracket feet, replaced brasses, old refinish, minor imperfections, 35-3/4" w, 18-1/2" d, 56" h 7,500.00

New England, c1790, cherry, flat molded cornice above case fitted with six graduated drawers with incised beading, bracket feet, replaced brasses, old refinish, imperfections, 35-1/2" w, 17-1/2" d, 55" h 5,175.00

New England, c1800, maple, cornice molding, case with six thumb-molded graduated

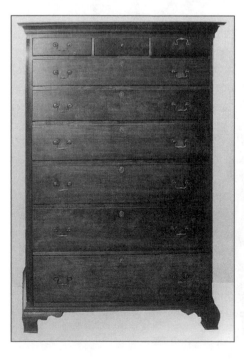

Tall Chest, Chippendale, Chester County, Pennsylvania, c1780, walnut, molded cornice, dovetailed top, overlapping drawers, three short drawers over six graduated long drawers, flanked by quarter columns, resting on ogee bracket feet, Ernest F. Hagen label, 42" w, 20" d, 71" h, $6,050. Photo courtesy of Alderfer Auction Company, Hatfield, PA.

drawers, bracket base with central drop, old refinish, old replaced brass, 40-1/2" w, 20" d, 55" h 9,200.00

New England, late 18th C, carved curly maple, molded cornice, seven thumb-molded long drawers, bracket feet, 40-1/2" w, 17-1/2" d, 65-1/2" h 9,500.00

New Hampshire, early 19th C, birch, reddish brown finish, molded cornice with relief carved frieze, dovetailed case with six graduated drawers, detailed bracket feet, carved sunburst on center drop, replaced brasses, 36" w, 19-1/4" d, 62-1/4" h 6,900.00

Pennsylvania, c1765, walnut, flat coved top, three small and five graduated wide-lip molded drawers, straight bracket feet, imperfections, 39" w, 61" h 4,000.00

Pennsylvania, c1800, cherry, applied top molding, two short over five graduated molded line-inlaid drawers, squiggle inlay across top and down stiles, chamfered and fluted quarter columns, scalloped bracket feet, orig hardware, one board sides, two horizontal boards on back, orig finish and brasses, poplar secondary wood, 41-1/2" w, 21" d, 58-1/2" h 7,500.00

Pennsylvania, Chester County, late 18th C, cherry, cornice cove molding above single drawer, visually divided into three, over split drawer, four graduated drawers below, flanked by quarter engaged fluted columns with capitals and bases, molded base, four brackets on platforms characteristic of Octorara, (area between Chester and Lancaster counties), imp "T. Stock-ton" on backboard, old surface, casters added, minor imperfections, 38" w, 21-3/8" d, 66-3/4" h 19,550.00

Rhode Island, late 18th C, cherry, flat molded cornice above case fitted with seven thumb-molded graduated drawers, bracket feet, orig brass bail pulls, old red stained finish, minor imperfections, 36-3/4" w, 19-1/2" d, 62-1/2" h 7,475.00

Classical: Tall chests of this period, c1800 to 1830, often exhibit more decoration in the form of applied moldings or carvings.

Pennsylvania or Ohio, c1825, tiger maple and cherry, rectangular top, case of two cockbeaded short drawers, deep drawer with walnut veneered border flanked by saw-tooth carved panels, four graduated cockbeaded drawers below flanked by vase and ring turned engaged columns, turned feet, turned wood pulls, old refinish, minor imperfections, 42-3/4" w, 22" d, 56" h.......2,760.00

Rhode Island, late-18th C, carved tiger maple, cornice with dentil molding, case of seven graduated thumb-molded drawers, molded tall bracket base with central drop, top drawer with fan-carving, orig brasses, early surface, 38" w, 18-3/4" d, 63-3/4" h.........27,600.00

Federal: Federal tall chests are straight chests. Look for slightly overhanging cornices and various sized drawers. Feet will be small splayed styles, including the fashionable sweeping French foot that became popular during this period.

America, c1790-1810, walnut, molded overhanging cornice, three narrow drawers over five graduated wide drawers flanked by narrow fluted quarter columns, oval brasses, French bracket feet, restored, 42-1/8" w, 22-3/4" d, 64-5/8" h...........................6,440.00

Pennsylvania, c1800, inlaid figured maple, molded overhanging cornice, case with three short drawers over five graduated long drawers, splayed feet, shaped apron, orig drawer brasses and escutcheons, 41-1/2" w, 22-1/2" d, 63" h.................................8,750.00

Hepplewhite: Hepplewhite tall chests feature inlay as a predominate design future. Most Hepplewhite tall chests feature large drawers.

America, inlaid walnut, banded inlay on top molded edge, six dovetailed drawers with oval line an border inlay, scrolled bracket feet, cherry secondary wood, old replaced eagle brasses, edge repairs to drawers, 37-1/2" w, 21-1/4" d, 46" h....................................2,420.00

Pennsylvania, walnut, orig wood facade and line inlay, nine dovetailed drawers with applied edge beading, chamfered corners with fluting and molded cornice, ogee feet, old worn finish, replaced brasses with ghost image of oval brasses, 41" w, 60-3/4" h 3,850.00

Queen Anne: Queen Anne tall chests feature molded cornices over long drawers. Look for a more sturdy style of foot rather an the del-

Tall, Queen Anne, curly maple, molded cornice, dovetailed case, six graduated overlapping drawers, bandy legs, duck feet, old finish, orig brasses, minor damage to veneer overlap, 36" w, 19" d, 54" h, $12,100. Photo courtesy of Garth's Auctions, Inc., Delaware, OH.

icate cabriole legs often associated with the Queen Anne period. Look for finely figured decorative woods to add interest to the chest.

America, 18th C, cherry, molded cornice, dovetailed case with seven overlapping dovetailed drawers, bracket feet, orig brasses, four replaced keyhole escutcheons, chestnut secondary wood, old mellow finish, age cracks, old pierced repair, minor restoration to feet, 36" w, 19-1/2" d, 51-3/8" h 4,250.00

America, 18th C, curly maple, molded cornice, dovetailed case, six graduated overlapping drawers, bandy legs, duck feet, old finish, orig brasses, pine secondary wood, minor damage to veneer overlap, 36" w, 19" d, 54" h 12,100.00

Sheraton: Tall chests from this period are simple, straight lines, but often found with turned feet. The hardware used was generally also plainer, but usually included pulls and escutcheons for locks and keys.

Country, curly maple veneer and cherry, cove molded cornice, eight dovetailed drawers, paneled ends, turned feet, refinished, some edge damage, replaced wood pulls, inlaid shield shaped escutcheons old replacements, minor repair to drawer edges, 40" w, 21-1/2" w, 67" h......................4,375.00

Cradles

Cradles represent a specialized form of furniture that easily comes to mind when thinking about antique furniture. Yet, few cradles fall neatly into the different period styles. Why? Because most were made by craftsmen or loving family members, not necessarily patterned after the designs of the day, but more or less each one is created individually. And, because cradles are so durable, many are passed down from generation to generation. While this tradition is wonderful, it keeps the number of cradles made down significantly. And, with fewer made, fewer are available to collect. However, many are sold every year through auction and in antiques shops, antique shows and flea markets all around the country. Here is a sampling of what styles, woods, and prices to expect.

See Children's Furniture for other examples of children's bedding.

Chippendale

Birch, canted sides, scalloped headboard, turned posts and rails, refinished,
37-1/2" l...400.00

Bentwood, mixed woods, five spindle ends, patent 1869, replaced cushions, 37" l, 31-1/2" h, $400.

Country

America, c1780-1809, mahogany, arched paneled hood, shaped sides with cutout handles, shaped arched footboard, molded base, shaped rockers with scrolled ends, dovetail and tenon construction, 21" w, 44" l,
29" h...675.00

America, found in Michigan, early, hooded, mahogany with old dark finish, flame veneer on top board of hood, dovetailed shaped footboard, mortised rockers with scrolled ends, Chippendale-style brasses on ends, renailing, veneer repair, 40" w, 18" d, 26-1/2" h....................330.00

America, poplar, old worn green paint, dovetailed, shaped rockers and scalloped ends with heart cutouts, wear and edge damage,
39" h...365.00

America, hooded
   Birch, dovetailed, cutout rockers, scalloped ends, 41" l................................525.00
   Cherry, mortised sides, scrolled detail, sq corner posts, turned finials, scrolled rockers, old dark finish, nailed repairs,
40" l..265.00
   Mahogany, dovetailed case, scrolled detail on foot and hood, cutout rockers, pine bottom board, brass end handles, old, possibly orig finish, minor old repair, 44" l..............1,210.00
   Pine, scalloped hood sides, plain bonnet top, orig finish 450.00
   Walnut, dovetailed, scalloped sides, hand holds, brass knobs, heart cutout in headboard, large rockers, 43-1/2" l............400.00

America, cherry, mortised sides, scrolled detail, sq corner posts, turned finials, scrolled rockers, old dark finish, nailed repairs, 40" l.............275.00

America, curly maple, fiddle back figured cherry panels, sq posts, turned finials, mortised and pinned rails, cutout designs in rails, oak rockers, 38-1/4" l...................................250.00

America, poplar, open style, central cutout sides and ends, hand holds, trestle rockers, old dark finish, 41" l....................................275.00

New England, 18th C, painted pine, arched hood continuing to shaped and carved dovetailed sides, rockers, old light green paint, old repairs, 40" l 300.00

New England, early 19th C, grain painted, pine, yellow ochre and burnt umber painting simulating tiger maple, 37-1/2" w, 19-1/4" d, 25-1/2" h 425.00

Pennsylvania, late 18th C, dovetailed, refinished curly maple, cut-out hearts, age cracks and shrinkage.............. , 41" 1,550.00

Pennsylvania, 19th C, walnut, scrolled back and sides, shaped rockers, old refinish, repaired crest, 39" l, 18-1/4" d, 21" h 250.00

Primitive, cherry, sq corner posts, turned acorn finials, shaped sides and ends with heart cutouts, shaped rockers, old soft worn finish, some edge damage, 35" l, 16" w, 20" h 275.00

Rustic, twig construction, rocker base, unsigned, 33" l, 22" d, 22" h 100.00

Victorian

America, brass, late 19th/early 20th C, brass, tall net hook over spindled rectangular crib, swing section with locking mechanisms, bent tubular loop frame, feet missing, hook detached, 41-1/2" l, 19-3/4" w, 41" h 750.00

America, cast iron, painted black, wooden slat bottom, finial missing, 37" l, 21" d, 36" h..200.00

America, walnut, sausage-turned spindles 360.00

Eastlake, 1875, walnut, paneled headboard, footboard, and sides, scrolling crest above short turned spindles, platform support, orig finish, dated..495.00

French Restauration, c1835-40, swing, mahogany, swan neck drapery post, 50-3/4" w, 22-1/2" d, 74-1/4" h 2,000.00

Renaissance Revival, c1860-85, walnut, shaped canopy frame, turned slatted sides, scrolled crest, shaped rockers 950.00

Windsor

New England, c1800-20, bamboo turned spindles, worn finish................................850.00

Cupboards

Cupboards are closets and storage units. A quick review of early architecture will reinforce that the early settlers were more concerned with putting a roof over their heads than with furniture or styles, and particularly closets. A simple cupboard usually did the job, along with a chest of drawers or perhaps a blanket chest. That was all the storage needed for their small wardrobes. The huge walk-in closets of today's modern homes would certainly astound our ancestors.

However, even the simple cupboards can be broken down into several different classifications as seen here. Many are defined by their usage, such as a linen press or kitchen cupboard. Others were for the storage of clothing, like armoires, and wardrobes.

Within these classifications, many of the cupboards are very stylistic and display elements of a particular period. Wall and corner cupboards often are rather vague in their design, having been crafted for function and often to fit a particular space. The generic term "Country" serves as a fitting style for many of these cupboards. Few are signed or identified with a specific cabinet maker. However, types of woods used and other clues help identify the region where they originated and perhaps the time frame.

Often architectural styles dictated how high or wide a cupboard would be, what kinds of materials would be used in its construction. Craftsmen who had a ready supply of poplar used that, while New England furniture makers often used the native pine. Cupboards that were made in several different types of woods are commonly found and usually were painted or stained to even out their coloration originally. The term "cupboard door" refers to a simple door created with a flat center section and molded perimeter frame. The term "married" refers to a cupboard where the top and base were combined, sometimes bridging two generations or different time frames.

Armoire

As the name implies, an armoire is a large cupboard and the form was first popular with French furniture makers. A few American styles include large cupboards which served as clothing storage. Listings for several European armoires are included for comparison purposes and to remind collectors that many European forms are sold and used by Americans and Canadians.

Art Deco, teak, architectural form cornice, ebonized trim, center applied ebonized stepped plaque, two raised paneled doors with ebonized trim, two drawers over geometrically shaped apron with ebonized trim, small ebonized stepped block feet, 39" w, 21-1/2" d, 79" h..650.00

Art Nouveau, teak, molded arched crest over plain frieze, pair of paneled doors, glazed panels at top, plinth base, 46" w, 16-1/2" d, 85" h..750.00

Classical
New York, c1835, mahogany, bold projecting molded Roman arch cornice, two paneled doors flanked by tapered veneered columns, ogee bracket feet, 74" w, 31" d, 94" h
....3,200.00

Pennsylvania, Philadelphia, early 19th C, mahogany, reeded cavetto molded cornice, Gothic arched frieze, paneled and acanthus carved doors, four carved and turned columns, dolphin carved front feet, 72" w, 25" d, 96" h.. 12,400.00

Empire-Style, America, mahogany, rectangular outset top over front with pair of outset frieze drawers surmounting pair of paneled doors, sliding shelves, plinth base, turned short feet, 43" w, 27-1/2" d, 60" h....................650.00

French Restauration, New York, c1830, mahogany, flat top with cornice molding, two doors, bird's eye maple lined interior, concealed drawer below, ribbed blocked feet, 56" w, 19-1/2" d, 90" h.........................2,800.00

Victorian

Eastlake, America, c1840, walnut, bold double ogee molded cornice, two arched paneled doors, shelved interior, plinth base, ogee bracket feet, 62" w, 24" d, 89" h 1,400.00

Gothic Revival, America, c1840, mahogany, molded cornice with carved crest, ogee molded and mirrored door, fitted interior with three string banded shelves, one drawer in molded plinth base, bracket feet, 35-1/4" w, 15-1/2" d, 70" h 4,500.00

Naturalistic Revival, New Orleans, c1850, attributed to Prudent Mallard, mahogany, shaped crest with two finials, mirrored door, interior fitted with drawers and shelves, satinwood inlay, scrolled skirt 12,500.00

Renaissance Revival

America, c1865, walnut, molded cornice over single mirrored door, interior now fitted with lift top cedar chest, 90-1/2" w, 53" d, 85-1/2" h 1,800.00

America, c1880, rosewood, arched molded cornice, rectangular mirrored door, long drawer, flattened bun feet, 51" w, 23" d, 98" h 3,750.00

European, oak, quarter sawed figure, curved cornice with applied moldings, and carved crest, two paneled doors with applied urns and foliage, two dovetailed drawers, turned pilasters and feet, break down construction, 59-3/4" w, 25" d, 96" h... 1,870.00

Chifforobe

What a wonderful name for a cupboard to store clothes, hats, and accessories. American furniture designers of the 20th century added mirrors to these handy armoire type cupboards, giving their furniture one more function.

Art Deco, 1935, herringbone design waterfall veneer, arched center mirror, dropped center section, four deep drawers flanked by tall cupboard doors, shaped apron 450.00

Chimney Cupboard

A slender type of cupboard, made to fit next to a chimney.

Country, pine, cornice, dovetailed case, paneled door, open shelf, green wash repaint, base recut, 14" w, 25-1/2" d, 64-1/2" h 400.00

Console Cupboard

A console is a more formal cupboard that is not as big as an armoire, but impressive stately.

Classical, c1820, rosewood, fitted with frieze drawer, inset medallions of Napoleon and Josephine, two paneled cupboard doors, flanked by free standing columns with ormolu capitals and bases, bun feet, 35-1/2" w, 13-1/2" d, 33" h 2,100.00

Corner Cupboards

Corner cupboards are often thought as massive pieces of furniture. Many were made in two or more sections. Many were made to fit the particular corner of a home, causing them to be quite individual in design and size. Because most were designed for use in dining rooms or kitchens, doors with glass panes allowed display of the owner's pretty china, an easy way to discreetly display wealth and good taste.
Corner cupboards tend to fall into a few furniture styles, but more are classified as "Country" as they combine elements from different furniture periods with innovations of the craftsman who created them.

Centennial, c1875, carved walnut, concave pine interior shell, fluted pilasters, three shaped shelves over single double-arched paneled door, molded base, 49" w, 19" d, 95" h.. 5,200.00

Chippendale

Maryland, mid-18th C, two sections, walnut, upper section with dentil molded cornice, pair of glazed doors with eight panes, lower section with double drawers over double paneled doors, ogee bracket feet, 48" w, 24" d, 87" h..................................... 6,500.00

Maryland, mid-18th C, two sections, walnut, upper section with molded cornice, arched double doors with keystone ornament, three drawers over pair of paneled cupboard doors, rat tail hinges, ogee bracket feet, two interior scalloped shelves, 48" w, 26" d, 88" h.................................... 13,200.00

Pennsylvania, attributed to Lancaster County, mid-18th C, two sections, cherry, upper section with broken arch pediment with carved foliage, shell, and rosettes, carved finials on fluted plinths, door with

Corner Cupboard, Chippendale, Pennsylvania, attributed to Lancaster County, mid-18th C, two pieces, cherry, upper section with broken arch pediment with carved foliage, shell, and rosettes, carved finials on fluted plinths, door with twelve panes, arched top rail, base section with raised panel doors, three dovetailed drawers, ogee feet, pine and poplar secondary wood, replaced brasses and hardware, old mellow finish, repairs and restoration, 44-1/4" w cornice, 102" h, $9,350. Photo courtesy of Garth's Auctions, Inc., Delaware, OH.

twelve panes, arched top rail, base section with raised panel doors, three dovetailed drawers, ogee feet, pine and poplar secondary wood, replaced brasses and hardware, old mellow finish, repairs and restoration, 44-1/4" w cornice, 102" h..................9,350.00

Pennsylvania, early 19th C, carved cherry, scrolled molded pediment flanking fluted keystone with flame finial, arched door flanked by reeded columns, three serpentine-shaped painted shelves, recessed panel doors also flanked by reeded columns, single shelf base interior, cyma curved skirt, old refinish, hardware changes, minor patching, 41-1/2" w, 17-3/4" d, 95" h...............9,200.00

Pennsylvania, last quarter 18th C, walnut, broken swan neck pediment centering urn finial, two eight pane glazed doors, three shelves over two paneled cupboard doors, ogee bracket feet, early painted interior, pediment repaired, pulls missing, one pane cracked, 52" w, 23-1/2" d, 96-1/2" h..................2,185.00

Pennsylvania, late-18th C, two sections, poplar, upper section with glazed arched doors, interior of one bowed and two serpentine shelves with plate rails, lower case of raised panel doors, serpentine skirt, flaring bracket feet, old surface, imperfections, 51" w, 25-1/2" d, 67" h...................................3,700.00

Southern, walnut, dentil molded cornice, arched mullioned upper door with fleur-de-lis style moldings, raised panel lower door, interior scalloped shelves, 39" w, 17" d, 72" h 6,750.00

Virginia, Giles County, early-19th C, walnut, one piece, applied dentiled cornice, two doors with three raised panels each, applied molded frieze over two raised paneled doors, canted corners, bracket feet, yellow pine and poplar secondary woods, replaced hinges, refinished, minor repairs, 46" w, 27" d, 91" h 3,600.00

Chippendale-Style, America, c1780, architectural, painted, shell carved, molded cornice with flanking stop fluted columns centering molded arch with keystone and stop fluted shell niche, three scalloped shelves flanked by fluted pilasters above one door, only central shelved portion with shell is period, rest of cabinet is new, 46" w, 15" d, 85-1/2" h......1,380.00

Country

America, first half 19th C, architectural, curly maple, arched cornice with molded details, carved rosettes, turned finials, arched upper paneled cupboard doors over paneled cupboard base doors, ogee feet, old refinishing, finials, upper sections of goosenecks, and feet replaced, 44-1/2" h, 99-1/2" h 10,450.00

Corner Cupboard, Country, America, reeded detail attributed to Hackensack, NJ, pine, two pieces, dovetailed case, upper section with molded cornice with geometric and relief band at frieze, pair of paneled doors, lower section with single dovetailed drawer over another pair of doors, reeded stiles, top interior with serpentine shelves with cutouts for spoons, bracket feet, red finish, old worn dark blue repaint over earlier cream color, 41-1/2" w, 45" d, 85-3/4" h, $15,400. Photo courtesy of Garth's Auctions, Inc., Delaware, OH.

America, first half 19th C, poplar, one-piece construction, molded cornice, paneled doors, wide stiles, cutout feet, old dark cherry finish, 45-1/2" w, 74" h 1,210.00

America, first half 19th C, poplar, outset ogee molded cornice with canted ends over front with shaped shelves, valanced surround, surmounting drawer and pair of doors with raised and fielded panels, opening to shelf, canted stiles, imperfections, 45" w, 24" d, 79" h 1,200.00

America, 19th C, painted pine, two sections, upper section with coved cornice top, two tall doors, base section with two shorter doors, corner bracket feet, painted red, imperfections, 46" w, 22" d, 84" h 600.00

America, mid-19th C, cherry, front with six-pane astragal door opening to shelves, flanked by canted stiles, lower section with pair of sunken panel doors, shelf interior, imperfections, 42" w, 29" d, 75" h 900.00

America, mid-19th C, pine, molded cornice, top single door with twelve panes of old glass, base with double paneled doors, perimeter molding, bracket feet, refinished, repairs to feet, 44" w, 84-1/4" h 3,685.00

America, mid-19th C, pine, one-piece construction, stepped out cornice and dentil molding, applied molding around top door, double doors in base with two inset panels, molded trim, bracket feet, rose head nail construction, some renailing, old dark varnished finish, hinges and back foot replaced, 44-1/2" w, 27" d, 81" h 5,500.00

America, late-19th C, pine, tall and narrow, one-piece construction, perimeter molding, top door with geometric arrangement of glass, paneled bottom door, scalloped apron, old green repaint, interior painted red, repairs, perimeter molding replaced, 27" w, 67-1/2" h 1,165.00

America, reeded detail attributed to Hackensack, NJ, pine, two sections, dovetailed case, upper section with molded cornice with geometric and relief band at frieze, pair of paneled doors, lower section with single dovetailed drawer over another pair of doors, reeded stiles, top interior with serpentine shelves with cutouts for spoons, bracket feet, red finish, old worn dark blue repaint over earlier cream color, 41-1/2" w, 45" d, 85-3/4" h....... 15,400.00

Maryland, Frederick, c1825, red and black grain painted decoration, poplar, two sections, upper section with applied molded cornice over two arched doors with ten lights each, lower section with applied molded frieze over two paneled doors, scalloped bracket feet, canted corners, later interior paint, 53" w, 23" d, 94" h 9,500.00

Ohio, late 19th C, curly maple, cove molded cornice, four paneled doors with applied butternut cutout decoration, two small dovetailed drawers, orig cast iron thumb latches with porcelain knobs, wire nail construction, pine and poplar secondary woods, 45-1/2" w, 81" h 3,750.00

New York State, c1830, cherry, two sections, upper section with glazed door, three shelved interior, lower case with drawers above recessed paneled doors, one shelf interior, refinished, old replaced pulls, 43" w, 21-1/4" d, 88" h.................................4,200.00

Pennsylvania, c1800, cherry, two sections, upper section with overhanging cornice with applied ebonized gadroon molding, over two double arched glazed doors with orig panes, three interior shelves, brass pulls and hinges, base section with two faux drawers flanking central drawer over two gadrooned crotch mahogany paneled doors, 49" w, 25-3/4" d, 87" h................................6,440.00

Pennsylvania, c1800, walnut, two sections, upper section with molded cornice with applied dentil molding, chamfered corners, double cathedral arched doors with walnut mullions, each with eight orig glass panes, base section with two paneled doors, ogee bracket feet, brass H-hinges, replaced hardware, some repairs to feet, 48" w, 24" d, 90" h......10,650.00

Pennsylvania, c1800-25, cherry, two sections, upper section with molded overhanging cornice, single glazed door with twelve orig panes, lower section with two paned doors, wooden knobs, bracket feet with scalloped skirt, doors detached, 40" w, 20" d, 83-1/2" h 4,375.00

Pennsylvania, c1810, poplar, old bluish-gray repaint, one piece, beveled cornice, doors with stepped raised panels, cutout feet, 42-1/2" w, 83-3/4" h 2,860.00

Pennsylvania, late 18th/early 19th C, pine, step molded cornice over two triple paneled cupboard doors, scalloped skirt, bracket feet, orig cast iron hinges and lock mechanism, 44-1/2" w, 23-1/8" d, 85-1/2" h............ 2,250.00

Pennsylvania, first quarter 19th C, pine, two sections, upper section with overhanging cornice, open case with three shelves, lower case with three drawers, alternating with four light wood inlaid bull's eyes, over two paneled cupboard doors flanking three false drawers, bone inlaid escutcheons, larger ring brasses, floor of case replaced, 63-1/2" w, 20-1/4" d, 80" h...............4,100.00

Shenandoah Valley, late-18th C, yellow pine, flat molded cornice above arched opening, three shaped shelves, two raised panel cupboard doors below, framed with applied molding, wrought iron hinges appear to be original, blue, green, and yellow wash, 41" w, 22" d, 89-1/2" h 2,990.00

Corner Cupboard, Empire, Ohio, attributed to Perry or Fairfield County, cherry, burl veneer and figured veneer, bowfront, elaborate molded cornice with applied moldings, arched double doors each with ten panes of old glass, paneled doors, one nailed drawer, turned pilasters with rope, pineapple and herringbone carving, paw feet, poplar secondary wood, replaced brasses, old mellow finish, butterfly shelves in top, 55" w, 103" h, $8,250. Photo courtesy of Garth's Auctions, Inc., Delaware, OH.

Southern States, c1850, mahogany, one piece, arched crown over mullioned glass door, butterfly shelf interior, base with solid paneled door, bracket feet, repairs, 36" w, 24" d, 79" h 1,500.00

Empire, Ohio, attributed to Perry or Fairfield County, cherry, burl veneer and figured veneer, bow front, elaborate molded cornice with applied moldings, arched double doors each with ten panes of old glass, paneled doors, one nailed drawer, turned pilasters with rope, pineapple and herringbone carving, paw feet, poplar secondary wood, replaced brasses, old mellow finish, butterfly shelves in top, 55" w, 103" h..8,250.00

Federal

America, c1800, cherry, two sections, upper section with later swan-neck pediment, twin glazed lattice doors, three open shelves, lower section with single drawer flanked by two mock drawers over twin panel doors, circular brass pulls, straight bracket feet, 52" w, 26" d, 94" h 4,500.00

America, c1800, pine, flat cornice top, two glazed doors and two paneled doors, step molded base, 45-1/2" w, 15" d, 69-1/2" h 1,750.00

Middle Atlantic States, c1790-1820, walnut, three painted shaped shelves, single glazed arched door, single shelf behind recessed paneled door flanked by fluted columns, old darkened surface, replaced hardware, imperfections, some restoration, repairs, 48" w, 22-1/2" d, 88" h 2,950.00

Middle Atlantic States, c1820, tiger maple, molded projecting cornice, two glazed doors open to three-shelved interior, over two recessed panel doors with single shelf interior, scrolled skirt, old surface, height loss, 54" w, 91" h......................................8,625.00

New England, late-18th C, pine, barrel-back, flat molded cornice, cupboard door with raised panel opening to three shaped shelves, cupboard door below framed by applied molding, orig wrought iron butterfly hinges on doors, natural color, minor imperfections, 46" w, 20-1/2" d, 93-1/2" h 3,450.00

New England, late-19th C, pine, molded projecting cornice, long paneled door over

Corner Cupboard, Hepplewhite, Southern, attributed to VA or the Piedmont, one piece, walnut, inlay, broken arch pediment with molded cornice, double top doors each with eight panes of glass, paneled doors, scrolled apron, bracket feet, stringing, diamonds, and vining foliage with fan in cornice and geometric design in rosettes, old soft finish, scrolled front shelves in upper section, yellow pine and poplar secondary wood, minor edge damage, 48-5/8" w, 94" h, $18,700. Photo courtesy of Garth's Auctions, Inc., Delaware, OH.

paneled base door, applied moldings, shaped interior shelves, old finish, minor imperfections, 40" w, 22" d, 83" h....................2,950.00

New England, c1800, pine, glazed door opening to two shaped shelves, above cupboard door with four recessed molded panels, both with cockbeaded surround, flanking panels, cutout feet, old refinish, front bracket missing, 48" w, 22" d, 84" h.............3,450.00

New England, early 19th C, pine, flat molded cornice above case with glazed door, three interior shelves, projecting lower case of two cupboard doors with cockbeaded panels on base with applied molding, old refinish, replaced hardware, imperfections, 57" w, 29-1/2" d, 88-3/4" h 1,725.00

Ohio, Perry County, cherry and curly maple, ebonized trim, six dovetailed drawers with turned pulls, paneled doors, turned quarter columns, bracket feet, old varnish finish, 46" w, 50" h 3,300.00

Pennsylvania, Lebanon County, c1830, paneled cherry, two sections, upper section with cove molding above two glazed and mullioned doors, shelved interior, base with two paneled doors, bracket feet, 51-3/4" w, 82-1/4" h 2,400.00

Hepplewhite

America, cherry, two sections, figured wood veneer on door panels, drawers, and cornice, molded cornice, upper section with double doors, each with eight panes of old glass, arched top lights, three drawer fronts with chamfered edges, center drawer dovetailed, two flanking faux drawers, paneled base doors, orig brass "H" hinges, other hardware replaced, old dark finish, bracket feet are old replacements, top interior covered in old worn yellow-green brocade, minor repairs to cornice, 54" w, 86" h 3,850.00

America, cherry with inlay banding around base, waist and top, inlaid fan in apron, line inlay with invected corners on doors, cove molded cornice, paneled doors with molded edge stiles and rails, cut-out feet and scrolled apron, one piece, old refinishing,

Corner Cupboard, Sheraton, PA, c1830, softwood, two double arched eight pane doors, over two drawer and two door base, turned feet, orig brownish-red varnish, 37" d, 87" h, $4,675. Photo courtesy of Alderfer Auction Company, Hatfield, PA.

replaced feet, repairs, 42-1/4" w, 82-1/2" h 3,300.00

America, curly maple, two sections, upper section with cove molded cornice, dovetailed case, double top doors each with eight panes of old glass, lower section with paneled doors, French feet, interior with pale yellow repaint, replaced hardware, old refinishing, minor edge damage, 49" w, 83" h 8,500.00

Country, walnut with inlay, molded cornice, top door with twelve panes of old glass, single dovetailed drawer over single paneled door, scalloped apron, French feet, refinished, replaced feet and hinges, repairs, inlay is later addition, 42" w, 23" d, 96-1/4" h 2,860.00

Southern, attributed to VA or the Piedmont, one piece, walnut, inlay, broken arch pediment with molded cornice, double top doors each with eight panes of glass, paneled doors, scrolled apron, bracket feet, stringing, diamonds, and vining foliage with fan in cornice and geometric design in rosettes, old soft finish, scrolled front shelves in upper section, yellow pine and poplar secondary wood, minor edge damage, 48-5/8" w, 94" h 18,700.00

Queen Anne, Connecticut River Valley, cherry, one piece, molded old replacement cornice, two raised panel tombstone panels over two square panels on upper raised doors, molded mid strip, base two square over two rectangular panel doors, fluted stiles, base molding pine backboards attached with rose head nails, old mellow refinishing, some repairs, 46" w at cornice, 42-3/4" w, 79-1/2" h................................4,500.00

Court Cupboard

The term "Court" refers to a large, stately wall-type cupboard. The style was found in the William and Mary period and later enjoyed by the Victorians.

Centennial, Hale and Kilburn, Philadelphia, c1870, carved oak, 17th C style, central trapezoidal cupboard over long drawer, open bottom shelf, floral marquetry cupboard and side panels, general wear, worn drawer runners, 46-1/2" w, 20-1/2" d, 46" h 650.00

Victorian, Renaissance Revival, walnut, good detail, applied moldings, turned, and fluted pilasters, elaborate molded peaked cornice, paneled doors with applied carving, two dovetailed drawers, bun feet, 59" w, 23-1/4" d, 104" h..2,475.00

Hanging Cupboard, Corner

Hanging corner cupboards reflect a limited number of furniture styles and like their full size namesake, they often are identified as "Country." The more diminutive size of a hanging corner cupboard decreases the amount of storage space they afford to a user, but their charm often resides with the carving found on the crest or cornice.

Chippendale

America, late 18th C, pine, front with six pane astragal door opening to shelved interior, flanked by paneled, canted stiles, cavetto molded base, 32-1/2" w, 23" d, 38-1/2" h 900.00

Country, late 18th/early 19th C, pine, scrolled crest and base, two shelves, old refinishing, interior has some worn old blue paint, 17-3/4" w, 35" h..........................770.00

Pennsylvania, c1780, walnut, molded cornice over double paneled door with shelved interior over two open shaped shelves, repairs, 30" w, 17" d, 56" h 3,750.00

George III, last quarter 18th C, inlaid mahogany, corner, outset molded cornice with canted ends, front with crossbanded frieze, similarly banded tracery door with twelve panes, glazing bars with boxwood stringing, interior with three shelves, raised on outset molded base, 31-1/4" w, 19" d, 44-1/2" h 1,800.00

Hanging Cupboard, Wall

Small hanging cupboards were made to hang on the wall. Such placement kept their precious contents out of harm's way and away from insects and animals. Some have rods or hooks to hang show towels. Most of these small cupboards do not fall into any one particular furniture style. Many are dated by the hardware style. Also see Boxes, Wall and Cabinets, Wall.

Country, walnut, dovetailed top, single paneled mullioned door, rat tail hinges, scalloped lower case, 20" w, 11" d, 35" h............6,000.00

Country, walnut, tombstone door, scalloped skirt, lower drawer and shelf door wedge mortised, 26" w, 13" d, 35" h 6,850.00

Jelly Cupboards

Jelly cupboards are useful pieces of furniture with lots of storage. The name goes back to the time when jellies, jams, and other preserves were "put up" for later usage and needed to be stored in a cool, dark place. The roomy interiors of jelly cupboards fit that need. Shelves are deep and usually spaced so that they could accommodate large canning jars. Some jelly cupboards also include drawers, useful for storing linens, utensils, and other items needed in a kitchen setting. Most jelly cupboards fail to fall into a particular furniture style. They were made simply by local craftsmen to fill a home maker's storage needs.

Jelly Cupboard, pine, molded edge top forms lid to secret compartment, two paneled doors with beaded detail, solid ends, cutout feet, wrought iron strap hinges, old mellow refinishing, 38-3/4 w, 18" d, 44" h, $950. Also shown are Rockingham sugar bowl (with damage) $95, cow creamer, $220, lion, $880; and yellow ware teapot with blue and green sponge dec, (hairlines) $220. Photo courtesy of Garth's Auctions, Inc., Delaware, OH.

Country, decorated, pine, orig reddish brown grained decoration, molded cornice with worn black paint, two doors with inset panels and cross hatch decoration, similarly decorated side panels, mortised joints on doors, molded base with worn black paint, bracket feet, one shelf missing, repairs to feet, 45" w, 17" d, 66" h 5,390.00

Country, pine, molded edge top forms lid to secret compartment, two paneled doors with beaded detail, solid ends, cutout feet, wrought iron strap hinges, old refinishing, 38-3/4" w, 18" d, 44" h 950.00

Country, pine, old red paint, molded cornice with overhanging top board, single door with four raised panels, rat tail hinges, high cutout feet with scrolled apron, applied base molding, 46-1/2" w x 16" d cornice, 41-1/2" w, 68-3/4" h 4,950.00

Country, poplar, molded edge top with crest, two dovetailed drawers, paneled doors, paneled ends, turned feet, refinished, minor edge damage, age cracks, 39-1/2" w, 20-1/2" x 42" top, 53" h 625.00

Country, walnut, dovetailed gallery, two raised panel doors, one linen fold drawer, solid sides, wooden pulls, scalloped apron, 47-1/2" w, 19" d, 48" h 700.00

Country, walnut, molded cornice, one board door with beaded edge, simple cutout feet, 29" w, 16" d, 51-3/4" h 1,200.00

Country, walnut, old red and green graining, square corner posts, tapered legs, mortised and pinned construction, two panels in each of two doors, three panels in each end, breadboard ends missing from top, hardware removed, 48-1/2" 2, 21-1/2" d, 51" h 1,650.00

Empire, poplar, pine secondary wood, double door top with molded cornice and four dovetailed spice drawers, base with paneled doors, molded center stiles, paneled ends, two dovetailed drawers, replaced brass drawer handles, 47" w, 18-3/4" d, 85-1/2" h 2,750.00

New Jersey, early 19th C, pine, painted, paneled and carved, molded overhanging top, cupboard with applied moldings, fluting, and raised paneled cupboard doors, bottom drawer, shaped base, three shelved interior, old red wash, replaced hardware, minor imperfections, 40-1/2" w, 17-1/4" d, 48" h 4,200.00

Ohio, c1830, cherry, refinished, restoration, 43" w, 15" d, 48" h 650.00

Pennsylvania, Smoketown, 19th C, pine and poplar, old yellow graining over red, high gallery back, two dovetailed drawers, paneled doors, one board ends with cutout feet, old replaced wooden pulls, old brass latches on doors, 40" w, 13" d, 47-1/2" h..............4,000.00

Pennsylvania, 19th C, butternut, painted, two doors, shelved interior, chamfered corners, cutout bracket feet, old red paint finish, 37" w, 20" d, 65-1/2" h 2,300.00

Southern, yellow pine, molded cornice, two raised panel doors, adjustable interior shelves, old refinishing, may have been built-in, one corner rounded, other squared, clipped cornice and base board, some edge damage, 42" w, 11" d, 56-3/4" h......................................275.00

Kas or Schrank

A kas, or schrank, is a large cupboard, similar to an armoire or wardrobe. Usually the difference between these types of cupboards is the decoration. A kas will often have painted decoration, while an armoire or wardrobe does not. The term also depends on the region of the country where the piece originated and the language of the region. On the East Coast, the Pennsylvania Germans made and used a kas, while those living in areas where the French influenced their culture, would store their clothes in an armoire.

Country, pine, orig red paint, molded edge base, paneled doors set in beaded frames, one board ends, molded 21-1/2" x 64" cornice, open interior with cast iron hooks, 62" w, 20" d, 76-3/4" h..2,000.00

New York Hudson River Valley, 19th C, cherry, heavy cornice molding over paneled doors, two shelved interior, base with single paneled drawer, heavy turned feet, replaced pulls, refinished, restored, 62" w, 21" d, 69-3/4" h...3,000.00

New York, Long Island, c1730-80, cherry, pine, and poplar, architectural cornice molding, two raised panel thumb-molded doors flanked by reeded pilasters, applied moldings, single drawer, painted detachable disc and stretcher feet, replaced hardware, refinished, restored, 65-1/2" w, 26-1/4" d, 77-1/4" h 4,500.00

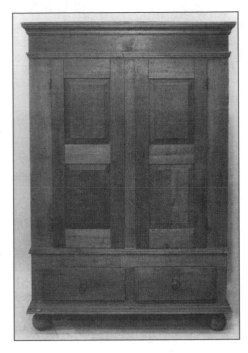

Kas, Country, Ohio, cherry, old soft finish, wood peg construction, applied moldings at cornice, waist, and base, dovetailed case, two raised panel doors, two dovetailed drawers, turned front feet, interior with wooden garment hooks, later adjustable shelves, feet replaced, edge damage, 49" w, 20-1/4" d, 7 7-1/4" h, $2,825. Photo courtesy of Garth's Auctions, Inc., Delaware, OH.

Ohio, cherry, old soft finish, wood peg construction, applied moldings at cornice, waist, and base, dovetailed case, two raised panel doors, two dovetailed drawers, turned front feet, interior with wooden garment hooks, later adjustable shelves, feet replaced, edge damage, 49" w, 20-1/4" d, 77-1/4" h 2,825.00

Pennsylvania, Bucks County, c1750-80, walnut, stepped overhanging cornice, two raised paneled cupboard doors, shelved interior, paneled sides, mid-molding, two short drawers below flanked by diamond appliqués, base molding below, bracket feet, orig brasses and wrought iron lock, small repair to left corner of cornice, 75" w, 26" d, 77" h 8,000.00

Pennsylvania, c1770, figured walnut, overhanging cornice, two raised paneled cupboard doors, flanked by and centering paneled stiles, three short drawers below, ogee bracket feet, 86" w, 28" d, 84" h 45,000.00

William and Mary, New York state, c1730-60, gumwood, paneled doors, interior with three shelves, under-hung divided drawer over single drawer, applied moldings, turned pull, front turned ball feet, old refinish, restoration, repairs, 60-3/4" w, 18-1/4" d, 77-1/2" h 4,200.00

Kitchen Cupboards

Kitchen cupboards are wonderful 20th C American inventions that were designed to save busy homemakers time and energy in the kitchen. Another common name for kitchen cupboards is "Hoosier" referring to a well-known brand name. A young homemaker could choose what features were most important to her when ordering her kitchen cupboard. She might decide to include a flour sifter and bin in one compartment, a spice rack in another. A tin-lined bread drawer and pull-out cutting board were popular accessories. An enameled top that pulled out at just the right height helped with the kitchen chores. Kitchen cabinets were often factory painted, but again the choice of colors was an option for the homemaker. All this choice has turned into a wonderful assortment of kitchen cupboards available in today's antiques market.

Oak, scalloped cornice over three cupboard doors, two glazed over two larger paneled doors, outset lower section with aluminum-lined work surface, over cupboard door flanked by three graduated drawers, 39-1/2" w, 28" d, 71-3/4" h..650.00

Oak, one long cupboard door with flour sifter, two small cupboard doors with slag glass inserts over two large cupboard doors with spice racks built into door frame, pull out white enameled top, one large cupboard door with interior shelf, two graduated drawers over bread drawer, tapered legs, refinished............................950.00

Painted, light green, one long cupboard with flour sifter, two small cupboard doors over tambour door, spice rack on back wall, pull out white enameled top, two small cutlery drawers over large cupboard door in base, wire rack and slide out bottom tray, short tapered legs, 36" w, 28" d, 72" h..................................450.00

Linen Press

A linen press serves the function its name describes. Popular in the Chippendale period and later periods with elegant styling, the form now is found in a modified form to serve as entertainment centers, etc. A true linen press will have a covering of doors to disguise the interior shelves or plain drawers. Some linen presses also have drawers in the base for addi-

tional storage. Expect to find interesting legs and feet on linen press forms, as they belong to the types of styles where those design elements were important to the furniture makers.

Arts & Crafts, Greene & Greene, fine grain mahogany, three graduated drawers with flaring horizontal pulls, decorated with detailed ebony inlay, two doors with vertical pulls decorated detailed ebony inlay along side ebony inlaid escutcheons fitted with orig keys, both orig Greene & Greene handmade keys of ebony and polished steel, signed four times, with burned signature "Sumner Greene, His True Mark," square peg construction, orig finish, from Bush-Bolton House, Pasadena, CA, c1905, 25-1/4" d, 72-1/4" l, 35" h 220,000.00

Chippendale

Canadian, pine, old reddish-brown flame graining, two sections, upper section with molded cornice, double doors, decorative scrolled panels, lower section with five dovetailed, paneled ends, bracket feet, wear and edge damage, 49-1/2" w, 21" d, 75-1/2" h.. 4,750.00

Country, pine and walnut, cornice molding, dovetailed case, paneled doors, turned feet,

Linen Press, country, poplar, molded cornice, two raised panel doors, two dovetailed drawers, bracket feet, orig hardware including batwing brasses and wrought iron H-hinges, engraved brass escutcheon and iron lock, old red finish, chestnut secondary wood, repairs, foot facings and cornice replaced, 41-3/4" w, 17" d, 73" h, $4,400. Photo courtesy of Garth's Auctions, Inc., Delaware, OH.

molded base, two dovetailed drawers in bottom interior, orig paint with red wash, 42" w, 75" h 1,200.00

Country, poplar, molded cornice, two raised panel doors, two dovetailed drawers, bracket feet, orig hardware including bat wing brasses and wrought iron H-hinges, engraved brass escutcheon and iron lock, old red finish, chestnut secondary wood, repairs, foot facings and cornice replaced, 41-3/4" w, 17" d, 73" h 4,400.00

New York, Hudson River Valley, c1780, gumwood, two-part, top with molded cornice, arched raised panel cupboard doors, conforming panels on either side of doors, two drawers over two long graduated drawers in base, bracket feet, replaced brasses, refinished, repairs, 48" w, 17" d, 74" h 3,500.00

Pennsylvania, c1770-1800, cherry, overhanging dentil molded cornice, two arched paneled doors flanked by chamfered fluted corners, interior with four shelves, lower section with three wide graduated drawers, replaced bat wing brasses, ogee bracket feet, 48-3/4" w, 20-1/4" d, 75" h.....10,080.00

Pennsylvania, c1770-1800, mahogany, overhanging step molded cornice over two paneled doors, lower section with two narrow drawers over single wide drawer, ogee bracket feet, later butterfly brasses, black script "C. Wiegand, Norristown" written on top of lower section, 48-1/4" w, 25" d, 77-1/4" h..6,725.00

Virginia, eastern, late 18th C, mahogany, two sections, top section with applied molded cornice over two paneled doors opening to reveal six graduated pullout shelves, lower section with applied molded frieze over two short drawers over two long drawers with cockbeading, ogee bracket feet, orig finial and brasses, poplar secondary wood, 49" w, 19-1/2" d, 84" h...............................12,500.00

Federal, New York, c1820, mahogany inlaid, top section with arched molding above inlaid frieze flanked by ball finials, two cupboard doors with applied molding opening to mahogany, cedar, and pine linen drawers, lower case with two cockbeaded short drawers, three graduated long drawers, flaring French feet joined by valanced skirt, old finish, 48" w, 22" d, 87-3/4" h................................9,775.00

George III, late 18th/early 19th, mahogany, rectangular dentil molded cornice over pair of plain doors, shelved interior, base with three cockbeaded drawers, bracket feet, some restoration, 48-1/4" w, 23" d, 82-1/2" h 2,300.00

Georgian, c1810, mahogany, molded lunette cornice above two paneled doors, lower section fitted with two short drawers over two long graduated drawers, bracket feet, 47-1/2" w, 21-1/4" d, 81" h 3,200.00

Georgian-Style

c1840, mahogany, molded cornice above two doors, each inset with shaped highly figured panel, lower section with two short drawers over two long graduated drawers, shaped bracket feet, 48" w, 22-1/2" d, 81" h 2,200.00

c1860 and later, walnut, molded cornice above two doors, each inset with shaped panel, lower section with three long graduated drawers, all with herringbone banding, bracket feet, 39-1/2" w, 21" d, 84" h.................2,500.00

Hepplewhite

Middle Atlantic States, mahogany, line and band inlaid, molded cornice, double blind cupboard doors, fitted interior, base with three long drawers, scalloped skirt, straight scalloped feet, refinished, 49" w, 19-1/2" d, 81" h 7,700.00

New York, mahogany, figured mahogany veneer and ebony inlay, removable cornice with curved molding with inlay and ball finials, double doors with five pull-out interior shelves, five dovetailed drawers, high French feet, scrolled apron, good old finish, pine secondary wood, repairs to cornice, center finial missing, age crack in left door, 46-1/2" w, 88" h 8,800.00

Queen Anne-Style, c1860 and later, walnut, molded domed cornice above two paneled doors, lower section with four long drawers, bun feet, veneered with oyster panels, side brass carrying handles, 46-1/2" w, 27" d, 85" h.......................................2,500.00

Regency, c1820, mahogany

Irish, garland form pediment above two doors, each inset with shaped panels,

Linen Press, Hepplewhite, New York, mahogany, figured mahogany veneer and ebony inlay, removable cornice with curved molding with inlay and ball finials, double doors with five pull-out interior shelves, five dovetailed drawers, high French feet, scrolled apron, good old finish, pine secondary wood, repairs to cornice, center finial missing, age crack in left door, 46-1/2" w, 88" h, $8,800. Photo courtesy of Garth's Auctions, Inc., Delaware, OH.

shelved interior, lower section fitted with three long graduated drawers, flanked on either side by rounded fluted pilasters, bracket feet, 48-1/4" w, 22" d, 95" h......................3,300.00

Molded cornice, two highly figured paneled doors, flanked by turned pilasters, lower section with two short drawers over two long graduated drawers, shaped bracket feet, 47-1/2" w, 20-1/2" d, 78" h 2,450.00

Molded over-hanging cornice, two paneled doors, opening to sliding shelves, lower section fitted with two short drawers over two long graduated drawers, splayed bracket feet, 52-1/2" w, 23" d, 87-1/2" h.......3,750.00

Sheraton-Style, c1840, mahogany, dentillated cornice above two doors, each inset with oval panel, lower section with four short drawers, bracket feet, 58-1/2" w, 26-1/2" d, 79" h..1,800.00

Victorian

America, Georgian taste, c1880, mahogany, molded cornice above two doors, each inset with highly figured panels, lower section fitted with two short drawers over two long graduated drawers, turned toupie feet, 48" w, 22" d, 82-1/2" h 1,500.00

America, second half 19th C, maple, superstructure with wooden screw surmounted by acorn finial, stand with frieze drawer, square-section legs, imperfections, 24-3/4" w, 14" d, 50-1/2" h 300.00

Pewter Cupboards

Pewter cupboards are easily identified by two distinctive features. They usually have a step-back where the top cupboard joins the base. The other feature is a plate rail that served to hold plates vertically. Few furniture styles included this type of cupboard as it usually was designed for kitchen use and not thought highly enough of to be made in a fancy wood or form.

Country

America, pine, molded cornice, open shelves, shaped sides, two paneled doors, cutout feet, mellow refinishing, 53-1/2" w, 80" h 4,200.00

Canadian, pine, light blue and red repaint, open top with slightly bowed shelves, applied reeded molding cornice with fretwork frieze, open base with beaded frame, three drawers, one drawer replaced, replaced bottom shelf and backboards, 51" w, 71" h 2,400.00

Pewter, Country, stepback, attributed to Ohio, poplar, old red finish, molded cornice, beaded edge stiles, top with three shelves, door with four raised panels, cutout feet, simple apron, replaced cornice, 35-1/2" w, 14" d, 79" h, $3,900. Also shown are several pieces of European pewter, large charger valued at $440. Photo courtesy of Garth's Auctions, Inc., Delaware, OH.

New England, c1820, grain painted, orig simulated burnt sienna mahogany and mustard graining, four open shelves, three small drawers over two banks of two graduated drawers, wooden knobs, 61" w, 14-1/8" d, 71-3/4" h 4,200.00

Pennsylvania, Lebanon County, c1770, painted blue, red, and buff, pine, two sections, upper section with overhanging cornice, two open shelves flanked by scrolling sides, projecting base below with molded edge, one long drawer with raised panel cupboard door, shelf interior, molded base, bun feet, paint of later date, 48" w, 15-1/4" d, 79" h 2,250.00

Stepback, attributed to Ohio, poplar, old red finish, molded cornice, beaded edge stiles, top with three shelves, door with four raised panels, cutout feet, simple apron, replaced cornice, 35-1/2" w, 14" d, 79" h 3,900.00

Stepback, pine, beaded board front, one door, interior shelf, middle shelf of top section cutout for spoons, ends have scalloping at middle section and cutout feet, old refinishing, cut-down, restorations, old alternations, 53" w, 18" d, 63-1/8" h 1,320.00

Stepback, pine, molded cornice, two small paneled doors at top, two longer doors in base, cutout feet, old refinishing, nut brown color, 48-1/2" w, 17-1/2" d, 75" h 1,100.00

Stepback, pine, shallow top section with three removable shelves, molded plate bar across bottom with spoon cutouts, base with two doors with inset panels, refinished, old nut brown color, reconstruction with additions, 48" w, 20-3/4" d, 76" h 1,265.00

Stepback, poplar, open top with perimeter molding, four shelves, base with two raised paneled doors, cutout feet, imperfections, 39" w, 16" d, 79" h 900.00

Stepback, poplar, two sections, upper section with cornice molding, two six glass pane doors, two shelves, open pie shelf; base section with two drawers over raised panel doors, one shelf interior, short turned feet, 56" w, 20" d, 87" h 2,250.00

William and Mary, early 18th C, found near Gettysburg, PA, pine and poplar, open shelves with cutouts for spoons, plate rails, molded cornice with scalloped rail, paneled doors with rat tail hinges, cutout and scalloped ends, bracket feet, apron drop, portions of feet restored, wear, age cracks, edge damage, old refinishing, some old red repaint, 56" w, 61-1/2" x 12-1/2" d cornice, 56" x 20" base, 80-3/4" h 7,000.00

Pie Safe

After baking for hours, a pie safe was called into service to store pies and all kinds of baked goods. This special cupboard usually had tin panels with punched holes for ventilation or even screened panels to allow for cooling of the delicious baked goods, while keeping them out of harm's way and away from insects, or sticky fingers.

Pie safes were quite the rage a few years ago and reproductions do exist, so look carefully for signs of age and wear. Layers of paint will usually attest to the long life and usefulness of this form.

Country

Butternut and poplar, dovetailed case, corner and base moldings, tin paneled doors with star flower and bird dec, old worn green

Pie Safe, country, 19th C, pine, single long drawer over six punched tin panels with fruited urns decoration, $1,650.

over red paint, orig cast iron latch, porcelain knob, removable batten, insect damage, 48-1/2" w, 72" h 900.00

Pine and poplar, sq posts with turned feet, two dovetailed drawers, punched tin panels with circular designs, refinished, 36-1/2" w, 22" d, 46-1/2" h 1,400.00

Pine, Pennsylvania, large molded overhanging cornice above lozenge/tongue stippled molding, three open shelves with plate guards above two door cabinet with tin back, bracket feet, minor old repairs, 54-3/4" w, 15" d, 72-1/2" h 450.00

Poplar, America, second half 19th C, outset molded top over pair of doors, each set with punched tin panel decoration with four phylfots, shelved interior, sides with similar panels decorated with star motifs, molded base raised on square section stile legs, 40-3/4" w, 17" d, 60-1/4" h 3,200.00

Poplar, attributed to Rich Brothers Shop, Wythe County, Virginia, c1830-40, one board top, two dovetailed drawers, two doors, punched tin panels with urn and tulip, hears and stars, side tins with repeating motif, turned legs, 50-1/2" w, 18-1/2" d, 54" h 5,000.00

Poplar, attributed to east Tennessee, worn old red paint, tin panel on each side, two pairs on each door with soldered seams, stylized urns of flowers and oak leaves, turned feet, 53" w, 48" h 1,650.00

Poplar, attributed to Zanesville, OH, area, twelve punched tins with snowflake designs, joined with solderless crimped seams, stripped of orig paint, later red wash 1,980.00

Poplar and Walnut, paneled construction, sq corner posts, rectangular slightly overhanging top, one long drawer, two doors each with three punched tins with star designs, high feet, solid paneled ends, layers of old paint, some damage to tins, 38-1/2" w, 16-1/2" d, 54" h 440.00

Poplar and white pine, Ohio, c1860, light brown paint decoration, two drawers over two paneled doors, two circular vents on each side, 38-1/2" w, 15-1/2" d, 54-1/2" h 600.00

Yellow Pine, eastern North Carolina, mid 19th C, red wash, three board tongue-and-groove top, two doors with two tins each, tin motif of central compass with star in each corner, each side with two tins, some worm damage, dry scraped, 52" w, 22-1/2" d, 65" h 950.00

Yellow Pine, Virginia, 19th C, painted, pierced, punched, shaped gallery above two decorated tin doors, three shelved interior above angled tapering feet, old green paint, paint loss, tin discoloration, other imperfections, 45" w, 17" d, 49" h..................1,955.00

Walnut, double doors with three punched tin panels with star, circle, and heart designs, two dovetailed drawers, cutout feet, refinished, 42-1/4" w, 48-1/2" h..................950.00

Walnut, Pennsylvania, first half 19th c, rectangular top, two short drawers, two cupboard doors, each mounted with three punched tin-panels depicting quarter round spandrels centering diamond motif, sq tapering legs, 41" w, 17-3/4" w, 53-1/2" h 2,900.00

Stepback Cupboards

Stepback cupboards are similar to pewter cupboards, but generally are larger. They may include doors with glass panes. Their shelves may be grooved to hold plates rather than a plate rail. The name is derived from the fact that the top section is narrower than the base, giving a step look at the mid section. Like corner, pewter, and wall cupboards, many fall in the a generic "Country" style, rather than a specific design style.

Country

Middle Atlantic States, early 19th C, two sections, upper section with painted poplar, flat molded cornice with applied beading above two glazed hinged doors with molded muntins, three shelves; base section with projecting base of two cupboard doors with recessed panels, cutout feet, refinished, some old paint, imperfections, 48-3/4" w, 86" h 3,800.00

New England, 18th C, primitive, two sections, upper section with three shelves with plate groove; base section with two drawers, two panel doors, traces of orig red paint, 56-1/2" w, 23-1/2" d, 81" h..............1,700.00

Pennsylvania, Hanover, Rupp Family, c1850, poplar and white pine, old varnish, mustard paint decoration on applied upper and lower half turned columns and two drawer fronts, two doors with six glazed panes each, interior with three shelves and spoon notches, pine shelf over two paneled doors, turned feet, 52" w, 22-1/2" d, 87" h 9,750.00

Pennsylvania, Mennonite, one piece, top section with twelve dec frosted panes of glass, two interior shelves, plate rack, bottom with two paneled door with one shelf interior, orig finish, pie shelf, simple cut out base and cornice, 42" w, 16-1/2" d, 80" h................2,000.00

Pennsylvania, two sections, pine and poplar, upper section with flat top with cove molded cornice, two paneled doors, shelf interior, turned quarter columns, pie shelf; base section with three small dovetailed overlapping drawers, two paneled cupboard doors, turned quarter columns, straight apron, bracket feet, wood knob handles, brownish-red paint traces, repainted black trim, 55" w, 22" d, 84" h 4,500.00

Pennsylvania or Ohio, c1840, walnut, two sections, upper section with applied molded

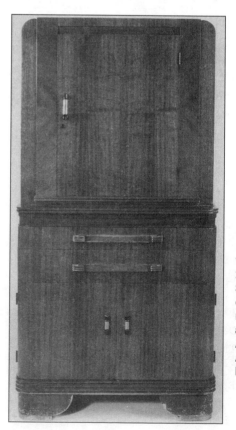

Stepback, Art Deco, c1935, veneered wood, chrome pulls, rectangular single door compartment on top, two long drawers over cabinet doors on base, interior glass shelves missing, nicks, wear to veneer, 29-3/8" w, 60" h, $1,200. Photo courtesy of Skinner Auctioneers and Appraisers of Antiques and Fine Art Boston and Bolton, MA.

cornice, two doors with eight glazed panes each, flanked by chamfered corners with lambs tongue, lower section with pine shelf, two board top, three drawers over two paneled doors, paneled sides, turned feet, poplar, and hardwood secondary woods, 52" w, 20" d, 93-1/2" h.................................4,500.00

Pennsylvania or Ohio, early 19th C, two sections, walnut, upper section with flat molded cornice above two glazed doors, two interior shelves, projecting base with two molded cupboard doors, cutout feet, 35-3/4" w, 16" d, 62" h...2,500.00

Federal, 19th C

Cherry, projecting cornice, pair of glass doors, three aligned paneled doors over pair

of cupboard doors, bracket feet, 63" w, 19" d, 84" h...2,500.00

Pine, flat cove molded cornice over two glazed lattice doors, lower section fitted with four paneled doors, molded base, 66-1/2" w, 16-1/2" d, 86" h...............................1,460.00

Sheraton

America, cherry, beveled cornice, paneled doors, one dovetailed drawer with cockbeading, high turned feet, poplar secondary wood, refinished, 41" l x 15-1/4" d cornice, 37-3/4" w, 89-1/4" h.........................3,650.00

Pennsylvania, Montgomery or Bucks County, c1830, poplar, cornice with matchstick molding, top with two six-light glazed doors, three light center panel, step shelf interior, above six spice drawers, base with three cockbeaded drawers over two blind doors, turned feet, 58" w, 21" d, 86" h
....7,250.00

Wall Cupboards

Wall cupboards are usually massive pieces of furniture with storage for dishes and objects that were useful in a kitchen or dining room. Most wall cupboards were made in two sections, allowing for ease in moving them since they can be quite heavy because of their bulk. Early craftsmen made these cupboards to take every day use. Today when you feel the sides of these large cupboards they often still display the soft shapes left by hand planing. Molded cornices help to left them right up to the ceilings of early homes. Shelved interiors might include a plate groove and even cutouts for which to display spoons. Why? Owning silver spoons was a sign of wealth and what a wonderful way to show them off. While exteriors might be finished with natural varnishes, many were stained, painted, or grained to imitate fine woods. Interiors were painted and often repainted because of years of continued use. Doors with glazed panes or paneled, commonly referred to as blind, are typically found on the top section. Sometimes a pie shelf is created where the top rests on the base. Drawers and more cupboard doors complete the cupboard. Many are found with short feet to help keep them off the floor.

Stepback, country, decorated, pine and poplar, orig red flame graining on yellow ground, solid red panels, cove molded cornice, three dovetailed drawers, pie shelf, paneled doors, one board ends with cutout feet, minor repairs, mismatched latches, 54" w, shelf is 20-1/2" d, 57" w, 84" h, $6,875. Photo courtesy of Garth's Auctions, Inc., Delaware, OH.

Few wall cupboards fall into distinct furniture styles. Often a style is attributed by the cornice, feet, or time frame.

Canadian, 19th C, painted, stepback, upper section with pair of paneled cupboard doors, three interior shelves, two drawers, lower section with pair of paneled cupboard doors, two interior shelves, allover orig blue paint, turned wooden knobs, minor imperfections, 53-3/4" d, 17-3/4" d, 86-1/2" h 7,200.00

Chippendale

Ohio, early 19th C, cherry inlaid, flat molded cornice, door with flush cockbeaded panel inlaid with two symmetrically arranged

Wall, Country, Ohio, cherry and curly maple, two sections, molded cornice, paneled doors, two silver drawers, pie shelf, three drawers in base, turned feet, refinished, old replaced brasses, 49" w, 19-1/4" d x 52-1/4" w shelf, 87-3/4" h, $7,700. Also shown are creamer, $465, plate $720, waste bowl, $495, and miniature cup and saucer, $550, all in blue spatterware Fort pattern. Photo courtesy of Garth's Auctions, Inc., Delaware, OH.

leafy branches, rectangular escutcheon, interior with three shelves, flanked by ring-turned columns, flat molded base, 19-1/2" w, 7-1/2" d, 27-1/4" h.............................1,495.00

Pennsylvania, walnut, two sections, upper section with step molded cornice over two doors with eighteen old glass panes, rat tail hinges, candle drawers, chamfered corners, rectangular pie shelf, lower section with three drawers over two paneled cupboard doors with mid supports, scalloped straight bracket feet, minor early repair, replaced drawer and hardware, 72" w, 20" d, 85" h...................22,100.00

Country

America, cherry and walnut, two sections, upper section with plain cornice, double doors each with six panes of old glass, pie shelf, base section with single long dovetailed drawer, paneled doors with raised panels, bracket feet, applied pressed moldings, replaced cornice and hardware, repairs, 53" w, 19-3/4" d, 82-1/4" h 2,310.00

America, found in Rhode Island, pine, old gray paint, molded cornice, two raised panel doors, single dovetailed drawer, cutout front foot bracket, one board ends with cutout feet, red and blue paint showing through at points of wear, replaced brass H-hinges and bails, repainted interior, imperfections, modifications due to hardware replacement, 36-1/4" w, 21-1/2" d, 73" h 5,775.00

America, pine, old red stain, stepback, molded cornice, raised panel doors set in beaded frame, 36" w, 80" h 2,100.00

America, softwood, red repaint, two sections, upper section with cove molded cornice, double doors each with four panels, pie shelf, lower section with three dovetailed drawers over paneled doors, bracket feet, interior painted blue, repairs, replaced feet, 59-3/4" w, 82" h 2,745.00

Maine, mid-19th C, grained pine, molded top, paneled door, four turned ball feet, orig simulated crotch mahogany graining in ochre and red brown, turned wooden pull, minor imperfections, 41-1/2" w, 17-1/4" d, 85" h 4,850.00

New England, c1850, Gothic influence, shaped gallery above three glazed doors, arched panels flanked by conforming side panels, pained red-brown, 23-1/2" w, 9" d, 23" h 600.00

New England, 18th C, grain painted, yellow pine, painted red, upper and lower doors, shelved interior, wooden latches, cornice, mid-section and base with molding, turned bulbous feet, butterfly hinges, 41-1/4" w, 20" d, 6301/2" h 7,200.00

Ohio, pine, cleaned down to old red, top case dovetailed, beveled cornice, raised panel doors, cutout feet, one board ends, minor edge damage, bottom board of top case signed "J. W. Ogden, Urbana, Ohio," 43-1/2" w, 88-3/4" h 2,200.00

Ohio, walnut, two sections, upper section with molded cornice and frieze, two glass paneled doors, perimeter molding, lower section with paneled doors, perimeter molding 59-3/4" w, 18" d, 90" h 1,200.00

Pennsylvania, c1840, red painted poplar, two sections, upper section with overhanging cornice above two glazed doors, shelved interior, projecting lower section with three short drawers, two raised panel cupboard doors, turned tapering legs, ball feet, orig Sandwich glass drawer pulls............................18,000.00

Empire, married, two sections, mahogany flame-grain veneer, beaded molding, scrolled feet and pilasters, upper section with molded cornice, double doors with Gothic tracery, six dovetailed drawers, old worn finish, some wear, veneer damage, 44" l x 145" d cornice, 39-1/2" w, 93-1/2" h...............................900.00

Federal

Middle Atlantic States, cherry, two sections, upper section with molded cornice over pair of glazed doors with six lights each, applied geometric decorated panels, stepback, pie shelf, base with three drawers over pair of paneled cupboard doors, replaced brasses, early repairs, 69" w, 21" d, 88" h................58,500.00

Pennsylvania or Ohio, c1830, cherry, molded top above two beaded small drawers, similar glazed door opens to interior space flanked by recessed panel sides, turned legs ending in small ball feet, refinished, imperfections, 28" w, 13-1/2" d, 25" h 1,850.00

Pennsylvania, c1840, poplar, blind (closed face), pair of cupboard doors with arched panels, four small drawers over two drawers, paneled lower cupboard doors flanked by turned columns, refinished with traces of orig paint, two drawer pulls missing, replaced hinges and glass, 53" w, 18-1/2" d, 85-1/2" h 2,500.00

Pennsylvania, c1850, married, poplar, upper section with bold cornice, two doors with six panes of glass, pie shelf, base section with three drawers over two door cupboard, flanked by carved columns, turned feet, minor imperfections, 54-1/2" d, 20" d, 84" h 2,675.00

Pennsylvania, Soap Hollow, c1861-65, poplar, two sections, orig red and green paint, red and yellow striping, gold and silver stenciled decoration with birds, etc., upper section with molded cornice, double doors each with six panes of old glass, center panel with three panes, over pie shelf, base section with three dovetailed drawers over two doors and center section, all with raised panels, dovetailed bracket feet, turned quarter columns on both sections, bottom rail of upper section with stenciled label "Manufactured by Peter K. Thomas," pieced repair to cornice, two drawer fronts replaced, touch-up repair to paint, 63-3/4" w, 86-1/2" h...........................35,200.00

Painted, New England, mid to early 19th C

Pine, double fielded panel door, interior of five shelves, orig bright blue paint, paint surface imperfections, 28" w, 14-1/2" d, 79-3/4" h 5,520.00

Pine, flat molded cornice above cock-beaded case of two shelves, projecting base with single cupboard door, painted white with salmon red interior, loss to height, 54-3/4" w, 15-1/2" d, 70" h....................................920.00

Pine, flat molded cornice above interior of three shelves bordered with molded surround, cupboard door below enclosing three shelves, old blue gray paint, replaced iron H-hinges, imperfections, 47-3/4" w, 18" l, 72-1/2" h 2,645.00

Pine, two paneled doors, interior of three shelves, cyma-curved skirt, old Spanish brown paint, height loss, surface imperfections, 48" w, 18" d, 60" h.................2,300.00

Queen Anne Style, English, late 19th/early 20th C, walnut, burl walnut, and polychrome dec, molded cornice over shelves, central cabinet door and drawer, base with drawers, cabriole legs, pad feet, shrinkage, wear to polychrome, 42-3/4" w, 17-1/2" d, 70-1/2" h 4,900.00

Shaker

Mount Lebanon, NY, 19th C, painted pine, two doors, numbered and labeled shelved interior, old light green paint, interior unpainted, some shelves missing, 23-3/4" w, 7-1/2" d, 40-1/2" h 1,610.00

Mount Lebanon, NY, c1850-60, painted poplar, two drawers above two recessed panel doors, opening to four shelves interior, arched base, old light gray paint, surface imperfections, 36-3/4" w, 16-1/2" d, 73" h 2,760.00

Slant Back, New England, late 18th C, pine, flat molded cornice above beaded canted front flanking shelves, projecting base with single raised panel door, old refinish, doors missing from top, imperfections, 37-1/2" w, 18" d, 73" h 2,300.00

Wardrobe

Wardrobe is the common name for a large cupboard designed to hold clothes. Each geographical region put their distinctive signature on hand made wardrobes.

Arts and Crafts, Gustav Stickley, New York

Oak, No. 920, c1910, rectangular top over two paneled doors, copper V-pulls, interior fitted with two open compartments over four long drawers over two open shelves, red decal, paper Craftsman label, some wear and small losses to wood at top edge, 34" w, 16-1/2" d, 59-3/4" h 14,950.00

Oak, two paneled doors over two drawers, orig hardware, inverted V-toe board, five shelves interior, unsigned, some restoration, 44" w, 23" d, 78" h 7,800.00

Country

America, one piece, pine, simple detail, molded cornice, raised panel door, beaded edge stiles, shelves and wood hooks in interior, worn dark brown finish, 75-3/4" h 600.00

America, one piece, poplar and pine, flat cornice, one door with two vertical inset panels with Rockingham glazed pottery knob,

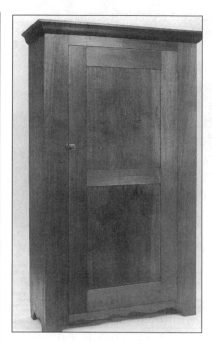

Wardrobe, Country, Ohio, attributed to Delaware County, walnut, molded cornice, one paneled door, scrolled apron, cutout feet, one interior shelf, orig hooks removed, brass latch added, old soft finish, one end of cornice cut to fit corner, 41-3/4" w, 77-1/2" h, $1,870. Photo courtesy of Garth's Auctions, Inc., Delaware, OH.

one dovetailed drawer with turned wooden knobs, molded base, interior fitted with fourteen small cast iron hooks and replaced shelf, old brown repaint, age crack in door, 38" w, 19" d, 83-1/2" h 525.00

Country, variegated marble top, double curved doors, serpentine front, seven drawers, scroll feet, gilt metal mounts, 36" w, 48" h 675.00

Ohio, attributed to Delaware County, walnut, molded cornice, one paneled door, scrolled apron, cutout feet, one interior shelf, orig hooks removed, brass latch added, old soft finish, one end of cornice cut to fit corner, 41-3/4" w, 77-1/2" h 1,870.00

Missouri, walnut, molded cornice, paneled door, one-board ends, flat pilasters with carved pine capitals, sq cutouts in top, pine secondary wood, 33-1/2" w, 20" d, 63" h 1,450.00

Classical, middle Atlantic states, 1840, mahogany veneer, two recessed panel doors, similar sides, interior with veneered drawers, base with platform feet, small interior drawers added, 65" w, 26" d, 79-1/2" h 3,200.00

William IV, c1840, mahogany, concave molded cornice above three long doors, central one mirrored, others paneled, two right doors opening to pull-out shelves and three long drawers, left door opening to hanging space, plinth base, 69" w, 23" d, 81-1/2" h 1,500.00

Desks

A desk is a furniture form that appears throughout most of the furniture styles. Functioning as a command center for early households, a well appointed desk served as a place to organize finances, write letters, and keep track of important documents. The furniture craftsmen who created these masterpieces used some ordinary woods, as well as some more exotic woods, like bird's eye maple. Use of inlays helped exhibit wealth and style.

The term "slant front" or "slant lid" mean the same thing and it describes the flat writing surface that folds down from the top to a comfortable writing height. By closing the front and perhaps locking it, important papers could be secured. Secret compartments and drawers were also built into some desks.

A "fall front" denotes a board that lowers from the top to a writing surface, it may or may not fit on a slant like a slant front. Some fall fronts, especially in the Arts & Crafts era, and on butler's desks were not slanted. A "knee hole" desk refers to a desk with a flat working surface, usually supported by two banks (or piers) of drawers or legs, allowing the user to sit with their knees under the desk top. A "lady's desk" is usually more diminutive and allowed a lady to sit with her legs under the working surface. She also had some compartments at her disposal, but often not as many as on a slant front desk. A "Davenport" is often a smaller version with fold-out working surfaces. A "butler's" desk has generally a smaller writing surface and fewer interior compartments. The butler was probably using the desk for simple record keeping or perhaps only writing instructions to others and not using the space for long correspondence. A "secretary" is a desk with a high bookcase top.

When purchasing an antique desk, look for signs of wear, pull out the slant front supports and see if the front rests flat on them. Look for signs of replaced hardware by examining the interior of drawers. Any holes not being used for current hardware may be a clue to the location of earlier hardware. Check to see if the height of the writing surface is comfortable. Perhaps the feet have been altered, check them carefully too. If purchasing a roll top or tambour closing desk, check to see that the top moves well. Any leather or felt covered surfaces should show some signs of wear. It is not unusual to find some repairs or restorations to early desks. Adjustments to the value of a particular desk will be determined by these factors, as well as the style, coloration, and overall appeal to the buyer.

Also see Secretaries, Boxes, and Tables for other forms of desks.

Aesthetic Movement

Desks from this brief furniture style are elaborate creations that reflected the exciting designs of the time. The provenance of one of these examples is enhanced by the original bill of sale.

America, c1885, lady's, ebonized cherry, Oriental influenced fretwork, panels and carving, three small aligned drawers over inset writing surface, three graduated drawers, 36" w, 20-1/4" d, 48" h 3,500.00

New York, Herter Brothers, Washburn Commission, mahogany, fall front, top section: shelf with gallery top supported by turned and blocked posts, back panel with decorated gold threaded material; middle section: slant lid, two supporting pull-out arms, central panel of marquetry inlaid with garland of flowers ending in bows, interior with two drawers, five cubbyholes, supported by two turned front legs, two bottom section with shelf and paneled back, missing orig writing surface, raised panel back, needs restoration, commissioned by Hon. William Drew Washburn for MN Greek Revival house, copy of orig bill of sale, 30" w, 20" w, 53-1/2" h 9,000.00

Art Deco

Desks from the Art Deco period, c1920 to c1945, reflect the changing furniture styles.

Look for sleek lines, usage of new materials, like metal, and exposed frames.

Frankl, Paul, Frankl Studios, New York, c1928, known as "Puzzle Desk," Chinese red lacquered body, four silver-leaf drawers with whimsical silver metal pulls, beveled mirrored top, fully restored, 40" w, 24" d, 28" h 16,000.00

McArthur, Warren, manufactured by McArthur Industries, 1930s, orig laminate top with upper gallery, anodized aluminum frame, some wear, 50" w, 37" d, 33" h 5,500.00

Art Nouveau

Furniture of the Art Nouveau period reflects the love of nature, flowers, and sweeping lines found in Art Nouveau accessories, prints, etc. This example may be American made, but since it is unsigned, it is difficult to tell. It was sold through an American auction house and is a good example of desks found in the Art Nouveau style.

Style of Louis Majorelle, c1900, rectangular top, leather inset over central drawer flanked by double drawers with brass mounts, stylized pine cone motifs, molded legs, 51" l, 29-1/2" w, 29" h 6,900.00

Arts & Crafts

Desks from the Arts & Crafts period are becoming more popular. Their plain lines and handy storage drawers make these desks

Arts & Crafts, Limbert, Grand Rapids and Holland, Michigan, c1910, No. 1141, oak, rectangular overhanging top, two drawers, corbel supports, lower median shelf, branded mark, minor stains and wear, 48" w, 32-1/4" d, $1,750. Photo courtesy of Skinner Auctioneers and Appraisers of Antiques and Fine Art Boston and Bolton, MA.

practical and useful. Prices are increasing for examples by the major designers of the period that still have the original finish, hardware, and are identified by labels.

Lifetime Furniture, Grand Rapids, MI

No. 105, rectangular top over single drawer, orig copper hardware with bookshelf on side, two slats on opposite side, refinished, branded mark, top shortened, 38" w, 25" d, 29" h 950.00

No. 8567, drop-front, single drawer and shelf, orig hammered copper hardware, fitted interior, double keyed-tenon construction, orig finish, decal, minor stains on top, 33" w, 16" d, 45" h 1,400.00

Limbert, Charles P., Grand Rapids and Holland, MI

No. 718, c1912, central pen tray, flanked by letter holders over two drawers with V-pulls, median shelf, branded mark, 36" w, 20" d, 37-3/4" h, stains, joint separation 1,100.00

Drop-front, gallery top and interior, single drawer, square hammered copper pulls, orig finish, branded mark, ring stain to top, 33" w, 18-1/4" d, 34-1/2" h 1,250.00

Drop-front, hammered trim lock, open shelf, glass cabinet door and cutout bookshelves to right side, some wear to orig dark finish, paper label, 33-1/2" w, 13-1/8" d, 49" h 5,000.00

McHugh, oak, partners, four drawers on each side, Mackmurdo feet, X-design applied to sides, orig dark finish, one knob replaced, 56" w, 37" d, 29" h 1,300.00

Roycroft, East Aurora, NY, drop-front, strap hardware, single drawer with large copper oval pulls, pull-out supports, Mackmurdo feet, gallery interior, orig finish, carved orb and cross mark, large chip to back of top, 38-1/4" w, 19" d, 44" h 8,000.00

Stickley Brothers, Grand Rapids, MI, No. 6515, oak, slant front, copper strap hinges, over single drawer, orig oval copper hardware, four tapered posts on shoefoot base, cleaned orig finish, unsigned, 30" w, 15" d, 47" h 1,900.00

Stickley, Gustav, New York

No. 550, c1902, slant front, three drawers, two cabinet doors with orig copper strap hardware, flush tenons at sides, orig finish, sgd, red decal, changes to lid supports, 33" w, 14" d, 48" h 9,900.00

No. 650, rect top, single drawer, lower median shelf, paper label, worn rails, drill holes on top, roughness, 36" w, 24" d, 30" h 920.00

No. 706, designed by Harvey Ellis, drop-front, overhanging top, paneled front inlaid with copper, pewter, and wood floral decoration, full gallery interior and lower shelf, faintly visible mark on back, two splints to back boards, new finish to top, 30" w, 13" d, 44" h 28,000.00

No. 728, oak, drop front, fitted interior, one horizontal drawer, under-tier shelf, red Gustav Stickley decal mark in drawer, 30-1/4" w, 13-1/2" d, 43-1/4" h 775.00

No. 729, fall-front, two half drawers over three full drawers, orig iron hardware, slab sides with through-tenon construction, fitted interior, red decal and paper label, orig finish, 37" w, 15" d, 45" h.....................3,850.00

Kneehole, nine drawers, chamfered sides and back, keyed through-tenon lower shelf, faceted wooden pulls, refinished top, orig dark finish base, replaced lock in center drawer, red decal, 53" l, 30" d, 30" h......................5,500.00

Arts & Crafts, Gustav Stickley, New York, kneehole, nine drawers, chamfered sides and back, keyed through tenon-lower shelf, faceted wooden pulls, refinished top, orig dark finish on base, red decal, replaced lock, imperfections, 53" w, 30" d, 30" h, $5,500. Also shown is table lamp with scalloped leaded glass shade, $1,300. Photo courtesy of David Rago Auctions/RagoArts.com, Lambertville, NJ.

Arts & Crafts, L. & J. G. Stickley, Fayetteville, New York, postcard, curved backsplash and plate rack, single drawer with round wooden pulls, light over-coat to orig reddish brown finish, "The Work of L.& J. G. Stickley" label, stain on lower shelf, 34" w, 20" d, 34-1/4" h, $1,200. Photo courtesy of David Rago Auctions/RagoArts.com, Lambertville, NJ.

Partner's, c1902, flat rectangular top, central drawer, pullout writing surface, four drawers on either side, wooden pulls, lower shelf with kneehole, V-board sides, prominent key tenons, mirrored on opposing side, large red signature, retailer's mark, minor older surface nicks, waxed finish, 60" l,. 40" d, 30" h......................................7,200.00

Stickley, L. and J. G., Fayetteville, NY

Chestnut, fall-front, full gallery interior, chamfered back, lower shelf area with open sides, shoe feet, new ebonized finish, Onondaga Shops, unmarked, 32-1/2" w, 14-1/2" d, 48" h...700.00

Oak, fall-front, gallery top, two drawers, gate leg and two lower open shelves, medium finish, branded L & J. G. mark, stain, minor roughness, 31-1/2" w, 9-3/4" d closed, 21-3/4" d open, 35" h 1,840.00

Postcard, curved backsplash and plate rack, single drawer, round wooden pulls, light over-coat to orig reddish brown finish, "The Work of L. and J. G. Stickley" label, stain on lower shelf, 34" w, 20" d, 34-1/4" h...............1,200.00

Unknown Designer

Fall-Front, c1912, oak, floriform strapwork, interior fitted with drawers and letter compartments, two split drawers over two long drawers, refinished, 36-1/4" w, 17-1/2" d, 45-3/4" h 1,840.00

Fall-Front, orig copper strap hardware, slab sides with double keyed-tenon construction, heart cutout at top, oval cutout at bottom, orig finish, 31" w, 12" d, 48" h.....................1,200.00

Rectangular top, 1916, oak, through posts over single drawer, round wood pulls flanked by book compartments with vertical slats, round revealed plugs, unsigned, 48" w, 28" d, 29" h 800.00

Chippendale

Chippendale desks feature several elements that were popular with both American and English furniture makers. As the period began, the style was fairly simple, with a slant lid being the most predominate feature. As the style evolved, more carving and more elaborate interiors can be found. Other design elements found in the Chippendale period include serpentine front and block fronts. A serpentine front has a bow in the center while a block front has a linear block design. An oxbow front is a reverse serpentine, where the bow turns inward. Numerous subtle design elements give clues as to where a piece was made. Massachusetts desks usually have any cockbeading applied directly to the case while Pennsylvania desks will have the cockbeading on the drawer fronts, not the case.

America, c1775, slant front, painted, maple and pine, rectangular top over slant lid, dovetailed case, hinged slant lid, fitted interior with five dovetailed drawers, four dovetailed overlapping drawers, bracket feet, old red paint, replaced brasses, pine secondary wood, 37" w, 18-1/2" d, 41-3/4" h 12,100.00

America, c1780-1800, slant front, walnut, rectangular top over slant lid, fitted interior with six drawers, six pigeonholes and cockbeaded prospect door, over case with four graduated cockbeaded drawers, ogee bracket feet, rebuilt interior drawers, replaced lid, replaced brasses, new feet, 37" w, 20" d, 41" h 1,495.00

America, third quarter 18th C, slant front, birch, hinged lid, fitted interior, with eight drawers and pigeonholes, dovetailed case, four dovetailed cockbeaded drawers, bracket feet, old refinishing, pine secondary wood, replaced brasses, some damage to feet, repairs, 39-3/4" w, 17-1/2" d, 31-1/2" writing height, 41-1/2" h 2,475.00

America, third quarter 18th C, slant front, maple, rectangular top over flush-paneled and molded slope opening to arrangement of small drawers and valanced pigeonholes centered by prospect door, over four graduated drawers with overlapping molding, molded base with ogee-molded claw and ball feet, 42-3/4" w, 21-1/2" d, 42-3/4" h 3,800.00

America, last quarter 18th C, slant front, mahogany, rectangular top over slant lid, fitted interior with central fan carved deep drawer over

Chippendale, America, c1775, slant front, painted, maple and pine, rectangular top over slant lid, dovetailed case, hinged slant lid, fitted interior with five dovetailed drawers, four dovetailed overlapping drawers, bracket feet, old red paint, replaced brasses, pine secondary wood, 37" w, 18-1/2" d, 41-3/4" h, $12,100. Also shown are two pairs of English Queen Anne brass candlesticks, $440 per pair, decorated miniature blanket chest, pine, green over black paint, diamond and initials "T. S.," bracket feet, 12-3/4" w, 7-1/4" d, 7-1/2" h, $1,210. Photo courtesy of Garth's Auctions, Inc., Delaware, OH.

small drawer flanked on either side by pull out secret compartment, three pigeonholes over two drawers, another deep fan carved drawer, all over two drawers, lower case having four graduated drawers with orig butterfly brasses, claw and ball feet, 40-7/8" w, 20-3/4" d, 43" h 5,265.00

Connecticut, c1780, slant front, cherry, rectangular top over slant lid, interior of central prospect door flanked by two valanced compartments and two drawers, two projecting short drawers, case with four graduated thumb-molded drawers, ogee bracket feet, replaced brasses, old refinishing, restoration, 30" w, 21" d, 41-3/4" h.........................2,185.00

Connecticut, late 18th C, block front, mahogany, slant front lid, fitted tiered interior with nine dovetailed drawers, pigeonholes, two pull-out letter drawers with fluted columns, flame carved finials and door with blocking and fan carving, dovetailed case, four dovetailed drawers, conforming apron, bracket feet, replaced brasses, old refinishing, feet replaced, repairs to case, 41-3/4" w, 21-1/2" d, 42-3/4" h 3,850.00

Country, slant front, maple, rectangular top over slant lid, dovetailed case, four dovetailed overlapping drawers, fitted interior with thirteen dovetailed drawers, ogee feet, orig brasses, refinished, replaced interior, repairs to feet and drawers, 40" w, 19-1/2" d, 43-1/2" h 1,100.00

Delaware River Valley, c1770, slant front, walnut, interior of central prospect door with recessed thumb-molded tombstone panel opening to valanced two-drawer interior flanked by document drawers with engaged columns and four valanced compartments and four short drawers, case with four thumb-molded graduated drawers, flanked by reeded quarter columns, ogee bracket feet on platforms, orig Chippendale brass pulls and escutcheons, old finish, minor imperfections, provenance: made for Captain John Lambert, Revolutionary War captain for whom Lambertville, NJ, was named....................25,300.00

Maryland, c1770, slant front, cherry, rectangular top over slant lid, fitted interior with valanced divided pigeonholes each over two small drawers over one longer drawer, central prospect with scalloped trim flanked by reeded columns, spiral quarter columns, two small drawers over three graduated drawers, ogee bracket feet, some early repairs, 39" w, 23" d, 43" h...8,800.00

Maryland, c1770, slant front, walnut, rectangular top over slant lid, blocked and stepped interior with valanced pigeonholes, center prospect with six small block front drawers flanked by reeded columns, eight additional drawers under pigeonholes, interior slides flanking two drawers over three graduated drawers, ogee bracket feet, minor early repairs, 38" w, 20" d, 41-1/2" h.............9,350.00

Massachusetts, Boston, c1750-70, block front, mahogany, carved slant lid, interior with fan carving, end-blocked concave and serpentine drawers, open compartments and prospect door flanked by capitals with flame finials, case with block graduated drawers, molded base with central drop, four claw and ball feet, orig brasses, old refinishing, 41" w, 22-1/2" d, 44-1/2" h..50,000.00

Chippendale, Massachusetts, late 18th C, slant front, oxbow, mahogany inlaid, lid opens to interior of small drawers with valanced compartments flanking prospect door with quarter fan inlays and stringing, single interior drawer, case of reverse serpentine drawers with cockbeaded surrounds, molded base, ogee feet on platforms, old surface, imperfections, 42" w, 21" d, 42" h, $6,900. Photo courtesy of Skinner Auctioneers and Appraisers of Antiques and Fine Art Boston and Bolton, MA.

Massachusetts, c1760-80, slant front, maple, two-stepped interior, four balanced compartments, fourteen drawers, case with four thumb-molded graduated drawers, bracket feet, old refinishing, minor imperfections, 35" w, 19-3/4" d, 41-1/2" h 4,200.00

Massachusetts, Boston area, c1770, slant front, mahogany, rectangular top over slant lid, interior with tombstone prospect door flanked by document drawers with columns, opening to three small drawers, one fan carved, others end-blocked, scrolled compartment dividers, serpentine small drawers, case with cockbeaded surround, four long drawers, molded base with shaped bracket feet, central double pendant, old dark surface, orig brasses, repairs, 37" w, 19-1/2" d, 42" h 11,500.00

Massachusetts, c1780, oxbow slant front, mahogany, interior of small drawers, valanced compartments, flanking prospect door with small drawers behind, case with four graduated cockbeaded drawers, light finish, replaced brasses, 41-7/8" w, 22" d, 43-1/2" h 4,200.00

Massachusetts, c1780, slant front, birch, rectangular top over slant lid, shaped interior with ten compartments and small drawers, cockbeaded case with four graduated drawers, bracket feet, replaced brasses, old refinishing, imperfections, 40" w, 21-1/4" d, 44-1/4" h 1,955.00

Massachusetts, Boston, c1770-80, slant front, mahogany, rectangular top over slant lid, interior with central concave fan carved prospect door opening to three concave drawers, flanked by baluster fronted document drawers, three valanced compartments, blocked drawers, fan carved drawer above two concave drawers, case with four graduated thumb-molded drawers, bracket feet, replaced brasses, old refinishing, imperfections, 39-1/2" w, 19-1/2" d, 42-1/4" h 37,600.00

Massachusetts, Boston, c1770-80, slant front, mahogany, oxbow serpentine, fall front opens to interior of central tombstone paneled prospect door flanked by document drawers with baluster fronts, three valanced compartments, three drawers, above cockbeaded case fitted with four graduated drawers with blocked ends on gadroon-carved ogee bracket feet, shaped beaded platforms, brasses appear to

Chippendale, New England, c1780, slant front, tiger maple, fitted interior, four graduated thumb-molded drawers, brass bail handles, eagle escutcheons and oval lock plates, straight bracket feet, 38" w, 19-3/4" d, 41" h, $3,600. Photo courtesy of Samuel T. Freeman & Co., Philadelphia, PA.

be orig, old refinishing, minor imperfections, 41" w, 23" d, 43-1/8" h 26,450.00

Massachusetts, Concord, c1780-90, slant front, maple, rectangular top over slant lid, three thumb-molded drawers over case with slant lid, interior with valanced small compartments, two document drawers, five small drawers, case with four graduated thumb-molded drawers, molded base, high shaped bracket feet, old refinishing, imperfections, inscribed "the property of Merriam, the first settlers of Concord," 35" w, 18" d, 47-1/2" h 17,250.00

Massachusetts, western, c1780, slant front, cherry, fall front opens to interior of five valanced compartments and drawers, case fitted with four graduated drawers with incised cockbeading, molded dovetailed bracket feet, replaced brass pulls, old refinishing, minor imperfections, 37-1/2" w, 18" d, 40" h 3,200.00

Massachusetts, c1785, block front, carved mahogany, rectangular top over slant lid, fitted interior with fan carved prospect door flanked by

Chippendale, New England, late 18th C, slant front, cherry, thumb-molded slant lid with narrow band inlay and center plain oval medallion, compartmented interior with small drawers and pigeonholes, flat top with dovetailing, base with pull-out support slides, four slightly graduated long drawers with maple stringing, rectangular and square banding above scrolled apron, slightly curved square bracket feet, 39" w, 18-1/2" d, 41-1/2" h, $2,300. Photo courtesy of Butterfields.

document drawers with flame carved finials on columns and valanced compartments plus fan carved concave drawers, blocked cockbeaded case with four graduated drawers, shaped center pendant, carved cabriole legs ending in claw and ball feet, old refinishing, replaced brasses, minor imperfections, 41-3/4" w, 22" d, 44-1/4" h...27,500.00

Massachusetts, c1785, slant front, cherry and tiger maple, fitted interior with central molded door flanked by document drawers, valanced compartments and drawers, four long thumb-molded drawers, bracket feet, center drop pendant, old refinishing, old replaced brasses, minor imperfections, 36-5/8" w, 18-3/4" d, 41-5/8" h 4,650.00

Massachusetts, 18th C, slant front, reverse serpentine, carved mahogany, two-stepped interior of valanced compartments and small drawers, case with four graduated scratch

beaded serpentine drawers, conforming molded base with central drop, frontal ball and claw feet, shaped bracket rear feet, old refinishing, repairs, 42" w, 22" d, 44-1/2" h..............5,175.00

Massachusetts, late 18th C, slant front, oxbow, mahogany inlaid, lid opens to interior of small drawers with valanced compartments flanking prospect door with quarter fan inlays and stringing, single interior drawer, case of reverse serpentine drawers with cockbeaded surrounds, molded base, ogee feet on platforms, old surface, imperfections, 42" w, 21" d, 42" h......................6,900.00

Massachusetts or New Hampshire, late 18th C, slant front, carved birch, rectangular top over slant lid, two-tier interior of valanced compartments and small drawers flanked by fan carved central drawer, case of four thumb-molded drawers, shaped bracket feet, refinished, repairs, 38-1/2" d, 19" d, 42-1/2" h........3,800.00

Massachusetts or New Hampshire, late 18th C, slant front, wavy birch, rectangular top over

Chippendale, New England, c1770-90, slant front, tiger maple, rectangular top, slant lid opens to fitted interior with six scalloped pigeonholes surrounding two central drawers, uppermost fan carved over three shallow drawers, case with four graduated wide drawers on molded bracket feet, restored, replacement butterfly brasses, 40" w, 19-3/8" d, 42-1/2" h, $4,200. Photo courtesy of Samuel T. Freeman & Co., Philadelphia, PA.

slant lid, interior of open compartments and two small drawers, four thumb-molded drawers, molded shaped bracket base, old refinishing, replaced brasses, restoration, 36" w, 17" d, 42-1/2" h..2,100.00

New England, c1760-80, maple, slant front, interior with fan-carved concave drawer, conforming drawer below flanked by shaped valanced compartments above shaped drawers, two projecting compartments, case with four thumb-molded graduated drawers, bracket feet, replaced pulls, old finish, imperfections, 35-3/4" w, 17" d, 40-3/4" h 5,175.00

New England, c1770-90, slant front, tiger maple, rectangular top, slant lid opens to fitted interior with six scalloped pigeonholes surrounding two central drawers, uppermost fan carved over three shallow drawers, case with four graduated wide drawers on molded bracket feet, restored, replacement butterfly brasses, 40" w, 19-3/8" d, 42-1/2" h 4,200.00

New England, c1780, slant front, maple, interior of eight valanced compartments, two document drawers, five drawers, case with four thumb-molded graduated drawers, bracket feet, replaced brasses, refinished, 35" w, 18-1/8" d, 41-1/2" h...3,800.00

New England, c1780, slant front, maple and tiger maple, rectangular top over slant lid, inlaid interior of seven valanced compartments and three drawers, case of four thumbnail-molded graduated drawers, bracket feet, replaced brasses, old refinishing, alternations, including inlay on interior, 38" w, 17-3/4" d, 43-3/4" h...3,900.00

New England, c1780, slant front, walnut and cherry, rectangular top, fall front opening to interior of central valanced compartment flanked by half engaged columns, document drawer, four small drawers and compartments, cockbeaded case with four graduated drawers, bracket feet, replaced brasses, old refinishing, repairs to base, 30-3/4" h writing surface, 18-3/4" w, 36" h....................................3,800.00

New England, c1790, slant front, mahogany, rectangular top over slant lid, fitted interior with nine drawers, eight valanced compartments, case with four incised cockbeaded graduated drawers, bracket feet, old

Chippendale, Pennsylvania, Philadelphia, c1770-80, slant front, walnut, rectangular top, architecturally fitted interior of eight serpentine fronted drawers, eight pigeonholes with scalloped moldings, central serpentine door flanked by fluted half columns enclosing three small drawers, entire compartment pulls out to reveal secret drawers behind, lower case with four wide graduated thumb-molded drawers, orig butterfly brasses, ogee bracket feet, some losses and replacements to feet, 41-1/4" w, 23-1/4" d, 44-1/2" h, $22,400. Photo courtesy of Samuel T. Freeman & Co., Philadelphia, PA.

refinishing, old oval brasses, 39-1/4" w, 18-1/2" d, 42" h.................................4,500.00

New England, 18th C, slant front, maple, walnut stepped interior with valanced compartments above small drawers, some with end blocking, central convex end blocked drawers with flanking document drawers with turned columns, case with four thumb-molded graduated drawers, bracket base, replaced brasses, old refinishing, repairs, 35-1/4" w, 19-1/2" d, 40" h..3,450.00

New England, mid 18th C, slant front, tiger maple, rectangular top over slant lid, two-stepped interior with valanced compartments over small drawers, central one flanked by document drawers and tiger columns with capitals and bases, molded step above three additional small drawers, over four thumb-molded drawers, molded bracket base, central drop, some replaced brasses, old refinishing, 35" w, 19-1/2" d, 44-1/4" h 6,325.00

New England, late 18th C, slant front, cherry, thumb-molded slant lid with narrow band inlay and center plain oval medallion, compartmented interior with small drawers and pigeonholes, flat top with dovetailing, base with pull-out support slides, four slightly graduated long drawers with maple stringing, rectangular and square banding above scrolled apron, slightly curved square bracket feet, 39" w, 18-1/2" d, 41-1/2" h..2,300.00

New England, late 18th C, slant front, tiger maple, two-tiered interior, valanced compartments, small drawers, carved central drawer flanked by document drawers with turned columns, four graduated drawers, replaced brasses, refinished, restoration, 36" w, 18" d, 39" h..2,550.00

Pennsylvania, Berks County, Oley Valley, c1770, slant front, carved and figured walnut, hinged molded lid, interior fitted with eight valanced pigeonholes, six short drawers, center prospect door concealing four graduated short drawers, case with four graduated thumb-molded long drawers, flanked by fluted quarter columns, ogee bracket feet, 40-1/4" w, 22-1/2" d, 43-1/4" h 9,995.00

Pennsylvania, Philadelphia, c1770-80, slant front, walnut, rectangular top, architecturally fitted interior of eight serpentine fronted drawers, eight pigeonholes with scalloped moldings, central serpentine door flanked by fluted half columns enclosing three small drawers, entire compartment pulls out to reveal secret drawers behind, lower case with four wide graduated thumb-molded drawers, orig butterfly brasses, ogee bracket feet, some losses and replacements to feet, 41-1/4" w, 23-1/4" d, 44-1/2" h......22,400.00

Pennsylvania, c1779, attributed to Charles Combrooks, slant front, figured walnut, dovetailed case, fluted quarter columns, four overlapping dovetailed drawers, fitted interior with six dovetailed drawers, pigeonholes, two pull-out letter files, center door conceals three interior drawers and secret compartment, ogee feet, back signed in chalk, orig finish, old repairs, replaced brasses, 32-1/4" writing height, 40" w, 22" d, 44" h....................7,000.00

Pennsylvania, c1780, slant front, walnut, rectangular top over slant lid, fitted interior with eight valanced pigeonholes, six drawers, two document drawers, center compartment with four drawers, four lower drawers, reeded quarter columns, replaced feet, 30" h writing height, 39-1/2" w, 40-1/2" h..............................2,750.00

Rhode Island or Massachusetts, late 18th/early 19th C, slant front, cherry, rectangular top over slant lid, interior of small drawers, single open valanced compartment, case with four drawers with beaded edges, ogee bracket feet, inside top drawer stamped "D. Goodale 1791-1858," old refinishing, replaced brasses, repairs, 39-1/2" w, 20" d, 41-1/2" h 2,990.00

Rhode Island, Townsend Goddard School, Newport, late 18th C, fall front, carved mahogany, lid opens to interior of shell carved concave prospect door, two valanced drawers, two compartments and drawer, flanked by three valanced compartments above blocked drawer and shell carved drawers above two concave carved drawers, case fitted with four thumb molded graduated drawers, ogee bracket feet, replaced brasses, refinished, restoration, 38-3/4" w, 20-1/4" d, 42-1/2" h 18,400.00

Rhode Island, c1750, slant front, carved mahogany, rectangular top over slant lid, fitted interior with central concave prospect door, three concave carved drawers, flanked by two carved valanced drawers, two compartments, blocked drawer and shell carved drawer above two concave drawers, case with four thumb-molded graduated drawers, ogee bracket feet, orig brasses, old refinishing, 37" w, 19" d, 42" h..32,900.00

Rhode Island, c1770-80, slant front, mahogany, rectangular top over slant lid, interior of eight valanced drawers above compartments, four small drawers with central shell carved prospect door enclosing two valanced compartments and two blocked drawers, case with four graduated thumb-molded drawers, ogee bracket feet, replaced brasses, 38" w, 19" d, 41-1/4" h...2,415.00

Rhode Island, Newport, c1780-1810, oxbow, mahogany, inlaid, slant front, lid opens to interior of six cusped pencil drawers flanking document drawers, inlaid prospect door, opening to two-shelved interior, small drawers above reverse serpentine case of cockbeaded graduated drawings beginning with top arched drawer on molded conforming base, ogee bracket feet, old dry surface, orig brasses, imperfections, descended in family from orig owner Captain Daniel Stillwell, 40" w, 23-1/4" d, 42-1/4" h 13,800.00

Rhode Island, c1780, slant front, tiger maple, fitted interior, three graduated drawers, brass hardware, ogee bracket feet, 36" w, 18-1/4" d, 41" h..5,000.00

Rhode Island, 18th C, slant front, cherry and maple, two-tiered interior of small compartments and drawers, thumb-molded case ad four graduated drawers, shaped bracket feet, casters, replaced brasses, old refinishing, repairs, 36-3/4" w, 18-1/4" d, 40-1/2" h 2,675.00

Rhode Island, late 18th C, slant front, cherry, stepped interior of small drawers, central one with shaping, case of beaded graduated drawers, ogee bracket feet, orig brasses, old refinishing, restoration, 39" w, 20" d, 43" h.................3,800.00

Southern, attributed to North Carolina, slant front, yellow pine, hinged lid, fitted interior with pigeonholes, center door and two dovetailed drawers, four dovetailed drawers, bracket feet, refinished, repairs, foot replaced, interior restored, 42" w, 21" d, 41" h................1,650.00

Chippendale-Style

These examples show many Chippendale elements but is from a later time period.

America, block front, mahogany, kneehole, 36" w, 20" d, 29" h...................................750.00

America, slant front, cherry, graduated drawers, cabriole legs, 29" w, 15" d, 40" l......500.00

America, slant front, maple and walnut, rectangular top over molded fall-front opening to fitted interior, case with four graduated drawers with overlapping molding, outset molded base with shaped skirt continuing to bracket feet, 37-1/2" w, 18-1/4" d, 39-1/2" h 1,000.00

Chippendale to Federal Transitional

As styles evolved, some furniture designers cleverly blended the elements from one style into another. This desk is a good example of the popular Chippendale desk retaining its slant front, but the interior shows more Federal elements.

America, late 18th C, slant front, walnut, rectangular top, architecturally fitted interior with eight straight front drawers, eight pigeonholes, central compartment with solid walnut door, flanked by tapering rounded half columns, entire compartment pulls out to reveal secret compartments, case with four graduated thumb-molded drawers, straight bracket feet, replacement brasses, repairs to feet, 39-1/4" w, 21-1/2" d, 41-1/4" h 5,100.00

Classical

Classical desks exhibit the same types of curves and scrolls found on other Classical period furniture. By this time frame, the desk top is usually no longer a slant front, but instead a different kind of pull-out or slide-out writing surface. Expect to find fine woods and veneers.

New England, c1825, lady's, carved mahogany and mahogany veneer, rectangular top with hinged desk box, fitted interior of three drawers above recessed case of two drawers flanked by free standing columns on square plinths continuing to vase and ring turned feet, old refinishing, minor imperfections, 36-1/2" w, 19-1/2" d, 36" h 900.00

New England, c1825-35, mahogany veneer, projecting cornice above veneered frieze and glazed doors, opens to two adjustable shelves over three small drawers, fold-out fitted writing surface lifts to well with two drawers and open compartments, two recessed panel doors open to single shelved interior flanked by scrolled supports which end in leaf and paw carved front feet, replaced brasses, refinished, restoration, 40" w, 23-1/4" d, 81" h..............1,380.00

Colonial Revival

One of the most often seen forms of Colonial Revival furniture seen today are desks. These manufactured desks are often clever blendings of several periods and have been made in the 20th century.

Governor Winthrop-style, c1920, serpentine front, mahogany veneer, solid mahogany slant front, fitted interior with two document drawers, shell carved center door, four long drawers, brass pulls and escutcheons..................750.00

Edwardian

While primarily English in origin, Edwardian furniture usually dates to the beginning of the 20th century. By this time, differences in construction between England and America are fairly easy to identify. This example shows how an American furniture maker interpreted the style.

America, c1900, kneehole, mahogany, rectangular crossbanded top with central oval medallion, front canted corners, long frieze drawer, two banks of three drawers, center cupboard door, foliate marquetry decoration, 37-1/2" w, 31" h......................................600.00

Empire

A form of desk that is common in the Empire era is the butler's desk. The unique feature of these desks are a top drawer face that opens to reveal a fitted interior. When closed, the desk looks like a chest of drawers. These desks are generally rather high, and are impressive pieces of furniture.

America, first quarter 19th C, butler's, cherry and curly maple, poplar secondary wood, scrolled crest with turned rosettes, pull-out desk drawer with arched pigeonholes and three dovetailed drawers, three dovetailed drawers with applied edge beading, turned and carved pilasters, paneled ends, paw feet, old finish, some edge damage, 44-1/2" w, 23" d, 57-3/4" h..1,925.00

America, first quarter 19th C, butler's, various woods, rectangular top with outset paneled frieze drawer, fall-front, fitted interior with small drawers, valanced pigeonholes and writing surface, three long cockbeaded drawers flanked by split spindles, turned short legs, repairs, wear, 41" w, 21-1/4" d, 47" h....................425.00

America, first quarter 19th C, slant front, cherry, rectangular top over slant front, fitted interior with curly maple trim, six drawers, four more drawers behind center door, four dovetailed drawers with applied edge molding, turned legs, scalloped apron, clear lacy glass pulls on large drawers, small opalescent glass pulls on interior drawers, pine and poplar sec-

ondary woods, old refinishing, some edge damage, age cracks to lid, 39-3/4" w, 21-1/2" d, 48-1/4" h..2,400.00

Federal

Desks of the Federal period show some enhancements to their design from the earlier Chippendale examples. Why? Furniture styles in London were changing, too, and the slant front desks suddenly lost favor. Not wishing to be out of step, American designers started to modify their desk designs too. Many still used

Federal, lady's, two part, mahogany and figured mahogany veneer, top with double doors with crossbanded veneer, fitted interior with shelves on one side, pigeonholes and four drawers on other side, three dovetailed drawers with applied beading and hinged writing shelf, turned and reeded legs, old finish, old replaced brasses, edge damage and age cracks, 40" w, 22" d, 57" h, $1,925. Shown in front are two statues, left is a 22-1/2" h white alabaster young woman, sold for $385; right is a 24" h porcelain peasant girl with wooden shoes, marked "Amphora, Austria," some wear and chip, $460. Photo courtesy of Garth's Auctions, Inc., Delaware, OH.

the popular slant front, but other types of desks were stylish as well and many included a pull-out drawer, known as a "secretaire" drawer. Another form is known as a "cylinder" front and this occurs when a curved lid hides the fitted interior. Another important development was occurring in society that changed the size of desks. Women were becoming more educated and more wanted a desk to fit their needs.

America, c1790, slant front, mahogany, fitted interior with eight small drawers over valanced pigeonholes, center prospect with shell carving flanked by columns, four graduated long drawers, scalloped apron, bracket feet, old finish, signed "Sam Kline," inscribed on rear of small interior drawer, restoration, 42-1/2" w, 19-1/2" d, 44" h.......................................2,500.00

America, c1800, butler's, mahogany and bird's eye maple shaped rectangular top, hinged front, leather inset writing surface, three long drawers, flanked by reeded columns, reeded cylindrical feet, casters, orig brass hardware inscribed "W. J.," 46-1/4" w, 22" d, 43-1/4" h...............................2,500.00

America, c1820, slant front, cherry, fitted interior, four graduated thumb-molded drawers, circular brass pull hardware, ring turned bun feet, 39-3/4" w, 19-1/2" d, 45-1/4" h..............2,500.00

America, c1820, slant front, walnut, rectangular top over hinged slant lid, fitted interior, four long graduated cockbeaded drawers, shaped bracket feet, 39" w, 19-1/2" d, 41-1/2" h...............................4,750.00

America, first quarter 19th C, butler's, inlaid mahogany, outset rectangular top above front with secretaire drawer opening to fitted interior with small drawers, pigeonholes, document boxes, and secret compartments, over pair of doors opening to sliding trays, turned feet, imperfections, 41-1/2" w, 23" d, 44" h..................950.00

Massachusetts, c1780, oxbow slant front, mahogany and birch, slant lid opens to interior of seven drawers with inlaid stringing, seven valanced compartments, cockbeaded case of four serpentine drawers, conforming bracket feet, old oval brasses, refinished, 40" w, 19-1/2" w, 43-1/2" h.................................11,025.00

Massachusetts, c1790-1810, oxbow, slant front, mahogany and mahogany veneer, fall front opens to interior of five drawers and nine valanced compartments, case with four cockbeaded graduated drawers, flaring French feet, old oval brass pulls, old refinishing, imperfections, 42" w, 44" h................................4,600.00

Massachusetts, c1800, slant front, mahogany and mahogany veneer inlaid, rectangular top over slant lid, fitted interior with central prospect door flanked by three drawers, four valanced compartments, cased with four cockbeaded graduated drawers, flaring French feet, valanced skirt with stringing and crossbanding, old finish, old oval brasses, minor replacements, 41-1/2" w, 20" d, 42-1/2" h.......3,450.00

Massachusetts, c1810, tambour, mahogany inlaid, two drawers, reeded tapering legs, refinished, replaced brasses, minor imperfections, restoration, 37-1/4" w, 23-1/4" d, 41-3/4" h.................................3,500.00

Massachusetts, c1810, tambour, mahogany inlaid, top section with two tambour doors opening to two drawers and three valanced compartments, centering inlaid prospect door, all flanked by fluted pilasters, projecting lower section of fold-out writing surface, case of three graduated drawers with inlaid stringing and straight skirt joining square double tapering legs with inlaid stringing and cuffs, old finish, needs restoration..........................2,875.00

Massachusetts, c1820, tambour, tiger maple and mahogany inlaid, top section with cross-banded cornice board over two tambour doors, interior of nine valanced compartments over fifteen drawers with mahogany cockbeaded surrounds, center prospect door, pen and ink on paper "Commandments 10" within arched glass panel set in mahogany panel framed by tombstone stringing, lower section: fold-out writing surface, two cockbeaded long drawers, straight skirt joining block ring-turned tapering legs, old refinishing, replaced pulls, minor restoration, 39-1/4" w, 18-1/2" d, 54" h 17,250.00

Massachusetts, central, early 19th C, lady's, mahogany inlaid, cove-molded top above three drawers with inlaid floral vines, checkered veneer banding opening to three-section interior, end sections each with three drawers above openings flanking two central compartments over fold-out writing surface, cockbeaded bird's eye maple and mahogany veneer drawers flanked by colonettes above spiral carved engraved columns ending in turned feet, replaced brass, old surface, door inscribed "F. A. Butler, Deerfield, March 1864," legs pieced, other repairs, 40-3/4" w, 20-1/2" d, 54" h...4,325.00

Massachusetts, western, early 19th C, slant front, cherry, rectangular top over slant lid, interior of compartments and small drawers, over single drawer, turned legs, refinished, imperfections, 38-1/2" w, 18" d, 36-1/2" h...........1,265.00

Massachusetts or New Hampshire, c1800, lady's, mahogany inlaid, hinged top opens to valanced compartments, small drawers, felt-lined writing surface, three drawers outlined with tiger maple veneer, matching legs, replaced brasses, restored, 41" w, 20" d, 47-1/2" h...1,725.00

Massachusetts or New Hampshire, c1820, mahogany, bird's eye maple, wavy birch, setback top with center bird's eye maple door flanked by two smaller mahogany doors over three bird's eye maple drawers, fold-out top, slip supports, four graduated drawers in base, ring-turned feet, refinished, imperfections, 41-1/4" w, 20-1/2" d, 60-1/2" h 2,750.00

New England, c1780-1800, slant front, cherry, rectangular top, architecturally fitted interior with four thumb-molded drawers, four pigeonholes and central compartment with fan carved door flanked by square half columns and reeded pull out compartments, pull out molding reveals small drawer, lower section with five graduated thumb-molded drawers, scalloped skirt, straight bracket feet, later brasses, 39-1/2" w, 18-1/4" d, 41" h 5,380.00

New England, southeastern, c1800, slant front, inlaid cherry, fall front with inlaid cross-banding opening to interior fitted with one row of long drawers and one row of short drawers, valanced compartments, cockbeaded case of four graduated drawers with inlaid crossbanding, flaring French feet, 40" w, 18-1/4" d, 42-1/2" h..6,900.00

New England, c1820, cherry, cherry veneer, and poplar, top section with flat molded cornice, two cupboard doors with recessed reeded panels enclosing shelves, midsection with two doors with recessed reeded panels enclosing compartmented four drawer interior, projecting base with fold-out writing surface, case of long drawer, two cupboard doors, flanking bottle drawers, reeded pilasters continuing to turned legs, replaced brasses, old refinishing, minor imperfections, 39" w, 21" d, 80-1/2" h..5,175.00

New England, c1825, two glazed doors with four arched openings, shelved interior, two small drawers over three aligned long drawers, glass knobs, brass escutcheons, turned feet, old refinishing, replaced brasses, imperfections, 37-1/2" w, 18" d, 64" h................3,950.00

New England, early 19th C, desk over chest, cherry, narrow cornice molding above hinged recessed panel lid, opens to interior of open compartments and small drawers over green baize-lined writing surface, over stepped out surface with ovolo corners, ring-turned engaged columns ending in tapering ring-turned legs and feet, flanking three drawers with scratch beaded edges, old refinishing, replaced brasses, 39" w, 21-3/4" d, 53-1/4" h 3,800.00

New England, early 19th C, mahogany and mahogany veneer inlaid, top section shaped gallery above flat molded cornice, two glazed doors enclosing compartments and drawer, flanking door and small drawer; projecting base with fold-out writing surface, two cock-beaded short drawers, two graduated long drawers, four sq tapering legs, inlaid crossbanding, old refinishing, some restoration, inscribed "22 Geo. L. Deblois Sept 12th 1810," 37-1/8" w, 20" d, 51-1/2" 3,000.00

New England, early 19th C, slant lid, maple stained, slant lid opens to interior of valanced compartments, small beaded drawers, four graduated beaded drawers, scrolled skirt flanked by shaped French feet, old dark red stain, orig brass, 39-1/2" w, 20" d, 44" h 4,320.00

New England, southern, early 19th C, fall front, cherry inlaid, rectangular top over slant lid, interior of seven drawers and compartments, case of four graduated drawers with incised beading, inlaid whalebone escutcheons, turned wooden pulls, flaring French feet with inlaid stringing and crossbanding, old finish, imperfections, 39-1/2" w, 20" d, 44-1/2" h 2,185.00

New York State, c1790-1800, butler's, mahogany inlaid, rectangular top with string inlaid edge, case with deep drawer with two inlaid ovals set in mitered panels bordered by stringing, interior opens to fold-out writing surface, central prospect door inlaid with urn of flowers bordered by stringing, flanked by document drawers with inlay of simulated pilasters, three drawers above four valanced compartments, case with four inlaid graduated drawers, flaring French feet joined by cutout inlaid skirt, replaced brasses, imperfections, 46" w, 21" d, 44" h..2,550.00

New York State, early 19th C, slant front, mahogany veneer, inlaid, slant lid and three graduated drawers outlined in stringing with ovolo corners, interior of veneer and outline stringing on drawers, valanced compartments, prospect door opening to inner compartments and drawers, flanking document drawers, orig brasses, old surface, veneer cracking loss and patching, other surface imperfections, 41-1/2" w, 21-1/2" d, 44" h 2,550.00

Pennsylvania, early 19th C, slant front, walnut inlaid, slant front and cockbeaded drawers outlined in stringing, base with band of contrasting veneers, interior of small drawers above valanced compartments, scrolled dividers flanking prospect door which opens to two small drawers, three drawers, old refinishing, repairs, 40" w, 20" d, 44-1/2" h............3,550.00

Pennsylvania or New York, c1790, mahogany inlaid, slant front, string inlaid lid opens to multi-compartmented interior, center prospect door, case of four graduated drawers, inlaid stringing flanked by inlaid lambrequin corners, inlaid flaring French feet, old replaced brasses, refinished, repairs, 41-1/2" w, 20-1/4" d, 42-3/4" h..2,770.00

Southern New England, c1780-1800, slant front, wavy birch, lid opens to valanced multi-drawer interior, case of four gradated drawers with incised cockbeading on cutout base, replaced brasses, old refinishing, minor imperfections, 39-1/4" w, 19-1/2" d, 43-1/2" h 2,550.00

Federal-Style

This example shows a 20th century adaptation of the Federal period style. The term tambour

refers to a door that is made of up small pieces of wood fastened to a thin fabric backing.

America, 20th C, tambour, mahogany inlaid, tambour slides open to two drawers, six valanced pigeonholes, oval inlaid prospect door, lower section with hinged writing flap, two inlaid drawers, square tapered legs with bellflower inlay, branded mark with crown and flower emblem, some veneer missing, 36" w, 19" d, 44" h..635.00

George II-Style

This desk style remains popular. Elements found in this desk can be attributed to both American and English furniture makers.

America or England, mahogany and burl walnut, tripartite top fitted with tooled leather panels over belt of three burled and line-incised drawers, whole supported by cabriole legs with shell carved knees, claw and ball feet, 72-1/2" w, 38" d, 30-1/4" h 2,300.00

Hepplewhite

Desks from the Hepplewhite era of the early 19th century may include a slant front, but other stylistic elements, such as French feet make it Hepplewhite. Look for straighter lines and inlaid decoration.

America, slant front, cherry, rectangular top over slant lid, dovetailed case, four dovetailed drawers with edge beading, fitted interior with eight dovetailed drawers, two letter drawers and center door, scrolled apron, French feet, replaced brasses, old mellow refinishing, old pieced repairs, 41-1/2" w, 19" d, 35" h writing surface, 46" h 3,350.00

Massachusetts, Salem, early 19th C, lady's, mahogany, figured veneer, crossbanded mahogany inlays, figured satinwood, and stringing, two sections, upper section with three doors, three drawers, fitted interior of drawers and pigeonholes, lower section with fold down writing surface, three dovetailed drawers with applied edge beading, sq tapered legs, refinished, minor age cracks and veneer damage, brasses and hinges replaced, 42" w, 20-1/4" d, 53-1/4" h 2,750.00

Massachusetts, Salem, 1802, lady's, tambour, mahogany, inlay, two sections, upper section with tambour doors and center door with fitted interior, pigeonholes and five dovetailed drawers, stringing on drawers, top with stringing with husks on pilasters, center door has stringing with invected corners, and oval medallion of figured veneer and banded outline, lower section with fold down writing shelf, four dovetailed drawers, applied edge beading, bracket feet, pine secondary wood, refinished, inside backboards signed "Made in the year of our Lord and Savior Jesus Christ 1802, by Thomas R. Williams," minor repairs to feet, top slightly warped, replaced eagle brasses, 39" w, 20-1/4" d, 47-3/4" h 4,580.00

Pennsylvania, early 19th C, slant front, walnut, rectangular top, thumb-molded edge, string and quarter fan inlaid hinged slant front, fitted interior, four line inlaid graduated long drawers, oval brass handles, shaped skirt with banded inlay, French feet, 42" w, 45" h.........................3,000.00

Modernism Era

Desks of the Modernism Era continue to use materials introduced in the Art Deco period. Look for metal frames, other natural materials, and unusual shapes.

Modernism-Era, Heyfield Wakefield, maple, rectangular top over knee hole flanked on each side by bank of two drawers, canted legs, side chair with wooden back, slip seat, desk: 50" l, 22" w, 29-1/4" h, chair: 18" w, 20" d, 32-1/2" h, $400. Photo courtesy of Skinner Auctioneers and Appraisers of Antiques and Fine Art Boston, and Bolton MA.

Modernism-Era, George Nelson, Thin Edge, c1956, rosewood veneer front and sides, white laminate top and writing surface, black metal rolltop, white metal legs, label, 42" w, 25" d, 34" h, $6,000. Photo courtesy of Treadway Gallery, Inc. of Cincinnati, OH.

Baughman, Mylo, manufactured by Milo Baughman, 1950s, walnut veneer, two banks of drawers, floating top, dowel legs, wear, 60" w, 28" d, 31" h...1,980.00

Frankl, Paul, manufactured by Johnson Furniture Co., 1940s

Cream lacquered cork, seven drawers with wood and brass handles, book shelf, 60" w, 26" d, 29" h 2,400.00

Knee Hole, two-tone, brass pulls, tapered legs, 36" w, 24" d, 30" h......................950.00

Heyfield Wakefield, maple, rectangular top over knee hole flanked on each side by bank of two drawers, canted legs, side chair with wooden back, slip seat, desk: 50" l, 22" w, 29-1/4" h, chair: 18" w, 20" d, 32-1/2" h 400.00

Maloof, Sam, oak, rectangular top over two drawers, dowel detail to top and sides, branded "Design/Made Maloof," 60" w, 25" d, 29" h...5,000.00

Nelson, George, manufactured by Herman Miller

Drop-leaf, hinged rectangular top, three drawers, brushed chrome base, refinished, 40" w, 24" d, 30" h 825.00

Original black lacquer, red leather writing surface and drawer fronts, lift-up compart-

Modernism-Era, designed attributed to Gilbert Rohde, manufactured by Herman Miller, Zeeland, MI, walnut and brass, demilune shaped desk top, three cased compartments, above two side drawers with circular brass pulls and open side compartments, cylindrical brass feet, minor wear, 45-1/2" l, 24" d, 29-1/4" h, $1,150. Photo courtesy of Skinner Auctioneers and Appraisers of Antiques and Fine Art Boston, and Bolton MA.

ment, perforated metal basket, 54" w, 28" d, 41" h 6,500.00

Thin Edge, c1956, rosewood veneer front and sides, white laminate top and writing surface, black metal rolltop, white metal legs, label, 42" w, 25" d, 34" h....................6,000.00

Walnut and tan leather writing surface and upper cabinet, satin chrome base, perforated metal file basket, some wear, 54" w, 28" d, 41" h......................................4,400.00

Rohde, Gilbert, manufactured by Herman Miller, Zeeland, MI, walnut and brass, demilune shaped desk top, three cased compartments, above two side drawers with circular brass pulls and open side compartments, cylindrical brass feet, minor wear, 45-1/2" l, 24" d, 29-1/4" h...1,150.00

Robsjohn-Gibbings, T. H., c1940, burled wood, fleur-de-lis inlay, two doors, interior drawers, refinished, 56" w, 22" d, 29" h..................3,850.00

Unknown Designer, 1950s, rectangular formica top above two drawers, ebonized V-base, 40" w, 24" d, 30" h...................................100.00

Modernism Era, Pop

This example shows how the Pop influence has further expanded on the changing shape of furniture. The price of this example is influenced by a well known designer, documented manufacture, and excellent condition.

Calka, Maurice, produced by Leleu-Desahy, France, 1969, biomorphic form, white fiberglass, four drawers, 72" w, 42" d, 30" h 9,500.00

Postmaster

A postmaster desk was a working piece of furniture, probably made by a local craftsman to specifications of the user.

America, second quarter 19th C, pine, flat top, recessed center panel fall front writing surface, interior fitted with small letter compartments, vertical divisions, table base with two drawers, turned legs, 38" w, 22-1/2" d, 62" h...........900.00

Queen Anne

Desks of the Queen Anne period feature cabriole legs and some curves. Look for slant fronts and fitted interiors where the curves are also plentiful.

America, slant front, walnut, banded slant lid, fitted interior, faux frieze drawer, four drawer, bracket feet, 37" w, 22" d, 40" h..........2,950.00

Connecticut, Norwich area, c1730-50, slant front, maple, slant lid opening to interior of valanced compartments separated by scrolled dividers and small drawers, case of four graduated thumb-molded drawers, molded base with short cabriole legs ending in square pad feet, orig brasses, early surface, pieced feet, 33-3/4" w, 13-1/4" d, 41" h 6,325.00

Country, Connecticut, slant front, pine and maple, rectangular top over slant lid, fitted interior with four drawers, pigeonholes, base frame with mortised and pinned apron with deeply scalloped edge, one dovetailed drawer, turned tapered legs, duck feet, refinished, replaced legs, feet with edge damage, repairs, 29-3/4" h writing height, 32-3/4" w, 19" d, 38-1/2" h..........7,900.00

Country, slant front, maple, rectangular top over slant lid, fitted interior with pigeonholes with scrolled details, scrolled apron, turned legs, refinished, feet ended out, small repairs, 31-1/2" w, 20" d, 32" h............................880.00

Maine, northern, 19th C, slant front, maple, interior with valanced compartments above small drawers, end drawers separated by scrolled dividers, case of three thumb-molded drawers, molded bracket base with central drop pendant, old darkened surface, 35-1/2" w, 17-1/2" d, 40-1/4" h 5,175.00

Massachusetts, c1730-50, slant front, walnut, rectangular top over hinged slant lid, two inlaid stellate devices, interior of open valanced compartments above small drawers, stellate inlaid prospect door, flanked by turned columns, opens to interior with small drawer, case with four graduated line-inlaid drawers, bracket feet, replaced brasses, surface imperfections and repairs, 38" w, 19-1/2" d, 43" h 6,800.00

Massachusetts, Boston, c1750, block front, kneehole, carved mahogany, thumb-molded top with blocked front, conforming case, valanced drawer above arched raised paneled door opening to shelves flanked by tiers of short drawers, blocked molded bracket feet, old refinishing, old brasses, imperfections, 35" w, 19-1/4" d, 31" h 24,000.00

New England, c1750, slant front, walnut, valanced fitted interior, two drawers over two graduated drawers, center apron pediment, bracket feet, old refinishing, imperfections, 34-1/2" w, 19-1/2" d, 39" h 7,500.00

Pennsylvania, c1740-60, table top, walnut, lid opens to interior of valanced compartments above two drawers and well, case with trunnels on molded dovetailed bracket base, centering shaped pendant, refinished, restoration, 23-1/2" w, 14-1/2" d, 16-1/2" h 2,530.00

Vermont, c1750, slant front, tiger maple and cherry, interior with central fan-carved drawer, two valanced compartments flanked by molded document drawers, four valanced compartments, three drawers, case with four thumb-molded graduated drawers, bracket feet, replaced brasses, old refinishing, imperfections, and repairs, 36" w, 18" d, 41-1/2" h 3,220.00

Queen Anne-Style

The U-form stretcher of one of these desks gives an important clue in determining that it's not a period Queen Anne desk. The other example has the characteristic cabriole legs, but the faux leather front is of a later period design.

America, slant front, walnut, rectangular top with low backboard, hinged slope opening to fitted interior, front with two molded drawers, scrolled apron, baluster turned legs joined by molded U-form stretcher, 30-1/4" w, 15-3/4" d, 42-1/4" h.....................................300.00

English, late 19th/early 20th C, lady's, walnut, molded top, slant top, fitted writing compartment, faux leather book fronted doors, cabriole legs, pad feet, 25-1/4" w, 13" d, 39" h......................................1,850.00

School Type

It's easy to conjure up an image of an early child's school desk. While once very popular with decorators, this craze seems to have passed. If looking for this unique form of desk, watch for examples that show some wear, but not abuse and remember that ink stains are almost impossible to remove from wood.

America, 19th C, double, elm, rectangular top with two hinged writing surfaces, each opening to storage well, three square-section tapering legs, 33-3/4" w, 16-1/2" d, 26-1/2" h..................................300.00

America, late 19th C, single, cherry, rectangular top with curved bottom edges, worn ink well hole, cast iron side rails connect desk to seat, some wear to attached folding seat.....................................275.00

Shaker

The Shaker Community created some unusual desks. They were concerned with the convenience of the desk to the user. The Shaker style is unique in it's clean lines and lack of ornamentation.

Sewing, Canterbury, New Hampshire, 1860s, butternut and chestnut, gallery divided into thirds by frame and panel construction door, base with four drawers on right side, lowest with lock, front with sliding work surface above two recessed horizontal panels next to door of frame and panel construction, left side with two horizontal recessed panels, ring-turned tapering legs, refinished, 29" w, 24" d, 38-1/4" h...17,250.00

Trustees, c1830, cherry, shaped gallery above lift-top, tombstone compartmented interior, base with single drawer, straight skirt joining four turned tapering legs, old refinishing, 30-3/4" w, 20-1/4" d, 50-3/4" h 2,875.00

Sheraton

Sheraton desks are found more often with a rectangular top rather than the slant front. As with the Federal style of desks, the slant front was starting to fall out of fashion, but because styles were somewhat slow to change, many desks are found with this feature. Look for delicate inlay on Sheraton pieces.

America, 19th C, lady's, mahogany, rectangular top, brown leather writing surface, satinwood string inlay decoration, two drawers, sq tapered legs, 42-1/2" w, 22" d, 28-1/4" h 975.00

America, 19th C, rectangular top with inlay, one long drawer, two aligned drawers, sq tapering legs, ball feet, 42-1/8" w, 21" d, 30-1/2" h 500.00

Country, school master's, cherry, slant lid with pull-out supports, fitted interior with three dovetailed drawers, seven pigeonholes, one dovetailed drawer, turned legs, old mellow finish, one pigeonhole bracket missing, age cracks in lid, top board and crest replaced, 29-1/2" w, 22" d, 38" h 900.00

Maine, birch, slant front, three drawers, decorative inlaid skirt, tapering ridge feet, interior with five drawers and five cubbyholes, turned legs, refinished, 37-1/2" w, 19" d, 45" h 1,200.00

Victorian

The Victorians wrote letters and required elegant desks. Look for the Victorian's love of ornamentation to enhance this basic furniture form.

Victorian, partner's, c1900, cherry, rectangular tooled leather top over three drawers, two convenience slides, double pedestals, each fitted with three drawers flanked by reeded sides, bun feet, 67" w, 49" d, 32" h, $2,900. Photo courtesy of Samuel T. Freeman & Co., Philadelphia, PA.

Davenport

c1870, inlaid Pollard elm, rectangular top, fitted compartments above hinged slant front, two leaf-tip carved cabriole supports bracked by case fited with four drawers opposed by four faux drawers, turned feet, wood casters, 20-1/2" w, 21" d, 33-1/2" h 2,950.00

c1875, mahogany and ebonized, shaped and carved back rest, rectangular top over projecting, hinged slant front lid, fitted with three drawers, one short pencil drawer, four long side drawers, paneled front, flanked by turned pilasters, bun feet, 21-1/2" w, 25" d, 32-1/2" h 650.00

c1880, top fitted with lidded compartment, slant front writing surface, variety of drawers, bank of four drawers on either side, scrolling carved legs, 21" w, 21-1/2" d, 33-1/2" h 350.00

Lady's, early 20th C, inlaid mahogany, tambour top opening to interior fitted with pull-out writing surface, variety of drawers and cubby holes, single frieze drawer, inlaid with medallion and swags, sq tapering legs, 31-1/2" w, 21" d, 37" h 950.00

Partner's, c1860-70, walnut, tarred linen writing surface, each side with three drawers, two flanking cupboard doors, applied foliate corner moldings, general wear, some damage to moldings, 54" l, 35-1/2" d, 30-1/2" h 900.00

Roll Top, Boston, late 19th C, oak, rectangular top, retracting roll top, fitted interior, two pedestals, each with three short drawers, deep center drawer, 54" w, 35" d, 43-1/2" h 1,800.00

Side by Side, oak, mirrored top, griffin supports, left side fitted with curved glass door, right side with hinged writing surface, fitted interior, three drawers, animal paw feet, 44" w, 15" d, 74" h 2,750.00

Eastlake, lady's, walnut, two part, top section sits on pegs, top section with mirror with two columns supported shelves, fancy carving, pressed decoration; base section with double hinged writing surface with dec floral carving, writing surface with two panels of green felt, lifts to reveal compartment desk interior with two drawers, one side fitted with two long drawers, gallery shelf in base, decorative applied pieces, shoe foot base, metal casters, 31-1/2" w, 19" d, 57" h...........................1,150.00

Renaissance Revival, Boston, c1857, oak, carving attributed to Thomas U. Walter, stamped "Doe, Hazelton & Co./Manufacturers/ Boston, Massachusetts," brass plaque engraved "John Hill/New Jersey," provenance includes service at US Senate 17,500.00

William and Mary

Desks found in the William and Mary period are massive, and somewhat angular in their appearance. The front is usually a slant front with an interior that is fitted, but not nearly as elaborate as the later Queen Anne or Chippendale period desks.

Connecticut, early 18th C, slant front, tulipwood and oak, fall-front lid with raised panel, interior of four compartments, three drawers, well with sliding closure, double arched molded front, base with long drawer, four turned legs, joined by valanced skirt, shaped flat cross stretchers, turned feet, replaced brasses, old refinishing, minor imperfections, 24-3/4" w, 15" d, 42-1/2" h 17,250.00

Connecticut, early 18th C, slant front, walnut veneer, rectangular top over slant lid, valanced interior with two document drawers with columns above four drawers with burl veneer and well below, double arch molded case with two short drawers and two long drawers, molded base, turned feet, replaced engraved brasses, old refinishing, 35" w, 19-1/2" d, 40-1/2" h...........5,175.00

William and Mary-Style

This example shows most elements of the William and Mary period such as applied moldings and teardrop pulls. However, it was made with 20th century screws and nails.

American, 20th C, oak, seven dovetailed drawers, applied moldings, molded edge top, brass tear drop pulls, old finish, turned legs and stretchers, one pc of molding missing from drawer, 27-3/4" x 59" x 31" h..................500.00

Wooten

William S. Wooten was an interesting furniture maker who enjoyed a very popular following during the Eastlake craze of the Victorian furniture period. He was trained as a minister who established the Wooten Desk Co. in Indianapolis, Indiana, in 1870. His desk was so unique that the design was patented in 1874 and the company remained in business until the early 1890s. What made Wooten desks so interesting is that his designs were actually well organized offices, all contained in large desk frame. The desks were made in several grades, including "Ordinary, Standard, Extra, and Superior." Today, the more ornate designs are generally preferred. A Wooten is easily identified as it can completely roll close on casters, hiding the numerous documents files, drawers, and working surface.

America, c1880-84, Queen Anne pattern, walnut and maple, carved, turned, and incised three-quarter gallery, triangular carved hinged long document door, two carved and paneled bowed doors, incised carved drop front opening to fitted compartments, pigeonholes, and drawers, numerous vertical and horizontal divided compartment, four center drawers, interior of left door fitted with divided compartments, right door fitted with forty square storage boxes, sides paneled and incised with ebonized triangles, outstretched molded, canted, and carved legs, casters, two gallery finials missing, minor damage, 42-1/2" w, 71" h...........................12,500.00

America, c1880, walnut, standard grade, pierced three-quarter gallery above two arched doors opening to fall front secretary, door interior fitted on one side with pigeonholes, compartments on other side, fall front writing surface, fitted compartments over four drawers flanked by horizontal and vertical file slats, trestle supports on casters, 42-1/2" w closed, 71" h..6,500.00

Hall Furnishings

Hall furnishings include all the types of furniture that were made to be used exclusively in a hallway setting. Benches, chairs, hat racks, and hall trees all offered comfort or a place to put coats and hats. Like many other pieces of furniture designed for a specific use, some hall furnishings do not fall neatly into any one furniture period. Dating information is included with the descriptions when known but even those are often just estimates.

Hallways in great American manor houses were often gathering places for guests. When "calling," it was customary to be received in a spacious hall, where one's card could be placed in a calling card receiver, often held on a side table, perhaps a coat or hat were taken to be hung up. A chair or bench was offered for the waiting visitor or perhaps they were taken to a parlor to wait.

Hallways in later homes, such as those designed in the Victorian era, or the Arts and Crafts era, were destined to serve as an area to prepare to go out into the cold. Benches were used to put on one's boots, seats held storage areas for hats and gloves. The foyers in today's homes are small in comparison to the spacious areas of earlier architectural styles.

Only items specifically designed for use in a hall are included in this section. Refer to specific sections for other types of benches, chairs, mirrors, stands, and tables that may have also been used in a hallway.

Coat Racks and Clothes Trees

Even the simplest of halls usually included a place to hang a coat. Such furnishings are often called clothes trees which describes their spindly appearance. Costumers are another name given to clothes trees, and it was the name given by the original Arts & Crafts period designers. A coat rack generally has larger hooks and is more substantial to bear the weight of coats.

Arts & Crafts

Stickley Brothers, Grand Rapids, MI, costumer

No. 188, double posts with rounded tops, corbeled shoe-foot base having through-tenon construction, orig hooks, orig finish, 20" w, 19" d, 69" h 1,400.00

Double posts, ten hooks, orig dark finish and hardware, unmarked, 17-1/2" w, 14-3/4" d, 75" h 1,400.00

Stickley, Gustav, New York, costumer

No. 52, single tapered post, orig iron hardware, cleaned orig finish, branded signature, 24" w, 71" h 1,000.00

No. 53, double posts tapered at top, orig iron hooks, shoe foot base with through-tenon construction, unsigned, cleaned orig finish, 13" w, 22" d, 72" h 2,530.00

Unknown Designer

Coat Rack, copper and metal, rectangular patinated lattice strapwork with eight coat hooks, pierced copper riveted frame on beveled mirror, 48" w, 26-3/4" h............... 490.00

Costumer

Four tall bent vertical slats, joined by three graduated clip-cornered medial shelves, four angular and reticulated double brass hooks, orig drip pan missing from lower shelf, 12-3/4" w, 72" h 290.00

Single pole with long corbels, cruciform base, orig hooks, orig dark finish, 20" w, 20" d, 72" h 120.00

Classical, New England, maple turned and acanthus carved post, fifteen clothes supports, ball finial, scrolled legs, 79" h 1,450.00

Federal, New England, c1820-30, maple single post, acorn shaped finial, fourteen shaped pegs descending full length of post, ring turned shaped vase base, three scrolled legs, 70-1/2" h 1,400.00

Modernism Era, Charles Eames, manufactured by Tigrett, c1951, Hang-It-All, multicolored primary wooden balls, white enameled metal frame, 20" w, 6" d, 15" h 1,550.00

Hall Bench

A hall bench usually has a place to sit while putting on outer ware and many also contain a storage area.

Colonial Revival, Baroque-Style, American, 1910, cherry, shell carved crest over cartouche and griffin carved panel back, lift seat, high arms, mask carved base, paw feet, 39-1/2" w, 21-1/2" d, 51" h 700.00

Victorian, golden oak, quarter-sawn, center mirror with arched top, two pairs of four prong hooks above hinged seat, 35-1/2" w, 18-1/4" d, 75" h..995.00

Hall Chair

A hall chair is a chair with a wide seat, usually substantial in form. The Arts & Crafts designers were known for designing specific usage-type furniture.

Arts & Crafts

Michigan Chair Co., heavily carved back and posts, solid seat, arched slab base with keyed tenon construction, orig finish, signed with orig paper label, 26" w, 20" d, 39" h 600.00

Stickley Brothers, Grand Rapids, MI, six sided back with inlaid floral design, plank trapezoidal seat, orig finish, unsigned, 21" w, 19" d, 40" h 1,425.00

Hall Mirror

Most halls included a mirror, some large and others more in scale with the rest of the furniture of the hall. It is important to remember that the homeowner was trying to impress a visitor with the grand nature of his furnishings and the hall was often the place where first impressions were made. A well-proportioned mirror was an excellent way of subtly displaying one's good taste and sense of style.

Victorian, oak, architectural-style frame, columnar sides, raised on conforming base, 40" w, 16" d, 77" h...................................950.00

Hall Racks and Foyer Etageres

Large pieces of furniture, designed to hold a coat, and perhaps other accessories, graced many halls. Here are several examples of different furniture styles to show how tastes changed.

Aesthetic Movement, last quarter 19th C, cast iron, back-plate case with pierced filigree of foliage and fruit centered by arched mirror, issuing six hat-hooks, base with umbrella-stand raised on bracket feet, 21-1/2" w, 69-3/4" h..575.00

Black Forest, carved and polychrome, shaped mirror plate surmounted by carved winged dragon over jardiniere, flanked on one side by plant stand raised on columnar supports, other side with winged dragon over etagere with three open shelves, two with spindle galleries, one supported by twisted column, other with carved dragon, resting on carved cabriole leg in shape of mythological beast, reeded toupie form leg, polychrome dec, 45" w, 16-1/2" d, 92" h 3,500.00

Civil War, America, c1870, cast iron, painted and gilded, cast in half-round, uprights form bayonets, crisscrossed by pair of eagle headed sabers, two other sabers flanking, olive branches crossbar hung with rope twists and tassels as are sabers, small United States shield, shield shaped mirror plate, base with US mail pouches, acorns, tassels, and ribbons, rope twist hooks, 26" w, 73" h 6,500.00

Modernism Era, Jean Lucien, c1935, chromed aluminum structure, hat rack and disc shaped hat pegs over center mirror and umbrella rack, 37-1/2" w, 8" d, 70" h 800.00

Victorian

America, burl walnut, ball finials above paneled and shaped cornice, rectangular mirror flanked by turned garment holders, marble top drawer supported by turned legs, shaped base, painted metal plant holders, 29" w, 14" d, 93" h 1,400.00

America, cast iron, faux bamboo, central mirror, repainted, 72" h 650.00

America, mahogany, carved and molded detail, brass trim, six brass hooks, oval mirrors, red marble insert in base, 62-1/2" w, 85" h 1,950.00

Gothic Revival, c1855, oak, ornate arched open cut upper frame, hooks at side, white marble shelf, ornate open cut base flanked by umbrella racks....................................10,000.00

Renaissance Revival

c1870, walnut, flat molded cornice, shaped beveled mirror within molded framework, four hooks across top, two on each side, curvilinear umbrella holders, brown marble insert over paneled cupboard door base, 80" h 2,450.00

c1870, walnut, ornate carved cresting, shaped mirror within molded framework, drop columns at each side, candle sockets and candle shelves, white marble shelf, single drawer flanked by umbrella racks, orig brass pans 4,000.00

Rococo Revival, walnut, intricate carving, six small shelves, two large shelves, stained, mirror back, 46" w, 14" d, 90" h 2,000.00

Windsor, American, pine, bamboo turned, six knob like hooks, orig yellow varnish, black striping, 33-3/4" w 200.00

Hat Racks

A place to hang one's hat was important in hallway furnishings. These examples show how several different furniture styles adapted to provide a solution by using wall space rather than floor space.

Aesthetic Movement, America, fourth quarter 19th C, ebonized, center mirror, paneled supports, 30" h 350.00

Arts & Crafts, motto type, unknown designer, three horizontal slats, one overlapping slat with five orig pegs, inscribed, "May the hinges of friendship never grow rusty," orig finish, 29" w, 4" d, 20" h 475.00

Windsor, pine, bamboo turned, six knob-like hooks, orig yellow varnish, black striping, 3-1/4" l..225.00

Miniatures and Children's Furniture

One area of furniture that is always of interest to collectors is the furniture used by children. This furniture falls into several different categories. The first is furniture which may be duplicates of period pieces of furniture, such as beds and chairs, that children used. The second type of children's furniture is pieces of furniture made for children to play with. It is important to remember that dolls during the 18th and 19th centuries were often large by today's standards. Playtime may have found a child having tea with a beloved doll and a childhood friend of almost the same size. A third type, not covered in this book, are tiny creations made for use in doll houses.

The term "salesman's sample" is commonly used to refer to this type of furniture. However, unless some documentation is included, it is hard to attribute a particular piece of furniture as a sample.

Look for the same details in fine children's furniture as found in the adult sizes. Many examples of children's furniture were hand made. Those often are the most cherished, as they are unique in their construction. Today collectors enjoy grouping small-sized furniture as an interesting display accent. Others use this size of furniture to accompany their doll collections. And others continue the fine tradition of actually allowing children to use and play with this furniture.

Reproductions of miniatures and children's furniture exist. Look for signs of usage, and even damage, from years of little hands touching the piece of furniture. Repainted pieces are usually valued a little less, but more than likely tend to be authentic. Check for construction techniques that date to the period of the piece to help establish age and authenticity.

Beds

These beds vary from detailed miniatures to beds actually used for children. All are detailed and made of similar woods to those used for adult beds.

Country, youth, Pennsylvania, Berks County, first half 19th C, attributed to Jacob Leiby, paint decorated, scroll cutouts on head and foot boards, cannon ball turnings, 69-1/2" l, 39-1/2" h..900.00

Federal, tiger maple, turned posts, scrolled headboard, tester frame, 15" l, 14" h 1,500.00

Folding, stained wood, folds into footed box, replaced calico bed hangings and coverings, 13" l, 11" h...825.00

Sheraton, turned legs and posts, wooden slat railings, old green paint, 48" l, 29" w, 30-1/2" h..275.00

Victorian, Thomas Sheraton style, c1890-1900, turned mahogany, tester, 34" l, 18" w, 28" h..500.00

Bench

The following example was made by an unidentified itinerant craftsman. Today many examples of Tramp Art are being considered as folk art, as the types of construction and materials used were very creative and are often unique.

Tramp Art, old dark finish with dark green, upholstered arched back, two birds with "Gladys" on apron, initials "G. J." in leg posts, seat cushion missing, some damage, applied decoration incomplete on arms, 30" w, 17-1/2" d, 25-1/2" h..1,100.00

Blanket Chests

Miniature blanket chests are probably the hottest segment of this market right now. Collectors are seeking interesting examples and frequently display them stacked on one another. Look for features like tills and dovetailed cases, just like their full-sized counterparts.

Blanket Chest, Chippendale, Pennsylvania, attributed to Octarora Valley, Chester County, walnut, rectangular top with edge molding, dovetailed case with paneled facade, two overlapping dovetailed drawers, arch pillars with inlaid diamonds, band of maple Greek key molding over drawers, raised panels on drawers with orig brasses, bracket feet, orig finish, orig wrought iron strap hinges, interior till with lid, pine and popular secondary woods, 26-3/4" w, 15-3/4" d, 16-3/4", $34,100. Photo courtesy of Garth's Auctions, Inc., Delaware, OH.

Chippendale

Decorated, pine, old crusty gray paint, black daubed graining, dovetailed case, two dovetailed drawers, molded edge lid, ogee feet, interior till, old repair to hinge rail of lid, 16" w, 9-3/4" d, 11" h 24,200.00

Pennsylvania, c1770-90, probably Lancaster or Chester County, figured walnut, molded rectangular top, well with paper lined till, plain case, ogee bracket feet, 19" w, 10-1/2" d, 11-1/8" h..........................5,975.00

Pennsylvania, attributed to Octarora Valley, Chester County, walnut, applied edge molding on top, dovetailed case with paneled facade and two overlapping dovetailed drawers, arch pillars have inlaid diamonds, band of maple Greek key molding over drawers, raised panels and orig brasses on drawers, wrought strap hinges, bracket feet, interior till with lid, pine and poplar secondary woods, old finish (possibly orig), 26-3/4" w, 15-3/4" d, 16-3/4" h 34,100.00

Country, early to mid-19th C

Pine, old blue paint, dovetailed case, lid and base with molded edge, dovetailed

bracket feet, old repaired crack in rear foot, 21" w, 12" d, 15-1/2" h 8,800.00

Pine, old green paint, six board construction, lift top, interior till, wire hinges, hook fastener, 5-1/4" w, 3-1/8" d, 4-3/4" h.....1,955.00

Pine, old green over black paint, diamond and initials "T. S." in yellow, dovetailed case, lid with applied edge molding, bracket feet, interior divided missing, repaired break in lid at hinge rail, 12-3/4" w, 7-1/4" d, 7-1/2" h...........1,210.00

Pine, old olive paint, stenciled flowers in black and white, all over red ground, lid replaced, removable bracket foot base is later addition, 30-1/4" w, 13" d, 14-1/2" h 615.00

Pine, old red paint, crazed over varnish, molding around lid and base, interior till, tapered feet, fitted lock, 18" w, 8-1/2" d, 10-3/4" h 675.00

Pine, old red paint, worn white initials, "C. L.," dovetailed case, lid edge molding,

Ice Box and Miniature Blanket Chests, Front: Ice Box, red and tan paint decoration, softwood, cutout bracket feet, metal lining, part of orig lining, 23" w, 18" d, 24" h, $415; back: Grain painted, orig grain painted surface, cutout bracket feet, interior with glove box, replaced lock, 45" w, 19" d, 26"h, $1,045; on top: painted, mustard ground, grain painted lines throughout, painted brown marbleized panels bordered in black, fitted interior, bracket feet, 29" w, 13" d, 17-1/2" h, $990. Photo courtesy of Alderfer Auction Company, Hatfield, PA.

bracket feet, wire hinges, wrought iron hasp, 17" w, 8-3/4" d, 9-3/8" h 1,760.00

Pine, old worn dark green over light green, molded edge lid and lock, applied base moldings, high bootjack feet, name "Ernest E. Olin" penciled in lid, 14" w, 6-1/2" d, 10" h 650.00

Pine, orig yellow paint, black feet, dovetailed case, applied edge molding, molded bottom edge, turned feet, Pennsylvania, 15-1/4" w, 7-1/2" d, 9-1/2" h 5,225.00

Pine, reddish brown flame graining, yellow ground, red showing at point of wear, applied lid molding, well shaped bracket feet, Pennsylvania, 15-3/8" w, 7-3/4" w, 10" h 22,500.00

Pine, six board construction, stained brown, cut-out feet, wear, small piece missing from one back foot, 6-1/2" l, 3-1/4" w, 4" h 950.00

Poplar and pine, orig green and black paint, top edge of case with swag decoration, side boards extend to make runner feet, applied molding around base, replaced lid molding, found in Maine, 15" w, 9" d, 7" h 625.00

Poplar, gray repaint over red, dovetailed case, lid and base edge molding, turned feet, rehinged, repairs to hinge rail, 20" w, 9-1/2" d, 12-1/2" h 440.00

Poplar, orig blue paint with red, green, yellow and black striping, same colors repeated in band around lid and oval medallion at brass bail handles, minor wear, 17-1/2" w, 11-1/2" d, 8-1/2" h 5,100.00

Poplar, orig dark red graining, initials "G. D." finger painted on left side, dovetailed case, applied lid edge molding, bracket feet, glued repair to hinge rail of lid, 19-1/2" w, 13-3/4" d, 13-3/4" h 1,320.00

Poplar, orig blue paint with red, green, yellow and black striping, same colors repeated in band around lid and oval medallion at brass bail handles, minor wear, 17-1/2" w, 11-1/2" d, 8-1/2" h 5,100.00

Walnut, dovetailed case, applied lid edge molding and on bottom edge, turned feet, old soft finish, interior till, lid has nailed repair to hinge rail, 20-1/2" w, 12-3/4" d, 14-3/4" h 550.00

Walnut, dovetailed case, interior till, replaced feet, 30" w, 13-1/2" d, 17-1/2" h 575.00

Tramp Art, America, early 20th C, mahogany, chip-carved decoration, including a potted plant, horseshoe, and letters "B" and "V," swing wooden handles at sides, interior till, loss to decoration on one foot, 9-3/8" l, 4-1/2" w, 4-5/8" h 115.00

Bookcase

This miniature was probably made for usage in a nursery to keep small children's books in place.

Country, hand made, scalloped cornice over four open shelves, base with three drawers, Peter Hunt hand painted decoration 1,750.00

Boxes

Many types of miniature boxes can be found. These examples show a few different types. Also see Boxes.

Desk, slant lid, pine, American, 19th C, 8-1/2" w, 6-1/2" d, 4" h 400.00

Wall, America, early 19th C, pine, trapezoidal box with shaped backboard, wire loop hanger, rack in backboard, 5" w, 2-1/4" d, 6" h 1,495.00

Cabinet

This interesting example was made for use by a child so playtime might be able to imitate the styles and textures used by adults.

Modernism Era, Paul McCobb, manufactured by Winchendon, birch case, eight drawers, brass pulls, orig label, refinished, 36" w, 12" d, 9" h 885.00

Chairs

Children's chairs are numerous, as they were made in sets just as adult versions. Chairs made for use in schools, churches, and nurseries are probably the most common types of children's chairs. Some miniature chairs were used as advertising pieces and can be found with a store's name stenciled on the seat or back. Advertising pieces tend to be most valuable in the geographic region where the store name is easily recognized.

Adironack, arm, wooden lawn type, 27" h 95.00

Chippendale-Style, wing back, early 20th C, mahogany legs and stretcher base, worn floral upholstery, cross stretcher missing, leg chips, 10" h seat, 29" h....................................660.00

Classical, Middle Atlantic states, early 19th C, arm, shaped crest above horizontal splat, racked stiles joined to shaped arms continuing to vase and ring-turned supports, outward flaring legs, joined by turned stretchers, needlepoint seat, old refinish, 12-1/2" h seat, 23-1/2" h....................................980.00

Classical-Style, Boston, c1920, side, mahogany, paneled concave crests, horizontal splat joining raked stiles, upholstered slip seats, sabre legs, refinished, 14-1/2" seat, 28" h, price for pair...............................550.00

Ladderback, side

America, dark brown paint over red, scrolled arms, replaced woven tape seat, 18" h 330.00

America, dark brown finish, acorn finials, rush seats, one with orig bulbous front stretcher, price for pair, 28" h...........3,850.00

New England, late 18th/early 19th C, old black paint, turned finials, arched splats flanked by turned stiles with turned caps above front legs, imperfections, 9" h seat, 23" h 350.00

Modernism Era, side, Harry Betroia, manufactured by Knoll International, black and white construction, orig yellow seat pad, 16" w, 12" d, 24" h....................................250.00

Modernism Era, Pop, side, unknown designer, 1960s, cantilevered form, red molded plastic, 16" w, 14" d, 23" h....................450.00

Victorian

Arm, carved walnut frame with molded sides, carved seat rail with drop pendant, front cabriole legs, tufted gold upholstery, 16" w, 29" h....................................550.00

Side, c1850, wide crest rail, turned legs and rungs, orig dark surface, crushed red velvet upholstery, price for pr..............350.00

Windsor

New England, early 19th C, side, ash, pine, and maple, curved open back with arched and shaped crest rail over four rods, shaped slab seat raised on splayed turned legs, joined by turned box stretcher, bamboo turning throughout 200.00

New England, early 19th C, bow back, side, bowed crest and spindles, plank shaped seat, swelled legs joined by H-stretchers, old black paint, cracks in seat, paint loss, 8-1/4" seat, 20-1/2" h.........800.00

Pennsylvania, first half 19th C, low back, arm, grain painted and parcel gilt, reserve scrolling concave crest continuing to downswept arms, six bulbous turned supports, plank seat, ring-turned tapering legs joined by stretchers, all over graining in brown and ochre, gilt highlights..........................950.00

Chaise Lounge

This example was probably made for use in playtime, for a treasured doll to take a nap.

Victorian, upholstered, 31" l................895.00

Chest of Drawers

Small chests of drawers taught a child to be neat and tidy. When the chest was child sized, it may have only been used for a few years before the child outgrew the small scale. Chests of drawers used to hold a doll's wardrobe tend to be more heavily played with, as they sometimes remained in a child's room and were used for other purposes, such as jewelry or trinkets, as the child grew. Look for some of

Chair: Windsor, very worn red paint with black striping, bowed back, turned spindles, plank seat, turned legs and stretchers, price for set of four (one shown), 13-3/4" h seat, 27" h, $330.

the same design features found in full-sized chests of drawers.

Chippendale

Mahogany, two small drawers over two long graduated drawers, scalloped skirt, French feet, old restoration, 13-1/2" l, 9-1/2" h 750.00

Walnut, four drawers, scalloped skirt, brass pulls and escutcheons, 18" w, 11" d, 26" h 950.00

Chippendale-Style, black onyx in small brick like segments, inset brasses, four dovetailed drawers, labeled "Maitland Smith," 21-/2" w, 16" d, 26-3/4" h 1,650.00

Classical, Country

Cherry, curly maple drawer fronts, poplar secondary wood, three dovetailed graduated drawers, paneled ends, turned feet, turned walnut pulls, old refinishing, 19-3/4" w, 11-3/8" d, 19-1/2" h 2,100.00

Mahogany and mahogany veneer, three dovetailed drawers, applied and turned half columns, delicate turned feet, tapered rear feet, old brass pulls, pine and poplar secondary wood, minor veneer chips and wear, one replaced pull, 14-1/8" w, 9-3/8" d, 15" h 1,540.00

Mahogany, full turned columns, rectangular backsplash, outset top drawer over three graduated long drawers, large ball feet, round wooden pulls, paneled sides, 14-1/2" w, 8-1/2" d, 18" h 1,200.00

Mahogany, full turned columns, swell front drawer over three long drawers, ball feet, opalescent glass pulls, paneled sides, top stained, 13-1/2" w, 10" d, 15" h 1,980.00

Mahogany, reeded columns, larger top drawer over three graduated drawers, ball feet, brass pulls,14" w, 15" h 1,500.00

Cottage Style, poplar, orig red paint, white striping, three drawers, high back mirror with shelves, wire nail construction, minor water damage to paint on feet, 23-1/4" h 400.00

Decorated, pine, orig graining in imitation of rosewood, yellow striping in imitation of inlay, dovetailed case, lift lid with two false drawers, two dovetailed overlapping drawers, high feet, scrolled apron, minor repair to feet, minor wear

and edge damage, 9-1/2" w, 1 1/4" d, 12" h 1,595.00

Federal

Connecticut, c1790, cherry, rectangular overhanging top with molded edge, case with four incised beaded graduated drawers, inlaid quarter fans and stringing, ogee bracket feet, old refinish, 38-3/4" w, 18" d, 34-1/4" h 7,200.00

Country

Cherry, molded top edge, three dovetailed drawers, chamfered corners, cutout feet, simple base molding, old finish, poplar secondary wood, 12-7/8" w, 9" d, 12-3/4 h 715.00

Mahogany, inlaid, three drawers, hidden rear top drawer, laminated ball feet, glass knobs, 13" w, 11" h 2,200.00

Softwood, swell front, conforming shaped top, two small drawers over three long drawers, scalloped skirt, 11" w, 10-1/4" h 275.00

New England, c1825, mahogany, rectangular molded top, two small drawers over three long drawers, large wood knobs, brass escutcheons, rope turned columns, 16-1/2" w, 8-1/2" d, 18" h 1,750.00

New England, first quarter 19th C, pine, case with two short drawers, two graduated long drawers, cutout base, replaced brass pulls, old refinish, imperfections, 18-1/2" w, 9" d, 17-1/4" h 635.00

Pennsylvania, Philadelphia or New Jersey, c1800, maple, rectangular top with reeded edge, two short and three long drawers with incised decoration, shaped skirt, straight bracket feet, orig brass knobs, 14" w, 6" d, 13-3/4" h 2,750.00

French Restauration, walnut and mahogany, three drawers, rect white marble top, ribbon bordered drawers and turned feet...350.00

Hepplewhite, Country

Inlaid cherry, four dovetailed drawers, 19-3/4" w, 11-3/4" d, 22-1/2" h 450.00

Mahogany, six dovetailed drawers with applied edge beading and molded edge top, inlaid base around base, French feet, two drawers with inlaid diamond escutcheons, one with wood escutcheon, pine secondary

Chest of Drawers, Hepplewhite, serpentine, mahogany with inlay, five banded dovetailed drawers, scrolled apron, French feet, inlay consists of banding around base, fan in apron, banding around drawers, crossbanded top edge with stringing and banding, patera medallion on top, poplar secondary wood, top drawer with old pen and ink inscription "William Eaty, May 28, 1798," purchased in Fairfield County, OH, restored at Winterthur, 18-3/4" w, 13-5/8" d, 24" h, $30,800. Photo courtesy of Garth's Auctions, Inc., Delaware, OH.

wood, refinished, edge damage, old repairs, one side warped and split along back edge, 23-3/8" w, 10-3/4" d, 21" h 2,550.00

Sheraton, Country

Cherry, molded edge top, dovetailed drawers with applied edge beading, one board ends, turned feet, old finish, pine secondary wood, repairs to base, feet may be old replacements, replaced brass knobs, 10" w, 7-1/2" d, 12-3/8" h 450.00

Cherry and curly maple, five dovetailed drawers with applied edge beading, paneled ends, turned feet, refinished, replaced brass pulls 850.00

Mahogany, five drawers, reeded columns, beehive turned feet, paneled sides, 20" w, 13" d, 19" h 1,980.00

Poplar, old red finish, drawers with mahogany veneer, three dovetailed drawers, pan-

eled ends, turned feet, poplar secondary wood, mismatched clear lacy knobs, drawer fronts with holes from previous hardware, 13" w, 9-3/4" d, 17-1/2" h 550.00

Walnut, c1820, rectangular top, four graduated long drawers, paneled ends, turned feet, 19-1/4" h 975.00

Walnut, scrolled crest, two dovetailed drawers with cockbeading, turned legs, 15-3/4" w, 9-1/4" d, 16-1/2" h 750.00

Tramp Art, America, late 19th C

Fashioned from cigar boxes, shaped crest and apron, alligatored finish, right side base repair, 8-3/8" w, 4-7/8" h, 9-3/8" h 260.00

Hand Made, three drawers, small mirror, old white repaint, gold trim, wear, age cracks in top, 15-1/2" w, 8-3/4" d, 21-1/2" h 360.00

Crib

Antique cribs frequently come into the antiques marketplace. Examples tend to have many turned spindles, and some fold or dismantle easily for later storage. Caution should be used if using a vintage crib for a new baby, as they fail to meet today's safety standards.

America, pine, turned posts and spindles, shaped crest rail and foot rail, turned and tapered feet, casters 450.00

Crib Settee

This combination of a crib and settee was a clever adaptation of a popular Arts & Crafts style of furniture.

Arts & Crafts, L. and J. G. Stickley, Onandaga Shops, Fayetteville, NY, spindled sides and back, orig tacked-on leather seat, enhanced orig finish, one hole in leather, unmarked, 60" w, 20" d, 39" h 4,475.00

Cupboards

Small cupboards are typically children's play things and were probably used to hold miniature sets of dishes and similar items.

Display, Victorian, 19th C, maple, two glazed doors over two short and two long drawers, 18-1/2" w, 9-1/2" d, 32" h 750.00

Kitchen, Hoosier type, oak, zinc work surface, 28" w, 50" h 850.00

Stepback, pine, old worn reddish brown finish, paneled doors, open top, pigeonhole interiors, 24-1/2" w, 12-3/4" d, 25-3/4" h 950.00

Wall, Pennsylvania, mid 19th C, pine, peaked crest, shelf and two drawers, scalloped frame, two lower cupboard doors, replaced wooden pulls, 29-1/4" w, 14-1/2" d, 44-1/2" h..625.00

Desks

A well-to-do child probably used these examples of child-sized desks. Notice that they have the same design elements found on full scale desks, with slant fronts, fitted interiors, etc.

Federal, desk on frame, decorated, poplar, worn orig brown graining, top with two doors, six drawers, pigeonholes, slant lid, square nails with later nails added, base is well made replacement, found in North Lawrence, OH, 18-1/2" w, 18-1/2" d, 44-1/2" h 900.00

George III-Style, English or American, 19th C, hand crafted, mahogany, slant front, interior fitted with two small drawers, case with four graduated drawers, mounted on bracket feet, 13" w, 7-1/4" d, 16-1/2" h 360.00

Hepplewhite, slant front, inlaid cherry, dovetailed drawers, 21" w, 14" d, 28-1/4" h.......600.00

Queen Anne, New England, c1750, slant lid, maple, lid opens to compartmented interior, case of two thumb-molded graduated drawers, bracket feet, braces probably replaced, old refinish, restored, 19-1/4" w, 11-1/2" d, 20" h..2,550.00

William and Mary, painted pine, rectangular molded top, interior pigeonholes and small drawers, single long molded drawer, molded base, ball feet, painted red, front foot loose, losses to paint, 13" w, 9-1/4" d, 14-1/2" h...2,950.00

Jelly Cupboard

Here is an example of a hand-made cupboard made for a child to play with, perhaps so she could have one like just like Mother did.

Country, pine and butternut, old dark varnish stain finish, scrolled crest, two paneled doors, cutout feet, scrolled front apron, homemade tin hinges, front feet have repair, one door with old tin braces, 8-1/2" w, 4-1/2" d, 13-1/4" h 440.00

Linen Press

This miniature linen press has the same elements as a full-sized linen press. It was probably made to be used in a child's room or nursery to hold their clothes.

Victorian, 19th C, mahogany, two cupboard doors above projecting case with two frieze and three long graduated drawers, ogee bracket feet, 24" w, 13" d, 39" h 1,950.00

Rockers

Many children's rockers are found in the antiques marketplace. Most were made for a child to use. Some examples are found with advertising.

Advertising, Pennsylvania furniture store, c1900, painted red, gold stenciled letters, turned spindled back, plank seat 200.00

Boston Style, New England, painted and stenciled, wide decorated yoke, caned seat, five spindles on back, scrolled arms, turned legs and front stretcher, 18" w, 28" h......300.00

Classical, mahogany, vase-shaped splat, rush seat, scrolled arms, 22" h...............275.00

Rocker, Arts & Crafts, Gustav Stickley, New York, c1904-06, No. 345, three horizontal back slats, open arms, orig leather sea, red decal mark, finish enhanced, 18" w, 25-1/2" h, $900. Photo courtesy of Skinner Auctioneers and Appraisers of Antiques and Fine Art Boston and Bolton, MA.

Ladderback, old dry red surface, turned bell finials, shaped arms, splint seat with minor damage, 25-3/4" h....................................275.00

Shaker, Mount Lebanon, No. 1, orig dark finish, old tape seat and back, gold stenciled label on rocker "Shaker's Trademark Mt. Lebanon, N. Y. No. 1," some old touch up to finish, some remnants of white paint on seat and back, 29" h....................................955.00

Screen

This screen may have been created to lend privacy in a nursery setting. As with other small-scaled furniture, it closely imitates the style of its larger counterpart.

Victorian, three folding panels, oak and brass, sheered fabric..............................850.00

Secretary

What 19th Century child wouldn't have loved to have such an elegant piece of furniture?

Birch and pine, folk carved, craved dog finials, fitted interior, ornate foliate carved bookcase door over rolltop desk, fitted interior, two drawers, paw feet................................1,200.00

Stand

Perhaps this miniature stand was a salesman's sample, made to be taken from region to region or displayed in a furniture store. Whatever its original purpose, it is a wonderful example of this smaller-scaled furniture.

Sheraton, stripped walnut, applied gallery, one board top with age cracks, single dovetailed drawer with applied edge beading, turned legs, 15-1/4" sq, 24" h.................495.00

Stools

These small scaled foot stools were made for a child to rest his feet while seated in a chair sized correctly for their smaller frames.

Decorated

Country, orig light green paint, yellow and ochre striping, floral decoration, 6-1/4" l, 3-3/4" d, 2-3/4" h................................800.00

Pennsylvania, Landis Valley, mid-19th C, poplar, rectangular top, ogee shaped apron, bootjack legs, red, green, and black foliage, flowers, baskets, and tendrils, yellow ground, 8-3/4" w, 4" d, 3-1/2" h........1,995.00

Federal, New England, c1825, foot, mahogany, upholstered, vase and ring turned legs, 8" l, 7" d, 7-3/4" h.....................................115.00

Tables

Small children's tables were used in the nursery and usually surrounded by several chairs.

Dressing Table, Hepplewhite, 19th C, walnut, rectangular top, three hinged compartments, three drawers, tapered rectangular legs, bun feet, 10" h.............................1,250.00

Drop Leaf

Country, pine, top with hinged leaves, square butt joint, rounded corners, turned legs, old dark finish, 22-1/4" w, 14-1/4" d, 6-3/4" leaves, 21-1/4" h.....................................385.00

Sheraton, walnut, leaves with decoratively cut corners, one dovetailed drawer, turned legs, pine secondary wood, old finish, minor edge damage, hinges replaced, age crack on top, 23-1/2" l, 12-1/2" w, 10-3/4" l leaves, 19" h.....................................1,400.00

Work, Classical, rosewood and fruitwood, rectangular hinged top, compartmented interior, two sliding drawers, sq tapered legs, one handle missing, 10-3/4" h.......................750.00

Trunk

This small-sized trunk may have been used by a child during playtime to store a doll's wardrobe. Many examples of fashion dolls are found with their own trunks, outfitted with all the accessories and clothing needed to enjoy dressing and playing with the doll.

Southbridge, MA, first half 19th C, dome top, rectangular base, paper lined interior, top and side painted with feathers and swags, red, yellow, and white, black ground, 20" w, 10" d, 8" h..775.00

Mirrors

Mirror, mirror on the wall—what an important part of furnishings mirrors play in our lives. All furniture periods have included mirrors and as the manufacturing techniques improved, sizes expanded, too. It is usually acceptable for an antique mirror to show some signs of aging, loss of silvering, etc. While mirrors are commonly thought as a way to view one's image, they are also important decorative elements. Used to create the illusion of more spacious appearances, they also capture light and reflect it back into a room.

Some mirror-related terms:

Architectural - usually combines architectural elements of the design period, used to reflect light.

Cheval - large mirrors which are designed with a base and can be used in a free-standing position.

Dressing - used to view one's appearance, sometimes mounted on a base or used on a table top.

Eglomise - a type of painting on glass where the design is painted on the back and intended to be viewed through the glass.

Girandole - circular convex mirror.

Looking Glass - a small mirror used to view one's image.

Over Mantel - large mirrors used over a fireplace mantel, primarily used to reflect light into a room.

Pier - large mirror either hung over a pier table or hung at a level so one could view skirts and feet.

Scroll - a scrolled mirror frame, made to be hung on a wall.

Shaving - used to view one's appearance while shaving. Usually found on bases, sometimes with small drawers to hold accessories.

Wall - a mirror designed to be hung on the wall and used for either viewing of one's image or reflecting light.

Aesthetic Movement

Mirrors from this period are generally large and designed to be used in hallways or over mantelpieces. Their purpose was primarily decorative.

America, c1880, over mantel, gilt, central cornice supported by two small columns over frieze dec with scene of snake attaching bird in tree, mirror plate highly dec with leaves, orig label of L. Utler, 47 Royal St., New Orleans, 64" w, 6" d, 84" h 3,600.00

Art Deco

Art Deco mirrors are some of the first to use colored glass. This period also introduced metal frames. Because mirrors are small enough to be easily imported, a French example is included for comparison purposes.

America, craved fruit and foliage at crest and on sides, 31" l, 41-1/2" h 95.00

America, octagonal blue glass, clear inset, chrome screws, 28" sq 150.00

French, c1930, giltwood, frame closed at bottom and sides, carved chevrons, stylized sundials and Chinese scrolls, hung by gilt thread rope, tapered rect beveled mirror plate, 27" w, 37" h 1,500.00

Art Nouveau

Art Nouveau mirrors used flowing lines. This furniture period also embraced using other materials, such as iron, silver, and pewter in additional to the traditional wood frames found on mirrors.

Wrought iron, octagonal reticulated internal edge, upper part mounted by stylized fountain and floral ground, beveled edge mirror, stamped "E. Brandt" lower right corner, 43" l, 38-1/2" w 64,000.00

Arts & Crafts

Arts & Crafts mirrors were designed to be used to compliment the distinctive furniture style that was popular from c1895 to 1915. Many of these mirrors also served as hat racks. Look for simple framework and original finishes.

Boston Society of Arts and Crafts, 1910, carved wood, rect, carved and gilded frame, ink mark, initials, orig paper label, 11-1/4" w, 18-1/2" h 700.00

Limbert, Charles P., Grand Rapids, MI, oak, frame with geometric inlaid design over rect cane panel shoefoot base, recoated orig frame, orig glass, 20" w, 8" d, 22" h 600.00

Michigan Chair Co., Grand Rapids, MI, c1915, wall, shaped cutouts, center rectangular mirror, scalloped details, orig paper label, 35-1/2" w, 23-1/4" h................................200.00

Roycroft, East Aurora, NY, hall, six hammered hooks, orig hanging chains and glass, fine orig finish, unmarked, 50" x 36"....2,000.00

Stickley, Gustav, New York

Cheval, No. 918, Harvey Ellis design, peaked full length mirror supported by sculptural base, double arched stretchers, through-tenon construction, orig dark finish,

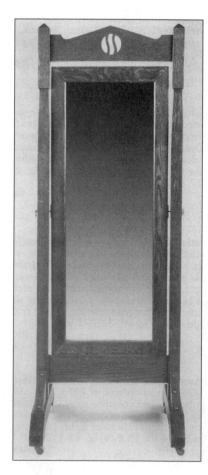

Arts & Crafts, cheval, attributed to California, c1912, oak, inverted V-shaped crest rail, circular wavy line cutout, rectangular swivel mirror, 27" w, 75" h, $1,725. Photo courtesy of Skinner Auctioneers and Appraisers of Antiques and Fine Art Boston and Bolton, MA.

sgd, 1904 black ink mark, 18" w, 17" d, 70" h 18,700.00

Table Top, c1912, swivel, arched rectangular frame, angled shoe feet, branded mark, 22" w, 21-1/2" h 690.00

Wall, c1909, No. 910, oak, arched frame, hand wrought iron hooks and chain, red decal, brown paper label, 35" w, 23-1/2" h 1,650.00

Unknown Californian Designer, cheval, c1912, oak, inverted V-shaped crest rail with circular wavy line cutout, rect swivel mirror, 27" w, 75" h 1,725.00

Unknown Maker, wall, oak, rectangular frame, unsigned, 31" w, 3/4" d, 40" h 175.00

Centennial

These examples of wall mirrors show how the designers of the 1870s were reminiscing about the earlier styles. The additional of eagles displayed their patriotism.

Chippendale-Style, America, third quarter 19th C

Carved giltwood, three carved eagles perched atop rocks and Rococo scrolls which continue down sides, intertwined with foliage and ripping nests, high relief carving, some repairs, 31" w, 59" h...............3,680.00

Mahogany, scrolled crest, pendant centering beveled mirror plate, 18-1/4" w, 35" h 75.00

Queen Anne-style, American, late 19th C, mahogany faced, scalloped, shell pendant, 32" h..250.00

Chippendale

The Chippendale period is filled with mirrors. During this time, they were used extensively to reflect candle light. Wealth and stature, plus one's political connections, could be demonstrated by elaborate crests on mirrors. Several English examples are included for comparison purposes, plus it is important to understand that mirrors were imported. American craftsmen then copied them and incorporated the latest designs in their work. It is often very difficult to tell where a mirror originated. Any original labels or markings add to the provenance, and, of course, the price.

America, c1820, pier, mahogany, rectangular mirror plate, surmounted by slip, conforming leaf carving, ring and block-turned frame, 21" w, 36" h 400.00

America, mid-18th C

Carved fretwork, mahogany, incised gilded scrolling and pierced phoenix at crest, orig glass and brass hanging hardware, old repairs to phoenix and carved gilt border, orig cedar backboard, chalked in 18th C script "sayDs," 22-3/4" w, 40" l.........3,590.00

Carved fretwork, walnut, gilt phoenix on crest, pinched corners, mirror peeling, repairs to framing, 21-1/2" w, 40" h 750.00

Carved fretwork, walnut, solid unadorned crest, molded border, orig glass and brass hanging hardware, 20" w, 44-3/4" l.....850.00

Scroll, cherry, old finish, repairs and restoration to ears and scroll work, old, possibly orig mirror glass with worn silvering, 12-1/4" w, 19-1/2" h 450.00

Scroll, hardwood, bird's heads designs, orig black paint, gilt decoration, label on back with "1911" and family history 925.00

Chippendale, c1780, mahogany fretwork, circular inlaid pinwheel in crest, molded border, orig glass, 11-3/4" w, 18-3/4" h, $425. Photo courtesy of Samuel T. Freeman & Co., Philadelphia, PA.

Scroll, mahogany, applied eagle, molded frame, old regilding to eagle, refinished, age cracks, one ear reglued, worn silvering, 14" w, 26" h 1,100.00

Scroll, mahogany, molded frame, old finish, old replaced ears, some edge damage, replaced mirror, Philadelphia paper label in very poor condition, 16-1/2" w, 30" h 420.00

Scroll, mahogany, molded frame, refinished, repairs, mirror replaced, 11-1/2" w, 19-3/4" h 225.00

Scroll, mahogany, molded frame with gilded liner, composition eagle in crest with old gilding, orig finish, orig mirror glass with minor wear to silvering, 19-3/4" w, 40-1/2" h...............3,575.00

Scroll, walnut, gilded composition Prince of Wales feathers in crest, two ears ended out, refinished, glass replaced, 13-3/4" w, 24-1/2" h 385.00

Wall, walnut, rectangular plate within ogee-molded crossbanded frame surmounted by pierced scroll fretted crest with center rosette, corners issuing further scrolls, suspending similarly fretted skirt, 20" w, 36-1/4" h 950.00

Wall, walnut and gilt gesso, scrolled frame, gilt gesso phoenix in pierced cresting above molded gilt incised liner, labeled "National Blake at 56 Cornhill (opposite the Statehouse) English, India & Hardware Goods," refinished, restorations, 22-3/4" w, 41" h..............2,985.00

America or England, c1790, carved mahogany, scrolled, incised, and pierced frame with foliate devices in crest, bracket enclosing molded liner, old refinish, replaced glass, imperfections, 18" w, 27" h.......650.00

America or England, late 18th C

Mahogany and gilt gesso, scrolled frame centering gilt carved phoenix in crest above molded gilt incised liner, old finish, old replaced glass, 18-1/4" w, 37" h 550.00

Mahogany and gilt gesso, scrolled frame with pierced crest and phoenix bird above molded gilt incised liner, old refinish, regilding, 16-1/2" w, 28-1/2" h 500.00

Mahogany and parcel gilt, scroll, carved gilt gesso shell and foliate device in crest above molded and gilt incised liner, minor imperfections, 18-3/4" w, 36" h........2,225.00

Chippendale, mahogany on pine, gilded liner, gilded phoenix, molded mirror frame, minor repairs, replaced glass, 14-1/2" w, 26" h, $3,575. Photo courtesy of Garth's Auctions, Inc., Delaware, OH.

Mahogany veneer on pine, scroll, gilded liner, some veneer damage, old veneer repair, 21" w, 39-3/4" h 2,400.00

Mahogany veneer on pine, scroll, regilded phoenix crest ornament and liner, orig mirror with very worn silvering, refinished, minor repairs, gilding on phoenix flaked, 17" w, 30-1/2" h 1,450.00

Mahogany veneer on pine, wall, carved moldings with old regilding, floral garlands and rosettes with phoenix finial, old mirror glass, some edge damage and old repair, 27-1/4" w, 57" h 11,450.00

Walnut veneer, scroll, 9-1/4" w x 15-3/4" h old mirror, 15-3/4" w, 26" h 425.00

Connecticut, mahogany, scrolled frame with symmetrical bird cut-out cresting above molded liner, labeled "C. Lyman, Middletown, Connecticut," 15-1/4" w, 24" h.............4,900.00

Country, scroll, mahogany veneer on pine, crown ornament and liner have gold repaint, considerable old repair, 31-3/4" h, 17-1/4" w 200.00

England, c1760, rococo carved giltwood, shaped scrolling frame surrounding trisected plate, 14-1/2" w, 38" h 1,000.00

England, late 18th C, walnut and parcel gilt, scrolled frame centering feathered plume, pierced crest above inlaid gilt incised liner, refinished, imperfections, 24-3/4" w, 43-3/4" h..........2,415.00

England, 19th C, walnut and parcel gilt, scrolled frame centering gilt foliate device, molded gilt incised liner, 21-1/2" w, 43" h 3,200.00

New England, c1780, inlaid mahogany, scrolled frame with pierced crest of gilt carved phoenix bird above string inlaid liner, 22-3/4" w, 46-1/4" h...2,300.00

New England, 1790, mahogany and parcel gilt, scrolled frame, center gilt gesso eagle in crest, molded gilt incised frame, regilded, 14-1/2" w, 29" h 250.00

New England, 1790, mahogany and parcel gilt, scrolled frame with pierced Prince of Wales feathered plume, molded gilt incised liner, restoration, 17-1/2" w, 34" h 250.00

New England, 1790-1810, mahogany and carved gilt, scrolled frame, pierced crest and carved phoenix bird above molded gilt incised liner, old finish, minor repairs, 17-1/2" w, 33-1/2" h..750.00

New England, 1790, mahogany on pine, gilded liner, gilded phoenix, good detail, molded mirror frame, minor repairs, replaced glass, 14-1/2" w, 26" h........................3,375.00

New England, late 18th C, mahogany and parcel-gilt, scrolled frame, pierced crest centering phoenix bird, molded gilt incised liner, restorations, 17" w, 30" h 520.00

Pennsylvania, Philadelphia, carved mahogany veneer fretwork, gilded phoenix in pierced crest, molded border with notched corners, gilded interior border, old beveled glass, old repairs to phoenix and fretwork, early 19th C label of Cabinetmaker Thomas Natt, Philadelphia on back, 26" w, 55" h...................7,280.00

Pennsylvania, Philadelphia, mahogany, scrolled frame enclosing molded liner and mirror glass, partial label of James Stokes, Philadelphia, March 15, 1810, 17-1/4" w, 33-1/2" h...2,760.00

Rhode Island, late 18th C, mahogany and gilt gesso, imperfections, 14" w, 8" d, 23" h..3,750.00

Chippendale-Style

The following mirrors all display some elements of the Chippendale style, but have been made after the 1790s.

Over Mantel, Chinese Influence, late 19th/

early 20th C, giltwood, topped by stylized columns, shaped surround with scrolls, acanthus, and rocaille throughout, Chinese-style birds on each side, 47-1/2" x 52" 2,415.00

Scroll

Curly maple, elaborate scrolls on crest, ears, and base, one ear cracked, small piece missing, worn silvering on mirror, old mellow finish, early 20th C, 21" w, 45" h.........660.00

Mahogany and mahogany veneer, scroll detail, darkened silvering, refinished, some age, but not period, 12-3/4" w, 21-3/4" h..330.00

Mahogany veneer, poplar secondary wood, old varnish finish, old repairs, backboard from clock, partial paper label, 19th C, 20-1/2" w, 38" h 550.00

Wall

Carved walnut, rectangular plate within molded conforming frame, surmounted by fretted scroll crest centered by carved eagle with outstretched wings, suspending similarly fretted skirt, 17-3/4" w, 34-1/2" h 230.00

Mahogany and parcel-gilt, 19th C, arched rectangular, beveled plate within conforming frame, surmounted by scroll crest centered by ho-ho bird, scrolled skirt centered by inlaid fan, 20" w, 35-1/2" h 700.00

Mahogany, gilded eagle finial, gilded egg and dart molded scalloped sides, some damage and repairs, 19-3/4" w, 44" h 375.00

Classical

Classical mirrors date to the c1800 to 1830 period. They are best identified as having scrolls, curves, and some naturalistic carvings.

America, 1795, over mantel, wirework crest, central urn, scrolling vines, rectangular mirror plate, pierced flower head pendant, 28-1/2" d, 59-1/2" h..2,950.00

America, c1820, over mantel, mounted eagle flanked by C-scrolls, mirror plate surrounded with molded and pierced scroll carved border, shell carved pendant, 31-1/2" d, 49" h..3,600.00

America, 1825-30, gilt gesso, two part, top section surmounted by eagle with outstretched wings, split baluster frame wit applied flanking foliate devices, lower section of split baluster

frame with acanthus leaves in relief, flora, corner rosettes and 4 applied flanking foliate devices, regilded, restored, 39" h, 82" h............... 4,900.00

America, c1830, mahogany, acorn drop cornice, turned and acanthus carved pilasters, reeded trim, orig reverse painting of house, trees, and sailboat, old finish, one brass corner rosette missing, 18" w, 32-1/4" h.............375.00

America, c1830-40, giltwood, four sq corners elaborated with foliate devices, repairs, losses, some regilding, 30" w, 26-1/2" h.............460.00

America, c1835, giltwood, architectural style, carved upper tablet, rectangular mirror plate, gilding retouched, 39" h 850.00

America, architectural, 19th C

Mahogany, acorn drop cornice, turned and acanthus carved pilasters, reeded trim, orig reverse painting of house, trees, and sailboat, old finish, one brass corner rosette missing, 18" w, 32-1/4" h 300.00

Mahogany and mahogany veneer, molded cornice, corner blocks, reeded columns, top with well executed old replaced reverse painted scene of house, trees, and fence, worn mirror, old dark finish, repairs, parts of moldings replaced, 19-3/4" w, 36-1/2" h........ 350.00

Pine, cove molded cornice, reeded pilasters, orig reverse painted top with steamer Ohio, old refinishing, pieced repairs at cornice 615.00

Two part, mahogany veneer, ebonized half columns with gold stenciled foliage, shiny varnish, replaced glass, 13-1/2" w, 26" h.....220.00

Two part, turned half column and corner block frame, old gold repaint, reverse painting of sailboat in red, blue, yellow, black and white, blue sky, flaking to water, orig mirror with worn silvering, 11-7/8" w, 22-1/2" h 220.00

America, 19th C, girandole, gilt gesso, eagle figure on foliate and grapevine cresting over circular molded frame, ebonized liner, flanking candle sconces, repainted, imperfections, 28-1/2" w, 41-1/2" h............................2,750.00

America or England, c1810-20, dressing, carved mahogany and mahogany veneer, cylinder top opens to reveal four drawers, centering one door, ivory pulls, above single divided long drawer, restoration, 19" w, 10-5/8" d, 32" h..1,610.00

America or England, c1810-20, girandole, gilt gesso, crest with eagle flanked by acanthus leaves, convex glass, ebonized molded liner with affixed candle branches, foliate and floral pendant, imperfections, 23" w, 35" h...5,175.00

America or England, c1820, dressing, swing, mahogany, rectangular, shaped cornice, half columns on sides, fitted single drawer, 17-1/2" w, 10" d, 29" h..300.00

England, early 19th C, giltwood, girandole, circular convex glass, reeded ebonized surround, carved eagle in flight on crest, carved acanthus leaves and floral pendant device, reglued, restored, 19" w, 39" h............2,645.00

Massachusetts, attributed to Boston, c1815, pier, carved giltwood, shell above leafage and cat o'nine tails crest, spiral and acanthus leaf carved ring turned columns punctuated by leaf carved squares at each corner, molded black liner, orig gilding, old glass, 36" w, 71" h..............21,850.00

New England, c1820, over mantel, gilt gesso, center panel flanked by two smaller rectangular mirror plates, ring-turned swirl-carved columns, minor imperfections, 69-3/8" w, 29-1/8" h 1,400.00

New England, c1825, mahogany and mahogany veneer, dressing, rectangular framed mirror, vase and ring turned supports, base with three short drawers, six turned legs, old refinish, imperfections, 22-1/2" w, 8" d, 27" h 300.00

New England, c1825, over mantel, carved gilt gesso, rect frame, acanthus leaf and spiral carved split balusters joining corner pieces, floral rosettes, reeded ebonized liner enclosed three-part glass, some regilding, 58-3/4" w, 38" h..2,425.00

Courting

A courting mirror is a small mirror used to view one's reflection. This example doesn't fall into any one particular design style. It also shows that inscriptions and labels lend to the provenance of mirrors.

America, wooden frame, reverse painted glass inserts and crest with bird and flowers, orig mirror glass with worn silvering, penciled inscription on back with "restored 1914," touchup to reverse painting, brass back corner braces, 10-7/8" w, 16-1/2" h 935.00

Federal

Federal mirrors are best considered as decorative elements, reflecting light while using some adornments like carving, and moldings on the mirror frames.

America, c1800, wall, giltwood, molded cornice, spherules, floral carved tablet over eglomise tablet, rectangular mirror plate flanked by double spiral turned columns, 19-1/2" w, 33" h...750.00

America, c1815-20, gilt gesso, molded cornice with applied balls above incised and molded frame, engaged columns flanking eglomise panel of American naval battle and mirror plate, some imperfections, 16" w, 35-1/2" h 1,610.00

America, 19th C, architectural, double spiral columns sides, flower heads and ribbon swag with bows on top, gilded, 56-1/2" h 3,000.00

America, 19th C, architectural, pine, orig dark finish, fluted frame, corner blocks, molded cornice, reverse painted scene of large building in black, white, red, blue, and green, flaked paint, old glass, 20-3/4" h, 12-1/2" w 150.00

America, first quarter 19th C, wall, giltwood and verre-eglomise, rectangular plate with verre-eglomise gilt landscape panel above, composite frame with reverse breakfront cornice mounted with spherules, raised on twisted turned columns, 17-1/2" w, 32-1/4" h.................................. 650.00

America, second quarter 19th C, giltwood, cornice with spherical decoration, reverse painted label flanked by reeded columns, rect-

Federal, c1830, gilt carved gesso, rectangular, ring turned and floral decorated frame, rosette corner blocks, 52-1/2" w, 31-1/2" h, $550.

angular mirror plate, labeled "Edward Lothrop, 53 Marlborough Street, Boston," imperfections, 13-1/2" w, 30" h 1,250.00

America, second quarter 19th C, grain painted, reverse painted glass panel over rectangular mirror plate flanked by fluted pilasters, 13-1/2" w, 22" h 600.00

America, mid 19th C, shaving, mahogany veneer on pine, oval beveled mirror with scrolled posts, four dovetailed drawers, edge and veneer damage, one foot missing, 24-3/4" w, 9-1/4" d, 29-1/4" h 300.00

America, mid 19th C, split baluster, eglomise fruit panel, orig gilding, one corner block missing, imperfections, paint loss, 30-1/4" h 300.00

America or England, 1810-20, girandole, gilt gesso carved, eagle with outstretched wings on rocky plinth, flanking foliate devices, circular frame with acanthus leaves, ebonized reeded liner with flanking candle sconces, foliate and floral drop pendant, regilding, 24" w, 43" h 5,475.00

Maine, c1815-20, gilt gesso, molded cornice with applied balls above two split balusters flanking tablet showing sailing vessel in harbor, mirror plate below, labeled "James Todd Portland Looking Glass Manufactory," 20" w, 31-1/2" h..1,955.00

Maine, c1825, giltwood, molded cornice with applied balls above tablet of cottage landscape, stenciled border, mirror flanked by spiral moldings, labeled "James Todd Portland Maine," minor imperfections, 10-3/4" w, 20" h 350.00

Massachusetts, c1807-19, attributed to Barnard Cermenati, wall, gilt eglomise, entablature with gilt spherules above reverse painted white panel with gilt eagle, swagged garland of flowers, 19-1/2" w, 36" h 3,350.00

Massachusetts, Boston, c1810, wall, gilt gesso, cornice with spheres above reverse painted tablet of two children dancing within a stenciled foliate and star border, mirror plate wit flanking molded spiral pilasters, labeled "Edward Lothrop #53 Marlborough Street, Boston," minor imperfections, 13-1/2" w, 30-1/2" h..2,250.00

Massachusetts, Boston, c1810, wall, split baluster, painted and gilded, black painted and gilt frame, reverse painted eglomise tablet of woman standing in courtyard against red draped background, flanked by blue above mirror plate, labeled "Bittle and Copper Burnish Guilders No. 28 Court St., Boston," some regilding, 20-1/4" w, 40-1/2" h 1,200.00

Massachusetts, c1810, wall, gilt gesso, cornice with applied spiral molding and foliate banding above eglomise tablet of castle ruins, white and blue background, over mirror plate flanked by fluted half columns, minor imperfections, 24" w, 45" h................................2,650.00

Massachusetts, c1815, wall, gilt gesso, cornice with applied spheres above central panel, applied water leaves and acorns, eglomise tablet of flower filled urn framed in silver on white background above mirror plate flanked by spiral molded pilasters, minor imperfections, 19-3/4" w, 44" h 2,850.00

Massachusetts, Boston, c1820, over mantel, gilt gesso, rect frame, central frieze of shell and grape vines in relief, mirror plate flanked by floral panes and mirrors, framed by spiral moldings, corner blocks with lions' heads, regilded, replaced mirrors, 56" w, 28" h 4,615.00

Massachusetts, c1820, wall, gilt gesso, molded cornice with applied spherules above eglomise tablet of cottage, mirror plate flanked by concave molding with applied spherules, minor imperfections, 23" w, 38-1/4" h 1,550.00

Massachusetts, Salem, c1825, wood and gilded gesso, cornice with spherical decoration, inset plaque with carved basket of flowers flanked by turned and combed columns, rectangular mirror plate, 18-1/2" w, 36" h 1,500.00

Massachusetts, Boston or North Shore, early 19th C, wall, gilt and eglomise, molded cornice with gilt spherules overhangs reverse painted tablet with light blue paint, white rect reserve with gilt urn and gilt flowerettes, imperfections and regilding, 22-1/2" w, 38" h 2,100.00

Massachusetts or New Hampshire, c1810, dressing, painted cream, red outline, gray pinstriping, painted foliate device in mustard brown and red, drawer with polychrome floral design, 17-3/8" w, 10" d, 19-1/4" h 1,400.00

New England, c1810, inlaid mahogany, rectangular string inlaid framed mirror, inlaid projecting base, single drawer, ogee bracket feet, old refinish, 14" w, 7" d, 15-1/2" h 230.00

New England, c1820, dressing, mahogany and mahogany veneer, rectangular inlaid mirror frame, turned supports, projecting boxed case, two short drawers, turned feet, refinished, 18-1/2" w, 7-1/2" d, 21-1/2" h.......400.00

New England, c1820, giltwood, rectangular frame, applied spiral moldings, landscape tablet with red roofed cottage, mirror glass base, imperfections, 10-1/2" d, 20" h...............175.00

New England, c1820, giltwood, rectangular frame, applied spiral moldings, orig eglomise panel with Perry's Victory, some tarnishing, some lifting on eglomise panel, 23" w, 43" h...1,870.00

New York, mid-19th C, giltwood, labeled "Parker and Clover Looking Glass and Picture Frame Makers 180 Fulton St. New York," molded cornice with applied spherules above eglomise table of girl in pasture landscape holding dove, mirror flanked by spiral carved pilasters, 13-3/4" w, 29-1/8" h 2,875.00

Federal-Style

These mirrors show several elements of the Federal period, but were not made in the c1790 to 1815 era.

America, gilt phoenix finial, swan neck pediment, oak branch swags, gilt borders, plaster phoenix, repaired, 28-3/4" w, 6-1/4" h 675.00

America, giltwood, round molded frame, convex mirror plate, surmounted by spread winged eagle, 31" h................................200.00

Hepplewhite

Hepplewhite mirrors take the straight form thought of as Hepplewhite and add curved supports to hold the mirror frames.

Dressing, England, c1780, mahogany inlaid, urn-form mirror on beaded shaped supports, turned whalebone finials and bosses, serpentine case with three drawers with turned ivory pulls, top with crossbanded border on ogee bracket feet, 16" w, 8" d, 23-1/2" h.........500.00

Scroll, mahogany veneer on pine, banded inlay, refinished, veneer repairs, old glass with some edge wear to silvering, back boards renailed, 24" w, 47" h 1,155.00

Shaving, mahogany with figured veneer

Bow front, shield shaped mirror, three

Hepplewhite, scroll, mahogany veneer on pine, banded inlay, refinished, veneer repairs, old glass with some edge wear to silvering, back boards renailed, 24" w, 47" h, $1,155. Photo courtesy of Garth's Auctions, Inc., Delaware, OH.

dovetailed drawers, ogee feet, old finish, orig glass with some silvering wear, orig ivory knobs and ornaments with some wear, minor edge damage and veneer repair, 17-3/4" w, 8" d, 23-3/4" h.....................................880.00

Bow front, shield shaped mirror, two dovetailed drawers, feet, posts, and mirror are old replacements, 17-3/4" h 225.00

Serpentine front, figured veneer facade and inlay, oval mirror with shaped posts, three dovetailed drawers, ogee feet, inlay consists of herringbone banding around drawer, mirror frame, and edge of case, inlaid ivory shield shaped key escutcheon, replaced brass pulls, minor repairs, feet replaced, 17-1/2" w, 8-1/2" d, 23-1/2" h...1,320.00

Queen Anne

The scrolling cabriole legs associated with this design style don't appear on mirrors, but the scrolling effect is still quite apparent. Mirrors of this period were used as decorative elements. Expect to find fine woods and moldings.

America, c1740-60, carved mahogany fretwork, solid unadorned crest, molded border, chamfered corners, replaced glass, 24-1/2" w, 51-1/2" h..3,650.00

America, c1750, walnut veneer on pine frame, fret arved pediment with central carved and gilded eagle, 15-11/16" l...................500.00

America, molded mahogany frame, old finish, old replaced mirror glass, 10" w, 11-1/4" h 550.00

America, walnut veneer, pine secondary wood, applied gilded carvings, scrolled crests and open frame with gilded liner, old mirror with some wear and flaking to silvering, age cracks in veneer, 13-1/4" w, 31-1/2" h 1,875.00

America, walnut veneer, pine secondary wood, applied gilded ornaments, molded frame, gilded line, scrolled crest, old beveled glass, brief biography of previous owner, Christian Meyer, attached to backboards, minor veneer damage, refinished, gilding redone, 19-1/4" w, 47" h..2,950.00

America, walnut veneer, pine secondary wood, scrolled crest, fretwork side garlands, gilded liner, old refinishing, regilding work and flaking, old damage and repairs, old mirror glass, 24-1/4" w, 39-1/4" h 3,950.00

England, c1730, japanned, molded frame with cockbeaded border, arched cornice, gilt lacquer designs of figures, birds, and flowers, enclosing two-part glass with cut designs of floral garlands, minor imperfections, 24" w, 54" h..31,100.00

England, 18th C, walnut, parcel-gilt, scrolled pierced crest with foliage device, molded gilt incised liner, two-part glass, restoration, 13" w, 32" h...575.00

New England, 18th C, black painted arched frame enclosing glass with beveled edge, stylized basket of flowers dec, 17-1/2" w, 16" h 700.00

Queen Anne-Style

A later mirror using Queen Anne elements and clearly showing an Oriental influence.

America or England, 19th C, japanned, rocaille carved cresting, serpentine front painted with Chinoiserie symbols, 18" w, 39" h...500.00

Queen Anne to Chippendale Transitional

These examples show how early craftsmen blended some elements from the Queen Anne period into the newly evolved Chippendale designs. The unadorned crest is definitely Queen Anne, while the use of veneers is the beginning of Chippendale.

America, c1750-70, carved highly figured walnut veneer fretwork, solid unadorned crest, molded border with chamfered corners, orig glass, orig brass hanging hardware, 21" w, 42" h..1,525.00

America, c1750-70, carved mahogany veneered fretwork, solid unadorned crest, molded border with chamfered corners, old glass...955.00

America, c1760-70, carved mahogany veneered fretwork, solid unadorned crest, gilt molded border with chamfered corners, orig glass, minor losses to veneer and molding, 22-3/4" w, 42" l 675.00

Sheraton

Sheraton mirrors date to the c1790 to 1810 period and reflect the same elements found in other Sheraton designed furniture.

America, mahogany, spiral turned split columns and bottom rail, inlaid panels of mahogany, rosewood, and cherry, architectural top cornice, split mirror, 24-1/2" w, 47" h......300.00

Massachusetts, Newburyport, c1808, architectural, gilt frame, reverse painting of eagle holding American shield, banner, and arrows in gold, white, and Union blue background, over mirror, minor flanking, small corner break to mirror, labeled "Barnard Cermentari," 18-1/4" w, 37-1/2" h 1,400.00

New York, Albany, architectural, gilded frame, eglomise painting, orig mirror glass discolored, replaced painting, old regilding with some flakes, 23-3/4" w, 41-1/4" h...........850.00

Sheraton-Style

Stylistically these mirrors reflect the designs of the Sheraton period, but were made early in the 20th century, years after the c1790-1810 period.

Architectural, mahogany frame, rosette dec, 32-1/2" h..200.00

Shaving, bow front

Cherry, inlay, turned posts and adjustable mirror, two dovetailed drawers, turned feet, old mellow refinishing, 16" w, 7-1/2" d, 19-3/4" h 250.00

Mahogany veneer on pine, line inlay, two dovetailed drawers, turned feet, adjustable mirror with turned posts, repairs and replacements, 18-1/2" w, 7-1/2" d, 23-1/2" h..... 150.00

Tramp Art

Tramp Art is design style with limited forms. The following examples were all created in America, c1900 and show how these unique American artists created mirror frames from left over scraps of wood and other materials.

Rectangular chip-carved frame, 5-3/4" w, 7-1/4" h..115.00

Rectangular chip-carved frame, ovolo corners, outer border of heart-shaped spandrels, old surface, 13-1/2" w, 16" h 635.00

Victorian

The Victorians loved their mirrors and used them as both decorations and for viewing. They added gilding, carving, and as many other decorative elements as they could.

Cheval, walnut, rectangular mirror plate, brass inlaid surround, spiraled supports with candleholders, curved legs, large brass feet, 71-1/2" h..1,695.00

Over Mantel, giltwood, domed cresting, frame carved with foliate swags, ribbons, and corbels, early 20th C, 43" w, 68" h 1,035.00

Wall, second half 19th C, bird's eye maple, rectangular mirror plate within conforming ogee-molded base, 27-1/4" w, 25" h 500.00

Wall, second half 19th C, giltwood and gesso, ornate, scrolled and leaf decoration, elaborate carved crest.........................1,450.00

Wall, second half 19th C, giltwood, carved and ebonized, shaped rectangular form, pierced floral cresting, sides set with carved paterae, yellow glass plates flanking central mirror plate, 27" w, 41-1/2" h...................750.00

Eastlake, pier, walnut, burl veneer, carved detail highlighted with worn gilding, shaped marble shelf over conforming paneled base, old finisk, 29-1/4" w, 13" d, 94" h............975.00

Gothic Revival, manner of Isaac Scott, c1870, over mantel, walnut and maple, arched crest with five finials, frame chip carved dec, side panels with aesthetic foliate dec, 60-1/4" l, 31" h..750.00

Renaissance Revival

American c1875, carved oak, pier, finely carved with game, putti, centered Ceres, glass shelves on sides, curved molded shaped base, 85" w, 124" h 9,200.00

America, third quarter 19th C, giltwood, over mantel, figural cresting with female face, floral and acanthus carving, 64" w, 74" h..1,725.00

Rococo Revival, c1860-80, pier

Carved, well executed, some repaired breaks and areas of regilding, 36-1/2" w, 94" h..1,200.00

Giltwood and composition, cresting carved with flutist within cartouche, frame elaborately carved in high relief with C-scrolls and foliage, minor restoration, 40" w, 77" h..3,450.00

Neo-Classical, Salem, Massachusetts, c1809-10, giltwood, molded cornice with outset corners, leaf molded frieze, white eglomise panel with gilt classical figures, surface imperfections, 20-1/4" w, 38-1/2" h, $1,750.

Miscellaneous

Because furniture plays such an important role in the lives of people, many specialized forms of furniture have been developed over the years. This section has a sampling of examples of different types of specialized pieces. Some have very serious purposes, others were for recreation.

Remember that buying antique furniture is an area where comparables are the best way to establish a price. This section is designed to offer some comparables in less traditional furniture collecting spheres.

Bin

Storage bins of every size and shape were used in general stores of by-gone eras. Today collectors include them in kitchens, keeping rooms, family rooms, and dens. They are most desirable when they contain some character of times long ago.

Double, store type, American, 19th C, slanted top with glass panel, new backing on glass panels 850.00

Checkerboards

Here is a minor form of furniture added just for fun. Today, checkerboards and other types of wooden game boards are collected and displayed as folk art. Note that the price of these colorful checkerboards is continuing to increase in value. However, as with other forms of desirable antiques, reproductions and newly made craftsmen checkerboards are available. Learn to look for signs of wear and take time to learn as much about the source of the checkerboard before making a purchase.

Pine, old black paint, red and yellow, wear, earlier paint underneath, 16-1/2" w, 20" h...2,145.00

Pine, old dark brown paint, green and yellow, 13" w, 13-1/4" h....................................1,870.00

Pine, old worn brown, white, and black paint, applied molded edge, hole for drawer, age cracks and edge damage, found in Maine, 15" sq...635.00

Pine, orig black and red stringing, stylized floral decoration on yellow ground, lid slides off revealing pine board inlaid with walnut, wooden checkers, found in Maine, 14" sq....................7,150.00

Pine, orig black paint with red and black square, yellow border, applied gallery, 14-1/4" w, 14-1/2" h...1,595.00

Pine, orig red and black paint, applied molded edge, 13-1/2" w, 13-3/4" h......1,760.00

Poplar, hardwood ends, old black, green, and yellow paint showing gray underneath, 13-1/2" w, 18-1/4" h.. 1,540.00

Drying Rack

Drying racks are folding racks used to dry items. Small racks were used to dry herbs and flowers. Other small racks were used to dry noodles and pastry. Larger racks were used outdoors to dry laundry. Most drying racks fold for storage when not in use.

Pine, natural finish, two section, each with three bars, 23" w, 30" h..........................200.00

Pine, natural finish, two section, mortised construction, age cracks, glued repair, 58-1/2" w, 38" h.. 60.00

Poplar, natural finish, three sections, folding, replaced hinges, 95" w, 60" h...................75.00

Dry Sinks

Dry sinks were important pieces of case furniture found in kitchens before the advent of indoor plumbing. Many are a combination of cupboard doors and drawers below a well used to hold a dishpan. Some feature metal linings in these wells, but usually they are of a later date. The addition of backsplashes and upper shelves offered a place to stash soap and other related items. Look for signs of wear, orig hardware, orig finish or grain painting.

America, mid-19th C, grain painted, simulated oak graining, cupboard top with two paneled doors, hood opening over dry sink, base with four graduated drawers and two cupboard doors, cast iron hardware, 54" w, 21-1/4" d, 78" h......................................1,650.00

America, second half 19th C, fruitwood, rectangular top with shallow well on left, work-surface and drawer on right, arched backboard, front with two sunken panel doors opening to shelf, stiles terminating in bracket feet, 46-1/4" w, 16-3/4" d, 38" h..650.00

America, second quarter 19th C, pine, case with peaked arched back panel, narrow shelf, quarter curved sides above work surface, base fitted with two doors, carved wood latches, flat base, 37" w, 17-1/2" d, 53" h....................900.00

America, second quarter 19th C, poplar, off center door with swing-out attached shelf, simple cutout feet, orig cast iron thumb latch, crest, stripped finish, 26" w, 18-1/2" d, 33" h........450.00

Dry Sink, Country, 19th C, pine, worn salmon paint, one board back with shaped ends, work surface and well, four drawers, two cupboard doors, $2,000. Also shown are a basket, $200, and wooden bowls, valued at $200-$250 each.

America, second quarter 19th C, walnut and poplar, pair of paneled doors, one drawer, old finish, dark green paint on interior of hutch top, orig cast iron latches with brass knobs, bottom end damage on feet, 52" w, 18-1/2" d, 49" h.....900.00

Chippendale, cherry, two paneled doors on top, rectangular sink over two paneled doors in base, 46" w, 23-1/2" w, 77" h..............1,250.00

New England, early 19th C, pine, rectangular splashboard with shelf, molded shaped sides above cockbeaded case, single cupboard door with recessed panel on cutout arched base, old surface with vestiges of red paint, replaced hinges and hardware, other imperfections, 44-1/2" w, 25" d, 41" h..1,035.00

Pennsylvania, Bucks County, c1820, painted, dovetailed gallery, single cupboard door base, painted green over blue, 34-1/2" w, 33" d, 32-1/2" h 3,995.00

Pennsylvania, York County, mid 19th C, pine, drawer on right, two door cupboard base, interior painted yellow, imperfections, 51-1/2" w, 20" d, 33" h..850.00

Etagerés

Large free-standing shelf units are called by this fancy French name. They were used in hallways, parlors, dining rooms, and other

Dry Sink, Country, found in Hardin County, OH, hutch top, walnut and poplar, partially removed old red and white paint, paneled doors, one nailed drawer, well with liner, pigeonhole shelf, applied moldings, base restored, 50" w, 18-1/4" d, 54-1/4" h, $770. Also shown are grotesque jugs, averaging $100 each, Photo courtesy of Garth's Auctions, Inc., Delaware, OH.

places where shelves could be accommodated. Also see Hallway Furnishings.

Country, New England, c1830, tiger maple, rectangular top, three short drawers, three shelves supported by block, ring-turned posts, turned legs, replaced brass pulls, old refinishing, 39" w, 12" d, 53" h 3,500.00

Victorian, mid-19th c, mahogany, top with pierced carved gallery and two shelves, scroll carved supports, base with single drawer and two shelves, vasiform reeded posts, flattened ball feet, 37" w, 15-1/2" d, 87" h 1,200.00

Foot Warmer

These wonderful inventions are often included as furniture forms, since their bodies are sometimes made entirely of wood. This example features a sliding panel allowing the user to insert warm coals into a tin container. Some other types of foot warmers have wooden frames and punched tin sides. Prices for those are generally higher when the tins feature a decorative motif.

Country, hardwood and pine, punched holes in case, sliding front panel, interior tin container for coals, wire bale handle, 10" w, 8-3/4" d, 6-1/2" h...215.00

Frames

Examples of picture frames are included here. Some display moldings that reflect the same types of moldings found on furniture forms.

Arts & Crafts, possibly by Slater Studios, New York, early 20th C, carved and gilded, rosette and ribbed corners enclosing fluted sections, flat interior panel, orig condition, remnant of paper label from William MacBeth, Inc., New York, on reverse, price for pair, 19" w, 21" h, $900. Photo courtesy of David Rago Auctions/RagoArts.com, Lambertville, NJ.

Look for frames that will compliment your decor and accommodate the size of object to be framed.

5-1/2" w, 8" h, Arts & Crafts, Roycroft, East Aurora, NY, tooled leather, embossed Glasgow roses, orb and cross mark, stand missing from back, some stains to surface 1,300.00

6-1/2" w, 9" h, Arts & Crafts, Roycroft, East Aurora, NY, tooled leather, embossed daisy motif, orb and cross mark, light wear to corners 1,500.00

7-1/2" w, 10" h, carved wood, America, 19th C, decorated with columns, trees, and letters "B" and "C," dark brown finish, minor wear 460.00

8" w, 10" h, bird's eye maple, gilded liner 125.00

8" w, 10-1/2" h, Tramp Art, old varnish finish, small piece of raised detail missing........165.00

8-1/4" w, 10-1/4" h, America, 19th C, grain painted, reverse ogee frame 1,380.00

8-3/4" w, 11" h, orig red and black decoration, back board missing, early mirror with old dark finish..200.00

9-1/4" w, 11-1/2" h, America, 1900, carved polychrome, horseshoe form, beaded border, carved grapevines flanking clasped hands, dated "1900" and "Leo" centering arched opening, stippled background, second frame with flowering vines and flowers, price for pair..............2,300.00

10-1/4" w, 12-1/4" h, pine, beveled, old red paint 90.00

10-3/8" w, 12-3/4" h, America, 19th C, carved pine, oval rope-twist design, red, white, and navy blue polychrome paint, very minor gouges and paint wear........................1,725.00

11-1/2" w, 13-1/2" h, bird's eye maple, ogee, gilded liner...175.00

12-1/2" w, 16-1/2" h, oval, cherry, folk-art carving with eagle and shield at top, feather detail at base and sides, old soft finish 785.00

12-3/4" w, 16-1/2" h, walnut, deep frame, black liner...95.00

13-3/4" w, 17-1/2" h, decorated, beveled, orig black paint, gold stenciling 330.00

13-1/2" h, 22-1/2" w, Arts & Crafts, intricate design, finely detailed inlay of multi-colored wood, holds two pictures, easel back, orig finish...1,400.00

14" w, 17-1/4" h, walnut, partly ebonized, etched, gilt slip within deeply molded cavetto outer frame, price for matched pair 250.00

14-1/2" w, 16-1/2" h, black enameled outer frame with incised white decorations, gray inner liner and thinner black inner liner, 8" x 10" opening 125.00

14-1/2" w, 16-1/2" h, double layer speckled frame, 8" x 10" opening.........................100.00

14-1/2" w, 16-1/2" h, oak outer frame, inner speckled frame, 8" x 10" opening.............95.00

14-1/2" w, 18-1/2" h, curly maple, beveled, old finish, one has small split, price for pair 635.00

17" w, 19" h, unknown Arts & Crafts period designer, gesso floral design, copper-like finish, holds 9-1/2" x 11-1/2" image............325.00

36-1/2" w, 11" h, Arts & Crafts, Roycroft, East Aurora, NY, wood, dark finish, holds six images in horizontal format, orig finish, orb mark.... 4,950.00

Game Boards

More fun and games for collectors. As with checkerboards, look for visually appealing combinations.

Pine, black and red checkerboard on one side, geometric pattern within circle on reverse, dark green ground, 19th C, some edge wear, 14" sq 7,475.00

Pine, old red, yellow, and black decoration, slide lid compartment with wooden checkers, minor edge damage, 21" w, 31-3/8" h..... 4,400.00

Game Board, early 1900s, painted checkerboard, molded rim, hole for hanging, minor age splits, $165.

Pine, old repaint, red and black checkerboard on one side, geometric design on other with black, white, and red flourish, white line border around checkerboard, signed "H. Petty," 13" x 13"..715.00

Pine, Parcheesi, red and orange, yellow and black striping, dark green ground, framed in black molding, minor paint wear, molding loss, 17-1/2" sq..7,475.00

Softwood, orig black paint, red ground, checkerboard on one side with edge striping, all rd on other side with black edge striping, dated "1880,"" 18-1/2" w, 24-3/4" h.....2,695.00

Mantle

This example of an architectural element is included as a point of reference. Many artifacts are removed from houses and other types of buildings before they are demolished. A mantle such as this one might be used in a room where a fireplace does not exist, but by adding such a wonderful wooden element, the whole room can take on a new dimension.

Victorian, Eastlake, c1875, carved oak, arched floral incised pediment, four shelves, four small mirrors surround central mirror, twist turned supports, spool turned galleries, stylized leaf craved fireplace surrounded by spoon turned columns and center fan carving, 60" w, 11-11/16" d, 104" h..............................1,200.00

Plate Rail

Plate rails are small racks made to hang on a wall and hold plates when not in use. This particular example is by a known furniture designer. Many more primitive examples exist and generally are priced in the $100 to $200 range, depending on their condition, ornamentation, and size.

Arts & Crafts, Gustav Stickley, No. 903, chamfered back with arched top, slated plat rail over corbelled lower shelf, inverted "V" bottom rail, orig finish, sgd with red decal, 48" w, 24" h...5,500.00

Pool Rack

Time for a little more fun. Racks, cue holders, and other types of furniture accessories are all associated with pool halls. Look for examples in good condition and with labels from major pool table manufacturers.

Arts & Crafts, Brunswick-Balke-Collender, c1912, inlaid mahogany, central mirror over ball rack, flanked by cue racks, liner and geometric wood and mother-of-pearl inlay, 48-1/4" w, 61" h 1,950.00

Shelves

Shelves of all sizes and shapes are available in the antiques marketplace.

America, 19th C

Hardwood, very worn red repaint, three shelves, square nail construction, old replacement to front corner, 33" w, 9-1/2" d, 35" h 440.00

Painted pine, three drawers, scalloped crests and ends, nailed drawers, two shades

Folk Art, hanging poplar, old dark finish, cutout floral crest, front molding on two shelves with punched zigzag design, second shelf longer than top shelf, some damage and repair to crest, 16 "w, 22" h, $550. Also shown are figural pottery whistles, $225-$250 each. Photo courtesy of Garth's Auctions, Inc., Delaware, OH.

of old green paint, 12-1/4" w, 4" d, 11-1/2" h 885.00

Painted pine, three shelves, arched rear supports, turned front supports, 16-1/8" w, 6-1/4" d, 19-1/4" h 750.00

Painted, red stain, scrolled crest, two shelves, cutout ends, 13-3/4" w, 6" d, 18-1/2" h 475.00

Primitive, corner, worn sage green paint over earlier coats of white and dark brown, dowel posts with simple carved finials, age cracks on all four shelves, molded repairs, 32" h 140.00

America, mid-19th C, marble rack, scalloped ends, three shelves, old green paint, 16" w, 4-5/8" d, 13-1/2" h 440.00

Folk Art, hanging poplar, old dark finish, cut-out floral crest, front molding on two shelves with punched zigzag design, second shelf longer than top shelf, some damage and repair to crest, 16" w, 22" h 550.00

Hanging

Corner, walnut, ornate jig saw work, star flowers and bird finials, old finish, 11-1/2" w, 20-1/2" h 250.00

Pine, old brown stain, two shelves, sliding dovetailed joint into ends, rounded top edge, 46-1/2" w, 8" d, 24" h 330.00

Ohio, found in Wayne County, walnut, old tan repaint, chip carved, porcelain button details, some edge damage, 17" w, 10-1/2" h...315.00

Middle Atlantic States, early 19th C, walnut, hanging, five graduated shelves flanked by scrolled sides, old refinished surface, 31-1/4" w, 6-1/2" to 10-1/2" d, 49-1/4" h.................1,100.00

Modernism-Era, Paul Evans, 1971, wall unit, gessoed wood and glass, three vertical supports of gessoed wood, surface decorated with various architectural textures in high relief, painted to simulate bronze, eight smoky glass shelves, middle support initialed "P. E. 71" at bottom, shallow chip to one shelf, 96" w, 17-1/4" d, 78-1/2" h 865.00

New England, early 19th C, dec pine, hanging, two pocket shelf, fanciful painted black on red ground, 11-5/8" w, 5-7/8" d, 14-3/4" h 980.00

New England, whale ends, walnut, three graduated shaped shelves, dovetailed base

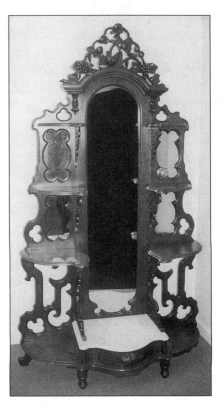

Victorian, c1870, étagère, walnut, grape and vine pierced carved crest over center mirror, flanked by three graduated shelves with pierced carved supports, single shaped drawer, marble base, turned feet, 48" w, 88" h, $3,300. Photo courtesy of Alderfer Auction Company, Hatfield, PA.

with two dovetailed drawers, old finish, ash and pine secondary wood, 24-1/8" w, 7-3/4" d, 38-3/4" h..2,750.00

Pennsylvania, pine, old worn finish, whale ends, found in Lancaster County, 31" w, 10" d, 30" h..660.00

Pewter, 18th C, oak, three shelves, cornice molding, well-shaped and carved top inside crest, each shelf with large opening flanking by two small openings, bottom with shaped extensions to sides, bead molded edges to shelves, shelf openings, 56" w, 6-1/2" d, 46-1/2" h.................1,150.00

Victorian, Gothic Revival, very worn dark graining, reverse cut mirror insert, age cracks in crest, some termite damage, 29" h 175.00

Spoon Rack

This type of wall mounted rack was used to hold a household's inventory of precious spoons. Today collectors use these racks as decorator items.

America, 19th C, blue-painted pine, stepped, hinged ends open to allow placement of spoons onto horizontal rods running through stepped central upright, tenoned into molded rectangular base, hinged latch keeps rack closed when in use, 6" w, 3-1/4" d, 7" h...........................550.00

Steps

Steps were created to assist with daily living. Many antique beds were constructed relatively high off the ground. The phrase "jump into bed" goes back to the times when beds were so high that the user actually had to leap into bed. While this sounds a little unlady-like, steps eliminated the necessity to do this. Library steps helped users to reach the upper shelves of tall bookcases. And sewing steps helped housekeepers reach to the tops of drapes and other probably bed frames. By keeping some of their sewing implements tucked into the steps, they could do minor repairs or stitches that would hold hangings in place.

Bed

Federal, 19th C, inlaid mahogany, 26" h 475.00

Victorian, English, third quarter 19th C, mahogany, each tread with leather-lined molded top, uppermost hinged and opens to storage well, middle tread hinged and slides open, short turned and tapered legs 1,700.00

Chair, George III, English, c1811, mahogany and caning, metamorphic, open armchair hinged at seat rail, back turning over to form set of library steps, damage to caning, minor losses, 36" h......................................8,625.00

Library

Georgian-Style, metamorphic, mahogany, folding out to 4 steps, brass casters, 36" w, 18" d, 21-1/2" h closed, 35" h open......800.00

Victorian, American, late 19th C

Mahogany, tooled inset leather, baluster feet, 17" w, 27-1/2" d, 26" h 1,400.00

Mahogany, tooled inset leather, bracket feet, 66-3/4" h 2,900.00

Sewing, Shaker, painted pine, nailed five-board construction, overhanging top, semi-circular cutout ends, bottom step set into dado in sides, painted light green, minor paint wear, 8-1/4" w, 15" l, 9-3/4" h...........................525.00

Table Swift

As the name implies, this weaving implement was used on top of a table. Other examples are known with attachments so that it could be secured to the edge of a table and then wound.

Shaker, Hancock, MA, c1850-60, maple and birch swift with translucent yellow wash, very minor imperfections, 29" d maximum extension, 24-1/2" h 450.00

Tea Cart

Tea carts are a style of furniture much more prevalent in English designs. However, for comparison purposes, a few examples are given here.

Arts & Crafts, Stickley Brothers

Glass lined tray top, lower shelf, slat sides, branded Stickley Brothers mark, new finish, 29" w, 17-1/4" d, 33" h, ...1,000.00

Removable tray over serving table, refinished, 32" w, 20" d, 29" h....................200.00

Tete á Tete

Need a place for a private conversation? A tete á tete might be just the piece of furniture you're searching for. It is basically two chair forms fastened together so that one person is sitting beside the other, but find their arms and legs pointing in opposite directions. They can talk, or perhaps kiss, but are separated from getting much closer by the frame. Again, a form of furniture much more popular in Europe and particularly France.

Massachusetts, Boston, early 19th C, painted faux bamboo turnings, crest rail above four spindles and splint seat, legs joined by double stretchers, old black paint, minor imperfections, 37" l, 17-1/2" d, 28" h 1,380.00

Tool Chest

This interesting chest is included to give a base line for the many type of wooden work chests found in the antiques marketplace.

Silversmith's, America, mid-19th C, walnut, dovetailed, lid with molded rim, molded base raised on low round feet, upper locking interior fitted with two removable trays above single locking drawer containing many silver-smithing tools, including stamps, gouges, files, treading tools, minor surface wear, one broken foot, 11" x 15" x 11" 2,760.00

Towel Rack

Towel racks are small racks made to hang on bedroom walls, often above a wash stand. Some are fitted with small mirrors or hooks in additional to the rods for hanging towels. This example is from the Victorian period, but many country examples are found in today's antiques marketplace. Expect to pay from $50 upward depending on the style, finish, and age of the towel rack.

Victorian, c1880, faux-bamboo, fitted with four hanging rods, turned supports 23" w, 7" d, 31" h...110.00

Wastebaskets

Designers in the Arts & Crafts movement wanted to meet all the needs of those who followed their ideals. These types of wooden wastebaskets are commanding higher and higher prices. Look for examples with orig labels, finishes, and unusual forms.

Lakeside Craft Shops, Sheboygan, MI

Octagonal form, eight slats supported by leather straps, orig finish, orig ring handles missing, 12" d, 16" h............................350.00

Tapered form, ftd base, twelve slats held together with replaced metal band, orig finish, paper label, handles missing, 15" h 325.00

Payne, chamfered sides, raised handles, oval cutouts, knob finials, orig finish, remnants of marks on bottom, some looseness, 11-3/4" sq, 16-1/2" h...325.00

Stickley, Gustav, similar to No. 94, fifteen slats attached with iron hoops, orig finish, unsigned, 12" d, 15" h.........................1,900.00

Unknown Designer

Flared form, four slats on each side, arched top rail, orig finish, attributed to Stickley Brothers, 14" w, 14" d, 15" h 650.00

Square form, mahogany, orig finish, 12" w, 16" d 500.00

Wine Cooler

Wine coolers are typically considered to be of English or European origin, but again the designers in the Arts & Crafts period created a form that complimented their furniture designs while fulfilling a unique function.

Arts & Crafts, Gustav Stickley, #553, tapered and slanted circular form, supported by copper bands, three footed base, orig copper hardware, orig finish, red box mark, 13" d, 15" h..9,350.00

Rockers

Rockers or rocking chairs show American ingenuity at its best. By adding curved rockers to an ordinary chair, the user could rock away for hours, creating a very simple pleasure indeed. Furniture makers soon latched onto this great idea and began to make rockers in addition to their chairs. Some Windsor makers even added rockers to their benches, creating a wonderful place for a mother or nanny to sit and rock a baby to sleep.

Aesthetic Movement

This example shows how the designers of the Aesthetic Movement used other materials to create an interesting rocker.

New York, c1850, wrought iron and brass, scrolled stiles form downward curving arm supports, joined by traverse at back, mounted upholstered leather cushion and arm pads 4,975.00

Art Deco

This Art Deco rocker takes the form one step higher in that a chair frame was created then carefully mounted to a platform that allowed movement, but did not have rockers as older styles did. This form is a little more compact and was the very latest in furniture styles, something those in the Art Deco period loved.

America, platform, late 19th C, oak and leather, allover geometric forms, square crest rail over trapezoid-shaped back with leather insert, flat arm over vertical down shaped supports, conforming seat with leather insert, rocks on cross-braced wire supports, 24-1/2" w, 23" d, 40-3/4" h 865.00

Art Nouveau

The floral-type capitals of this rocker help identify it as Art Nouveau. The use of native oak helps identify it as America. The "fumed finish" was a type of finish that was very popular in the late Art Nouveau period and warmly embraced by the Arts & Crafts designers.

American, c1900, oak, fumed finish, carved arms, saddle seat, three splats with floral type capitals 400.00

Arts & Crafts

The designers of the Arts & Crafts period loved rockers of all kinds. All the major designers and manufacturers included several designs in their lines. Some had hard seats, while others got softened a bit with cushions. Most Arts & Crafts rockers used the rocker form on the feet of the piece, but some also engaged the use of platforms. A Morris rocker is simply a larger form with the chair section similar to a Morris chair in styling. A sewing rocker is a small rocker, usually without arms, that sits relatively low, and was more comfortable for ladies to use.

Harden Furniture Co., Syracuse, NY

Oak, curved crest rail over four narrow and one wide vertical back slat, open arm with two side corbels, spring cushion leather seat, paper label, some stains and roughness, 27-1/4" w, 31-1/2" d, 37" h 550.00

Oak, deep floral carving at back and front legs, old rush seat, orig finish, unsigned, 33" w, 31" d, 34" h 2,650.00

Oak, tapering vertical slats on back and under curved arms, drop-in spring seat cov in brown leather, new dark finish, 27-1/4" w, 29-3/4" d, 35-1/2" h 475.00

Wave, two horizontal crest rails, wide central vertical slat flanked by two narrower slats, curved arms over four vertical side slats, skirt with through tenons, unsigned, seat missing, 29-1/2" w, 31-1/2" h, 36-1/4" h 1,495.00

Hubbard, Eldridge & Miller, Rochester, NY, c1910, oak, carved crest rail over five vertical slats, flat arms tapering toward back with corbel supports, five vertical slats, spring cushion seat, refinished in cordovan color, 28-1/2" d, 38" h..200.00

Karpen Furniture Co., Chicago, IL, square back with curved top leather panel, nine square cutouts under each upholstered arm, reupholstered brown leather back, seat, and arm rests, orig finish, unsigned, 29" w, 32" d, 37" h...2,800.00

Lifetime Furniture, Grand Rapids, MI, cutout crest rail, three vertical back slats, heavy plank front legs, refinished, seat missing, splint to arm, unmarked, 29-3/4" w, 27" d, 33-1/2" h....... 750.00

Limbert, Charles P., Grand Rapids and Holland, MI

No. 518, low deep form, open under arms, refinished, branded mark, 32" w, 29" d, 31" h 1,500.00

No. 580, oak, T-back design, orig recovered drop-in cushion, recent finish, branded, 24" w, 29" d, 34" h 150.00

Arm, arched top over five vertical slats, upholstered back, three slats under each arm, orig worn leatherette cushions, orig dark finish, 28" w, 30" d, 42" h.........1,850.00

Sewing, manufactured by Klingman & Limbert Chair Company, tall back, wide horizontal slabs at back, cane seat, carved seat rail, remnants of earliest paper label, 20" w, 18" d, 36-1/2" h....................................600.00

Sewing, T-back, single vertical back slat, tacked-on Japan leather seat, branded mark, 17-1/2" w, 27" d, 31" h 200.00

Sewing, wide horizontal back slat with two cutouts, recovered leather seat, refinished, unsigned, 18" w, 23" d, 30" h..............250.00

McHugh, heavy ladderback, orig rush seat, fine orig finish, unsigned, 24" w, 34" d, 37" h..1,120.00

Plail Brothers

Barrel, oak, spindles from broad top rail to seat, arched apron, dark brown leather seat, orig finish, remnants of paper label, 24-1/2" w, 32" d, 29" h.......................................2,750.00

Barrel, oak, slatted barrel back, D-shaped recovered seat, refinished, unsigned, 26" w, 28" d, 31" h.......................................2,500.00

Roycroft, East Aurora, NY

Open-arm, five vertical back slats, replaced tacked-on leather seat, orig finish, carved orb and cross mark, torn seat cushion, 26-1/2" w, 28" d, 35" h, ...1,200.00

Arts & Crafts, L. & J. G. Stickley, Fayetteville, NY, c1912, oak, curved crest rail over five vertical slats, straight sides with spring cushion seat, arched seat rail, minor wear, 18-1/4" w, 33-3/4" h, $375. Photo courtesy of Skinner Auctioneers and Appraisers of Antiques and Fine Art Boston and Bolton, MA.

Sewing, mahogany, five vertical back slats, replaced tacked-on leather seat, carved orb and cross mark, 19" w, 21" d, 33" h, ...900.00

Stickley Brothers, Grand Rapids, MI, No. 567, tall spindled back, rounded arms, narrow slats, drop-in spring seat covered in orig Japan leather, branded mark, paper label, missing pin caps, some wear, 29" w, 33" d, 35-1/2" h 1,650.00

Stickley, Gustav, New York

No. 303, c1904, sewing, oak, four horizontal back slats, canvas seat, wide seat rail, orig paper label, 14" w, 16" d, 33" h 650.00

No. 309, ladderback form, three horizontal slats, orig rush seat, orig finish, red decal, 25" w, 27" d, 32" h 725.00

No. 313, H-back, orig drop-in leather cushion, lightly cleaned orig finish, red decal, 25" w, 30" d, 37" h 990.00

No. 323, five slats under arms, recovered drop-in seat cushion, orig finish, red decal, 29" w, 36" d, 38" d 2,600.00

No. 323, five slats under arms, replaced drop-in seat cushion, old refinish, red decal, 29" w, 36" d, 38" h 1,980.00

No. 2627, sewing, early form, three vertical slats flanked by inside corbels at posts over old leather seat, orig finish, sgd, 17"w, 23" d, 29" h 495.00

Arm, five vertical back slats and corbels under flat arms, drop-in spring seat in red Japan leather, over-coated, unmarked, split to one rocker, 29" w, 32" d, 37" h 2,375.00

Arm, three vertical bask slats, tacked-on spring seat, orig red Japan leather, open arms with corbels, unmarked, 26-1/4" w, 29" d, 38-1/2" h 1,250.00

Five vertical back slats, drop-in spring seat covered in orig leather, corbels under each open arm, orig finish, branded mark, minor veneer loss at arms, post tops split, loose joinery, 27-1/4" w, 30" d, 37" h 1,395.00

Arts & Crafts, left: Stickley Brothers, Grand Rapids, Michigan, No. 567, tall spindled back, rounded arms with narrow slats, drop-in spring seat covered in orig Japan-leather, some over-coating to arms, wear to legs and runners, branded mark and paper label, missing pin caps, 29" w, 33" d, 35-1/2" h, $1,400; right: L. & J. G. Stickley, oak, tall back, six vertical back slats, drop-in spring seat, corbels under open arms, unmarked, refinished, 28-1/4" w, 30" d, 38" h, $700. Photo courtesy of David Rago Auctions/ RagoArts.com, Lambertville, NJ.

Five vertical back slats, recovered leather seat, refinished, 24" w, 27" d, 34" h 500.00

Flat arm, slatted sides, drop-in spring seat, red decal, reupholstered in back leather, refinished, wear to arms, 29" w, 30" d, 39-1/2" h 2,400.00

High backed, 5 vertical slats under each arm, corbels, loose seat cushion, branded mark, orig finish, arms recolored, 29" w, 30" d, 41" h 1,800.00

Sewing Rocker, H-back, plank back, drop-in seat, orig Japan leather, orig finish, branded mark, 16-3/4" w, 24" d, 34" h 400.00

Sewing Rocker, ladderback, orig rush seat, orig finish, branded mark, some wear, 16-3/4" w, 25" d, 31" h 450.00

Sewing Rocker, mahogany, tall spindled back, sling seat, red decal, some alligatoring to orig finish, 19" w, 28" d, 40" h 2,200.00

Sewing Rocker, Thornden, two horizontal back slats, orig rattan seat, orig finish, red decal, 18" w, 26" d, 31" h 600.00

V-back, five vertical back slats, orig tacked-on hard leather seat, orig medium finish, branded mark, 25-3/4" w, 20-1/2" d, 34-1/2" h 900.00

Stickley, L. and J. G., Fayetteville, NY

No. 413, Morris, oak, four horizontal back slats, branded "The Work of L. & J. G. Stickley," orig cushions in poor condition, 29" w, 34-1/2" d, 36" h 1,250.00

No. 451, c1912, concave crest rail over six vertical slats, shaped flat arm with corbels over six vertical slat, branded "The Work of L. & J. G. Stickley," scratches on arm, 28" w, 31-1/2" d, 38-1/2" h 1,380.00

No. 781-1/2, flat arm with five slats under each arm, arched seat rail, some wear to orig leather cushion, orig dark finish, sgd "The Work of L.& J. G. Stickley," 30" w, 36" d, 38" h 3,300.00

No. 831, Morris-type, adjustable back, open under arms, orig finish, sgd "The Work of...," back bar replaced, 30" w, 35" d, 38" h 1,500.00

Curved crest rail over five vertical slats, straight sides with spring cushion seat, arched seat rail, c1912, minor wear, 18-1/4" w, 33-3/4" h 375.00

Curved crest rail over slatted sides, orig drop-in spring seat, Handcraft label, new dark finish, 26-3/4" w, 26-1/2" d, 31" h 2,850.00

Six vertical back slats, open under arm recovered orig drop-in cushion, worn orig finish, sgd "The Work of L. & J. G. Stickley," 27" w, 27" d, 35" h 600.00

Tall back, six vertical back slats, drop-in spring seat, corbels under each open arm, refinished, unmarked, 28-1/4" w, 30" d, 38" h 900.00

Unknown Designer, oak

Adjustable Back, four horizontal back slats, flat arms over four side slats, orig dark finish, reupholstered back and seat cushions, c1916, 26-5/8" w, 34" d, 42-1/8" h 990.00

Curved and shaped crest rail over three horizontal slats, flat arms with cut corners,

Arts & Crafts, unknown designer, c1910, oak, curved and shaped crest rail over three horizontal slats, flat arms with cut corners, raised arm posts, web seat support, narrow side stretchers over wide seat rail, 25-1/4" w, 36" h, $575. Photo courtesy of Skinner Auctioneers and Appraisers of Antiques and Fine Art Boston, and Bolton MA.

raised arm posts, web seat support, narrow side stretchers over wide seat rail, c1910, finish lightened, missing seat cushion, 25-1/4" w, 36" h 575.00

Curved crest rail over four vertical slats, flat open arms, spring cushion seat, c1912, upholstery missing, 39" h 375.00

Curved crest rail over five vertical back slats, shaped arms with through tenons, long corbel supports, two side slats, medium brown finish, spring cushion seat, needs reupholstering, minor wear, 28" w, 30" d, 35" h 425.00

Sewing, curved crest rail over three vertical slats, shaped seat over lower side stretchers, c1912, some wear, 17" w, 24" d, 32" h 115.00

Young, J. M., Canton, NY, oak

Four curved horizontal crest rails, flat arm with short corbel supports, leather spring cushion seat, c1910, 28" w, 35" h 250.00

Four vertical back slats, drop-in spring seat, refinished, 28" w, 24" d, 36-3/4" h 300.00

Vertical side slats, corbels, new fabric covered loose back and seat cushions, enhanced orig finish, 30-1/4" w, 29-1/2" d, 32" h 1,200.00

Boston

Boston rockers are comfortable rockers, usually with high backs that sweep gently around the person. Look for a comfortable formed seat and scrolled arms. This truly American form often gets based from generation to generation since the rocker becomes a family favorite.

America, 19th C, grain painted, gilt stencil dec, scenic dec crest, rosewood grained seat 750.00

America, maple, spindle back 200.00

America, painted, brown background, gold, yellow, and green flowers and leaves painted on side crest rail, gold striping, large shaped seat with caned center, wear to paint on scrolled arms, recaned seat in delicate star pattern 295.00

Centennial

This example is a later form of a rocker style created for the Centennial, designed to incorporate styles of earlier furniture periods. It has some elements from Chippendale, and also Queen Anne.

America, c1880-1900, carved crest rail with scrolled ears, elaborate pierced and carved splat, S-curved arms carved with scrolled terminals, shell carved apron, carved knees with claw and ball feet on runners, orig blue upholstery, splat cracked on one, price for pr, 26" w, 35" d, 42" h..1,450.00

Colonial Revival

A manufactured rocker made by a popular American furniture maker. This shows how the Colonial Furniture Co. interpreted the early Windsor style.

Colonial Furniture Co., Grand Rapids, MI, Windsor-style, comb back, birch, mahogany finish, turned legs, 21" w, 17" d, 27-1/2" h......200.00

Country

Many rockers defy labeling as one particular furniture style and are grouped here under the generic Country heading. As you read through these descriptions, note that several contain damage, wear, etc. Most rockers were heavily used, many were used outside and left out in all kinds of weather, adding to the stress and wear they received. However, to some collectors it is this wear that shows use and they embrace that as part of the history or character of the chair.

America, early 19th C, decorated, writing arm, worn orig red and black paint, white striping, black stenciled detail, damaged woven splint seat, wear and minor age cracks in writing arm...........275.00

America, ladder back, maple, shaped arms, four slats, turned finials, turned front ring and arm posts, old refinishing, replaced woven splint seat, minor age cracks, 43" h 500.00

America, ladder back, half arms, four slat back, turned finials, old soft refinishing, replaced paper rush set, rockers worn flat, found in PA, 44-1/4" h 125.00

New England, c1830, grained and stenciled, rosewood graining, olive green stenciled crest, thumb-back, yellow striping, 15-1/4" h seat, 32-1/4" h..450.00

New York State, c1825, decorated, crest rail painted with red flowers, light green ground, arrow form uprights, shaped arms and turned legs, plank seat 2,450.00

Pennsylvania, Bucks County, early 19th C, painted, four rect concave splats joining turned stiles to scrolled arms, vase and ring supports, rush seat on ring turned legs joined by stretchers, on rockers, old green paint with black and yellow striping, imperfections, 16-1/2" h, 44-1/2" h...250.00

Hitchcock-Type

During the time when Hitchcock chairs were very popular, some were also made into rockers. Here is a typical example.

New England, mid-19th C, painted black, curved back with overhanging crest rail above panel of woven thongs, downswept scroll arms flanking similarly paneled seat, baluster-turned splayed legs joined by turned box stretcher, gilt highlights on black ground 400.00

Folk Art, country, made from parts of spinning wheel, caned seat, ring-turned spindles under arm and base, double turned stretchers, $125.

Queen Anne, old dark alligatored finish, urn shaped splat, bold turnings, old replaced splint seat, rockers old addition, 14-1/2" h seat, 40" h, $425. Photo courtesy of Garth's Auctions, Inc., Delaware, OH.

Ladderback

Ladderback rockers have straight backs just like the ladderback chair styles.

America, old red paint over black, three slat back with turned finials, shaped arms, turned posts, damaged old woven splint seat, wear to arms, 42-1/2" h......................................275.00

Modernism Era

Designers of modern furniture included several rockers in their lines. Some have been quite successful on the antiques marketplace. Look for examples in very good condition as any repairs or reupholstered elements decreases the values dramatically.

Eames, Charles, manufactured by Herman Miller, zinc struts, birch runners

Early gray Zenith shell, rope edge, orig label, some wear to runners, 25" w, 27" d, 26" h..1,500.00

Early yellow Zenith shell, rope edge, orig label, 25" w, 27" d, 26" h..................1,300.00

Orange fiberglass arm shell, 25" w, 27" d, 27" h..1,100.00

White fiberglass arm shell, 25" w, 27" d, 26" h..1,100.00

Yellow upholstered fiberglass shell, presentation tag, 25" w, 27" d, 26" h........750.00

Zenith shell, salmon fiberglass, rope edge, black wire struts, birch runners, c1950, 25" w, 27" d, 27" h..1,400.00

Gehry, Frank, Easy Edges, c1972, cutout form, corrugated cardboard, masonite edge, 41" w, 23" d, 25" h..............................4,000.00

Takeshi Nii, c1972, Ny X series, high back black canvas seat, wooden armrests, steel tube base, folds flat, 24" w, 28" d, 33" h............225.00

Queen Anne

Here is an example of a period arm chair that has had rockers added to create a rocking chair. By the damage noted on this one, it appears the chair was well used through the years.

Country, arm chair, urn shaped splat, bold turnings, old replaced split seat, rockers old addition, old dark alligatored finish, 14-1/2" h seat, 40" h..425.00

Rustic

Rustic rocking chairs appear in the antiques marketplace frequently. Many were made by small local craftsmen and have lasted through generations. Craftsmen today still create rockers using small trees and

Rustic, bentwood, early 20th C, back and seat of curved bent slats, bent twig arms and cross-bracing, mixed woods, 37-1/2" h and 41-1/2" h, price for pair $920. Photo courtesy of Skinner Auctioneers and Appraisers of Antiques and Fine Art Boston, and Bolton MA.

branches, molding them into shape while the wood is green and pliable.

America, late 19th/early 20th C, bentwood, shaped coiled back joined to bent arms on splint seat and legs, ached and coiled seat supports, old worn painted surface, small repair to back, 14-1/2" h seat, 41-1/2" h 920.00

Shaker

The Shaker communities were well known for making fine furniture and rockers were favorites. Being practical, the Shakers created several different styles of rocking chairs and conveniently numbered each one. Today, collectors delight in finding these numbered examples. Knowing the Shaker community that created a particular rocker helps increase the provenance and value.

New Hampshire, Canterbury, c1850, maple and birch, four arched slats joining turned stiles to scrolled arms, turned tapered supports continuing to turned legs on rockers joined by stretchers, old finish, 14-1/2" h seat, 43" h 7,500.00

New Hampshire, Enfield, c1840, maple and birch, three arched slats joining turned stiles to tape seat, turned legs joined by stretchers, old refinish, 17-1/2" h seat, 41" h 850.00

New York, Mount Lebanon, No. 5, worn orig finish, stenciled label on one rocker, old replaced blue and ivory woven tape back and seat, 37-3/4" h 725.00

Shaker, Mount Lebanon, New York, c1880-1930, finials, splats, shaped arms with mushroom caps, rush seat, old varnished surface, imperfections, 15" h seat, 41-1/2" h, $865. Photo courtesy of Skinner Auctioneers and Appraisers of Antiques and Fine Art Boston and Bolton, MA.

New York, Mount Lebanon, No. 7, arms, orig dark finish, "7" impressed on top slat, turned posts, three slat back, shawl bar, shaped arms with mushroom cap ends, replaced rush seat, 41" h..1,100.00

New York, Mount Lebanon, 1880-1930, production, finials, splats, shaped arms with mushroom caps, rush seat above rockers, old varnished surface, imperfections, 15" h seat, 41-1/2" h..865.00

Sheraton

This example of a Sheraton rocker shows how colorful these practical chairs could be. Many times rockers were made of many different types of wood. Some woods were used for their durability, others because they "turned" well. By painting, this mixture of woods could be hidden. Original decorations are now sought by collectors.

Country, decorated, worn orig red and black graining, yellow striping, gold stenciled fruit on colored bronze powder on shaped crest, spindle back, scrolled arms, S-curved seat, turned legs, wear to rockers, 39-1/2" h 250.00

Victorian

The Victorians loved rockers and had them in parlors, bedrooms, and on porches. Some innovations, like platform bases, were popular on rockers destined for parlors. Many are found covered in needlepoint or tapestry coverings.

Platform, mahogany, upholstered seat and back, carved and turned arms 350.00

Platform, walnut, padded back, arms, springs in seat, reupholstered in needlepoint with floral design, rose colored background, brass nailhead trim 425.00

Eastlake, America, late 19th C, mahogany platform, incised and pierced cresting over sq panel back, center, padded reeded arms, velvet seat upholstery, reeded supports 400.00

Renaissance Revival, George Huntzinger, NY, 1876, walnut, ring turned armrests and stretchers, cloth wrapped wire seat and back, dated, 21" w, 33" h 400.00

Wicker

Wicker rockers were popular for porches and

also used in living rooms and sun rooms. Most were painted originally and many have been repainted over the years. Look for signs of wear and be wary of any that show signs of breakage in the caning.

America, c1910, paper-twist type body, repainted rusty-brown, sq back with diamond weave pattern, woven skirt, scrolled arms with wrapped decoration, replaced seat cushions, price for pair of rockers and matching table with circular top 600.00

America, painted white, sq back, basket weave pattern over openwork back, rectangular arm-rests with wrapped braces, openwork sides, braided edge on basketweave seat and skirt, X-form stretcher, 32" w, 33" h.......................200.00

Windsor

Windsor rockers are quite popular now with col-lectors and found easily in the antiques market-place. Variations in the back, such as Bird Cage or Comb Back, determine the name of the type of Windsor. Although some Windsor rockers were original productions, many are chairs which have added rockers. Examples of rockers that were originally chairs are noted as "on rockers." Look for examples with good original decoration.

Arrow Back, orig ink graining, scrolled arms, widely splayed back 500.00

Windsor, Pennsylvania, comb back, mixed woods, scrolled crest rail, bulbous stretcher and arm supports, 27" w, 43" h, $1,275.00 Photo courtesy of Richard Opfer Auctioneering, Inc., Timonium, MD.

Bird Cage

New England, c1810, birdcage crest with seven spindles and turned arms, shaped seat, splayed bamboo-turned legs joined by stretchers on rockers, old refinish, 15" h seat, 37-1/2" h 500.00

New England, c1810, painted, birdcage crest, bamboo turned spindles, scrolled arms, shaped seat, turned legs joined by stretchers, on rockers, old red paint, imper-fections, 17" h, seat, 31-1/2" h............815.00

Bow Back, seven spindle back, saddle seat, old finish, repairs 250.00

Comb Back

America, crusty black repaint, yellow design on crest, alligatored finish, bamboo turnings, scrolled arms, step down crest, repairs to crest, 43-3/4" h 200.00

America, old dark green (black) repaint, yellow striping, crest dated "1769," comb ini-tialed "C," well shaped seat with incised groove around border, bamboo turnings, traces of scene in center, found in Vermont, 44" h 770.00

New England, c1810-15, rect splat above six spindles, barrel crest rail with applied scrolled arms, bamboo turned supports, shaped seat on splayed bamboo turned legs joined by stretchers on rockers, old red brown paint with yellow pinstriping, 15" h seat, 41" h 1,380.00

New England, c1820, shaped comb above six spindles continuing to crest and seven spindles on shaped and splayed bamboo turned legs joined by stretchers to rockers, orig apple green with gilt finial stenciled dec, 15-1/2" h, seat, 44-1/4" h back 900.00

New Hampshire, New Ipswich, early 19th C, old Spanish brown paint, natural arms, signed "J. Wilder," restoration, 13-1/2" h, 44" h 1,250.00

Spindle Back, America, c1850, grain painted, stencil dec, scrolled crest, tail spindle back, shaped seat, bamboo turned legs, box stretcher 450.00

Step Down Crest, old two tone black and dark repaint, white striping, spindle back, "S" curve arms, shaped seat, splayed base with rungs, repairs to seat, old split with nailed repair, 33-3/4" h.....................................525.00

Secretaries

The furniture form known as a "secretary" belongs in the large case classification. Secretaries are basically desks with the addition of a cupboard or bookcase-type top section. Found in almost every furniture style, secretaries are highly functional with detailed interiors full of drawers, pigeonholes, and document storage areas. The French term "secretaire a'abattant" is often used to describe a secretary, especially those with detailed interiors.

Many secretaries are made in two or more parts for ease of construction. Carefully examine both parts of a secretary to make sure that they are both of the same furniture period. A quick way to check this is to look for consistency in design elements and also construction techniques. The type of dovetail used in the top should be identical to the dovetailing found in the base. Drawers should show some signs of wear, as should doors and shelves. Cornices are sometimes a separate piece, being held on with a dowel or fitting well with moldings. Also see Bookcases and Desks.

Art Nouveau

Art Nouveau secretaries are one of the few periods that include leaded glass in the upper cases. Many examples of Art Nouveau secretaries found in the antiques market are of French origin.

America, mahogany, projecting molded cornice, pair of leaded glass doors over lower cabinet, slant font writing surface, small drawers and pigeonholes interior, three drawers, turned legs, bun feet, 36-1/4" w, 17-1/2" d, 83-1/2" h..1,650.00

Centennial

Since secretaries were a popular furniture form in the 18th century, they were also favorites of the furniture manufacturers who were creating "antique"-looking furniture of the 1875 era.

America, inlay mahogany, two sections, upper section with four drawers over six cubbyholes center, line inlay door opening to reveal two cubbyholes and large drawer, sliding tambour doors flanked by inlay panels with simulated columns; lower section with fold-over line inlay lid, two drawers with line inlay, diamond inlay on legs, some lifting to veneer, replaced cloth writing surface, 37-1/4" w, 19-3/4" d, 46" h 800.00

Chippendale

The Chippendale period of furniture offers many secretaries. Look for the same elements found in desks, such as oxbow, serpentine fronts, and slant fronts. The interiors are fitted with many different configurations.

America, 18th C, oxbow, mahogany, two sections, upper section with molded cornice, paneled doors with scrolled stiles and rails, one adjustable shelf, lower section with slant front lid, fitted interior, consisting of eleven dovetailed drawers, three with carved fans, two pull-out

Chippendale, America, 18th C, oxbow, mahogany, two pieces, upper: molded cornice, paneled doors with scrolled stiles and rails, one adjustable shelf, base: slant front lid, fitted int. consisting of eleven dovetailed drawers, three with carved fans, two pull-out letter drawers with half columns and turned finials, four dovetailed drawers with applied edge beading, serpentine apron and drop with central carved fan, ogee feet, orig brasses, old finish, minor repairs to feet, 40-1/2" w, 14" d, 66-1/2" h, $35,750. Photo courtesy of Garth's Auctions, Inc., Delaware, OH.

letter drawers with half columns and turned finials, four dovetailed drawers with applied edge beading, serpentine apron and drop with central carved fan, ogee feet, orig brasses, old finish, minor repairs to feet, 40-1/2" w, 14" d, 66-1/2" h 35,750.00

America, 18th C, slant front, cherry, two sections, upper section with bookcase top with paneled doors, adjustable shelves, molded cornice, lower section with slant front with fitted interior, pigeonholes and seven drawers, four dovetailed cockbeaded drawers, dovetailed bracket feet, pine and walnut secondary woods, refinished, replaced brasses, pierced repairs, replaced feet, 39-3/4" w, 31" h writing height, 80" h 4,250.00

Connecticut, 18th C, cherry, two sections, upper section with molded scrolled cornice with carved pinwheels above applied central ornament and recessed panel doors, interior with two shelves and scrolled dividers above desk interior of small valanced compartments with scrolled dividers flaking pinwheel carved drawer and small drawers arranged in two-step interior, lower section with case of graduated thumb-molded drawers flanked by fluted quarter engaged columns, bracket feet on platforms, some old brass, refinished, restoration, 39" w, 20-1/2" d, 91-1/2" h 35,650.00

Country, found in Vermont, butternut, old dark red finish, two sections, upper section with molded cornice, two inset paneled doors with scalloped crests, two dovetailed drawers, H-hinges, slant front with fitted interior consisting of five dovetailed drawers with brass pulls, one hidden drawer, eight pigeonholes, lower section with dovetailed case with four dovetailed cockbeaded drawers, dovetailed bracket feet, replaced brasses, pine secondary wood, wear to drawers, scrolled brackets on pigeonholes replaced, nailed repairs to feet, 37-1/4" w, 78-1/2" h 11,550.00

Massachusetts, c1770, block front, cherry, two sections, upper section with molded cornice, pair of arched and paneled doors, fitted interior, carved pilaster with stylized scrolls, lower molded section with thumb-molded hinged lid, fitted interior, four blocked and graduated drawers, bracket feet, 40-1/2" 2, 21-3/4" d,

Married! Chippendale mahogany top, late 18th C, with Classical maple chest of drawers, c1860, top section with outward curving cornice above two glazed and mullioned doors, chest having deep top drawer over three graduated drawers flanked by spiral fluted columns terminating in square plinths, baluster form turned replacement feet, 42-1/4" w, 28-2/3" d, 92" h, $2,300. Photo courtesy of Butterfields.

96" h 14,500.00

Massachusetts, c1770-1800, carved mahogany, three sections, scrolled pediment with carved rosettes, above upper section with cyma curved paneled doors flanked by pilasters, interior of open bookshelves surrounded by small valanced compartments and row of open pigeonholes, lower section with desk base with blocked and fan carved interior with small drawers flanking concave prospect door flanked by columns with turned finials on stepped bases, cockbeaded case, four graduated block front drawers, molded ogee bracket feet, replaced brasses, restoration, 40-3/8" w, 22-3/8" d, 95-1/2" h 15,950.00

Massachusetts, c1770-90, carved mahogany, three sections, upper scrolled and molded pediment above upper section with tympanum with projecting shell and arched raised panel doors flanked by fluted pilasters, candle slides, raised panel slant lid with blocked facade, molded conforming base, bracket feet, interior of upper bookcase divided into nine open compartments above four small drawers, interior of lower case with two fan-carved blocked drawers, similar prospect door, small blocked and plain drawers, scrolled compartment dividers, replaced brasses, old finish, restored, 39" w, 22" d, 93-1/2" h 19,550.00

Massachusetts, 18th C, walnut, banded inlay, dovetailed case, two sections, upper section with pull-out candle shelves, double doors with raised arched panels, broken arch pediment with urn and flame finial, interior with four dovetailed drawers and shelves with pigeonholes and removable partitions, one drawer signed in ink "Chloe Dunbar," lower section with slant front lid, fitted interior of eight dovetailed drawers, pigeonholes, two letter files with half columns, center door with one drawer and secret drawer, four dovetailed overlapping drawers, bracket feet, orig brasses, pine secondary wood, old finish, minor repairs, age cracks, finial replaced, 38" w, 21-1/2" d, 31" writing height, 93" h..........................19,000.00

New England, c1775, mahogany, two sections, upper section with broken pediment with brass urn finial crest, blind cupboard doors with scalloped trim, lower section with slant front desk over four graduated drawers, shaped ogee bracket feet, central fan drop, upper panels in doors replaced, 43" w, 23" d, 87" h..5,500.00

New England, c1780, cherry, two sections, upper section with flat cove molded cornice, two cupboard doors, molded recessed panels, projecting base with slant lid opening to interior of central prospect door flanked by three valanced compartments and drawers; lower section with case of four thumb-molded graduated drawers, bracket feet, replaced brasses, refinished, restored, 39-1/4" w, 20-1/8" d, 86" h..4,500.00

New England, southeastern, c1780, cherry, two sections, upper section with flat molded cornice, two cupboard doors with molded recessed panels, set into lower section with slant lid, opening to interior of central prospect door with two faux valanced compartments and drawer, three interior drawers flanked by four valanced compartments, two interior drawers, case with over four thumb molded graduated drawers, bracket feet, old brasses, refinished,

restored, 40-1/4" w, 18" d, 82" h 2,760.00

New England, 18th C, tiger maple, two sections, upper section with broken arch top, flame finials, arched blind doors, inlaid slant top, valanced pigeonholes, twelve drawers, two document drawers, lower section with dovetailed case with four drawer, reeded quarter columns, replaced bracket feet, 38-1/4 w, 22-1/2" d, 75-1/2" h 22,000.00

Pennsylvania, c1760-70, cherry, two sections, upper section with broken arch pediment, boldly carved floral rosettes, turned and carved finials, double doors each with seven panes of glass in geometric arrangement, fluted quarter columns, applied reeded detail, base: slant top lid with fully developed fitted interior of eight dovetailed drawers with serpentine fronts, center door with blocking and carved fan with five graduated drawers with serpentine fronts, eight pigeonholes each with hidden drawers and fan carving, two letter drawers with fluted columns and reeding, four overlapping dovetailed drawers, fluted quarter columns, ogee foot, orig eagle brasses, H-hinges, and latches, orig finish, minor repairs to feet and some replaced glue blocks, 38-1/4" w, 20-3/4" d, 90" h 88,000.00

Pennsylvania, c1765, bonnet top, walnut, two sections, upper section with swan's neck crest, carved rosettes, pair of arched hinged doors, interior adjustable shelves, small drawers and pigeonholes, candle slides, lower section with hinged molded lid, interior with small pigeonholes and drawers, center prospect door opening to small drawer and pigeonhole, four molded graduated long drawers below, bracket feet, staining to interior drawers, 37-1/2" w, 21" d, 96" h.......................20,000.00

Virginia, walnut, two sections, upper section with pair of blind cupboard doors, slant front desk base with fitted interior, six valanced pigeonholes over eight stepped drawers, center prospect with shell carved door over small drawer, flanked by reeded columns, four graduated drawers, ogee bracket feet, some lip damage, possibly married, 38" w, 22" d, 85" h..6,250.00

Chippendale-Style

These secretaries describe examples that

have several elements of the Chippendale style but are of a later time frame or contain elements of later furniture styles.

America, last quarter 19th C, two sections, upper section with glazed two door bookcase top, lower section with slant front desk with fitted interior, shell carved prospect door over four graduated thumb-molded drawers, leaf carved quarter columns, claw and ball feet, chips to feet, 37" w, 22" d, 79" h 1,150.00

Country, hand made, block front, fan carved lid, claw and ball feet, 35-1/2" w, 20-1/4" d, 91-3/4" h.................................2,950.00

New England, mahogany, two sections, upper section with broken arch pedestal over two arched paneled doors, fitted secretary interior with pigeonholes, six small drawers, lower section with fall front, stepped fitted interior, straight front, two small and two wide drawers, brass bail handle, escutcheons, lock plates, straight bracket feet, 42" w, 24" d, 93-3/4" h 3,200.00

Classical

Secretaries found in the Classical period generally have flat-molded cornices, rather than the high pediments found on Chippendale period secretaries. Moldings or muntins on glazed doors tend to more curving, some display a definite Gothic influence.

America, c1820-30, mahogany and mahogany veneer, two sections, upper section with two arched glazed twelve pane doors, right door opening to reveal four drawers over four pigeonholes, left side with shelves, front stiles carved with pineapple motif, lower section with three drawers over fold-out writing surface, slide supports, three long drawers, turned feet, poplar and white pine secondary woods, minor repairs, 44" w, 20" d, 69" h 2,500.00

America, c1820-30, mahogany, two sections, upper section with flat molded cornice over twin Gothic glazed lattice doors, three open shelves and cubbyhole section over three small drawers, lower section with fall front over three drawers, brass ring pulls flanked by ring-turned columnar sides, ebonized ball feet, 47" w, 19-1/2" d, 75-1/4" h.............................2,700.00

America, 1829, carved mahogany, two sec-

tions, upper section with projecting cornice, mullioned glazed doors, shelf interior, lower section with fall front drawer with fitted interior, carved rope turned half columns, front hairy paw carved feet, turned back feet, sgd and dated "Edward West, 1829," 51-3/4" w, 22" d, 93-3/4" h...............................5,650.00

America, c1830-50, secretaire a'abattant, mahogany, single drawer over fall front desk, interior fitted with urn and line inlaid drawers and architectural molding, exterior door and drawer fronts of veneered crocthwood flanked by marquetry panels and half columns, case with three drawers, ending in bun feet, 36-1/2" w, 16-1/2" d, 57" h 1,265.00

America, c1865-75, walnut, two sections, upper section with projecting molded cornice, pair of glazed doors, interior shelves, two short drawers, lower section with hinged fold-down writing surface, three graduated drawers, scrolled legs, turned wood pulls, 42" w, 18-1/2' d, 70" h.....................................1,200.00

America, early 19th C, mahogany, granite top, fall front enclosing later fitted compartment, gilt bronze mounts, veneer loss, 32-1/4" w, 18-1/4" h, 54-3/4" h 1,150.00

America, mid-19th C, diminutive, mahogany, two sections, upper section with pair of mullioned doors over pair of drawers; lower section with fold-out writing surface over classical columns, 44" w, 21-3/4" d, 68" h 700.00

Massachusetts, Boston, c1820-25, secretaire a'abattant, carved mahogany and mahogany veneer, marble top above cove molding, mahogany veneer facade flanked by veneered columns topped by Corinthian capitals, terminating in ebonized ball feet, recessed panel sides, fall front opens to desk interior over two cupboard doors, old refinish, 35" w, 17-1/2" d, 57-1/2" h................................16,100.00

Massachusetts, c1830, mahogany veneer, molded cornice, two glass doors, two small drawers below, fold-out writing surface, two long drawers in base, shaped front feet, turned back feet, refinished, 39" w, 18-1/4" d, 72" h....................................1,200.00

New England, c1830, mahogany and mahogany veneer, flat molded cornice above two glazed doors, Gothic arched mullions, shelved interior above three short external drawers on projecting base, fold-out writing surface, ogee molded long drawer, two cupboard doors, ogee bracket feet, refinished, 45-1/2" w, 25" d, 83-1/2" h 5,400.00

New York, c1830, mahogany and mahogany veneer, two sections, upper section with flat molded cornice above two glazed doors, three short drawers incorporating flanking column on square plinth, lower section projecting with fold-out writing surface, two cupboard doors with raised panels, flanking turned columns on ring-turned hexagonal tapering front feet, sides with recessed panels on rear stile feet, refinished, 45-1/2" w, 25" d, 93" h 7,500.00

Pennsylvania, Philadelphia, c1840, two sections, top section with molded cornice over two glazed doors over fall front writing surface enclosing fitted interior with six drawers and six pigeonholes; lower section with one shallow drawer over two deep drawers, book matched mahogany veneer, replaced brasses, rear feet reinforced, top molding repaired, 45-1/4" w, 20-1/2" d, 89-1/2" h 2,100.00

Classical, married example

These examples are included to illustrate how often large case pieces of furniture are used by succeeding owners. Perhaps the original Chippendale secretary base was damaged. So, in order to continue using the bookcase top section, a later Classical chest of drawers was added. To a collector of either period, this secretary probably would not be acceptable, but someone liked these examples well enough to buy them at an auction in 1999.

Classical maple chest of drawers, c1860, with Chippendale mahogany secretary top, late 18th C; top section with outward curving cornice above two glazed and mullioned doors, chest with deep to drawer above three graduated drawers flanked by spiral turned columns, square plinths, chest supported on baluster form turned replacement feet, 42-1/4" w, 20-3/4" d, 92" h 2,300.00

New England or New York State, c1825, mahogany and mahogany veneer, married, top section with flat projecting ogee molded cornice, two glazed doors with molded muntins

enclosing three shelves, base with hinged box desk, three recessed long drawers, flanked by turned columns, turned feet, old refinish, 36" w, 19" d, 79" h...2,990.00

Classical-Style

Here are two examples of secretaries which have elements of the Classical style, but were made later.

Late 19th C, gilt bronze mounted mahogany, rect top, fall front with fitted interior, over pair of recessed cupboard doors, flanked by columns, paw feet, 44-1/4" w, 23-1/2" d, 49-1/4" h...1,955.00

Early 20th C, variegated gray marble top, case fitted with frieze drawer over drop front secretary, three drawers below, block feet, ormolu mounts, 38-1/2" w, 18-1/4" d, 58-1/2" h...1,775.00

Colonial Revival

Like the Centennial style of furniture, furniture manufacturers have been imitating early Ameri-

can furniture styles. Colonial Revival is the name given to furniture made in the 20th century that reflects back to earlier styles, while Centennial refers to furniture made about 1875.

Colonial Desk Co., Rockford, IL, c1930, mahogany, broken arch pediment, center finial, two glazed mullioned doors, fluted columns, center prospect with acanthus carving flanked by columns, four graduated drawers, brass eagle, carved claw and ball feet, 41" w, 21" d, 87" h...1,000.00

Sheraton-Style, late, American, c1925, walnut and oak, projecting molded cornice, pair of glazed doors, fold-out writing surface, long drawer, turned tapering legs, 35" w, 1-1/2" d, 75" h..900.00

Federal

Secretaries are desirable forms of Federal furniture. Expect to find most secretaries as two sections, some with crests or molded cornices. Doors in the upper cases will open to shelves or may be fitted with glass doors. Expect to find fitted interiors with drawers, pigeonholes, and places to store documents. The writing surface is generally a fold-out or pull-out writing surface, although some examples are found with a slant front. The base usually consists of drawers.

America, c1800, cherry, two sections, upper section with restored molded cornice, two paneled doors open to nine slots with three removable shelves, slant front desk interior with four pigeonholes over two one drawer on each side of privacy door with oval burl veneer, opening to four drawers, lower section with four graduated cockbeaded drawers, scalloped skirt, repaired French feet, white pine and poplar secondary woods, period brasses, refinished, 39-1/2" w, 22" d, 92" h........................7,250.00

America, third quarter 18th C, mahogany, two sections, upper: shaped architectural pediment with gilt-metal ball and spike finials, cavetto cornice over crossbanded frieze, checker-banding, front with pair of thirteen-pane astragal doors, two adjustable shelves; base: outset fall-front opening, fitted interior, four graduated cockbeaded oxbow-fronted drawers, conforming molded plinth base, molded and spurred bracket feet, 44-1/4" w,

24-1/4" d, 93-1/2" h...........................17,000.00

America, early 19th C, lady's, two sections, mahogany, upper section with scrolled crest with reeded posts and brass finials, double door top with applied molding, lower section with hinged writing shelf, fitted interior, three dovetailed drawers with applied beading, turned feet, 37-1/2" w, 18" d, 65" h.....2,500.00

Maryland, Baltimore, c1800, inlaid mahogany, two sections, upper section with molded cornice, two glazed and mullioned cupboard doors, interior shelves, lower section with three short drawers over roll top, sliding leather inset writing surface, fitted interior, three long graduated drawers, shaped apron, splay feet, 47" w, 21" d, 86" h..8,000.00

Massachusetts, c1790, inlaid mahogany, two sections, upper section with shaped gallery with inlaid central panel above two molded glazed doors, shelved and valanced compartment interior, lower projecting base with fold-out writing surface, three cockbeaded inlaid graduated drawers, flanked by inlaid sq tapering legs, imperfections, 40" w, 19-1/4" d, 76" h...3,250.00

Massachusetts, c1790-1810, inlaid mahogany, two sections, upper section with hinged molded rectangular top opening to well, two cupboard doors with line and column inlaid panels, fitted interior, lower section with hinged and baize-lined folding writing surface, four graduated long drawers, replaced French feet, 40-1/4" w, 48" h.................................6,000.00

Massachusetts, Boston or North Shore, early 19th, mahogany inlaid, two sections, upper section with central panel of bird's eye maple with cross-banded mahogany veneer border and stringing joined to the plinths by a curving gallery above flat molded cornice, glazed beaded doors with Gothic arches and bird's eye maple panels and mahogany cross-banding and stringing enclosing shelves, compartments, and drawers; lower section with projecting section with fold-out surface inlaid with oval bird's eye maple panel set in mitered rect with cross-banded border and cockbeaded case, two drawers veneered with bird's eye maple panels bordered by mahogany cross-banding and stringing, flanked by inlaid panels continuing to sq double tapered legs, lower edge of case and leg cuffs with lunette inlaid banding, old finish, replaced brasses, imperfections, 41" w, 21-3/4" d, 74-1/2" h 9,775.00

Massachusetts, early 19th C, mahogany and mahogany veneer, two sections, upper section with bookcase top, shaped pediment over cupboard doors with arched glazed panels, two interior shelves, lower section with cylinder desk, fitted interior, two short drawers over two graduated long drawers, short ring turned baluster legs, old finish, minor imperfections, 39" w, 22" d, 42" h 9,500.00

New England, c1820, tiger maple, two sections, upper section with shaped cornice with block finials, two glazed cupboard doors with diamond shaped mullions, shelved and fitted interior with drawers, document shelves, and valanced pigeonholes, over three small drawers, lower base section with pullout drawer supports, three graduated long drawers, reeded legs, scalloped apron, 39-1/2" w, 19" d, 70" h 4,500.00

New England, c1825, cherry, two sections, upper section with molded cornice over two glazed and mullioned cupboard doors, interior shelves, lower section with projecting case, one long drawer, hinged drop-front, felt-lined writing surface, fitted interior, two cupboard doors, ring-turned legs, casters, 42-1/2" w, 22" d, 85-1/2" h 2,400.00

New England, c1830, mahogany veneer, two sections, upper section with molded cornice with scroll shaped pediment, two short glazed doors with rounded arches, two small drawers below with pull handles, lower base section with fold-out lined writing surface, three drawers, twist turned columns, turned legs, old refinishing, 37-1/2" w, 18-1/2" d, 68" h..............2,500.00

New Hampshire, early 19th C, bird's eye maple, two sections, upper section with scrolled gallery centering satinwood and cockbeaded plinth and urn foliage carved finial, flanked by reeded plinths and finials, cove molding and veneered frieze centering a satinwood panel, two glazed doors with reeded muntins and inlaid satinwood panels bordered by mahogany banding, two adjustable shelves, two cockbeaded drawers below with bird's eye maple veneer and mahogany cross-banded border, opening to multidrawer, valanced, and compartmented interior, lower section with case fitted with three cock-

beaded drawers, flanked by cockbeaded panels, vase and ring turned feet joined by scrolled apron centering a cockbeaded satinwood panel, replaced brasses, old refinish, imperfections, 40" w, 20" d, 83-3/4" h 10,350.00

Georgian

Georgian period secretaries are often difficult to tell their country of origin. Both English and American craftsmen used mahogany and similar construction techniques.

America or English, c1810, mahogany, two sections, upper section with swan's neck pediment with palmetto medallions over two astragal glazed doors, lower section fitted with slant front opening to inset gilt-tooled leather writing surface, drawers and cubby holes flanking central arched cupboard, over two short drawers over three long graduated drawers, bracket feet, 35-1/2" w, 18-1/2" d, 94-1/2" h.................3,600.00

Hepplewhite

Hepplewhite secretaries are usually identified by the use of inlay. If the top section doors are glazed, the mullions tend to be geometrical rather than the scrolling effect sometimes found in Classical period secretaries.

America, lady's, mahogany with inlay, two sections, upper section with cornice with brass finials, tambour section with fitted interior with dovetailed drawers, double doors with geometric arrangement of glass, lower section with fold-down writing shelf, three dovetailed drawers, considerable restoration, 39-1/4" w, 18-1/2" d, 74-3/4" h...1,800.00

America, two sections, upper with walnut and figured walnut veneer with inlay, pine and poplar secondary wood, top: removable cornice with high goosenecks, keystone and turned finials, double doors with adjustable shelves, stringing inlay with invected corners and inlay on cornice, lower base section with slant front lid, fitted interior, with pigeonholes and ten dovetailed drawers, center door, four dovetailed drawers with applied edge beading, bracket feet, old finish, period replaced brasses, pieced repairs, some edge damage, replaced finials, 39-5/8" w, 11" h x 42-1/4" cornice, 21" d x 40-1/2" w base, 90" h 20,900.00

New England, late 18th C, butler's, inlaid mahogany, three shelves in cupboard top, butler style drawer and two long drawers in base, 40-3/4" w, 67-1/2" h............................3,200.00

Modernism Era

Secretaries from this period are unusual. Most furniture designed in the Modernism Era is low and sleek, rather than the vertical height associated with most secretaries.

Gilbert Rohde, manufactured by Herman Miller, c1940, upper bookcase with drop front desk over four doors, carved wooden pulls in burl and paldio veneers, refinished, 66" w, 15" d, 72" h...2,600.00

Queen Anne-Style

This example shows some elements of the Queen Anne-style, with the use of astragal glazed doors, but the ball feet and scalloped box stretcher are from a later period.

America, late 19th C, mahogany, double domed cornice above two astragal glazed doors, lower case fitted with slant-front top, fitted with drawers and cubby holes, two long graduated drawers, turned trumpet legs, ball feet, joined by scalloped box stretcher, 35" w, 19" d, 83" h...2,500.00

Regency

This style is usually associated with English furniture makers, but this example was made in New Hampshire. Having a signature adds to the provenance of this secretary.

New Hampshire, c1830, cherry, mahogany, veneer, two sections, upper section with doors, two interior shelves, six drawers, and three compartments, lower section with writing surface, double lift lids, rear lid opening to reveal nine drawers, five divided compartments, two central drawers flanked by nine drawers, fully turned columns with ropetwist detail, stamped "Chas Dennett" on interior, white pine secondary wood, old finish, 38-1/4" w, 20-1/2" d, 83" h.............4,250.00

Sheraton

The following examples exhibit elements from the Sheraton design style, but all are dated a little later than the c1790 to 1810 that is most closely associated with Sheraton. This helps to reinforce that styles often continued even when a new style was becoming fashionable in other parts of the country.

America, c1820, mahogany, drop front, two drawers, fitted interior with twenty-eight pigeonholes, four ledger slots, three small drawers 850.00

Ohio, East Liverpool, c1880, cherry, two sections, upper section with bookcase top with molded cornice, paneled doors, adjustable shelves, lower base section with dovetailed case, three dovetailed drawers, fold-down slant front, fitted interior, four pigeonholes, two dovetailed drawers, turned feet, old brown graining, replaced brasses, 34" w, 19-1/4" d, 76-1/2" h...2,500.00

West Virginia, Monroe Country, c1825, walnut, two sections, upper section with molded cornice over pair of banded cupboard doors, dovetailed shelves, slant front, interior with central graduated drawers, four pigeonholes on each side, lower case with slides, three graduated drawers, bracket feet, yellow pine and poplar secondary woods, refinished, minor repairs, 37-1/4" w, 18" d, 85" h............3,750.00

Victorian

The massive style of furniture usually associated with the Victorian period is carried out to extremes with secretaries. Examples will often feature large pediments and cornices, scrolling mullions on glazed doors. Bases can have either drawers or cupboards or both. It should be noted that by the time that secretaries were created for this time period, they could be "ordered" through local furniture stores. The future owner could select from several different styles of cornices, tops, and bases, allowing for some interesting combinations.

America, cherry, arched pediment, scrolled carving over glass doors, six drawers, slant front desk over two aligned drawers over two long drawers, bracket feet, 40-1/2" w, 22" d, 88" h..1,650.00

America, mahogany, cavetto molded platform top, leaf carved edge, ogee molded drop front, fitted rosewood veneered interior, with marquetry floral scrollwork inlay, three gradated drawers, rocaille carved skirt, short cabriole legs, upturned feet, 39" w, 23" d, 65-1/2" h 4,250.00

America, maple and cherry, rectangular top, projecting cornice, sq case, glazed doors, slant front deck with carving, three long drawers, turned knobs, bracket feet, 39" w, 22" d, 84" h 650.00

America, walnut, figured veneer panels, two sections, upper section with shaped cornice over two glazed doors, lower section with cylinder roll front opening to two fitted interior drawers, over long drawer and pair of cupboard doors, 47" w, 25" d, 95" h 2,975.00

America, c1840, two sections, mahogany, upper section with ogee cornice surmounting carved frieze, arched glass doors with applied foliate carved decoration, lower section with slant front, fitted interior, one serpentine and two large drawers with applied foliate carved

Victorian, Eastlake, burl walnut and mahogany, shaped cornice over pair of glazed cupboard doors, cylinder front, writing surface with fitted interior, single drawer over two doors, shaped base, 27" w, 22" d, 66" h, $1,800.

decoration, shaped skirt with applied foliate decoration, bracket feet, 44-1/4" w, 20" d, 94-1/2" h 5,000.00

America, two sections, walnut, top: crown molding cornice, two glazed doors with burl and walnut buttons; lower base section with burl cylinder roll with two drawer walnut interior, pigeonholes, slide-out writing surface, base: three long drawers with burl dec, tear drop pulls, refinished, 40" w, 23" d, 86" h 1,850.00

Eastlake, America

Burl walnut and mahogany, two sections, upper section with shaped cornice, pair of glazed cabinet doors, cylinder front, writing surface, lower base section with two doors, shaped apron, 27" w, 22" d, 66" h 1,500.00

Walnut, two sections, upper section with carved crest over two glazed doors, flanked by turned pilasters, cylinder with veneered panels, fitted interior, lower base section with long drawer over two small drawers and cupboard door, 41-1/2" w, 22-1/2" d, 95" h 2,200.00

Gothic Revival, c1870, walnut, galleried top over slant lid, interior fitted writing compartment over drawer over cabinet doors and drawers, molded base, 36" w, 20-1/4" d, 63-1/2" h 2,415.00

Renaissance Revival

America, c1860, walnut, burl veneer, turned and carved ornaments, hand carved bust of Shakespeare finial, three dovetailed drawers, dovetailed upper case with mirrored door, bird's eye maple fitted interior, base with turned legs and stretcher, 46-1/2" w, 22" d, 91-1/2" h 3,750.00

America, c1865, walnut, two sections, upper bookcase section, S-curved pediment with center applied grapes and foliage carving, two arched and molded glazed doors, shelved interior, three small drawers with applied grapes and foliage carved pulls; lower section with fold-out writing surface, two short drawers over two long drawers with oval molding and applied grapes and foliage carved pulls, matching ornamentation on skirt, 48" w, 21" d, 95" h 5,000.00

Sideboards

Sideboards are large case pieces of furniture usually reserved for service in a dining room setting. Their multiple cupboard doors hold accessories and some are fitted with special racks to hold wine bottles. Drawers are for storage of silver and linens. The top of a sideboard often doubled as a buffet or server, resulting in the other common name for sideboards.

Arts & Crafts

Arts & Crafts furniture makers included servers in their dining room suites. Look for original hardware and interesting plate racks, as well as mirrors and decorative accents. As with any other furniture of this period, the price is enhanced by knowing the original maker, finding a decal, brand, or label. Original finish also adds to the value. An English Arts & Crafts server is included for comparison purposes.

Liberty, English, 2" thick oak construction, top cabinet with bi-fold doors concealing geo-

Arts & Crafts, Limbert, Grand Rapids and Holland, Michigan, c1907, No. 1453 3/4, oak, rectangular plate rack over central mirror, conforming rectangular top, two central drawers flanked by cabinet doors over long drawer, branded mark, 48" l, 19" d, 52-5/8" h, $2,185. Photo courtesy of Skinner Auctioneers and Appraisers of Antiques and Fine Art Boston and Bolton, MA.

metric leaded glass windows, flanked by open shelves, over two drawers and two cabinet doors, slat legs, hand-wrought iron strap hinges, attributed to custom design after Liberty's Cullodon dresser, some restoration, 90" w, 30" d, 80" h............................13,200.00

Limbert, Charles P., Grand Rapids and Holland, MI

No. 1453-3/4, c1907, rectangular plate rack over central mirror, conforming rectangular angular top, two central drawers flanked by cabinet doors over long drawer, branded mark, 48" w, 19" d, 52-5/8" h.....................................2,185.00

No. 1445, three drawers flanked by two cabinet doors with orig copper strap hinges and hardware over one full drawer, arched and notched toe-board and orig plate rail,

Art Nouveau, carved backsplash, medial shelf over rect top, flanking side cabinets with applied Art Nouveau style floral decoration, interior shelf, brass pulls, eight reeded and shaped feet, refinished, wear, 49-1/4" l, 24-1/2" d, 40-1/4" h, $1,200. Photo courtesy of Skinner Auctioneers and Appraisers of Antiques and Fine Art Boston, and Bolton MA.

through-tenon construction, orig finish, 60" w, 23" d, 46" h 5,500.00

Ebon-Oak, backsplash, two shelves, orig finish, branded mark, minor split to post, 36" w, 16-1/2" d, 38-1/2" h, ...2,000.00

Oak, c1910, oblong top, mirrored back above case, three short drawers flanked by paneled cupboard doors over long drawer, cooper pulls and strap hinges, sq legs, chamfered tenons, branded mark, 49-1/2" w, 53-1/2" h 900.00

Oak, two half drawers flanked by two cabinet doors over one full drawer, orig copper hardware, mirrored back, orig finish, branded mark, 48" w, 20" d, 48" h 2,240.00

Roycroft, East Aurora, NY

Mahogany, mirrored backsplash, three small drawers flanked by two cabinets with leaded glass doors, over single large linen drawer, orig finish, carved orb and cross mark, casters, 60-1/4" w, 25" d, 54" h........................9,850.00

Plate rack, single drawer with oval pulls, 2 cabinet doors with leaded glass fronts and round copper pulls, carved orb and cross mark, new dark finish, 42" w, 20-1/4" d, 45" h, ...12,000.00

Arts & Crafts, in the style of Shop of the Crafters, c1915, oak, whole rectangular canted form, long mirror with arch, rectangular overhanging top, two short drawers above two cabinet doors, single long drawers, unsigned, some damage, 42" l, 19-1/4" d, 37-1/2" h, $1,265. Photo courtesy of Skinner Auctioneers and Appraisers of Antiques and Fine Art Boston and Bolton, MA.

Shop of the Crafters-Style, c1915, oak, whole rectangular canted form, long mirror with arch, rectangular angular top, two short drawers above two cabinet doors over single long drawer, unsigned, 42" w, 19-1/4" d, 37-1/2" h, some damage 1,265.00

Stickley Brothers, Grand Rapids, MI, No. 8507, plate rack, four rounded posts, three small drawers flanked by two paneled doors, over long linen drawer, new medium-dark finish, metal tap, 54" w, 23" d, 45" h 3,850.00

Stickley, Gustav, New York

No. 814-1/2, three drawers flanked by two cabinet doors over single long drawer, orig copper hardware, lightly cleaned orig finish, branded signature, 66" w, 24" d, 49" h 9,000.00

No. 816, long drawer over three central

Arts & Crafts, Roycroft, mahogany, mirrored backsplash, three small drawers flanked by two cabinets with leaded glass doors, one large linen drawer, casters, orig finish, carved orb and cross mark, 60-1/4" l, 25" d, 54" h, $8,500. Shown on Turkish Kilim rug, pair of silver Arts & Crafts candlesticks and American art pottery ftd bowl. Photo courtesy of David Rago Auctions/RagoArts.com, Lambertville, NJ.

drawers flanked by two doors, arched apron, signed with red decal, partial paper label, refinished, restored veneer on sides, 48" w, 18-1/4" d, 45-1/4" h............................4,750.00

Plate rack, chamfered back and sides, three drawers with heavy faceted wooden pulls, large red decal, new finish, 59-1/4" w, 24" d, 44-1/4" h..............................14,000.00

Plate rack, three small drawers, two cabinet doors, strap hardware, single long linen drawer, orig reddish-brown finish with some cloudiness, some loss of veneer, side pull holder missing, paper label, 66" w, 24" d, 48-1/2" h...6,000.00

Stickley, L. and J. G., Fayetteville, NY

No. 734, two cabinet doors flanking three center drawers, all over one long drawer, orig copper hardware, plate rail, re-coated orig finish, sgd "The Work of L. and J. G. Stickley," 48" w, 20" d, 44" h.............4,375.00

No. 738, c1912, oak, plate rail, rectangular top, two center drawers flanked by two cabinet doors, strap hinges, branded mark, minor stains, 60" w, 20" d, 46" h......2,400.00

Plate rack, six small drawers, two cabinet doors over linen drawer, arched apron, orig medium finish, Handcraft label........4,250.00

Plate rack, two cabinet doors flanking four drawers, single long linen drawer, sgd "The Work of L. and J. G. Stickley," replaced plate rack, stains on top, 72" w, 25" d, 49-1/4" h..5,500.00

Plate rack, two drawers, two shelves, orig finish, "The Work of L. and J. G. Stickley" decal, 48" w, 22" d, 49" h..................3,950.00

Unknown Designer

Mahogany, Viennese influence, peaked back rail with horizontal design in pierced brass, two drawers, orig brass hardware, refinished, Chicago retailer's tag, 42" w, 20" d, 44" h.......................................2,500.00

Oak, c1916, gallery shelf with mirror, two half drawers, two doors over central long drawer, orig finish, unsigned, 54" w, 20" d, 55-1/4" h, some stains and roughness to veneer...500.00

Oak, in style of Gustav Stickley, two drawers and hammered iron faceted pulls and back plate, lower shelf with wide slab legs and

through-tenon construction, old refinishing, minor chips, 48" w, 20" d, 40" h..........3,500.00

Oak, three drawers flanked by two cabinet doors, orig brass hardware and mirrored back, worn orig finish, 52" w, 22" d, 51" h..500.00

Centennial

This Chippendale-style sideboard shows how furniture makers of the Centennial period envisioned this functional piece of furniture.

Chippendale-Style, America, late 19th C, mahogany, block front with shell carving, four drawers, front cabinet doors, gadrooned apron, cabriole legs, claw and ball feet, 68" w, 24" d, 40" h...950.00

Classical

Classical sideboards show how more elaborate this style became as it developed through the years of 1805-1830. The style is typified by scrolling, but many of these sideboards include carving on their column-type supports, legs, and feet. Tops of many Classical sideboards are either rectangular or rectangular with angular features. Look for additional work surfaces in the form of pull-out slides during this time period.

America, c1830, carved mahogany, rectangular angular top, single large drawer flanked by heavily carved panels, resting on carved base, thick pillar supports top, quadrapedal base, carved lions' paws feet with casters, orig pressed glass pulls, facing surfaces veneered, imperfections, 45" w, 18-3/4" d, 33-1/2" h 750.00

America, c1845, mahogany, three drawers over four drawers, mahogany veneer front on center drawer, two pull-out working surfaces above two smaller drawers, four mahogany turned front posts, four front hairy paw feet, two turned rear feet, glass pulls, 73" w, 24" d, 42" h...750.00

America, mid-19th C, carved mahogany and mahogany veneer, center drawer with inset shelf, central doors with relief carved fan, four Ionic columns across front, drawer over raised panel door at each end, paw feet with acanthus leaves at cuffs, old dark worn finish, pine secondary wood, minor veneer wear, imperfections, 68" w, 24" d, 47" h 2,325.00

America, mid-19th C, mahogany, molded backsplash over rectangular angular top, three drawers and three recessed cupboard doors flanked by columns, ball feet, 59-1/4" w, 21-3/4" h, 48" h 2,415.00

America, mid-19th C, mahogany, pair of molded drawers over recessed full width drawer, cupboard door below, flanked by scrolling columns, scroll feet, 47" w, 22-1/2" d, 48-1/2" h..950.00

America, mid-19th C, mahogany, rectangular faux-marble top surrounded by brass gallery, three short drawers above two paneled doors centered by two small drawers, flanked by pineapple carved columns, paw feet, 54" w, 22" d, 56" h..850.00

Massachusetts, c1800, bow front, mahogany and mahogany veneer, shaped top with outset corners, two long center drawers flanked by small doors over two cupboard doors flanked by two small drawers, carved capitals above fluted columns, old refinishing, old brasses, imperfections, 47-1/2" w, 22-1/4" d, 42" h 4,750.00

Massachusetts, Boston, c1826, mahogany and mahogany veneer, rectangular angular top, ogee molded drawer, two cupboard doors with flat mitered borders, flanking scrolls, scrolled legs, old finish, minor imperfections, 40" w, 18-1/2" d, 34" h..........................1,725.00

Middle Atlantic States, 1840-45, carved mahogany and cherry veneer, rectangular top over mahogany veneered drawer, two recessed panel doors opening to one shelf interior, flanked by veneered scrolled supports, veneered base, old refinishing, hardware changes, splashboard missing, 40" w, 18-3/4" d, 40-1/8" h..2,550.00

New England, c1802, mahogany and mahogany veneer, veneered peaked backboard, scrolled gallery, rectangular top with rounded edge, case of two cockbeaded short drawers, two cupboard doors, paneled sides, turned feet, old refinishing, replaced brasses, 58" w, 21" d, 44" h..............................4,200.00

New York, c1825, carved mahogany and mahogany veneer, rectangular angular top, case with two cockbeaded short drawers and long drawer with banded borders flanked by applied gothic panels above vase and ring turned spiral carved legs joined by medial shelf, cast brass casters, replaced pulls, old refinishing, minor imperfections, 30" w, 16-1/4" d, 33-1/2" h..2,100.00

New York, c1830, carved mahogany and mahogany veneer, leafage carving flanking central basket of fruit over two small corner drawers above classical columns flanking a central drawer above compartment flanked by side recessed paneled doors, one shelf interior, carved paw feet, old refinishing, orig glass pulls, minor imperfections, 60" w, 21" d, 50-1/2" h..4,200.00

Philadelphia, c1830, carved mahogany and mahogany veneer, backboard outlined in brass inlay, center brass floral device, conforming top, three convex veneered drawers above brass inlaid paneled cabinet doors, flanked by Ionic columns on carved front feet, casters, old refinishing, 71" w, 23-1/2" d, 45" h 9,990.00

Colonial Revival

This example of a Chippendale-style sideboard differs from the Centennial example in that it includes more up-to-date features, such as wine drawers, but carries through the styling with claw and ball feet.

Chippendale-style, c1920, mahogany, center bow front over two frieze drawers, two deep drawers flanked by two wine drawers, central section flanked by two drawers over curved cupboard doors, claw and ball feet, 46" w, 18" d, 40-1/2" h 1,750.00

Federal

Sideboards of the Federal period are probably the most sought after by collectors and command the highest prices for this type of furniture. Mahogany and other fine woods were used. Look for decorative inlay on the top, front, and legs. Forms include several variations, bow front, serpentine front, and straight front, where the name is derived from the shape of the front and usually the top corresponds. Legs vary from the tapered square legs to reeded legs, with the tapered square legs being more typical.

America, c1800-10, bow front, mahogany, banded and strung edge, inlaid stiles with pendant bellflowers, tapered sq legs, 53-3/4" w, 40" h 24,000.00

America, c1810, bow front, mahogany, shaped rectangular top, slightly projecting center section, one long drawer over two cupboard doors, flanked by two deep cellarette drawers flanked by two short drawers over two cupboard doors, flanked by fluted columns, ring-turned cylindrical tapering legs, 72" w, 23" d, 40-1/4" h 2,400.00

Connecticut, Hartford, c1790, serpentine front, inlaid mahogany, serpentine top with line inlay and crossbanding, conforming case with drawers and central cupboard doors, sq tapering line inlaid legs witch cuff inlays, old finish, old replaced brasses with American shield and anchor, 77" w, 28-1/2" d, 42" h 35,000.00

Maryland, Baltimore, c1790-1800, serpentine front, inlaid mahogany, serpentine top and front with inlaid edge, conforming shaped case with central drawer above cupboard doors, inlaid ovals bordered by stringing, flanked by cupboard doors, four square tapering legs with conforming inlay continuing to inlaid cuffs, old refinishing,

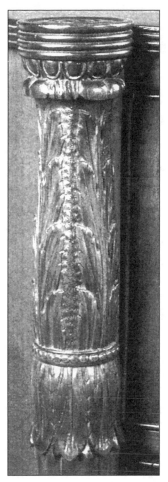

A close-up detail of the sideboard's carving.

minor imperfections, 75-1/2" w, 29" d, 39" h 31,050.00

Maryland, Baltimore, c1815-25, mahogany veneer, paneled, top with inlaid molded edge, three cockbeaded drawers and four recessed paneled doors opening to shelved interiors separated by fluting and stop fluting, reeded tapering and turned legs, old refinishing, replaced brasses, veneer cracks and losses, 72" w, 25" d, 45" h 3,800.00

Massachusetts, Boston, c1785-1810, bow front, inlaid mahogany, D-shaped top with banded edge, mahogany veneer between maple stringing, case with three cockbeaded drawers, four cupboard doors, flanked by turned and reeded legs topped by stringing in outline, old surface, replaced brasses, imperfections, 61-1/4" w, 23-1/4" d, 29" h 8,625.00

Massachusetts, Boston, c1790, inlaid mahogany, rectangular top with ovolo corners, conforming case with two central drawers inlaid with ovals within mitered frames flanked

Federal, Massachusetts, Salem, c1815, carved mahogany veneer, mahogany top with reeded edge, flanked by engaged columns topped by carved concentric circles above carved leafage on stippled ground over reeded legs ending in ring-turned feet, three cockbeaded drawers above central cupboard doors, flanked by end drawers, replaced brasses, old refinish, imperfections, 53" w, 24-1/2" d, 42-1/2" h, $8,625. Photo courtesy of Skinner Auctioneers and Appraisers of Antiques and Fine Art Boston and Bolton, MA.

by rectangles formed by cross-banding and stringing, arched apron, flanked by drawers and cupboards, tapering legs on casters, replaced brasses, old finish, repairs, loss of height, 68-1/2" w, 27" d, 38" h..............1,850.00

Massachusetts, c1790, bow front, inlaid mahogany, shaped top, center long drawer over pair of cupboard doors, flanked by shaped drawer over single cupboard door, sq tapered legs, old refinishing, minor imperfections, 59-1/2" w, 25-1/2" d, 43" h..9,250.00

Massachusetts, Boston, c1790-1805, bow front, inlaid mahogany, shaped top with inlaid edge, three drawers, two end cupboards, all cockbeaded and outlined with veneer and stringing, arched skirt, square tapering legs, outlined in stringing, ending in spade feet, replaced brass, old refinishing, minor repairs, 70" w, 28" d, 40" h..............................10,350.00

Massachusetts, c1810, bow front, inlaid mahogany, shaped top outlined in inlay, conforming case with central drawer with reserve, flanked by end drawers outlined in Greek key inlays, two central cupboard doors with beaded ovals, flanked by cupboard doors, legs with bellflower inlays on front of the upper and lower sections, replaced brasses, old surface, 71-1/2" w, 26-1/2" d, 42" h......................................21,850.00

Massachusetts, Boston, c1810-20, mahogany, maple, and rosewood veneer, two-tiered case, demilune superstructure, maple inlaid panels surrounded by cross-banded rosewood veneer above cockbeaded end drawers, small central drawer flanked by end cupboards, six-ring turned tapering legs, case with concentric turnings, reeding, cockbeading, and scenic landscape jointed on underside of arched opening, old surface, replaced pulls, replaced leg, veneer loss, later landscape painting, 74-1/2" w, 24-1/2" d, 44-3/4" h 9,200.00

Massachusetts, c1815, bow front, inlaid mahogany, top with bowed front and ovolo corners, conforming case with two cockbeaded central short drawers flanked by wine drawers, two cupboard doors, contrasting inlaid stringing on quarter engaged ring-turned reeded posts continuing to reeded legs, old refinishing, restored, 44-1/4" w, 21-1/2" d, 39-1/2" h 5,250.00

Massachusetts, Salem, c1815, carved mahogany veneer, mahogany top with reeded edge, flanked by engaged columns topped by carved concentric circles above carved leafage on stippled ground over reeded legs ending in ring-turned feet, three cockbeaded drawers above central cupboard doors, flanked by end drawers, replaced brasses, old refinishing, imperfections, 53" w, 24-1/2" d, 42-1/2" h 8,625.00

Massachusetts, Boston area, early 19th C, bow front, inlaid mahogany, elliptical top with inlaid edge, overhanging case of veneered cockbeaded drawers, end cupboards outlined with stringing, having central bone inlaid escutcheons, central hinged butler's desk drawer opening to interior of small drawers and open compartments with felt-lined writing surface, above working drawer, arched skirt outlined with patterned inlay, square tapering legs outlined with stringing, ending in cuff inlays, orig surface, replaced brasses, imperfections, 62" w, 24" d, 41" h.............................14,950.00

Massachusetts, early 19th C, mahogany and maple veneer, two-tiered shaped tops with beaded edges, cockbeaded drawers outlined in rosewood veneer and stringing with end cabinets on turned mahogany legs, replaced brasses, imperfections, 69-5/8" w, 26-1/2" d, 43-3/4" h...5,600.00

Federal, Middle Atlantic States, c1790-1810, mahogany inlaid, serpentine front, three drawers over two doors flanking central cupboard doors, all with elliptical and circular line inlay, crossbanded inlay along apron and square tapered legs, ending in crossbanded cuffs, 72-3/4" w, 21-7/8" d, 40-1/2" h, $10,350. Photo courtesy of Samuel T. Freeman & Co., Philadelphia, PA.

Middle Atlantic States, c1780, block front, mahogany and satinwood inlays, two board top, two central drawers, lower drawer with inlaid conch shell, flanked on each side by single large drawer, six reeded and turned tapered legs, white pine secondary wood, ivory escutcheons, replaced brasses, old refinishing, 72-1/2" w, 23-3/4" d, 38" h 12,450.00

Middle Atlantic States, c1790, mahogany and cherry inlaid, overhanging top with canted corners and serpentine front, central cockbeaded door inlaid with cherry panel with quarter fan inlays and mahogany mitered border, cockbeaded wine drawer with three-drawer facade at one end, three cockbeaded graduated drawers on other, ends with cherry veneered panels, four sq inlaid tapering legs ending in molded spade feet, lower edge of case with molding, old finish, minor imperfections, 48-1/2" w, 21-5/8" d, 37" h 19,950.00

Middle Atlantic States, c1790, mahogany and mahogany veneer, small center drawer over pair of recessed cupboard doors, flanked by pair of cupboard doors, sq tapered legs with bellflower inlays, kite-shaped escutcheons, restoration, 55-1/2" w, 25-1/2" d, 38-1/2" h 10,250.00

Middle Atlantic States, c1790-1810, serpentine front, inlaid mahogany, serpentine top, three drawers over two doors flanking central cupboard doors, all with elliptical and circular line inlay, crossbanded inlay along apron and square tapered legs, ending in crossbanded cuffs, 72-3/4" w, 21-7/8" d, 40-1/2" h 10,350.00

Middle Atlantic States, c1815, bow front, inlaid mahogany, shaped top, conforming case with long center drawer over recessed pair of cupboard doors, flanked by small drawer over door, pedestal with drawer over cupboard door with arched inlay, turned reeded legs, ball feet, old refinishing, minor imperfections, 78-1/2" w, 25-3/4" d, 45" h 6,250.00

New England, c1790, bow front, mahogany and mahogany veneer, overhanging top with shaped front, conforming case, central pullout surface, bowed cockbeaded drawers, two cupboard doors flanked by concave drawers and cupboard doors, six sq tapering legs, replaced brasses, old refinishing, imperfections, 64" w, 20-1/8" d, 37-1/2" h 5,500.00

New England, Southern, c1790-1810, cherry, inlaid, trapezoidal shaped top, center long drawer over pair of large inverted cupboard doors, flanked by smaller doors, smaller drawers over single cupboard doors on each end, oval and circular inlays, oval brasses, ivory shield shaped escutcheons, straight tapering legs with bellflower inlay, crossbanded cuffs, 72" w, 15-1/4" d, 42-1/4" h.......15,000.00

New England, c1800, bow front, inlaid mahogany, shaped top with inlaid edge, conforming case with single central drawer flanked by two small end drawers over four cupboard doors and two sectioned bottle drawers, facades outlined in stringing with ovolo corners, six sq tapering legs with cuff inlays, replaced hardware, refinished, some restoration, 67-1/2" w, 21" d, 41" h 11,500.00

New England, c1810-20, mahogany, fluted edge, breakfront top, back and side rails with S-curved ends, extending over conforming base, center curved side center drawer, two flanking smaller drawers with wide outline bands, four doors with triple line inlays, two center doors slightly recessed, raised columns with similar inlays and supported on tapered square feet, raised bands, 74" w, 25" d, 40" h 3,200.00

Federal, New England, c1810-20, mahogany, fluted edge, breakfront top, back and side rails with S-curved ends, extending over conforming base, center curved side center drawer, two flanking smaller drawers with wide outline bands, four doors with triple line inlays, two center doors slightly recessed, raised columns with similar inlays and supported on tapered square feet, raised bands, 74" w, 25" d, 40" h, $3,200. Photo courtesy of Butterfields.

New Hampshire, Portsmouth, c1800-15, bow front, mahogany and flame birch veneer, shaped top with inlaid edge, three drawers outlined in crossbanded mahogany veneer and stringing over two central cupboard doors flanked by sectioned bottle drawer and end cabinets above six double tapered cuff-inlaid legs, front legs with bellflower, old surface, replaced pulls, imperfections, 68-3/4" w, 26" d, 41-5/8" h..............................18,875.00

New York City, c1780-1800, inlaid mahogany, straight front, recessed central cupboards and bowed ends, conforming top with veneered edge, three drawers with stringing in outline, each front leg topped by book inlay, outlined in stringing to cuff inlays, oval inlays in double-line stringing, replaced brasses, refinished, imperfections, 71-1/2" w, 26-1/4" d, 41-1/2" h 23,000.00

New York, c1800, bow front, mahogany, drop center, raised cavetto molded plinth sides with cockbeaded drawer and cupboard doors, bow front with long drawer and two cupboard doors, two compartmented bottle drawers, turned and reeded legs, brass capped feet, 78" w, 27" d, 51-1/2" h.................................6,775.00

New York, c1800, bow front, painted and inlaid mahogany, oblong top, case with two convex cupboard doors, two center convex drawers, bookend and line inlaid dies, line inlaid sq tapering legs, crossbanded cuffs, front painted in 19th C polychrome with classical motifs including griffins, bacchanalic figures, masks, and garlands, repairs, losses to veneer, 68" w, 27-1/2" d, 39-1/4" h 5,000.00

New York, c1800, serpentine front, inlaid mahogany, oblong top, two small convex drawers, pair of cupboard doors and bottle drawers, central hinged door, tombstone inlaid dies, line inlaid sq tapered legs, crossbanded cuffs, 73" w, 28" d, 44" h..17,500.00

Rhode Island, c1800, bow front, mahogany and mahogany veneer, shaped top over four drawers over four cupboard doors, sq tapering legs, chalk inscription "Hilliker," old refinishing, old replaced brasses, imperfections, 69" w, 25-1/4" d, 41" h 4,000.00

Vermont, Rutland, c1825, cherry, rectangular top with ovolo corners and inlaid edge, outset columns with colonettes above reed-

ing on turned feet, central fitted hinged butler's desk drawer over two long drawer, all outlined in beading enclosing mahogany crossbanded veneer, orig surface, replaced brasses, imperfections, 46-1/8" w, 21-3/4" d, 44" h 6,500.00

Virginia, 1790-1810, walnut and yellow pine, molded rectangular top, cockbeaded case with end drawers, right drawer visually divided into two drawers, left with two working drawers, central cupboard cockbeaded door, four square tapering legs, old brass pulls, old refinishing, repairs, inscription on drawer reads "Virginia Hunt Board, early 19th cent. from family of Admiral Todd, Naval Commander prior to and during the Civil War, Virginia," 56" w, 22" d, 39" h..5,520.00

Federal-Style

The following examples are Federal-style sideboards, made well after the period ended, but each have some elements relating to the 18th century Federal style of furniture.

America, mid-19th C, inlaid mahogany, shaped rectangular top, inlaid edges, center section with two short cockbeaded drawers over one cockbeaded cupboard door flanked by two cockbeaded cellarette drawers, flanked by reeded half columns, flanked by two short, cockbeaded drawers, over two cockbeaded cupboard doors, flanked by reeded three-quarter columns, reeded cylindrical tapering legs, 73-1/4" w, 24" d, 40" h.........................4,500.00

America, late 19th C, mahogany, top with outset rounded corners, shaped splashboard with ebonized accents, two frieze drawers, turned tapered legs, 51" w, 19-1/2" d, 44-3/4" h..800.00

America, late 19th C, mahogany, rectangular top, straight front, three cockbeaded drawers, oval brass bail handles, thistle decorated escutcheons, flanked by two small drawers, twin panel doors, shaped apron, sq tapering legs, 66" w, 21-1/2" d, 36-1/2" h.............750.00

Hepplewhite

Hepplewhite sideboards are second in popularity to those from the Federal period. Possibly it's the same clean lines that appeal to collec-

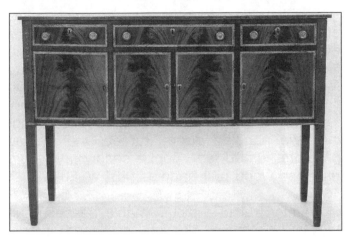

Hepplewhite, America, mahogany with figured mahogany veneer with inlay, four doors and three dovetailed drawers, stringing and banding with foliage designs on posts and banding around edge of doors, drawers, and top, sq slightly tapered legs, replaced eagle brasses, minor repairs, 54" w, 18-3/8" d, 38" h, $11,000. Photo courtesy of Garth's Auctions, Inc., Delaware, OH.

tors. Expect to find more and larger inlay on Hepplewhite examples.

America, c1780, serpentine front, mahogany, serpentine top, three drawers, two cupboard doors, one decanter drawer, sq tapering legs, banded feet, 61" w, 25-1/4" d, 39-1/2" h..5,475.00

America, c1800, serpentine front, mahogany, serpentine top, four aligned drawers, center shaped cupboard doors flanked by two small panels, flanked by reverse shaped cupboard doors, sq tapering legs, fan inlays at corners of all doors, stringing and other inlay, 75-1/2" w, 40" h 6,500.00

America, bow front, mahogany and mahogany veneer with inlay, bowed center section with conforming doors and dovetailed drawer, two flat side doors, sq tapered legs, banding and stringing with bell flowers on legs, corner fans on doors and drawers, reworked, repairs, replaced brasses, 58-1/4" w, 18-1/2" d, 37-3/4" h..2,200.00

America, mahogany with figured mahogany veneer with inlay, four doors and three dovetailed drawers, stringing and banding with foliage designs on posts and banding around edge of doors, drawers, and top, sq slightly tapered legs, replaced eagle brasses, minor repairs, 54" w, 18-3/8" d, 38" h..........11,000.00

America, serpentine front, mahogany, oblong top, serpentine top, conforming frieze with three cockbeaded drawers, central recessed cupboard doors flanked by conforming doors, sq tapered legs with crossbanded cuffs, 66" w, 28" d, 41" h..3,950.00

America, serpentine front, mahogany, serpentine top, conforming case, five dovetailed drawers, double doors, banded inlay around top edge and feet, stringing on drawers, doors, posts, and legs, corner fans on doors, sq legs, old replaced brasses, old finish, some leg banding missing, minor age cracks, veneer damage, 67" w, 27-1/2" d, 42-3/4" h 4,850.00

Maryland, mahogany, rectangular top, one long drawer, four sq tapered legs, bellflowers, spiral ovals, line, and band inlay, areas of inlay missing, replaced brasses, 39" w, 19" d, 32-1/2" h..12,100.00

Maryland, mahogany, serpentine front, oval band and rectangular panel inlay, pair of cupboard doors, central drawer over two smaller cupboard doors, six sq tapered legs with banded cuffs, refinished, 71-1/2" w, 22-1/2" d, 39-1/2" h..24,200.00

New York, mahogany and figured mahogany veneer with inlay, serpentine case, five dovetailed drawers, double doors, stringing and banding with husk and bookend inlay on tapered legs, diamond escutcheons, old brasses, minor veneer repairs, drawers lined with green felt, 71" w, 30-1/4" d, 40-1/4" h..............................12,650.00

Hepplewhite-Style

These examples show other names for sideboards. "Demilune" refers to a gently bowed top. A Hunt Board refers to another important function of a sideboard, especially in Southern society.

Demilune, satinwood and inlaid mahogany, shaped top, conforming frieze, sq tapering legs with bellflower inlay, 68" w, 19-1/4" d, 33-1/2" h..800.00

Hunt Board, Southern, hand made, poplar, ash, and birch, brownish stain repaint, two nailed drawers, applied beading, molded top edge, high sq tapering legs, 49-3/4" w, 21-1/2" d, 48-3/4" h..600.00

Landstrom, bow front, mahogany, shaped top, two graduated drawers flanked by cupboard doors, one sq tapering legs, spade feet, 72" w, 23" d, 37-1/4" h..........................2,000.00

Modernism Era

Modernism Era designers also included a sideboard in their dining room suites. During this period, look for shaped woods as well as the use of metals and plastics.

Nakashima, George, New Hope, PA, c1960, walnut, rectangular angular top, three sliding doors, interior fitted with two compartments flanking four central drawers, right hand compartment drilled for stereo, 75" w, 24" d, 30-1/2" h...6,900.00

Unknown Designer, 1940s custom made, orig finish

Chinese red lacquer, two doors, brass trim, Lucite handle, 60" w, 21" d, 37" h........2,200.00

White lacquer, two doors, three drawers, brass, and Lucite hardware.............1,875.00

Wormley, Edward, manufactured by Dunbar

Light mahogany, central compartment flanked by two doors with ebony and walnut fronts, hinged corner doors, plinth base, brass "D" pulls and keys, orig "D" tag, 80" w, 18" d, 31" h.......................................1,800.00

Light mahogany, three drawers with four woven front sliding doors, interior drawers and shelf, brass legs, some wear to finish, 82" w, 18" d, 36" h 1,800.00

Wright, Frank Lloyd, manufactured by Henredon, mahogany, one cabinet, eight drawers, Greek Key rim, 66" w, 20" d, 35" h 3,000.00

Sheraton

Sheraton sideboards tend to be more rectangular in form than Federal sideboards. The time frames are quite similar with Sheraton dating to about 1790 to about 1810. Remember that the name of this style was derived from the designs used by Thomas Sheraton, a famous English furniture designer. Therefore, the sideboards included in this style have a more English flare to them. Look for some inlay, use of fine woods, as well as innovative closures such as tambour doors. Some the following examples appear to be late for this period, but it's important to remember that the design styles often overlapped. Sheraton's influence was felt for many years.

America, first quarter 19th C, mahogany, bowed crossbanded top, central drawer and tambour door flanked by satinwood line and fan inlaid cupboards, sq tapering legs, spade feet, 63" w, 24" d, 35" h........................6,500.00

Country, curly maple, scalloped edge gallery top, five dovetailed drawers with applied beading, two paneled doors, turned and reeded pilasters, turned feet, poplar secondary wood, replaced wood pull handles, 48" w, 20-3/4" d, 43" h..5,750.00

Country, walnut and curly maple, beaded edge top, four dovetailed drawers, scalloped aprons, turned legs, line inlay around apron and drawer fronts, old varnish finish, replaced glass pulls, wear and edge damage, one heart inlay missing, large water stain on top, 69-1/2" w, 21-1/2" d, 43-1/2" h..5,500.00

Georgia, c1820, walnut, two board top, three drawers, central raised panel door flanked by two large drawers, six sq tapered legs, yellow pine secondary wood, 48-1/2" w, 20" d, 43" h..7,500.00

Kentucky, c1820, walnut, two board top, three center drawers flanked by one drawer over pair of cupboard doors, scalloped skirt, orig paper label in drawer reads "Will R. Lake, Georgetown, KY," yellow pine secondary wood, 59-1/2" w, 21" d, 36-1/2" h 4,950.00

Kentucky, c1830, cherry, three drawers over four doors, turned feet, orig pulls, poplar secondary wood, refinished, 73" w, 20-1/2" d, 45" h..3,500.00

Southern, c1800-20, butler's, figured walnut veneer, single board top over central pull out fitted desk with fold down writing surface over arched apron flanked on either side by shallow drawer over deep drawer, six turned cylindrical tapering legs, brass rosette pulls, some veneer chipping, 74-3/4" w, 22-3/4" d, 38-3/4" h 3,360.00

Victorian

Sideboards of the Victorian era illustrate how designers of that time felt bigger was better, higher was even better. And, the usage of marble tops, mirrors, carving, and other types of ornamentation were popular. Woods and finishes tend to be dark, adding to the heavy appearance of these sideboards.

America, late 19th C, carved walnut, upper section with floral carved top over beveled mirror flanked by single door cabinets, lower section with marble top, five fitted drawers, flanked by two doors, 48" w, 23" d, 84" h 2,995.00

English, third quarter 19th C, carved mahogany, reverse breakfront, rectangular angular top with rounded corners, recessed serpentine central section, arched and molded back board, carved with scrolling foliate and flower heads, center pierced rocaille, conforming frieze drawer flanked on each side by pedestal, each with paneled door, shaped panel carved with fruit swag, opening to drawer and shelf, outset molded plinth, 90-1/4" w, 29-1/2" d, 65-4/5" h..2,000.00

Eastlake, rosewood, inlaid ebony door, ebonized and gilded moldings, incised carved leaf decorations enhanced with gold, 51-3/4" w, 22-3/4" d, 60" h 4,000.00

Gothic Revival

America, c1840, mahogany, carved scrolled gallery top, two lotus molded drawers, two cupboard doors, twist reeded columns, paw feet, 51-1/2" w, 23" d, 52-1/4" h 3,375.00

New York, Kimbel & Cabus, c1875, design No. 377, walnut, galleried top over two cupboard doors over open self over slant front over central drawer over open well flanked by two cupboard doors, galleried base shelf, bracket feet, 39-1/4" w, 17-3/4" d, 73" h 9,775.00

Renaissance Revival, America, third quarter 19th C

Cherry, curled mahogany drawer fronts, burled arched panel doors..................900.00

Mahogany, shaped rectangular top, three aligned drawers, two cabinet doors, heavily carved acanthus leaves and shell form dec, 46" w, 27" d, 99" h 3,500.00

Walnut, burl walnut, marquetry, and gilt incised, shaped backsplash with oval marquetry panel, shaped case with drawer over door enclosing shelf, molded base, turned feet, 49-1/2" w, 19" d, 57" h 4,025.00

Walnut, upper section with carved scroll and fruit decoration over mirrored back, lower section with marble top, three fitted drawers, double doors, carved fruit pulls, 60" w, 21" d, 54" h 4,200.00

Walnut, marquetry, and parcel gilt, shaped top with removable statuary stand, cabinet door with floral marquetry, plinth base with shaped feet, minor damage, 50-1/4" w, 22" d, 51-3/4" h 3,750.00

Sofas and Settees

Sofas, settees, love seats, couches and settles all offered seating. Settees and love seats are the smallest of this group. Sofas and couches are longer and often more generous in the seat. Settles are often considered benches since they lack upholstery. Some settees and sofas were originally part of parlor groups and may include matching arm chairs, rockers, straight chairs in numerous multiples. Early settees and sofas were often included in the inventories of old estates and frequently were listed as part of the bed chamber furnishings. Why? Because during early periods, it was fashionable for the lady of the house to receive some special guests in her bed chamber and small scale entertaining, such as tea, was often done in these rooms. Other sofas were listed as part of the hall furnishings, particularly when the hall was large or the person living there was important enough to receive many callers. Sofas are rarely found in inventories before 1820 as the form was not popular to after that time. Also see Benches.

Parlor Suites

Art Nouveau: *Art Nouveau parlor furniture carried the theme of nature and scrolls to the designs and often the fabrics used for upholstery.*

America, c1904-10, mahogany and birch, settee and side chair, each labeled "Karpen Guaranteed Upholstered Furniture Chicago-New York," foliate carved crests, center maiden's head, 53" l, 26" d, 40-1/2" h settee, 23" l, 23" d, 40-3/4" h chair 3,000.00

Empire-Style: *This interesting parlor suite was made in the early part of the 20th century, and includes elements relating to the popular Egyptian revival. Elements giving it the Empire name include the foliate carved crests and the paw feet.*

America, early 20th C, carved walnut, settee and two fauteuils, all with padded backs surmounted by foliate carved crest, arms supported by carved sphinx heads, square legs ending in paw feet, 37" h fauteuils, 67" l, 22" d, 38" h settee 3,550.00

Victorian: *Most of the existing parlor suites from the late 1880s were made during the Victorian era. Parlors at that time period were areas where one's culture and wealth was displayed and an extensive parlor suite was certainly a way to accomplish this.*

Renaissance Revival

America, c1880, carved walnut, five pieces, settee and four side chairs, settee with three button-back chair backs with architectural frames surmounted by leaf carved crests, out-curved arms with padded elbow rests, reverse serpentine front, over-stuffed seat raised on turned tapering legs with casters, incised decoration and burr-wood panels throughout, 61" l sofa 1,995.00

America, c1880, carved walnut, two pieces, sofa and side chair, sofa with padded and slightly arched rectangular back flanked by architectural posts suspending carved tassels, padded over-scroll arms, over-stuffed reverse-serpentine fronted seat, shaped conforming rails raised on turned tapering legs, mounted throughout with rosettes and burr-wood panels, 62" l sofa 1,200.00

Rococo Revival, John Henry Belter, NY, c1860, laminated and carved rosewood, Rosalie pattern, undulating cresting with flowers, leaves, and trailing fruit and vines, serpentine seat rail similarly carved, molded cabriole supports, blue silk upholstery, 73-1/2" l 5,175.00

Settees

Art Deco: *Art Deco settees were designed for intimate conversation. Look for sleek lines and the introduction of metal frames.*

America, attributed to Warren McArthur, c1930, tubular aluminum frame, sheet aluminum seat and back supports, removable vinyl cushions, 68" l 5,750.00

Centennial: *Centennial furniture makers were accustomed to the idea of settees, but few historical examples existed, so they developed the form based on their own interpretations.*

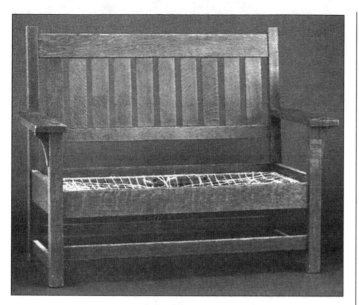

Arts & Crafts, settee, Gustav Stickley, New York, slatted back and corbels under lower arms, unmarked, bottom of legs shaved, new dark finish, 47-1/2" l, 23-3/4" d, 38-1/4" h, $1,100. Photo courtesy of David Rago Auctions/ RagoArts.com, Lambertville, NJ.

Chippendale-style, c1880-1915, mahogany, carved triple chair back, ornately carved crest rail and slats, upholstered seat, scrolled arms, claw and ball feet 1,100.00

Classical: *By the Classical period, settees were a popular form. Look for scrolling forms, such as shaped arms, serpentine front rails, curved legs. Exposed wood frames usually are mahogany.*

America, c1850, mahogany, serpentine front, carved crest, transitional rococo design elements, 82" l 600.00

America, 19th C, mahogany, scroll arm, turned top rail terminating in acanthus carved scrolls, fruit and foliate carved paw feet, 75" l, 26" d, 32-1/2" h 2,200.00

Massachusetts, Boston, 1820-30, mahogany veneer, rolled crest above arms with down-turned terminals, scrolled arm supports, three turned tapering legs, refinished, de-upholstered, minor imperfections, 89-1/4" l, 21" d, 19" h seat, 35" h....................................500.00

New York, c1820, mahogany, cornucopia carved crest rail interrupted by crotch mahogany veneered central rail, cornucopia carved arms, comma shaped arm supports, crotch mahogany veneered front rails, cornucopia carved legs ending in claw feet, spool turned rear legs, orig finish, striped beige upholstery, 92-1/4" l, 23-1/2" d, 39-1/4" h..............2,240.00

Colonial Revival: *Another example of furniture makers taking a style and adapting it to a furniture form rarely found in that historical period. This type of furniture was valued by interior decorators of the day for those clients who wanted that "early American look."*

William and Mary style, America, c1930, loose cushions, turned baluster legs and stretcher, 48" l 750.00

Empire: *The furniture designers of the Empire era created settees again with intimate conversations in mind, as they seated only two people. Adding to the allure of the form, many designated them as "canapés" in their catalogs. The usage of this French term helped to convey one's sophistication.*

America, first quarter 19th C, carved mahogany, padded rectangular back with over-scroll crest rail and downswept ends, over stuffed seat with rope-carved rails continuing into acanthus-capped lyre-form over-scroll padded arms, winged lion-law feet, 63-1/2" h 750.00

America, late 19th/early 20th C, mahogany and parcel-gilt, curved and padded back, reeded frame continuing into arms with swan-form supports, overstuffed seat, sabre legs 400.00

America, late 19th/early 20th C, mahogany, curved backs, each armrest ending on ram's head, hoof-foot feet.............................2,100.00

Federal: *Not many settees date to this era, but those that do show a more gentle use of curves than their earlier Chippendale predecessors.*

America, c1790-1815, mahogany, shaped crest rail, over triple shield back, pierced splats, over-upholstered seat, molded sq tapering legs, pink and beige floral silk upholstery, 52" l 950.00

Massachusetts, North Shore, c1800-15, inlaid mahogany, gently arched upholstered back, flanked by molded sloping arms, reeded baluster turned supports, bowed upholstered seat, turned and reeded tapering legs, headed by inlaid rectangular panels outlined with patterned stringing, old break and repair to one leg, 71" l, 26" d, 34-1/2" h 17,500.00

Pennsylvania, Lehigh County, c1820, mustard painted and polychrome dec, shaped tripartite crest on turned supports centering pierced baluster-form splats, downswept scrolling arms, plank seat, ring-turned tapering legs joined by stretchers, decorated in yellow, red, green, and white and black highlights, fruit and flowers on ochre ground, 76" l 1,400.00

French Restauration: *As the name implies, this furniture style takes its influence from French furniture. Look for scrolling elements and use of dark, expensive woods.*

New York, c1835-40, carved mahogany, scrolling back extends to form arms, orig upholstery removed.............................1,500.00

New York City, c1840, rosewood, arched upholstered back, scrolled arms outlined in satinwood terminating in volutes, rectangular seat frame with similar inlay, bracket feet, 80" l, 27" d, 33-1/2" h...1,200.00

Sheraton: *Sheraton cabinet makers took the Federal style and returned it to a boxier back. The upholstered squared backs and seats usually featured upholstered arms and detached arm supports which usually continued to form the legs.*

America, c1835, pine, half spindle back, flat crest rail, turned legs and stretchers, 72" l 400.00

America, inlaid mahogany, open arms with fluted posts, seat rail with swag design inlay, ivory colored upholstered back, sides, and seat, fluted tapering front legs, turned feet, 51" l 1,750.00

America, mahogany frame, turned arm posts and legs, beaded frame, worn old slate blue silk damask upholstery, repairs to frame, 72" l 1,400.00

America, repainted white, black, red, and gold decoration, shell and vintage decorated crest, scrolled arms, turned arm supports, pierced rail back, balloon shaped rush seat, turned legs, outward curved feet, 50" l 1,400.00

Victorian: *Victorians loved their love seats and settees. These small scale sofas offered seating for just two people, but it was done in elegance and with comfort. Look for padding and comfortable seats.*

America, carved rosewood, c1870, shaped and padded back, two arched end sections joined by dipped section, each with pierced foliate crest, over upholstered serpentine front seat, flanked by scroll arms, conforming rail continue to cabriole legs, frame leaf carved 850.00

America, carved walnut, foliate carved arched crest rail, incurving sides, short carved arms, short cabriole legs, wooden casters, blue upholstery, wear, 64-1/2" l, 31" d, 41-1/8" h 300.00

America, wrought and cast brass, lion finials on back posts, red and gold brocade seat cushions and upholstered back, 48-1/2" l...825.00

Gothic Revival, America, c1850, carved walnut, shaped crest rail surmounted by center carved finial, stiles with arched recessed panel and similarly carved finials, upholstered back and seat, open arms with padded armrests and scrolled handholds, carved seat rail, ring turned legs, ball feet, 67-1/2" l, 23-1/2" d, 49-3/4" h...800.00

Renaissance Revival, America, c1875, carved walnut, triple back, each having carved crest and ebonized plaque inlaid with musical instruments, red floral damask upholstery 1,200.00

Rococo Revival

Mahogany, late 19th C, molded pierced floral crest in Art Nouveau taste, reupholstered in wine tufted velvet, 58" l, 29" d, 44" h 1,200.00

Rosewood, laminated curved backs, Stanton Hall pattern, attributed to J. & J. Meeks, rose crest in scrolled foliage and vintage, tufted gold velvet brocade reupholstery, age cracks and some edge damage, 65-1/2" l..............5,500.00

Wicker: *Wicker settees were usually made en suite. Designed to be used in sun rooms and conservatories, they were often painted and cushioned with bright print fabrics.*

America, tightly woven rectangular back, inverted triangle-dec, tightly woven arms, rectangular seat with woven diamond herringbone pattern, continuous braided edging from crest to front legs, turned spindle apron, 43" l, 36" h 500.00

Sofas

Aesthetic Movement: *Aesthetic Movement sofas feature carving, as well as scrolled elements. They spanned the time from the late Victorian era to the more angular Art Deco and Arts & Crafts period.*

America, late 19th C, top rail centered by carved cartouche, flanked by finials, scrolled arm rests, half-scroll legs, casters, as found condition, 61" l, 23-1/2" d, 41" h 650.00

Art Nouveau: *Art Nouveau sofas often were included in parlor suites. However, during the years these suites often are divided up. This example is attributed to a well-known designer, which enhances its value.*

Carlo Bugatti, attributed to, 1900, ebonized wood, rectangular back, mechanical seat, slightly scrolling rectangular arms, parchment upholstery, painted swallows and leafy branches, hammered brass trim, four block form feet, 68-3/8" l 1,900.00

Arts & Crafts: *Arts & Crafts settees and sofas are generally boxy in appearance and include long, low, and feature slatted backrests. Many are designed with slats and/or corbels under the arm supports. The addition of leather seats helped to soften the seating.*

Harden Furniture Co., Syracuse, NY

Three slats under each rounded arm, twelve back slats, rounded crest rail, drop-in spring seat, through-tenon construction, wear to medium finish, orig paper label, 80" l, 27" d, 35" h 3,250.00

Four slats under lower, wavy arms, eleven vertical slats, straight crest rail, drop-in spring seat, through-tenon construction, orig dark finish, orig paper label, 54" l, 24" d, 38" h 3,800.00

Limbert, Charles P., Grand Rapids and Holland, MI

No. 939, oak, eleven back slats, corbels under arm, recovered orig drop-in cushion, branded, refinished, 75" l, 27" d, 40" h 800.00

No. 1657, arched top rail, fifteen back slats, three slats under each arm, seat missing, refinished, branded mark, 70" l, 27" d, 38" h 2,500.00

Drop arm, broad vertical slats, three sq cutouts on back, one sq cutout under each arm, alternating with plain and sq cutout slats on back, webbed seat, orig dark finish, branded mark, 68" l, 26" d, 40-1/2" h 4,750.00

McHugh, heavy ladder back form, double chair back, orig rush seat, Mackmurdo feet, fine orig finish, unsigned, 46" l, 25" d, 40" h 900.00

Stickley, Gustav, New York

No. 165, c1902-03, even arm, four tapering posts centering three sets of repeating slightly flared back slats, reupholstered, red decal, 60" l, 26" d, 40" h 12,000.00

No. 208, c1905, straight rail over nine back slats, carved seat frame, 79-3/4" l, 31-31-1/2" d, 28-3/4" h..10,000.00

Stickley, L. and J. G., Fayetteville, NY

Broad vertical back and side slats, cloud lift apron and sides, new dark brown leather seat cushion, orig dark finish, branded "The Work of L. and J. G. Stickley," 54-1/4" l, 24" d, 36" h 4,250.00

Lower open arms and thirteen back slats, drop-in spring cushion, skinned original finish, 53" l, 22-3/4" d, 36-1/4" h 1,350.00

No. 295, c1910, slanted head rest, headboard and footboard with four horizontal slats centered by single wider slat, webbed support on slanted headboard, spring cushion seat, Handcraft decal, 72-1/2" l, 28" d, 22" h 1,150.00

Oak, drop-arm form, twelve vertical slats to back and orig drop-in spring cushion, recovered in brown leather, refinished, unsigned, 65" l, 25" d, 36" h 1,800.00

Unknown Maker, America, 1916, No. 331, oak, drop arm, tapered posts, joining horizontal crest rail over twelve vertical back slats, flat arms over four vertical slats, cordovan colored simulated leather seat with storage box supported by new corner blocks, manufacturer's no. 331 mark, finish light medium brown, original darker, wear, 72" l, 30" d, 39-3/4" h.................................700.00

Centennial: *As with settees, the Centennial furniture makers called upon their design skills to create sofas that would blend with older styled furniture.*

Chippendale-Style

America, late 19th C, mahogany, shaped camel back, rolled arms, single cushion seat, chamfered legs, stretcher, gold damask upholstery, 77" l 900.00

America, late 19th C, mahogany, shaped back, rolled arms, yellow velvet upholstered seat, gadrooned apron, cabriole legs with carved knees, claw and ball feet, 62" l 1,500.00

Duncan Phyfe-Style, Centennial, mahogany, reeded lyre frame, carved crest with foliage, cornucopia, etc., reeded legs, paw feet, old finish, old reupholstery, 78" l, $1,430. Photo courtesy of Garth's Auctions, Inc., Delaware, OH.

Duncan Phyfe-Style, mahogany, reeded lyre frame, carved crest with foliage, cornucopia, etc., reeded legs, paw feet, old finish, old reupholstery, 78" l.................................1,430.00

Chesterfield: *A Chesterfield is best recognized for its rounded back and leather covering. This example is an American adaptation of the popular English style.*

America, 20th C, brown leather, minor damage, 68" l, 29" h....................................1,750.00

Chippendale: *Few examples of Chippendale sofas exist. However, expect to find a bowed back and rectangular seat. Feet tend to be carved and often include the claw-and-ball-type foot, so popular with this period.*

Country, step down back with step down arms, bowed front with large down filled cushions, eight molded carved legs, cup caster feet, reupholstered, 76" l, 32" d, 36" h 3,000.00

Maryland, Baltimore, c1810, mahogany, marquetry and inlay cornucopias, floral and fine patterns, 70" l, 29" d, 35" h...........4,200.00

Massachusetts, c1825, carved mahogany and mahogany veneer, carved palmette and scrolled ends, ogee molded frame, foliate carved ring-turned legs, casters, old finish, imperfections, backs added, price for pair, 66" l, 27" d, 26" h.............................2,400.00

New York, c1770, mahogany, camel back, shaped crest, outward scrolling arm supports and seat, sq molded legs, flat stretcher, 80" l 10,000.00

New York, c1820-25, mahogany, concave carved crest rail e ding in carved eagle heads,

upholstered back and seat, scroll arms extending into convex molded seat rail, carved and applied wing returns, lion's paw feet, 85" l, 37-1/2" h....................................8,500.00

Chippendale-Style: *These sofas are examples of how 20th century furniture designers are creating sofas to compliment Chippendale-styled furnishings. They used more up to date furniture construction techniques and fabrics.*

Camel back, worn olive upholstery with red flower design, 20th C reproduction, 80" l 2,255.00

Mahogany, arched back flanked by scrolled arms, sq molded legs, upholstered in ivory silk, 20th C reproduction, 78" l, 29" d, 35" h 250.00

Classical: *Classical sofas are long and gracious. Expect to find elaborate carving, and rich coverings.*

America, c1830, mahogany, carved cornucopias, acorns, oak leaves, and acanthus leaves, basket of flowers finial, refinished, gold brocade reupholstery, 83" l.......................1,850.00

America, c1840, box style, mahogany, upholstered arms, scroll feet, 65-1/4" l, 32" h 825.00

America, c1840, lyre form, mahogany, mahogany veneer, reeded crest, pineapple finials, carved acanthus leaves and flowers on arms, paw feet with applied and relief craved cornucopia returns, old finish, reupholstered in gold velvet, 77" l, 27" d, 35" h 1,450.00

America, first quarter 19th C, straight mahogany veneered crest rail, out scrolling molded arms, "J" feet, blue medallion and stripe upholstery, 86" l, 21-1/2" d, 30" h... 1,120.00

America, first quarter 19th C, undulating molded crest rail interrupted by mahogany veneered center, out scrolling molded arms, cornucopia carved claw feet, red upholstery, 87-1/2" l, 23" d, 36" h 1,575.00

America, late 19th C, mahogany, box type, scroll arms and legs, molded skirt, later green velvet upholstery, 82" l, 29" h, 33" h 1,500.00

Massachusetts, Boston, c1820, carved mahogany veneer, rolled brass trim outlines leafage carvings, punch work ground, red velvet upholstery, old refinish, minor imperfections, 84" l, 35" h 2,000.00

Middle Atlantic States, 1805-20, carved mahogany and bird's eye maple veneer, Grecian style, scrolled and reeded arm and foot, punctuated with brass rosettes, continuing to similar reeded seat rail with inlaid dies, reeded saber legs flanked by brass flowerettes, brass paw feet on castors, old surface, 75" l, 14-1/2" h seat, 35" h 3,680.00

New England, 1820-40, carved mahogany veneer, cylindrical crest ends, leaf carved volutes, upholstered seat and rolled veneer seat rail, leaf carved supports, carved paw feet, 92" l, 16-1/2" h seat, 34-3/4" h 1,650.00

New York, c1815-20, box style, carved mahogany and rosewood, carved eagle brackets, brass inlay, paw feet, cherry and pine secondary woods, slightly reduced, orig damaged brocade upholstery..............................2,400.00

New York, c1825-40, mahogany, straight cylindrical crest rail with scrolled arms, paw feet with wing brackets, red upholstery, minor losses to feet, repairs to crest rail, 63-1/2" l, 24-1/4" d, 36-3/4" h..2,645.00

Duncan Phyfe: *Mr. Phyfe was a well-known New York furniture maker who worked in the time frame of Sheraton furniture. He was greatly influenced by the English furniture designs of the day.*

New York, mahogany, crest with fluted panels and swag drapery with ribbons and tassels, reeded scrolled arms, turned and reeded arm posts and legs, old worn and faded upholstery, 60-1/4" l...12,650.00

Federal: *Few sofas date to this period, but when found, it is usually apparent that the cabinet maker was trying to soften the harsher Chippendale lines with more curves, and the use of tapered legs. A crest rail offered another area for decoration and shaping.*

America, late 18th C, figured mahogany frame, crest and scrolled arms with single inlay, scrolled legs, brass paw feet, repairs to frame and front legs, old finish, new silk brocade upholstery, 71-1/4" l.............................2,500.00

America, late 18th C, upholstered, curved arched back, molded arms descending into turned legs, square reeded tops, tucked red velvet upholstery, 80-1/2" l, 30" d, 37-1/4" h 2,465.00

Massachusetts, c1810-15, inlaid mahogany, slightly arched crest continuing to downward sloping sides and reeded arms, swelled vase and ring turned reeded posts on bird's eye maple and string inlaid panels, ring turned reeded tapering legs, joined by slightly bowed frame, old surface, imperfections, 78" l, 25" d, 37-1/2" h..8,625.00

Massachusetts, c1815, carved mahogany, minor imperfections, 77" l, 29" d, 35" h 2,000.00

Massachusetts, c1815, shaped reeded crest rail continuing to scrolled arms on vase and ring-turned posts, fluted panels, reeded paneled seat rail joining ring-turned reeded frontal legs, raked rear legs, 78" l, 32" d, 33" h 1,695.00

Massachusetts, Salem, 19th C, carving attributed to Samuel McIntire, acanthus and floral carved arms and crest with swag, arrows, floral medallions and punched background, turned arm posts, eight sq tapering legs, pale blue upholstery, minor small repairs, 76-1/2" l..................10,350.00

Massachusetts, 19th C, inlaid mahogany, arched veneered crest continues to reeded arm supports, bowed seat, frontal reeded and turned legs, real square raking legs, old refinish, restoration, 79" l, 15-1/2" h seat, 37" h 1,725.00

New England, c1815, reeded arm supports, gently bowed seat rail, sq tapering molded legs, upholstery removed, 79" w, 36-1/2" h......2,750.00

New Hampshire, c1815, carved mahogany, upholstered, straight crest continuing to shaped sides with carved arms on vase and ring reeded and swelled posts and cockbeaded panels, bowed seat rail, vase and ring-turned legs with cockbeaded rectangular inlaid dies, old finish, minor imperfections, 78" l, 24" d, 17" h seat, 34" h back 2,415.00

Pennsylvania, Philadelphia, c1815, carved mahogany, slightly arched crest, upholstered back flanked by leaf carved terminals, semi-exposed seat rail with flower head carved dies, reeded tapering legs, restoration to legs and crest, 74-1/2" l.....................................2,750.00

Hepplewhite Style: *Hepplewhite sofas generally are more curved in the back, giving an almost cabriole feel to the design.*

America, 19th C, mahogany, boldly banded inlay in two colors, lyre arms with brass rosettes, rounded edge stretchers, sq tapered

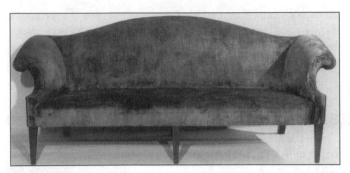

Hepplewhite, camel back, mahogany, upholstered, six legs, simple line inlay on three front legs, 84" l, 33" d, 37" h, $18,700. Photo courtesy of Richard Opfer Auctioneering, Inc., Timonium, MD.

legs, reupholstered in floral stripe brocade, 79" l 1,870.00

Modernism Era: *The designers of the Modernism Era have taken this seating form to new shapes, colors, and materials. Some designs are starting to command high prices, particularly when signed, well documented, or are still sporting the original fabrics and finishes.*

Frankl, Paul, manufactured by Directional, c1966, sculptural bronze exterior in abstract design, orig gray fabric, 60" l, 36" d, 24" h..850.00

Heywood Wakefield, three seat bentwood maple frame, cushions reupholstered in vintage fabric, refinish, 73" l, 33" d, 30" h 650.00

Kagan, Vladimir, 1950s, biomorphic cushions, reupholstered in linen fabric, solid walnut base, 96" l, 44" d, 29" h.....................15,000.00

Nelson, George, Marshmallow

Custom made for the ConEdison Building, New York City, 1958, extended version in orig Alexander Girard multicolored Naugahyde cushions, brushed steel and black metal frame, one cushion reupholstered, 104" l, 32" d, 29" h, one of two produced, sold by Treadway Gallery, Inc. Dec. 1998....................................66,000.00

Manufactured by Herman Miller, 1957, circular cushions in orig Alexander Girard striped red, purple, black, green, and gray fabric, black enameled and brushed steel frame, accompanied by orig sales receipt, some wear, 52" l, 32" d, 30" h 15,400.00

Manufactured by Herman Miller, 1957, circular cushions in orig Alexander Girard, sample version, made to illustrate range of Alexander Girard fabrics available, eighteen cushions each in a different fabric, satin

chrome and black enamel frame, 51" l, 32" d, 30" h 15,400.00

Nelson, George, manufactured by Herman Miller, Steel Frame, reupholstered seat and back, blue fabric, white laminate table, steel frame, 46" l, 30" d, 27" h 375.00

Saarinen, Eero, manufactured by Knoll International, c1948, Womb Settee, organically molded fiberglass shell, reupholstered in blue wool, chrome metal legs, 52" l, 34" d, 36" h......2,500.00

Unknown Designer, 1940s custom made, rectilinear upholstered form, orig blue lacquered wood base, needs to be reupholstered, 91" l, 32" d, 26" h 900.00

Wormley, Edward, manufactured by Dunbar, V-form, reupholstered in light blue ultra-suede, walnut base, 108" l, 48" d, 32" h 1,750.00

Modernism Era, Pop: *Pop designers have taken the ground-breaking work of the early era and interpreted the form into unusual shapes and styles.*

Harcourt, Geoffrey, manufactured by Artifort, c1973, Cleopatra, foam and metal frame, orig purple wool upholstery, casters, 74" l, 34" d, 26" d..3,500.00

Klaug, Ubald, distributed by Stendig, c1960, Terraza, two piece sculptural form, off-white leather, label, each section 60" l, 36" d, 27" h...1,900.00

Matta, manufactured by Knoll International, c1968, Malitte seating system, five piece stackable upholstered foam cushions, black and orange, wear to fabric, 62" l, 25" d, 61" h 2,000.00

Regency: *This period is a reflection of the English styles popular from c1812 to 1830.*

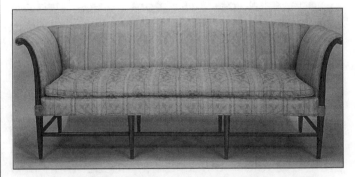

Hepplewhite-Style, mahogany, banded inlay in two colors, lyre arms with brass rosettes, square tapered legs, rounded edge stretchers, reupholstered in floral stripe brocade, 79" l, $1,870. Photo courtesy of Garth's Auctions, Inc., Delaware, OH.

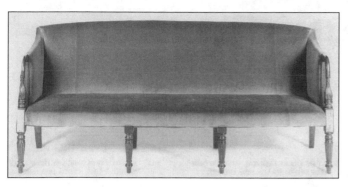

Sheraton, Massachusetts, c1810, mahogany, upholstered, slightly bowed crest rail, reeded arm supports with satin wood panels, straight apron front, four reeded tapering legs, peg feet, 76" l, $3,500. Photo courtesy of Samuel T. Freeman & Co., Philadelphia, PA.

These examples are included to show how this period was embarking on a new design.

America, mahogany reclining arms form chaise, black and white striped upholstery, carved, 58-1/2" l 1,700.00

Irish, c1820, carved mahogany, padded back and out-scrolled arms joined to cushioned seat, bulbous reeded feet ending in casters, 83" l, 31-1/2" d, 29" h 2,650.00

Victorian: *The Victorians took their sofas and stuffed the backs, seats, arms, and some even include padded rests for a weary head. When the wood frame was exposed, it generally was dark woods that were carved or enhanced as the Victorians loved to do. Expect to find coverings ranging from horsehair to velvets and brocades.*

America, c1890, camel back, reupholstered, turned legs, 60" l 750.00

America, mid-9th C, carved mahogany, shaped crest rail, arched pediment, acanthus carved arm supports, later velvet upholstery..1,200.00

America, third quarter 19th C, carved walnut, arched and padded back continuing into down-swept arms, serpentine-fronted over-stuffed seat with conforming rail continuing into cabriole legs, frame molded and leaf-carved throughout, 70-3/4" l.............................1,400.00

America, third quarter 19th C, carved walnut, tri-arched padded back with flower-carved crest rail, continuing into over-scroll padded arms with back-curved supports, serpentine fronted over-stuffed seat with conforming rails continuing to cabriole legs, frame molded throughout, 55-1/2" l, price for

pair 900.00

America, third quarter 19th C, simulated rosewood, back centered by button-upholstered oval panel surmounted by flower and cabochon crest, flanked on each side by curved oval similarly upholstered chairback continuing into over-scroll arms, serpentine fronted over-stuffed seat with shaped rails continuing into cabriole legs, fame molded throughout and carved with acanthus leaves, 65" l 750.00

Eastlake, c1870-80, walnut, two elaborately carved detailed back supports separated by shaped pillar, C-shaped arms, kidney shaped seat, peg feet with casters, re-upholstered, 67" l, 25" d, 43" h 750.00

Renaissance Revival, second half 19th C, carved walnut, padded rectangular back surmounted by anthems crest, flanked by baluster-turned posts, arms with elbow rests, bowfronted over-stuffed seat, turned legs with casters, frame paneled, mounted with bosses, 64-1/2" l..850.00

Rococo Revival, John B. Belter, carved rosewood, triple back, carved central rose and fruit on sides, scroll band underneath, carved segmented scroll, tufted back red silk upholstery, brass caster feet, old restoration to central crest, worn seat fabric, 62" l, 42" h 4,500.00

Victorian, c1875, carved mahogany, elaborate shell and floral carved shaped crest rail, seat back and arm rests covered in salmon velvet, floral carved shaped apron, leaf carved scroll feet terminating on casters, price for pair, one shown, 77" l, $2,100. Photo courtesy of Samuel T. Freeman & Co., Philadelphia, PA.

Stands

Most furniture styles include some kind of specialized stand. Often these are named to represent their function. Stands are found in almost all kinds of wood and some incorporate an interesting use of metal, leather, and marble.

Baker's Rack

A baker's rack or stand was originally a metal stand made to be used in a kitchen or bakery. It was designed to hold heavy pots, trays, and all the other types of utensils commonly found in a kitchen.

America, wrought iron, 48" w, 14-1/2" d, 84" h 500.00

Bird Cage Stand

Most bird cages are designed to be hung from a stand. This example shows how the Victorians adapted wicker for this purpose.

Wicker, painted white, tightly woven quarter moon shaped cage holder, wrapped pole standard, tightly woven conical base, 74" h 225.00

Book Stand

Book stands were popular in several different furniture periods. The idea was that an open book could be placed on the stand for reading. Many times heavy reference books, such as dictionaries, were placed on this kind of stand.

Arts & Crafts

Roycroft, East Aurora, NY, Little Journals, mahogany, two shelves fastened to side with keyed through-tenon s, orig finish, Roycroft metal tag, 26" w, 14" d, 26" h 900.00

Stickley, L. and J. G., slanted book shelf above four shelves, through-tenon construction at sides, sgd "The Work of L. & J. G. Stickley," orig finish, 28" w, 13" d, 36" h 7,250.00

Unknown Designer

Mahogany, double V-shaped trough over two wide shelves, five slats at sides,

Book, Arts & Crafts, Stickley Brothers, Grand Rapids, Michigan, oak, gallery top, three open shelves, three sided spindles, medium brown finish, branded "Stickley Bros. Co., 4708," refinished, wear, 26-3/4" w, 12" d, 38-1/2" h, $1,100. Photo courtesy of Skinner Auctioneers and Appraisers of Antiques and Fine Art Boston, and Bolton MA.

work orig finish, 22" w, 20" d, 30" h 500.00

Oak, in the style of Gustav Stickley, V-shaped top rail over lower shelf, through-tenon construction, refinished, 32" w, 10" d, 29" h 800.00

Victorian

Cast iron and oak, old worn bronze colored paint on iron, labeled "Thomas & Thomas," 36" h 330.00

Walnut veneer, end pieces set with pate-sur-pate plaques of cupids playing badminton, Bettemann's patent, sold by Shreve Crump and Low, 16" l 600.00

Chafing Dish Stand

Here is an example of a stand with a very specific use. It was designed as part of a dining room suite where it was probably a very useful piece of furniture.

Arts & Crafts, L. and J. G. Stickley, Fayetteville, NY, rectangular top, lower shelf with extended shelf supported by long corbels, orig finish, unsigned, minor wear to top, 18" w, 12" d, 28" h..2,900.00

Chamber Stands: See Wash Stands

Coffin Stands

Here is a type of stand that dates back to early furniture periods. Before the advent of funeral homes, wakes were held at the deceased's home. Stands such as these performed a sad, but useful purpose. Look for these to be sold as pairs or sets of four. Several years ago, some interior decorators had favored these for use as coffee table supports when putting a large sturdy piece of glass on top of the supports. This practice gave a new application to something that has certainly become outdated.

Folding, sawhorse type, turned legs, old black paint, price for pair, 21-3/4" h........150.00

Tripod, turned wooden legs and stretchers, old worn red and black paint, set of four, 39-3/4" h..250.00

Crock Stands

Crock stands are sturdy pieces of primitive Americana made to hold several crocks at a time. These working stands were usually painted. Today's collectors enjoy them to display not only crocks, but also plants and other small objects.

Folding, poplar, worn red paint, three shelves with decorative brackets, turned back legs, 41" w, 32" d, 49-1/2" h.................1,210.00

Primitive, five stepped shelves, old green repaint, late wire nail construction, 38" w, 30" d, 31" h..195.00

Primitive, weathered pine, green over paint, shaped ends, stepped shelves, square and round nail construction, added support blocks, 40" w, 11-1/4" d, 22" h............................325.00

Drink Stand

The Arts & Crafts period designers created a small stand with a top designed to hold a glass or small decanter. The shelf below could hold other bar-ware type articles.

Arts & Crafts, L. and J. G. Stickley, circular top and shelf, cross-stretchers, "Work of ..." decal, skinned orig finish, old stains, filled holes on top, 18" d, 29" h........................950.00

Dumbwaiter

A dumbwaiter is a stand designed to hold dishes or plates in a dining room setting.

Georgian, late, papier-mâché, c1825-1830, oval, mounted on later crimson-lacquered and parcel-gilt faux bamboo stand, chip at edge of gallery, 23-1/2" w, 29-3/4" h, 21-1/2" h..........1,800.00

Queen Anne-Style, walnut, three circular shelves, splayed legs, pad feet, 21" d, 39" h.. 300.00

Easel

American easels can be very plain and practical or scrolling and decorative as the two examples below. Plain easels have a relatively low dollar value in the antiques marketplace.

Aesthetic Movement, America, c1875-80, attributed to Kimbel and Cabus, NY, ebonized, damage to one foot, 70-1/2" l..............1,800.00

Victorian, Gothic style, America, c1872, oak, swiveling pierced stand, tracery-carved top rail, rotating on platform base, molded sq legs joined by stretchers, adjustable racks missing, stamped "1738," price for pair, 31" w, 87" h..5,500.00

Lamp or Light Stands

A lamp or light stand could be considered the later edition of candlestands. Its function was to hold a lighting source. Look for this type of stand primarily after kerosene and electricity was introduced. Also see Candlestands.

Arts & Crafts

Limbert, No. 260, rect top, lower shelf, four

drawers with hammered copper pulls, orig finish, paper label, minor buckling to veneer at side bottom, 17" w, 15-1/2" d, 36" h....2,900.00

Unsigned, c1916, circular top, four legs, lower cross stretcher with through tenons, 13" d, 30-1/8" h, top water damage and wood separation 990.00

Chippendale, eastern Massachusetts, 18th C, maple and oak, circular top, chamfered octagonal post and cross base, old natural color, imperfections, 13" d, 24-1/2" d........................ 1,955.00

Federal, New England, late 18th/early 19th C, painted cherry, circular top mounted on rectangular post, triangular chamfered platform, three splayed turned feet, old blue gray paint over earlier red wash, imperfections, 12-1/4" d, 24-3/4" h..1,150.00

Federal-Style, mahogany, molded rect top, two drawers, sq-section tapered legs, 18-1/4" w, 18" d, 28" h..800.00

Magazine Stands

Magazine stands were popular with English designers and are often called Canterburys. It was the Arts & Crafts period of American furniture making that really embraced this style of stand.

Magazine, Arts & Crafts, unknown designer, slatted sides and back, single drawer, three lower shelves, over-coated finish, 21" w, 14" d, 42-1/2", $700. Also shown is Van Briggle Pottery vessel, $2,400. Photo courtesy of David Rago Auctions/ RagoArts.com, Lambertville, NJ.

Arts & Crafts

Lakestand Craftshop, three vertical slots under back, containing five square cut-offs with arched and cut-out side, recent finish, unsigned, 14" w, 10" d, 38" h...........1,100.00

Limbert, Charles P., Grand Rapids and Holland, MI

No. 300, four shelves with canted sides, circular cutout with single vertical spindle, re-coated orig finish, branded mark, 20" w, 14" d, 37" h 1,200.00

No. 301, two shelves with one wide slat at sides, arched toe-board, orig finish, branded mark and numbered, 16" w, 10" d, 29" h 1,200.00

Michigan Chair Co., two cabinet doors with cross cut-out design over three open shelves, arched toe board, refinished, 20" w, 12" d, 44" h..700.00

Roycroft, East Aurora, NY

Slatted sides and back, apron, three shelves, orig dark finish, carved orb and cross mark, 32-1/2" w, 15-1/2" d, 38-1/2" h 7,500.00

Solid tapered sides, rounded top, three shelves, orig dark finish, carved orb and cross mark, 14" w, 12" d, 37-1/2" h....................................8,500.00

Stickley Brothers, Grand Rapids, MI

No. 4602, five shelves, slatted sides and back, orig finish, taped on Stickley Bros. paper label, 15-1/2" w, 12" d, 47" h...1,450.00

No. 4804, mahogany, four shelves, three slats at side and back, cutout gallery, orig finish, paper label, 20" w, 15" d, 36" h...4,500.00

Three shelves, slatted sides, skinned orig finish, metal tag, 16" w, 13" d, 31" h..900.00

Stickley, Gustav, New York

No. 72, designed by Harvey Ellis, overhanging rectangular top, arched apron, sides flanking three shelves, orig finish, Craftsman paper label, 21-1/2" w, 12-3/4" d, 41-3/4" h......................7,900.00

No. 79, four shelves, arched toe-board, slab sides with cutouts at top, through-tenon construction, light re-coat over orig finish, paper label, 14" w, 10" d, 40" h 1,750.00

No. 506, c1902, square beveled top, four shelves, arched rail and paneled sides, refinished, 16" w, 14" d, 39" h 4,400.00

No. 514, similar to, three shelves, leather and tack facing under inverted "V" top, paneled sides, orig dark finish, unsigned, 15" w, 14" d, 35" h 4,250.00

Stickley, L and J. G., Fayetteville, NY

No. 45, four shelves, arched toe-board, arched side-rails, cleaned orig finish, branded "The Work of L. and J. G. Stickley," 21" w, 12" d, 45" h 2,450.00

No. 46, four shelves, three slats to each side, arched toe board, lightly re-coated orig finish, Handcraft decal, 21" w, 12" d, 42" h..2,100.00

No. 345, gallery top, four shelves, chamfered back, skinned finish, Onodaga Shops oval label, 19" w, 12" d, 45-1/2" h 2,000.00

Arched apron, four shelves, tapered sides, top and bottom mortised through sides, orig finish, Handcraft decal, 18" w, 14-1/2" d, 42" h 2,375.00

Chamfered back, arched backsplash and stretchers, four shelves, orig light finish, Handcraft decal, 19" w, 12" w, 45" h 2,400.00

Slatted sides, four shelves, worn orig finish, Handcraft label, repairs, 21" w, 12" d, 42" h..2,000.00

Three vertical slats to each side, four shelves, orig finish, "The Work of L. and J. G. Stickley" decal, repairs, 21" w, 12" d, 42" h..1,950.00

Tobey Furniture Co., four shelves with replaced leather and tacks on facing, Tree of Life carving at each side, refinished, unsigned, 14" w, 14" d, 44" h...........1,200.00

Unknown Designer

Four shelves joined by cutout sides flaring to base, oak, c1916, sq top, stamped "1885D," 13" sq top, 42" h, stains, roughness 460.00

Four shelves, slab sides, through-tenon construction, cutout design at top, orig finish, 17" w, 13" d, 26" h 575.00

Single drawer, three lower shelves, slatted

sides and back, over-coated finish, 21" w, 14" d, 42-1/2" h...................................800.00

Three shelves, through-tenon construction, slab sides with heart shaped cutouts at top, refinished, 20" w, 13" d, 40" h..... 350.00

Tramp Art, hanging type, orig dark finish, brass tacks, 15" w 85.00

Music Stands

Music has played an important part in lives of people for generations. It was once quite stylish to give musicals in their homes and to do this properly an elegant music stand was needed to complement the rest of the decor of the music room.

Arts & Crafts, Stickley Brothers, Grand Rapids, MI, similar to Gustav Stickley No. 570, mahogany, four shelves, arched supports on sides, tapered legs, refinished, 20" w, 15" d, 39" h..2,200.00

Victorian

Gilt iron, openwork scrolled lyre work, two scrolling candelabra arms, adjustable column, scroll tripod feet, electrified, 54-1/2" h..275.00

Oak and mahogany, checkered line inlaid lip, tapered reeded standard, circular platform, four stylized animal legs, 19th C..1,700.00

Newspaper Stand

Since the Victorian's loved specialized forms of furniture and daily newspapers were also becoming part of every day life, it is only natural that a newspaper stand was developed during this period.

Victorian, carved walnut, relief carved urn and flower decoration, tripod base, carved lion's paw feet, 24" h 450.00

Night Stands

Night stands are stands found in bedrooms. Just as we use night stands today, these stands held clocks, lamps, and whatever else was needed close at hand during the night. The other function for night stands is found in a hallway, at the top of stairs, and then their primary function was to hold a candle or lamp. Because the usage is so general, it is often difficult to def-

initely identify a stand as a night stand.
Also see Side Stands and Tables.

Arts & Crafts

Stickley, Gustav, New York, c1912, sq top, single drawer, circular wooden pull, lower median shaft, branded mark, 16" w, 16" d, 28-1/2" h 575.00

Unknown Designer

Flush top, two short drawers over two full width drawers, sq faceted wooden pulls, open space above lower sq shelf, 18" sq top, 28-1/2" h 1,100.00

Rectangular top, one drawer over open space over small cabinet, sq faceted wooden pulls, tapered legs, new dark finish, repair to top, 17" w, 16" d, 29-3/4" h 850.00

Country, Pennsylvania, Soap Hollow, dated 1875, painted red-orange on cherry, overhanging top, single drawer, four ring-turned slightly swelled legs, drawer stenciled "1875" flanked by initials "RF," 21-3/4" w, 22" d, 29" h 2,000.00

Federal

America, c1800, bird's eye maple, rectangular top, single drawer frieze, round base pull handles, ring-turned tapered legs, 20-1/8" w, 14-3/4" d, 28" h 1,425.00

New England, c1810, tiger maple, rectangular top, sq tapered legs, old refinishing, imperfections, 18-1/2" w, 15" d, 23-1/4" h 1,465.00

Hepplewhite, attributed to Chillcothe, OH, walnut, two board top, one dovetailed overlapping drawer, scalloped apron, splayed base, sq tapering legs, refinished, top loose, 16-1/4" w, 17-1/4" d, 26-1/2" h 1,450.00

Modernism Era

Nelson, George, manufactured by Herman Miller, birch veneer, three compartments, pull-out shelves, price for pair, 17" w, 14" d, 40" h 1,200.00

Unknown Designer, 1940s, two drawers, side cutouts, orig blue lacquer, silver plate and brass hardware, price for pair, 24" w, 21" d, 26" h..........................800.00

Sheraton, early 19th C, mahogany, stepped rectangular top, open shelf, sq tapered legs, spade feet, 15" w, 12" d, 36" h 750.00

Victorian, Renaissance Revival, America, c1865-75, walnut, marble top over single drawer, cupboard door below, finished on all four sides, 21" w, 20-1/2" d, 29-1/2" h 500.00

Pedestal

A pedestal is an unusual stand that is more aptly described by its shape rather than its usage. It is easy to imagine a statue or bust resting on an elegant pedestal or perhaps a lovely plant. Whatever the usage, a pedestal tends to be a functional stand.

Aesthetic Movement, Kimbel & Cabus, New York, c1876, ebonized and parcel gilt, 41" h...1,200.00

Arts & Crafts

Limbert, Charles P., Grand Rapids and Holland, MI

No. 269, oak, sq top, tapered column, sq base, orig finish, branded signature, 12" w, 12" d, 35" h.........................1,200.00

Overhanging square top, full length corbels, four footed base, cleaned orig finish, branded mark, 16" sq, 36" h 2,800.00

Unmarked, style of Greene and Greene, circular top, four sided cut-out column, flaring base, refinished top, alligatored finish on base, 15-1/4" sq, 37-3/4" h, ...1,200.00

Biedermeier-Style, birchwood, circular white-fleck black marble top over narrow frieze raised on three pilasters dec with black banding joined by central shelf, concave plinth and pad feet, pr, 40-1/2" h............................. 800.00

Empire-Style, early 20th C, burl walnut, circular top supported by three scrolling supports headed by ebonized and gilt maiden's heads, ending in hoof feet on a tripartite base to ball feet, 11" d, 39" h..............375.00

Tramp Art, polychromed in green and black paint, squared top and base, elaborate decoration on square column, 12-1/2" w, 12-1/2" d, 25" h...995.00

Plant Stands

Plant stands were important decorative accessories in several furniture styles. Look for plant stands to have a plain top over a more ornate pedestal and usually are supported by sturdy legs as a base. Always look for signs of water

Plant, Arts & Crafts, Roycroft, paneled box, tapered posts, orig finish, carved orb and cross mark, 13-1/2" sq, 28-1/2" h, $4,250. Photo courtesy of David Rago Auctions/ RagoArts.com, Lambertville, NJ.

damage and dents or chips as this type of stand was easily tipped over.

Art Nouveau-Style, brass, oval onyx marble inert on top surrounded by alabaster flambeau finials, platform stretcher below, 19" w, 34" h 595.00

Arts & Crafts

Limbert, Charles P., Grand Rapids and Holland, MI

Ebon-oak line, overhanging top, four caned panels on each side, recent finish, branded signature, 14" w, 14" d, 34" h 2,100.00

Square top over arched apron, flaring legs, supported by floor stretchers, orig finish, branded signature, 12" sq, 17" h.........890.00

Paine Furniture Co., circular top with orig leatherette covering, sides tacked, pedestal base, four long corbels, four slender legs, orig dark finish, metal tag, 12-1/2" d, 31" h 650.00

Roycroft, East Aurora, NY, paneled box, tapered posts, orig finish, carved orb and cross mark, 13-1/2" sq, 28-1/2" h 4,500.00

Stickley Brothers, Grand Rapids, MI, square overhanging top, lower shelf, refinished top, orig finish on base, 18" sq, 32" h 995.00

Stickley, Gustav, New York

No. 9, Damascus, octagonal Grueby tile with green matte glaze, supported by eight angled legs, arched stretchers, refinished, unsigned, 18" w, 18" d, 21" h 22,000.00

Early form, splayed legs supported by flared and vertical keyed-tenon stretcher, notched rail, orig finish, early red decal, 14" w, 14" d, 26" h........................5,500.00

Unknown Designer

Faceted posts, inset copper drip-pan, single drawer, lower shelf, orig finish, few water stains, 12-1/4" sq, 30" h 300.00

Overhanging top above caned panel on each side, orig finish, 16" w, 1" d, 29" h 325.00

Square top over squared stem, refinished, 12" w, 42" h.. 450.00

Square top over tapered stem, corbelled pedestal base, refinished, 12" sq, 29" h..275.00

Classical, mahogany, octagonal top, carved standard, four splayed saber legs, price for pair, 48-1/4" h...495.00

Country

America, burl ash top, turned ash column,

Plant, Arts & Crafts, unknown designer, faceted posts, inset copper drip-pan, single drawer, lower shelf, orig finish, few water stains, 12-1/4" sq, 30" h, $250. Photo courtesy of David Rago Auctions/ RagoArts.com, Lambertville, NJ.

three cast iron branch legs, 10-1/2" d,
33-1/4" h 225.00
New England, last half 19th C, painted
pine, three demilune graduated shelves,
rectangular supports, chamfered legs on
casters, joined by stretchers, old green paint,
37" w, 18-1/2" d, 40" h 520.00
Fernery, wicker, painted white, tightly
woven, rect well, wrapped braced legs, X-form
stretcher, 25-1/2" w, 18-1/2" d, 32" h......300.00
Queen Anne-Style, carved mahogany, circular top, reeded acanthus carved pedestal, tripod base, 23" d, 40" h.............................200.00
Victorian
America, circular top, walnut and other
woods, arched supports, ball trim, middle
shelf conforming gallery on bottom shelf, old
dark worn finish, claw and ball feet, some
damage, 36-1/4" h 300.00
America, marble top, walnut base, three cutout legs, turned column, refinished, 12-1/2" d,
34-1/2" h 175.00
New York, c1875, attributed to George W.
Hunzinger, walnut, painted cream color, gilt
highlights, turned center column with large
round ball and teardrop pendant, four turned
legs extend from base of ball, turned rods
extend upward from each leg and terminate in
small circular disk stands, these rods are also,
supported by small turned rods extending from
center column, four smaller disks are supported
by angled rods, creating eight spaces for flower
pots, 37-1/4" w, 55-1/2" h 2,300.00

Sewing Stands

Sewing stands were designed to hold a lady's
sewing implements, some included a basket,
pin cushions, thread holders, etc. in their
design. Some furniture periods referred to
these diminutive stands are work stands, espe-
cially when they contain a storage area for a
sewing project that was being worked on daily.
Arts & Crafts, Roycroft, East Aurora, NY,
lift-top panels, two deep side storage areas,
flanking three small drawers, round wooden
pulls, carved orb and cross mark, refinished,
30" w, 16-1/2" d, 29" h.........................4,250.00
Classical
America, black lacquer and gilt Chinoise-

Sewing, Federal, New York, c1815-20, mahogany veneer, top
with molded veneered edge, two veneered drawers, spiral
carved legs, turned feet, casters, replaced brasses, old refinish, minor imperfections, 21" w, 16" d, 29-1/2" h, $1,840.
Photo courtesy of Skinner Auctioneers and Appraisers of
Antiques and Fine Art Boston and Bolton, MA.

rie decoration, case with pullout work bag, lift
lid, fitted tray, turned legs, paw feet, several
interior lids missing, 23-1/4" w, 16-1/2" d,
29-1/2" h 1,250.00
New England, c1820, cherry and mahog-
any veneer, rectangular top with outset corners, two drawers, opalescent glass pulls,
ring-turned columns extend to legs, refinished, minor imperfections, 18" w, 17-1/2" d,
29" h 1,200.00
Country
Painted floral motif, lift lid, octagonal, hoof-
type feet, 9-1/2" d, 23" h..................2,100.00
Primitive oak and mixed wood, tiered basket stand, lower shelf, swing handle, chip
carved "A. S. 1913," some slight discoloration, 11" w, 29-1/2" h...........................200.00
Federal
America, c1830, bird's eye maple, rectan-

gular top with mahogany inlay, two drawers, circular bras pull handles, ring-turned tapered legs, brass casters, 22-1/4" w, 15-1/2" d, 28" h 1,575.00

Massachusetts, c1790, bird's eye and tiger maple veneer, rect bird's eye veneered top outlined with mahogany veneer and half-round molding, two bird's eye maple veneered drawers with bone escutcheons, ring-turned tiger maple tapering legs, small turned ball feet, imperfections, veneer cracks and losses, 20-1/2" w, 16-3/4" d, 30-1/4" h 2,990.00

Massachusetts, North Shore, early 19th C, mahogany inlaid, figured mahogany veneered top, four turret corners topped by turned discs above colonettes flanking two cockbeaded drawers surmounting turned pedestal with four scrolled and curving legs, brass paw feet on casters, sun fading, minor repair, replaced brasses, 17-1/4" w, 19-1/2" d, 30-1/2" h 1,610.00

New York, 1815-20, mahogany veneer, molded veneered edge above two veneered drawers, spiral carved legs ending in turned feet, casters, replaced brass, old refinish, minor imperfections, 21" w, 16" d, 29-1/2" h 1,850.00

Federal-Style, inlaid mahogany, rectangular top over front with three graduated drawers, top drawer with fitted tray, flanked on each side by faceted box, each with conforming hinged lid, raised on turned tapered and reeded legs with ball feet, imperfections, 28-1/2" w, 14" d, 29" h...150.00

Sheraton

America, mid 19th C, bird's eye maple, rectangular top, single drawer frieze, brass lion's head mask ring pull handles, shaped terminal supports joined by shaped stretcher, flaring legs, brass paw casters, 20-1/2" w, 18-1/2" d, 29" h 1,575.00

Massachusetts, Boston, c1800, mahogany, serpentine front, two drawer, ring-turned brass pulls, flanked by spool-turned reeded tapering legs, diminutive brass casters, 17-1/4" w, 17-1/4" d, 29" h 2,650.00

Tramp Art, dark orig finish, well at top with handles on each side, large rectangular pin-

cushions on front and back, four molded legs, applied sawtooth trim, shelf at base, lid missing, 18-1/4" w, 13-1/4" d, 27" h 420.00

Victorian, c1870, burl walnut, lift lid, mirrored top end, bird's eye maple interior, single drawer, apron fitted with pullout yard basket, twin arched terminal supports, shaped stretcher, caster feet, 21-1/2" w, 15-1/2" d, 29-1/2" h..500.00

William IV, c1830, mahogany, top with folding drop leaves, two banded drawers, one compartmented, with pull-out green velvet storage compartment below, circular standard on concave base raised on scrolling toes, 17" w closed, 30" open, 19-1/4" d, 30" h 2,000.00

Shaving Stands

Shaving stands are clever inventions designed to hold the implements one needed for daily grooming tasks, including shaving. A mirror is an important part of this type of stand. Many stands were made to tilt to suit the comfort of the user. Also see Mirrors.

Classical

America, c1820, mahogany inlaid, Grecian pediment over tilting mirror flanked by circular columns with carved capitals, rectangular base with rounded corners, two over two line-inlaid drawers with orig drop brass bails, block feet, veneer missing in several places, 22-1/2" w, 12" d, 36-1/2" h...................400.00

New England, c1830, figured mahogany veneer, circular mirror in V-shaped support, two graduated circular tiers, over with double lift lids, columnar support on scrolling tripod legs, some veneer loss, repairs, 63" h 1,325.00

Federal, mahogany, two drawers, bracket feet, 18-3/4" w, 9-1/4" d, 19-1/2" h 325.00

Folding, shelf folds, mirror slides up and down, brass candle arms with later electric candles, orig casters, old finish, 14-3/4" d, 49-1/2" h..450.00

Queen Anne, mahogany, shaped molding to support wash bowl, turned wood soap bowl, two small triangular drawers, tripod feet 495.00

Sheraton, first quarter 19th C, mahogany, rectangular mirror rotates on turned supports with acorn finials, bow front with three drawers, glass knobs, turned bun fee, one foot missing, 22-3/4" w, 7-7/8" d, 22-1/2" h 460.00

Victorian

Mahogany, circular mirror, round surface with drawers, carved support, three leaf carved feet, 56" h 495.00

Walnut, canted rectangular top with molded edge, foliate carved crest and adjustable support, single tier with drawer, fluted standard supports bowl, tripod base, paw feet, 15" d, 62" h 600.00

Side Stands

The definition of a side stand is a small stand or table used for many purposes. Usually a side stand has a drawer and overhanging top. Also see Night Stands, Side Tables, and Work Tables.

Classical, French, early 20th C, square onyx top with cloisonné rim, four bronze columns, sq base, paw feet 3,220.00

Country, maple and pine, one board pine top, molded edge along bottom of deep apron, splayed legs with well executed ring turnings, age cracks in top, legs repegged, one foot chipped, 29-3/4" h 490.00

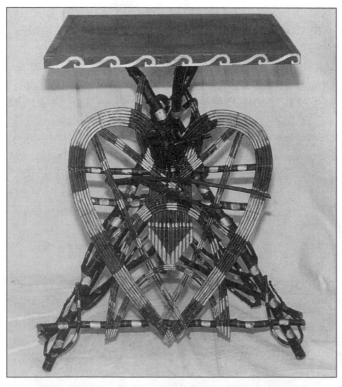

Side, Adirondack folk art twig style, square molded top, heart motif, $950.

Side, Chippendale, New England, c1780, cherry carved, rectangular overhanging top, four Marlborough molded legs joining beaded straight skirt with drawer, old finish, top warped, other imperfections, 14" w, 21-1/2" d, 27-1/2" h, $2,530. Photo courtesy of Skinner Auctioneers and Appraisers of Antiques and Fine Art Boston and Bolton, MA.

Decorated, poplar, worn orig red flame graining, one board top, single dovetailed drawer with chamfered edges, turned legs, some surface damage to top, 19-3/4" w, 20" d, 27" h 300.00

Empire, late, Pennsylvania, decorated, cherry, and poplar, orig red and black graining, one board top, single dovetailed drawer, turned legs, 22" w, 22-1/2" d, 30" h 4,400.00

Federal

Massachusetts, c1800, mahogany and cherry, overhanging serpentine top with canted corners, straight skirt with drawer joining four sq tapering legs, old brass pull, refinished, minor imperfections, 20-1/4" w, 15" d, 28-1/2" h................................2,100.00

Massachusetts, c1800, mahogany, square top with rounded edges, single drawer, straight skirt, four sq tapered legs, old refinishing, old brass, minor imperfections, 16" w, 16" d, 29" h.......................................1,150.00

Massachusetts, western, c1800, cherry inlaid, bow front, cockbeaded crossbanded single drawer with flanking wavy birch panels, refinished, replaced knob, minor imperfections, 17-3/4" w, 26-1/2" h...........2,750.00

New England, c1810, birch bird's eye maple, rectangular overhanging top, over drawer, straight skirt joining four square tapering legs, old red paint, imperfections, 20-1/2" w, 17" d, 28-1/4" h...............1,380.00

Pennsylvania, cherry, orig brown sponged vinegar graining, gold striping old brown over-varnish, two board top, two decal designs on single dovetailed drawer, turned legs, poplar secondary wood, porcelain pull, 22" w, 23-1/2" d, 30" h 2,200.00

Rhode Island, c1825, cherry, bird's eye maple, and mahogany veneer, rectangular overhanging top with applied beaded edge, drawer with bird's eye maple veneer and mahogany crossbanding, four vase and ring-turned legs continuing to tapering feet, old finish, imperfections, 20" w, 19" d, 27-3/4" h 690.00

Hepplewhite, country

Birch and chestnut, two board top, one dovetailed drawer with divided interior, square tapered legs, old varnish finish, top has been reattached, 21" w, 19" d, 28-1/2" h 525.00

Birch, one board top, one dovetailed drawer, sq tapered legs, old worn finish, age crack in top, replaced brass pull, 14-1/2" w, 15-1/2" d, 26" h 325.00

Cherry, one board top with ovolo corners, single dovetailed drawer with edge beading, square tapered legs, old refinishing, drawer interior with old yellow tinted varnish, poplar secondary wood, replaced brass pull, 17-1/2" w, 17-3/4" d, 27" h 1,100.00

Cherry, one board top with applied gallery, single dovetailed drawer, square tapering legs, old finish, orig brass ring handle and floral escutcheon, 24-1/2" w, 24-3/4" d, 28-1/4" h 2,975.00

Cherry, two board top, one dovetailed drawer, sq tapered legs, refinished, top replaced, drawer repaired, replaced brass, 17-3/4" w, 19-3/4" d, 27-1/2" h 300.00

Hardwood, one board top with cut ovolo corners, one dovetailed drawer, mortised and pinned apron, sq tapered legs, old dark worn finish, top reattached with old large head nails, 18" w, 18-1/2" d, 26" h 1,100.00

Poplar, orig red and black graining, yellow and green striping, gold stenciled floral design on dovetailed drawer, one board top, sq tapering legs, some wear, 17" w, 18-3/4" d, 28-1/5" h 4,320.00

Walnut, three board top, mortised and pinned apron, scalloping on four sides, sq

tapered legs, old worn refinishing, replaced top, 19-1/2" w, 19-1/2" d, 27-1/2" h 350.00

Sheraton, Country

Cherry and mahogany veneer, serpentine case, one board figured cherry top, two conforming dovetailed drawers with applied beading, turned legs, old finish, colorless glass lacy glass pulls, poplar secondary wood, age cracks on top, one drawer pull chipped, lock removed, some veneer damage, 20" w, 20-1/2" d, 28" h 1,100.00

Cherry, old black and red graining, one dovetailed drawer, turned legs, pine secondary wood, lock mortise pieced in wood, top old replacement, 18-1/2" w, 16-3/4" d, 28-1/4" h 300.00

Cherry, two board top, one dovetailed drawer, slender turned legs, refinished, edge damage and wear, 19-3/4" w, 19-3/4" d, 26-1/4" h 500.00

Mahogany and mahogany veneer, cast with rounded corners, two dovetailed drawers, rope carved legs, turned feet, pine and poplar secondary woods, refinished, replaced brass pulls, repairs to veneer, 19" w, 15-1/2" d, 26" h 495.00

Mahogany veneer, two dovetailed drawers, dragon edges Arnold top, molded edge drawers, orig glass knobs, some veneer chips, 21" w, 18" d, 29" h 600.00

Smoking Stands

Smoking stands were created to hold a smoker's accessories, and usually contained an ashtray. Some had compartments for tobacco or pipes and matches. The Adirondack style includes some cleverly made smoking stands which use small logs and unfinished pieces of wood. Because this style was quite popular a few years ago, many modern craftsmen have created their own versions. Look for signs of wear and usage when purchasing a vintage smoking stand. When the stand includes doors and more elaborate fittings, they are generally called a smoking cabinet. See Cabinets, Smoking.

Adirondack, circular top with fixed and carved smoking set, three legged base with pine pole construction, orig finish, ashtray missing, 9" d, 31" h 240.00

Art Deco, cork construction, chromed metal base, 14" d, 22" h 225.00

Tabourets

A tabouret is a small side stand that was popular with the Arts & Crafts period designers. This small stand could easily be moved from room to room and used as a side stand, small table, stool, or to hold a lamp or other accessories. As with other Arts & Crafts period furniture, a design identified as being made by a specific designer helps to increase the value. In addition any marks, brands, decals, or original labels or tags also held the price to rise. Finding a vintage tabouret with the original finish is also a plus and adds to the value.

Arts & Crafts

Brooks, similar to Limbert No. 259, octagonal top over splayed slat sides, rectangular cutouts, refinished, unsigned, 20" w, 20" d, 28" h 9,000.00

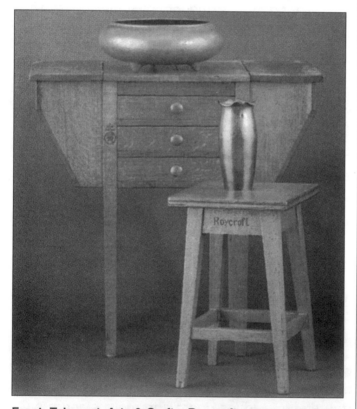

Front: Tabouret, Arts & Crafts, Roycroft, square top, flaring tapered legs, carved "Roycroft," refinished, 12" sq top, 18-1/2" h, $1,100; rear: Sewing Stand, Roycroft, lift-top panels over two deep side storage areas, flanking three small drawers with round wooden pulls, carved orb and cross mark, refinished, 30" w, 16-1/2" d, 29" h, $3,750. American art pottery also shown. Photo courtesy of David Rago Auctions/RagoArts.com, Lambertville, NJ.

Limbert, Charles P., Grand Rapids and Holland, MI, No. 251, octagonal top over splayed slab sides, rectangular cutouts, branded signature, refinished, minor damage to top, 17" w, 17" d, 24" h 2,000.00

Roycroft, East Aurora, NY

12" square, 18-1/2" h, square overhanging top, flaring tapered legs, refinished, carved "Roycroft" 1,400.00

15" square, 20-1/2" h, square overhanging top, four sided plank base, keyhole cut-outs, carved orb and cross mark, refinished 4,750.00

15-1/2" square, 21-1/2" h, square overhanging top, orig brown tacked-on leather, apron carved "Roycroft," flaring legs, refinished............................2,100.00

Stickley, Gustav, New York

Circular overhanging top, cloud-lift cross-stretchers, orig finished, branded "Ali Ik Kan," 15-3/4" d, 14" h.........1,000.00

No. 603, circular top, notched cross-stretchers, orig finish, branded mark, paper label, minor wear to top, 18" d, 20" h 1,100.00

Stickley, L. and J. G., Fayetteville, NY

No. 558, octagonal top, exposed leg joints, red and yellow decal, nick, some roughness, 17" h.............................400.00

No. 558, octagonal top, through -post legs over arched cross-stretchers, refinished, branded mark, 15" d, 17" h................ 995.00

No. 559, octagonal top, exposed leg joints, refinished with faux stain, 20" h 800.00

No. 560, cutout corner top, arched stretchers, orig finish, Handcraft decal, 16" w, 16" d, 18" h.............................1,540.00

Clip-corner, legs mortised through top, arched cross-stretchers, orig condition, branded mark, 15" sq, 17-1/2" h 950.00

Clip-corner overhanging top, arched stretchers, orig dark finish, Handcraft label, 16" sq, 18" h.......................1,650.00

Unknown Designer

Mahogany, circular top, lower shelf with cross-stretchers, refinished, 14" d, 18" h 375.00

Tabouret, Arts & Crafts, L. & J. G. Stickley, Fayetteville, NY, octagonal, arched cross-stretchers and legs mortised through top, orig finish, branded "The Work of L. & J. G. Stickley," minor water damage, reglued board, 18" sq, 20" h, $1,600. Photo courtesy of David Rago Auctions/ RagoArts.com, Lambertville, NJ.

Oak, octagonal top, four flared legs with cutout and exposed screw construction, refinished, 17" w, 17" d, 18" h 200.00

Trunk Stand

Today when we travel, we grab a suitcase or two and expect to find a place designated to hold our bags when we arrive at our hotel. Our ancestors were no different, but they often traveled with large trunks since their stays were of a longer duration.

Arts & Crafts, Limbert, Charles P., Grand Rapids and Holland, MI, rectangular top with six horizontal slats, orig finish, branded mark, 26" w, 16" d, 18" h 1,150.00

Umbrella Stands

A few furniture periods include wooden umbrella stands. Most umbrella stands were pottery, but a few of the Arts & Crafts designers included them in their designs. Because the Victorians

and later the followers of the Arts & Crafts movement wanted everything in a special place, umbrella stands were one way to accomplish this need for order. Also see Hall Furnishings.

Arts & Crafts

Lakeside Crafters, octagonal, wooden slats hinged with leather strapping, orig finish, replaced leather strapping, 10" d, 26" h 700.00

Stickley, Gustav, New York

No. 55, four tapered posts with divided top, drip-pan missing, refinished, unsigned, 20" w, 12" d, 34" h 275.00

Uncataloged version, twelve vertical even slats, exposed nailheads, orig finish, red decal, 28-1/2" h....................11,000.00

Victorian

America, shaped and carved crest, molded marble top, single drawer flanked by two circular openings, turned feet, 34" w, 13" d, 35" h 195.00

Gothic Revival, oak, rectangular grid top supported by four arched top columnar legs with recessed arch design, rectangular base with fitted metal tray, medium brown finish, some minor splitting, 34" w, 12-1/2" d, 29-1/2" h 525.00

Valet

This form of stand is used to hang a gentleman's clothes to assist him in dressing. It is form more often found in English furniture styles, but this example is American and is in deed based on an English style.

Regency-Style, mahogany, hanging form, two drawers, lower rack, spiral carved legs to cabriole end supports, pad feet, 19-1/2" w, 10" d, 48-1/2" h..275.00

Wash Stands

Wash stands are a larger stand found in a bedroom. The form was designed to hold a wash bowl and pitcher and the accompanying accessories, such as a soap dish, toothbrush holder, smaller pitcher, shaving mug, etc. A lower shelf might hold a chamber pot or large slop jar. Before the days of indoor plumbing wash stands were a necessity. Some include small vertical pieces on the back, known as backsplashes. Very elabo-

rate wash stands may have cutouts for the individual pieces and even towel bars on the sides. As the age of machine made furniture came into being, many wash stands were made to be one of the matching pieces in a bedroom suite. Earlier furniture styles had more of a simplistic design to this functional piece of furniture.

Arts & Crafts

Limbert, Charles P., Grand Rapids and Holland, MI, ash, orig copper top and back, towel rack, orig green finish, unsigned, from Old Faithful Inn, Yellowstone National Park, 43" w, 18" d, 42" h 7,125.00

Stickley, Gustav, New York, No. 626, two half drawers over two paneled doors, towel bar, red decal, orig wood knobs replaced with V pulls, refinished, 40" w, 21" d, 44" h 4,950.00

Chippendale, Middle Atlantic States, walnut, scalloped skirt under rectangular top, central drawer, shaped cross stretcher, 14" w, 30-1/2" h...475.00

Classical

America, c1850, mahogany, marble backsplash with shelf, shaped rectangular marble top, single long projecting drawers, two cupboard doors, shaped block feet, 33" l, 20" d, 38-1/2" h 450.00

Wash, Chippendale, walnut, shaped backsplash and sides, rectangular top with cutout for bowl, two drawers, scrolled self, turned legs, 37-1/2" w, 18-1/2" d, 36-1/2" h, $275.

America, first quarter 19th C, cherry and bird's eye maple, corner, molded convex top with scalloped backboard supporting small corner shelf, baluster turned supports, conforming under-tier with two small drawers flanked by central dummy drawer, ring and twist-turned legs, bun feet, 24-1/2" w, 18" d, 38-1/2" h 550.00

New England, 1825-35, mahogany veneer, scrolled supports, attached dressing glass over two small drawers above long drawer, four ring-turned tapering legs, restoration, 36-1/2" w, 19-1/4" d, 63-1/2" h..............................2,645.00

Vermont, attributed to, c1825, paint dec and gilt stenciled, scrolled splashboard above pierced top with bow front and sq corners, conforming skirt with two flanking small drawers painted black with gilt cornucopia and Greek key dec, scrolled sides joining medial drawers with vase and ring turned legs, orig lighter blue-green paint, apple green striped borders, 18-1/2" w, 15" d, 37-1/4" h 2,300.00

Country

Cherry, three board top, one dovetailed drawer, mahogany veneer, turned legs, top old replacement, 18" w, 19-3/4" h.......395.00

Corner, New England, early 19th C, mahogany and bird's eye veneer, shaped gallery, medial shelf with drawer, poplar secondary wood, refinished, minor repairs, 23" w, 16" d, 41" h 1,750.00

Decorated, Wythe County, Virginia, c1840, two board top and backsplash, red field, black squiggle decoration, single walnut drawer, four sq tapered walnut legs, similar paint decoration on lower shelf, poplar secondary wood, 21" w, 16" d, 34' h 625.00

Painted, second quarter 18th C, green foliate decoration, yellow ground, shaped backsplash over rectangular top, circular cutout, ring-turned cylindrical tapering legs joined by short stretcher, one drawer, 18" w, 16" d, 40" h 350.00

Pine, galleried top, hinged fall front door, simple cabriole legs, old brown repaint, 33" w, 19-1/2" d, 36" h..................................425.00

Federal

America, c1810-30, mahogany, corner, molded backsplash, veneered bowfront with three circular washbowl and implement cutouts, turned spindles atop shelf with one drawer, turned legs with cutout stretcher, ball and peg feet, 24" w, 16" d, 38" h 675.00

America, c1815, mixed woods, molded top edge, tapered legs, lower central drawer, 15" w, 28-1/2" h 250.00

Connecticut, c1800, cherry, square overhanging top with applied beaded edge above a straight skirt with cockbeaded and string inlaid drawer, joining square tapering string inlaid legs, refinished, minor imperfections, 19" w, 18-3/4" d, 28" h 1,380.00

Connecticut, c1800, mahogany, square top with circular molded opening surrounded by applied scrolled decorative element above four square supports continuing to beaded medial shelf with drawer and shaped cross stretchers, central molded platform, old finish, imperfections, 16" d, 15-3/4" d, 30-1/4" h 700.00

Maryland, attributed to Annapolis, mahogany, line inlaid top, central inlaid drawer, inscribed underneath, line inlaid straight slightly tapered legs with crossbanded cuffs, refinished, 15-1/2" w, 32" h 850.00

Massachusetts, c1800, mahogany and mahogany veneer inlaid, top with bowl cutout, small shelf on backsplash, single drawer, tambour door, sq tapered legs, old refinish, replaced brasses, minor imperfections, 18-1/2" w, 18-1/4" d, 41" h 1,595.00

Massachusetts, North Shore, c1815-25, carved mahogany, shaped splashboard, veneered cabinet door flanked by ovolu corners, carved columns of leaves and grapes on punchwork ground, ring turned tapering legs, brass casters, old replaced brasses, old refinish, minor restoration, 21-1/2" w, 16" d, 35-5/8" h 2,300.00

New England, c1815-25, mahogany, shaped splash-back flanking quarter round shelves, pierced top, turned supports joining valanced skirt and medial shelf with drawer, vase and ring-turned legs, old brass pull, refinished, 20-1/2" w, 16" d, 47" h 2,100.00

New York, c1820, mahogany and mahogany veneer, shaped gallery above rect top, four vase and ring-turned legs joined by medial shelf with two short drawers, brass pulls, refinished, 33-1/2" l, 16-3/4" d, 34" h 1,100.00

New York State, early 19th C, mahogany, replaced pulls, refinished, imperfections, 22" w, 17" d, 42" h.. 495.00

New England, early 19th C, painted and dec, dec splashboard above wash stand top with round cut-out for basin, medial shelf with drawer below, orig yellow paint with green and gold stenciling and striping, paint wear, imperfections, 18-1/4" h, 1" d, 39-1/4" h......... 350.00

New Hampshire, Portsmouth, c1800, mahogany inlaid, shaped splashboard with center quarter round shelf, pierced top with bow front, square string inlaid supports continue to outward flaring legs with patterned inlays, medial shelf, satinwood skirt, small center drawer with patterned inlaid lower edge, shaped stretchers with inlaid paterae, old finish, minor imperfections, 23" w, 16-1/2" d, 41" h................................5,750.00

Hepplewhite

America, c1820, corner, mahogany, fitted top with backsplash, shaped cross-stretcher, flared leg with pad feet, 23" w, 16" d, 43-1/2" h...975.00

Country, cherry, square overhanging top, one drawer, splayed fluted legs, X-stretcher, 18" w, 27-1/2" h 1,430.00

Massachusetts, Salem, corner, bow front, curly maple, dovetailed high crest with shelf, molded detail on bowed edge, top with cutouts for bowl and jars, mid shelf with one dovetailed drawer, trefoil bottom shelf, sq legs, outward curving feet, old finish, 21" w, 43-1/2" h..3,250.00

Shaker, Enfield, Connecticut, South Family, c1820-30, double ogee shaped sides flanking work surface, backsplash above two recessed paneled doors, each opening to two shelved interior, old light brown paint, short shelf and 4" backsplash later additions, surface imperfections, 38-1/2" w, 18" d, 45-1/2" h.........4,600.00

Sheraton

America, c1820, decorated pine, orig white paint, red and green striping, turned legs and posts, dovetailed drawer, crest with corner shelves, cutout for bowl, white porcelain knobs, 20-1/4" x 16-1/4" x 32-3/4" h...... 250.00

America, c1820-40, mahogany, rectangular top with two inch rim over one drawer, shaped shelf front, block and ring turned legs ending in peg feet, 22" w, 16-3/4" d, 30" h 525.00

America, c1825-40, mahogany, rectangular top with cutout for bowl and accessories, dovetailed gallery with two corner shelves, turned legs and posts, base shelf with single dovetailed drawer, old finish, pine secondary wood, age cracks in top, replaced brass pull, 19-1/2" w, 15-1/2" d, 32-1/4" h 350.00

America, early 19th C, mahogany, rectangular top with splashboard, scrolled front supports, baluster shaped turned rear supports, bottom shelf with fitted drawer, four turned legs, 22" w, 15-3/4" d, 36" h 650.00

America, early 19th C, painted and stenciled, two tiers, backsplash in yellow and brown stripes, fruit stenciling, 24" w, 36" h 450.00

America, early 19th C, pine, top with gallery and bowl cutout, one dovetailed drawer, turned supports and legs, old mellow refinishing, old replaced gallery, 17-3/4" w, 16-1/4" d, 30" h 425.00

Sheraton-Style, c1850, mahogany, hinged top lifting to compartment fitted for washing implements, front fitted with two false drawers above single drawer, sq feet, 19-1/4" w, 16" d, 30" h 1,100.00

Tramp Art, America, 19th C, five tiers, swivel mirror at top, four drawers, lift-top compartment, allover chip-carved raised panel dec, shaped mirror inserts, minor wear, 30-1/2" h 1,150.00

Victorian, Gothic Revival, late 19th C, walnut, marble top, incised carved blocked panels, splashboard, drop pulls, 31" w, 17" d, 37" h 650.00

What-Not Stand

Understanding and appreciating the Victorian's love of clutter, it's easy to understand why they liked small whimsical stands and shelves to hold their treasures.

Victorian, late 19th C

Painted black, single drawer, gilt classical designs and pin striping, turned legs, minor imperfections, 19"w, 17-3/4"d, 54" h 975.00

Walnut and rosewood, corner type, four

graduated serpentine shelves, twist turned supports, 26" w, 16" d, 45-1/2" h 275.00

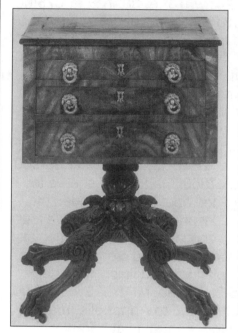

Sewing, Classical, c1820, mahogany, rectangular top over straight front fitted with writing desk drawer over two drawers, brass lion mask head ring pulls, acanthus carved standard, four acanthus carved legs, paw feet with casters, 23" d, 17" d, 32" h, $1,000. Photo courtesy of Samuel T. Freeman & Co., Philadelphia, PA.

Side (Stand), Federal, Pennsylvania, Pennsylvania German, c1790, pine, maple framed slate top, splayed block and spool turned legs, one deep drawer with carved "H.A" and "1790" on front, shaped apron on two sides, box stretcher, missing two stretcher boards, 39" x 33" top, 27-1/2" h, $2,465. Photo courtesy of Samuel T. Freeman & Co., Philadelphia, PA.

Stools

Stools are found in many future styles. Designed to be practical, many are found with painted finish. Expect to find signs of usage, as many stools have served generations of users.

Bar

When the advent of small entertaining bars in homes and "rec" rooms became all the vogue, it was time to also design bar stools to accompany this new form of furniture. Stools are usually high enough to allow the user to comfortably sit and converse with the bartender and others seated in the same area.

Adirondack, Old Hickory, rustic design, woven splint back and seat, pine pole frame, orig finish, price for pair, 16" w, 12" d, 9" h...600.00

Modernism Era
Alvar, designed for Artek, c1954, "X," each leg of five laminated ash pieces jointed at seat, leather upholstery, traces of orig label, price for pair, 18-1/2" w, 18" h...450.00

Weinburg, Fred, attributed to, c1955, metal and naugahyde, circular seats, two pink, one white, one gray, design raised on angular black rod base with circular foot rest, price for set of four, 31" h 1,100.00

Windsor, worn old reddish-brown finish, yellow striping, 33" h....................................770.00

Child's

Many children have enjoyed the privilege of their own stools that enabled them to reach objects that may have been too high. This example is unusual with its tree trunk base. Expect to pay $25 and upward for ordinary examples of 19th century children's stools and even less for 20th century examples.

Country, carved and painted wood, mushroom, tree trunk pedestal, tripod legs, 7-1/2" d, 9" h..375.00

Folding

A stool designed to be used as extra seating was crafted by the firm of L. and J. G. Stickley. This particular stool is known by its number. Other ordinary folding stools would be in the $25 range if found with upholstery in very good condition. Make sure all mechanical parts are functioning before trying to sit on one of these early forms.

Arts & Crafts, L. & J. G. Stickley, Fayetteville, NY, No. 399, recovered leather seat, signed, "The Work of L. & J. G. Stickley," 18" w, 16" d, 15" h...2,785.00

Foot

A place to rest one's weary feet causes these little stools to be very popular in many furniture periods. As the styles of furniture evolved, so did the decorations and finishes on stools.

Arts & Crafts
Roycroft, East Aurora, NY
Inset green vinyl seat, refinished, carved orb and cross mark, new seat, 17" l, 12" w, 14-1/2" h.............................900.00

New chocolate brown tacked-on leather top, tapered feet, carved orb and cross mark, 15" w, 9" d, 9-3/4" h 700.00

Foot, Country, pine, five-board construction, 17" l, 6-3/4" w, 9" h, $48.

Stickley Brothers, Grand Rapids, MI, smoker's, drawer, orig chocolate broth Japan leather seat, skinned finish, unmarked, 21" w, 13-1/2" d, 18" h.....................895.00

Stickley, Gustav, New York

No. 301, arched seat rail, orig worn leather and tacks, refinished, unsigned, 20" w, 16" d, 15" h..........................800.00

No. 302, c1906, leather top, short flaring feet, red decal and paper label, 12-1/4" d 450.00

Low form, replaced seat, orig finish, branded mark, 16" w, 12" d, 9" h 400.00

Oak, dark brown orig leather, flared sq feet, partial paper label, wear, older splintered wood, loss to one leg, 12" l, 12" w, 5" h..490.00

Stickley, L. and J. G., Fayetteville, NY

No. 391, rectangular form, orig leather, orig finish, Handcraft decal, 19" w, 14" d, 18" h..450.00

Rectangular form, new tacked-on leather top, arched apron, orig finish, unmarked, 19" w, 15" d, 16" h......1,400.00

Rectangular form, worn leather upholstered top, branded "L. & J. G. Stickley," 19-1/4" l, 16-1/4" d, 13-3/4" h..........550.00

Tobey Furniture Co., concave side over cross-stretcher base, replaced leather, refinished, 17" w, 17" d, 16" h.....................350.00

Unknown Designer

Leather covered top, splayed sides with teardrop cutouts, recovered top, refinished, 26" w, 17" d, 18" d.................425.00

Oak, rectangular top, sq legs joined with box stretcher, brown leather upholstery, nailhead trim, 20-1/4" w, 16-1/4" d, 15" h..775.00

Chippendale, c1790, mahogany, brass studded ochre leather top above double-hinged ratchet mechanism for adjusting height and angle, brass-bound sq legs joined by box stretcher, 25-1/2" w, 16" d, 14" h.........1,350.00

Chippendale-Style, carved mahogany, rectangular, padded drop-in seat with shaped rails, cabriole legs with claw and ball feet, carved shell work and acanthus foliage.............575.00

Classical

American, c1845, mahogany, acanthus carved bracket feet, pale blue velvet upholstery, 18" w, 15" d, 9-1/2" h.................175.00

America, early 18th C, mahogany, ogee molded frame, round legs, 17" w, 23" d, 10" h..125.00

Boston, c1835, mahogany and mahogany veneer, rect concave over-upholstered top, conforming veneered frame, scrolled legs terminating in applied bosses, joined by vase and ring turned stretcher, old refinish, 25" w, 17" d, 16" h.....................................1,380.00

New York, c1830-35, mahogany and mahogany veneer, rect concave top on conforming frame, Grecian cross legs joined by vase and ring turned stretcher, 19" w, 14-1/2" d, 17" h..750.00

Country, cherry, cutout feet mortised through top, orig finish, edge wear, 12-3/4" w, 7" d, 7-1/4" h..200.00

Decorated

Alligatored red, yellow, and green paint, gold and black stenciled buildings, flowers, and "E. H" on top, scalloped apron and legs, minor edge wear, two scalloped points missing on apron, 14" l, 6" w, 6-7/8" h 770.00

Cherry, inlaid stars on top, orig finish, alligatored surface, 11-3/4" w, 5-7/8" d, 5-3/4" h..495.00

Poplar, old worn brown paint, gold striping, splayed turned legs, old added dowel rod rungs, 13-3/4" l, 9" d, 9" h....................275.00

Splayed turned legs, rect top, old dark green paint, yellow and green, "F" and flowers, 7-1/2" x 13-1/2"..............................85.00

Empire

America, second quarter 19th C, mahogany, overstuffed tapestry top, serpentine sides, molded conforming rails, scrolled feet with castors 150.00

America, mid 19th C, mahogany, floral needlepoint work upholstery over cove-molded frame, ogee bracket feet, 22" w, 20" d, 18" h...475.00

Mission, Oak, rectangular, arched skirt, four vertical slats per side, 20-1/4" l, 14" d, 16" h 350.00

Queen Anne, America, mid 19th C, rosewood, needlepoint seat, cabriole legs, 17" w, 17" d, 14" h..450.00

Victorian

Mahogany, floral needlepoint upholstery, 17-1/2" h..............................125.00

Walnut, finger carved, green velvet upholstery..250.00

Windsor

Oval, splayed base, old dark green repaint, 14" l, 10" w, 10-3/4" h 250.00

Rectangular, old worn red and black grain painting, yellow striping, splayed base, turned legs, nailed repair to one end, 10-3/8" l, 9" w, 7-1/2" h..................................220.00

Garden

This interesting stool was made to be carried out to the garden for the user to sit on while accomplishing garden chores, such as weeding or planting.

Unknown designer, Japanese influence, octagonal top over eight curved sides, cutouts at center, orig finish, 11" w, 11" d, 17" h................200.00

Joint or Gout

One of the folk remedies to lessen the pain of swollen joints or gout was to elevate the aching limb. Small stools were called into service for this job.

Victorian, America, c1880, walnut, upholstered, rocking top, 19" l, 21" h 275.00

William and Mary, attributed to MA, early 18th C, rect molded overhanging top, four splayed block vase and ring turned legs, turned feet joined by molded skirt and stretcher, old refinish, minor imperfections, 24" w, 16" d, 23" h 8,050.00

Milking

Probably the second most common form of stool is the kind associated with a farmer or milkmaid sitting beside a cow, milking away. Most of these stools are identified by three legs. Common examples start in price about $25 and go upwards depending on the wood used, condition, and style.

Country, primitive, three legs, heart cutout handle, relief carving, old dark finish......275.00

Ottoman

Ottomans are recent additions to the world of furniture design. They are usually designed to accompany a lounging chair or perhaps a small sofa. Ottomans are usually big enough so that someone can comfortably seat on the top, or rest one's tired feet.

Modernism Era

Eames, Charles, manufactured by Herman Miller, black leather, rosewood plywood shell, 26" w, 21" d, 18" h....................450.00

Nelson, George, manufactured by Herman Miller, Coconut chair

Original black wool upholstery, chrome metal base, re-foamed, 23" w, 18" d, 10" h 2,200.00

Original blue naugahyde, chrome base, orig upholstery label, 24" w, 19" d, 16" h...5,225.00

Saarinen, Eero, manufactured by Knoll International, Grasshopper, upholstered seat, molded birch legs, unmarked, 24" w, 17" d, 16" h...750.00

Victorian, tufted rect seat, mahogany turned and tapered legs, 26" w, 19" d, 16-1/2" h...200.00

Piano and Organ

A common type of stool is the round variety used to provide seating for someone playing a piano or organ. The more ornate the stool, the higher the value is. Look for examples that have working mechanisms to raise and lower the top.

Classical, late, America, c1840, rosewood, columnar, swivel top..............................275.00

Victorian

America, circular, upholstered top, ebonized stem, three fancy metal legs.......200.00

America, mahogany, round upholstered swivel seat turned baluster standard, round base, scrolled feet, 20" h....................225.00

Seating

Another common type of stool is one that is used for seating. Some of these are primitive in nature, being made of materials at hand and often to fit into a specified location. Look for a broader top on a stool designed to be used for seating. Often these handy stools are put into use for standing on their sturdy tops to reach a little higher.

Seating, Sheraton, country, curly maple, oval bentwood seat frame, old rush seat, turned and tapered legs, turned ball feet, double front and back stretchers, old mellow finish, 15" w, 11-1/2" d, 16-1/4" h, $1,980. Photo courtesy of Garth's Auctions, Inc., Delaware, OH.

Country, primitive, Southern pine, mortised, central hand grip, partial paint, 19" w, 17" h 450.00

Modernism Era
　　Castiglioni, Achille, manufactured by Zanotta, Mezzadro, metal tractor set, one in black, one in orange, cantilevered chrome and wood base, imp marks, price for pair, 20" w, 22" d, 20" h 850.00
　　Eames, Charles, manufactured by Herman Miller, Time-Life, turned walnut form, concave seat, 13" d,15" h................1,450.00

　　Saarinen Eero, manufactured by Knoll International, circular upholstered seats, white enameled base, orig label, 15" d, 16" h 850.00
　　Wormley, Edward, manufactured by Dunbar, matched set of three, tufted cushion, bleached mahogany X-base, needs to be reupholstered, 24" sq, 16" h 2,200.00
Victorian
　　America, poplar and hardwood, one board round top, turned legs, red stain, 16" h 200.00
　　America, walnut, finger carved, green velvet upholstery 275.00
　　Massachusetts, L. Postauka & Co., Cambridgeport, adjustable, reupholstered seat, orig label, patent date April 4, 1871....385.00

Thebes

A Thebes stool is a romantic interpretation of stools found in ancient times. The two examples shown below show the difference in value between a stool in refinished condition and one in "as found" condition.

Aesthetic Movement, attributed to Liberty & Co., c1884, mahogany
　　Concave slatted seat over spindled seat rail, turned legs, refinished, 17" sq, 15" h.. 1,400.00
　　Square slatted top, turned legs joined by spindle supports, "as found condition," some scuffing, 17" w, 17" d, 14-1/2" h.......3,450.00

Vanity Stool

Like a piano stool, a small seat was designed to allow a lady to sit at her vanity table to apply make-up, etc.

Arts & Crafts, Gustav Stickley, New York, No. 301, orig rush seat, tapered legs, orig finish, branded signature, 20" w, 16" d, 18" h.....2,750.00

Tables

Tables are present in every furniture style. Because tables served a very useful purpose, they were treasured and frequently designed to serve a particular function. As furniture styles evolved and wealth increased, more and more of these specialized forms became fashionable. From humble beginnings, such as a table that turned into a chair by the fireplace, to the elaborately inlaid card tables of the 18th century to the eclectic coffee tables of the late 20th century, many examples can be found.

It was a simple table for the early settlers, one that functioned for food preparation and serving, as well as a gathering place in the early homes. During the Federal decorating style, it was popular to keep all furniture, including tables, pushed against the wall of a room, so that the room could be multi-functional. Many tables from this period, including card, game, and tea tables, are hinged to help fold them even more compactly. As decorating styles continued to evolve, more tables were introduced into the main part of a room, whether a dining room or living room. Tables to hold lamps, and even telephones became popular as those wonderful inventions invaded American's lifestyle and decorating themes.

To determine the age and style of a table, look carefully at all the elements, but pay close attention to the legs and feet. Often these are the easiest to identify. A rectangular top was popular in many of the design styles, but claw and ball feet are distinctly Chippendale. While brasses are more ornamental than functional on tables, it also gives clues as to age, if original to the table. Examination of construction techniques, nails, screws, etc. will often lead to more dating clues.

When purchasing an antique table, be sure to examine it carefully, checking for original parts, legs, leaves, and hardware. Often table legs are shortened over the years, sometimes leaves develop warps or may also be shortened.

Architect's Tables

This type of table was created for professional architectures and was not designed for use in a home setting. Today, collectors include them as they are interesting shapes and often made of fine woods.

Georgian, in the manner of Thomas Sheraton, c1820-25, inlaid mahogany, top surface marred, interior under lift-up drafting surface split, 43-1/4" w, 27" l closed, 27-3/4" h 1,760.00

Victorian, cast iron frame, oak drawing board, adjustments for height and tilt, pedestal with adjustable arm, oak shelf, cubbyhole, tripod feet, old worn cream-colored paint on base with red striping, old worn and stained varnish finish, 21" x 26" board 1,200.00

Breakfast Tables

Breakfast tables are typically small tables used to serve breakfast in either a bedroom or sitting room. They are found in most design periods that were present during the era of big households and full staffs. Later design periods often dropped this style when breakfasts were served in the kitchen, dining room, etc. Also see Drop-Leaf and Pembroke Tables.

Chippendale
New England, late 18th c, mahogany top with two drop leaves, single drawer in apron, sq legs, X-stretcher, old refinishing, repair to top, 29" w, 19-3/4" d, 28" h 750.00

Rhode Island, Newport, walnut, tilt square top with notched corners, scroll carved legs, tripod base with elongated claw and ball feet, old refinishing, top and hinge block old replacements, 34-1/2" top, 27" h 2,200.00

Classical
America, c1820, mahogany, rectangular top, two shaped drop-leaves, single molded edge drawer, four turned drops at each corner, foliate carved pedestal, four down curv-

Breakfast, Classical, New York, c1825, carved mahogany, rectangular top with two drop leaves with shaped corners, convex aprons flanked by rosewood panels with brass inlaid stringing and turned pendants, turned acanthus leaf-carved support, four acanthus leaf-carved legs ending in hairy paw feet, old refinish, minor imperfections, 24-3/4" w, 39-1/2" d, 29-1/4" h, $920. Photo courtesy of Skinner Auctioneers and Appraisers of Antiques and Fine Art Boston and Bolton, MA.

ing acanthus and lion paw carved legs, 38" l, 28" h 750.00

America, c1825, carved mahogany, circular tilt-top, molded segmented veneered top with crossbanded frieze, elaborately turned baluster form standard carved with bands of foliage, rectangular platform base with concave sides, cased corners, raised on winged lion-paw feet with casters, 43" d, 31" h 2,300.00

America, late 19th, mahogany, associated variegated circular rose marble top, acanthus carved pedestal with quadruped base ending in paw feet, 50" w, 50" d, 31" h 2,675.00

Massachusetts, c1820, carved mahogany and mahogany veneer, rectangular drop leaf top, straight skirt, two cockbeaded drawers, turned and spiral carved column, rectangular platform, four scrolled legs with brass rosettes, cast brass hairy paw feet, 18" w, 42" d closed, 28" h............................2,250.00

New York, c1815-25, carved mahogany and mahogany veneer, one working and one faux drawer, scalloped D-form leaves, outswept legs with leaf carving, old refinishing, 37-1/2" w, 25" d, 28-3/4" h...............4,450.00

New York, c1820, mahogany and mahogany veneer, 38-1/2' w, 47" d, 28" h 950.00

New York, c1825, carved mahogany, rectangular top with two drop-leaves with shaped corners, convex aprons flanked by rosewood panels with brass inlaid stringing and turned pendants, turned acanthus leaf carved support, four acanthus leaf carved legs ending in hairy paw feet, old refinish, minor imperfections, 24-3/4" w, 39-1/2" d, 29-1/4" h 920.00

Pennsylvania, Philadelphia, early 19th C, hinged top, skirt with drawer, carved pedestal base, carved paw feet, 48-3/4" w, 28" h 1,850.00

Federal

America, first quarter 19th C, mahogany, molded rectangular top with rounded front corners, single drop-leaf, baluster turned standard, quadruped base, reeded downswept legs, lion paw caps with casters, 54" l, 44-1/2" d, 28-1/2" h.............................850.00

Massachusetts, Boston, c1810, mahogany and satin wood inlaid, top with elliptical front half serpentine ends, dart inlaid edge, conforming skirt of satin wood panels with edge of crossbanding and geometric inlay, inlaid dies top of crossbanding and geometric inlay, inlaid dies top reeded tapering legs, swelled feet, old finish, minor imperfections, 36-1/2" w, 29" h 17,250.00

New England, c1800, cherry, serpentine shaped top, shaped skirts, flanked by sq tapering molded legs, refinished, imperfections, 17-1/2' w, 35" d, 27-1/2" h......1,450.00

New England, c1800, inlaid mahogany, single drawer, D-shaped leaves, sq tapered legs, old refinishing, minor imperfections, 21-1/4" w, 35" d, 29" h 1,950.00

New England, c1810, tiger maple, rectangular overhanging top, drop-leaves with ovolo corners, straight skirt joining four square tapering legs, old finish, 36-1/4" w, 18" d closed, 27-1/2" h 3,800.00

New England, early 19th C, cherry, serpentine leaves flank single drawer, refinished, replaced pull, repairs, 36" w, 19" d, extends to 57" l, 29" h.........................750.00

New England, early 19th C, maple and cherry inlaid, rectangular hinged top with ovolo corners, square tapering legs outlined in stringing, ending in triangular inlay, top with old surface, base with old refinish, surface imperfections, 36" w, 15" d, extends to 34-1/2", 49" h.....................................2,645.00

New York, attributed to Duncan Phyfe, c1820, carved mahogany, oval top with molded edge, D-shaped drop leaves, frieze drawer, opposing faux drawer, four leaf carved supports resting on fluted plinth, four leaf carved downswept legs, brass paw feet, 51" w extended, one leg repaired, 39" d, 28-1/2" h...2,450.00

New York, attributed to William Whitehead, New York City, c1792-1800, inlaid mahogany, line inlaid top with hinged leaves, stringing banding the edge above oval inlaid frieze, one with working and one with false drawer, square tapering inlaid legs which begin with twelve point paterae and continue with V-shaped and looped stringing in conjunction with three point bellflowers and terminate in cuff inlays, old surface, repaired brass pulls,

A closer view of the detail on the breakfast table.

minor imperfections, 31-1/8" w, 19-3/4" d closed, 40" d open, 28" h 118,000.00

New York, c1800, mahogany inlaid, mahogany top and leaves with stringing in outline, flanking square tapering legs topped by inlaid ovals with floral motifs above husk inlays with teardrops and ovals, ending in cuff inlays, old refinish, drawer with old brasses, one pieced leg, other imperfections, 21-1/2" w, 31-1/2" d, extends to 40", 29" h..........................7,475.00

South Carolina, Charleston, c1790-1800, mahogany and kingwood inlaid, top with large oval veneered central reserve banded in kingwood veneer and stringing, outlined with meandering inlaid vine with leaves and berries, skirt with one faux and one working drawer inlaid with flowerette at each corner, two others flanking central lozenge of stringing over front square tapering legs topped with twelve-point paterae above three-point husks which descent toward cuff inlays over brass casters, old refinish, missing or replaced brasses, veneer loss and imperfections, 31-1/4" w, 19-5/8" d, 10" d leaves, 28-12" h..............................266,500.00

Breakfast, Federal, New York, c1800, mahogany inlaid, mahogany top and leaves with stringing in outline, flanking square tapering legs topped by inlaid ovals with floral motifs above husk inlays with teardrops and ovals, ending in cuff inlays, old refinish, drawer with old brass, one pieced leg, other imperfections, 21-1/2" w, 31-1/2" d, extends to 40", 29" h, $7,475. Photo courtesy of Skinner Auctioneers and Appraisers of Antiques and Fine Art Boston and Bolton, MA.

Federal, late, America, c1800, mahogany, drop-leaf, rectangular top with rule-jointed leaves, square section tapering legs, 40-1/2" l, 39-1/4" w, 28-1/4" h...............................450.00

Georgian-Style, early 20th C, mahogany, round top with walnut banding, vasiform standard on four splayed reeded and acanthus carved legs, brass paws on casters, 63" d, 30" h.......................................950.00

Hepplewhite, walnut, drop-leaf, rectangular top, leaves with rounded corners, line inlaid frieze, sq tapering legs, 46-1/2" l, 27-1/2" h...........600.00

Sheraton, America, c1830, mahogany, rectangular top and drop-leaves, shaped corners, apron drawer, rope-carved legs, ball feet..............650.00

Card Tables

During the times when elegant entertaining often included playing card games, it was quite a necessity to have a beautiful table to serve this sole purpose. Many card tables have folding tops, often to facilitate placing them near the exterior walls, when that style of decorating was popular. As cabinet makers developed the form, more elaborate styles of tops evolved, leaving the plain rectangular version behind as D-shapes, ovolo corners, etc. became fashionable. Also see Games Tables.

Arts & Crafts, Gustav Stickley, New York, two side drawers with faceted wooden pulls, stretchers mortised through legs, keyed through-tenon center stretcher, orig finish, early red box decal, minor stains on top, 30" w, 18" d, 28-3/4" h 20,000.00

Chippendale

Massachusetts, c1750-80, inlaid cherry, rectangular top, fluted edge, undercut inner top with central inlaid stellate device, two paterae on frieze, sq molded legs, frontal brackets, side opening drawer, old surface, imperfections, 31-1/4" w, 29-1/4" h 6,750.00

Massachusetts, c1760-75, mahogany, hinged top with molded edge, straight beaded skirt, four Marlborough legs, orig surface, repairs, 33-1/2" w, 16" d, 29-1/4" h 1,265.00

Pennsylvania, Philadelphia, c1755-90, attributed to Thomas Afleck, mahogany, rectangular top with molded edge, apron with applied gadrooned molding, one overlapping dovetailed drawer, Marlborough legs with inside chamfer, orig brasses, refinished, pine and poplar secondary woods, minor damage to moldings on feet, gadrooning, and drawer overlap, pierced repair to leaf at hinges, 36" w, 17-3/4" d, 28-1/4" h...............6,550.00

Pennsylvania, Philadelphia, c1760-80, carved mahogany, rectangular hinged top, outset rounded corners, recessed baise covered surface, corner candle pockets, conforming apron, center beaded molded short drawer, acanthus carved cabriole legs, claw and ball feet, minor repairs and restoration, 33-3/4" w, 32-1/2" d, 28-3/4" h.......72,500.00

Pennsylvania, c1780, mahogany, rectangular top, skirt with cockbeaded frieze drawer, bracketed sq legs, Marlborough feet, orig brasses, brackets restored, 33-1/4" l, 17-1/2" w, 28-3/4" h 3,250.00

Rhode Island, Newport, c1764-1809, John Townsend, mahogany, serpentine top with edge fluting on top leaf, conforming apron with gadrooned edge bead, fretwork brackets, sq legs with stop fluting, secret drawer in apron, refinished, corner bracket replacements made by Kahl Gabrian, minor edge damage, short age cracks in top, 34-1/4" w, 17" d, 27-3/4" h 27,500.00

Rhode Island, Newport, c1780, mahogany, rectangular folding top with fluted and molded edge, conforming cockbeaded frame joined to square tapering legs by pierced brackets, refinished, restoration, 32" w, 15-1/2" d, 29-3/4" h..........................5,500.00

Rhode Island, Newport, c1780-1800, mahogany, shaped top with slightly outset corners, single center long drawer, straight reeded legs, branded "N. Hoyt," 33-1/2" w, 17-1/4" d, 28-1/2" h..........................6,750.00

Chippendale-Style, mahogany rectangular top, rounded corners, shaped apron, acanthus carved cabriole legs, claw and ball feet, 37" w, 17-1/4" d, 29" h 850.00

Classical

America, mahogany, rectangular molded top, carved and molded frieze, carved baluster form supports, four paw feet, casters, as found condition, 36" w, 17-1/2" d, 29" h.......... 800.00

Card, Classical, Massachusetts, Boston, c1835, mahogany veneer, rectangular top with veneered edge above skirt, square tapering pedestal over shaped veneered platform, flattened ball feet, casters, old refinish, minor veneer loss, 37" w, 17-1/2" d, 29" h, $460. Photo courtesy of Skinner Auctioneers and Appraisers of Antiques and Fine Art Boston and Bolton, MA.

Massachusetts, c1820, carved mahogany and mahogany veneer, shaped top with beaded edge, conforming skirt with beaded lower edge, four acanthus carved ring-turned spiral carved legs, old refinishing, 35-1/2' w, 17-1/2" d, 29-1/4" h 1,925.00

Massachusetts, c1820, mahogany and mahogany veneer, rectangular molded top, D-shaped leaves with outset corners, ring-turned and fluted legs, price for pair, 38" w, 17" d, 29-1/4" h.................................4,500.00

Massachusetts, Boston, c1825, attributed to Issac Vose and Son, carved mahogany veneer, rectangular top swivels above skirt with scrolled ends, tapering pedestal with acanthus leaf carving in outline, shaped veneered pedestal base with additional leaf carving, carved paw feet on casters, old refinish, 36" w, 17-3/4" d, 29" h 3,800.00

Massachusetts, Boston, mid 18th C, mahogany veneer, rectangular top with veneered edge over skirt, square tapered pedestal over shaped veneered platform, flattened ball feet, casters, old refinish, minor veneer loss, 17-1/2" d, 36" w, 29" h............................600.00

New England, mid 18th C, carved mahogany veneer, rectangular tops with beaded edges, short skirt with beaded edges, acanthus leaf and spiral carved legs on casters, old refinish, minor imperfections, 35" w, 17-1/2" d, 30" h 1,380.00

New York City, c1800-15, carved mahogany and satinwood veneer, rectangular top with canted corners, pivots over satinwood skirt, cyma carved deeply incised legs with flanking applied wood carved ornamentation, legs terminate in leafage carved ankles above carved animal paw feet, old refinishing, 37-1/2" w, 18-3/4" d, 28-1/2" h 7,200.00

New York State, c1830, mahogany veneer, fold-over top, canted corners, carved pedestal, animal type legs, paw feet, casters, old refinish, 35-3/4' w, 18-1/2" d, 29-1/4" h 1,250.00

Ohio, walnut, hinged scalloped edge top, apron with applied moldings, turned and paneled legs, 31-1/2" w, 15-1/2" d, 28-1/2" h 495.00

Pennsylvania, Philadelphia area, c1825, mahogany carved and veneer, rectangular folding top, conforming frieze with beaded edge, carved support with acanthus leaves and basket of fruit, shaped concave platform and acan-

Card, Classical, New England, mid-18th C, carved mahogany veneer, rectangular tops with beaded edges, short skirt with beaded edges, acanthus leaf and spiral carved legs on casters, old refinish, minor imperfections, 35" w, 17-1/2" d, 30" h, $1,380. Photo courtesy of Skinner Auctioneers and Appraisers of Antiques and Fine Art Boston and Bolton, MA.

thus leaf scroll and paw carved feet, refinished, 38" w, 18-1/2" d, 30-1/4" h....................4,900.00

Pennsylvania or New York, c1815, carved mahogany and mahogany veneer, lyre-form, brass lyre strings, cast feet, old refinish, imperfections, 35-1/4" w, 17-3/4" d, 29-1/2" h..2,400.00

Colonial Revival, Hepplewhite, late 19th C, walnut and mahogany, serpentine sides, bow front, inlaid and cross banded apron, 36" w, 17" d, 29" h..1,350.00

Federal

Massachusetts, c1790, attributed to Jacob Forster, mahogany, rounded fold-over top, straight apron with inlaid decoration, sq tapered legs, 36" w, 18" d, 29" h 3,500.00

Massachusetts, c1790, mahogany inlaid, folding top with inlaid border and crossbanded edge above conforming frame with three patera within rectangles formed by crossbanding and stringing, carved lower edge joining four square tapering legs inlaid with crossbanding and stringing, old refinish, imperfections, 35-3/4" w, 17-1/2" d, 29" h 3,565.00

Massachusetts, c1790, mahogany inlaid,

Card, Federal, Massachusetts, c1810, mahogany inlaid, folding top with half-serpentine ends, square corners, elliptical front, inlaid edge, conforming base centering tiger maple rectangular panel, cross-banded mitered border with dark inlaid lower edge, four legs with inlaid dies and swelled vase and ring turnings, old refinish, needs repair, 37-1/2" w, 17" d, 29" h, $1,850. Photo courtesy of Skinner Auctioneers and Appraisers of Antiques and Fine Art Boston and Bolton, MA.

folding top, half serpentine ends elliptic front and square corners, conforming base centering an inlaid panel bordered by geometric stringing and crossbanding with crossbanded lower edge joining four square tapering legs, crossbanded panels in the dies continuing to inlaid cuffs, refinished, minor imperfections, 35-3/4" w, 17" d, 30" h.......................2,875.00

Massachusetts, c1790, mahogany inlaid, rectangular folding top with ovolo corners and inlaid edge, conforming inlaid frame centering satinwood oval, four double tapering legs with satinwood and string inlays continuing to stringing and cuffs, refinished, restoration, 35-3/4" w, 17-3/4" d, 29" h.................1,400.00

Massachusetts, Boston, c1790, mahogany and bird's eye inlaid, serpentine top with outset corners, conforming bird's eye maple veneered skirt with central flame birch veneer oval reserve, mahogany veneered panel flanked by reeded front legs stopped by colonettes, ending in ring-turned swelled feet, old refinish, minor surface blemish, 36" w, 17-3/4" d, 28-1/2" h...............4,900.00

Massachusetts, Newburyport, c1790, mahogany inlaid, shaped top above skirt with central veneered oval patera in rectangular panel flanked by square double tapering legs topped by rectangular dies bordered by patterned inlay, cuff inlays, refinished, 36" w, 17-1/2" d, 28-1/4" h 3,565.00

Massachusetts, c1790-1800, mahogany inlaid, folding top, half serpentine ends, elliptic front, crossbanded edge above conforming frieze, oval panel bordered by geometric band within mitered rect, cross banded skirt joining four square double tapering legs with stringing and inlaid cuffs, old finish, minor imperfections, 36-1/4" w, 17" d, 28-7/8" h.......6,750.00

Massachusetts, Boston, attributed to Seymour Workshop, c1800, mahogany inlaid, small drawer behind one of two hinged fly rails, old surface, minor imperfections, 39-3/4" w, 19-1/4" w, 28-3/4" h 9,500.00

Massachusetts, c1800, mahogany inlaid, folding top with half serpentine ends, elliptical front with incised beaded edge, conforming frame centering satinwood oval panel within mitered rectangle bordered by inlaid stringing and checkered band, four double tapering legs with inlaid cuffs joined by beaded skirt, old refinish, minor imperfections, 36" w, 18" d, 28-1/2" h 1,725.00

Massachusetts, c1800, mahogany inlaid, shaped top with inlaid edges, frieze with similar inlay, square tapering legs outlined with stringing, topped with satinwood dies, old refinish, 35-1/2" w, 18" d, 28" h 2,185.00

Massachusetts, c1800, tiger maple, folding top with half serpentine ends, elliptic front and square corners above conforming skirt joining four square tapering legs, old refinish, minor imperfections, 36" w, 16-3/4" d, 28-1/2" h.......................1,840.00

Massachusetts, North Shore, c1800, mahogany and flame birch veneer, serpentine top outlined in patterned inlay, ovolo corners above skirt with two rectangular inlaid panels, flanking central oval above reeded and ring-turned legs with carved and veined leafage, old refinish, very minor imperfections, 36" w, 16-7/8" d, 30" h...7,475.00

Card, Federal, Massachusetts or New Hampshire, c1910, birch and mahogany inlaid, birch bowed top with blocked ends, serpentine sides, mahogany veneer drawer outlined in stringing, square tapering legs, orig brasses, refinished, imperfections, 36" w, 16" d, 30" h, $920. Photo courtesy of Skinner Auctioneers and Appraisers of Antiques and Fine Art Boston and Bolton, MA.

Card, Federal, New England, early 19th C, mahogany inlaid, demilune, shaped folding top with conforming skirt, tapering legs with banded cuffs, some re-veneer, 36-1/2" l, 18" d, 29-1/2" h, $1,265. Photo courtesy of Skinner Auctioneers and Appraisers of Antiques and Fine Art Boston and Bolton, MA.

Massachusetts, c1810, mahogany inlaid, folding top with half-serpentine ends, square corners, elliptical front, inlaid edge, conforming base centering tiger maple rectangular panel, crossbanded mitered border with dark inlaid lower edge, four legs with inlaid dies and swelled vase and ring turnings, old refinish, needs repair, 37-1/2" w, 17" d, 29" h 1,850.00

Massachusetts, c1810-15, mahogany inlaid and carved, top with half-serpentine ends, square corners, elliptical front and crossbanded edge above conforming crossbanded skirt joining four vase and ring-turned reeded legs ending in turned tapering feet, old refinish, imperfections, 36" w, 17-1/2" d, 27-3/4" h..........................3,220.00

Massachusetts, Boston or North Shore, early 19th C, cherry inlaid, bowed top with square ends, undercut lower top over paneled veneered frieze with inlaid ovals, ring-turned tapering chip carved legs, partially refinished, repairs, 36-1/2" w, 17-1/2" d, 29" h 3,200.00

Massachusetts or New Hampshire, c1810, birch and mahogany inlaid, birch bowed top with blocked ends, serpentine sides, mahogany veneer drawer outlined in stringing, square tapering legs, orig brasses, refinished, imperfections, 36" w, 16" d, 30" h 920.00

Massachusetts or New Hampshire, c1810-15, mahogany inlaid, folding top with elliptic front, ovolo corners, crossbanded edge, conforming frame centering inlaid satinwood oval within a mitered mahogany rectangle flanked by satinwood veneer and mahogany crossbanded borders continuing around quarter-engaged vase and ring-turned reeded legs ending in peg feet, old refinish, some imperfections, 34-3/4" w, 18" d, 29-1/2" h 4,150.00

New England, c1800, inlaid mahogany, demilune, hinged top with edge of inlaid stringing, confirming base, three string inlaid lozenge panels, four sq tapering legs with string inlay and cuffs, old refinishing, restoration, 36" w, 17-3/4" d, 29-1/4" h 1,465.00

New England, early 19th C, mahogany inlaid, demilune, some re-veneer, imperfections, 36-1/2" w, 18" d, 29-1/2" h 1,265.00

New Hampshire, Portsmouth, c1800, carved and inlaid mahogany, serpentine top

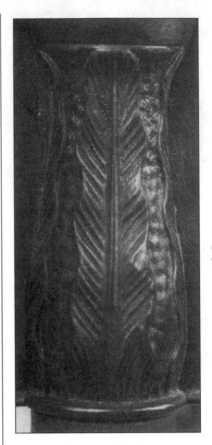

Detail of water leaves carving on Federal card table.

Card, Federal, New Hampshire, Portsmouth, c1800, carved and inlaid mahogany, serpentine top with ovolo corners, skirt with inlaid central reserve in a rectangular panel flanked by reeded legs, topped by carved water leaves on punchwork ground, ending in swelled feet, old surface, imperfections, 36-1/4" w, 17-1/2" d, 30" h, $5,175. Photo courtesy of Skinner Auctioneers and Appraisers of Antiques and Fine Art Boston and Bolton, MA.

with ovolo corners, skirt with inlaid central reserve in a rectangular panel flanked by reeded legs, topped by carved water leaves on punchwork ground, ending in swelled feet, old surface, imperfections, 36-1/4" w, 17-1/2" d, 30" h 5,175.00

New Hampshire, c1800, mahogany, rectangular hinged top, geometric banding inlay and stringing, sq tapered legs, refinished, 35-1/8" w, 18" d, 28-3/4" h 1,926.00

New Hampshire, c1810, inlaid mahogany, scalloped D-shaped hinged top, reeded legs, old refinishing, imperfections, 38" w, 16" d, 30" h 3,750.00

New Hampshire, c1810, mahogany and wavy birch inlaid, shaped hinged top, ring-turned legs, old finish, minor imperfections, 39" w, 19-1/2" d, 29-1/4" h 2,450.00

Rhode Island, c1760, inlaid mahogany, hinged top, elliptical front, square corners, crossbanded edge, conforming frieze of central oval panel flanked by shaped panels defined in stringing, four square tapering legs, dies with contrasting panels above banding, leaf device and stringing, old refinish, restorations, 34-3/4" w, 17-1/2" d, 28-3/8" h 2,300.00

Rhode Island, c1790, inlaid mahogany, hinged veneered top with ovoid corners and diagonally banded edge, veneered and crossbanded frieze with ovals, interrupted line stringing on mitered rectangular over straight tapered legs continuing to inlaid cuffs, old surface, imperfections, 38-1/2" w, 19" d, 29-1/2" h 1,850.00

Georgian, c1765-1770, carved mahogany, fold-over, interior covered in green baize, fitted with four piece wells, fly-leg action, paw feet, 36-1/2" w, 16-3/4" d closed, 28-3/4" h 3,500.00

Hepplewhite

America, mahogany with inlay, demilune, hinged top with edge inlay, curved apron with banded inlay, square tapered legs, repairs, apron as veneer damage, old replaced top, some pierced repairs, 35-1/2" w, 27-1/4" h 400.00

America, mahogany with inlay, demilune, inlaid stringing on edge of top, apron, and legs, banding on edge of apron and feet, sq tapering legs, swing leg support, 34-1/8" w, 17" d, 28-1/4" h 1,950.00

America, mahogany and figured mahogany veneer with inlay, exaggerated serpentine apron with ovolo corners, square tapered legs, two swing legs support hinged lid, stringing and bell flower inlay in legs, banding and stringing on apron and posts, stringing on edge of top, old finish, some loss of height to feet, added brass casters, minor repairs at hinges, initials "W. P." carved inside apron, 35-1/2" w, 17-1/2" d, 27" h 3,850.00

America, mahogany with inlay, chestnut secondary wood, serpentine top, serpentine apron, square tapered legs, banding and stringing inlay on legs, figured veneer apron with banding, stringing and inlaid eagle in oval, banded inlay on top edge, refinished, opaque red stain on underside of top and apron, 35-3/4" w, 18-3/8" d, 28-1/2" h 4,675.00

America, mahogany with inlay, serpentine top, conforming apron, square tapered legs, stringing and banding around apron and

rectangles with invected corners dissected by stringing on flame figure veneer, stringing on top edge, sgd "J. Wilson," three board leaf replaced, veneer repair, 35-3/4" w, 28-3/4" h 3,025.00

Maryland, mahogany, demilune flip top, oval leaf, bellflower and line inlay, top has conch shell inlay, sq tapered legs with spade feet, areas of inlay missing some veneer, 35-1/2" w, 17" d, 30" h 18,200.00

Maryland, mahogany, D-shaped top with line and band inlay, later eagle inlay on top, four sq tapered legs with crossbanded cuffs, 36" w, 17-3/4" d, 29-1/2" h 2,750.00

Maryland, mahogany, oval leaf, bellflower and line inlay, sq tapered legs with spade feet, some inlay checking, 36" w, 17-1/2" d, 29" h 4,650.00

Massachusetts, Boston, mahogany, cut-corner top, cut-corner apron, sq tapered legs, banded inlay on top, stringing on legs, unusual stylized feather or wheat deign with rectangles on all four posts and top, refinished, pierced repair to top, age cracks, provenance, includes documentation that reputes table belonged to Joseph Barlett, signed of Declaration of Independence, 35-3/4" w, 17-1/2" d, 28-1/8" h........6,500.00

Middle Atlantic States, mahogany, D-shaped top with oval and bellflower inlay, four sq tapering legs with crossbanded cuffs, 36" w, 18" d, 29-1/2" h 7,200.00

New York State, mahogany with good figure, curved serpentine top, conforming apron, sq tapering legs, stringing inlay on legs, banding at feet, bottom edge of apron, and edge of top, old finish, very minor veneer damage, small patch to one hinge, 35" w, 17" d, 28-3/4" h 3,950.00

Pennsylvania, Philadelphia, c1790-1810, inlaid mahogany, recessed rounded corner hinged top, diamond form banding, conforming apron having side panels with incurvate corner rectangular stringing, front with similar stringing encased in rectangular banding, centered by shell pattern body covered tureen, tapered square legs headed by oval medallions of arched flowers and leaves, 36" w, 18" d, 29" h 8,625.00

Rhode Island, Newport, demilune, inlaid mahogany, pine secondary wood, figured veneer apron with banded inlay forming rectangles with pattern in center of each, top edge with matching banded inlay, square tapered legs with banded inlay, two swing legs, two secret drawers in back of apron, old finish, some loss of height to feet, 36" w, 17-3/4" d, 26-1/2" h...........................2,640.00

Queen Anne, America, second quarter 18th C, mahogany, demilune fold-over top, molded and hinged top opening to polished surface, further storage well, conforming frieze raised on cabriole legs with pointed pad feet, secondary wood oak, 30" w, 17" d, 28" h 3,450.00

Sheraton

America, 19th C, mahogany, demilune flip top, walnut banding, two paneled supports, platform base, pin line inlay, splayed legs, brass paw caster feet, 35-3/4" w, 17-1/2" d, 28-3/4" h...1,950.00

Country, cherry, curly maple and mahogany veneer apron, hinged top with D-shaped leaves, turned legs, reeded detail, 36-3/4" l, 18-3/4" d, 29" h................................1,250.00

Massachusetts, North Shore, c1810, mahogany, mahogany veneer, satinwood inlay, serpentine front, cutout corners, tilt top with herringbone inlay, lower top with beveled edge, four reeded and tapered legs, white pine secondary wood, repair to top, 35-1/2" w, 17-1/2" d, 29-1/2" h.........4,750.00

Massachusetts, Salem, mahogany, serpentine top, conforming apron, string and banded inlay on apron, figured satinwood veneer on rounded corners, stringing on top edge, turned and reeded legs, refinished, 36-1/2" w, 17-1/2" d, 29-1/2" h.......10,200.00

Center Tables

A center table is defined as a table used in the center of a room, or hall, and which is generally more formal, placed to display one's wealth and good taste.

Adirondack, Rittenhouse, circular top over splayed turned pine legs, orig finish, unsigned, 30" d, 30" h..475.00

Aesthetic Movement

America, last quarter 19th C, giltwood, ala-

Center, Aesthetic Movement, in the manner of E. W. Goodwin, late 19th C, mahogany, circular overhanging top, lower hexagonal medial shelf, six hexagonal legs, 38-1/4" d, 28-3/4" h, $1,840. Photo courtesy of Skinner Auctioneers and Appraisers of Antiques and Fine Art Boston and Bolton, MA.

baster columns and plaques, galleried shelf, 29-1/4" w, 18-1/2" d, 31-1/2" h.........1,800.00

America, last quarter 19th C, giltwood, inset onyx rectangular top, painted and gilded Renaissance-style frieze, minor imperfections and losses, 55" w, 35" d, 30-1/2" h......................................2,600.00

America, last quarter 19th C, walnut, inset onyx rectangular top, carved spoke-like devices on side, sq tapered legs, turned stretcher, 24" w, 16" d, 29-1/4" h 1,200.00

New York, manner of E. W. Goodwin, late 19th C, mahogany, circular overhanging top, lower hexagonal median shelf, six hexagonal legs, 38-1/4" d, 28-3/4" h...........1,840.00

Arts & Crafts

Limbert, Charles P., Grand Rapids and Holland, MI, No. 158, McIntosh influenced design, double oval form, rectangular cutouts at wide lower cross stretcher base, orig finish, unsigned, 48" w, 36" d, 29" h 9,900.00

Tobey Furniture Co., circular top, four splayed legs, cross stretcher base with keyed-tenon construction, top refinished, base with orig finish, height probably altered, 36" d, 28" h...900.00

Center, Classical, Boston, Massachusetts, c1835-45, carved mahogany veneer, Carrara marble top, veneered apron with two working drawers, tapered pedestal on shaped veneered pedestal, scrolled carved feet on casters, replaced brasses, old surface, veneer losses and patches, old replaced marble, 35-3/4" d, 29" h, $4,025. Photo courtesy of Skinner Auctioneers and Appraisers of Antiques and Fine Art Boston and Bolton, MA.

Unknown Designer, oak, round top, four sq legs joined by cross stretchers, exposed tenons, pyramidal center finial, 40" d, 30" h 1,950.00

Centennial, Chippendale-Style, c1876, mahogany, beveled black marble top, scalloped apron with carved knees and returns, cabriole legs, claw and ball feet, two knee returns missing, 49" l, 31" w, 29-1/2" h........................1,725.00

Classical

America, c1840, mahogany, scalloped brown marble top over conforming apron, flaring octagonal pedestal on trefoil feet, 39" w, 32" d, 29" h.................................2,200.00

America, 19th C, mahogany, variegated green and white marble top, veneered skirt, acanthus carved and turned standard, four acanthus carved paw feet, 43" d, 29" h 2,900.00

Massachusetts, Boston, c1835-45, carved mahogany veneer, Carrara marble top, veneered apron with two working drawers, tapered pedestal on shaped veneered pedestal, scrolled carved feet on casters, replaced brasses, old surface, veneer losses and patches, old replaced marble, 35-3/4" d, 29" h 4,025.00

Federal-Style, mahogany, circular quarter veneered top, paneled frieze with drawer, baluster-form standard, tripod base with downswept legs, block feet, casters, 30-1/2" d, 27-1/2" h...650.00

Victorian

America, mid 19th c, walnut, shaped, veined marble top, carved skirt with mythological masque and floral leaf decoration, cabriole legs and floral leaf decoration, cabriole legs with carved floral knees, leaf carved stretcher with leaf carved bulbous finial, 30-1/2" w, 30-1/2" d, 30" h...............2,500.00

Gothic Revival, New York, c1840-50, carved rosewood, hexagonal marble top, six standards on shaped base, casters, 41-3/4" l, 31" h...28,500.00

Renaissance Revival, third quarter 19th C, walnut, burl walnut, marquetry, part ebonized, shaped molded top above conforming frieze, carved trestle supports joined by stretcher, 45" w, 26" d, 28-1/2" h.........................3,750.00

Rococo Revival, New York, walnut with burl veneer, molded relief carved and turned details, shaped white marble top, labeled "Taylorson & Sill, Corning, N.Y.," one apron drop missing, 29-3/4" l, 20-3/4" d, 80" h.........450.00

William and Mary, oak, rectangular top, straight frieze, baluster turned legs joined by fluted box stretcher, 38-1/2" l, 29" h 1,950.00

Chair Tables

This unique 18th century form of table transforms into a chair by tilting the top to form the back of a chair. Because of their primitive nature, chair tables do not fall into any particular furniture style.

New England, 18th C, red painted pine, scrubbed top tilts above base, shoe feet, top has been squared at ends, other minor imperfections, 42-1/2" w, 43-1/4" d, 26-1/2" h................ 1,380.00

New England, late 18th C, painted maple and pine, square overhanging breadboard top, four square chamfered tapering posts joined by two horizontal rails continuing to square legs joined by medial square seat and box stretchers, old red paint, some loss to height, 46-3/4" w, 44-1/2" d, 27-1/2" h 5,175.00

Chair, New England, late 18th C, pine round scrubbed top tilts over dark green painted plank seat, painted green square arm supports and legs joined by square stretchers, old mellow color on top, old green paint, imperfections, 42" w, 44" d, 28-3/4" h, $4,025. Photo courtesy of Skinner Auctioneers and Appraisers of Antiques and Fine Art Boston and Bolton, MA.

New England, late 18th C, pine and tiger maple, round top tilts above plank seat, block and baluster turned legs joined by stretchers, refinished, restoration, 52" d, 26-1/2" h...........4,890.00

New England, late 18th C, pine round scrubbed top tilts over dark green painted plank seat, painted green square arm supports and legs joined by square stretchers, old mellow color on top, old green paint, imperfections, 42" w, 44" d, 28-3/4" h 4,025.00

New Jersey, early 19th C, painted pine, rectangular top, reeded bench seat, joining double demilune cutout ends with exposed tenons, old red paint, minor imperfections, 35-3/4" w, 76" l, 27" h.......................................9,775.00

Chamber or Dressing Tables

A chamber table is a form very similar to a small sideboard or server. When the table was used as a lady's dressing table, it is proper to call it either a chamber or dressing table. One of the Chippendale examples below has exquisite carving attributed to one of the most prominent carvers of the Federal period, Samuel McIntire. His detailed carvings remain as hallmarks of his craftsmanship and skill. Also see Stands, chamber.

Aesthetic Movement, c1890, maple, rectangular mirror above rectangular molded top, three drawers with silvered Art Nouveau hardware, square tapering legs joined by shaped shelf stretcher, 38" w, 19" d, 55" h 900.00

Arts & Crafts

Limbert, Charles P., Grand Rapids and Holland, MI, #492-1/2, arched mirror base cabinet with single drawer, orig copper hardware and through-tenon construction, orig finish, replaced pins on mirror support, branded signature, 36" w, 24" d, 56" h.....................800.00

Stickley, Gustav, New York

No. 919, Vanity, Harvey Ellis influenced design, swivel mirror with exposed butterfly joints, two drawers, orig wooden pulls, arched rail and bowed sides, orig finish, branded signature, 36" w, 18" d, 55-1/2" h 3,500.00

Harvey Ellis design, overhanging rectangular top, two drawers with round wooden pulls, tapered legs, red mark, new dark finish, nick to pull, 36" l, 18" d, 54-1/4" h to top of mirror..............2,250.00

Harvey Ellis design, overhanging rectangular top, two drawers, wooden pulls, arched apron, mirror set in frame with butterfly joints, new finish, red decal, 36" w, 18" d, 54" h 3,600.00

Chippendale

Massachusetts, c1790-80, painted birch, rectangular overhanging top with molded edge and shaped corners, straight cockbeaded skirt and long drawer joining four square beaded and chamfered legs, pierced brass pull (may be orig), old black painted surface, imperfections, 28" w, 17" d, 28" h 5,750.00

Massachusetts, c1793-1806, carving attributed to Samuel McIntire, Salem, mahogany veneer on white pine, serpentine front and sides, ovolo front corners with turned discs over two long drawers, lower with central arched blind tambour flanked by delicate grape clusters and leaves on punchwork decorated ground above ring-turned reeded and tapering legs ending in turned feet, brasses appears to be original, old refinish, minor imperfections, 36-5/8" w, 18-1/8" d, 35" h...........................112,500.00

Chamber, Chippendale, Pennsylvania, Philadelphia, c1760-75, carved mahogany, rectangular top with molded edge overhanging case with quarter engaged fluted quarter columns, four thumb-molded drawers, center drawer with concave shell-carved device on stippled background flanked by applied carved tendrils, scrolled skirt, cabriole legs with shell carved scrolled knees, ball and claw feet, orig brasses, old refinish, minor losses, patches to drawer fronts, 35" w, 20" d, 29" h, $13,800. Photo courtesy of Skinner Auctioneers and Appraisers of Antiques and Fine Art Boston and Bolton, MA.

Pennsylvania, Philadelphia, c1760-75, carved mahogany, rectangular top with molded edge overhanging case with quarter engaged fluted quarter columns, four thumb-molded drawers, center drawer with concave shell-carved device on stippled background flanked by applied carved tendrils, scrolled skirt, cabriole legs with shell carved scrolled knees, ball and claw feet, orig brasses, old refinish, minor losses, patches to drawer fronts, 35" w, 20" d, 29" h 13,800.00

Detail of shell carving on Chippendale chamber table.

Classical, Baltimore, Maryland, c1850, Charles Hale, flame mahogany, rectangular mirror plate swivels between turned uprights, rectangular case with two short drawers over projecting rectangular surface, single long drawer, ring-turned cylindrical tapering legs, 38" l, 19-1/2" d, 59" h 3,000.00

Federal, Salem, Massachusetts, 1815-25, figured mahogany veneer, rectangular top with ovolo corners above colonettes extending to tapering reeded legs, turned ball feet flanking two matched mahogany veneer cockbeaded drawers above beaded skirt, orig eagle

Chamber, Federal, cherry, mahogany veneer, stepback top drawers and beveled edge mirror with lyre posts, five dovetailed drawers, turned legs, refinished, replaced brass pulls, pine secondary wood, 33" w, 16-1/2" d, 57-1/4" h, $1,320. Also shown are two clear flint bar bottles, $110. Photo courtesy of Garth's Auctions, Inc., Delaware, OH.

stamped brasses, old finish, restored, 40-1/2" w, 18-3/4" d, 36-1/2" h 4,860.00

French Restauration, c1840, mahogany, white marble top mounted with oval swing mirror suspended between swan head supports, frieze drawer fitted with sliding writing surface and brass inkwells, 28-1/4" w, 16-1/2" d, 52-1/2" h..1,550.00

Hepplewhite, New York State, mahogany, serpentine top, conforming apron, edge beading, sq tapering legs, minor veneer damage to apron, 42" w, 20" d, 30-1/4" h 1,750.00

Queen Anne

Delaware Valley or New Jersey, c1740-60, carved walnut, overhanging molded rectangular top above case of four short thumb-molded drawers and four cabriole legs ending in carved Spanish feet, joined by valanced apron, replaced brasses, old refinish, imperfections, 26" w, 19-3/4" d, 29-1/2" h 10,925.00

Massachusetts, Boston, c1730-50, walnut, thumb-molded overhanging top with shaped front corners, case with one long drawer over three small drawers, central one with lunette, flat arched skirt, drop pendants, four cabriole legs, high pad feed, replaced brasses, old refinish, repairs, 34-1/2" w, 21" d, 30-1/2" h...............................10,350.00

Massachusetts, c1740, walnut veneer, overhanging top with thumbnail molding, four matched panels of crotch veneer outlined in herringbone veneer, case with five similar drawers with cockbeaded surrounds, arcaded skirt with applied cockbeading, drop pendants, cockbeaded skirt, cabriole legs, pad feet, old refinish, old replaced brasses, 29" w, 18" d, 31" h 12,750.00

Massachusetts, c1750, mahogany, overhanging chamfered edge top, central concave carved drawer, flanked by small drawers, valanced concave carved skirt, two acorn drop pendants, four foliate-carved knees, four claw and ball feet, replaced brasses...17,750.00

Middle Atlantic States, possibly Maryland, walnut, notched top, center small drawer flanked by deeper drawers, valanced concave carved skirt, acorn pendant drops, cabriole legs, pad feet, 28" w, 21' d, 28" h.........3,000.00

Rhode Island, 1790s,. mahogany, shaped hinged leaves, straight skirt, turned cabriole legs ending in small high pad feet, refinished, repaired, 48-1/2" w, 35-1/2" d, 28" h............................2,100.00

Sheraton

Country, decorated, hardwood and poplar, old yellow repaint, brown and black striping, scrolled crest, two drawers in scrolled backsplash, long drawer, ring-turned legs, 34" w, 17" d, 39" h.................................350.00

Vermont, c1835-45, bird's eye and tiger maple veneer, dressing mirror with tiger maple frame flanked by scrolled supports above two short drawers, projecting base with single long drawer on four ring-turned square legs ending in turned feet, replaced pulls, refinished, imperfections, 36-3/4" w, 19" w, 58" h..1,100.00

Sheraton-Style, English, 19th C, lady's, painted satinwood, rectangular top with serpentine front edge, outset rounded corners, conforming front with central drawer over arched kneehole, flanked on each side by two further drawers, interspersed by outset columnar stiles with gilt foliate capitals continuing into turned, tapered, and fluted legs with casters, painted with floral arabesques, inlaid rosewood crossbanding, 47-3/4" w, 22" d, 30-1/2" h 4,500.00

William and Mary, Massachusetts, c1720, walnut veneer, two deep drawers, small center drawer, shaped X-stretcher with finial, replaced brasses, top re-veneered, minor imperfections, 33-3/8" w, 23" d, 40" h..........................4,200.00

Chess Tables

Modern designers have enjoyed creating special usage tables just as 18th and 19th century craftsmen did.

Arts & Crafts, Gustav Stickley, New York, No. 419, c1901, leather top over vertical stretcher, keyed-tenon construction, remnants of game board pattern on orig leather top, orig finish, unsigned, 39" w, 27" d, 26" h................ 11,000.00

Modernism Era, Isamu Noguchi, manufactured by Herman Miller, c1948, Model IN-61, ebonized plywood with inset plastic markers, fixed top on wooden dowels, two piece base, 22" w, 26" d, 19" h............................37,500.00

Coffee Tables

The use of a small, lower table as a coffee table did not become popular until the Art Deco period. The Modernism Era designers carried the concept to new shapes.

Art Deco

Deskey, Donald, manufactured by Deskey-Vollmer, 1927, flat band steel with original black vitrolite top, 24" sq, 15" h......... 15,000.00

McArthur, Warren, manufactured by McArthur Industries, 1930s, glass top, anodized aluminum frame, orig rubber feet, label, 24" sq, 20" h 3,500.00

Arts and Crafts, Limbert, Charles P.,
Grand Rapids and Holland, MI, No. 164, square top over flared legs, inverted V-apron, refinished, unsigned, cut-down, 34" w, 33" d, 19" h 850.00

Modernism Era

Aaltop, Alvar, manufactured by ICF, plate glass top, bentwood birch frame, 27" sq, 18" h 100.00

Brown Saltman, 1960s, black and white laminate top, lift-up compartments, walnut frame, minor wear to wood, 41" sq, 16" h.........500.00

Butler, Lew, manufactured by Knoll International, c1950, black and white laminate top, walnut base, 38" w, 34" d, 16" h 375.00

Eames, Charles, manufactured by Herman Miller CTM, circular ash plywood top, four chrome legs with screw-in footpads, 34" d, 16" h..950.00

Surfboard, elliptical form, black Formica, wire strut base, 89" w, 29" d, 10" h 3,550.00

McCobb, Paul, manufactured by Calvin, circular white glass top, brass base, 42" d, 15" h 450.00

Mont, James, circular red lacquer top, silver-leaf edge, ebonized base, refinished, 48" d, 14" h..50.00

Nelson, George, manufactured by Herman Miller, round walnut veneer top, brushed steel frame, 41" d, 14" h 770.00

Noguchi, Isamu, manufactured by Herman Miller, triangular glass top with early pale green edge, ebonized wood base, 50" w, 36" d, 16" h....................................1,300.00

Platner, Warren, manufactured by Knoll International, c1966, steel rod hourglass shape, circular glass top, 16" d, 18" h..................550.00

Robsjohn-Gibbings, T. H., manufactured by Widdicomb, plate glass top with polished corners, light walnut and brass base, 45" sq, 12" h 2,100.00

Schultz, Richard, manufactured by Knoll International, c1960, Petal, white lacquered segmented top, metal prong base, some wear to top, 42" d, 15" h 550.00

Unknown Designer, 1940s custom made
Circular white marble top, orig blue lacquered wood base, 40" d, 15" h......100.00
Rectangular glass top, black lacquered base, 58" w, 36" d, 19" h..............1,875.00

Unknown Designer, 1950s style, in the manner of Noguchi, triangular plate glass top, ebonized legs, 40" w, 29" d, 14" h......... 100.00

Wegner, Hans
Manufactured by Andr. Tuck, Denmark, rectangular top, chrome base, impressed mark, 47" w, 22" d, 15" h..................300.00
Manufactured by Carl Hansen, Denmark, triangular teak top, tapered teak dowel legs, label, 26" w, 26" d, 17" h 600.00

Wirkkala, Tapio, manufactured by Asko, rectangular top with inset laminate birch designs, tapered laminated dowel legs, marked, very minor wear to top, 39" w, 24" d, 16" h 2,800.00

Wright, Frank Lloyd, manufactured by Henredon, mahogany, hexagonal, Greek Key trim along sides of top and stretcher, 22" w, 22" l, 17" h 1,250.00

Wormley, Edward, manufactured by Dunbar
Black laminate top, light mahogany triangular frame, green tag, 34" sq, 17" h 500.00
Flip-top, dark mahogany, white laminated shelf, two drawers, 40" w, 17" d, 26" h...850.00
Rectangular dark mahogany top, perforated magazine holders on bentwood legs, green tag, 64" w, 23" d, 20" h 1,300.00

Sheaf of Wheat, circular terrazzo top, light walnut base, gold metal tag, 38" d, 20" h 700.00

Modernism Era, Scandinavian, Danish, Copenhagen, c1950, walnut, long rectangular top with rounded corners, tapered cylindrical legs, sgd with metal tag "Illums Bolighus," circular metal tag "fd," 60" l, 19-3/4" w, 16" h 635.00

Console Tables

Console tables are small tables generally used against a wall, primarily as an accent table.

Adams-Style, early 20th C, inlaid mahogany, demilune top, inlaid urn and satinwood banding above frieze inlaid en suite, square tapering legs with bellflower inlay, matched pair, 35-1/2" h, 17-3/4" d, 29" h 1,100.00

Art Moderne, attributed to Lorin Jackson, c1942, rectangular top, horseshoe shaped mahogany base, Lucite winged torch, medallion on center of mirrored back, two stylized Egyptian columns support mirrored one drawer top, applied Lucite Minoan frieze, 48" w, 20" d, 33-1/2" h.................................7,900.00

Arts & Crafts

Lifetime Furniture, Grand Rapids, MI, narrow bow front top, single center drawer, six legs, long corbels, orig finish with minor wear, paper label, 67" l, 22" d, 31" h.............7,500.00

Unknown Designer, trestle, long narrow top and lower shelf, new finish, replaced toe to one side, 96" l, 24" d, 29-1/2" h.........2,300.00

Chippendale-Style, mahogany, marble rectangular top, scroll carved frieze, chamfered square legs, 48-1/2" w, 36" d, 27-1/2" h...............1,750.00

Federal-Style, attributed to middle Atlantic states, 19th C, demilune, mahogany, D-shaped top, conforming apron, sq tapering legs, 44-1/2" w, 22-1/2" d, 28" 600.00

Georgian-Style, mahogany, serpentine top, conforming frieze fitted with one small central drawer, tapering square legs, 45-1/4" w, 21-3/4" d, 36" h 750.00

Hepplewhite, Maryland, mahogany, inlaid paneled and rectangular forms, lower strings of flowers, cut concave corners, repairs to bottom of top, 44-1/4" w, 19-1/2" d, 32" h 32,900.00

Modernism Era

Frankl, Paul, manufactured by Johnson Furniture Co., cream lacquered cork, square cutouts, mahogany shelf with removable magazine tray, 71" w, 21" d, 28" h...3,300.00

Unknown Designer, 1940s, custom made Bleached oak, two tiers, tapered legs, brass trim, in the style of Robsjohn-Gibbings, two 57" w, 21" d, 28" h.....................2,200.00

Lacquered, rectangular top, lattice trestle base, white lacquer, 57" w, 18" d, 36" h 1,875.00

Victorian

Empire Revival, America, c1890-1900, mahogany, D-shaped top, baluster base with three scrolled feet, 46" w, 22-1/2" d, 29-3/4" h..550.00

Renaissance Revival, c1875, matching mirror, carved walnut, rectangular top, two long drawers, carved baluster legs, heavy cast brass bail handles, mirror: step molded cornice over mask and floral vine carved frieze, mirror flanked by fluted columns topped by leaf carved capitals, 71" w, 16" d, 115" h 2,760.00

Dining Tables

Dining tables are those which were used in large dining rooms and capable of seating many people comfortably. Many dining room tables sold today were actually part of three section tables, with the center section being a plain drop leaf table with matching shaped extensions, Finding all three sections together adds greatly to the value. Other banquet-type tables were

Dinette Suite, Art Deco, National Chair Co., Boston, MA, c1938, cut-corner table on U-shaped fluted base, extension leaves, four stepped panel-back chairs with plank seats, chair backs stenciled, wear to finish, 42" w table, 34" h chairs, $350. Photo courtesy of Skinner Auctioneers and Appraisers of Antiques and Fine Art Boston, and Bolton MA.

Dining Room Suite, Victorian, c1900, mahogany, eleven chairs with wide shaped crests and scrolled back splats, trapezoidal seats, scrolled legs, low front stretcher, sideboard scrolled backsplash with applied cresting, doors and drawers, matching long mirror with applied cresting, circular table with leaves, heavy scrolled legs connected to shaped pedestal base, $12,075. Photo courtesy of Jackson's.

made as two part tables, especially during the Federal period. Long dining room tables are one furniture form that was overlooked as American homes started to have smaller dining rooms and less formal dining arrangements.

Adam-Style

Carved mahogany, banded top, three pedestals, each of triangular form, scrolling acanthus carving, scrolled terminals, bun feet, two leaves, 132" w, 48" d, 30" h 4,200.00

Mahogany, rounded rectangular top with rosewood banding and satinwood stringing, three triangular pedestals with acanthus carving, ball feet, two leaves, 138-1/2" l, extends to 188", 48" d, 30" h 3,550.00

Art Deco

America, c1930, burled walnut, double rectangular top, pedestal base, open geometric design, 54" l, 22" d, 31" h ...13,850.00

Europe, c1938, Thuya and rosewood, rectangular top with cut corners in veneer over eight-paneled cone shaped pedestal, waisted pedestal above flared panel base, six side chairs with dropped crest rail, tapered angular back splat above tapered panel legs, navy suede seats, minor wear, 59" l, 49" d, 31-1/2" h table, 37-1/2" h chairs 4,600.00

Arts & Crafts

Indiana Hickory Furniture Co., early 20th C, hickory, circular top, bentwood and log

supports, branded manufacturer's mark, retailer's metal tag "Paine Furniture Boston," 47-1/2" d, 28-3/4" h.............................975.00

Limbert, Charles P., Grand Rapids and Holland, MI

No. 419, circular top, four leaves, five legs, over-coat to orig finish, branded Limbert mark, 48" d, 31" h 2,600.00

No. 424, architectural form, circular top, series of eight legs joined by arched stretchers, octagonal center leg, three orig 12" leaves, refinished, sgd, 60" d, 29" h 14,300.00

No. 1480-C-54, circular flush top, central pedestal, four through-tenon trestle legs, two 12" leaves, skinned finish, veneer patch to section of apron, branded mark, 54" d, 28" h 3,250.00

No. 1487, circular top, intricate base with strong Prairie School design, orig finish, branded mark, four orig leaves and case, 54" w, 29" h 8,250.00

Circular top, split-pedestal, four footed base, rack of four leaves, orig finish, restoration to one foot, branded mark, 54" d, 29" h..3,400.00

Roycroft, East Aurora, NY, mahogany, circular, extension, overhanging top, split ped-

Dining, Arts & Crafts, Gustav Stickley, New York, c1910, No. 634, round table top, center square pedestal joined to four square post legs, flared cross stretchers, through tenon joinery, six leaves, refinished, wear, marring, 54" d, extends to 120", 30" h, $6,900. Photo courtesy of Skinner Auctioneers and Appraisers of Antiques and Fine Art Boston, and Bolton MA.

estal base, orig finish, carved orb and cross mark, four leaves, padded covers, 48" d closed, 29-3/4" h..............................9,000.00
    Stickley Brothers, Grand Rapids, MI, oak
        Circular top supported by square center post on cruciform base, refinished, unsigned, 48" d, 30" h..................1,500.00
        Circular top with corbeled pedestal base, c1916, metal label, five leaves in orig box, refinished, 54" d, 11" w leaves, 29-1/2" h 4,025.00
    Stickley, Gustav, New York
        No. 632, circular top, five tapered legs, three orig leaves, refinished, some veneer loss, 48" d, 29" h..........................1,980.00
        No. 634, c1907-12, oval top, four heavy sq posts with large center post, cross stretchers with through tenons, six leaves, paper label, 54" l, 54" w, 30" h, ... 11,500.00
        No. 634, c1910, round top, center square pedestal joined to four square post legs by flared cross stretchers through tenon joinery, six leaves, refinished, wear, marring, 54" d, extends to 120", 30" h 6,900.00
    Unknown Designer
        Circular top, split pedestal, four shoe feet, casters, orig finish, unmarked, 48" d, 30-1/2" h 1,500.00
        Veneered circular extension top and apron, shoe feet, three leaves, refinished, small veneer edge chips, 48" d, 29-1/2" h 600.00

Chippendale
    Massachusetts, c1770, carved mahogany, overhanging rectangular drop-leaf top with rounded corners and molded edge, scrolled apron joining four carved cabriole legs, claw and ball feet, refinished, restoration, 47" w, 46" d open, 28" h 2,415.00
    Massachusetts, c1770, carved mahogany, circular overhanging drop-leaf top, scrolled skirt joining four cabriole legs ending in carved claw and ball feet, old refinish, repairs, 47" w, 46-1/4" d, 28" h 4,600.00
    Massachusetts, c1780, carved walnut, rectangular overhanging drop-leaf top, four cabriole legs ending in claw and ball feet joined by cutout apron, refinished, imperfections, 47-1/2" w, 47" d open, 48" h..............2,100.00

    New England, c1780, mahogany, drop-leaf, rectangular overhanging drop-leaf top, four molded straight legs joined by cutout skirt, old refinish, minor imperfections, 47-1/4" w, 47" d open, 27-3/4" h 1,150.00
Classical
    America, c1840, mahogany, two sections, rectangular top, rounded corners, rectangular drop leaf, cushion molded frieze, ring turned tapered legs, 76" l extended, 30" h 950.00
    New England, c1820, carved mahogany and mahogany veneer, rectangular overhanging top with rounded leaves, lyre-form supports centering a carved fan with applied brass rosettes, molded shaped outward flaring legs ending in cast brass hairy paw feet, joined by straight beaded skirt, two drawers, vase and ring-turned and beaded square medial stretchers, old refinish, 50" w open, 51-1/2" d, 28-3/4" h............................2,990.00
    New York State, c1820-30, mahogany carved drop leaf, rectangular hinged top, leaves with corner shaping, leaf-carved tapered legs ending in ring-turned feet, casters, imperfections, 38" w, 23" d, 29" h......................690.00
    New York State, 1820s, mahogany carved drop-leaf, rectangular hinged top, long leaves with beaded edges fall over straight skirt, four acanthus leaf carved and turned legs ending in brass caps with casters, old refinish, imperfections, 47-1/2" w, 18" d, extends to 61" l, 29" h.........................865.00
Classical, late
    c1890, mahogany, circular top, molded frame, ring-turned pillar rests on splayed legs ending in heavy paw feet, includes three 13-3/4" w leaves, 54" round, 27-3/4" h 1,475.00
    Late 19th C, mahogany, extension, square rope edge top, circular fluted pediment with rosette carving on leaf carved splayed legs with carved claw feet, extra center brace, five extra leaves, fully extended: 48" w, 124" l 4,100.00
    Late 19th C, mahogany, flip-top, rectangular swivel flip top, block form single pedestal platform base, scroll feet, 46" w, 23-3/4" d, 28" h 365.00
Federal
    America, c1800-20, mahogany inlaid, rect-

angular top with reeded edge, two crotch-wood veneer drawers with banded inlay, line inlay on square tapered legs with banded inlay cuffs, 46" w, 24" d, 30" h 850.00

America, first quarter 19th C, mahogany, rectangular top with rounded corners, conforming molded frieze, turned, tapered, and reeded legs headed by acanthus carved panels ending in brass caps with casters, 48" l, 42-1/2" w, 29" h 850.00

America, first quarter 19th C, mahogany, two part banquet-type, figured wood in apron and top, each section has five turned and reeded legs, swing legs to support leaf, old finish, minor repairs, price for two piece table, 22" w, 47-3/4" l, 22-1/4" leaf, 28-3/4" h, extends to 88-1/2" l..........................1,870.00

New England, early 19th C, cherry, drop-leaf, rectangular hinged leaves, straight skirts, square tapering legs, refinished, repairs, 50" w, 14" d, 53" extended, 29" h 1,265.00

New England, early 19th C, cherry, drop-leaf, rectangular hinged leaves, straight skirts, swing ring-turned tapering legs, old mellow surface, minor imperfections, 45" w, 19" d, 62-1/2" l extended, 30" h 990.00

New England, early 19th C, mahogany inlaid, D-shaped hinged leaves, single drawers, reeded legs ending in small turned ball feet, refinished, losses, cracks, 26" w, 22-1/2" d, 48-1/2" extended, 29" h..........................460.00

New England, first quarter 19th C, mahogany, three sections, center section with rectangular top, long rectangular leaves, six

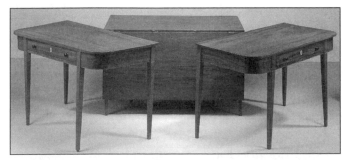

Dining, Federal, New England, c1800-25, three sections, mahogany, center section having six geometric banded tapering square legs, matching inlay at bottom of apron, two matching rounded corner extension tables with later fitted apron drawers, 120" l extended, 48" w, 29-3/4" h, $4,320. Photo courtesy of Butterfields.

geometric banded tapering square legs, matching inlay at bottom of apron, two matching rounded corner extension tables having later fitted apron drawers, overall length 120", 48" w, 29-3/4" h 4,350.00

Virginia, early 19th C, mahogany veneer, three sections, two "D" ends flanking rectangular center section with two hinged drop leaves, square tapering legs, old surface, imperfections, provenance; family descent from origin in Smithfield, VA, Isle of Wright County, owner was Sarah Folk Wilson, who married John Goodnow Wilson, lived at family home, Mantura, which burned in 1885, this table and one other piece of furniture were saved, (sold by Skinner's, Oct 24, 1999) 48" w, 21-1/2" d center section, each "D" 24", extends to 85-1/2" l, 28-3/4" h 12,650.00

Federal, late, early 19th C, America, various woods, rectangular top with rule-jointed leaves, plain frieze with single drawer, turned legs with tulip-turned feet, 62-1/2" l, 46-3/4" w, 29-3/4" h 350.00

Federal-Style

Cherry, rectangular top, turned double pedestals, two leaves, down-curving legs ending in brass caps, 66" l, 42" w, 28" h 950.00

Inlaid mahogany, extending, rectangular top with rounded corners and reeded edge, conforming frieze similarly reeded, raised on square-section tapering legs joined by serpentine end stretchers, satinwood cross-banding throughout, three leaves, 48" w, 93" l, 30" h 900.00

Mahogany, extending, rectangular top with rule-joined leaves and rounded corners, baluster-turned end supports with downswept square-section legs with brass caps, one leaf, 36" w, 64-1/4" l, 28-1/2" h 575.00

Mahogany, extending, rectangular top, two leaves, 47-1/2" d closed, 23" w leaves, 30" h..1,555.00

Mahogany, molded rectangular top with rounded corners, each end support with molded downswept legs terminating in brass caps, joined by turned pole stretchers, 130-1/4" l, 42" w, 28" h 400.00

Mahogany, twin pedestal, extending, rectangular top with rounded corners and reeded edge, turned, ring-turned tapering pedestal raised on tripod base with molded downswept legs ending in brass caps and casters, two leaves, 43-1/2" w, 119-1/2" l, 29-3/4" h 2,000.00

Walnut, three piece, central portion with two drop leaves, two end sections form ellipses when connected to central leaves, connected by wood pegs, four legs on each end piece, six on central portion, all legs square tapered with line inlay at neck and cuff, end sections appear to b 19th C, center section of later manufacture, 46" w, 112" l extended, 29" h.................2,150.00

Georgian, c1790, drop-leaf, mahogany, rectangular top, two rectangular leaves, tapering circular legs ending in claw and ball feet, 42" w, 21" d, 61" open, 28-1/2" h 1,100.00

Georgian-Style

c1870, carved mahogany, rounded top with rosewood and satinwood banding, raised on two pedestals, each with fluted and floral-carved standard, four splayed like-carved and beaded legs ending in Greek key pattern feet, 88" l, 47-1/2" d, 30" h.........................3,300.00

c1890, mahogany, ovoid banded top raised on two pedestals, each with vasiform standard on three splayed legs ending in brass paws on casters, one 21-1/2" leaf, 62" w, 39-1/2" d, 29-1/2" h...................900.00

Hepplewhite

America, early 19th C, mahogany, two D-shaped ends on rectangular drop leaves, sq tapering legs, spade feet, 96" l, 56" w, 28" h 2,400.00

Maryland, mahogany, two D-shaped ends, swing leg support, oval, band, and line inlay, custom fashioned strip inset to fill in and butt two ends when not fully extended, refinished, 99" l extended, 46" w, 29" h 7,700.00

Modernism Era

Eames, Charles, manufactured by Herman Miller, rectangular walnut plywood top, folding chrome legs, refinished, 54" w, 34" d, 29" h 950.00

Juhl, Finn, manufactured by Bovirke, 1953, rectangular top, two pop-up leaves, oval teak legs, 59" w, 35" d, 29" h 250.00

Knoll, Florence, manufactured by Knoll International

Elliptical plywood top, chrome pedestal base, 78" w, 49" d, 29" h..............1,500.00

Elliptical oak veneered top, chrome X-base, minor edge damage, 78" w, 48" d, 28" h..1,210.00

Nelson, George, manufactured by Herman Miller, Swagged-Leg, circular laminate top with walnut edge, chrome and walnut frame, label, 48" d, 29" h 2,300.00

Noguchi, Isamu, manufactured by Knoll International, white laminated top, chrome struts, black enamel base, 48" d, 29" h 2,400.00

Rohde, Gilbert, manufactured by Herman Miller, circular pickled veneer top, tubular metal legs, two leaves, minor wear, 48" d, 28" h 1,540.00

Robsjohn-Gibbings, T. H., manufactured by Widdicomb, radiating walnut veneer top, dowel legs, three leaves, label, 48" d, 29" h 2,310.00

Saarinen, Eero, manufactured by Knoll International, circular white laminate top, white cast aluminum pedestal base, 36" d, 29" h 775.00

Wegner, Hans, Denmark, c1950, walnut, rectangular top, semi-circular drop-leaves, wide rectangular drop-leaf insert 865.00

Woodard, 1960s, circular glass top, extruded aluminum base, 44" d, 29" h 550.00

Wormley, Edward, manufactured by Dunbar

Circular dark mahogany top, tapered legs, three leaves, 50" w, 29" h....1,900.00

Rectangular walnut top, curved sides, tapered slab legs, brass foot, three leaves, refinished, 72" w, 42" d, 29" h 3,750.00

Wright, Frank Lloyd, manufactured by Henredon, mahogany, rectangular top, Greek Key trim along sides of top and stretcher, 63" w, 42" l, 29-1/2" h 1,250.00

Neoclassical, New York, c1805, mahogany, three-part, center section with two hinged leaves, shaped veneered platform with four reeded curving legs ending in brass paw feet on casters, four spiral curved and ring-turned columns, two flanking sections each with D-shaped end with single hinged drop-leaf above pedestal form conforming to center section, skirt punctuated by rectangular dies above turned pendants, bottom edge outlined in veneer, refinished, minor patch in top, 53-3/4" w, 163-1/2" l, 30" h 68,500.00

Queen Anne

Connecticut River Valley, cherry and birch, painted red, minor imperfections, 40-1/2" w, 36" d, 28-1/2" h 21,000.00

Massachusetts, 18th C, maple, rectangular top overhanging drop-leaf, hinged top with molded edge above scrolled skirts, cabriole legs ending in pad feet, old surface, imperfections, 42" w, 13-1/2" d, 41-1/2" l extended, 28" h 6,325.00

New England, mid 18th C, maple, rectangular top overhanging D-shaped drop-leaves, hinged leaves, scrolled skirts, cabriole legs ending in pad feet, old refinish, imperfections, 42" w, 13" d, 27-1/2" d 4,310.00

New England, late 18th C, mahogany, square overhanging drop-leaves, four cabriole legs with arris knees, pad feet, cutout apron, old refinish, imperfections, 47" w, 46" d, 27-3/8" h................................2,760.00

New England, late 18th C, painted, orig blue-green paint, rectangular top, single

Dining, Queen Anne, Massachusetts, 18th C, maple, rectangular top, drop leaves with molded edge, scrolled skirts, cabriole legs, pad feet, old surface, imperfections, 42" w, 13-1/2" d, 41-1/2" extended, 28" h, $6,325. Photo courtesy of Skinner Auctioneers and Appraisers of Antiques and Fine Art Boston and Bolton, MA.

long drawer, tapered legs, pad feet, early turned pull, minor repairs, 43" w, 24-1/4" d, 26-1/4" h..15,950.00

Pennsylvania, Philadelphia, c1780, walnut, rectangular top with drop leaves, cabriole legs, trifid feet, 51-1/4" l extended, 42" w, 27-1/4" h....................................4,650.00

Rhode Island, c1750-70, maple, circular drop-leaf top, straight apron joining four block turned tapering legs ending in pad feet, old refinish, imperfections and restorations, 41" w, 42" d, 26-1/2" h 1,610.00

Queen Anne Style, America, walnut, oval, molded circular top extends with two leaves, molded conforming frieze, cabriole legs with pad feet, 88" l, 44" w, 28-3/4" h..............650.00

Sheraton, country, cherry, curly maple drop-leaf top, figured cherry veneer shaped aprons, turned and rope carved legs, casters, refinished, price for pair, 44-1/2" w, 62" l extended, 30-1/2" h.................................4,200.00

Sheraton-Style, late 19th/early 20th C, mahogany, central portion with two drop leaves, each D-form end with drop leaf, two separate leaves, reeded legs, gate leg on one end detachable, 71" l, 48" w, 29" h 2,990.00

Victorian

America, walnut, two 10" l drop leaves, 34" l, 10" w, 29" h 500.00

Eastlake, oak, shaped rectangular top, shaped quatrefoil pedestal, casters, 37-1/2" d, 29" h..750.00

Morris & Co., designed by George Jack, c1890, mahogany and inlay, rectangular top with ebony and holly herringbone inlay on sides, shaped legs with stylized foliage inlay, joined by hayrake stretcher, tapered feet, 96" l, 37" w, 28-3/4" h 19,550.00

Dressing: See Chamber or Dressing Tables

Drop-Leaf Tables

A drop-leaf table may be a dining table or any other table form that has at least two drop leaves of matching size and shape. Breakfast tables, dining tables, Pembroke tables, and even some work tables have drop leaves. Because this name is so common among auc-

tioneers and antique dealers, as well as collectors and decorators, the name continues to be used to describe tables of many different furniture styles. Look for signs of normal wear, especially to leaves and tops. Many tables have had "improvements" made to them over the years, perhaps to remove a warp in a leaf, perhaps to update leaves to a more modern look. It is generally to the buyer's discretion whether these "improvements" are simply repairs or added character to the table. Also see Breakfast tables, dining tables, Pembroke tables, and work tables.

Arts & Crafts

   Stickley Brothers, Grand Rapids, MI, rectangular top, two 9" leaves, refinished, unsigned, 29" w, 14" d, 30" h...........1,250.00

   Stickley, L. and J. G., Fayetteville, NY, No. 553, gate-leg drop-leaf, two narrow lower shelves, shoe foot base, refinished, unsigned, 42" dia. open, closed 42" w, 15" d, 30" h 2,500.00

Drop-Leaf, Chippendale, Rhode Island, 18th C, mahogany, rectangular top, two hinged rectangular drop leaves, shaped frieze, six chamfered square legs, 47-3/4" w, 62" l open, 28" h, $3,500.

Centennial, late 19th C, mahogany, rectangular top with drop leaves, vasiform pedestal with leaf carved knees and four hairy paw feet, 46" w extended, 29-1/8" h......................490.00

Chippendale, America

   Cherry and walnut, replaced one board top and leaves, square butt joints, scalloped aprons with replaced drops, maple swing leg supports, cabriole legs, claw and ball feet, refinished, 48" w, 15-3/4" d, 15-3/4" l leaves, 27-3/4" h...935.00

   Curly maple top and apron end, cherry base, old dark finish, square legs with mortised and pinned stretchers and apron, dovetailed drawer in one end, age cracks in top, table was originally longer, feet have plugged holes from removed casters, minor repairs to rule joint, 68-1/4" l, 18-1/2" w, 8-1/2" l leaves, 26" h........................3,300.00

   Massachusetts, mahogany, round drop leaves, cabriole legs, claw and ball feet, replaced top, 50" l, 50" w, 27" h.......2,200.00

Classical

   America, c1840, walnut, hinged rectangular top, two drop-leaves, conforming apron, octagonal pedestal, quatrefoil plinth base, scrolled feet, casters, 60-1/4" w, 42" d, 28-1/2" h 500.00

Drop-Leaf, Arts & Crafts, Gustav Stickley, New York, beveled ground top, cutout gothic arches, X-gatelegs, small red box decal, light over-coat to orig dark finish, 30" d, 28-1/2" h, $4,750. Photo courtesy of David Rago Auctions/RagoArts.com, Lambertville, NJ.

Drop-Leaf, Federal, New England, early 19th C, maple and cherry inlaid, rectangular hinged top with ovolo corners, square tapering legs outlined in stringing, ending in triangular inlay, top with old surface, base with old refinish, surface imperfections, 36" w, 15" d, extends to 34-1/2", 49" h, $2,645. Photo courtesy of Skinner Auctioneers and Appraisers of Antiques and Fine Art Boston and Bolton, MA.

New England, c1820, mahogany, rope turned legs, 41-3/4" l, 48" w open, 28-1/2" h 500.00

New York State, c1815, mahogany, rectangular top, round leaves, beaded skirt with drawer, four ring-turned reeded legs ending in swelled feet, cast brass hairy paw feet, refinished, restored, 36" w, 57" l open, 28-3/4" h 1,925.00

Federal

New England, early 19th C, mahogany, old refinishing, imperfections, 49-1/2" l, 48" w, 29" h 1,250.00

Rhode Island, c1800, mahogany, oval drop-leaf top, conforming cockbeaded base joining four square tapering legs, old refinish, very minor imperfections, 34-3/4" l, 20" d closed, 29-3/4" h 2,550.00

Hepplewhite, country

Cherry, drop leaf top with cut corners on leaves, one dovetailed drawer, sq tapering legs, old brass pull, old mellow refinishing, one board top with repaired crack through center, 36" w, 21" d, 10-3/4" l leaves, 28-1/4" h 490.00

Maple, curly top, scrubbed one board top and leaves, mortised and pinned construction, base with old dark (black) paint, square tapered legs, leaves warped, top with age crack, 16-1/2" w, 40" l, 12-1/4" leaves, 29-1/4" h 900.00

Hepplewhite-Style, country, 19th C, pine, old brown graining, top opens to circle, single dovetailed drawer, squae tapered legs, worm holes, wear, touch-up repair to paint, 40-3/4" w, 19-1/2" l, 10-3/4" leaves, 29-1/4" h 1,320.00

Queen Anne

America, c1750, birch, one board top and rounded one board leaves, scrolled apron and swing legs, cabriole legs, duck feet, old dark finish on base, top refinished, repairs and old restoration, 41-1/2" w, 14" d, 15-1/2" d leaves, 28-3/4" h................................1,850.00

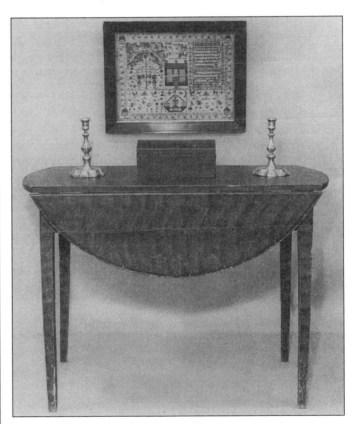

Drop-Leaf, Hepplewhite-Style, 19th C, found in Maine, country, pine, old brown graining, top opens to circle, one dovetailed drawer, sq tapered legs, worm holes, wear, damage, touch-up to paint, 40-3/4" d, 10-3/4" leaves, 29-1/4" h, $1,320. Also shown are $2,310 sampler; pr Continental pewter candlesticks, $275; painted green dome top box (age crack in lid) $300; and pewter charger, $200. Photo courtesy of Garth's Auctions, Inc., Delaware, OH.

America, c1750, mahogany, oval hinged top, flat arched apron, six tapered gate legs, raised pad feet, 62-1/2" l, 28" h 2,875.00

America, c1750, maple and pine, scrubbed one board rectangular top, scrolled apron, cabriole legs, duck feet, old dark finish on base, top and leaves are old replacements, repairs to feet, 48" w, 15-3/4" d, 15-1/4" l leaves, 28" h..........................380.00

America, c1750, walnut, rectangular top, scalloped base, cabriole legs ending in trifid feet, top has been enlarged and married to base, new hinges, miscellaneous repairs and additions, 59-1/4" l extended, 44" w, 28-3/4" h 490.00

Country, cherry and pine, orig dark red finish, one board top with sliding supports for leaves, well turned legs, stretcher base with button feet, age cracks in top, 16-1/2" w, 36" l top, 26-1/8" h 22,000.00

Country, maple and other hardwoods, tapered legs with duck feet, swing legs, refinished, repairs, top reattached, 41-3/4" l, 14-3/4" leaves, 26-1/4" h 2,450.00

Country, maple, scalloped apron on ends, cabriole legs with duck feet, old dark refinishing, restoration, 42" w, 13-1/2" d, 14" leaves, 27-1/4" h 2,975.00

Country, maple with curly top, cabriole legs with curved ankles, small duck feet, swing legs, top rubbed down to old soft finish, edge damage and wear, hinges replaced, traces of

Drop-Leaf, Queen Anne, New England, late 18th C, maple, hinged leaves flank straight skirts, cabriole legs, pad feet, refinished, repairs, 54" w, 16" d, 52" l extended, 27" h, $1,150. Photo courtesy of Skinner Auctioneers and Appraisers of Antiques and Fine Art Boston and Bolton, MA.

old red on underside, leaves warped, 1-3/4" w, 13-3/4" l leaves, 26" h 3,850.00

Maryland, walnut or mahogany, oval inlaid drop leaves with line inlay, swing leg, pad feet, 42" l, 42" d, 28" h 12,750.00

Massachusetts, maple, one board top, leaves open to form enlarged oval, slender tapered legs with duck feet, two swing legs, old mellow refinishing, some damage and repairs to rule joints, stains on top, 41" l, 14-3/4" leaves, 25-3/4" h 2,420.00

Massachusetts, mid to late 18th C, rectangular top, hinged square leaves flanking straight beaded skirt with beaded edges, cabriole legs ending in pad feet, early surface, minor imperfections, 44" w, 15-1/2" d, extends to 42-1/2" l, 27-1/2" h 4,600.00

New England, c1740-50, walnut, rectangular top, square posts transitioning to circular tapered legs, penny feet, top is married to base, straightened, replaced hinges, feet repaired, 47-1/2" w, 47-3/4" extended, 29-1/2" h 1,050.00

Rhode Island, late 18th C, maple, painted, hinged leaves fall to flank straight skirt, ring-turned tapering legs end in turned feet, orig surface, scrubbed top, faint gray-green painted surface, rough condition, 42" l, 14-1/2" d, 26-3/4" h 5,465.00

Queen Anne-Style, early 20th C

Walnut, banded top with two rounded leaves, raised on tapering circular legs, pad feet, 11" w closed, 31" w open, 17" d, 25" h 275.00

Walnut, rectangular top, altered gate leg mechanism, scalloped apron, trifid feet, restorations to feet, 41" w, 17" d, 28-1/8" h ... 500.00

Sheraton, America, c1800-10

Cherry, D-shaped drop leaves, shaped frieze, scissors-like supports, fluted legs, 39" l, 51-1/2" extended, 28" h 1,750.00

Cherry, single drawer, gate leg, 41" l, 19-1/2" d, two 20-1/4" l leaves,29-1/2" h 375.00

Curly maple, two board top, one board leaves, well shaped turned legs, old worn finish, slight warp to leaves, 16-1/4" w, 37-3/4" l, 13-1/2" leaves, 28-1/2" h 1,350.00

Mahogany, one board top and leaves, turned legs, scrubbed top, old dark finish on

Drop-Leaf, Sheraton, attributed to Charleston, SC, flame mahogany, rectangular top, two leaves, ring turned legs, peg feet, $775.

Farm, New England, early 19th C, overhanging rectangular pine top, drawer with divisions, X-shaped sawbuck base, orig pull, old refinish, minor imperfections, 45" w, 28-1/4" d, 28-1/2" h, $750. Photo courtesy of Skinner Auctioneers and Appraisers of Antiques and Fine Art Boston and Bolton, MA.

base, one swing leg with old pinned repair, age cracks in leaves, 42" w, 18-1/2" d, 19-1/2" l leaves, 29-1/2" h 385.00

Victorian, country, c1880, pine, rectangular top above frieze fitted with two drawers, two board drop leaves, square legs joined by H-form stretcher, 54" w, 29-1/2" d, 30" h....500.00

William and Mary, Connecticut, early 18th C, cherry, overhanging oval drop leaf top, four splayed block vase and ring-turned legs, butterfly support, turned feet, joined by beaded apron with thumb-molded drawer, old refinishing, restored, 40" w, 35-1/4" d, 25-1/2" h...2,650.00

Drum Tables

A drum table is a center-type table with a round or octagonal top.

Classical, mahogany, octagonal top, four working and four faux drawers in frieze, circular pedestal, shaped platform base, C-scroll feet, 28" d, 27-1/2" h 750.00

Federal, mahogany and maple, circular star inlaid top, four frieze drawers, foliate carved vase-form standard, reeded out-swept legs, brass hairy paw feet with casters, 22" d, 28" h...5,750.00

Farm Tables

A farm table is a simple table, often with a breadboard top, and supported on a sawbuck

base. These tables are not associated with any one furniture style, but blend nicely with many country styles.

Country

New England, early 19th C, overhanging rectangular pine top, drawer with divisions, X-shaped base, orig pull, old refinish, minor imperfections, 45" w, 28-1/4" d, 28-1/2" h
....750.00

Ohio, poplar and chestnut, old gray wash, scrubbed three board top with chamfered edge, removable sawbuck legs, chamfered corners, 79-1/2" w, 34" d, 29" h 1,120.00

Pine, one board top with breadboard ends, molded edges, cross stretcher with beaded edges, base old replacement, old nut brown refinishing, pierced repairs, 40-1/2" l, 19-1/2" d, 26-1/2" h 550.00

Pine, two board breadboard top, old worn finish, cleats holding top to base replaced, 30-1/2" w, 47-1/2" l, 29" h 660.00

Sheraton-Style, cherry and maple, oval top on rectangular base, drop leaves, turned legs on squashed ball feet, repair to one leaf, 56" l, 41" w, 28-5/8" h 300.00

Folding Table

Folding tables that were meant for occasional use are a more recent invention. Several companies manufacturing them during the Victorian period and after that time.

Victorian, Renaissance Revival, Gates Manufacturing Co., Philadelphia, PA, patent 1877, cherry, rotary, adjustable sliding top, two drawers, adjustable support, four paw feet, each drawer with orig paper label 650.00

Games Tables

Games tables are small tables designed to be used to play parlor games, such card games, chess, backgammon, etc. They are usually constructed with a shaped top so that those who use these tables can sit comfortably to play the game of their choice. Some game tables have interior wells to store pieces. Expect to find signs of usage around the edges of these tables and especially to any playing surface. Also see Card Tables and Chess Tables.

Arts & Crafts, Stickley Brothers, Grand Rapids, MI, No. 324, table: hexagonal top, arched apron, six legs, stacked cross stretchers at base, keyed-tenon construction; six matching chairs: arched back with hand hold cutout, molded plank seat, three leg base, sgd with metal tag, numbered, all refinished, table: 41" d, 29" h, chairs: 14"w, 14" d, 28" h 3,750.00

Chippendale
Pennsylvania, c1750-80, mahogany, rectangular top, single drawer with scrolled line, cockbeaded frame, square molded straight legs, replaced brasses, 35" w, 17" d, 29" h 920.00

Pennsylvania, c1760-80, walnut, rectangular molded top, single bead molded drawer with brass bails and key escutcheons, bead molded frame, square molded straight legs, one leg swings to support leaf, one patch repair, 35-3/4" w, 17-1/2" d closed, 29-1/2" h 3,250.00

Pennsylvania, Philadelphia, c1760-80, mahogany, rectangular molded top, one line beaded drawer, molded apron, square legs, Marlborough feet, orig brasses, 36" w, 17-1/2" d, 29-1/4" h..........................9,200.00

Classical
America, c1820-40, carved mahogany, swivel lift top, oval shaped games surface, compartment for playing pieces, single drawer, four turned and reeded legs, 19" horizontal crack on top, 25-1/4" w, 15-3/4" d, closed, 28-3/4" h.................................495.00

America, c1830, figured mahogany veneer octagonal top, resting on molded frame with veneered edges, heavily carved and turned pillar rests on circular carved base with quadripedal legs, legs carved at top with brass rosettes, tapering to brasses lions' paw feet, ending in casters, 37-1/2" w, 18-1/2" d, 30-1/2" h.........................1,625.00

America, c1840, mahogany, reeded fold-over top, supported by acanthus and spiral turned legs, 36" w, 17-1/2" d, 29-1/2" h 500.00

Massachusetts, Boston, early 19th C, mahogany, hinged top with molded edge, scrolled skirt, pedestal with carved leaf decoration, stepped plinth base, scrolled feet with casters, 34-3/4" w, 25-1/2" d, 27-1/2" h 1,500.00

New England, c1820, carved mahogany, tiger-maple crossbanded borders, brass inlaid stringing, solid lyre-form standard, outswept carved legs, refinished, 35-1/2" w, 17-1/2" d, 28" h.................................2,950.00

New England, c1825, painted poplar, square top with painted black and red checkerboard design, above straight skirt continuing two working and two false drawers, four vase and ring-turned legs ending in ball feet, old painted surface probably original, paint shows evidence of considerable use, 18" w, 16-3/4" d, 28-3/4" h...........................1,100.00

New York, c1815, mahogany, shaped top, brass Classical figural decorated apron, lyre form standard, four acanthus carved flaring legs, brass paw feet and casters, 35-3/4" w, 18" d, 29" h....................................14,000.00

Empire, first quarter 19th C, mahogany, fold-out hinged molded rectangular top with rounded corners, opens to polished surface over ogee molded frieze, square-section bluster-form standard raised on molded square platform base, scroll feet and casters, secondary wood white pine, 34-1/2" w, 17" d, 29-1/2" h............. 1,750.00

Federal
America, c1810, mahogany, serpentine top, reeded tapered legs, ball feet, 35" w, 17-1/4" d, 30" h...............................1,250.00

Massachusetts, attributed to Boston or Salem, c1805, inlaid mahogany, rectangular folding top with half serpentine ends, ovolo corners, elliptical front and crossbanded string inlaid edge, conforming frame centering oval figured panel within rectangle bordered by stringing and banding, flanked by rosewood panels bordered by stringing and figured wood banding, dies with figured panels above ring-turned swelled reeded legs ending in tapering feet, refinished, 33-3/4" w, 17-1/2" d, 28-3/4" h...........................5,750.00

Federal-Style

America, mahogany, demilune form top, pinstripe inlay decorated apron, eagle and bellflowers inlay, sq tapered legs, 36" w, 17-1/4" d, 30" h...950.00

Massachusetts, late 19th C, birchwood inlaid mahogany, shaped serpentine top with cross banded inlay, outset corners above checkered inlaid frieze, turned reeded legs, peg feet, 36" w, 18" d, 30" h 720.00

Hepplewhite, late 18th C, satinwood, leather inset top, sq tapering legs, 35" w, 35" d, 28" h...2,750.00

Neoclassical, America, mahogany, angular top, leaf carved standard, downswept legs, brass paw casters, 34-3/4" w, 17" d, 28-1/4" h.....595.00

Sheraton, Massachusetts, c1800-20, mahogany, bowed top with reeded edge, inlaid tombstone panels, reeded legs, ball and peg feet, minor repairs, 35-1/2" w, 17-1/4" d, 29" h 920.00

Victorian

America, late 19th C, walnut and burl walnut, hinged rectangular top with rounded edges, felt lined interior, shaped supports joined by turned stretcher, scrolled feet, casters, 36" w, 17-1/4" d, 28-1/4" h............900.00

America, late 19th C, walnut and yew wood, inset chess and checkerboard, 36" w, 19-1/8" d, 26" h.....................................775.00

Rococo Revival, c1875, walnut and burl walnut, hinged rectangular top, carved frieze, cabriole legs, 35-1/2" l, 18" d, 25" h 575.00

William IV, second quarter 19th C, mahogany and inlay, rectangular top with chess/checkers board on top, felt lined verso, base enclosing backgammon board, plain frieze with

Gate-Leg, William and Mary, New England, 18th C, maple, oval hinged top, heavily turned gated maple base, single drawer, old refinish, restoration, 13-1/2" d, 29" h, $4,830. Photo courtesy of Skinner Auctioneers and Appraisers of Antiques and Fine Art Boston and Bolton, MA.

egg and dart molding, pedestal base, foliate collar, quadripartite base on carved turned feet on casters, shrinkage, minor veneer loss, 24-1/2" w, 24-1/2" d, 28-1/4" h 2,100.00

Gate Leg Table

A gate-leg is the common name for a table with an additional pair of legs used to support a drop leaf. To quality as a true gate leg, the leg must be mortised into the apron of the table.

William and Mary

Massachusetts, early 18th C, maple, oval drop-leaf top, six block vase and ring-turned legs joined by molded apron with drawer and block, vase and ring-turned stretchers, refinished, imperfections, 52-1/4" l, 41-1/2" w, 22" h...9,775.00

New England, 18th C, maple, oval hinged top, heavily turned gated maple base, single drawer, old refinish, restoration, 13-1/2" d, 29" h...4,830.00

New England, 18th C, maple, half round leaves on butterfly-shaped supports, straight skirt, block, baluster, and ring-turned legs, turned feet, square stretchers, refinished, minor imperfections, 14" w closed, 38" w extended, 36-1/2" d, 25-1/4" h.............................19,550.00

Harvest Tables

A harvest table is similar to a farm table or work table. The term generally refers to a sturdy table with a long top. Some harvest tables have added drop-leaves.

Country, curly maple top, maple base, replaced top and leaves with bold curl and breadboard ends, pegged construction, one dovetailed drawer, turned legs, feet, and stretcher base, feet ended out, drawer and leaf supports added, 73-1/2" w, 24-1/2" d, 11-1/4" leaves, 28-1/2" h 3,200.00

Empire, central Massachusetts, c1820-30, red painted pine, two board top with breadboard ends, straight skirt, ring-turned tapering legs ending in ball turned feet, orig red paint, imperfections, 96" l, 32" w, 29-1/4" h 9,775.00

Federal, Massachusetts, c1800, pine and maple, long rectangular top with two drop laves, sq tapered legs, old refinishing, 114" l, 35-1/4" w, 26-1/2" h..............................6,750.00

Hutch Tables

A hutch table serves two functions: It can be used as a table and also provides storage in the well beneath the seat. Like chair tables, hutch tables are primitive tables and do not fall within any particular furniture style. Because hutch tables were important decorator-type tables during past generations of antique collecting, many reproductions and fakes are found today in the marketplace. Look for genuine signs of aging, usage, and shrinkage of the wood.

Country, curly maple, bold figure, square nail construction, two board top with slight warp, cutout feet, orig triangular shaped extenders added to front feet, mellow old refinishing, old restoration and reconstruction to base, 60" w, 39-1/2" d, 29" h 1,925.00

Country, pine, two board top, old worn yellow and brown graining, black striping, paneled edges, hinged seat in base, 56" l, 30" h... 1,870.00

New England, late 18th C, painted, scrubbed pine circular top, early red paint, imperfections, shoe feet, stretcher, 53" w, 37" d, 28-1/4" h 6,500.00

New England, late 18th C, painted, scrubbed pine rectangular top, old color above old dark red base, locking compartment in base, minor imperfections, 44-1/4" w, 35-3/4" d, 29" h........6,800.00

New York State, northern, late 18th C, painted, scrubbed circular top over old red base, shaped sliding stretcher type key, shoe feet, imperfections, 43-1/2" w, 32" d, 26" h....................4,750.00

Pennsylvania, early 19th C, pine, rectangular top hinges on two sides with demilune tops, cutout feet joined with medial shelf with exposed tenons, old surface, 54" w, 35-3/4" d, 29-3/4" h...1,380.00

Vermont, pine, birch, and poplar, two board breadboard scrubbed top, single dovetailed drawer, mortised and pinned construction base, shoe feet, traces of old red finish, age cracks in top, 41-3/4" w, 37-3/4" d, 28-3/4" h 4,200.00

Lamp Tables

Lamp or Light tables are small tables used to hold a lamp. Before the advent of electricity, candles or oil lamps on candle stands were used to provide lighting in a room setting. Once electricity became popular, it was then necessary to have a table to hold the new invention. Also see Candle Stands and Light Stands.

Arts & Crafts

Limbert, Charles P., Grand Rapids and Holland, MI

No. 148, circular top, splayed legs, wide square cutout cross stretchers, orig finish, branded mark, 30" d, 29" h 5,500.00

Circular top, broad cross stretchers, square cutouts, orig reddish-brown finish, branded mark, some stains on top, 30" d, 29" h...5,500.00

Stickley Brothers, Grand Rapids, MI

No. 2500, circular top over cross stretcher base, through-tenon construction, old refinishing, unsigned, 24" d, 29" h 1,100.00

Circular top, legs mortised through top, square apron, circular shelf on cross stretchers, new finish to top, orig finish to base, unmarked, 24" d, 30" h..........950.00

Circular top, orig tacked-on burgundy leather top with floral tacks, lower clip-cornered shelf, cross stretchers, new finish to base, unmarked, 26" d, 29-1/2" h 1,400.00

Stickley, Gustav, New York

No. 611, square clip-corner top, lower shelf on cross stretchers, cleaned orig finish, large paper label, some stains to top and shelf, 24" sq, 29" h 1,850.00

Circular top, sq and arched apron, flaring plank legs, keyed through-tenons, arched cross stretchers, unmarked, new finish, filled in hole on edge, 40" d, 28-3/4" h 4,250.00

Stickley, L. and J. G., Fayetteville, NY

Circular overhanging top, lower circular shelf, arched cross stretchers, unmarked, refinished, chip to one leg, 24" d, 29-1/4" h...850.00

Clipped corner, arched cross stretchers, refinished top, orig base, metal tag from "H. S. Barney Co., Schenectady, N.Y.," 24" sq, 29" h....................................900.00

Unknown Designer, circular top, lower shelf over cross stretchers, new dark finish, 29-1/4" d, 29" h.....................1,700.00

Library Tables

Library tables are broad-topped tables with plenty of room to spread out books, maps, and other types of reading materials found in a library. Look for the library table form in periods where it was fashionable to have a specific room designed as library in one's home. Other furnishings in such a room might include a

Library, Arts & Crafts, Gustav Stickley, New York, No. 614, c1912, oak, rectangular top, two drawers, hammered copper pulls, lower median shelf with through tenons, branded mark, 42" w, 29-1/2" d, 30" h, $2,100. Photo courtesy of Skinner Auctioneers and Appraisers of Antiques and Fine Art Boston, and Bolton MA.

desk, chairs, lamps, bookcases, lots of shelves with books, and perhaps a ladder or stool to be able to reach the higher bookshelves.

Aesthetic Movement, attributed to carver William Fry, Cincinnati, OH, oak, rectangular overhanging top, two dovetailed drawers, trestle base with rope carving, relief carving, grotesque head pulls, damage to one drawer, 43" l, 26-1/2" d, 30" h 825.00

Arts & Crafts

Limbert, Charles P., Grand Rapids and Holland, MI

No. 153, turtle-top, overhanging contoured top, single blind drawer, lower shelf mortised through trestle legs, four square cut-outs, fine orig finish, branded mark, 47-3/4" l, 30" d, 29-1/2" h.............9,500.00

No. 164, two drawers with orig copper pulls, full length corbels on legs, refinished, signed with copper plate, 48" w, 34" d, 29" h................................1,600.00

No. 1132, rectangular top over blind drawer, lift-top writing surface, wear to orig finish, branded mark, 42" w, 26" d, 29" h 1,750.00

Single drawer, overhanging rectangular top, pair of square brass pulls, orig finish, branded mark, minor wear to top, 42" w, 29-3/4" d, 29" h 1,500.00

Single drawer, overhanging rectangular top, square hammered copper pulls, arched apron, orig finish, branded mark, 48" w, 28" d, 29" h........................1,650.00

Single drawer, raised rectangular top, arched apron, ebony inlaid squares to casing, string inlay on legs, orig finish, branded mark, ink stains on top, 42" w, 26" d, 29-3/4" h 1,600.00

Single drawer, rectangular top, orig copper hardware, inset caned panel, shaped slab legs with cutout design, orig finish, branded mark, 42" w, 24" d, 29" h 1,750.00

Two drawer, overhanging top, long corbels, over-coat to dark finish, branded Limbert mark, 48" l, 34" d, 29" h..........1,300.00

Roycroft, East Aurora, NY, oak

No. 018, mahogany, massive form, two drawers, orig copper hardware, five vertical slats to each side, keyed-tenon lower shelf, Mackmurdo feet, orb signature, orig finish, minor surface wear, 48"w, 30" d, 30" h..............................6,000.00

Apron, lower shelf, Mackmurdo feet, skinned finish, carved orb and cross mark, 30" w, 22" d, 27-3/4" h 4,000.00

Single drawer, two oval copper pulls, flaring plank sides with Moorish cut-outs, carved orb and cross mark, new dark finish, 59-1/2" l, 30" d, 30" h 3,250.00

Shop of the Crafters, No. 335, cut-corner top over slab sides, intricate inlaid design in ebony and lighter woods, rectilinear cutouts above cross stretcher base, numbered, top refinished, orig finish to base, some veneer loss, 36 w, 36" d, 29" h 2,850.00

Stickley Brothers, Grand Rapids, MI

No. 2680, overhanging rounded rectangular top, three drawers, large brass escutcheons and pulls, through-tenon lower shelf, over-coated finish, unmarked, 60" l, 36" d, 30" h 2,500.00

No. 2784, rectangular top, single drawer, orig wooden knobs, three vertical slats to sides, arched top rail, through-tenon construction, refinished, unsigned, 40" w, 26" d, 30" h..........................750.00

Overhanging rectangular top, single drawer, two slatted shelves on either side, lower shelf, orig finish, marked "Quaint Furniture/Stickley Bros. Co./Grand Rapids, MI," 44" 2, 28" d, 30-1/4" h 1,250.00

Prairie Design, rectangular top, lower shelf supported by two legs on each side, full length corbels, refinished, Quaint metal tag, 40"w, 26" d, 39" h........1,700.00

Stickley, Gustav, New York

No. 456, rectangular top, two hidden drawers, lower shelf with flush tenon construction, orig finish, early red decal, minor distress to top, 36" w, 24" d, 29" h 12,100.00

No. 614, c1912, oak, rectangular top, two drawers, hammered copper pulls, lower median shelf with through tenons, branded mark, 42" w, 29-1/2" d, 30" h...........2,100.00

No. 636, c1902, circular, orig tacked-on leather top, flaring plank legs, arched apron and cross stretchers mortised with keyed through tenons, orig finish, large red box decal, 48" d, 30" h.........22,500.00

No. 653, rectangular top over single drawer, orig iron hardware, orig finish on base, top refinished, red decal, 48" w, 30" d, 29" h 1,985.00

Hexagonal, arched and stacked stretchers mortised through six legs, keyed through-tenons, refinished top, orig ebonized finished on base, partial label, 55" d, 30" h...4,750.00

Rectangular top, full-sized, two drawers, long corbels, cast iron butterfly pulls, arched through-tenon construction, orig finish, large early red decal, some scratches on top, 59-1/2" l, 35" d, 30-3/4" h 30,950.00

Stickley, L. and J. G., Fayetteville, NY

No. 597, overhanging rectangular top, narrow lower shelf, mortised with keyed through tenons, orig dark finish, Handcraft label, some wear to top, 40" w, 28" d, 29" h..1,600.00

Overhanging rectangular top, single drawer, long corbels, lower shelf, orig finish, Handcraft decal, some rings on top, 42" l, 28" d, 29" h 1,500.00

Overhanging rectangular top, single drawer, copper pulls, long corbels, "The Work of L. and J. G. Stickley" label, new finish, 42" w, 28" d, 29" h 1,300.00

Overhanging rectangular top, two drawers, copper pulls, lower shelf, orig dark finish, Handcraft decal, three small drilled homes in one leg, some splits to lower shelf and leg top, 48" l, 30-1/4" d, 29-1/2" h....................1,600.00

Unknown Designer

Large architectural form, rattan with oak inset top, bookshelves at each side, suspended lower shelf all with oak inset surfaces, refinished, repainted, 72" w, 36" d, 30" h..4,400.00

Oak, rectangular top, c1912, single drawer, hammered copper pulls, lower median shelf with through tenons, arched side stretchers, stains, wear, 48" w, 30-1/4" d, 30" h 525.00

Oak, rectangular top, single drawer on each side, one drawer with lift-up writing surface, refinished, 38" w, 25" d, 30" h 500.00

Centennial, c1876, walnut, inlay and medallions 8,000.00

Victorian

America, late 19th C, oak, octagonal faux marbleized top, molded rim with foliage and hammered motif, inset drawer with egg and dart border, support with turned finial center, lion's head scroll feet with caters, 53" w, 31-1/2" h 2,900.00

Renaissance Revival, c1875, walnut, felt inset top, 38" l, 23-1/2" w, 28-1/2" h 500.00

Occasional Tables

Occasional tables are small tables used to hold bric-a-brac, perhaps lamps, or magazines. Another name for this type of useful table is "end tables," especially when found in pairs. Like coffee tables, this form of table did not become popular until the 20th Century, when decorating and entertaining styles changed dramatically. A few examples exist from earlier furniture styles, but these small tables were probably called side or work tables. Also see Side Tables and Work Tables.

Aesthetic Movement

Rohlfs, Charles, rectangular top, four sq legs, signed and dated 1905, 23-3/4" l, 18" w, 28-1/2" h 950.00

Unknown Designer, brass mounted rosewood and mixed metal, spider-web inlay on top corner, minor imperfections, 20" w, 20" d, 27" h 8,925.00

Arts & Crafts

Limbert, Charles P., Grand Rapids and Holland, MI, octagonal top over splayed legs, spade cutouts supported by cross stretchers and double keyed tenons, some wear to orig finish and corners, unsigned, 45" d, 29" h 2,750.00

Roycroft, East Aurora, NY, oak, overhanging rectangular top, lower shelf, Mackmurdo feet, carved orb and cross mark, refinished, 30" w, 22" d, 28" h 4,750.00

Stickley, Gustav, New York, No. 644, round top, four cut-in leg posts, offset cross stretcher, base with through tenons, paper label, refinished, stains, 30" d, 28-3/4" h, ...2,070.00

Federal, first quarter 19th C, cherry, outset rectangular top, frieze with drawer, turned,

tapered, and reeded legs, 17-1/4" w, 17-1/4" d, 28-1/2" h..1,000.00

Georgian-Style, America, c1930, carved mahogany, shallow apron carved in blind Chinese fret, conforming plate glass top, 19" d, 27-1/2" h..200.00

Louis XVI-Style, giltwood and marble top, gray veined white marble oval top, pierced foliate frieze suspending floral swags, turned and fluted legs joined by X-form stretcher, 29-1/2" l, 22" w, 23" h 200.00

Modernism Era

Evans, Paul, 1970, circular glass top, sculpted base, sprayed metal exterior, sgd and dated, 42" d, 25" h 260.00

Frankl, Paul

Manufactured by Directional, c1966, sculptural bronze exterior, black laminated top, price for set of three, 16" h, 16" h 1,300.00

Manufactured by Johnson Furniture Co., two tiered design, cream lacquered cork top, dark mahogany Greek key frame, price for pair, 36" w, 33" d, 24" h 650.00

Mathsson, Bruno, manufactured by Karl Mathsson, 1940s, rectangular birch top, molded birch legs, label, 29" w, 20"d, 21" h 850.00

Nelson, George, manufactured by Herman Miller, circular white laminate top, white pedestal base, orig label, some wear, 17" d, 22" h 250.00

Platner, Warren, manufactured by Knoll International, bronzed finished rod construction, orig glass top, 16" d, 18" h..........850.00

Robsjohn-Gibbings, T. H., manufactured by Widdicomb, 1955

Circular walnut veneered top, walnut dowel base, double cross stretchers, orig label, 30" d, 24" h...........................885.00

Square walnut veneered top, walnut dowel base, double cross stretchers, orig label, 30" sq, 22" h 950.00

Rohde, Gilbert, manufactured by Herman Miller, pair, two tiers, dark finish, tapered leatherette wrapped tapered legs, single drawer, 29" w, 16" d, 27" h 1,450.00

Saarinen, Eero, manufactured by Knoll International, white circular laminate top, white pedestal base, label, 20" d, 21" h 285.00

Unknown Designer, manufactured by Dunbar, Berne, IN, post war, rectangular top over single drawer, leathered covered drawer pulls, four legs with leather capped feet, light brown finish, metal tag, minor loss, 19" w, 17" d, 25" h 200.00

Pembroke Tables

The term "Pembroke Table" is usually used to describe a small drop-leaf table with or without a drawer. A Pembroke table was customarily found in a bedroom or upper sitting room. The name "Pembroke" hastens back to the Federal furniture style and reflects on the custom of the day to have one's breakfast served on a small table in a bedchamber. A Pembroke is generally smaller than a breakfast or drop-leaf table. Also see Breakfast Tables and Drop-Leaf Tables.

Chippendale

America, cherry, two board top, beaded apron, dovetailed drawer with brass knob, square legs with inside chamfer and beading, mellow finish, maple and poplar secondary woods, 35-1/2" l, 21-1/2" d, 7-3/4" leaves, 28" h 3,200.00

America, cherry, poplar secondary wood, one dovetailed drawer, drop-leaf top with cut ovolo corners on leaves, square molded legs,

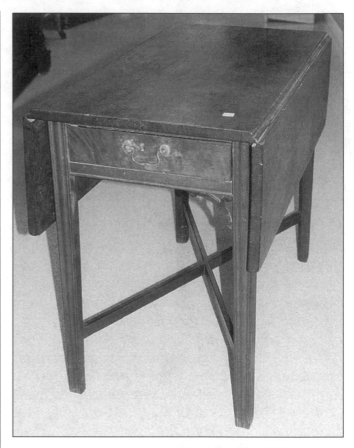

Pembroke, Chippendale, Philadelphia, PA, c1780, cherry, single drawer, fretwork arches on apron, tapered legs, cross-stretcher base, orig hardware, 34" l, $1,980. Photo courtesy of Alderfer Auction Company, Hatfield, PA.

orig brass bale, old mellow refinishing, 34-1/2" l, 8-1/2" leaves, 28-1/2" h......2,310.00

America, mahogany, drop-leaf top, one dovetailed drawer, square tapered legs with inside chamfer, cross stretcher base, old finish, replaced brasses on drawer, repair to cross stretcher, 20" w, 33" l, 9-1/2" l leaves, 28" h 1,550.00

Connecticut River Valley, c1780, mahogany, exotically grained drop leaf top, four sq legs with inside chamfered corners, joined by straight skirt, drawer, shaped flat cross stretchers, old finish, orig brasses, top slightly warped, 35" w, 34-3/4' d, 27" h 3,875.00

Massachusetts, Cape Cod, mahogany, rectangular drop-leaf top, single dovetailed cock-beaded drawer, square molded legs with inside chamfer and cross stretcher, old finish, old brass bale, poplar and oak secondary woods, added steel angle braces to underside

Pembroke, Chippendale, country, shaped drop leaves, single drawer with wooden knob, tapered legs with peg feet, $300.

of top, minor stains on top, 10-3/4" l leaves, 20-1/4" w, 31-3/4" w, 28-3/4" h............3,575.00

New Hampshire, Portsmouth, late 18th C, cherry, rectangular drop leaf top overhangs straight skirt with drawer, four sq beaded legs, inside corner chamfered to shape and pierced cross stretchers, refinished, repairs, 35" w, 21-1/2" d, 27-3/4" h...............2,610.00

Pennsylvania, c1750-80, highly figured mahogany rectangular top, two drop leaves, single drawer with line beading and brass bail handle, straight molded legs with chamfered interior corners, crossed X-form stretcher, 20-1/2" w, 29" d, 27-1/2" h.................2,585.00

Pennsylvania, c1780, mahogany, rectangular top, two drop leaves, single drawer, square tapering legs with chamfered interior corners, joined by X-form stretcher, orig brass pull, repairs to stretcher and top, 37" w, 30-1/2" d, 28" h.........................550.00

Federal

America, 1790-1800, walnut, rectangular top with two leaves, single drawer with replaced pull, square tapered legs, banded inlay on frame and on legs 3" from bottom, 20" w, 34" d, 29" h.............................1,020.00

Detail of leg on Federal table.

Pembroke, Federal, eastern Virginia, c1800-13, mahogany inlaid, top with stringing in outline, two inlaid drawer facades, one working, one faux, square tapering legs with inlaid circles and stringing in outline, old refinish, minor imperfections, 37" w, 22" d, 47-3/4" extended, 27" h, $3,800. Photo courtesy of Skinner Auctioneers and Appraisers of Antiques and Fine Art Boston and Bolton, MA.

Massachusetts or Connecticut, c1800, cherry, serpentine drop leaf top, frieze drawer, string inlay, lower edges of alternating inlay squares joining four sq double tapered legs inlaid with oval paterae, stringing and icicle motif continue to sawtooth cuffs, refinished, 20" w, 39-1/2" d, 28-3/4" h.................3,500.00

Massachusetts, c1800, inlaid mahogany, rectangular drop leaf top with ovolo corners, single drawer, straight skirt joining four sq tapering legs with stringing inlay, refinished, old brass pull, 35-3/4" w, 19" d, 28-1/2" h...1,650.00

New England, c1800, mahogany, rectangular drop leaf top, straight apron, drawer with incised cockbeading, four square tapering legs, orig oval brass pull, old finish, minor imperfections, 20" w closed, 31" d, 29" h...........1,725.00

New England, c1810-15, mahogany inlaid, rectangular overhanging top, rounded leaves, straight skirt with drawer, lower inlaid edge continuing to four vase and ring-turned reeded tapering legs, old refinish, imperfections, 36" w, 18-3/4" d, 28-1/2" h.....1,955.00

New Jersey, early 19th C, mahogany inlaid, rectangular top outlined in inlay, shaped leaves also outlined, faux and working drawers with same outlining, flanked by inlays above square tapering legs outlined with stringing and double band of cuff inlays, orig brasses, old surface, 32" w, 20" d, 27-1/2" h..........................3,800.00

New York, c1790-1800, mahogany inlaid, rectangular top, shaped drop-leaves bordered by stringing, crossbanded skirt, working and faux birch veneered drawers, bordered by stringing, four square tapering legs inlaid with wavy birch panels in the dies above stringing and inlaid legs, refinished, some fading, 20-1/2" w, 30-1/2" d, 28-1/2" h............2,300.00

New York, c1790-1810, mahogany inlaid, rectangular line inlaid top flanked by ellipti-cally shaped leaves, line inlaid veneered drawer, one false drawer, crossbanded inlay on frame, square tapered legs with line inlay and crossbanded cuffs, orig hexagonal stamped brass pulls on drawer and false drawer, 20-1/2" w, 32" d, 28" h 6,750.00

New York, c1800-20, mahogany, rectan-gular top with double elliptical leaves, single cockbeaded drawer flanked by inlaid veneer tombstone panels, reeded legs with ring turnings at neck tapering to bulbous peg feet, brass casters, 24-1/2" w closed, 35-3/4" d, 28-1/4" h..........................1,400.00

New York, c1810, mahogany, rectangular top, two shaped drop leaves, single drawer, orig pull, casters, old refinish, shaped leaves extend to 32-3/4" l, 30" w, 18-1/4" d, 27-1/4" h..1,400.00

New York, c1815, mahogany veneer, mahogany rectangular top with hinged rounded leaves, flanking one faux and one working drawer, each with cockbeaded skirt, spiral carved legs ending in ring-turned feet, old refinish, replaced brasses, 23" w, 36" l, 28-1/2" h..1,150.00

Rhode Island, c1800, cherry inlaid, oval drop-leaf top with incised beaded edges, con-forming skirt with drawers, lower edge inlaid with contrasting stringing, joining four square tapering legs with icicle inlay, stringing, and banded cuffs, orig bail brasses, old refinish, 36-3/4" x 32-3/4" top, 27-3/4" h...........7,475.00

Southeastern United States, c1790-1800, mahogany inlaid, oval drop-leaf top bordered in inlaid stringing on conforming skirt, drawer

and lower edge of geometric banding, four square tapering legs, dies inlaid with ovals, ebony dots and stringing continuing with bell flowers, stringing, and cuffs, replaced brass pulls, old refinish, minor imperfections, 37" w, 29-1/2" d, 28-1/2" h...............3,335.00

Virginia, eastern, c1800-13, mahogany inlaid, top with stringing in outline, two inlaid drawer facades, one working, one faux, square tapering legs with inlaid circles and stringing in outline, old refinish, minor imper-fections, 37" w, 22" d, 47-3/4" extended, 27" h 3,800.00

Georgian-Style, c1860, mahogany, two frieze drawers, raised on turned circular stan-dard, four splayed legs ending in bass caps on casters, 25-1/2" w, extends to 48", 32-1/4" d, 29" h..1,100.00

Hepplewhite

America, cherry, one board top, mortised and pinned apron, one dovetailed drawer, cross stretcher, sq tapered legs, imperfec-tions, 31" w, 18-1/4" d, 28-1/2" h 750.00

America, cherry, serpentine drop leaf top, serpentine end aprons, conforming drawer, sq tapering legs with inside chamfer, stringing inlay on legs and aprons with fans and oval pat-erae, fretwork brackets, refinished, 35-3/8" w, 16-3/4" d, 8-3/4" l leaves, 28" h............7,200.00

America, inlaid mahogany, drop leaf top, banded inlay on top, single dovetailed drawer, sq tapered legs, inlay stringing and banding on legs, curved end aprons, old worn finish, edge inlay damage, old repairs, replaced brass knob, 32" w, 17-3/4' d, 10-1/4" l leaves, 28-3/4" h 950.00

America, maple and birch, one board curly birch top, bird's eye figure in legs, apron, and drawer front, square tapered legs, single dovetailed drawer, one board leaves with rounded corners, refinished, top reattached, glue blocks added, 36" w, 12" leaves, 28-1/2" h 900.00

Maryland, Baltimore, attributed to school of Levin Tarr, mahogany, line and band inlay top, bellflower, ovals, line and band inlaid tapered legs, rounded drops, provenance from Harford County, MD, family, 33" l, 43" open, 28-1/2" h.......................62,750.00

New England, mahogany, inlay, shaped drop leaves, single drawer, sq tapered legs, white pine and poplar secondary woods, refinished, repaired, 21" w, 33" d, 28" h..... 1,250.00

Sheraton, country

Cherry, one board top and leaves, one dovetailed drawer, well shaped turned legs, old finish, poplar secondary wood, replaced wood knob pull, 36" w, 18-1/2" d, 13" l leaves, 30" h...450.00

Cherry and curly maple, drop-leaf, shaped leaves, turned legs, 35-1/2" w, 18" d, 12" l leaves, 28-3/4" h.................................500.00

Mahogany, rectangular top with demilune drop leaves, single drawer frieze, reeded tapered legs, brass casters, 41" l, extended, 36" d, 29-3/4" h................................1,975.00

Maple, folding apron wings, turned legs, old finish, 36-1/4" w, 17-1/4" d, 28" h........ 1,450.00

Victorian, America, maple, red top, two 10" w leaves, two aligned frieze drawers, baluster turned legs, 17-1/2" w, 28" h.....................650.00

Pier Tables

Pier tables are elaborate creations designed to allow a lady to gaze into the mirrored back and see that her skirts were in proper order. Pier tables were commonly placed in halls and public spaces of grand houses to facilitate this usage. The form is found only in very formal styles.

Classical

Massachusetts, Boston, c1820-35, mahogany veneer, carved, rectangular white marble top, gilt carvings of flowers tied with ribbons, center carving of cupids and wreath, mirrored back, columns with gilding, shaped base, 45-1/2" w, 16-7/8" d, 19-1/4" h................4,250.00

Middle Atlantic States, c1830-40, carved mahogany, figured mahogany veneer splashboard supported by marble columns topped by carved Ionic capitals with ring-turned bases, marble top, two convex veneered drawers, similar columns flank platform with concave front, backed by mirror and pilasters, old refinish, 37-1/2" w, 19" d, 41" h......................................3,750.00

New York, c1835-40, mahogany veneer, figured veneer frieze about square tapering columns ending in molded bases, flanking shaped

Pier, Classical, New York, c1835-40, mahogany veneer, figured mahogany veneer frieze above square tapering columns ending in molded bases, flanking shaped veneer platform with flat columns in rear flanking pier glass, old refinish, marble top missing, veneer cracking and loss, $2,070. Photo courtesy of Skinner Auctioneers and Appraisers of Antiques and Fine Art Boston and Bolton, MA.

veneer platform with flat columns in rear flanking pier glass, old refinish, marble top missing, veneer cracking and loss 2,100.00

Pennsylvania, c1830, mahogany veneer, carved, rectangular marble top, carved Doric capitals on columns as supports, D-shaped shelf with conforming apron, plain back, reeded bulbed feet, 40" w, 22" d, 40" h............1,500.00

Pennsylvania, c1840, attributed to William Alexander, Sharpsburg, carved mahogany and mahogany veneer, brass-inlay stringing and rosettes, acanthus-leaf and grapevine-carved frontal supports, paw feet, rectangular mirror flanked by turned and fluted supports, framed with black and gilt foliate designs, medial shelf with inset oval marble panel, remnants of paper label, old refinish, minor imperfections, 42-1/8" w, 18-7/8" d, 40" h 14,500.00

Hepplewhite, c1790, mahogany, serpentine top above conforming frieze fitted with one drawers, raised on molded tapering square legs, 30-1/2" w, 16" d, 32-1/2" h..........1,980.00

Rent Tables

Rent tables are rare. They were made with numerous drawers to store records of a land-

lord's tenants. The one included here is interesting for it's unique combination of woods, plus the maker signed it and dated it and even included the area of Ohio where he worked.

Ohio, cherry, oak, curly maple, and walnut, revolving octagonal top with four dovetailed drawers, lyre pedestal with applied circle, four part base, scrolled feet, old refinishing, some edge and veneer damage, one drawer bottom signed "James Anderson maker, Hamilton Co., Harrison, Ohio 1857," 26" d, 29" h 3,000.00

Side Tables

Side tables are small tables used to hold accessories, lamps, or small objects. Most furniture styles include a small table whose function varied depending upon the room it was used in. Also see Occasional Tables and Side Stands.

Art Deco, Warren McArthur, manufactured by McArthur Industries, c1930, black lacquer top, tubular anodized aluminum frame, orig rubber feet, damage to top, 24" w, 18" d, 31" h 4,250.00

Art Deco-Style, America, late 20th C, wrought iron, rectangular glass top, metal frame with striations, scrolled legs and cross stretchers, gray metal finish, corner of glass chipped, 32" l, 20" d, 18" h....................175.00

Side, Arts & Crafts, New York, rectangular top over medial shelf, pegged tenons exposed through shaped sides extending to base, wear, repair to foot, refinished, 36-1/4" l, 24-1/8" d, 28-1/4" h, $2,300. Photo courtesy of Skinner Auctioneers and Appraisers of Antiques and Fine Art Boston, and Bolton MA.

Art Moderne, attributed to Lorin Jackson, c1942, Lucite, oval glass top, circular skirt with applied rosettes, four tapering legs, price for pair, 21-1/4" d, 25-3/4" h 4,800.00

Arts & Crafts

Limbert, Charles P., Grand Rapids and Holland, MI, c1807, oak, oval lower shelf, cross-member base, sq cutouts, orig dark finish, branded mark, 47-1/2" l, 36" d, 29-1/4" h 3,950.00

Unknown Designer, New York, oak, trestle, rectangular top, medial shelf with pegged tenons exposed through shaped sides extending to base, wear, repair to foot, refinished, 36-1/4" l, 24-1/8" d, 28-1/4" h 2,300.00

Chippendale

Massachusetts, c1780, red painted birch, overhanging top, half serpentine ends, serpentine front, straight skirt, thumb-molded Marlborough legs, orig red paint, imperfections, 24" d, 15-1/2" d, 26" h............2,185.00

New England, c1780, carved cherry, rectangular overhanging top, four Marlborough molded legs joining beaded straight skirt with

Side, Chippendale, Massachusetts, c1780, birch, rectangular overhanging top with half serpentine ends, serpentine front, straight skirt, thumb-molded Marlborough legs, orig red paint, imperfections, 24" w, 15-1/2" d, 26" h, $2,185. Photo courtesy of Skinner Auctioneers and Appraisers of Antiques and Fine Art Boston and Bolton, MA.

drawer, old finish, top warped, other imperfections, 14" w, 21-1/2" d, 27-1/2" h.........2,530.00

Classical

Massachusetts, c1825, mahogany and mahogany veneer, rectangular top with scrolled gallery above conforming case with long drawer, circular brass pulls, four ring-turned column supports, concave platform, turned legs, old refinishing, 39" w, 18-3/4" d, 30" h 2,950.00

New England, c1825, mahogany and mahogany veneer, circular marble top, top supported by center pedestal and three C-shaped supports, scrolled shaped base, casters, 24" d, 30" h 6,250.00

Federal

Massachusetts, c1810-15, mahogany, square overhanging top, straight beaded skirt and single drawers, four ring-turned reeded tapering legs, brass casters, refinished, minor imperfections, 19-1/4" sq, 27-1/2" h 1,840.00

Middle Atlantic States, c1820, curly maple, square top, single cockbeaded drawer, square tapering legs, 19-1/2" l, 19-1/2" w, 29-1/4" h 1,500.00

New England, c1790-1800, mahogany and birch, figured mahogany overhand, figured birch drawer, four square tapering legs, straight skirt with drawer, old refinish, minor imperfections, 17" w, 17-1/2" d, 27-3/4" h..........2,875.00

Side, Federal, Massachusetts, c1810-15, mahogany, square overhanging top, straight beaded skirt and single drawers, four ring-turned reeded tapering legs, brass casters, refinished, minor imperfections, 19-1/4" sq, 27-1/2" h, $1,840. Photo courtesy of Skinner Auctioneers and Appraisers of Antiques and Fine Art Boston and Bolton, MA.

New England, c1800-10, tiger maple, overhanging square top with ovolo corners, straight skirt with drawer joining four square tapering legs, replaced brass pull, old refinish, very minor imperfections, 19-3/4" x 19-1/2" top, 28" h..............................4,350.00

New Hampshire, c1820, maple and birch, rectangular overhanging top with ovolo corners, straight skirt with drawer, joining vase and ring-turned tapering legs, replaced brasses, refinished, 20-1/2" w, 18-1/2" d, 29-1/2" h......700.00

Federal, Late, c1800-1825, cherry, poplar secondary wood, molded rectangular top, frieze drawer, turned and ring-turned legs, bun feet, 20-3/4" w, 29" h..............................250.00

Georgian, c1820 and later, mahogany, rectangular top with molded edge, frieze fitted with two drawers, square tapering legs, 39-1/4" w, 20" d, 35-1/2" h 675.00

Hepplewhite, Southern, walnut, one board top, mortised and pinned apron, fretwork corner brackets, applied molding around edge of apron, one dovetailed drawer with figured drawer front, banded inlay, orig oval brass with emb thistles, sq tapering legs, yellow pine secondary wood, refinished, minor repairs, stands, and age cracks, 23-1/2" w, 19-1/2" d, 28-1/4" h................ 1,250.00

Mission, oak, three-quarter gallery, two open shelves, slat form, supports, sq legs, 15-3/4" w, 12-1/4' d, 31" h......................850.00

Modernism Era

Eames, Charles, manufactured by Herman Miller, ESU 100, black laminated top, zinc frame, primary blue masonite panel, 24" w, 16" d, 21" h 2,210.00

Frankl, Paul, manufactured by Johnson Furniture Co., cream lacquered cork top above dark mahogany shelf on triangular legs, some wear, 30" w, 18" d, 21" h 350.00

Noguchi, Isamu, manufactured to Knoll International, circular white laminate top, wire struts and birch wood base, label, 24" d, 20" h 4,400.00

Unknown Designer, manufactured by Dunbar, Berne, IN, post war, what-not, circular top over shelf above single drawer, three tapered shaped legs, light brown finish, metal tag inside drawer, minor wear, 20-1/2" d, 26-1/2" h.............................550.00

Wormley, Edward, manufactured by Dunbar, Janus, sculptured dark mahogany frame, Tiffany glass tile top, brass feet, gold metal tag, crack to one tile, 15" sq, 23" h 2,900.00

Neoclassical, c1865, rosewood, variegated marble top, incised carved molded edge, burled skirt with applied medallions and shield, central stylized urn standard, plinth base, four scrolling gilt decorated palmetto legs, flattened ball feet, 24" d, 29" h...........................6,500.00

Queen Anne

Pennsylvania, c1750, walnut, rectangular top, plain skirt, splayed turned tapering legs, pad feet, 20-1/2" l, 19-3/4" w, 28-1/2" h 6,850.00

Rhode Island, c1760, mahogany, molded oblong top, shaped skirt, turned tapering legs, pad feet, 40-1/4" l, 21" w, 26" h...........7,000.00

Tramp Art, New England or New York, late 19th/early 20th C, carved woods, projecting square top, medial shelf, square legs with applied multi-layered shaped and chip carved decorations, old varnish finish, 16" w, 15-3/4" d, 26" h 700.00

Victorian

America, carved mahogany, shaped marble top, foliate carved apron, cabriole legs joined by X-stretcher with center finial, 31" w, 22" d, 29" h..575.00

Renaissance Revival, c1860, rosewood, gilt incised, circular black marble top, leaf-carved frieze and pedestal with geometric inlay, foliate-carved tripod base, tiger-paw feet, trefoil base on carved bun feet, losses to two feet, 19" d, 30-3/4" h 6,750.00

William and Mary, late 17th C

Marquetry, walnut, inlaid rectangular top, molded edge, one long drawer, later barley-twist legs, shaped inlaid center stretcher, ball feet, 42-1/2" l, 24-1/2" d, 33" h 1,750.00

Walnut, rectangular top with molded edge, frieze drawer, ring and baluster turned legs, joined with waved cross stretcher, ball feet, 27" l, 26" h 4,200.00

William IV, c1840, pine and mahogany, rounded rectangular top raised above plain frieze, turned circular legs, bulbous toupie feet, 54" w, 21" d, 29" h.................................465.00

Sofa Tables

Sofa tables are narrow tables made to be placed behind a sofa. This type of furniture arrangement was particularly popular in homes with large rooms where furniture was placed in the center of a room, rather than around the perimeter. By including a table behind a sofa, a lamp and other small accessories could also be placed there.

Classical

Massachusetts, Boston, c1825, mahogany and mahogany veneer, rectangular overhanging top with rounded leaves, straight skirt with two short drawers and square tapering support, serpentine platform with canted corners, suppressed ball feet, old turned wooden pulls, refinished, minor imperfections, 57" w, 24" d, 30" h..............1,850.00

New York, c1820-25, carved mahogany and mahogany veneer, rectangular drop-leaf top with reeded edge above ogee molded frame of two short drawers, shaped supports with Ionic capitals and applied banded panels, molded plinths and outward flaring legs ending in brass hairy paw feet joined by square molded tapering stretcher, old refinish, some imperfections, 41" w, 19-1/2" d, 30" h 3,000.00

Regency-Style, English, satinwood, rosewood crossbanded, ebony inlaid, silvered hardware, trestle supports ending in caps on casters, 37-1/2" w, 23" d, 29-1/2" h.....2,990.00

Tavern Tables

Tavern tables are a popular type of table with collectors and decorators. Tavern tables typically have a rectangular top, an apron, four legs and a stretcher connecting the legs for added stability. Many examples of tavern tables exist, possibly because this type of table was popular and taverns were known to use many small tables for dining, games, etc. Tavern tables have been copied for generations by craftsmen so it is not unusual to find stylized examples of many of the historical furniture periods. Before buying a vintage tavern table, look for signs of wear, perhaps repairs, and a desirable patina.

Chippendale

Country, cherry, rectangular top, one wide drawer, one small drawer, block and ring-

Tavern, Chippendale, 18th C, tiger-maple, breadboard top, single long drawer, scalloped apron, ring turned tapered legs, $750.

Tavern, Federal, Massachusetts or New Hampshire, 18th C, maple rectangular overhanging top with breadboard ends, single thumb-molded pine drawer, turned tapering legs ending in double ball turned feet, old refinish on base, old scrubbed top, very minor imperfections, 41-1/2" w, 28" d, 27" h, $2,760. Photo courtesy of Skinner Auctioneers and Appraisers of Antiques and Fine Art Boston and Bolton, MA.

turned legs, stretcher shelf, brass bail handles, escutcheons, lock plates............650.00

Country, pine, two board top with breadboard ends, mortised and pegged apron with edge bed, stretcher base, square slightly splayed legs with molded corners, old nut brown finish, repairs to beading, top is old replacement, 31" w, 21-3/4" d, 28" h ..715.00

New England, late 18th C, cherry, old refinish, restoration, 27-3/4" w, 20-1/4" d, 22-3/4" h 1,750.00

Colonial Revival, Wallace Nutting, William and Mary-Style, c1930, No. 637, maple, rectangular removable top, one large drawer, heavily turned legs with ball/peg feet, massive H-form stretcher, branded mark and paper label, some staining to top, 49-3/4" w, 30-1/4" d, 30-1/4" h 1,250.00

Federal

Country, hardwood and pine, turned legs, mortised and pinned apron and stretcher, scrubbed finish, repaired, 38-1/4" l, 28" h
....300.00

Massachusetts or New Hampshire, 18th C, maple rectangular overhanging top with breadboard ends, single thumb-molded pine drawer, turned tapering legs ending in double ball turned feet, old refinish on base, old scrubbed top, very minor imperfections, 41-1/2" w, 28" d, 27" h 2,760.00

New England, c1790-1810, painted pine and maple, rectangular overhanging top, straight skirt joining four square tapering legs, old red paint on base, imperfections, 46" w, 28" d, 28" h 2,550.00

New England, southeastern, c1800, maple, rectangular overhanging breadboard top, straight skirt, thumb-molded drawer joining four squared tapering legs, old surface with vestiges of dark brown paint, 36" w, 25" d, 27-3/4" h................................2,875.00

Pennsylvania, 18th C, poplar, rectangular overhaging top, straight beaded skirt, large and small drawers, four block, vase, and ring-turned legs continuing to turned feet, joined by box stretchers, replaced brasses, old refinish, restored, 54" w, 29" h............................ 980.00

Hepplewhite, country, maple and pine, scrubbed pine breadboard top, mortised and pinned maple apron, sq tapered maple legs, traces of old red paint on base, 37-1/2" l, 26-1/2" h..800.00

Queen Anne, country

Maple and birch, one board pine top with scrubbed finish, breadboard ends, dovetailed drawer with beaded edge and brass pull, turned legs with button feet and stretcher base, old worn red finish, two posts have age cracks, top with added square nails, 22-1/2" w, 18-1/2" d, 25" h 4,675.00

Maple base, one board pine top with breadboard ends, one dovetailed drawer with pine front, turned wooden pull, stretcher base with turned legs, ball feet, old refinishing, feet ended out, age cracks in top, 41-1/4" w, 22-1/2" d, 27-1/2" h.........1,760.00

Maple, brown over earlier red, two board top with molded edge, notched corners, dovetailed drawer, turned legs, button feet, pine secondary wood, old replaced engraved brasses in orig holes, some restoration to top, glue blocks replaced, 19" w, 30-1/2" l, 25-7/8" h...........................1,925.00

Maple, oval two board top, mortised and pinned apron, cut-out detail, tapered legs with duck feet, old reddish stain on base, wear and repair to feet, old repairs, 30-1/2" x 22" top, 26-3/4" h..............................3,355.00

Maple, two board top with notched corners, mortised and pinned apron, tapered legs, duck feet, top cleaned, old red on base, old finish with stains, minor age cracks in top, 36" l, 26-1/2" w, 27-1/2" h.........5,500.00

Pine, worn old red, one board top with molded and cut corners, turned tapered legs, worn button feet, 30-1/2" w, 23" d, 27" h 1,100.00

Queen Anne-Style, country, hardwood and pine

Oval two board top, turned legs, molded stretcher, made up out of old parts, 29-1/2" l, 21-1/4" w, 25-3/4" h 495.00

Two board top with breadboard ends, mortised and pinned apron, one dovetailed drawer, turned legs, duck feet, old mellow refinishing, some restoration, 42-1/2" w, 28-1/2" d, 28" h................................1,100.00

William and Mary

New England, c1740, maple, rectangular overhanging top with thumb-molded edge above single drawer, baluster turned legs joined by square stretchers, turned feet, old refinish, replaced wood pulls, very minor imperfections, 40" w, 19" d, 29" h 6,900.00

New England, c1750, maple and pine, round overhanging top, plain apron, turned legs, box stretcher, varnish over old red paint, 34-1/4" d, 25-1/2" h...............7,500.00

New England, 18th C, maple and pine, rectangular overhanging top, straight skirt with thumb-molded drawer, four block vase and ring-turned legs continuing to turned feet, joined by box stretchers, old refinish, some imperfections, 37-1/2" w, 26" d, 26-1/2" h 2,100.00

New England, mid-18th C, maple and pine, rectangular overhanging breadboard top, block, vase and ring-turned splayed legs joined by straight molded skirt, box stretcher, turned feet, old surface, imperfections, 21-3/4" w, 15" d, 25" h 2,530.00

New England, mid-18th C, painted birch and pine, oval overhanging top, four splayed vase and ring-turned legs continuing to turned feet, joined by straight apron and box stretchers, painted black, imperfections, 33" l, 24" d, 17" h..............................8,100.00

New England, mid-18th C, painted maple and pine, rectangular overhanging breadboard top, straight apron with thumb-molded drawers, block, vase, and ring-turned legs ending in turned feet, square stretchers, later red paint, imperfections, 44" w, 25-1/4" d, 28-1/2" h...4,320.00

New England, Southeastern, 18th C, overhanging rectangular top, four block turned legs ending in turned feet, joined by straight skirt with drawer, old finish, minor imperfections, 41-3/4" w, 28" d, 27-1/2" h..................2,990.00

Tavern, William and Mary, New England, mid-18th C, maple and pine, rectangular overhanging breadboard top, block, vase and ring-turned splayed legs joined by straight molded skirt, box stretcher, turned feet, old surface, imperfections, 21-3/4" w, 15" d, 25" h, $2,530. Photo courtesy of Skinner Auctioneers and Appraisers of Antiques and Fine Art Boston and Bolton, MA.

Pennsylvania, 1770-1810, walnut, rectangular top, molded skirt, three molded drawers, ring-turned legs, box stretcher, flattened ball feet, 29" w, 30" h 6,000.00

Tea Tables

Tea tables constitute one of the most desirable of the high end antique table categories. Their elegance is well defined in their design, from the top to the turned pedestal to the sweeping bases. And, since tea was a very popular past time, it was almost a requirement for early American manors to have a fine tea table. The tradition carried forward into modern furniture styles, each style interpreting the form with their own characteristics. Before purchasing an antique tea table, examine it closely for signs of age, wear, repairs, and the condition of the finish. As with many popular forms of furniture, copies of tea tables have been made for generations. Tea tables listed below are by period first, then the stylistic copies associated with that period.

Arts & Crafts

Limbert, Charles P., Grand Rapids and Holland, MI, No. 110, circular top, cross stretchers, tapered legs, cleaned orig finish, branded mark, stains on top, 22" d, 25" h 400.00

Roycroft, East Aurora, NY, circular top, deep apron, cross stretchers, Mackmurdo feet, over-coated finish, carved orb and cross, 36" d, 30" h, ...4,250.00

Stickley, Gustav, New York

No. 604, circular top, arched cross stretcher, orig finish, red decal, some wear to top, 20" d, 26" h 1,600.00

No. 654, circular top, arched cross stretcher, orig finish, paper label, some wear to top 1,700.00

Young, J. M., overhanging circular top, arched apron, skinned finish, paper label, board separation at top, 36" d, 28" h 475.00

Centennial, Chippendale-Style, c1876,
mahogany, circular tilt-top with molded pie crust rim, carved pillar with leafage and ring decoration, heavily carved tripod legs, claw and ball feet, orig tilt-top mechanism and brass hardware, 34" d, 29-3/4" h 2,365.00

Chippendale

America, c1770-90, walnut, tilt-top, circular top with raised rim, birdcage revolving base, turned pillar with large bulbous central portion, series of rings, cabriole legs, pad feet, orig brass locking hardware, iron brace underneath securing base, old repairs to tilt mechanism, 33-1/2" d, 28-1/2" h 965.00

America, mid-18th C, mahogany, quatrefoil shaped two board tilt top with thumb-molded edge, turned column, tripod base with cabriole legs and snake feet, refinished, sun bleached finish, refastened cleats, 31-1/2" x 33-1/4" top, 28-3/4" h 1,925.00

America, mid-18th C, mahogany, circular tilt top, single plank top with molded edge, baluster turned standard, molded downswept tripod legs, pointed pad feet, reduced in height, 34" d, 21-1/4" h 325.00

America, mid-18th C, mahogany, pine three board top, turned column with scalloping on bottom edge, tripod base, snake feet with carved ridge on center from ankle down, old alligatored finish, 30" d, 30" h 1,210.00

Tea, Chippendale, attributed to John Goddard, Newport, Rhode Island, c1760-90, carved mahogany, molded top with contoured cleats, turned pedestal, cabriole legs, carved five-toed pads, old refinish, minor repair, 32" d, 28" h, $3,450. Photo courtesy of Skinner Auctioneers and Appraisers of Antiques and Fine Art Boston and Bolton, MA.

England, late 18th C, carved mahogany, circular top supported on dovetailed mahogany box open at both ends, rotated above pedestal with carved diamonds enclosing scratch carving details, tripod base with acanthus leaf carving on knees, claw and ball feet, old surface, repairs, 32-1/4" w, 31-3/4" d, 29" h 2,415.00

Massachusetts, c1780, mahogany, tilt-top, serpentine top, vase and ring-turned post, tripod cabriole leg base ending in pad feet on platforms, old refinish, imperfections, 30" x 31" top, 29" h 1,610.00

New England, 18th C, apple wood, tilt-top, serpentine top, cabriole leg base, pad feet, refinished, one foot pierced, 35" w, 34" d, 27-1/4" h 460.00

Pennsylvania, Philadelphia, c1735-50, mahogany, scalloped top tilts and turns above birdcage support, turned column pedestal over knees symmetrically carved with shells and husks on cabriole legs, ball and claw feet, old finish, imperfections, 32" d 343,500.00

Pennsylvania, c1740-60, turned walnut, rectangular two board top, beaded frieze, splayed ring-turned baluster form legs, box stretcher, ball feet, 30" l, 21" d, 28-1/4" h 7,775.00

Pennsylvania, c1760, mahogany, birdcage tilt-top, swelled pedestal over cabriole legs, pad feet, refinished, imperfections, 21-3/4" d, 27-3/4" h 2,185.00

Pennsylvania, c1770, walnut, bird cage with turned posts, one board top, pie-crust edge, turned column, tripod base, carved walnut knees with oval and bellflower, claw and diamond shaped ball feet, old finish, repairs to base of column where legs join, repairs to bird cage, minor age cracks, 26" d, 28" h 4,400.00

Pennsylvania, c1780, walnut, circular molded top, birdcage platform, vase and ring-turned post, tripod cabriole legs, paneled knees, pad feet on platforms, old refinishing, minor imperfections, 35-1/2" d, 28-1/2" h 2,500.00

Rhode Island, c1780, cherry, circular tilt-top, urn turned support, tripod cabriole leg base ending in pad feet, old refinish, some imperfections, 31-1/2" d, 28" h 650.00

Rhode Island, Newport, mahogany, round one board dish top, turned column, tripod base, snake feet, old mellow finish, restoration includes period repairs, 23-1/2" d, 27-5/8" h 3,575.00

Rhode Island, Newport, Santo Domingo mahogany, two board top, turned column, tripod base, carved knees, elongated claw and ball feet, old finish, repairs to hinge block, 33-1/2" d, 27-1/2" h 8,250.00

Chippendale-Style, tilt-top, circular top with shaped and molded pie crust edge, birdcage with turned colonettes, baluster turned standard raised on leaf-capped downswept leg with claw and ball feet, 33-3/4" d, 29-1/4" h 1,100.00

Classical

America, carved mahogany demilune fold-over top, hinged top opens to polished surface, baluster turned acanthus carved standard raised on rectangular platform base with concave sides, canted leaf capped lion paw feet with casters, 36-3/4" w, 18-1/4" d, 29-1/2" h 650.00

New York State, 1820s, carved mahogany, shaped tilt-top, turned and carved pedestal, leaf-carved hairy legs and paw feet, old surface, casters missing, repairs, 27-1/2" w, 20" d, 27-5/8" h 990.00

New York State, early 19th C, mahogany, rectangular scalloped edge top, molded skirt, vasiform support with lotus leaf motifs, acanthus carved legs, hairy paw feet, 30" w, 21" d, 28" h 1,200.00

Federal

Maryland, last quarter 18th C, inlaid mahogany, demilune fold-over top, hinged top opens to polished surface, conforming frieze edged with banding and raised on square-section, tapering legs with inlaid cuffs, boxwood stringing throughout, secondary woods oak and white pine, 36-3/4" w, 18" d, 29-3/4" h 2,750.00

Massachusetts, c1800, mahogany inlaid, octagonal tilt-top bordered with inlaid geometric stringing and crossbanding, vase and ring-turned post and three shaped legs inlaid with geometric banding, old refinish, imperfections, 23-1/4" w, 16-1/4" d, 29" h 2,990.00

Tea, Federal, Massachusetts, late 18th C, maple and pine, oval top, four block splayed turned legs, joined by straight apron, old refinish, imperfections, 31-1/4" w, 24-1/2" d, 27" h, $2,875. Photo courtesy of Skinner Auctioneers and Appraisers of Antiques and Fine Art Boston and Bolton, MA.

Massachusetts, late 18th C, maple and pine, oval top, four block splayed turned legs, joined by straight apron, old refinish, imperfections, 31-1/4" w, 24-1/2" d, 27" h 2,875.00

New England, c1805, birchwood and mahogany, octagonal top with inlaid edge, petal carved urn standard, inlaid and shaped down-curving legs, 16" w, 30-1/2" h 9,900.00

New York, c1810, mahogany, tilt top, double elliptic top, vase and ring-turned support, three reeded outward flaring legs on ball feet, 26" x 21-3/4" top, 26-3/4" h 1,495.00

Federal-Style, inlaid walnut, fold-over, rectangular top with inset rounded corners, conforming frieze raised on square section tapering legs, boxwood stringing, price for pair, 36-1/2"l,. 25-3/4"w, 30-1/4" h 800.00

Queen Anne

America, mahogany, two board porringer top with candle shelves, mortised and pinned apron with simple cutout detail, slender tapered legs terminate in slightly curved ankle with duck feet, old dark finish, repairs,

top and pullout candle shelves are old replacements, 25-1/2" x 32-1/2" top, 26-1/2" h 4,125.00

America, maple, oval overhanging top, four block turned tapering legs, pad feet, straight skirt, old refinish, minor imperfections, 32-1/2" w, 26" d, 25-3/4" h 3,250.00

Massachusetts, 18th C, figured cherry, tilt-top, three board top, pedestal base, cabriole legs, arris pad feet, refinished, restoration, 31" d, 26-1/2" d 1,150.00

Massachusetts, 18th C, mahogany, tilt-top, dish top with molded edge, urn shaped pedestal, cabriole legs, pad feet, refinished, restoration, 37" d, 28-1/2" h.............2,300.00

Massachusetts, coastal northern, or New Hampshire, c1730-60, mahogany, molded tray top overhangs straight molded frieze, scrolled skirt, cabriole legs, scrolled knee returns, pad feet on platforms, old refinish, imperfections, 30" w, 19-1/2" d, 27-1/2" h 41,400.00

New England, 18th C, maple and pine, rectangular breadboard overhanging top, valanced apron with drawer joining four cabriole legs, pad feet, old refinish, top of different origin, other imperfections, 38-1/2" x 26" top, 27" h 2,875.00

New England, mid-18th C, maple, overhanging oval top, valanced apron, four block turned tapering legs, button feet, old refinishing, 28" w, 21-3/4" d, 26" h 3,875.00

New England, late 18th C, maple, overhanging oval top on four block turned tapering legs ending in pad feet on platforms joined by valanced skirt, old refinish, minor imperfections, 32-3/4" w, 26-1/4" d, 27-1/2" h.............5,475.00

Pennsylvania, c1730-80, walnut, rectangular one board top, shaped apron, cabriole legs, sq feet, orig finish on top, 35" w, 25" d, 27-1/2" h 24,000.00

Rhode Island, late 18th C, cherry, tilt-top, circular top, birdcage platform, vase and ring-turned support, tripod cabriole base, pad feet on platforms, old surface, minor imperfections, 33" d, 29-3/4" h 1,610.00

Virginia, Williamsburg, mid 18th C, walnut, inlay top overhanging slightly shaped skirt, four cabriole legs with shell carvings, bellflowers below, deeply carved elongated

Tea, Queen Anne, Massachusetts, 18th C, figured cherry, tilt-top, three board top, pedestal base, cabriole legs ending in arris pad feet, refinished, restoration, 31" d, 26-1/2" h, $1,150. Photo courtesy of Skinner Auctioneers and Appraisers of Antiques and Fine Art Boston and Bolton, MA.

flanking scrolls above paneled trifid feet, old surface, 27-1/2" w, 17-3/4" d, 29-1/4" h 7,550.00

Victorian, late 19th C, papier-mâché, tilt top, minor chips and imperfections, 23-1/2" d, 28-1/2" h...350.00

Telephone Tables

Here again is a style of table that only came into being after the invention of another object, this time the telephone. Some telephone tables and stands are almost whimsical in their form, with built-in cupboards for storage of the telephone or books, a place to write, and some even included a bench for seating while talking on the telephone. Also see Telephone Stands.

Arts & Crafts

Limbert, Charles P., Grand Rapids and Holland, MI, overhanging rectangular top, pull-out covered drawer with arched front, lower shelf, branded mark, refinished, rectangular stain to top, chip on bottom shelf, 24" w, 22" d, 29" h 1,395.00

Stickley, Gustav, New York, No. 605, square top, lower shelf, orig finish, red decal and paper label, 14" w, 14" d, 29" h........... 1,400.00

Unknown Designer

Small cabinet, single drawer, paneled sides, sq copper Limbert pulls, new finish, unmarked, 17-1/2" sq, 36' h.........1,300.00

Square top over shelf, orig finish, 16" w, 16" d, 30" h 200.00

Tile Tables

Another unique form, designed to highlight the wonderful decorative tiles of the Arts & Crafts period. The tables were probably designed to be used as side tables. The examples shown below reinforce the importance of provenance and having a marked piece. The first table is by a well-known designer, signed, and with the original finish. The lovely signed Grueby tiles add considerably to the value. The second example is by an unknown maker with unsigned tiles.

Arts & Crafts

Stickley, Gustav, New York, twelve inset William Grueby tiles with matte green glaze, arched apron, lower shelf with double keyed-tenon construction, orig finish, red decal, 24" w, 20" d, 26" h......................................55,000.00

Unknown Designer, four matched incised multicolored tiles, curved iron base, 16" w, 16" d, 20" h...200.00

Tray Tables

The idea of being able to eat one's dinner while enjoying a favorite television program caught on quickly. Today tray tables are not as popular as they once were, but still can be found in many different styles. The form actually goes back to the old English butler's serving table, where the top was a tray designed to fit on a wooden base.

Arts and Crafts, unknown designer, mahogany, folding, lift-up circular top, base with dual cross stretcher construction, refinished, 25" d, 19" h..1,760.00

Modernism Era, Knoll International, 1940s, webbed stool, removable molded plywood top, 25" w, 19" d, 17" h 600.00

Trestle Tables

Trestle tables are another example of a table form becoming the name for a table. The use of such a table is often dictated by the location, being a library, dining, or kitchen area. The long narrow tables were a departure from the usual table style and appealed to some buyers.

Arts & Crafts

Limbert, Charles P., Grand Rapids and Holland, MI, triple corbels on each side, lower shelf mortised through legs, orig medium finish, unmarked, 49-3/4" w, 28" d, 29-1/4" h 2,895.00

Stickley, Gustav, New York

No. 637, rectangular top, lower stretcher with double keyed-tenon construction, refinished, paper label, 48" w, 30" d, 28" h 1,550.00

Overhanging rectangular top, thick lower shelf mortised with keyed-through tenons, over-coat to orig dark finish, large red decal, 48" w, 30" d, 28-1/4" h 2,450.00

Stickley, L. and J. G., Fayetteville, NY, Mousehole, stretcher mortised through cut-out plank sides, keyed through-tenons, refinished top, orig finish to base, unmarked, 48" w, 32" d, 29" h 3,375.00

Unknown Designer, plank top, lower shelf mortised with through-tenons, orig reddish-brown finish, some alligatoring to top, 95-1/2" l, 29" d, 31" h.......................3,750.00

Mission, oak, rectangular top, three corbels at sides, applied belt and vertical rectangular cutout, unsigned, refinished top, 50" w, 28" d, 29" h...900.00

William and Mary, Hudson River Valley, early 18th C, pine, rectangular cleated top, scroll upright supports join with molded board stretcher, trestle feet, 96" l, 30-1/4" h.......................8,750.00

Work Tables

Work tables are small tables used as work surfaces in various rooms of early homes. Work tables found in the kitchen served as places to prepare food, perhaps later to hold food before serving in the dining room. Other work tables were used in living rooms, bedrooms, libraries to hold whatever activity was important to that particular area. As the importance of the room increased, and the public display of one's wealth and good breeding, the more elaborate work tables, and furniture in general, became. Most work tables of the Chippendale and Federal periods were plain. As the style of furniture became more refined in the Classical period, work tables also received more attention, more details, and more decoration.

Chippendale

Country, attributed to Maine, maple, birch, and pine, orig red finish, scrubbed one board top with bread board ends, single dovetailed drawer with brass pull, beaded corners on legs, apron, and stretcher base, age cracks, 50-1/4" w, 29-3/4" d top, 26" h 3,300.00

Country, attributed to Vermont, decorated, pine, old green paint, yellow striping on drawer and legs, two board pegged top with scrubbed surface, dovetailed drawer, small brass pull, 35-7/18" w, 23-3/8" d, 27-3/4" h 2,475.00

Country, maple, chestnut, and birch, old brown finish, two board breadboard top, single dovetailed drawer, scalloped edge apron, square legs with molded corners and inside chamfer, cross stretcher, chestnut secondary wood, top loose and has age cracks, 38-1/2" l, 25-3/4" d, 27-3/4" h 880.00

New England, c1820-25, carved mahogany and mahogany veneer, rectangular top with shaped leaves and molded edge, two drawers, four ring-turned spiral-carved posts, trestle feet with carved rosettes and concave paneled legs ending in cast brass hairy paw feet, joined by ring-turned spiral-carved medial stretcher, old refinish, minor imperfections, 18-1/2" w, 18" d, 29-3/4" h.......................1,150.00

New York, c1815-25, mahogany and mahogany veneer, rectangular top inlaid with sections centering a circular panel with ovolo corners, quarter-engaged ring-turned posts ending in acorn pendants flanking two graduated drawers, vase and ring-turned spiral-carved support on rectangular platform, outward flaring beaded legs, applied brass rosettes, ending in brass casters, old circular brass pulls, refinished, imperfections, 30" w, 14" d, 29-1/2" h.................................1,265.00

Pennsylvania, walnut, turned legs with square feet, removable three board top, single overlapping dovetailed drawer, stretcher base, molded edge apron, old finish, edge damage, old repairs, wear and knife marks on top, 29-3/4" w, 54-1/2" l, 26-1/2" h 3,300.00

Classical

America, c1825, mahogany, dual demilune ends with hinged covers for compartment, one drawer over one double false drawer, reverse of central portion has three false drawer fronts, turned pillar with central urn motif resting on quadruped tapered legs, brass paw feet, most body surfaces veneered, orig hardware, minor repairs, 25-1/2" w, 13-1/2" d, 29" h 900.00

America, early 19th C, mahogany, rectangular top, two 11" w D-form drop leaves, two serpentine drawers, turned legs, casters, 19" w, 25" d, 29" h 500.00

America, early 19th C, curly maple, top with mahogany crossbanded veneer edge, applied cherry edge banding, two dovetailed drawers, apron with corner posts and turned drops, turned column, four curved legs with mahogany ball feet and rosettes, replaced drawer pulls, interior dividers missing, minor repairs, mismatched turned feet, refinished, 18" w, 18" d, 28-1/2" h 1,450.00

Maryland, Baltimore, second quarter 19th C, stamped "From Thomas D. Hiss/Cabinet Maker/No. 47 W. Pratt St./Balto" on inner left side of drawer, plum-pudding mahogany, outset rectangular top over frieze with paneled drawer, right-hand side with candle slide, lyreform end supports raised on concave platform stretcher, scroll feet and casters, imperfections, 22-1/4" w, 20" d, 28-1/2" h......... 1,200.00

Maryland, Baltimore, second quarter 19th C, pine and poplar ebonized, scratch floral and urn decoration to exposed wood surface, rectangular top with slightly rounded corners, decorated apron with single drawer, squared pedestal support, shaped base, scrolled feet, some blemishes, 19-1/2" w, 18" d, 28" h 1,760.00

Maryland, mid 19th C, painted, octagonal top, floral decoration, central fitted drawer, lyre base, brass rosette and ball capped feet, some paint loss and flaking, 22" w, 15-1/2" d, 29" h.................................2,200.00

Massachusetts, Boston, c1825, carved mahogany and mahogany veneer, hinged rectangular top opens to interior with work surface and compartments, case with rounded drawer, recessed drawer below, flanked by acorn pendants, turned acanthus carved post and four shaped acanthus carved legs, paw feet, casters, old finish, 22-1/2" w, 17-1/2" d, 33" h 1,250.00

Massachusetts, Boston, c1830, attributed to Issac Vose, Jr., carved mahogany and mahogany veneer, rectangular top with rounded leaves, two drawers, top drawer fitted with adjustable work easel, lower drawer with two faux drawer facade, molded pedestal shaped platform with carved scroll feet, old refinishing, minor imperfections, 22-1/2" w, 19" d, 30" h 1,975.00

Massachusetts, Boston, c1830, carved mahogany and mahogany veneer, rectangular top with canted corners, half rounded edge, conforming case with two drawers and bag drawer, foliate carved ring-turned columns, concave shaped platform and four turned feet, old finish, old brasses, 22-1/2' w, 17" d, 31-1/2" h..............................14,000.00

Massachusetts, c1830, mahogany and mahogany veneer, square top, rounded beaded drop leaves, four vase and ring-turned legs on casters, three half-round veneered drawers with turned pulls, old refinish, 18-1/2" w, 18" d, 29" h 575.00

New York, upstate, c1830-40, mahogany veneer, drawers, 27" w, 15-3/4" d, 29" h 950.00

Country

Missouri, cherry, three board top, one dovetailed drawer with cockbeading, orig turned wooden knobs, turned legs, old refinishing, worn surface, 34-1/2" w, 48" d, 27-1/2" h..300.00

Ohio River Valley, c1840, walnut, inlaid geometric designs and hearts, glass knobs, old finish, some loss to inlay, 20" w, 16-1/2" d, 29" h 3,200.00

Pennsylvania, second half 18th C, walnut, rectangular removable top, two apron drawers, turned legs with stretchers........2,000.00

Federal

America, first quarter 19th C, mahogany, outset rectangular top with molded edge, front with two graduated drawers flanked by reeded stiles, turned tapering ring-turned legs, 22" w, 16" d, 29" h.......................950.00

Massachusetts, c1790, mahogany and satinwood inlaid, octagonal top, inlaid edge, satinwood veneered conforming skirt, center bag drawer with geometric inlaid lower edge, four sq tapered legs, old refinishing, replaced pulls, imperfections, 19-3/4" w, 16-1/4" d, 29" h.......................2,200.00

Massachusetts, Boston, c1800, mahogany, flame birch veneer, shaped octagonal top, single drawer, straight tapered legs, spade foot, X-shaped stretcher, casters, 20" w, 18-1/4" d, 28-1/2" h...............2,750.00

Massachusetts, c1815, mahogany veneer, rectangular top, case with three graduated drawers flanked by reeded panel legs, casters, replaced brasses, refinished, restored, 22-1/4" w,. 18-1/4" d, 32-1/2" h........2,875.00

Massachusetts, western, c1820, cherry and bird's eye maple, rectangular bird's eye maple overhanging top, bird's eye maple drawer, cherry straight apron joining four ring-turned swelled legs ending in peg feet, replaced pull, old refinish, imperfections, 20" w, 19-1/2" d, 27-3/4" h 1,495.00

New England, c1820, mahogany and mahogany veneer, rectangular top, two cockbeaded graduated drawers and straight cockbeaded skirt joining front delicate vase and ring-turned legs, ball feet, old refinish, minor imperfections, 18" w, 15-1/2" d, 28-1/4" h.....................2,100.00

New England, c1830, mahogany, smooth lift top with rounded edge and turquoise felt writing surface, two semi-cylindrical open compartments, two dovetailed drawers, one large, one smaller with nine part divided interior, continuous reeding, slender turned and reeded legs, old added brasses, pine sec-

ondary wood, old finish, 23-3/4" w, 12-3/4" d, 28-5/8" h 3,600.00

New York or Philadelphia, c1815, carved and veneered mahogany, projecting rectangular case with flanking hinged tops, astragal ends, cockbeaded compartmented drawer, deep drawer below on vase and ring-turned legs, tapering feet, refinished, replaced brasses, minor imperfections, 24-1/2" w, 13-1/4" d, 28-1/2" h 2,530.00

Pennsylvania, Pennsylvania German, c1790, pine, maple framed slate top, splayed block and spool turned legs, one deep drawer with carved "H.A" and "1790" on front, shaped apron on two sides, box stretcher, missing two stretcher boards, 39" x 33" top, 27-1/2" h.....................2,465.00

Pennsylvania, c1810, pine, old worn brown paint over red, removable three board top with replaced pegs, two dovetailed drawers, turned wood pulls, turned legs with chips, age cracks, 54" w, 36" d, 30-1/2" h... 1,760.00

Federal, late, c1800-25

Cherry and bird's eye maple, drop-leaf, rectangular top, rule-jointed leaves, plain frieze with drawer, turned square section legs, turned and tapering feet, 37-1/4" l, 22-1/2" w, 28-3/4" h, ...400.00

Cherry and bird's eye maple, rectangular top with rounded corners, rule-joined leaves, frieze with two drawers, lower drawer with fitted interior, turned and tapering legs, 37-1/4" l, 23-3/4" w, 26-1/2" h 600.00

Cherry and tiger maple, outset rectangular top over front with two drawers, spiral-turned legs, tulip form feet, 23-1/2" w, 18-1/2" d, 26-3/4" h 650.00

Federal-Style, mahogany, outset rectangular top with molded edges, frieze with drawer, raised on turned tapering ring-turned legs, 18" d, 25" w, 30" h...................................450.00

Hepplewhite

Country, maple, pine breadboard top, mortised and pinned apron, one overlapped dovetailed drawer, sq tapered legs, refinished, replaced top set on hinges to enable it to top, traces of old red paint, 46-1/2" w, 28-1/2" h 800.00

Country, pine and chestnut, removable two board top, one dovetailed drawer that is hidden in apron, under-edge finger hold, mortised and pinned apron with beaded edge, slightly splayed square tapered legs, refinished, 39-1/4" w, 31" d, 30-1/4" h 770.00

Country, walnut and other woods, old worn brownish gray finish, two board top, apron with two dovetailed drawers, square tapered legs, casters, 67-1/2" l, 31" d, 29-3/4" h 1,870.00

Pennsylvania, pine, removable breadboard top, square tapered legs, two overlapping dovetailed drawers, mortised and pinned apron, refinished top, old red on base, feet ended out, old wrought iron braces on one corner, 78-1/4" l, 36-1/2" d, 30" h 2,100.00

Queen Anne, Chester County, Pennsylvania, walnut, pine top, two drawers, beaded skirt, splay legs, replaced top and drawer runners, 51" w, 32" d, 29-1/2" h.................1,650.00

Sheraton, America, 19th C

Mahogany, figured mahogany veneer, two dovetailed drawers with third drawer front that holds work bag frame, turned and rope carved legs with spool turned posts, replaced brasses, old finish, top drawer fitted, lift-up writing surface, old replaced legs, 17" x 18-1/4" top, 8-1/4" leaves, 29-3/4" h 725.00

Mahogany, pair of drawers supported by turned pedestal, quadruped base, 19" w, 16-1/2" d, 30-1/2" h 550.00

Poplar, old red finish, one board top, single dovetailed drawer, well shaped turned legs, mortised apron, 40-1/4" w, 26" d, 29" h 2,530.00

Regency, c1810, lacquered, Chinoiserie taste, canted top opening to storage space, delicate square legs, whole cream colored with polychrome and gilt figural landscape, floral and avian dec, 12-1/4" w, 10" d, 28-1/2" h....................900.00

Victorian, French, c1870, lady's, rosewood, superstructure fitted with drop-front opening to variety of drawers and cubbyholes, lower section fitted with single frieze drawer over pull-out storage well, tapering square legs ending in casters, whole with inlaid scrolling patterns, 24" w, 16" d, 42" h 1,320.00

Victorian-Style, carved mahogany, top with ebonized banding lifting to removable compartmented storage drawer, demilune drawer below, sunburst pattern, vasiform standard, three splayed acanthus carved legs ending in scrolled toes, 23-1/2" w, 15-1/2" d, 31" h 550.00

Writing Tables

Arts & Crafts

Roycroft, East Aurora, NY, mahogany, slatted sides, two drawers with hammered copper pulls, lower shelf mortised with keyed through-tenons, Mackmurdo feet, orig finish, carved orb and cross mark, 48" l, 30" w, 30" h 5,000.00

Stickley, Gustav, New York

No. 657, rectangular top over twelve spindles at each side with through-tenon construction, orig finish, red decal, some stains, 48" w, 30" d, 29" h...4,750.00

Chippendale-Style, carved mahogany, trisected inset leather top, central frieze drawers flanked by two drawers, cabriole legs headed by acanthus carving, scrolled toes, 54" w, 39" d, 30" h..1,550.00

Federal

Country, early 19th C, yellow-pine, outset rectangular chamfered top over frieze with drawer, delicately turned tapering legs with ball feet, old refinish, imperfections, 25" w, 36-1/2" l, 28-1/2" h..............................600.00

Pennsylvania, Philadelphia, c1815, mahogany, fitted top, interior with compartments, fluted tapered legs, casters, old finish, 24' w, 17-1/2" d, 28-3/4" h.........7,525.00

Georgian-Style, carved mahogany, top with gadrooned edge, inset glass surface, central drawer flanked on either side by two drawers, cabriole legs headed by acanthus carving, claw and ball feet, 61" w, 40-1/2" d, 30-1/2" h..1,450.00

Sheraton Style, early 20th C, mahogany, top with molded edge and inset red gilt-tooled leather writing surface, frieze fitted with two drawers to one side, raised on fluted tapering legs, spade feet, 71-1/2" w, 42" d, 31" h 2,200.00

Victorian

America, late 19th C, mahogany, rectangular green gilt tooled leather top with beveled edge, gadrooned molding, two drawers, baluster turned carved legs, 46" w, 29-1/4" h 1,450.00

Glossary

Acanthus: Scalloped leaf decoration. May be applied or carved.

Aesthetic Movement: Furniture style greatly influenced by the Japanese taste, c1875-1914. Popular in America, but more prevalent in England.

Anthemion: Carved flat ornament, resembling honeysuckle flower and leaf.

Architectural Mirror: A wall mirror that combines architectural elements of the design period, used to reflect light.

Arrow-Back: Form of chair back from the late Windsor period, identified by row of flat flaring back stiles that narrow from wider point-type top to slender base.

Art Deco: Furniture style dating from approximately 1920-1940.

Art Furniture: Furniture style dating from approximately 1875-1914.

Art Nouveau: Furniture style dating from approximately 1896-1914.

Arts and Crafts: Furniture style dating from approximately 1895-1915.

Ball Foot: Turned round foot. Similar to a bun foot, but rounder.

Balloon-Back: Form of chair back shaped like a hot-air balloon, rounded at the top, tapering toward seat.

Baluster: Turned vertical post, with vase or column-form shaped outline.

Banding: Term used to describe edging design.

Barrister Bookcase: A common name for the stacking bookcases with glass fronts, popularized in the Victorian era.

Bellflower: Floral decoration. May be applied or carved.

Bentwood: Term used to describe furniture with an element that was permanently bent through a mechanical process, such as steam or pressure. Well-known designers include Samuel Greeg and Michael Thonet. Other manufacturers of Bentwood furniture were Jacob and Joseph Kohn; Philip Strobel and Son; Sheboygan Chair Co.; and Tidoute Chair Co.

Bergère: Upholstered chair with rounded back, closed arms, and loose seat cushion.

Bird-Cage: Support element of a tilt-top table, generally two blocks separated by columns.

Block: Support element of many furniture forms. Used to increase support or guide drawers, area to apply glue, etc.

Block and Vase: Decorative turning that combines a square and vase element.

Block Foot: Rectangular or square plain feet.

Bootjack Feet: Term used to described arched foot created by cutting away some of a side or foot board.

Boss, Bosses: Decorative applied ornament(s), often round or oval.

Bow Front: Term used to described a chest with a slight swell, or bow, in the center.

Box-Stretcher: A structural configuration on the base of a chair that has a bar from leg to leg.

Bracket: Term used to describe curved segment that connects a leg to a seat rail, etc. A bracket can be a functional structural segment, as well as aesthetic.

Bracket Foot: One of the simplest of furniture feet, shaped like a bracket, usually with a mitered corner. Variations include a plain bracket foot, a molded bracket foot, or a scrolled bracket foot.

Brasses: Term used to describe metal hardware.

Brass Inlay: Term used to describe technique where thin sheets of different colored brass are laid in a slightly recessed area to create a pattern or design.

Broken Arch Pediment: Term used to described a triangular or curved pediment that features an open area at the upper most point.

Bun Foot: Term used to describe a turned foot that features a flattened ball, sometimes on a small square or rectangular shoe or pad.

Butterfly: Term used to describe a shaped element used as a hinge or support.

Button Foot: Term used for a small, flattened ball feet.

Butler's Desk: A compartment and writing surface found on some desks and sideboards for use by a servant.

Cabriole Leg: Elegant leg style that curves outward at the knee and tapers inward at the ankle.

Caning: Strips of rattan woven to create a seat or back.

Capital: Top section of a column, used to determine style, usually decorative in form.

Carving: Term used to describe technique that craftsmen used to create designs by using chisels and other implements to sculpt designs.

Case: Term used to describe the box-like body of a piece of furniture, particularly chests, cupboards, or other storage type pieces of furniture.

Centennial Revival: Furniture style dating from approximately 1875-1915.

Chamfer: Term used to describe a beveled or cut-off corner or edge.

Cheval: A large mirror, designed with a base and can be used in a free-standing position.

Chinoiserie: Decoration featuring American or European interpretation of Oriental motifs.

Chip Carving: An intricate geometric style of carving.

Chippendale: Furniture style dating from approximately 1755-1790.

Circa: Common term used to reflect the theory that dates given are approximate and can be a few years early or later than the dates shown, i.e. c1850 could be as early as 1845 or as late as 1860.

Classical: Furniture style dating from approximately 1805-1830. Less commonly known as Empire.

Claw and Ball Foot: This style of foot features a carved claw grasping a round ball. Many variations exist, some being more detailed than others.

Club Foot: Foot with a slightly pointed toe, usually thick and substantial.

Cockbeaded Molding: Type of molding where a thin beaded edge is the design element.

Colonette: Term used to describe a small column, often an applied type of decoration.

Colonial Revival: Furniture style dating from approximately 1915-1940.

Continuous Arm: Term used to describe an arm that extends from one side to another without breaking for a crest across the back. Commonly found on Windsor chairs, settees, bentwood, and other types of chairs.

Cornice: Top horizontal molding commonly found on case furniture.

Country: Furniture style dating from approximately 1790-1850.

Crest Rail: The top rail on the back of a chair.

Cross Stretcher: Base stretcher that intersects another stretcher at right angles, also referred to as X-stretcher.

Cupboard Door: Term used to refer to a simple door created with a flat center section and molded perimeter frame.

Cut-Out Feet: Construction term used to describe a piece of furniture with a solid side piece, where the feet are simply cut out from the side piece.

Dentil Molding: Form of molding that reflects the architectural style of using small rectangles, generally separated by evenly spaced open areas.

Dot-and-Dash Piercing: Type of pierced trim created by alternating circles and sets of horizontal lines.

Dovetails: Joint formed as two pieces of wood are fitted at right angles with interlocking flaring tenons.

Drapery: Carved or inlaid decoration resembling swagged cloth.

Dressing Mirror: A mirror used to view one's appearance, sometimes mounted on a base or used on a table top.

Duncan Phyfe and Phyfe-Types: Furniture style dating from approximately 1795-1840.

Eagle Brasses: Hardware made in the form of a spread-wing eagle, usually made of brass.

Eastlake: Furniture style dating from approximately 1870-1890, part of the Victorian era.

Eglomise: A type of painting on glass where the design is painted on the back and intended to be viewed through the glass, often found as decoration on mirrors.

Egyptian Revival: Furniture style dating from approximately 1870-1890; part of the Victorian era.

Elizabethan Revival: Furniture style dating from approximately 1850-1915; part of the Victorian era.

Empire: Furniture style dating from approximately 1805-1830. More commonly known as Classical.

En Suite: Term used to indicate that furniture is a matching part of a set, or suite.

Escutcheon: Small decorative brass, metal, or ivory plate used on the outside of a keyhole. Also may be called a "Key Plate."

Fall Front: Term used to describe a board that lowers from the top to a writing surface.

Fan Back: Type of Windsor chair back with a rectangular crest rail over a flared, straight-sided back.

Federal: Furniture style dating from approximately 1790-1815.

Festoon: Carved decorative element, sometimes consists of a fruit or floral motif, similar to a drapery.

Finial: Decorative element found as an ornament on top of a case or pediment. Names such as "flame finial" or "corkscrew finial" indicate the three-dimensional shape of the finial.

Fluting: Term used to describe horizontal channel carving.

Foliate: Decoration that resembles leaves. May be applied or carved.

Foot Board: Section of bed frame where user commonly puts feet. Can be paneled, turned, or have elements to support canopy frame.

French Foot: Style of foot with concave curves.

French Restauration: Furniture style dating from approximately 1830-1850.

Fretwork: Decorative element composed of intersecting lines, can be made with molding or actually cut into the piece.

Gadrooning: Term used to describe swirled or curved fluting, usually an edging.

Gateleg: Extra leg designed to help support table leaf. Support mechanism to attach to table that allows leg to swing freely often resembles a simple gate.

Girandole: A circular convex mirror.

Gothic Revival: Furniture style dating from approximately 1840-1860, part of the Victorian era.

Grisalle: Term used to describe painting in tones of gray, usually used on interiors or as a background for other types of decoration.

Graduated Drawers: Term means the drawers which are different in size from one to another, usually the smallest drawer is in the top, the next slightly larger, etc.

H-Stretcher: A H-configuration of structural rails found on the base of many chairs.

Hairy Paw Foot: Foot carved to depict an animal's hoof with details such as hair and claws found on many examples. Usually wider at the base than the smaller hoof foot.

Hand-Cut Dovetails: Joints made by dovetails that were individually cut by the craftsman. Many are typified by slight inconsistencies in the making.

Head Board: Section of bed frame where user commonly puts head. Can be paneled, turned, or have elements to support canopy frame, often framed by decorative bed hangings.

Hepplewhite: Furniture style dating from approximately 1790-1810.

Hoof Foot: A foot that is carved to resemble an animal's hoof.

Incised Decoration: Term used to describe technique used by craftsmen that created designs, usually lines and geometric shapes, that are not very deeply carved into the wood.

Inlay: Term used to describe technique where thin sheets of different colored woods are laid in a slightly recessed area to create a pattern or design.

Ivory Inlay: Term used to describe technique where thin pieces of ivory are laid in a slightly recessed area to create a pattern or design.

Japanning: Technique using Oriental lacquer work on a wood base, consisting of many layers of varnish and color. Some decorated examples have motifs of figures, animals, and florals are created in gesso, gilded or silvered, before the lacquer work layers are applied.

Joining: Term used to describe the process of using mortise and tenon joints to create sturdy furniture.

Klismos: Chair form inspired by the ancient Greeks. It is identified by a crest rail, curving uprights, and tapering saber legs. The form was popular in some of the Victorian Revival periods as well as early Classical periods.

Knee Hole Desk: A desk with a flat working surface, usually supported by two banks (or piers) of drawers or legs, allowing the user to see with their knees under the desk top.

Lady's Desk: Desk of more diminutive proportions, which allowed a lady to sit with her legs under the working surface. Davenport Desk: A smaller version of a desk with fold-out working surfaces.

Looking Glass: A term used to describe a small mirror used to view one's image.

Louis XVI Revival: Furniture style dating from approximately 1850-1914; part of the Victorian era.

Machine-Cut Dovetails: Joints formed that have consistently even and tight fitting angles. Some later machine-made dovetails are rounded rather than angular.

Marlborough Leg: Style of leg where the leg is square, may be fluted, generally ends in a blocked foot.

Marquetry: Term used to describe inlay arranged in a specific motif, such as floral or landscapes.

Married: Term used to describe a piece of furniture where the top and base were combined, sometimes bridging two generations or different time frames.

Medallion: Round, oval, or spherical ornament, usually applied.

Mission, Prairie: Furniture style dating from approximately 1900-1920.

Modernism-Era: Furniture style dating from approximately 1940 to 1960.

Modernism Era, Pop: Furniture style dating from approximately 1960 to present.

Molded Bracket Foot: Bracket foot with additional molding as a decorative element on the foot or at the connection with the case.

Molding: Decorative piece of wood used for ornamental purposes.

Mortise and Tenon Joint: Joint created when the tenon, a small tab-like extension, is fitted into a square or rectangular opening, known as a mortise. Sometimes a mortise and tenon joint has a wooden peg to securely fasten the joint. When a mortise and tenon joint is visible to the viewer, it is called an "exposed mortise and tenon."

Naturalistic Revival: Furniture style dating from approximately 1850-1914; part of the Victorian era.

Neoclassic or Greco-Roman: Furniture style dating from approximately 1790-1815.

Neo-Greek Revival: Furniture style dating from approximately 1855-1885; part of the Victorian era.

Ogee: Term used to describe a molding shaped like the letter "S." Also called a cyma curve.

Ormolu Mount: Term used to describe the technique where gilt-covered metal mountings are used as decorative or functional elements.

Overlapping Drawer: Term indicating a slight extension on the face of the drawer that covers the drawer opening tightly when closed, thus overlapping the case.

Over Mantel Mirror: A term used to describe large mirrors used over a fireplace mantel, primarily used to reflect light into a room.

Over-Upholstered: Upholstered section that appears to be overstuffed.

Oxbow Front: Another name for a reverse serpentine-shaped front.

Pad Foot: Term used to describe a small rounded foot that rests on a platform or small base.

Palmette: Decorative carving in the shape of a palm leaf or fan.

Patera: Term used to describe a oval or round motif with segments that radiate from the center.

Pediment: Upper most section of a case style of furniture.

Period Brasses: Term used to describe hardware that is original to the piece, usually used only when the hardware is made of brass, but sometimes this phrase is used to denote any period metal hardware.

Period Hardware: Term used to describe hardware that is original to the piece, dating from the time of manufacturing.

Piecrust Edge: Term used to describe edge of a circular form that resembles the edge of a pie.

Pier Mirror: A large mirror either hung over a pier table or hung at a level so one could view skirts and feet

Pilaster: Column with a flat or rectangular side, used for ornamental purposes only.

Plinth: Term used to describe base of column.

Queen Anne: Furniture style dating from approximately 1725-1810.

Reeding: Term used to describe vertical channel carving.

Replaced Hardware: Term used to describe hardware that is not original to the piece. May not be stylistically accurate.

Reproduction Hardware: Term used to describe hardware made to look like antique or period hardware.

Restauration: Term used to describe a predominately French furniture style dated about 1830-50. It features simple lines, and light woods.

Renaissance Revival: Furniture style dating from approximately 1850-1880; part of the Victorian era.

Ring Turning: Term used to describe molding or legs turned on a lathe, with small rings as part of the design element.

Rococo Revival: Furniture style dating from approximately 1845-1870; part of the Victorian era.

Roll Top: Type of somewhat flexible closure used to close a desk where a sliding section moves up and behind the fitted interior of the desk. Usually made like a tambour, but often of large dimensioned wood and consequently can be more rigid than a standard tambour.

Rosette: Rose-like round ornament, sometimes divided into small segments or petals.

Saber Leg: Type of chair leg that tapers and curves. Shape resembles a cavalry saber.

Sack Back: Type of Windsor chair where the back is rounded.

Saddle Seat: Type of seat where wood is carved to gently fit user comfortably.

Scallop: Term used to describe decorative carved or applied element that resembles a shell.

Scroll: Decorative element consisting of swirls.

Scrolled Bracket Foot: Bracket foot with a scrolled design at the sides.

Scroll Mirror: A scrolled mirror frame, made to be hung on a wall.

Secondary Wood: Term that refers to the wood used on the interior of the drawers, perhaps the back, or areas that are unseen.

Secretaire a'abattant: French term used to describe a secretary, especially those with detailed interiors.

Secretary: Term used to describe a desk with a high bookcase top.

Serpentine Front: Term used to describe a more shaped top, often having several curves.

Shaker: Furniture style dating from approximately 1800-1914.

Shaving Mirror: A small table-top mirror, used to view one's appearance while shaving. Usually found on bases, sometimes with small drawers to holding accessories.

Shell Carving: Term used to describe decorative carved elements that resemble shells or scallops.

Sheraton: Furniture style dating from approximately 1790-1810.

Side Rail: Chair side rails extending from the crest rail to seat.

Six-Board Construction: Term used to describe a blanket chest made from six boards, one for the top, front, back, bottom, and sides.

Skirt: Connective piece often found between table legs and table top. May be scalloped or plain or contain a drawer opening.

Slant Front: Term that describes a flat writing surface that folds down from the top to a comfortable writing height. Also known as a slant lid.

Slant Lid: Term that describes a flat writing surface that folds down from the top to a comfortable writing height. Also known as a slant front.

Snake Foot: Term used to describe a small rounded foot, often carved with eyes or other reptile-like details.

Spade Foot: Term used to describe small trowel-shaped foot.

Spanish Foot: Term used to describe sweeping carved scrolling foot.

Spindle: Turned rod used as a support element in chairs, bird cage supports, etc.

Spool Turning: Term used to describe turned element where lathe is used and end result is a series of spools or rounded elements.

Stretcher Base: The structural members that extend from chair leg to chair leg, adding stability.

Stringing: Term used to describe inlaid wood that is usually lighter than base wood. Can be found used either horizontally or vertically.

Swag: Decoration similar to drapery or festoon, to give the illusion of draped fabric.

Tambour: Technique whereby thin strips of wood are glued to a cloth backing, retaining some flexibility. Frequently used as doors or other types of enclosures.

Teardrop: Type of hardware shaped like a pendant, usually with a brass or metal backplate and turned wooden teardrop.

Tester: Term used to describe bed frame with a canopy.

Thumb-Molded: Type of molding where edge is smooth, as though a thumb has carefully smoothed out the edges.

Trifid Foot: Delicate foot that is carved to resemble three toes.

Vasiform Splat: A decorative splat, usually found on chairs, shaped like a vase.

Veneer: Thin layer of wood glued to less expensive wood base.

Victorian: Furniture style dating from approximately 1840-1890, contains many sub-styles.

Wall Mirror: A mirror designed to be hung on the wall and used for either viewing of one's image or reflecting light.

William and Mary: Furniture style dating from approximately 1690-1730.

Windsor: Furniture style dating from approximately 1750 to present.

X-Stretcher: A type of chair base configuration that has elements which go across the base and the stretcher bars cross, sometimes joined together. Also referred to as a cross-stretcher.

Index